Modernization of China's Agricultural Production Organizations

Series on Chinese Economics Research*

(ISSN: 2251-1644)

Series Editor: Fan Gang *(Peking University, China)*

This series aims at publishing top-quality research works on Chinese economics and finance. Since the reform in 1978, the Chinese economy has experienced three decades of unprecedented rapid growth and countless volumes have been written to explain the phenomenon. The series offers the best of the research works done by economists who specialized in Chinese economics and finance.

The topics covered in this series are diverse, e.g. main drivers of economic growth, growing income disparity, rent-seeking behaviors, financial regulations, financial market, state-owned enterprises, food security, developmental strategy, RMB reform and service industry.

Published:

Vol. 25: *Modernization of China's Agricultural Production Organizations*
by Cao Yang
translated by Dong Ming and Li Xue

Vol. 24: *A Theoretical Analysis, Performance Evaluation, and Reform Solution of the Health Care System in China*
by Sheng Hong, Zhang Lin and Qian Pu

Vol. 23: *China's Industrial Policy Transformation: Theory and Practice*
by Huang Hanquan

Vol. 22: *The Great Transformation: Supply-side Structural Reform*
by Ma Xiaohe

Vol. 21: *China's Economic Development Strategies: Transformation and Innovation*
by Liu Rui

Vol. 20: *China's Rural Labor Migration and Its Economic Development*
by Liu Xiaoguang

Vol. 19: *Environmental Economics Research and China's Green Development Strategy*
by Zhang Youguo

*For the complete list of volumes in this series, please visit
www.worldscientific.com/series/scer

Series on Chinese Economics Research – Vol. 25

Modernization of China's Agricultural Production Organizations

Yang CAO
Central China Normal University, China

Translated by
Ming DONG
Xue LI
Zhejiang Gongshang University, China

World Scientific

NEW JERSEY • LONDON • SINGAPORE • BEIJING • SHANGHAI • HONG KONG • TAIPEI • CHENNAI • TOKYO

Published by

World Scientific Publishing Co. Pte. Ltd.
5 Toh Tuck Link, Singapore 596224
USA office: 27 Warren Street, Suite 401-402, Hackensack, NJ 07601
UK office: 57 Shelton Street, Covent Garden, London WC2H 9HE

Library of Congress Cataloging-in-Publication Data
Names: Cao, Yang, 1955– author.
Title: Modernization of China's agricultural production organizations /
Yang Cao, Central China Normal University, China ;
translated by Ming Dong, Xue Li, Zhejiang Gongshang University, China.
Other titles: Dang dai Zhongguo nong ye sheng chan zu zhi xian dai hua yan jiu. English
Description: New Jersey : World Scientific, [2023] | Series: Series on Chinese economics research, 2251-1644 ; vol. 25 | Includes bibliographical references and index.
Identifiers: LCCN 2022030888 | ISBN 9789811242267 (hardcover) |
ISBN 9789811242274 (ebook) | ISBN 9789811242281 (ebook other)
Subjects: LCSH: Agriculture--Economic aspects--China. | Agriculture, Cooperative--China.
Classification: LCC HD2097 .C37313 2023 | DDC 338.10951--dc23/eng/20220812
LC record available at https://lccn.loc.gov/2022030888

British Library Cataloguing-in-Publication Data
A catalogue record for this book is available from the British Library.

Sponsored by Chinese Fund for the Humanities and Social Sciences

当代中国农业生产组织现代化研究
Originally published in Chinese by China Social Sciences Press

For any available supplementary material, please visit
https://www.worldscientific.com/worldscibooks/10.1142/12418#t=suppl

Desk Editors: Sanjay Varadharajan/Lixi Dong

Typeset by Stallion Press
Email: enquiries@stallionpress.com

About the Author

Cao Yang is a professor and doctoral supervisor at the School of Economics and Business Administration, Central China Normal University. He has been a visiting scholar at the University of Queensland and the University of Cambridge. He is a member of the Academic Committee, Central China Normal University and director of the Academic Committee of School of Economics and Business Administration.

He has published five monographs in Chinese, including *The Choice of History — The Development History of Market Economy*, *Study on Contemporary Chinese Rural Microeconomic Organization Form*, etc. In addition, he has published five English papers in international journals such as *Asian Economic Journal*, and more than 70 papers in Chinese in domestic journals such as *Economist*, *Economic Perspectives* and *Chinese Rural Economy*.

About the Translators

Dong Ming was a professor of translation at Zhejiang Gongshang University (ZJSU) before she retired in 2020. She graduated from Shanghai International Studies University (SISU) with a Master's degree in English and American Literature in 1989. She has authored three translation monographs *Spatial-Temporal Translation Studies*, *A Philosophical Perspective of Translation Studies* and *Translation: Creative Treason*, and tens of papers on translation theories, language and culture, English teaching, etc. She has translated solely or collaboratively *Learning Revolution in the Information Age — Using Hanghzou as an Example, Wen Jiabao's Journals of Geology, A Bright Shared Future, Hangzhou, A Glimpse of Hangzhou, Remembrances of the West Lake, 100 Heroes of China's Bamboo Industry, In Search of the South Song Empire* and *History of Xiling Seal Engravers' Society*.

Li Xue is a translator and English teacher. Li Xue graduated from Shanghai International Studies an University (SISU) with a Master's degree in English Language and Literature in 2006. Since then she has been teaching courses to undergraduates in Zhejiang Gongshang University (ZJSU). As an outstanding and aspirational teacher with high personal standards, she has won teaching awards in the "ZJSU Creative Teaching Competition" in 2017 and the third prize in the "National Micro-course Competition" in 2019.

She has always dedicated her academic focus to translation theories and practice, published over 20 papers and translated works including

The Sword of King Arthur (2005), *Super Sad True Love Story* (2012) and *The Jewels in China's Crown* (2018). She has also presided over many academic projects, including *On the Translation — Introduction of Hongloumeng from the Perspective of Paratext* (2019) and *On the Creative Treason of Translators* (2011).

Disclaimer

The author, Prof. Cao Yang, is solely responsible for all the contents in this book. Anyone claiming copyright for any part of the text/illustrations used in this book is advised to contact ycao55@163.com. The Publisher is not responsible for any potential copyright violation in this book.

Contents

Chapter 1

Introduction

1.1 Reform and Opening-Up: The Most Distinctive Feature in the Contemporary China

As to the term "contemporary era", people tend to have many different definitions. Contemporary China here refers specifically to China since the reform and opening-up. In history, "era" is used to define a relatively long and important period of time, distinctive from its previous times, and is thus time-defining. Therefore, "era" in itself has the connotation of "to replace" and "to update".

China's reform and opening-up is, undoubtedly, time-defining. It is a choice crucial to China's destiny. Hu Jintao noted in the political report of the 17th Congress of the Communist Party of China (CPC) that "the most distinctive feature of the new era is reform and opening-up. From villages to cities, from economic field to other fields, the process of comprehensive reform is unfolding itself irresistibly. From sea coastal areas to river coastal areas, border areas, from eastern region to middle and western region, the door of opening-up has opened with great resolution. The unprecedented great reform and opening-up has largely inspired tens of millions of people's initiatives in transforming a planned economy with intense concentration into a socialist market economy with immense vitality, transforming a closed and semi-closed economy into an all-round open one."[1] *Decision of the CPC Central Committee on Some Major*

[1] Hu Jintao. *To Uphold High the Great Banner of Socialism with Chinese Characteristics and Strive for the New Victory of Building a Well-off Society in an All-round Way — Report on the Seventeenth National Congress of the Communist Party of China.* Beijing: People's Publishing House, 2007, p. 1.

Issues Concerning Comprehensively Deepening the Reform adopted at the third plenary session of the 18th CPC Central Committee further states that "reform and opening-up is a great new revolution by the people of all ethnic groups under the guidance of CPC, and it's the most distinctive feature of the contemporary China. During the 35 years since the third plenary session of the 11th CPC Central Committee, our Party has been determined to carry on reforms on economic system, political system, cultural system, social system, eco-civilization system and party building system with great political courage, constantly expanding opening-up with great resolve, profound change, wide and unprecedented influences and great achievements."[2]

The start of this important historic era is marked by several milestone events. The "big contract", starting from the rural area, initiated the great historic turn on the economic level, whose effect can be described in the saying "one tossed stone stirs up thousands of ripples". The disintegration of the people's commune system under the impact of "big contract" indicates the organizational foundation of planned economy in vast rural areas has been dismantled. In the wake of "villages encircling cities", the focus of reform has gradually changed from rural areas to urban areas, as planned economy has been replaced by market economy.

The great change, or transformation in the contemporary China, is not confined to economic sphere only. It is an all-round change and transformation. Kornai, a renowned Hungarian scholar, believes "transformation is a big, manifold concept, including even some minor transitions. I don't see eye to eye with people who equate transformation as the change from planned economy to market economy. Transformation is not restricted to the economy only, but includes aspects like lifestyles, cultures, political and legal systems, all of which might be synchronized, or be in a cause-and-effect relation with each other."[3] Lang defines transformation as "a controlled, self-fulfilling social and cultural process leading to fundamental changes in politics, law, technology, management, organization and

[2] *Decision of the CPC Central Committee on Several Major Issues Concerning the Comprehensive Deepening of Reform.* Beijing: People's Publishing House, 2013, p. 1.

[3] Kornai, J. *By Force of Thought — Irregular Memoirs of an Intellectual Journey.* Cambridge, Massachusetts and London, England: The MIT Press, 2005.

social structure, which is also reflected on those individuals and groups in the social environment and organizations, i.e., changes in their core values, thinking and behavioral processes."[4] In essence, transformation of contemporary China is a comprehensive revolution in economy, society, politics, culture, even people's values, thinking modes and lifestyles.

The process of transformation is not a universal benefit increase of "Pareto improvement". Reform is essentially a readjustment of people's economic and social interests, which will inevitably bring about new fluctuations in the pattern of social interests. The beneficiaries under the traditional system, especially those who benefited from the "institutionally monopolized gains" endowed by the traditional system, will suffer absolute or relative losses in the course of reform; new interest strata and groups will also bring about new contradictions and conflicts of interests. Social wealth is truly increasing at an unprecedented speed. In the past over 30 years since reform and opening-up, GDP has been growing at a pace of over 9% annually on average. In 2010, the aggregate GDP in China's mainland was RMB39.8 trillion yuan, surpassing Japan and becoming the second largest economy in the world with great improvement in overall national strength. "China's economy now has a global influence and is no longer a 'price taker' in the world economy." "China is no longer a marginal participant. Rather it has entered the central stage of the world economic and financial system."[5] However, at the same time, interest conflicts between different social groups have also increased sharply. For example, individual income disparity marked by Gini coefficient has reached a historic high since the founding of the People's Republic of China (PRC). According to a study by the World Bank, the Gini coefficient in China's mainland was 0.20 in the early 1980s, 0.42 in 1993, 0.437 in 1999 and 0.496 in 2006. By international standards, that above 0.4 is the "Gini coefficient warning line", indicating a large individual income disparity. Besides, according to data provided by the

[4]Lang, R. *The Transformation of Organizations in East Germany and Eastern Europe: Unsolved Questions and Problem Areas for Research*. Munich: Mering Hampp, 1996.

[5]Lin Chonggeng and Spencer, M. *Medium-and-long-term Development and Transformation of China's Economy: Thoughts and Suggestions from an International Perspective*. Beijing: CITIC Press, 2011.

National Bureau of Statistics (NBS),[6] Gini coefficient of China's mainland was 0.491 in 2008, reaching its highest point. Although it later dropped down year by year, it remained above 0.4. In 2013, Gini coefficient was 0.4743. "China has become one of the countries with the most serious income disparity in Asia," Asian Development Bank said in its 2008 report *Emerging Asian Regionalism — Partnership for Shared Prosperity*.

With the rapid growth of national wealth, the country is becoming richer and stronger. However, due to the widening individual income gap and the sharpening of various social contradictions, the individual sense of well-being and index of happiness have not increased accordingly. The "happiness-income myth", or the so-called "Easterlin Paradox" once haunted developed countries such as the United States and Europe, is now emerging in China. More specifically, since the reform and opening-up, the national well-being and happiness index has experienced "rising first and falling later" trajectory, which is not synchronized with the continuous growth of national wealth and national income.[7] Facts both at home and abroad have shown that it is more difficult to continuously improve people's sense of happiness and satisfaction than to continuously raise national income and national wealth. Robert Kennedy once said, "Even if we've managed to eliminate fiscal deficits, we are facing a more challenging task — satisfaction deficits."[8]

Needless to say, contemporary China as a whole is an open, pluralistic society. "We face unprecedented development opportunities as well as risks and challenges." Various interest groups have different reflections on the contemporary China as well as different expectations for the future. Charles Dickens said in his *A Tale of Two Cities*, "It was the best of times,

---

[6] The data of the NBS are different from those of the World Bank. The Gini coefficient data provided by the NBS are: 0.479 in 2003, 0.473 in 2004, 0.485 in 2005, 0.487 in 2006, 0.484 in 2007, 0.491 in 2008, 0.490 in 2009, 0.481 in 2010, 0.477 in 2011, 0.474 in 2012 and 0.473 in 2013.

[7] He Lixin and Pan Chunyang. Understanding China's "Easterlin Paradox": Income Gap, Unequal Opportunities and National Well-being. *The World of Management*, No. 8, 2011, pp. 11–22.

[8] Sandel, M. *Justice: What's the Right Thing to Do*. New York: Farrar, Straus and Giroux, 2010.

The major symbol of the start of modernization is the industrial revolution. Therefore, in early theories, modernization was often equated with industrialization, and a "modernized country" was also known as an "industrialized country". This relatively narrow concept of modernization has brought about drawbacks, the most serious being the "industrialization-only" tendency of some developing countries, which had led to agricultural depression, environmental deterioration and extreme imbalance of economic development. *The Dictionary of Modern Economics*, edited by David W. Pierce, reads: "industrialization refers to the industrialization process of developing countries, which take the development of industry as overall developing strategy. In the early post-war period, and in fact until the early 1960s, many economists believed that industrialization was the optimal way for underdeveloped countries to develop their economies, and many of their governments accepted this assertion and formulated strategies giving priority to industrial development. The result is only a few countries achieved their goals (mainly those implementing export incentive policy), while most countries fell into the distressing economic chaos."[10] Gerald M. Meier, renowned economist of Development Economics, remarked: "Although many underdeveloped countries focused on the sophisticated industrialization in their initial plans, they are now reflecting and reevaluating the role of industrialization." Other scholars, however, have not been confined by the narrow concept. For example, Professor Zhang Peigang, forerunner in Development Economics of China, defined industrialization in his doctoral dissertation at Harvard University in 1945 as "the continuous change of a series of basic production functions", which "can include both industrial development and agricultural reform".[11] Nevertheless, industrialization lays particular stress on the process of economic modernization, so modernization entails

"people's concept on modern times, which has changed with beliefs and are promoted by science, is such as the belief in the ever progressing of knowledge and the ever developing of society and moral improvement."

[10]Pearce, D. W. *The MIT Dictionary of Modern Economics*. Cambridge: MIT Press, 1987.

[11]Zhang Peigang. *Agriculture and Industrialization*. Wuhan: Huazhong University of Science and Technology Press, 2002, pp. 64–65.

industrialization, while industrialization does not necessarily entail modernization, nor can it be equated with modernization.

At the same time, since the process of world modernization originated in Western Europe, the so-called "classical modernization theory" led by early Western scholars defined modernization as "westernization". They believed that the process of modernization of all countries would follow the "unilinear evolution"[12] of the Western developed countries. The so-called "the country that is more developed industrially only shows, to the less developed, the image of its own future." For example, Lerner defines "modernization" in *Encyclopedia of International Social Sciences*, Volume 6 as "the dissemination of systems and values from Western Europe and North America to other parts of the Europe after the 17th century, and to the rest of the world from the 18th to the 20th century." The equation of modernization with "westernization" has brought disastrous consequences in the practice of developing countries: traditional culture and civilization has withered, but modern civilization is not established either. As Marx commented on the British colonial rule over India, "the loss of his old world, with no gain of a new one, imparts a particular kind of melancholy to the present misery of the Hindoo, and separates Hindostan, ruled by Britain, from all its ancient traditions, and from the whole of its past history."[13] People in developing countries have gradually

---

[12]Whether Marx agrees or disagrees with the historical view of "unilinear evolution" is a controversial issue in the academic circle. On the one hand, Marx wrote, "the country that is more developed industrially only shows, to the less developed, the image of its own future." (Marx, Karl. *Capital: A Critique of Political Economy*. Moscow: Progress Publishers, 1956.) On the other hand, Marx criticized Russian populist Mihelovsky for misinterpreting his ideas. Marx said: "He feels himself obliged to metamorphose my historical sketch of the genesis of capitalism in Western Europe into an historico-philosophic theory of the general path imposed by fate upon every people, whatever the historic circumstances in which it finds itself, in order that it may ultimately arrive at the form of economy which will ensure, together with the greatest expansion of the productive powers of social labour, the most complete development of man. But I beg his pardon. (He is both honouring and shaming me too much.)" (Marx, Karl and Engels, Frederick. Letter from Marx to Editor of the Otecestvenniye Zapisky, *Karl Marx Selected Works in Two Volumes*. London: Lawrence and Wishart Limited, 1947.)

[13]Marx, K. The Rule of Britain in India. *Karl Marx Selected Works in Two Volumes*. London: Lawrence and Wishart Limited, 1947.

realized the fallacy of equating modernization with "westernization" in practice and theory, and thus have started the exploration and practice of diversity of modernization adhering to their respective national conditions.

In China, "since the defeat of the Opium War in 1840, Chinese pioneers sought truth from the western countries with great efforts".[14] So China's early exploration on modernization followed the "westernization" road. Some radical scholars followed Japan's example of "leaving Asia for Europe" and advocated "total westernization". However, "the master always bullies his disciples". "Westernization" cannot help China realize modernization, for neither can it "make the people rich and the country strong", nor can it "make the country rich and the army strong." Failures and setbacks have taught us a good lesson, and Chinese people, under the leadership of CPC, have taken a difficult and exploring road to modernization with Chinese characteristics since the beginning of the 20th century. In this sense, after the reform and opening-up, contemporary China has entered a milestone era, inheriting the past and ushering in the future, forging ahead on the long road of modernization with Chinese characteristics. President Xi Jinping believes: "To realize the goal of building a well-off society in an all-round way, building a prosperous, strong, democratic, civilized and harmonious socialist modern country, and realizing the Chinese dream of the great rejuvenation of the Chinese nation are to prosper and strengthen the country, to revitalize the nation, and to increase people's sense of happiness, which deeply reflects not only the ideals of the Chinese people today, but also the glorious tradition of the unremitting struggle of our predecessors."[15]

Diverse Roads or Diverse Modernizations?

As the English saying goes, all roads lead to Rome. There is only one Rome, but the roads to get there are diverse. The same can be said of modernization.

---

[14]Mao Zedong. On People's Democratic Dictatorship. *Selected Works of Mao Zedong*, Vol. 4. Beijing: People's Publishing House, 1991, p. 1469.

[15]Xi Jinping. "Speech at the First Session of the Twelfth National People's Congress." *People's Daily*, March 17, 2013.

Diverse modernization means that modernization itself is pluralistic, which means it is uncertain. In other words, different people have different Romes in their minds, and there are numerous ways to reach there.

I advocate diverse roads of modernization, but I don't agree with its various interpretations, for it may lead to the vulgarization or secularization of modernization. Those run counter to the essence of modernization may be labeled as modernization, just like the various and even bizarre modernizations we see in the world today.

Modernization, after all, is not a dough that can be kneaded at will. It has a basic definition, connotation, common values and ideals of human civilization, for example, the development of science and technology, the abundance of social wealth, a sound legal system, democratic politics and social harmony, and of course the most important of all, "the full and free development of man".

1.3 What Is the Intrinsic Quality of Modernization?

What is the intrinsic quality of modernization? Or, in other words, why do we have to achieve it?

Modernization is not about machinery, equipment, high-rise buildings, GDP, GNP or material wealth. Industrialization, urbanization and high-tech are only the external forms of modernization rather than the essence of it. Meanwhile, we are not modernizing for the sake of modernization itself. Amartya Sen, the 1998 Nobel Prize winner in economics, known as "the Conscience and the Mother Teresa of Economics", criticized the "narrow view of development"[16] in which GNP, personal income increase, industrialization and even modernization are regarded as the ultimate goal of development in his masterpiece Development as Liberty. He believes that the intrinsic quality of development is expanding people's substantive freedom. Undoubtedly, GDP, GNP, material wealth, per capita income, industrialization, urbanization and so on are all important in the process of modernization, but they are important only because they provide basic material guarantee for expanding people's substantive freedom. "Broadly

[16]"The narrow view of development believes development means the growth of gross national product (GNP), the increase of personal income, industrialization, technological progress, or social modernization, etc." (Sen, A. *Development as Freedom*. Palatine: Anchor Books, 2000.)

speaking, development is increasingly seen as the expanding of freedom in choice and action."[17]

In my opinion, the ultimate value and goal of modernization we are pursuing should be what Marx and Engels called "the full and free development of man". The essential meaning of modernization is the process of expanding "the full and free development of man". It should be noted that "man" here not only refers to "each" but also to "all". In the words of Marx and Engels, "the free development of each is the condition for the free development of all".[18] At the same time, only "each" get "full and free development", "full and free development" of "each" can be effectively guaranteed and sustained. This is because as long as there are people, though small in number, deprived of the opportunity of "full and free development" in the society, no one can guarantee he himself or his descendants would not be deprived of the opportunities. "Only by emancipating the whole human mankind can the proletariat finally emancipate himself", which embodies not only Marx's broad humanistic sentiments, but also the essence of Marx's human liberation and human liberty.

In Marx's Theory of Human Development, "Free" Development is More Essential and Crucial than "Full" Development

If we try to summarize Marx's theory on "human development" in a comprehensive, complete and accurate way, it should be "the full and free development of man". The "man" here refers to not only "each" but also "all", though first of all it is "each". In fact, without individual freedom, we cannot talk about the freedom of mankind, nor about the so-called freedom of the society as a whole. This is just as Marx said: "If each man is not liberated, the whole society cannot be liberated."

Obviously, Marx's theory of "human development" has two basic qualifiers: one is "free" and the other is "full". Comparatively speaking, which one is of an essential meaning? Which one is more important? I think it's "free" rather than "full".

First, from the perspective of teleology, "free" is of a higher level than "full". To some extent, full development is for the sake of free development, or as Amartya Sen put it, to enhance people's capability to realize substantive freedom. Perhaps, some people may wonder if we can put it reversely — free development is for the sake of full development?

[17]Meier, G. and Stiglitz, J. eds. *Frontiers of Development Economics: The Future in Perspective*. Oxford: Oxford University Press, 2000.

[18]Marx, K. and Engels, F. Manifesto of the Communist Party. *Karl Marx Selected Works in Two Volumes*. London: Lawrence and Wishart Limited, 1947.

My answer is definitely no. In Marx's theoretical system, to achieve each and all's freedom is the ultimate goal of human civilization development, but he's never put full development to that superiority. Secondly, free development is the basic premise of full development (it should be noted that "basic premise" does not mean free development serves for full development.) Marx' full development, as is mainly opposed to the involuntary old-style division of labor, leads to the "alienation" of labor. Marx believed: "as long as man remains in natural society, that is, as long as a cleavage exists between the particular and the common interest, as long, therefore, as activity is not voluntarily, but naturally, divided, man's own deed becomes an alien power opposed to him."[19] How can we achieve full development, which, in Marx' opinion, means each can become accomplished in any branch he wishes, society regulates the general production and thus makes it possible for me to do one thing today and another tomorrow.[20] It is opposite to the abnormal, partial development bound by old-fashioned division of labor. Marx believes that one of the major ways is to increase man's free time gradually. He stressed, "the time which society is bound to devote to material production is shorter, and as a consequence, the time at its disposal for the free development, intellectual and social, of the individual is greater in proportion "[21] In other words, only when people can dispose of their own time and develop themselves freely can the so-called full development be realized.

There is a theoretical tendency in China that most articles only explore "full development" of human beings, but intentionally or unintentionally avoid "free development", or replace "full and free development of man" with "full development of man" when talking about Marx's theory of human development. What's the reason behind? The fundamental reason lies in the fear of "freedom" in Chinese academia for a long time. It should be said that the ultimate goal and theoretical essence of Marxist social revolution is to form the real basis of a higher form of society, a society in which the full and free development of every individual forms the ruling principle. Full,[22] or in other words, to set up "community of freemen". From the perspective of ultimate goal, all Marxist doctrines can be understood as "the doctrine of liberating the whole mankind". From the perspective of word origin, "liberation" and "liberty" are cognate. Unfortunately, this Marxist thought has been forgotten or even misinterpreted intentionally or unintentionally for quite a long time. At the stage when the proletariat were trying to seize power, it is understandable and urgent that people put more emphasis on "class" and "class struggle". At the early stage of socialist construction, people had no existing socialist model to follow. It was also hard to avoid regarding public ownership and planned economy as the essential characteristics of socialism in the exploratory period. However, the essential feature of

[19] Marx, K. and Engels, F. *German Ideology*. Moscow: Progress Publishers, 1956.
[20] *Ibid.*, 1968.
[21] Marx, K. *Economic Manuscripts of 1857–1858*. Moscow: Progress Publishers, 1959.
[22] Marx, K. *Capital: A Critique of Political Economy*. Moscow: Progress Publishers, 1956.

communism is, after all, the "full and free development of man" rather than the long-term "class struggle" between "one class" and "the other", or the planned economy that restricts individual autonomy and liberty, or controls everything by the state administration. "The community of freemen" highlights first "free" and then "community". The recent criticism of the "over-debate on community of freemen" or "unusual enthusiasm on community of freemen" shows exactly how the fine thoughts of the community of freemen have been neglected, even distorted for such a long time. In some people's view, emphasizing "man's freedom" means "capitalist liberalization". Professor Du Guang of the Party School of CPC Central Committee once remarked that "Marxist theory of freedom is the most urgently needed theory in our society at present. A key fact is that people generally harbor a deep fear for "anti-liberalization". Even in the famous song *Unity is Power* which has been popular for over half a century, "forge ahead towards freedom" has been changed to "forge ahead towards victory". It can be seen how serious this "fear of freedom" is.

Perhaps there is another reason why "full and free development of man" was replaced by "full development of man". In the traditional concept of political economy, "full development" seems to deny the division of labor, specialization and therefore, the market economy. However, Marx' "full development" in its original sense denies only the division of labor out of compulsion, but not the division of labor out of volition, that is, the division of labor based on "liberty". In fact, "full development" does not mean that people do everything, or labor division, social division and production specialization will perish. The essence of "full development" is that people can freely engage in the work that they want to. It also implies people can freely reject the work that they do not want to, which, obviously includes division of labor and specialization. On a deeper level, "full development" is only a by-product of "free development". We must not put the cart before the horse, replacing the higher level of "free development" with "full development".

Excerpt from Cao Yang's "The Role and Value of 'Freedom' in Marx' 'Human Development' Theory",

Economic Dynamics, No. 1, 2012

The scientific "people-oriented" development concept, put forward by the CPC Central Committee, has inherited and developed the essence of Marx' human liberation and human liberty. First of all, the fundamental goal of "people-oriented" development must be defined as "full and free development of man". It has scientifically answered the question of "for whom" development is, or, "for whom" modernization actually is. Secondly, "people-oriented" concept has also clearly defined the fundamental driving force of development, i.e., development must rely on the initiative and creativity of the broad masses of the people. It has scientifically answered the question of "by whom" development should be promoted, i.e., "by whom" modernization should be promoted. "People" is not only the ultimate purpose, but also the fundamental motivation of development. Only the unity of "for whom" and "by whom" can constitute the complete content of "people-oriented" concept. As is noted in *The Political Report of the Eighteenth Congress of CPC*, "people-oriented" concept is the core of the in-depth implementation of the scientific outlook on development. Achieving, maintaining and developing the fundamental interests of the overwhelming majority of people is the starting point and destination of all the work of the Party and the state. In short, development is for people, by the people and the achievements should be shared among people.

The "Easterlin Paradox" that the growth of national wealth is not synchronized with the growth of National Happiness Index (NHI) in contemporary China is due to the fact that China's economic development over the past three decades has deviated from the fundamental purpose of the scientific people-oriented concept to some extent. The political achievement's view which overstresses GDP has blurred our developing goals. Fundamental development goals like people's sense of well-being, NHI, the full and free development of each as well as of all, unfortunately, have been overshadowed and replaced by the growth rate of GDP, the index of total industrial output value and the high-rise buildings of urbanization. The practice of development has repeatedly shown that,[23] if we do not start from the fundamental goal of the development of freedom and

[23]As to the harm of GDP-only concept, some foreign experts also have profound insights. For example, Robert Kennedy said in his 1968 campaign for the Democratic presidential candidate: "At present, our annual gross national product is over $800 billion. However, it includes air pollution, cigarette advertising and rescue costs for cleaning up highway accidents. It includes the special locks we use to lock doors, windows and prisons where burglars are locked up. It includes the destruction of mahogany and the natural miracles lost in the upheaval. It includes naphtha bombs and nuclear warheads, police armored vehicles used to suppress urban riots. It also includes... television programs that glorify violence in order to sell toys to our children." (Sandel, M. *Justice: What's the Right Thing to Do*. New York: Farrar, Straus and Giroux, 2010.)

happiness of "people" (all the people, not a minority group), behind the rapid growth of "GDP" may lurk the extreme disparity of individual income, the predatory exploitation of resources and the high consumption and pollution.

It is true that, unlike GDP, GNP and industrial gross output value, the sense of happiness, NHI and the full and free development of every man and the whole mankind are hard to quantify accurately. Therefore, in a so-called mainstream economics framework which is overstressing "mathematics" and "models", in a government administrative model that is boasting of "digital management", the essence of development can easily be marginalized in the name of prioritization, or easily be replaced by some "instrumental" figures. However, as Basu said, "a vaguely defined but broadly inclusive goal is always better than one that is rigidly defined but morally ungrounded."[24]

Under the guidance of "people-oriented" scientific concept of development, our modernization research and practice should focus on people rather than GDP, avoiding mistakes like "seeing things but not people". Ancient Chinese philosophers emphasized that "man is the most precious in the heaven and earth" and that man is superior to thing. Following this thread of thinking, it is safe to say that the so-called issue of "agriculture, countryside and peasants" is essentially the issue of peasants. It is an issue of man. Therefore, agricultural modernization and rural modernization must revolve around peasants, which is the entity and motive force of development. However, we cannot focus our research on the isolated, "atomized" individuals, because after all, man is a social being, a "real historical man" (Marx). Without the macro-environment of economy and society, human beings are just "high-level animals". Even within the framework of western mainstream economics, Mark Grannovetter remarked that rational "economic man" is not "an individual in a vacuum", and when making maximization decisions he will inevitably be influenced by the social network in which he is "embedded" in.[25]

---

[24]Meier, G. and Stiglitz, J. eds. *Frontiers of Development Economics: The Future in Perspective*. Oxford: Oxford University Press, 2000.

[25]Granovetter, M. Economic Action and Social Structure: The Problem of Embeddedness. *The American Journal of Sociology*, Vol. 91, No. 3 (1985), pp. 481–510.

Therefore, "people-oriented" concept is a suitable perspective for the study of modernization process of agriculture, rural modernization process, the modernization process of peasants and the modernization of agricultural production organizations, for agricultural production organization is the carrier and basic level for peasants to carry out various economic and social activities, which connects with a single "peasant" as an "ego" at one end, and a group of "peasants" as a "bigger ego" (us) at the other.

1.4 Agriculture: From Tradition to Modernization

With regard to agriculture, the definition in *Ci Hai* is "the social production sector that utilizes the living functions of plants and animals to obtain agricultural products through man's cultivation". Since "food is the rule of the people" and "the production of means of subsistence is the very first condition of their (direct producers') existence and of all production in general",[26] agriculture is the most ancient and important basic industry in human society. Other industries and sectors of social production have been separated from agriculture successively. It should be noted that early agriculture itself is a multi-functional entity. Agriculture is not only an industry but also a culture, a way of production and life. The root of the word "agriculture" in English is "culture". On the one hand, from the perspective of word formation, agriculture is the culture of land (soil, earth). In ancient China, it was called "*she ji*", "*she*" was "God of Earth" and "*ji*" was "God of Grain", vividly illustrating agriculture was the foundation of a nation, and why traditional culture was also called "farming culture". On the other hand, ancient agriculture, highly integrated with nature, not only benefited from, but also was controlled by, natural forces. From a positive perspective, it was "harmony between man and nature", human activities were compatible with nature and production was integrated with ecology and life. From a negative perspective, it was "feeding on heaven", human beings becoming slaves of nature. All earlier modes of production were essentially

[26] Marx, K. *Capital: A Critique of Political Economy. Op. cit.*

conservative.[27] In Schultz's words, "traditional agriculture should be regarded as a special type of economic equilibrium",[28] with the following characteristics: (1) the technological condition remained unchanged for a long time; (2) if factors of production were used as sources of income, the motivation to acquire and hold such factors of production would remain unchanged for a long time; (3) due to the above reasons, the supply and demand of traditional factors of production were also in a stagnant equilibrium for a long time. Therefore, the land productivity and labor productivity were very low, the agricultural residue was sparse, most of the social labor force were engaged in agriculture, but the increase of food was still often unable to catch up with the growth of population and therefore human society had long been trapped in the so-called "Malthus trap".

Industrialization originated in the West promoted social division of labor and industrial differentiation, while modern science and technology liberated agriculture from the rigid constraints of nature and improved social productivity, including agricultural productivity. The great progress of agricultural production in industrial society fundamentally liberated mankind from "Malthusian Trap" in which population grew at a geometric level while means of subsistence, with grain as its major part, grew at an arithmetic level. Meanwhile, it brought unprecedented increase in agricultural labor productivity, thus greatly reducing agricultural and rural population and accelerating the urbanization process. However, too busily engaged in conquering the nature, man has been revenged for neglecting the nature, which has caused a series of new contradictions and problems: the distinctive and colorful original ecology of agriculture has gradually disappeared in the global landscape; the healthy connections between agriculture and nature, environment and ecology have been cut off. Marx said capitalist production "on the one hand concentrates the historical motive power of society; on the other hand, it disturbs the circulation of matter between man and the soil... it therefore violates the conditions

[27] *Ibid.*

[28] Schultz, T. W. *Transforming Traditional Agriculture.* Chicago: University of Chicago Press, 1983.

necessary to lasting fertility of the soil."[29] In addition, industrialization transforms agriculture and industrializes its production, but the originally multi-functional agriculture is gradually rendered single-functional and narrow-scoped. Agriculture has become in a narrow sense "planting + aquaculture", even a simple "agricultural workshop" within the framework of "big industry". Due to the misguidance of "industrialization only" strategy, the function of agriculture has been passively affiliated to industrialization for quite a long time. It seems that the only purpose of agriculture is to provide food, raw materials, labor, market, capital and foreign exchange for industrialization.[30]

The marginalization of agriculture and its being passively affiliated to industrialization have brought about the decline in the status of agriculture, for it has been regarded as an inevitable disadvantaged industry in modern industrialized society for quite a long time. However, agriculture is the foundation of the whole national economy. "The production of means of subsistence is the very first condition of their (direct producers') existence and of all production in general."[31] Therefore, it is unimaginable and unsustainable for modern society to operate without a strong modern agriculture as its solid foundation.

Traditional Agriculture, Modern Agriculture and "Malthusian Trap"

At the end of 18th century and the beginning of 19th century, renowned British economist Thomas Robert Malthus put forward his famous population theory, in which he notes there is a basic trend in the growth of human population and means of subsistence, i.e., food-based means of subsistence only increases in an arithmetic progression, while population increases in a geometric progression. Therefore, in order to maintain the balance between means of subsistence and human population, we can only rely on the so-called "positive checks" (increase in deaths) such as war and plague, or "negative checks" (decrease in

[29] Marx, K. *Capital: A Critique of Political Economy. Op. cit.*

[30] "As Lewis told us, at first, the main task of the agricultural sector was to provide resources for industrialization — to release labor, accumulate and transfer capital and earn foreign exchange." (Adelman, Alma. Misunderstandings in Development Theory and Their Implications for Policy, Meier, G. and Stiglitz, J. eds. *Frontiers of Development Economics: The Future in Perspective*. Oxford: Oxford University Press, 2000.)

[31] Marx, K. *Capital: A Critique of Political Economy. Op. cit.*

fertilities) such as moral restraint (abstinence) and late marriage. Undoubtedly, this is a horrible and pessimistic perspective of human society.

Although Malthus' theory on demography was criticized for a long time in China, the trend he described did exist in the traditional agricultural society. In traditional agricultural society, due to the stagnation of technology, the growth of food, especially grain, was very slow on the whole, truly in an arithmetic progression; while the growth of human population was relatively fast due to many reasons of economy, culture, society and technology. Therefore, in the traditional agricultural society, hunger, famine, war and riot recurred in the human history. Marx once argued that "the reform of agriculture, and hence the question of property based on it, is the alpha and omega of the coming upheaval. Without that, Father Malthus will turn out to be right."[32] Obviously, the agriculture Marx referred here was traditional agriculture. From this we can see that Marx did not totally deny Malthusian Theory. Mabel Ping-Hua Lee, Chinese-American scholar, wrote in his English edition of *History of China's Economy* that the history of traditional agricultural China was a strong proof of Malthusian Theory.[33]

After the Industrial Revolution, the rapid development of science and technology, modern agriculture and the change in people's mode of production and lifestyle, especially the change in the concept of reproduction, have unchained us from "Malthusian Trap" on the whole, and we have even seen the so-called "anti-Malthusian trend" in which the means of subsistence such as food increase in a geometric progression, while human population increases in an arithmetic progression, even zero growth and negative growth have emerged in some countries. So has mankind ever been got rid of famine and "Malthus trap"? Perhaps not. According to *Brief Statistics on World Population 1979* by Census Bureau of the United States, at the end of the 1960s, 56 developing countries had a faster population growth than food growth; by the 1970s, the number of such countries had increased to 69. In 2008, a report by Food and Agriculture Organization of the United Nations (FAO) remarked that 37 countries in the world were facing a food crisis, and some countries in Asia, Africa and Latin America were experiencing widespread unrest because of food shortages.

What is the reason that modern society still lingers in the shadow of "Malthusian Trap"? It is not because of the lack of technological means to increase food production, nor the lack of land resources, but the deviation of institutional arrangements in today's world. Amartya Sen offers another explanation from the perspective of relation between democracy and famine, in which he believes in modern democratic countries, large-scale famine is unlikely to occur.[34] Another solution is China's rural household contract system, which has basically solved the problem of food and clothing.

---

[32] Marx, K. Letters of Marx to Engels (August 14, 1851). *Karl Marx & Frederick Engels: Collected Works*. Intl Pub Co. Inc, 1996.

[33] Mabel Ping-Hua Lee. *The Economic History of China*. New York: AMS Press, 1969.

[34] Sen, A. *Development as Freedom*. Palatine: Anchor Books, 2000.

1.5 Division of Labor and Integration: The Longitudinal View Based on the Whole Industrial Chain of Modern Agriculture

What is modern agriculture? *Policy on China's Agricultural Science and Technology*, issued jointly by 10 commissions and ministries including State Science and Technology Commission and the Ministry of Agriculture in 1998, divides the connotation of modern agriculture into three aspects: pre-production aspect, including agricultural machinery, fertilizer, water conservancy, pesticides, plastic film, etc.; mid-production aspect, including planting (including seed industry), forestry and animal husbandry (including feed production) and aquatic industry; post-production aspect, including processing, storage, transportation, marketing, import and export trade technology of agricultural products, etc. We can see from above that modern agriculture is no longer confined to the traditional agricultural production sectors such as planting and breeding, and also includes secondary industry like means of production industry and processing industry, as well as the tertiary industry like transportation, technology and information services. It means modern agriculture has expanded from the simple primary industry to the secondary and the tertiary industry, forming a longitudinal and closely linked industrial system or industry chain with agricultural products as the core.

Historically, early agriculture, with self-sufficient natural economy as the entity, had a very short production-consumption chain, processing "from field to table". Most of the agricultural products were self-produced and self-consumed, which could be directly served "from field to table" with very simple household processing. A small number of agricultural surplus products were mainly sold through market, and the relatively simple processing was mainly carried out by manual workshops, and its transportation was not complicated. At the same time, the vast majority of the means of production, like seeds, farm manure and natural enemies for pests, were supplied by nature or peasants' households. Such agricultural production tools as hoes, ploughs, harrows and water wheels were provided by rural handicraft industry, which was essentially dependent on agriculture. Therefore, strictly speaking, there was no agricultural industry chain based on the deepening of internal division of labor in early natural economy agriculture. In other words, agriculture was an industry, but it had not formed an industrial system.

In the era of industrialization, the commercialization and marketization of agricultural products had accelerated, promoting the division of labor within agriculture. Agricultural machinery, fertilizers, pesticides, film, seeds, feed, processing of agricultural products, storage and transportation, sales, even agricultural technology and information had developed into independent sectors successively. From field to table, there were many links to go through, which means that the industrial chain of agriculture was growing.

The extension of agricultural industrial chain caused by the deepening of internal division of labor had greatly improved the efficiency of agricultural production and changed the structure of production and employment in which the number of direct producers in the mid-production field was decreasing, while the number of indirect producers in the secondary and tertiary sectors before and after production had increased substantially. As Marx has stressed, "'that the number of labourers employed' is not 'in proportion to the wealth of the state', that relatively more workers are employed in an industrially undeveloped country than in one which is industrially developed... Arts are cultivated, and civilization is extended."[35] For example, the current direct producers of agriculture in the United States are about 2% of the total labor force, but the indirect producers related to agriculture account for nearly 15%.[36]

It should be emphasized that the deepening of the division of labor within agriculture, and the extension of the agricultural industry chain have also made the division and distribution of agricultural surplus, or agricultural profits, among departments and stakeholders more and more complex. The famous "smile curve theory", put forward by Shi Zhenrong,

---

[35]Marx, K. *Theories of Surplus-Value*. Firebird Pubns, 1971.

[36]Agriculture and related industries in the United States are collectively referred to as the food and fiber system. According information (Xuan Xingyun and Wang Chunfa. *Perspective of Agricultural Modernization in Western Countries,* 1998), in 1990s, the number of employers in American agriculture and related industries was 23,200,000, of which only 3,200,000 were directly engaged in agricultural production, while the remaining 20,000,000 were employed in agricultural services and other related industries.

founder of Taiwan Acer Group, compares the industrial chain to a curve of a smiling mouth with both ends up. We can see from the curve the added value is more reflected in the two ends of the industrial chain and less in the middle (see Figure 1.1). If we apply the curve to the agricultural industry chain, the two ends are prior- and post-production industry, while the middle represents mid-production industry. As direct producers, most peasants are in the field of production, their added value being the lowest, and often at a disadvantage in the division of agricultural profits. It means that peasants, as direct producers of agriculture, have less income than employees in the secondary and tertiary industries of indirect producers of agriculture, and agricultural surplus in the mid-production area is far less than that in the prior and post production areas. As some scholars have said, "if we calculate the comprehensive benefits of the industry from basic production to final consumption, agriculture is still one of the most promising and profitable industries."[37] The so-called "disadvantaged agriculture" mainly refers to the mid-production area (which is nevertheless regarded as the main part of agriculture), i.e., the comparative benefits of "mid-production" agriculture is low, which brings about the low comparative benefits of producers (peasants).

In order to offset the "disadvantageous" status of "mid-production" agriculture and improve the income level of direct producers (peasants), it is necessary to carry out "integration of interests" on the basis of the deepening of internal labor division, so that agricultural surplus and comprehensive benefits can be shared rationally within the three areas. The management and operation of agricultural industry chain, originated in the United States in the 1950s, is such a kind of innovation on the integration of interests, promoting the longitudinal integration and development of modern whole industry chain.

The management and operation of the agricultural industry chain, adhering to call of modern agriculture for "division" and "integration", based on the principle of market and meanwhile transcending it, is to integrate pre-production, mid-production and post-production industry into an organic "community of interests" with the aim to obtaining and

[37] *Ibid.*

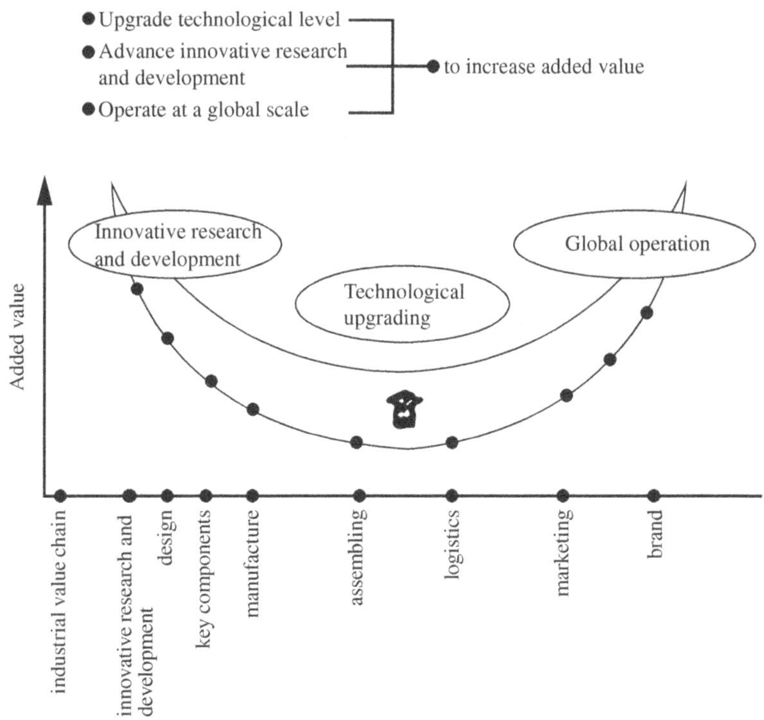

Figure 1.1. Smile curve theory

sharing maximum added value of agricultural products. The core elements here are: (1) maximizing the added value; (2) sharing benefits.

How to maximize the added value? First, we need to extend agriculture industrial chain to extend agriculture value chain. To extend industrial chain is to extend the processing chain instead of the circulating chain of agricultural products, to increase the proportion of intensive processing and deep processing so as to maximize the added value. In modern society, with the liberation of women and the increase of leisure time, it is possible and necessary to extend industrial chain to the traditional family food processing and consumption process. Such examples include ready-to-eat foods, semi-finished products, pre-packed clean vegetables, etc. According to *The 11th Five-Year Development Program of the National Food Industry*, China is rich in food resources, the output of agricultural products such as grain, oil, vegetables, fruits, meat and aquatic products ranks first in the world, but the degree of food processing and value adding is relatively low. In terms of processing capacity, the proportion of processed food in consumer food in China is only 30%, far below the level of 60–80% in developed countries. Among them, our processed vegetables account for only 30%, compared with over 90% in developed countries such as the EU, the United States and Japan. Our processed citrus is only about 10%, compared with over 70% in the United States and Brazil. China's citrus processing capacity is only about 10%, while the United States and Brazil reach more than 70%. Our meat factory slaughter rate only accounts for about 25% of the market turnover, meat products account for only 11%, while the European Union, the United States, Japan and other developed countries have reached full factory slaughter rate, meat products account for 50%. In terms of output value, in 2005, the ratio of gross output value of food industry to total output value of agriculture in China was only 0.5:1, compared with 2.0–3.7:1 in developed countries.

Second, maximizing the added value can also increase the breadth of the agricultural industry chain, i.e., to improve the level of comprehensive utilization, and to form an efficient and sustainable circular economy. Circular economy is a kind of economic development mode based on material recycling and comprehensive utilization. Compared with the traditional one-way linear mode of "resources-agricultural products-waste discharge", circular economy forms a feedback process of "resources-agricultural products-renewable resources", which also means the agricultural industry chain will become a circular industry chain with broader connotation, and a multi-channel industrial link will be established. Practice has shown that agricultural circular economy is conducive not only to maximizing the added value but also to the ecology and environment of the whole society, as well as improving peasants' way of production and lifestyle. Agricultural circular economy in a narrow sense mainly refers to the recycling of resources in agriculture, forestry, animal husbandry and fishery, like the internal recycling mode of "rice-vegetable-fish (shrimp)-duck", external recycling mode between planting and breeding of "pig (feces)-biogas (fertilizer)-corn (feed)". Agricultural circular economy in a wider sense refers to the recycling of resources in the primary, secondary and tertiary industry related to agriculture, i.e., the recycling within the whole agricultural industry system. The large agricultural circular economy of Daohuaxiang Group in Yichang, Hubei Province in Case 1–1, is a five-level circular industrial chain of "green planting-food processing-total mixed feed-scale farming-organic fertilizer".

[Case 1.1] "Big Agriculture" Circular Economy of Daohuaxiang Group, Yichang, Hubei Province

Daohuaxiang Group, located in Longquan Town, Yichang City, Hubei Province, is a National Key Leading firm of agricultural industrialization and the first batch of demonstration firms of processing industry in agricultural product of China. It is also the first firm of over RMB10 billion yuan in the "Four Batches" project of agricultural product processing industry in Hubei Province and the pilot firm of circular economy in Hubei Province.

With the view of "big agriculture" and core values of green ecology, the Group has constructed a new "five-level circular industrial chain" of green planting-food processing-total mixed feed-scale farming-organic fertilizer. The "five-level recycling industry chain" has the planting industry (corn, rice, konjac, sweet potatoes, etc.) as the input end, liquor, corn pulp, konjac food, edible alcohol, ethanol made through intensive processing during which added value is also increased. Waste materials such as distiller's grains, corn sticks, straw, potato dregs are processed into complete mixed feed for milk (vegetable) ox, pigs and other household uses like raising chickens, ducks, fish; the manure of livestock is recycled to make organic fertilizer, and sold to peasants for green agriculture planting, so that a complete circular economy chain of agricultural industrialization featuring the development of "green and safe food" is formed.

"Big agriculture" circular economy not only prospers Daohuaxiang Group but also drives the large-scale planting, specialized production and ecological development of local agriculture. The operation mode of "the Group + base + peasant household" has greatly increased peasants' income. Meanwhile, Longquan Town, where Daohuaxiang Group is located, used to be a backward village with a population of fewer than 1,000, but now it has become a modern town with over 10,000 permanent residents and perfect infrastructure of schools, hospitals, supermarkets and hotels.

Field investigation by the author and relevant information provided by Daohuaxiang Group.

Compared with maximizing the added value of agriculture, a more challenging problem perhaps is how to share benefits among direct and indirect producers of agriculture, i.e., all stakeholders in the agricultural industry system. It is closely related to the theme of the book, namely, the organizational form and structure of agricultural production and its corresponding benefit distribution mechanism, which will be discussed in later chapters of the book.

1.6 Function and System: The Lateral View Based on Versatility of Modern Agriculture

From the longitudinal point of view, modern agriculture is an integrated industrial system (agricultural industry chain) with agricultural products as the core, while from the lateral point of view, it is a multi-functional broad-sense agriculture. Agricultural versatility means that agriculture has not only economic functions but also ecological, social and cultural functions, which, in a sense, is a return and affirmation of the ancient systematic agriculture (agriculture is not only an industry but also a culture, a mode of production and life) at a higher level, a new understanding and orientation of agriculture under the new historical conditions.

In the final analysis, the versatility of agriculture is decided by the increasing diversity of demand on agriculture in the modern society. With the development of social economy, people's demand on quality of life is not limited to the satisfaction of material wealth but also the satisfaction of intangible wealth. People need a quiet environment, fresh air and pluralistic culture. Urban residents want to have a different experience of rural life. Therefore, the systemic function of agriculture, especially the non-economic function, is becoming more and more important. In March 1998, the United Nations Organization for Economic Cooperation and Development (UNOECD) states in the communique of the Conference of Ministers of Agriculture that agriculture has a wider range of functions besides providing agricultural products, and it also outlines the versatility of agriculture: "agricultural activities, going beyond the basic function of providing food and fibre, aim at creating a landscape, a favorable environment for land conservation, sustainable management of renewable natural resources and the protection of biodiversity." In September 1999, the Food and Agriculture Organization (FAO) of the United Nations remarked at the International Conference on the Multifunctional Characteristics of Agriculture and Land that the basic function of agriculture is to provide food and raw materials for society, but in the context of sustainable rural development, agriculture has multiple objectives and functions in economic, environmental, social and cultural aspects. In 2007, *Opinions of the CPC Central Committee and the State Council on Actively Developing Modern Agriculture and Solidly Promoting the Construction of a New Socialist Countryside* stressed: "Agriculture has functions of not only food supply, but also raw material supply, employment, income increase, ecological protection, sightseeing, leisure, and cultural inheritance, etc.," from which we can see in addition to providing agricultural products, peasants' employment and salary, modern agriculture in a broad sense has many more functions, such as regulating climate, protecting and improving environment,[38] maintaining ecological balance and biodiversity, sightseeing and leisure, maintaining the original rural lifestyle, preserving the rural cultural diversity heritage and inheriting traditional history and culture.

From the perspective of versatility of contemporary agriculture, modern agriculture is no longer confined to traditional planting and aquaculture. It includes not only pre-production, mid-production and post-production services and processing industries in the agricultural industry chain but also many new agricultural forms. For example, creative agriculture, ecological agriculture, circular agriculture, carbon sequestration agriculture, leisure agriculture, tourism agriculture and so on. Therefore, the modern agricultural production organization in this book includes all kinds of micro-economic organizations which are adapted to versatility of agriculture (see Table 1.1).

New Agricultural Forms Rising Globally

Creative agriculture is not only an economic activity but also a high degree of agricultural civilization, with its goal to endow agriculture with rich cultural connotation and

---

[38] *World Development Report 2008: Agriculture for Development* by the World Bank states that "Agriculture is using (often abusing) natural resources, which has both positive and negative impact on the environment. Agriculture is currently the largest user of water resources, which leads to water shortage. To a considerable extent, agriculture has initiated groundwater depletion, agricultural chemical pollution, soil fertility decline and global climate change (agricultural greenhouse gas emissions account for 30% of the total). But agriculture has also fulfilled environmental functions through carbon sequestration, watershed management and biodiversity conservation."

Table 1.1. Functions of agricultural versatility in different areas

Environmental function	Social function	Food safety function	Economic function	Cultural function
Global				
Maintain ecological environment	Stabilize society	Ensure global food safety	Enhance economic growth	Promote cultural diversity
Alleviate climate change	Eliminate poverty		Eliminate poverty	
Maintain biological diversity				
Region/country				
Maintain ecological environment	Reduce the side effects of blind rural population flow to cities	Guarantee food supply	Guarantee work force employment	Preserve cultural tradition
Conserve water and soil	Guarantee alternative social welfare	National food safety	Economic buffer	Unique cultural characteristics
Maintain biological diversity	Form social capital	Food hygiene and safety		Reflection on the role of agriculture
Maintain air quality				
Local				

Maintain ecological environment	Stabilize rural community through agriculture and rural employment	Regional and farmer food safety	Employment influence on the secondary and tertiary industry	Develop tourism through landscape and culture
Conserve water and soil	Family value and influences on members of different genders			Original knowledge, tradition and technology
Maintain biological diversity				
Discharge and manage pollution				

Source: Ni Hongxing. *Non-Trade Concerns and Agricultural Trade Liberalization*. Beijing: China Agricultural University Press, 2003.

creativity so that consumers can experience and feel the wonder and joy of it. Creative agriculture has given agricultural production and products more emotional and cultural connotations: the beauty of color, shape, taste, quality, aesthetics and soul. At the same time, creative agriculture also creates "intelligent agriculture" and "happy agriculture", which helps make the countryside a beautiful, individualized, landscape-and-tourism-oriented place so as to attract tourists to experience rural life, return to nature, and create a new lifestyle of green civilization. This new characteristic agriculture, which integrates scientific, technological and cultural elements into agricultural production, further expands agricultural functions and enhances agricultural added value. It initiated in developed countries in the late 1990s and has achieved remarkable results, especially countries like the Netherlands, Germany, the United Kingdom and some other European countries.

Tourism agriculture, also known as "leisure agriculture", is a type of comprehensive agriculture, in which tourists are not only provided with accommodation, leisure and recreation, but also encouraged to go sightseeing, pick fruits, experience farming and rural life, as well as enjoy pastoral pleasure. Sightseeing agriculture, a new type of agriculture for rural development, is the utilization of rural equipment, space, production sites, products, business activities, natural ecology, natural environment, rural human resources, etc., with an aim to bringing the function of leisure tourism into full play through strategic planning, increasing people's experience in rural areas and agriculture, improving tourism quality, increasing peasants' income as well as enhancing the sound development of agriculture.

Urban agriculture was first proposed by some American economists in the 1950s and 1960s. It refers to the operation of agriculture, forestry, animal husbandry, aquatic production, agricultural business activities, rural culture and farm life through the utility of rural landscape, natural ecology and environmental resources in urbanized areas so as to provide places for people to tour around, experience agriculture and understand the countryside. In other words, urban agriculture is an industry that integrates production, life and ecology of agriculture.

Eco-agriculture refers to the agricultural development mode that follows the laws of ecology and eco-economics, methods of system engineering and intensive management of modern science and technology are applied on the premise of protecting and improving ecological environment. Eco-agriculture is an agricultural eco-economic complex system, which integrates agricultural ecosystem and agricultural economic system to achieve the greatest overall ecological and economic benefits. Eco-agricultural models include raising fish and duckweed in rice-field, the intercropping of grain, fruit and medicine crops, the combination of agriculture, forestry and animal husbandry, the combination of grain, mulberry (feed of silkworms) and fishery, the combination of breeding, raising and adding, and the multi-level comprehensive utilization of organic wastes such as chicken manure for feeding pigs, pig manure for feeding fish, etc. The production of eco-agriculture is based on the sustainable utilization of resources and the protection of ecological environment. According to the principles of coordinated adaptation of organism and environment, optimum combination of species, efficient operation of energy and material, and balance of input and output, the production of eco-agriculture is organized by means of system engineering, relying on the input of modern science, technology and social and economic information.

Carbon sequestration agriculture refers to the process, activity or mechanism of absorbing and fixing carbon dioxide in the atmosphere by means of afforestation, forest management, deforestation reduction, forest vegetation protection and restoration, combined with relevant rules with carbon sequestration trading. Afforestation and reforestation carbon sequestration project in the Clean Development Model (CDM) is the only cooperation mechanism between developed and developing countries in the field of forestry under the framework of *Kyoto Protocol*. It works under the principle that the obligation of reducing carbon dioxide emissions can be offset by forest carbon sequestration, and the compensation of the value of forest ecological benefits can be realized through the market. According to the regulations, developed countries help developing countries achieve sustainable development by providing them with funds and technology, while developed countries fulfill their obligations under *Kyoto Protocol* by purchasing "certified emission reductions" from developing countries. The Youth Afforestation Project to combat desertification in Aohan Banner, Inner Mongolia, Northeast China, is the first "carbon sequestrating" afforestation project in China under CDM of *Kyoto Protocol* and partially funded by foreign parties. During the first five-year period of validity, the project has invested \$1.53 million and afforested 3,000 hectares of desert land in Aohan Banner.

— Selection and collation of relevant information based on Baidu website

Different Interpretations of Post-Modernization Trend of Thought on Modern Agriculture

Just as the way post-modernization trend of thought criticizes modernization, it also has different interpretations on modern agriculture.

From the perspective of post-modernization, modern agriculture is a factory-type and large-scale agricultural production mode based on modern rationality and Newtonian science, which applies mechanical and linear modern technology to agricultural production activities, uses a large number of high-intensity farming systems as well as generally uses high-level inorganic chemical inputs for large-scale single-species continuous farming. Therefore, postmodernism has a critical attitude towards modern agriculture. Postmodernism believes modern agriculture follows the thinking mode of dualistic opposition in which man separates from nature and man separates from man, so despite its great achievements, it inevitably leads to at least eight kinds of drawbacks: (1) exploitation of land; (2) hidden hazards to health; (3) huge consumption of oil; (4) pollution on the environment; (5) disaster to the ecology; (6) misinterpretation of economics (externalities); (7) social destruction and (8) cultural erosion. Obviously, modern agriculture understood by post-modern trends of thought is not the same as modern agriculture discussed in this book.

Tan Xuewen. Modern, Postmodern and Eco Agriculture — International Symposium on the Development of "Two Types of Rural Areas" and Eco-Agriculture, Fifth International Symposium on the Comparison of Agricultural Modernization in China. *China's Rural Economy*, 2010(2).

1.7 Agricultural Modernization and Modernization of Agricultural Production Organizations

Agricultural modernization is closely linked with modern agriculture, and in a sense, the former is cause and the latter result. Therefore, some scholars believe "the core of agricultural modernization is to constantly replace traditional factors of production with modern ones, and to transform traditional agriculture to modern agriculture."

Just as people's understanding of modern agriculture is a gradually deepening process, people's understanding of agricultural modernization also deepens through constantly revising the past, partial misconceptions. For quite a long time from the founding of the PRC to the reform and opening-up, people had restricted agricultural modernization to the level of production technology, especially production tools, agricultural modernization had been equated "four modernizations" in machinery, electronics, water conservancy and chemical technology, a true reflection of people's understanding of modern agriculture in that historical period when they focused on the simple process of production and agriculture was only limited to the narrow sense of "small agriculture", i.e., planting and aquaculture. In my opinion, there is a deeper reason behind. During that period, we had a blind "sense of superiority in ownership" or "sense of superiority in social system". We believed people's commune system and planned economy at that time were superior to those of western developed countries, while what we lagged behind was only production technology and tools, namely the so-called "contradiction between advanced production relations and backward productivity". There seemed no need to study the modernization of production organizations, since we believed our production systems organizations were so-called "advanced production relations".

After the reform and opening-up, we are constantly extending the connotation and denotation of agricultural modernization with the deepening of people's understanding of modern agriculture, especially with the expansion of international vision brought about by the opening-up to the outside world. Generally speaking, the definition, expression and reflection of agricultural modernization in this period were "all flowers blossoming" (to put it another way, there was "no consensus"). In addition to the traditional "four modernizations", there were commercialization, specialization, marketization, scientification, intensification, scale, industrialization, socialization, ecology, gardening, standardization, organization, just to name a few. In my limited reading scope, there were more than 30 ways of expressions of agricultural modernization by Chinese scholars. Now only two of them are introduced as follows. One is the "Seven Modernizations" summarized in an article in *Farmer's Daily*: Mechanization of production process, scientific production technology, intensive growth mode, marketization of business cycle, socialization of production organization, high optimization of production performance and intellectualization of workers; the other is the nine aspects summarized by Huang Zuhui: modernization of agricultural economic structure, modernization of agricultural infrastructure and production, modernization of means, science and technology, industrialization of management, socialization of services, modernization of laborers, modernization of resources and environment, modernization of peasants' living and consumption.[39]

Scientific research tends to be comprehensive, or cumbersome. Therefore, it is necessary for scientific research to "grasp the big and let go of the small" or "grasp the big together with the small". There is no need to cover all aspects. According to Marx's theoretical analysis framework, productive forces and production relations are the two basic aspects to grasp agricultural modernization. The most obvious defect in the theory and practice before China's reform and opening-up was that we had neglected or obscured production relations, the root of which was the sense of superiority of ownership and system that we blindly boasted of at that time.

---

[39]Huang Zuhui, Lin Jian and Zhang Dongping. *Agricultural Modernization: Theory, Process and Approach*. Beijing: China Agricultural Publishing House, 2003, pp. 5–6.

The modernization of agricultural production organization is the core of the modernization of agricultural production relations.

Firstly, organization is the collection of individuals at the social level, and the essence of modernization is the modernization of individuals, with "the full and free development of man" as the ultimate goal. The modernization of organizations provides the crucial institutional and organizational guarantee for the full and free development of man. In North's words, "it is the success or failure of human organizations that determines whether society is progressing or retrogressing."[40]

Secondly, institutional change with organizational change as its core is the basic condition not only to ensure the smooth introduction, diffusion and re-innovation of "exotic" advanced science and technology, but also to induce "endogenous" technological innovation and progress. From the historical facts of economic development, few developing countries have completely rejected advanced technology from developed countries. The government of the Qing Dynasty adopted a closed and conservative attitude to the outside world, but it advocated the strategy named "western learning for use", in which "western learning" was not western culture or social system in the context at that time, but pure technology and tools. "Western learning" was grafted onto the "body" of "Chinese learning", which unfortunately failed to bear the fruit of modernization as practice has shown. Since the body remained unchanged, the use had nowhere to demonstrate, or it could be demonstrated distortedly. As Lu Xun once sneered bitterly: "Westerners use gunpowder to make bullets against the enemy, but we Chinese use them as firecrackers to worship God; Westerners use compass to navigate the world, but we Chinese use them to see geomantic omen; Westerners use opium as medicine, but we Chinese use them as food. Same things can be used in such different ways!"[41] Moreover, within a rigid, closed and backward framework, people lacked the intrinsic motivation and demand for technological innovation progress. Even if advanced technology was introduced from outside,

---

[40] North, D. C. *Structure and Change in Economic History*. New York: W. W. Norton & Company, 1982.

[41] Lu Xun. *Advantages and Disadvantages of Electricity, Pseudo-Freedom Statement*. Beijing: People's Literature Publishing House, 1995, p. 9.

it was unlikely to facilitate development, or change the production and economic structure of the whole society. It has proved that without the modernization of organization and system, the modernization of technology and tools cannot be realized and promoted smoothly.

Thirdly, with a global outlook we can easily see that the biggest difference of agricultural development in each country does not lie in technology or tools, but in production organization. For example, the degree of mechanization in the Soviet Union used to be as high as that of the United States. However, its labor productivity and output lagged far behind. The fundamental reason lied in the production organization. From China's practice, the main drawback is not technology alone, either. In fact, China's hybrid rice, oil crops and refined farming methods are in a leading or advanced position in the world. The biggest contradiction facing China's current agricultural modernization is the contradiction of small production and large market, small production and large society. In other words, the organizational form cannot adapt to the development of market economy.

Finally, from the perspective of division of knowledge in modern society, the focus of social sciences scholars, especially that of economic researchers, should be on the production relations and systems, with the form of production organization as its core. Of course, Marx has long before remarked that the study of production relations cannot be isolated from productive forces. According to the theories of modern institutional economics, institutional change and technological change are closely related. In conclusion, the focus of philosophy and social science research should be on production relations and system, while the technological problems should be left to experts and scientists of natural sciences.

1.8 The Basic Content and Framework of the Book

This book is composed of seven chapters (see Figure 1.2).

Chapter 1 Introduction. It explains the keywords in the title of the book — "Contemporary China", "modernization" and "agriculture". It expounds the significance of the study, basic content and framework of the book, and outlines the innovation of the book and future research directions.

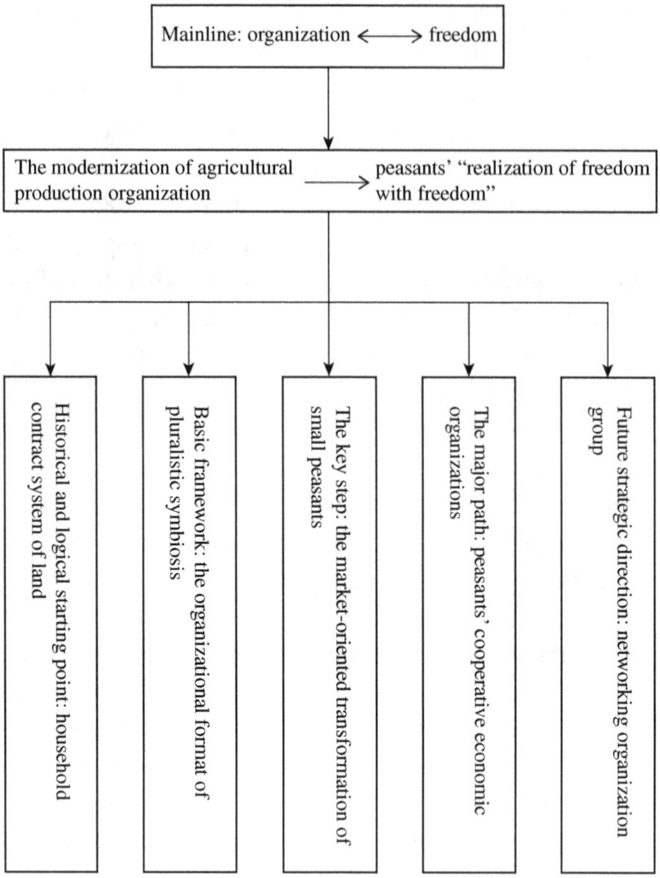

Figure 1.2. Basic framework of the book

Chapter 2 The Basic Analytical Framework: Freedom and Organization. In a sense, this chapter serves as the outline of the book and the research work on the modernization of agricultural production organizations in contemporary China by the research group.

I, as the chief expert in winning the bid of "Research on the Modernization of Agricultural Production Organizations with Chinese Characteristics" at the end of 2007, am fully aware of the significance of the subject and the responsibility on our shoulders. The so-called "major" topic, of course, needs a strong "problem awareness" (I dare not say "solution") of the major issues in the process of social and economic development. But we also need a theoretical insight and analysis framework on innovation and breakthroughs, so a major idea ("outline") is urgently needed to lead the research of this topic, which should be inclusive, contemporary and universal to a certain extent at the same time. Otherwise, we may be baffled by the endless problems in real life, unable to find the crux of solving them, let alone the direction of the future. If we follow the general empirical method, or adopt one or two modern popular quantitative models, econometric analysis and other tools, we still doubt whether such an arrangement could grasp the core of the modernization of contemporary China's agricultural production organization. In this regard, we agree with Nicholas Georgescu Rogan in that the key part of human social history is the story told in plain language and that, in the research of human society with the highest degree of complexity, mathematics, econometrics and computer simulation methods are relatively simple methods, while historical, comparative, institutional and hermeneutic approaches are probably the real sophisticated ones in economics.[42] Furthermore, as Whitehead said, "If science does not want to degenerate into a mess of special hypotheses, it must be philosophically grounded and its foundations must be thoroughly criticized."[43]

Isaac Newton said "if I have seen further than others, it is by standing upon the shoulders of giants." The "full and free development of man" and the "to realize freedom freely" by Karl Marx, "development as freedom" by Amartya Sen all give me great inspiration and enlightenment. In addition, I feel indebted to Du Runsheng, one of the major participants and leaders of China's rural economic reform, for his book entitled *Du Runsheng's Account on Major Events in the Decision-Making of China's Rural System Reform*. Du put it bluntly: peasants should be "free men".[44] Starting from these creative sources, I have come to realize although the

---

[42]Foster, J. and Metcalf, J. S. eds. *Frontier of Evolutionary Economics*. Cheltenham: Edward Elgar Pub, 2001.

[43]*Ibid.*

[44]Du Runsheng. *Farmers Should Be "Free Man" & Du Runsheng's Account on Major Events in Decision-Making in China's Rural System Reform*. Beijing: People's Publishing House, 2005, p. 197.

modernization of organizations is like a myriad of threads, in the final analysis, organizations should be the path and platform for people's "realization of freedom with freedom" rather than tools and shackles!

Based on the above understanding, the second chapter mainly discusses the relationship between freedom and organization, trying to clarify the theme of the topic and the book: the criterion for modern organization is to expand "the full and free development of man" and to improve the "capability" to achieve "substantive freedom". The main contents include: what is freedom, what is organization, how an organization can expand the space of individual freedom, and how it can be alienated as a tool to restrict individual freedom; how to evaluate and criticize the relevant theories of western mainstream economics, and how to think and explore Marx's thought of "the community of free men".

Chapter 3 The Historical Context and Internal Logic of the Transition of Agricultural Production Organizations in Contemporary China: Interpretation Based on Peasants' Freedom. By adopting the analytical method of integrating history and logic, we firmly grasp the major line of "organization-freedom". From the perspective of "realization of freedom with freedom" by peasants, we emphasize that the household contract system of rural land is the historical and logical starting point of the modernization of agricultural production organizations in contemporary China.

The chapter first analyses the people's commune system, pointing out it is essentially a collective security guarantee for the basic subsistence right at the expense of the peasants' self-management and free choice, which was rational in a specific context. The fundamental reason for its disintegration is low efficiency caused by the narrow space of choice and the "double-way lock-in" between peasants and the commune. Therefore, the most lasting and far-reaching significance of reforms on rural economic system and household contract system is not the decentralized management of peasants, but the broader and more inclusive organizational and institutional platform it has provided for peasants' "realizing freedom freely". The platform has given peasants two basic and fundamental rights in the process: one is the "right of land contractual management" guaranteed by law, the other is the "freedom of labor". Moreover, the household contract system does not completely deny the reasonable factors in the people's commune system. In fact, the equitable contracting of community land has inherited and extended the collective security guarantee for the basic right to subsistence. At the same time, peasants' freedom is not sufficient and complete in contemporary China, for the dual economic and social structure as well as the corresponding institutional arrangements have restricted peasants' "realization of freedom with freedom" as well as their capability to do so in many ways. Therefore, the basic direction of rural economic and social system reform and even the national economic and social system reform in China is to further expand the institutional space for peasants' free realization of freedom.

Chapter 4 Pluralism and Symbiosis: The Basic Framework of Agricultural Production Organizations in Contemporary China. The chapter expounds the idea that the basic framework of agricultural production organizations in contemporary China is pluralism and symbiosis based on the peasant household economy and intertwined with various forms of economic organizations. This symbiotic organizational framework has not only been the result of peasants' free choice since the reform and opening-up, but also provided a broader stage of organization and system for peasants' further diversification of free choices.

This chapter explores the significance of symbiosis theory, pointing out symbiotic evolution is another evolutionary path, which is the evolution of "win–win cooperation" and "multi-win cooperation" rather than schemes of "winner takes all" "who beats whom" or "who destroys whom". Its basic premise implied is to recognize pluralism, diversity and heterogeneity of the objective world. The major part of this chapter is a series of real-life cases obtained by the author and members of the research group through field investigation and literature search. The cases are collected nationwide, covering eastern, central and western part of China. Each case is representative (not an isolated one), but none of them can cover, include or replace all the others, illustrating the diversity, heterogeneity and complexity of the forms of agricultural production organization in contemporary China. It needs to be noted that the work of the author and the research group is to discover rather than invent the distinctive production organization forms in the colorful real life; to discover rather than invent the blending and cooperation between various production organizations, as well as the contradictions, conflicts, interests coordination and integration in the process of cooperation. At the same time, it should be noted that the cases studied in this chapter cannot cover all the forms of production organization, which further shows the basic characteristics of diversity, and further proves that household management, collective management, cooperative management and firm management are taking shape in China's rural areas.

Chapter 5 Transforming Small Farming: The Key to the Modernization of Agricultural Production Organizations in Contemporary China. This chapter outlines two concepts and two paths of "transforming small peasants", namely, collectivizing and marketizing. Collectivizing is essentially to eliminate small peasants, while marketizing is to transform small peasants into "nodes" in the modern and market-oriented network, substituting traditional peasant economy with modern peasant system.

This chapter analyses the different types of small peasants and two different ways of transforming them, with the focus on how to carry out market-oriented transformation in contemporary China. This chapter points out that the transfer of agricultural labor force, the substantial reduction of the numbers of peasants and the promotion of urbanization are the prerequisites for market-oriented transformation; land transfer is the gradual process toward moderate scale operation by small-scale market-oriented peasants with Chinese characteristics, and it is based upon the separation of three rights, namely, right of ownership, contract and management. The specialization and scale operation in agricultural production is an important measure to transform small peasants. The chapter answers such major questions in reality as how to promote agricultural mechanization on the basis of peasants' household economy, how to promote advanced agricultural technology, and "who will till the soil in the future agriculture".

Chapter 6 Who Organizes Peasant Cooperative Organizations and Whom to Organize? This is an unavoidable question in the modernization of agricultural production organizations in contemporary China.

This chapter first answers the question of "whether market-oriented small peasants need cooperative organizations". Secondly, it points out that the main difficulty in the development of farmer cooperative economic organizations is not lack of demand, but rather lack of supply: the scarcity of "entrepreneurs" (organizers); the organizational and operational costs of farmer cooperative organizations are also high. This chapter analyses the unique role of the government as "organizer", but at the same time emphasizes the bottom line and boundary of government-led cooperation: inviolable peasants' right of free choice. As for the popular viewpoint that peasants' cooperation is "the alliance of the weak", this chapter gives out a basically negative answer, stressing that the organizer of professional cooperative is the relatively strong party in rural economic and social life; the members are mainly specialized peasants and market-oriented peasants instead of poor peasants; the establishment of cooperative economic organizations is conducive to the emerging of rural middle class.

Chapter 7 Networking in the Modernization of Agricultural Production Organizations in Contemporary China. This chapter addresses the question of "how to guide agricultural modernization with information technology" at the organizational and institutional level.

This chapter first provides definitions of "network" and "networking organization group". Secondly, it explains the internal relationship between modern network, networking organization and "modern peasant economy" by referring to cases of the Netherlands, Russia, etc., and also points out that the "bottleneck" of agricultural modernization is not improper micro-economic organization but the lack or imperfection of modern network and networking organization. Since the reform and opening-up, the organizational form of agricultural production in China has undergone a historic transformation from the "uniformity" of the people's commune system to the "diversity" based on the farmer's household economy and symbiosis of various forms of micro-economic organizations; the further development direction is to gradually move towards networking based on diversity. Establishing networking organization is the concrete embodiment of "guiding agricultural modernization by information technology" at the organizational and institutional level. So "uniformity–diversity–networking" is the historical track of the modernization development of agricultural production organization in contemporary China.

1.9 Innovation of this Work and Direction for Future Research

Innovation is the vitality as well as essence of theoretical research. However, it is not easy to achieve innovation for the following reasons: firstly, it is confined by the cognitive ability of researchers (including individuals and the team); secondly, it is influenced by the external environment in both the complexity and uncertainty of the external environment and the "framework" formed by the interaction of various systems, rules, customs and ideologies. People are always eager to explore the unknown space and domain freely, but they are also restricted by various "unfreedoms" consciously or unconsciously, just like we are still eating the "steamed bread" our predecessors or counterparts have eaten, treading on the path that our predecessors or counterparts have tread. At present, so much low-level repetition and academic "bubble" have proved real innovation is Of course, "innovation" should not be regarded as a "mysterious palace" that only a few can dabble in. New theories and viewpoints are innovation, so are new perspectives and methods. In a sense, new materials and new data are also innovation. Wagner & Berger states there are four ways of developing a theory: first, elaboration, i.e., elaborating the original theory by constructing new ones; second, proliferation, i.e., drawing on ideas and methods from other fields to create a new theory; third, competition, i.e., putting forward a new or even contesting argument for the established one and creating a new theory; fourth, integration, i.e., formulating a new theoretical model on the basis of two or more established ones.[45] Chinese scholar Zhu Yongxin has a broader understanding of "new": "When some concepts are mentioned again as they are gradually forgetting, they are new." "When some concepts were said in the past and applied into practice today, they are new." "When some concepts have been clarified from obscurity and become vivacious, they are new."

[45] Wagner, D. G. and Berger, J. "Do Sociological Theories Grow?", *American Journal of Sociology*, Vol. 90, No. 4 (1985), pp. 692–728.

"When some concepts are introduced from the old context to the new for inheritance and innovation, they are new."[46]

The innovation of this book from a macro viewpoint is to build a theoretical framework for understanding the modernization of agricultural production organizations in contemporary China from the perspective of peasants "realization of freedom with freedom", or enhancing their "capability" to realize "substantive freedom", neither of which is, admittedly, the originality of our research group or me. However, within my limited reading scope, it's innovative to comprehensively and systemically analyze the agricultural production organization in contemporary China and formulate a basic theoretical framework by drawing on the works of Karl Marx or Amartya Sen concerning "freedom".

The theoretical framework of research, or the innovation of research perspective centers on the concept of "organization and freedom", and relative viewpoints and conclusions are drawn thereafter.

(1) As a long-term stable institutional arrangement of man's cooperative behavior and relationship, organizations should be regarded as an effective means to guarantee and realize individual freedom, expand the space of individual freedom rather than restrict individual basic freedom. Therefore, the ultimate criterion of organizational modernization is to expand the "all-round and free development of man" and enhance people's "capability" to achieve "substantive freedom".

(2) Retrospect on the people's commune system from the perspective of freedom. The people's commune is a collective guarantee organization for peasants' basic right to subsistence at the cost of peasants' free choice. The underlying reason for its disintegration is the inefficiency caused by lack of freedom. The consequence of depriving or restricting peasants' right to freedom of choice is peasants' basic right to subsistence cannot be guaranteed in the long run, or, the basic problem of food and clothing cannot be solved.

[46] Wang Yao. Education is a Poem. *Reading*, Vol. 3, 2012, pp. 96–101.

(3) Recognize the essence of rural land household contract system from the perspective of freedom. The most far-reaching, enduring and essential significance of household contract system of land lies not in the decentralized management, but in the fact that it provides a relatively broad and inclusive organizational and institutional platform for peasants to realize their freedom with freedom, which is the most important theoretical basis to maintain the "long-term stability" of the system and "stay clear of deviations".
(4) Interpretation of "right to freedom of property" and "right to freedom of labor" based on household contract system of land from the perspective of peasants' freedom. Household contract system grants peasants two basic but vital rights: one is "right to freedom of property", the most important of which is "land contractual right" guaranteed by law; the other is "right to freedom of labor".
(5) Because the state protects the rural household contract system "permanently", and does not allow any organizations (including village collective organizations) to infringe on the peasants' right to land contractual management, which are essentially a "legal private right" based on the collective ownership but surpassing collective ownership and protected by law.
(6) Peasants have the freedom of "no tilling" without giving up the right of land contractual management, which is a very important freedom in that peasants can choose to engage in agriculture, or choose not to engage in agriculture. This is a significant progress in the process of peasants' free development compared with the "unfreedom" of the people's commune system which binds the peasants on the land. At the same time, the non-abandonment of the right to land contractual management gives peasants the freedom to return to agricultural production in case they failed in other businesses, for they have the freedom of "trial and error". It is precisely because of the guarantee of the right to land contractual management that peasants can be more confident and resolute in engaging in non-agricultural industries and enjoy the "freedom of no tilling".
(7) Transforming from the unfreedom of labor in the commune system to the freedom of labor under the household contract system of land is one of the major measures for peasants' "realizing freedom

freely". Only when the broad masses of peasants have a complete control over their own labor, will there be a large-scale transfer of agricultural labor force, as well as various forms of agricultural production organizations, like hundreds of flowers blooming. At the same time, the realization of "labor freedom" of Chinese peasants is a gradual historical process. Laborers' total control over their own labor is only the prerequisite to realize "labor freedom", and more importantly, a free economic and social environment is needed to enable workers to achieve "labor freedom" with freedom.

(8) Understanding the basic framework of agricultural production organization in contemporary China from the perspective of peasants' freedom. "Pluralistic symbiosis" based on the independent complementarity, cross-cutting integration and mutual development of family-based household management, collective management, cooperative management and firm management is the basic framework of agricultural production organization in contemporary China. The premise of "pluralistic symbiosis" is diversity and difference, and its essence is benefit symbiosis, so it does not exclude competition or evolution. However, this kind of competition and evolution are not the ones described in the sayings like "you die so that I live" "who defeats whom" "who kills whom" "winner takes all". The "symbiotic evolution" is a kind of universal evolution in which all kinds of organizations in the group benefit. Fundamentally speaking, the organizational framework of pluralistic symbiosis is not only the inevitable result of peasants' free choice under the impetus of market mechanism, but also provides a broad and inclusive organizational and institutional space for peasants to realize their freedom freely.

(9) Understanding "market-oriented transformation of small peasants" from improving the "capability" to realize "substantive freedom". Unlike collective transformation, market-oriented transformation is not to eliminate small peasants, but to transform the traditional peasant economy into a modern one so as to enhance peasants' "capability" to achieve "substantive freedom". Therefore, in the wake of market-oriented transformation of small peasants, we should enforce land transfer based on the "separation of rights", namely, ownership, contract and management, which is of

distinctive Chinese characteristics. Furthermore, in response to question like "who will till the soil and how", we should enhance specialized and mechanicalized agricultural production so as to engage modern peasants in modern agriculture.

(10) Understanding farmer cooperation from the perspective of expanding peasants' freedom. Market-oriented peasants need cooperation, but the fundamental purpose of cooperation is to enhance the "capability" of peasants to achieve "substantive freedom", rather than lose or restrain freedom. Therefore, peasants have the right of choice on cooperation, which is the bottom line for government guidance and cannot be deprived of or infringed on.

(11) Understanding the significance of constructing and improving rural modernization network and building rural networking organization group from the perspective of peasants' freedom. At present, peasants' weak capability to realize substantive freedom can be mainly attributed to the lack or imperfection of modern network and networking organization groups rather than "improper micro economic organizations". Constructing and improving modern network for agriculture and rural area, constructing and improving networking organization groups for agriculture and rural area are, in essence, to build a new agricultural operating system in pace with modern market economy, information economy and network economy. It's also a key prerequisite to peasants' "capability" to realize "substantive freedom". Uniformity-pluralism-network is the historical trajectory of agricultural organization in contemporary China.

(12) Understanding "agricultural modernization led by information technology" from the macro historical perspective of improving peasants' freedom. The 18th National Congress of CPC put forward the idea of "agricultural modernization led by information technology" with the stress on "led by", which should not be partially understood as "every village is connected with telephone and every household has access to the Internet". It's more about the profound and full changes brought about by information economy and network economy on agricultural production organization. The transformation of production organization from "pluralism" to "networking" and the building of a new agricultural management system fully have

illustrated "information technology leading agricultural modernization" and modern networking economy leading the profound and full changes of production organization modes.

This book also draws on ideas and methods from fields besides economics and management, such as "symbiosis" from biology, and "network" from physics and sociology, which have broadened our research horizon, provided new research ideas, and drawn new conclusions. Of course, these references and introductions are not our innovation, but the research path through which we use such methods, or the object and scope of research are distinctive from others.

As to policy suggestions, our major innovation is the strategic priority transfer of agricultural production organization, as termed as "to stabilize household contract system of rural land, and to facilitate market-oriented, pluralistic symbiosis of agricultural production organization with focus on building networking organization group of agriculture and rural area". We believe that since the reform and opening-up, the organizational form has undergone a historical transformation from the "uniformity" of the people's commune system to the "diversity" based on the peasant household economy; the further development direction is from "diversity" to "networking", from diverse "microeconomic rebuilding" to "establishing networking organization group" and speeding in building a new agricultural management system.

In specific, this book has proposed such policy suggestions:

(1) Further stress the sanctity and inviolability of peasants' right to land contractual management, and give peasants more freedom in the transfer, transaction and inheritance of land contract. Therefore, it is necessary to amend the current *The Law of the People's Republic of China on Land Contract in Rural Areas*; to allow peasants to "sell outright" the right to land contractual management after entering the city, exchanging it for urban social security right. Meanwhile, we can experiment with methods like "one son/daughter inheritance of right to land contractual management".

(2) Further reform the household registration system of "urban–rural divide", give peasants full freedom of residence and migration.

The government can neither forbid nor coerce peasants' entry into cities and become "new citizens".

(3) Land transfer on the basis of peasants' free choice is the road of moderate scale management of agriculture with Chinese characteristics according to the principle of "separation of three rights" — namely, rights to ownership, contract and management. It should be encouraged to carry out active diversified exploration on the premise of market operation. However, practice has shown there are great uncertainties and risks in the process of "industrial and commercial capital going to rural area", transforming family agriculture into factory agriculture, and peasants into agricultural workers. So we must be very meticulous in doing so.

(4) Under our specific constraints of resources and institutions, the specialization and scale operation of links in the production chain are key to the market-oriented transformation of small peasants, which is also an important part of the construction and improvement of agricultural social service system. The government should introduce positive incentive policies to guide the development of various specialized service organizations in rural areas.

(5) The criterion of agricultural mechanization is the coverage of farm machinery services in all aspects of the overall agricultural production, as opposed to the number of farm machinery a single farmer owns. Therefore, the subject of mechanization is specialized and market-oriented machinery services, and what the majority of peasants need to purchase is services rather than machines. So policies need to be adjusted toward providing subsidies to those who purchase services instead of machines; at the same time, policies should also favor the development of machinery professional households, cooperatives, service firms and other social service organizations.

(6) Two basic ways to cultivate professional peasants are either by promoting land transfer, cultivating specialized peasants, developing family farms or promoting the specialization of production links, cultivating and developing various types of specialized agricultural production organizations. On the issue of "who will till the soil" in the future, in my opinion, the fundamental way out is to cultivate professional peasants on the basis of free choice rather than confine

the existing agricultural labor force on the land forcibly. We should also allow non-peasants, urban citizens and college students to become "professional peasants".

(7) The main obstacles to the development of rural cooperative economic organizations is the scarcity of "organizer" resources and the high organizational and operational costs. In order to smooth its development, it is necessary and reasonable for the government to provide policy support, i.e., to grant proper "policy benefits". At the same time, rural cooperative economic organizations should learn from the successful experience of firms and joint-stock companies. At this stage, it may become improbable to apply "international standards" on economic cooperative organizations and "organizers".

(8) Peasants' professional cooperatives are not "the alliance of the weak". There's inherent logical rationality in taking specialized peasants rather than poor peasants as the entity of the organization. The main function is to promote specialized and commercial production, and the main beneficiaries are the relatively wealthy specialized peasants. Therefore, the function of fostering rural middle class is actually greater than that of poverty alleviation, so cooperatives should be more accurately positioned.

(9) Peasants' professional cooperatives or other similar cooperative economic organizations only provide an alternative for peasants' cooperation, which is not the only or exclusive form of organization. Peasants' cooperation should be allowed to take on many forms. Therefore, on the premise of acknowledging its merits, there's no need to generalize or elevate their functions. At the same time, by joining a cooperative, members only merge part of their economic functions rather than "become a complete cooperative man", which means members shouldn't be tied down by the cooperative.

(10) The experience of developed countries like the Netherlands and the United States has shown the efficiency of the modern small-scale farming system is attributed to a mature, well-developed modern network and networking organization group behind it. "Diversified" organizations do not necessarily form a comprehensive competitive advantage with complementary functions; the "diversified"

organizational structure may also stagnate in the decentralized state for a long time, bringing in no organizational synergy at all. Therefore, the key is to build a networking organization group with complementary and mutually beneficial functions, resource and benefit sharing so that it will create "returns of network economy" peculiar to modern network economy. Therefore, the future path lies in the transition from diversification to networking.

(11) As modern network is essentially a social public product with strong external reliance, "government-guidance" is a natural and inevitable feature in its construction and improvement. However, government-guidance does not equal to government-dominance. Under the guidance of the government, peasants, firms, various types of cooperative economic organizations and the whole society must be mobilized to build a cohesion. Hence, the guidance of the government and the cohesion of relevant economic stakeholders are the two prongs for the building and improving the modernization network in China.

(12) Because the social mechanism of trust is a kind of public goods with obvious positive externalities, the government bears crucial responsibility for its establishment and improvement. The government should act as the main system supplier, act as the "moral preacher" and "moral benchmark" of integrity.

In the initial stage of our research, we felt quite capable and fully charged. However, with the deepening of the research, more problems emerged, some of which were beyond our scope of capability. This book has raised some questions and hopefully answered part of them, but there are still more questions that have not been raised, or answered, or the answers are far from satisfactory. For example, how to measure the "capability" to realize "substantive freedom"? How to coordinate "market-oriented transformation of small peasants" and the urbanization process? Especially how to build and improve the networking organization of agriculture and rural area? There are too many unknown areas to be explored. In the following years, I will make further studies on the three issues mentioned above in the hope that experts in the academic circles, especially young scholars, will make joint efforts.

Chapter 2

The Basic Analytical Framework: Freedom and Organization

Abstract

As a long-term stable institutional arrangement of people's cooperative behavior and relationship, organizations play a fundamental role in the effective guarantee, realization and expansion of individual's freedom, as well as enhancing the "capability" of individuals to realize "substantive freedom".

2.1 What Is Meant by Freedom?

In contemporary world, no word appears to be more sacred than "freedom", no word is more confusing, either. Montesquieu, famous French Enlightenment thinker, said that "No word contains more connotations and leaves more impressions on people's consciousness than freedom."[1]

Kant, the famous German philosopher, believes freedom, as an existential human nature, is *a priori* that needs no proof.[2] That is to say, freedom is human nature; man was born free. This natural human ontological freedom is the basis of all freedoms.[3] Marx agreed with Kant in that "freedom

[1] Montesquieu. *The Spirit of the Laws*. Cambridge: Cambridge University Press, 1989.

[2] Kant said, "It is not necessary for me to prove freedom theoretically because it satisfies our purpose to believe that freedom is the basis on which rational beings are placed in their concepts in view of their actions." (Han Shuifa. *Kant Biography*. Beijing: Hebei People's Publishing House, 1997.)

[3] Malinowski disagrees with the view of natural liberty. He believes that "no individual is a person with natural liberty either in the sense of individual or in the sense of genealogy."

is so much the essence of man that even its opponents implement it while combating its reality."[4] He suggests that "the whole character of a species, its species-character, resides in the nature of its life activity, and free conscious activity constitutes the species-character of man."[5] Arendt put it more abruptly: "Being and freedom are the same thing."[6]

Freedom is pivotal, and it is hard to understand and measure it in practice, too. Lincoln once remarked, "We are never offered a clear definition of freedom."[7] After reading large volumes of literature, Akton sighed, "Freedom is a concept with two hundred definitions."[8] In Kant's opinion, common understanding of freedom is misleading, ambiguous and even self-conceited. Therefore, it cannot be put in the phenomenal world, but can only be put in the ontological world together with "the existence of God" and "immortality of soul". It is "thing-in-itself",[9] which is beyond the scope of human pure reason. Despite such profound philosophical language, freedom is just as Basu said when he talked about the concepts of human development and comprehensive development: "Everyone seems to agree, but few know what it actually means."[10]

In order to enable people to grasp freedom in real life so that freedom is not a vague and purely metaphysical concept,[11] many scholars regard

---

No one can be born free (Malinowski, Bronislaw. *Freedom and Civilization.* Bangalore: Mysore Press, 2014).

[4]Marx, K. Proceedings of the Sixth Rhine Province Assembly. *Karl Marx & Frederick Engels: Collected Works.* New York: Intl Pub Co. Inc, 1996.

[5]Marx, K. *Economic and Philosophic Manuscripts of 1844.* Eastford: Martino Fine Books, 2011.

[6]Arendt, H. *The Freedom to Be Free: From Thinking Without a Banister.* New York: Vintage Books, 2018.

[7]Malinowski, B. *Freedom and Civilization.* Bangalore: Mysore Press, 2014.

[8]Acton. *Freedom and Power.* Scotts Valley: Create Space Independent Publishing Platform, 2013.

[9]Kant believes that we can only recognize the phenomena that thing-in-itself reveals to us, while thing-in-itself is unknowable (Yu Wujin. *Practice and Freedom.* Wuhan: Wuhan University Press, 2010.)

[10]Meier, G. and Stiglitz, J. eds. *Frontiers of Development Economics: The Future in Perspective.* Oxford: Oxford University Press, 2000.

[11]"When Baker commented on Kant's tendency to separate and oppose the phenomenal dimension of human beings from the dimension of "thing-in-itself" (or ontology), he wrote

human needs and their satisfaction as a basic yardstick in practice.[12] According to Marx and Engels, material life, in one form or another, depends on the developed needs, and the generation of these needs, like their satisfaction, is a historical process itself. "Needs being the vocation of all human beings".[13] Therefore, the degree of satisfaction reflects the degree of freedom, satisfaction is "the new evidence of man's essential power, as well as the new enrichment of human essence".[14] Amartya Sen, the 1998 Nobel Prize winner in economics, summarized "substantive freedom" as "capability". What is meant by "capability"? In Sen's words, "a person's capability is the combination of various possible functioning that a person may accomplish." Capability, therefore, is a kind of freedom, a substantive freedom to realize the combination of various possible functioning (or, in plain words, the freedom to realize different ways of life).[15] And he says, "Substantive freedom includes the basic capability to live free from hardships — hunger, malnutrition, treatable diseases and premature mortality — as well as freedoms to be literate, numerate and to enjoy political participation, etc." Sen also believes that his view of freedom can be traced back to Aristotle's exposition on "life quality" and Smith's exposition on "life necessities".[16] "According to Adam Smith's analysis, what

---

with humor: "We bear the freedom of the ontological human beings, but we hang the phenomenal human beings." (Yu Wujin. *Freedom of Practice*. Wuhan University Press, 2010.) Professor Haldan believes: "The primary essence of how to conduct scientific research is comparability... If the study of freedom has any practical effect, it must be solved well." (Malinowski, Bronislaw. *Freedom and Civilization*. Bangalore: Mysore Press, 2014.)

[12] Marx and Marcuse also took "free time" as a measure of individual freedom. Freedom means that people have more and more "free time" at their disposal. In Marx's words, "Increasing free time means increasing the time for the full development of the individual." According to Marcuse, "What determines the content of human existence is not working time, but free time." (Yu Wujin. *Practice and Freedom*. Wuhan University Press, 2010.)

[13] Marx, K. and Engels, F. *German Ideology*. Moscow: Progress Publishers, 1968.

[14] Marx. *Economic and Philosophic Manuscripts of 1844*. Eastford: Martino Fine Books, 2011.

[15] Sen, A. *Development as Freedom*. Palatine: Anchor Books, 2000; *Ibid*.

[16] Sen ignored Marx. In fact, Marx among the earliest scholars to link "ability" with "freedom". Marx once said that the key of human being's transition from "the kingdom of necessity" to "the kingdom of freedom" lies in "the development of human ability".

is a 'necessity' in a society depends on what is needed to provide minimum freedom," said Sen.[17] Malinowski has a similar point here. He believes that freedom of existence is the eternal foundation of free expansion and the basic condition of all other freedom. Freedom of existence is two-pronged: one is freedom of security, or freedom from fear, the other is freedom of prosperity, or freedom to satisfy one's needs.[18] He believes "true freedom ... is the increasing control, efficiency and intensity of individuals over themselves, the environment, artificial creation and natural resources."[19] Rawls has a more detailed analysis of "basic goods" (which is called "classical analysis" by Sen): "Basic goods include income, but also include other general 'means'. Basic goods are general means to man's goals, including rights, freedoms, opportunities, income, wealth and self-esteem."[20]

To understand and grasp freedom in practice by linking human needs with the "capability" of realizing such needs can avoid talking about freedom in vain. Freedom must have substantive content (what Sen calls "substantive freedom") rather than a superficial and formal right. For example, a poor man, deprived of basic capabilities,[21] has various formal freedoms of shopping, driving and traveling which no one can interfere with, but in fact the freedoms for him are only a mirage, or castle in the air, which cannot be realized at all. Therefore, substantive freedom is a kind of free volition, a right on his own will, and the entity must have the capability to choose independently. In this sense, freedom has both the ontological value that "man is the supreme essence of man" and the significance (practicality) which can be developed concretely in real life.

The original text is as follows: "On the other side of the realm of necessity, the development of human ability as an end itself, the realm of freedom, begins." (Marx, K. *Capital: A Critique of Political Economy*. Moscow: Progress Publishers, 1956.)

[17] Sen, A. *Op. cit.*

[18] Malinowski, B. *Freedom and Civilization.* Bangalore: Mysore Press, 2014.

[19] *Ibid.*

[20] Sen, A. *Op. cit.*

[21] Sen "sees poverty as a deprivation of basic viable abilities rather than just low incomes" (Sen, A. *Op. cit.*). Roosevelt also argues "people in poverty are not free people." (Sandel, M. *Justice: What's the Right Thing to Do.* New York: Farrar, Straus and Giroux, 2010.)

If we grasp freedom from the perspective of capability of human needs and satisfaction, it is obvious freedom in reality is manifold, for man's needs and their satisfaction are hierarchical. Engels once divided human needs into three levels: survival, pleasure and growth; Maslow, famous American psychologist, divided human needs into five hierarchies: physiological, safety, social, esteem and self-actualization. Generally speaking, lower levels of needs should be satisfied before people pursue higher levels, which means the realization of freedom in reality is also a historical, continuous, infinite process evolving from low to high levels. Marx said, "the satisfaction of the first need (the action of satisfying, and the instrument of satisfaction which has been acquired) leads to new needs; and this production of new needs is the first historical act."[22] However, it should be noted that the process of the hierarchical realization of freedom must not be understood mechanically and rigidly. The hierarchical nature of freedom does not mean that people cannot pursue higher levels of freedom until their primary needs are met. In fact, people in hunger also have basic esteem needs, primitive people also crave to show their talents and personality in various ways. It is absolutely wrong to regard freedom as a luxury, or to believe not until we are financially well off can we talk about freedom and enjoy freedom. Freedom itself is a fundamental human right. Article One of *The Universal Declaration of Human Rights* opens with a clear statement: "All men are born free, equal in dignity and rights."

Although freedom is human nature, an ever-chasing goal and practice of human society, "man was born free but always fettered," as Rousseau put it. "Fetters" are constraints and confinement, or unfreedoms, which means freedom is often limited and relative.

Why is it? It comes first and foremost from man himself. Although man is a conscious, rational and advanced animal evolved from the realm of animals, his cognitive and behavioral abilities are quite limited. Man is not free as to what he can't understand or control in the nature. In this sense, man is not the master of nature, but the slave of it. In the view of Hegel, German master of dialectics, freedom is the recognition of inevitability. Only by recognizing and grasping the laws of nature can man achieve

---

[22] Marx, K. These on Feuerbach, *The German Ideology*. Moscow: Progress Publishers, 1968.

freedom. Engels remarked: "Hegal was the first to state correctly the relation between freedom and necessity. To him, freedom is the insight into necessity... Freedom therefore consists in the control over ourselves and over external nature, a control founded on knowledge of natural necessity; it is therefore necessarily a product of historical development. The first men who separated themselves from the animal kingdom were in all essentials as unfree as the animals themselves, but each step forward in the field of culture was a step towards freedom."[23] Therefore, man advocates science, regarding knowledge as the path toward freedom. As Qi Liang put it, "thanks to the association of human freedom with the understanding of the world, the western world has been worshipping knowledge and science for over two thousand years. They are convinced as long as they persist in their intellectual pursuit, they can become as almighty as God with their motto, 'knowledge is power', which seems to bring them both almightiness and liberty."[24]

From another perspective, like happiness, the subjective feeling of freedom largely depends on the individual vision as well as external environment. A frog living in the bottom of the well felt free and satisfied before he got a glimpse on the outside world. But once he leapt out of the well, entering the "upper world" from the narrow "well bottom", he would feel confused, bewildered, unhappy and unfree. Is there any likelihood that he would return to the "happiness" and "freedom" in the bottom of the well by intentionally ignoring or forgetting the outside world?! Malinowski said, "Freedom consists in the width of vision and effectiveness of action."[25] The transition of freedom from a narrow horizon to unfreedom from a wider horizon and then to freedom from a wider horizon has in itself shown that freedom is relative and limited, and the transition itself shows the evolution and elevation of freedom. In a sense, vision itself is part of freedom.

---

[23]Engels, F. *Anti-Dühring: Herr Eugen Dühring's Revolution in Science.* Moscow: Progress Publishers, 1947.

[24]Qi Liang. *Western Liberal Tradition.* Guangdong: People's Publishing House, 2003.

[25]Malinowski, B. *Freedom and Civilization.* Bangalore: Mysore Press, 2014.

People's freedom is always restricted and confined, with the major constraints coming from the social sphere.[26] Human beings have dual attributes of both naturalness and sociality, with sociality being key factor in his separation from the realm of animals. Marx said, "Man is a political animal in the most literal sense: he is not only a social animal, but an animal that can be individualized only with society."[27] Therefore, "the human essence is no abstraction inherent in each single individual. In its reality it is the ensemble of social relations."[28] Man by making up a society is stronger and freer than other animals; however, his behavior is also regulated by a set of rules, systems and customs. Rousseau remarked that "What mankind loses by social contract is his natural freedom and unlimited access to everything he wants and procures; what he gains is social freedom and entitlement to everything he owns. In order to balance gains and losses without making mistakes, we must distinguish between natural freedom, limited only by individual strengths, and social freedom, bound by public welfare."[29] In a word, human's natural and social attributes determine that human's freedom will inevitably be restricted and bound by the established natural and social conditions.

Restrictions from the social level are both necessary and crucial, without which human beings would be trapped in the "Hobbesian jungle" of "war against all", slaughtering each other and ultimately destroying human beings altogether. Here, the purpose of restrictions is to better protect mankind's freedom, i.e., "everyone's" freedom, and to expand the real space of freedom. In this sense, "freedom comes from compliance with rules."[30] Therefore, freedom is not an individual's free will, or doing anything without restrictions. Hobbes once said that absolute freedom means

---

[26]Prof. Yu Wujin believes that freedom is not embodied in the relationship between man and nature, but only in the relationship between man and man, i.e., freedom is only an ontological category, not an epistemological category. I don't agree with this viewpoint, but insist on the Hegelian tradition of "freedom is the recognition of inevitability" in the category of epistemology.

[27]Marx, K. *A Contribution to the Critique of Political Economy*. Franklin Classics, 2018.

[28]Marx, K. These on Feuerbach, *Op. cit.*

[29]Rousseau, J.-J. *The Social Contract*. Washington, DC: Henry Regnery Company, 1954.

[30]Malinowski, B. *Op. cit.*

that everyone can get what he wants, but it doesn't exist in reality. The bottom line of freedom in modern society is neither to infringe on the freedom of others nor to build one's own freedom on the unfreedom of others.[31] In Locke's words, "Reason, or natural law, teaches reason-compliant mankind that man is created equal and independent, no one can infringe upon the life, health, liberty or property of others."[32] That is to say, human's real freedom is based on the recognition of the freedom of others. When Yan Fu, famous thinker and translator in the late Qing Dynasty and early period of Republic of China, translated the title of John Stuart Mill's masterpiece *On Liberty* to *On the Boundary of Rights (Qun Ji Quan Jie Lun).* He saw the boundary of freedom keenly by saying "man's freedom should be based on the boundary of others." Kant pointed out that "does freedom mean I can do whatever I want to?" If so, it is too superficial. He continues to argue "freedom means I can undo whatever I don't want to," which is real freedom. In Kant's view, freedom is not only a kind of individual right but also the basis of individual responsibility (responsibility to others and the society). "To Kant, self-respect and respect for others come from one and the same principle."[33] It is clear freedom and discipline are consistent here.[34] Hoffe said "the restriction on freedom exchanges for the guarantee on freedom, while the abandonment of freedom exchanges for the entitlement on the right of freedom."[35]

Unfortunately, many rules and systems in human society are not meant to better protect everyone's freedom or expand the real space of freedom,

---

[31] Hobbes, T. *Leviathan*. Eugene: The University of Oregon Press, 1999.

[32] Locke, J. *Two Treatises of Government*. Scotts Valley: CreateSpace Independent Publishing Platform, 2015.

[33] Sandel, M. *Justice: What's the Right Thing to Do*. New York: Farrar, Straus and Giroux, 2010.

[34] Ancient Greek philosophers like Socrates, Plato and Aristotle did not like "liberty", for they believed that personal freedom did not necessarily lead to virtue or conscience. If people are free to live according to their own will, rather than follow saints' teachings or the nobles' rules (examples), it is likely to lead to widespread degeneration. Kant links freedom and self-discipline, which has better solved the worries of ancient Greek philosophers about liberty.

[35] Höffe, O. *Political Justice: Foundations for a Critical Philosophy of Law and the State*. Hoboken: Wiley, 1995.

the restriction on freedom doesn't succeed in exchanging for guarantee of freedom, or the freedom of a few is procured at the expense of that of the majority, and one's own freedom is based on the unfreedom of others. Tocqueville said, "A tyrant himself does not deny the virtue of liberty, but he wants to monopolize it, believing nobody else deserves it. Therefore, the difference lies not on the opinions on freedom but the respect for others."[36] Marx also has a sharp exposition of this: "No man combats freedom; at most he combats the freedom of others. Hence every kind of freedom has always existed, only at one time as a special privilege, at another as a universal right."[37] Is it the freedom of "one", "the minority", or of "each", "all"? Whether freedom is a privilege of the minority or a universal right of everyone is the major, fundamental divergence of the opinions on freedom. Marx and Engels believed "the free development if each is the condition for the free development of all."[38] In Milton's Law, "universal freedom brings about economic growth benefiting all mankind".[39] The most significant substantive progress of human social freedom is the expansion of its universality.

Freedom, in its initial sense in the West, means to get rid of the coercion of others and the society, to liberate from personal attachment and realize the independence of personality. Therefore, "liberty" and "liberation" are cognate words.[40] Marx said, "Every emancipation is a restoration of the human world and of human relationships to man himself," which equals the realization of man's liberty. Cassirer said, "Human culture as a whole can be called the process of continuous self-liberation."[41]

---

[36]Tocqueville, A. de. *The Old Regime and the Revolution*. Chicago: The University of Chicago Press, 1998.

[37]Marx. Proceedings of the Sixth Rhine Province Assembly, *Karl Marx & Frederick Engels: Collected Works*. Intl Pub Co. Inc, 1996.

[38]Marx, K. and Engels, F. Manifesto of the Communist Party, *Karl Marx Selected Works in Two Volumes*. London: Lawrence and Wishart Limited, 1947.

[39]Quoted from Xiao Guoliang. Company Contemplation, *Reading*, No. 2, 2011.

[40]There are two basic words in English: freedom and liberty. Both of them caontain the meaning of free will, autonomy and liberation.

[41]Marx, K. On the Jewish Question, *Karl Marx & Frederick Engels: Collected Works*. New York: Intl Pub Co. Inc, 1996.

The process of human self-liberation is essentially the process of generation and expansion of universal liberty.

2.2 "Free to Realize Freedom": Freedom is Both the Purpose and Means

From the perspective of human self-liberation and human liberation, the generation of freedom is an infinite historical process with no end. Freedom is not only an ideal state but also a practice in real society. On the one hand, the realization of freedom requires man to constantly improve his cognitive ability, while the freedom of thoughts is the premise to enhance his cognitive ability; on the other hand, the freedom of each is the condition of freedom for all, but the realization of each's freedom also calls for a favorable environment and condition. From this perspective, freedom is the prerequisite and condition for the realization of freedom, as what Marx has put it, "Freedom includes not only what my life is, but equally how I live, not only that I do what is free, but also that I do it freely."[42]

"Realization of freedom with freedom" is not a meaningless word game of repetition but contains profound thought and philosophy. Freedom here is both an end and means. Sen expressed similar idea by saying "freedom is not only the primary end but also the principal means of development."[43] Freedom, as an end, is an ideal state that each (me) and all (us) have always been pursuing. The history of man's development is also the history of man's constant pursuit and realization of freedom. "Man himself is the supreme essence of man." Freedom as a means is an indispensable prerequisite for the realization of freedom. In a sense, "freedom" as a means is more important than the "freedom" as an end, for without the former the latter would be only a mirage or castle in the air.

---

[42]Marx, K. Proceedings of the Sixth Rhine Province Assembly, *Karl Marx & Frederick Engels: Collected Works*. Intl Pub Co. Inc, 1996. The translation version of 1995 is "Freedom includes not only what I live on, but also how I live, not only what I do freely, but also I do what I do freely" (see page 181). The author believes that the 1982 version can better reflect the essence of Marxist thought.

[43]Sen, A. *Op. cit.*

Sen calls freedom as a means "instrumental freedom". He emphasizes and examines five types of "instrumental freedom": (1) political freedoms; (2) economic opportunities; (3) social facilities; (4) transparent guarantees; (5) protective security. "The instrumental freedoms help people live more freely and improve their overall capabilities in this aspect, and the five types complement each other," Sen said.[44]

Individual freedom needs to establish the entity status of an individual, i.e., man has to be a "free man". "A free man" is an independent, autonomous and equal person in law. A slave cannot be a free man, he is only a tool that can speak. Smith's "economic man" is an independent and autonomous person in law, which is the foundation of modern civil society and modern market economy.[45]

Admittedly, the status of a free man granted by law may only ensure "formal freedom" rather than "substantive freedom". When talking about the trade of labor in capitalist society, Marx argues that capital-employed labor is "substantive unfreedom covered up by formal freedom". He continues to elaborate on it by saying "and this worker must be free in the double sense that as a free individual he can dispose of his labor-power as his own commodity, and that, on the other hand, he has no other commodity for sale, i.e. he is rid of them, he is free of all the objects needed for the realization of his labor-power."[46] Compelled by both the law of hunger and the law of survival, he has to sell his labor. In this sense, he is not free. Obviously, the latter kind of "free", namely "free of all the objects needed for the realization of his labor-power", is essentially "unfree". "To be free of all the objects" means that the basic economic and social conditions for safeguarding and pursuing individual freedom have been lost. As Sen has put it, there is no "capability" to realize individual's "substantive freedom". If we follow on in the logic, we are going to find a certain property right (rather than "to be free of all the objects") is the essential material basis and premise to protect individual freedom, and that individual

---

[44] *Ibid.*

[45] How to understand "economic man" in Smith's theory? Please refer to the paper "Thoughts on Several Questions of 'Economic Man Hypothesis' published by the author in the first issue of *Jianghan Forum* in 2009, pp. 46–50.

[46] Marx, K. *Capital: A Critique of Political Economy*. Moscow: Progress Publishers, 1956.

private ownership is the basic economic system guarantee for individual freedom. In this light, we may more accurately understand and grasp the profound meaning of Marx's controversial argument: "The capitalist mode of appropriation, the result of the capitalist mode of production, produces capitalist private property. This is the first negation of individual private property, as founded on the labor of the proprietor. But capitalist production begets, with the necessity of a natural process, its own negation. It is the negation of negation. This does not re-establish private property for the producer, but gives the producer individual property based on the achievements of the capitalist era, i.e., on co-operation and the possession in common of the land and of the means of production."[47] In my understanding, the individual private ownership here,[48] as opposed to "personal, labor-based private ownership", is based on large-scale social production; the individual private ownership here is also different from the capitalist private ownership owned by a few but deprived of the majority. It is "owned" by every individual (rather than abstract society), i.e., the general public. Generally speaking, universal freedom must be supported by universal individual ownership as its economic system.

It should also be stressed here that Marx has never denied the great historic progress of "free man" compared with slaves. From the perspective of the development process of human freedom, labor freedom of workers is more than "formal freedom". Even if a man has "freedom without possession", he's at least free to sell their own labor, free to choose employers, so it's still a major progress of substantive freedom compared with personal dependence and extra-economic coercion in which it's even impossible to choose employers. Sen emphasized the historic significance of this "formal freedom" in the process of human development[49] in his book *Development as Freedom*. In fact, he once quoted from Ramachandran, an Indian scholar, as saying, "Marx distinguishes

---

[47] *Ibid.*

[48] Some scholars (including Engels) have interpreted "personal ownership" here as personal ownership of consumer goods, which is not right. In the context, it is obvious that we are discussing the ownership of means of production.

[49] Unlike Sen, most Chinese scholars tend to emphasize the hypocrisy and deception of this "formal freedom".

between the formal freedom of the workers under capitalism and the real unfreedom of workers in pre-capitalist systems: 'the freedom of workers to change employers makes him free in a way not found in earlier modes of production.' The study of the development of wage labor in agriculture is important from another perspective as well. The extension of the freedom of workers in a society to sell their labor power is an enhancement of their positive freedom, which is, in turn, an important measure of how well that society is doing."[50] Of course, we can never be satisfied with this incomplete sense of "formal freedom". Socialist revolution is to change the situation of workers who have "freedom without possession", promote the further development and transcendence of freedom. It is not to change "free man" into another form of dependent unfree man.

A "free man" is a "social being" rather than a man totally of his own free will. As Sen put it, "the freedom each of us enjoys is inevitably regulated and restricted by the social, political and economic opportunities that we may have."[51] From this perspective, the free economic social environment is of decisive significance to the realization of freedom for free men. Sen has a famous saying: "Personal freedom is a social product in essence." The degree of social freedom also determines the degree of individual freedom. Cicero said, "Only when we become slaves of the law, can we become free."[52] But there are good laws and bad laws. Good laws guarantee freedom, while bad ones destroy it, both of which are a social product rather than a private outcome.

A free social environment is not uniform or unitary, but pluralistic, inclusive and open. Acknowledging the rationality of individual freedom means recognizing individual differences and pluralism of individual free choice on the basis of non-infringement on the freedom of others and common interests of society. Allowing everyone to choose freely does not guarantee (in fact, it is also impossible to guarantee) the correctness of every individual's choice, but society should make sure that individuals have the opportunity to pursue freedom and happiness, and even the opportunity and right to "trial and error", without which there will be no

---

[50] Sen, A. *Op. cit.*

[51] *Ibid.*

[52] *Ibid.*

real freedom. Therefore, only in a pluralistic, inclusive and open society can people enjoy freedom freely.

2.3 Who Gives Me Freedom: A Second Reflection on "Realization of Freedom with Freedom"

In specific, "realization of freedom with freedom" means that "free man" achieves freedom on the basis of non-infringement on the freedom of others and that of the society through free (but also self-disciplined) action in a free social and economic environment. However, in the historical process of human society, the freedom of vulnerable groups appeared to be granted by the enlightened and powerful elite groups, the unfree enslaved groups were liberated by the enlightened and powerful liberators. For example, the liberation and freedom of black slaves in the United States were attributed to the Civil War and *Emancipation Proclamation*, issued by President Lincoln. Therefore, human freedom in general is strived and gained by mankind as a whole, but individual freedom is not attributed solely to the individual's own strength.

The differences among individuals, groups and strata exist at any time throughout human history, which is often the root of one group depriving the freedom of another. Historically speaking, people striving for it were often the ruled group at the bottom of the social strata, accounting for the majority of the population. Those minority ruling group, indulged in excessive freedom rather than lack in it, tended to abuse freedom, ignoring and trampling on the freedom of others. In essence, the process of human civilization is the process of freedom evolving from the privilege of minorities to the sacred and inviolable right of the majority and ultimately the right of all. Although we cannot deny the important role played by enlightened elite[53] in the process of human liberation ("liberation" and

[53]Thomas R. Day provides a case study of the white elite during the liberation of black Americans, which is contrary to our conventional preconceptions. "On the issue of black rights, the attitudes of the public and the elite are very different," Day remarked. White people with the least rights and the least education oppose black rights most. Compared with white people with higher socioeconomic status, they are more reluctant to contact blacks, using the same public lounge, watching movies or eating together, or being

"liberty" being cognate words), with an aim to make freedom irreversible and inalienable, we must establish the social consensus and the institution for freedom, which requires interaction between the upper and lower classes, between the enlightened elites and the grassroots, especially the group deprived of freedom to liberate themselves.

History has shown that the freedom bestowed is not freedom indeed, or freedom complete. Since it can be bestowed, it can be rescinded as well. In this circumstance, the elite group who acted as the liberator tended to have a sense of superiority: if I gave you freedom, you should be grateful and content, or I shall take it back or restrict it, which would obviously become the hidden danger of real freedom. For example, black Americans saw the hope of freedom when Lincoln issued *Emancipation Proclamation*. However, as Martin Luther King said in his famous speech "*I Have a Dream*" in front of Lincoln Memorial in 1963, "but one hundred years later, black people still is not free. One hundred years later, the life of black people is still sadly crippled by the manacles of segregation and the chains of discrimination. One hundred years later, black people lives on a lonely island of poverty in the midst of a vast ocean of material prosperity. One hundred years later, black people is still languished in the corners of American society and finds himself an exile in his own land."[54] The real realization of African American freedom cannot rely solely on the external liberation of the elites (like Lincoln); more importantly, it needs the awakening of the black people themselves and the struggle of their own. Furthermore, true universal freedom requires broad social consensus and a solid social foundation. Real individual freedom can never separate from the freedom of the whole society. Martin Luther King was widely acclaimed in American society, for he long before had realized clearly that

---

neighbors. Those who are most concerned about racial discrimination are the wealthy, well-educated white people, who are also most willing to contact with black people. The political implications of this finding are obvious: white people with less education and income are more likely to oppose civil rights legislation and the improvement of black people's conditions in education, work, income and residence. In the white community, the more affluent and well-educated white people tend to support civil rights. (Dye, T.R. *Understanding Public Policy*. Upper Saddle River: Prentice Hall, 2007.)

[54] King, M.L. "A Speech in Front of Lincoln Memorial", *The Appreciation of Speeches by Famous Jurists*. Ji'nan: Shandong People's Publishing House, 1995.

the freedom of black people and white people are inseparable. "Their destiny is closely related to ours."[55] Therefore, black people's freedom could not be gained through depriving white people of their freedom, or through strategies like "violence for violence". The American Black Liberation Movement led by Martin Luther King was not to provoke the confrontation and conflict between black people and white people, but rather to work toward black and white people "joining hands as brothers and sisters".[56] In fact, Marx and Engels have similar ideas in that they believe only by liberating all mankind can the proletariat finally liberate himself.

True freedom cannot depend on others' bestowment, or solely on individual strength. "I" can only "emancipate myself" by integrating and forming "us". Lonely individuals are not free in society, and "loneliness" itself is a manifestation of social exclusion and unfreedom. Therefore, only through cooperation and organization can people obtain real substantive freedom. However, it is also possible for organizations to alienate themselves into powerful tools to suppress and restrict individual freedom. Organizations are undoubtedly a social product.

2.4 What Is Meant by "Organization"?

There are many definitions of "organization" with rich connotations. From the perspective of semantics, "organize" as a verb can be regarded as an action, coordinating and managing social and economic activities formed by individuals and groups. As a noun, "organization" mainly refers to a group, or a stable cooperative relationship formed by people for a certain purpose and governed by a certain set of rules. "Organizations are groups of individuals who interact under certain rules in pursuit of certain common goals," says George Hendricks.[57] According to James Mach and Herbert Simon, "organizations are systems for coordinating actions among individuals or groups with different preferences,

---

[55] *Ibid.*

[56] *Ibid.*

[57] Hendrikse, G. *Economics and Management of Organizations*. New York: McGraw-Hill, 2003.

information, interests or knowledge."[58] Of course, as a group, "organization" (noun) and "organize" (verb) are in fact inseparable. A group needs to be coordinated and managed. In other words, the organizer needs to organize it through action. Marshall regards organization as the fourth factor of production besides labor, land and capital. Organizers, regarded as entrepreneurs, provide "organization", a specific factor of production.[59] Kindelberg and Herrick further remarked that "a major difference emerges between organization and other elements: all other elements tend to replace each other, while organization is a complement rather than a substitute."[60] To be more specific, organization cannot be substituted by labor, land or capital. Organizations, as a factor of production, agglomerate other factors of production. Therefore, Latan defines an organization as a decision-making unit that controls resources.[61] In this book, I tend to adopt a broader definition, regarding organization as a relatively stable social cooperative group composed of a certain number of individuals (or legal persons), connected and bound by a certain institution (written or unwritten, formal or informal). Small groups, such as families, are common living organizations among relatives bound by marriage, consanguinity or adoption. "Family is the most early-born form of social and economic organization."[62] A country, as a large group, is "a politically organized society".[63] There are many different types of organizations in between with different functions, such as firms, cooperatives, political parties, schools, clubs and churches. Among them, there are not only economic organizations but also political, cultural, educational and religious organizations, etc. There are not only profit organizations but also

[58] Mach, J. and Simon, H. *Organization* (2nd edition). Hoboken: Wiley-Blackwell, 1993.

[59] Marshall, A. *Principles of Economics*. Warsaw: Andesite Press, 2015.

[60] Kindelberg, C.P. and Herrick, B. ed. *Economic Development*. New York: McGraw-Hill Education, 1977.

[61] "An organization is generally regarded as a decision making unit a family, a firm, a bureau by which resources are controlled." (Ruttan, V.W. "Can Economic Growth Be Sustained?" *The Collected Papers of Vernon W. Ruttan and Yujiro Hayami*. Oxford Scholarship Online, 2015.)

[62] *Cihai* (abbreviated edition). Shanghai: Lexicographical Publishing House, 1989.

[63] *Concise Encyclopedia of Britain*, Vol. 3. Beijing: China Encyclopedia Publishing House, 1985.

non-profit ones. In addition, in today's society, there are many transnational organizations and international organizations, e.g., transnational corporations, the United Nations, WTO and so on.

No matter they are economic or political organizations, or other types of social organizations, all of them have several common basic features. According to Stephen P. Robbins and Mary Kurt, "The term organization refers to an entity that has a clear goal, personnel and a sophisticated structure."[64] Goal, personnel and structure are regarded as the three primary elements of an organization. North summarizes the characteristics of the organization from the institutional level into three aspects: "Firstly, establishing a set of behavior restraint mechanism in the form of rules and regulations; Secondly, designing a set of procedures to detect violations and ensure compliance with rules and regulations; Thirdly, defining a set of moral and ethical codes of conduct that can reduce transaction costs."[65] Of course, these rules, regulations, procedures, moral and ethical codes of conduct may be written, formal, or only social conventions or subconsciousness among members of the organization or the place where the organization is located. But whether formal or informal, written or unwritten, without the rules, regulations, procedures, moral and ethical codes of conduct, it is difficult for any organization to operate normally, let alone grow steadily. Specifically, an organization should have the following five basic characteristics: firstly, a certain number of people (at least two, such as a monogamous family), which differs organizations from individual; secondly, a definite organizational goal, which is not a simple summation of individual goals of the members; thirdly, organizational charters or codes of conduct, which are the maintenance mechanism; fourthly, an organizer, or entrepreneur, who is the authoritative leader or leading institution; lastly, a certain organizational property, which is the basic material conditions on which the organization operates. Economic organizations differ from other social organizations in that its operation mode and rules are based on economic interests, or put it another way, economic organizations are the aggregation of economic entities with different interests.

---

[64] Marshall, A. *Principles of Economics*. Warsaw: Andesite Press, 2015.

[65] North, D.C. *Structure and Change in Economic History*. New York: W. W. Norton & Company, 1982.

In modern society, firms are the primary micro-production units as well as micro-economic organizations. Therefore, Theory of the Firm is the primary and key theory of economic organization in modern economics. However, modern economic organizations have more than one form besides firm, so organizational theory includes, rather than equates, theory of the Firm. Coase sees firm and market as two different ways of organization. Organization here can only be understood from the perspective of behavioral science. Market, in Smith's words, is an invisible hand. It is neither a real economic entity nor an organization in the strict sense of Robbins and Kurt's. Therefore, the relationship between market and firm is not parallel between one kind of organization and another, but the relationship of the ocean and the islands on it.[66] The "island", in Coase's words, lives in the "ocean" and is connected by the market.

2.5 The Most Essential Function of Organization: Expanding the Space to Advance Personal Freedom

Why do individuals need organizations? Or, more specifically from the economic level, why should individual labor be organized into "team production", individuals become members of firms (organizations)? Mainstream economists, especially neo-institutional school, who believes they have answered the question of "why do organizations exist" by opening the "black box" of firms, sees the question mainly in the light of efficiency and transaction costs. Coase believes that "the essential characteristic of firms is to replace price mechanism".[67] That is to say, firms save transaction costs and improve social and economic efficiency. According to Alchin and Demsetz, "team production will be adopted if team output exceeds the sum of individual output and is sufficient to offset the costs of organizing and restricting team members,"[68] which implies the existence

[66] Tan C. ed. *New Trends in Development Economics*. Wuhan: Wuhan University Press, 1999, p. 146.

[67] Putterman, L. and Kroszner, R.S. eds. *The Economic Nature of the Firm*. Cambridge: Cambridge University Press, 2001.

[68] *Ibid.*

of an organization is due to the fact that its revenue is higher than its costs.[69] There is no mistake in explaining the existence of an organization by using efficiency, transaction cost or organizational benefit. The question is why does an organization pursue efficiency and organizational benefit? Is there a deeper reason, or a higher goal behind it? If an organization is regarded purely as a tool pursuing efficiency and benefit, we are likely to ignore man and freedom, its highest essence. From the analysis framework of this book, as a long-term and stable institutional arrangement of people's cooperative behavior and relationship, the essential function of an organization is not efficiency, but the guarantee to more effectively safeguard and realize individual freedom, expand the space of individual freedom and enhance individual's capabilities for realization of freedom with freedom.

Individuals are only free in form rather than in essence. As far as the relationship between individual and nature is concerned, a single person cannot combat dangers from nature. "The first men … were in all essentials as unfree as the animals themselves."[70] In terms of the relationship between individual and society, it's improbable for a single person to cope with the complexity and uncertainty of human social environment. Marx states that "In the process of production, human beings work not only upon nature, but also upon one another. They produce only by working together in a specified manner and reciprocally exchanging their activities."[71] So the free space of individual is actually very narrow. Only by cooperating, relying on the collective (group) strength and forming an organization can man possibly overcome cognitive and behavioral limits. Marx and Engels believe that "only then will the separate individuals be put in a position to acquire the capacity to enjoy this all-sided production

---

[69] In my book entitled *Research on the Form of Rural Microeconomic Organizations in Contemporary China* published in 2007, I answered the question "Why does an economic organization exist" also by asserting that organizational benefits outweigh organizational costs. However, I was also aware of the importance of personal freedom at that time, and therefore included the loss of personal freedom in the organizational cost.

[70] Engels, F. *Anti-Dühring: Herr Eugen Dühring's Revolution in Science*. Moscow: Progress Publishers, 1947.

[71] Marx, K. and Engels, F. *Karl Marx Selected Works in Two Volumes. Op. cit.*

of the whole earth (the creations of man)."[72] According to Malinowski, "freedom does not exist in individual actions. Freedom exists only in organized groups where people achieve their goals and share the fruits of their work through collaboration based on an integrated common goal."[73]

Firstly, cooperation and organization can create "collective strength" that individual labor does not have, make up for personal physical limits, expand the space and time of labor, thus expanding the real space of individual freedom and enhancing the capability to achieve substantive freedom.

As a natural man, an individual is unable to complete many tasks due to his physiological limits. Therefore, an individual is not free. However, as a social being, man can use collective power, the power of cooperation and organization, to help him complete the work that is beyond him as an individual. In essence, it is expanding individuals' free space by means of collective, cooperative and organizational strength, enhancing individuals' capability to achieve substantive freedom. Marx states that "In such cases the effects of the combined labor could either not be produced at all by isolated individual labor, or it could only be produced by a great expenditure of time, or on a very dwarfed scale. Not only have we here an increase in the productive power of the individual, by means of co-operation, but the creation of a power, namely, the collective power of masses."[74] H.A. Simom also remarks that "since individual is limited in knowledge, insights, skills and time, organization has become a useful means to achieve human goals."[75] Xunzi, an ancient Chinese philosopher, gave a vivid example: "Man is not as strong as an ox, as fast as a horse, but cattle and horses are tamed to serve man. Why? Man can team work, while cattle and horses can't."

Secondly, cooperation and organization can deepen the division of labor and improve labor efficiency. While gaining "benefits of division of labor", we can also gain "economies of scale" that individual labor is incapable of, obtain "surplus of cooperation" and "benefits of

[72]Marx, K. and Engels, F. *German Ideology. Op. cit.*

[73]Malinowski, B. *Op. cit.*

[74]Marx, K. *Capital: A Critique of Political Economy.* Moscow: Progress Publishers, 1956.

[75]Simon, H.A. *Models of Man.* New York: John Wiley and Sons, 1957.

organization", which provide necessary material basis and premise for the full realization of individual freedom and the promotion of individual's capability to realize substantive freedom.

Smith said, "The greatest increase in labor productivity, as well as the greater facility, skill and judgment in the use of labor seems to be the result of division of labor."[76] The simplest economic organization, such as an agricultural household, is a division of labor in which men farm and women weave, utilizing their respective gender expertise. The more complex the economic organization, the more sophisticated and developed its professional division of labor. There are natural division of labor, social division of labor and division of labor within economic organizations. The division of labor within economic organizations is the basis of social division of labor and also its deepening and refinement. Compared with individual labor, cooperation and organization can better realize the specialization of division of labor, thus can more effectively utilize the comparative advantages of each member and improve the overall labor productivity. Smith once gave a vivid account of the pin manufacturing industry at that time. In his case, if there is no division of labor, "a skilled pin-making artisan, working alone rather than specializing in a particular procedure, couldn't possibly make 20 pins a day no matter who he is. It is likely he could not even make one pin." But after division of labor, "ten artisans can make 48,000 pins per day, i.e. 4,800 pins per person per day".[77]

In addition, it is self-evident that individual labor cannot generate economies of scale. Therefore, cooperation and organization are the prerequisite of economies of scale. Marshall has long recognized it by saying there was a close functional relationship between scale of production and economic returns, which indicates with the expansion of production and operation, there will be a decline in costs and an increase in returns. To put it in standard mathematical language, in a regular quasi-concave homogeneous production function, if the output elasticity of each factor input is greater than one, the production function has the characteristic of

[76] Smith, A. *An Inquiry into the Nature and Causes of the Wealth of Nations*. London: Methuen & Co., Ltd., 1904.

[77] *Ibid.*

increasing returns to scale, i.e., it has the potential of economies of scale, which come from the inseparability of many production processes, production facilities and fixed assets investment. Without a certain economic scale, the potential economic benefits cannot be realized. In addition, returns to scale come from the reduction of unit cost and the improvement of labor productivity with the expansion of economic scale. When talking about the rise of mass production, Chandler observed that we tended to equate the improvement of productivity and the reduction in unit cost with economies of scale. He distinguishes economies of scale and division income in organizational gains. He said, "economies of scale come from the ability to integrate and coordinate material flows rather than from the more specialized and further division of labor in factories."[78]

Thirdly, cooperation and organization provide a platform for contacts between individuals and the society, channels for knowledge exchange and complementation, thus it can enhance the cognitive and behavioral ability of individuals to achieve freedom.

John Stuart Mill wrote as early as the mid-19th century: "In the current situation of slow progress, the significance of people getting to know those who are different from them in ways of thinking and behavior is hard to imagine."[79] Individual labor is a kind of lonely work, in which individual workers are limited to their own experience and knowledge. Organizations bring together different individuals with diverse experiences, knowledge structures, ways of thinking and behavior, form complementary and intersected knowledge, which is one of the most efficient ways to enhance cognitive and behavioral abilities in the real world, and further realize freedom more fully.

Knowledge complementarity and intersection make knowledge resources shareable. If you exchange one goods for another, you'll inevitably lose one for the sake of another; if you exchange one kind of knowledge with another person, you two can share both without any loss. Obviously, sharing makes knowledge a special resource with "spillover

---

[78] Chandler Jr., Alfred. D. *The Visible Hand: The Managerial Revolution in American Business*. Cambridge: Harvard University Press, 1993.

[79] Meier, G. and Stiglitz, J. eds. *Frontiers of Development Economics: The Future in Perspective*. Oxford: Oxford University Press, 2000.

effect", i.e., social benefits associated with positive external economic effects. Knowledge can be spread from one person to another, from one group to another through cooperation and organization so that people's average skill level and knowledge stock are generally improved, and the whole society has higher labor productivity. New Growth Theory, represented by Romer and Lucas, is based on the spillover of knowledge and human capital. They believe knowledge and human capital, as special factors of production, has diminishing returns to scale in its own production but increasing marginal productivity as an input to production.[80]

Furthermore, knowledge complementarity and intersection are also crucial to generate new knowledge, promote innovation and human civilization. Peter Drucker, master on management, states that the unique feature of knowledge innovation nowadays is that it is seldom based on a single knowledge, but the aggregation of different kinds of knowledge. Exchanges of opinions, intersection and integration of knowledge will often inspire new ideas and knowledge, thus promoting the constant innovation and development of human knowledge.[81] Lazonik said, "Innovation is a social process, which requires the intentional participation of many people with diverse expertise and functions. Innovation requires collective organization because it is complex, cumulative and constant."[82]

Fourthly, cooperation and organization can produce and provide public goods to meet the public needs, which is a major prerequisite to enhancing individual's capability to realize substantive freedom.

Public goods, as opposed to private goods, is for all members of the society to consume and share. It is an indispensable social prerequisite and social security to ensure the full realization of individual freedom of all members and to enhance everyone's capability to realize substantive freedom. Sen's five types of "instrumental freedom" (political freedoms,

---

[80]Romer, P. "Increasing Returns and Long-Run Growth", *Journal of Political Economy*, Vol. 94, No. 5 (1986), pp. 1002–1037; Lucas, R. "North-Holland On the Mechanics of Economic Development", *Journal of Monetary Economics*, Vol. 22, No. 1 (1988) , pp. 3–42.

[81]Drucker, P.F. *Innovation and Entrepreneurship*. Sanford: Collins Press, 1993.

[82]Lazonick, W. "The Integration of Theory and History: Methodology and Ideology in Schum-Perter's Economics," in Magnusson, L. ed. *Evolutionary and Neo-Schumpeterian Approaches to Economics*. New York, Springer-Verlag, 1994, pp. 245–263.

economic opportunities, social facilities, transparency guarantees and protective security) are closely related to public goods. Sen remarked that "substantive public funding", like basic medical security and elementary education, "is crucial to the development and utility of man's capability", and these "social arrangements can be decisive in ensuring and expanding individual freedom".[83] As we all know, public goods are what private producers (let alone individual producers) unable or unwilling to produce or provide, so public organizations, especially the government, have special responsibilities in this regard.

Fifthly, the social security and punishment mechanism provided by organizations can protect the boundaries of individual freedom, and guarantee people's right to "realization of freedom with freedom" more effectively.

Everybody has the instinct and desire to pursue freedom and happiness, though some pursue freedom and well-being at the cost of others, violating the legitimate boundaries. Without a strong restrictive and punitive mechanism, the freedom of many people, especially the vulnerable groups in society, will be violated. Individual strength is quite limited in punishing those violating actions, as has been proved by practice, while an organization can make up for the limits and shortcomings of individuals, for as a "community of responsibility", it has stronger deterrence and punishment mechanisms.

Obviously, the state, as an "organization with legitimate violence", has a unique role in effectively protecting individual freedom. North remarked, as "an organization with comparative advantage in violence", "the basic services provided by the state are the primary rules of the game",[84] which, from a historical perspective, are better than the "Hobbesian jungle" type of irregular human cannibalism despite its bias toward the ruling class rather than universal benefit to all. In this sense, "almost all sets of rules are better than no rules at all".[85] In the modern society ruled by law, the rights of people transferred to the government are part of the rights

---

[83] Sen, A. *Op. cit.*

[84] North, D.C. *Structure and Change in Economic History*. New York: W.W. Norton & Company, 1982.

[85] *Ibid.*

necessary for organizing the state and government rather than all rights of the people. The government governs the country primarily by law. Therefore, law should embody public will and guarantee people's freedom. As Locke said, "the purpose of law is not to deny or restrict freedom, but to protect and expand freedom."[86] In Montesquieu's words, at the level of legal system and rule by law, the so-called freedom is "the right to do everything permitted by law". "In a country, i.e. a society with laws, freedom is merely an individual can do what he should do, and is not forced to do what he should not".[87] It can be seen that the purpose of the people's transfer of rights is to enable the state to better protect the people's basic freedom, i.e., "freedom can only be restricted for its own sake".

In a word, individuals need organizations. Although efficiency and utility are considered here, in the final analysis, the purpose is to expand the space of personal freedom and enhance the capability of individuals to achieve substantive freedom. If efficiency is regarded as the sole and ultimate goal of an organization, it will most likely lead to alienation of the organization.

2.6 The Alienation of Organization: Bound, Restriction and Imprisonment on Individual Freedom

The entry of "alienation" in *The Concise Encyclopedia of Britain* reads: "Although alienation is popular in the analysis of modern life, it has always been vague and ambiguous in meaning."[88] Yu Wujin argues: "In the study of Marxist philosophy, perhaps no concept is more controversial than 'alienation'. Some scholars regard it as the trace left from Marx's earlier thoughts, or a useless appendix that can be removed, while others regard it as the most important concept in Marxist philosophy."[89] I'm not going to elaborate on the concept of alienation. Rather I tend to adopt a

---

[86] Locke, J. *Two Treatises of Government*. Scotts Valley: CreateSpace Independent Publishing Platform, 2015.

[87] Montesquieu. *The Spirit of the Laws*. Cambridge: Cambridge University Press, 1989.

[88] *Concise Encyclopedia of Britain*, Vol. 9. Beijing: China Encyclopedia Press, 1986.

[89] Yu Wujin. *Practice and Freedom*. Wuhan: Wuhan University Press, 2010, p. 308.

most accepted definition in the academia: alienation is the object created in individual's activities, but it becomes an external and alien force, which in turn opposes and oppresses individual himself. *The Encyclopedia* explains in this way: "It can be understood that an individual loses contact with himself in one way or another."[90]

In my opinion, organizational alienation is an institutional arrangement, which was created in social activities and originally meant to expand personal space of freedom and enhance capability to realize substantive freedom, but it has turned out an external and alien force, and become a confinement, restriction or imprisonment on the basic freedom of individuals. It's particularly true for those organizers and theorists who push efficiency to the extreme and regard it as the only (or ultimate) goal of an organization, and limiting the individual freedom to the greatest extent is deemed the most powerful way to improve the so-called organizational efficiency.

Firstly, the coercive power of an organization is far greater than that of an individual, through which the organizer can deprive its members of their various rights, even basic personal freedom.

Joining an organization itself means giving up part of their freedom, otherwise, the organization cannot exist. Engels said, "how a society, even of only two people, is possible unless each gives up some of his autonomy?"[91] The abandonment or transfer of individual freedom, if out of volition, can be regarded as "the restriction of freedom trading for the guarantee of freedom".

However, it is undeniable that in human society, quite a number of organizations are coercive rather than voluntarily organized out of pursuit for the maximum interests by its members. It means some members have forcibly deprived others of their freedoms in the name of the organization. Both theory and practice have shown the coercive power of an organization is far greater than that of an individual. A man with a strong physique can only deprive a few people of their freedoms, while a weak scholar can easily deprive hundreds of their freedoms through coercive power.

---

[90] *Concise Encyclopedia of Britain*, Vol. 9. Beijing: China Encyclopedia Press, 1986.

[91] Engels, F. Frederick Engels to Friedrich Cuno, January 24, 1872, *Karl Marx Selected Works in Two Volumes*. London: Lawrence and Wishart Laimited, 1947.

Secondly, the division of labor within the organization promotes specialization and improves labor efficiency, but at the same time, it may deepen the alienation of labor, so individuals may become more dependent on the organization and finally enslaved by the organization.

Division of labor and specialization undoubtedly can greatly improve labor efficiency, but at the same time, they may also bring alienation of labor. Marx and Engels remarked: "as long as man remains in natural society, that is, as long as a cleavage exists between the particular and the common interest, as long, therefore, as activity is not voluntarily, but naturally, divided, man's own deed becomes an alien power opposed to him."[92] The division of labor and specialization may lead to partial development of human labor skills, while the overall developments of human facility and personality are restrained and suppressed. In the state of extreme specialization (or partialness), individuals can only specialize in "one skill" and excel in "one specialty", without which one cannot make a living. If this skill or specialty is solidified within an organization, the individual can only depend on it and become a slave of the organization in the real sense (not necessarily in the legal sense).

However, it should be noted that the division of labor does not necessarily lead to labor alienation. The underlying cause is social disintegration and labor-capital antagonism rather than division of labor. In social practice, socialization of capital, intellectualization of workers, enhancement of human capitals, expansion of space and ability for the free flow and choice by the laborers, construction and improvement of the system and mechanism of benefit sharing among stakeholders, reduction in the "imperative working time", increase in the "free time" of workers can all help eliminate or alleviate labor alienation.

Thirdly, the operation of any organization requires authority. Authority, as opposed to compliance, is based on power. One's own will must obey the will of others, and one's own action must obey the command of others. Especially for those organizations with strict hierarchy, it is iron law for the subordinates to obey the authority.

The authority of an organization arises from the objective need to organize joint activities and co-production. Marx remarked that "all

---

[92] Marx, K. and Engels, F. *German Ideology*. *Op. cit.*

labour in which many individuals co-operate necessarily requires a commanding will to co-ordinate and unify the process, and functions which apply not to partial operations but to the total activity of the workshop, much as that of an orchestra conductor."[93] Director labor, as is named by Marx, is the authority of the organization, which can ensure the smooth progress of division of labor, cooperation and efficiency of an organization. However, Marx also states that there is another side to the authority of organizations, namely supervision, which is based on the antagonism between organizers, managers and members of the organization. "The greater this antagonism, the greater the role played by supervision. Hence it reaches its peak in the slave system."[94] Within an organization, organizers and managers are usually in a strong position, whose power and authority can easily dismantle its restrictions, going far beyond the boundary of director labor. Once the power is highly concentrated and expanded, most members will lose their "ego". From the perspective of the history of human organizations, power tends to pursue greater power, and "freedom will be threatened whenever there is centralization and manipulation of power".[95] Therefore, as Malinowski said, "a clear distinction must be drawn between necessary authority and power abuse, the former is to guarantee freedom in an organization while the latter is bound to suppress activity and deny freedom."[96]

Finally, in order to ensure unified will, organizations often require unanimity in thought and speech, which is likely to stifle the ideological freedom of members of organizations.

It is undeniable that unanimity in thought plays an important role in improving efficiency. However, if it goes beyond the necessary boundaries of production cooperation or "director labor" and begins to penetrate into all aspects of the social life, it will greatly restrict the free space of the members, especially in freedom of thinking and imagination, thus killing the most important source of social innovation. Rosa Luxembourg, well-known early German female Marxist social activist, remarked in her

[93] Marx, K. *Capital: A Critique of Political Economy*. Moscow: Progress Publishers, 1956.

[94] *Ibid.*

[95] Malinowski, B. *Freedom and Civilization*. Bangalore: Mysore Press, 2014.

[96] *Ibid.*

article on the Russian Revolution in 1918: "since freedom is blocked, the public life of the country has become barren, sterile, monotonous and futile, for by abolishing democracy the source of all spiritual wealth and progress has been blocked." "Without free opinion confrontation, the life of any public institution will gradually languish and become an organ without soul, only the ghost of bureaucracy lingering."[97] British scholar Hodgson also said, "In the field of thinking, as in nature, diversity is the dynamic for evolution. When variety and diversity vanish, innovation and progress may slow down till a complete standstill sets in."[98]

2.7 Organization Achieves Security at the Price of Freedom? A Reflection on the Theory of Knight

Since organization is a restriction on individual freedom, why should individuals join an organization? Leaving aside the compulsory organization, why should individuals with "free man" status give up their freedom of labor and choose to work under the instruction and supervision of others? More specifically, why should workers be employed by firms rather than work on their own? Frank Knight's answer is that workers (employees) give up freedom for security.

Risk, Uncertainty and Profit, authored by Frank Knight in 1927, has been a major work in Western Theory of the Firm and Western economic theory. The basic premise of Knight's theory is the heterogeneity of individuals and the uncertainty of economic life.[99] Knight believes "people differ in their abilities to effectively control others and decide what to do themselves. Besides, individual diversity also plays a role in self-judgement, self-trust of power and tendency to act on one's own and 'take

---

[97] Xiao Guoliang. Contemplation on Company, *Reading*, No. 2, 2011.

[98] Hodgson, G.M. *Evolution and Institution: On Evolutionary Economics and the Evolution of Economics*. Cheltenham: Edward Elgar Pub, 1999.

[99] William Brett and Roger L. Ransom argue that "Knight's first contribution is to distinguish between risk and uncertainty" (Breit, W. and Ransom, R.L. *The Academic Scribblers*. Princeton: Princeton University Press, 1999.)

risks'."[100] According to Knight, only a few people in society are risk-biased, while most are risk-averse or risk-neutral. Due to the uncertainty of economic life, most risk-averse or risk-neutral people are willing to give up their freedom of labor for economic security. In Knight's words, "confident and adventurous ones assure suspicious and timid ones by guaranteeing a certain income in exchange of possession of the actual results."[101] In other words, entrepreneurs (organizers) as risk takers, gain the right to labor decision by taking on risks of risk-averse or risk-neutral employees (workers), and thus employees get insurance, economic security and a certain income. In a sense, Knight's theory inherits and expands Smith's theory on division of labor. In modern economics, it means that those risk-biased can take risks and those risk-averse or risk-neutral are granted safety.

Gary S. Becker shares similar ideas. In Becker's view, in traditional society, people face limited information and many uncertainties. In the absence of formal security system, family, or "group of relatives", becomes an efficient "insurance company" in "protecting its members against unforeseeable disasters".[102] It means family, as an organization, mainly provide security for all family members, and parents are equivalent to entrepreneurs who take risks.

From the broad sense of freedom, security is also a kind of freedom, and it's the most basic freedom of subsistence. Of course, individuals' free decision and free action are also a kind of freedom and from the hierarchy of freedom, it may be a freedom at a higher level. Therefore, from the perspective of the hierarchy of freedom, a more appropriate interpretation of Knight's theory is to exchange a higher level of freedom for the basic freedom of subsistence. Obviously, if people's freedom of subsistence cannot be realized, high-level freedom, such as the realization of self-worth, is an empty talk.

---

[100] Putterman, L. and Kroszner, R.S. eds. *The Economic Nature of the Firm*. Cambridge: Cambridge University Press, 2001.

[101] *Ibid.*

[102] Becker, G.S. *An Economic Analysis of the Family*. Dublin: Economic and Social Research Institute, 1986.

Knight's theory interprets the relationship between employers and employees as that of free exchange and choice on the basis of autonomy and free will due to different abilities and preferences. "Freedom for security" conforms to the principle of equal exchange of market economy. Nevertheless, Knight's theory cannot answer the question why some risk-biased proletarians can only be employed because they are "free to have nothing". In fact, those proletarians don't have much space for free choice. In Sen's words, they lack the capability to realize substantive freedom. "The law of hunger" and "the iron law of survival" urge them to become employed by others. Furthermore, where does people's difference in ability and preference come from? Is it derived from people's disposition and genes, or from the external economic and social environment? Knight and Marx differ in whether the division of labor between employer and employee is caused by possession of property (means of production) or the difference in personal abilities and preferences.

From a historical perspective, in the early stage of capitalism when the working class was mainly composed of physical proletarians who had no possession, Marx's analysis was indeed more inclusive and convincing. Workers had to sell their labor not because they were risk-averse or risk-neutral, but because they were "rid of everything". "The owner of labor-power, instead of being able to sell commodities in which his labor has been objectified, must rather be compelled to offer for sale as a commodity that very labor-power which exists only in his living body."[103] In criticizing Knight's theory, Coase stated that those who had a better judgment and knowledge could gain income by selling their judgment and knowledge without necessarily organizing firms. Here, "judgment and knowledge" could be sold as an independent commodity.[104] However, within the framework of Marx's theory, workers who were "free to have nothing" did not have the basic prerequisites and conditions for producing independent commodities. Even if they had the preference and courage to take risks, they could only sell their own labor as employees and could not become independent producers. In fact, the proletarians who were "free to have nothing" might be more willing and courageous to take risks than the

[103] Marx, K. *Capital: A Critique of Political Economy*. Moscow: Progress Publishers, 1956.

[104] Coase, R. "The Nature of the Firm", *Economica*, Vol. 4, No. 16 (1937), pp. 386–405.

bourgeoisie, because the proletarians "had nothing to lose but chains". Wasn't "putting on an uprising and becoming bandits" a more adventurous act than organizing firms?

In fact, Marx cannot explain why some people in modern society who are not "free to have nothing", such as white collar and gold collar workers, choose to be employees when they have the alternatives. It should be noted that in the period when the middle class gradually became the major social stratum, the process of intellectualization and socialization of capital was accelerating. Not all employees (workers) were "free to have nothing". Many of them were fully qualified to make free choices between independent production and being employed; or, in Marx's terms, they could either "sell commodities with their objectified labor" or "sell labor only existing in bodies". For example, many high-end professionals and technical personnel with doctoral or master's degrees have chosen to start their own businesses, become bosses (produce independently or employ others), or teach in universities or become engineers (be employed by others) in firms. The former is undoubtedly willing to take more risks and challenges, while the latter is more secure. Whatever choices they have made, the differences between their abilities and preferences will be shown.

2.8 Labor and Capital Can Be Substituted As the Homogeneous Factor of Production in Firm? A Criticism on the New Classical Theory of the Firm

From the classical economics with Adam Smith as its vanguard, the Theory of the Firm of Western mainstream economics has always been centered on efficiency.

Smith believes that firms are the product of division and cooperation of labor, and "the greatest increase in labor productivity, as well as the greater facility, skills and judgment in the use of labor seem to be the result of division of labor".[105] The inevitability and rationality of the firm is that it

[105] Smith, A. *An Inquiry into the Nature and Causes of the Wealth of Nations*. London: Methuen & Co., Ltd., 1904.

can promote the division of labor, improve production efficiency and produce more social wealth. Of course, it also brings profits to entrepreneurs and employment opportunities to workers. Indeed, Smith did not systemically and thoroughly examine the internal structure of the "black box" of firm, but he still saw the antagonism between labor and capital within the firm by saying "the interests of both sides are absolutely inconsistent", and he also remarked that the employer "occupies the advantageous position."[106]

Marshall, master of neoclassical economics, emphasizes the special role of organization as the fourth major factor of production, explores the role of entrepreneurs, economies of scale, market structure of firms, private partnerships, joint-stock companies, cooperatives and other extremely wide scope of issues with the core of firm efficiency (profit maximization), so he has laid down the foundation for a more comprehensive and systematic (or somewhat not profound in some aspects) Neoclassical Firm Theory, and promoting the quantification, modelling and "natural science" process of it.

The firm theory of neoclassical economics is undoubtedly Theory of the Firm. The entrepreneur is implicitly recognized as the personalized representative of the firm, while profit maximization is the sole purpose of the firm's production and operation. Starting from the scarcity of resources, using economic man, rational choice and complete market as basic assumptions, adopting the methods of "marginal increment" and "equilibrium analysis", the firm theory of neoclassical economics tries to prove that as long as a firm works by production function and cost function, output maximization can be achieved through optimal allocation of production factors under certain technological level and target cost. Or, under the condition of a certain target output, the optimal allocation of production factors can minimize costs, which is also the optimization of firm efficiency. Here, the input–output relationship of a firm is a purely technical relationship that has nothing to do with the decision-making behavior of its members (employees), which is criticized by evolutionary economist Hodgson: "Firms are more of a series of cost-benefit curves than an organization."[107]

---

[106] *Ibid.*

[107] Hodgson, G.M. *Evolution and Institution: On Evolutionary Economics and the Evolution of Economics.* Cheltenham: Edward Elgar Pub, 1999.

What is a firm? What is an organization? A firm or organization, in essence, is an economic entity with different individuals (or groups) and interwoven interests rather than a simple or complex combination of profit and cost curves. In the neoclassical Theory of the Firm, labor and capital can be substituted for each other. Lively laborers, cold inanimate machines and factories are regarded as homogeneous and undifferentiated factors of production. "People" in firms, especially workers in firms, have disappeared. What can be seen is the undifferentiated factors of production and the inanimate functional relationship. As James Mach and Herbert Simon put it, this theory "generally tends to see employees as inanimate tools for assigned tasks" and "as established factors rather than variable factors".[108] In fact, Marshall himself does not fully agree with this simplified standard function model. Marshall once reminded people of the essential difference between selling commodities and selling labor (In Marx's words, "selling commodities with their own objectified labor" and "selling labor only existing in his living body"). He states that "When a person sells his service, he has to go to the spot in person. For a brick seller, whether the brick is used to build a palace or a sewage is totally irrelevant to him. But for a man who sells his labor, since he is responsible for completing the task with certain difficulty, whether the workplace is favorable and colleagues friendly is directly relevant to him."[109]

The most representative of new classic firm theory applied to practice is scientific management, put forward by Frederick W. Taylor, father of management. Based on the principle of the highest output of a firm and the highest efficiency of each person, the theory has realized a series of standardized management, such as tool standardization, operation standardization, labor action standardization and labor environment standardization. While greatly improving the production efficiency of a firm, it also "regards man, a living creature, as a relatively simple machine for completing simple tasks".[110]

---

[108] Mach, J. and Simon, H. *Organizations*. Hoboken: Wiley-Blackwell, 1993.

[109] Marshall, A. *Principles of Economics*. Warsaw: Andesite Press, 2015.

[110] Mach, J. and Simon, H. *Op. cit.*

2.9 Firm is the Result of a Series of Contracts: A Criticism to the Firm Contract Theory of New Institutionalism

Coase, founder of New Institutionalism, strongly criticized Neoclassical Theory of the Firm. He believes Neoclassical Theory of the Firm is a far cry from reality, for it can explain neither the reasons for the existence of firms nor their boundaries and scopes, so firms are still a "black box" beyond total comprehension. Coase sets up New Institutionalism on the basis of transaction cost theory and tries to answer such key questions as the nature and boundary of a firm, with his focus still on efficiency, though. Where is the boundary between a firm and market? It depends on the comparison between market transaction cost and firm management cost with an aim to minimizing cost, or, maximizing benefit. According to Coase, "the definition we give is very close to that of real-world firms."[111]

As is mentioned earlier, if we see a firm as an efficiency maximizing organization, it's likely to neglect the position and role of individuals, especially employees. In the neoclassical Theory of the Firm, labor, as a dynamic factor of production, is degraded as something that could be substituted with capital. Man "is described as a relatively simple machine to accomplish relatively simple tasks".[112] However, as a criticism on neoclassical Theory of the Firm, New Institutionalism has not corrected its fundamental defect, which is "seeing stuff rather than people". On the contrary, it has gone even farther in this regard.

It is undeniable that Coase himself did see a significant difference between "selling commodities" (through market connection) and "selling labor" (hierarchy of firms). He states: "the essence of the legal concepts of employer and employee is 'direction'."[113] However, Coase regards firms as a kind of transaction organization, and his versatile concept of

[111]Putterman, L. and Kroszner, R.S. eds. *The Economic Nature of the Firm*. Cambridge: Cambridge University Press, 2001.

[112]Mach, J. and Simon, H. *Op. cit.*

[113]Putterman, L. and Kroszner, R.S. eds. *Op. cit.*

transaction cost[114] leads some of his followers to push the New Institutionalism to another extreme.

Some of Coase's followers are not satisfied with his theoretical interpretation of the firm as a market substitute. In their view, Coase didn't persist in the concept of transaction cost. Zhang Wuchang, for example, argues that "it is not entirely correct to say that firms replace markets. To be exact, it's one contract replaces another."[115] In other words, it is the factor market that replaces the intermediate product market. In the view of these economists, a firm is only a special form of market, and it's in essence a contractual organization, connection of a series of contractual relations.[116]

Since a firm is regarded as a series of contractual relations, the relationship between people in the firm, especially the relationship between capital and labor, is totally submerged in the vast ocean of all kinds of contracts. Alchin and Demsetz believe "firms do not own all their inputs, they do not have the right to command, mandate or regulate, either, which bears no difference from the ordinary market contracts between two individuals...What is meant exactly by saying 'directing workers and assigning tasks to them?' There's literally no difference from the direction of a consumer to his grocer and his assigned tasks ... The employee is assigned to print this document rather than that one in the same sense as the grocer is asked to sell tuna instead of bread."[117] The essential difference between selling products and selling labor stressed by Marx, and to some extent endorsed by Marshal and Coase, has been neglected by New Institutionalism. Is an advance or retrogression of the theory?

---

[114]"Transaction cost is considered a vague and imprecise concept, and there are concerns that it may be arbitrarily used to explain everything that analysts cannot explain with a more' rigorous' model."

[115]Zhang Wuchang. *Economic Interpretation*. Hong Kong: The Commercial Press, 2000, p. 363.

[116]Jensen, M. and Meckling, W. "Theory of the Firm: Managerial Behavior, Agency Costs, and Ownership Structure", *Journal of Financial Economics*, Vol. 3, No. 4 (1976), pp. 305–360.

[117]Alchian, A.A. and Demsetz, H. "Production, Information Costs and Economic Organization", *IEEE Engineering Management Review*, Vol. 3 (1975), pp. 777–795.

2.10 The Weight of Personal Freedom in an Organization

There is a common defect in both neoclassical Theory of the Firm and New Institutionalism, which can be depicted as "seeing stuff rather than people". More accurately, the so-called mainstream Theory of the Firm only maximizes the profits of entrepreneurs (or shareholders); its members, especially ordinary workers, are assimilated as homogeneous factors of production like machinery and factory buildings, submerged by homogeneous contractual links. Within such "non-humanistic" theoretical framework, "economics is bound to deviate from the concern for freedom".[118] No wonder William White, American sociologist, sighs in his book *Organizer* that "Individual is nothing, while organization is everything."

However, there are still some "non-mainstream" voices that still concern the role, status and weight of individual freedom in firms without neglection of efficiency.

Harry Dawes finds[119] "the desire for independence (which is often a major goal in a worker's life) is why high-income technicians are willing to run retail stores or sell insurances."[120] Running retail stores and selling insurance do not necessarily earn higher wages than being employed as technicians, and their income is far less stable, for they have to take risks on their own. So why do these high-income technicians prefer to run retail stores and do insurance work? The ultimate reason is "the desire for independence". Independence means more personal freedom and more voluntary action. Here, individual freedom weighs more than income difference and economic security.

In the study on slavery in the South before its abolishment, Fogel and Engelman found that the slave labor organization (manor) at that time was quite efficient for slave owners, and even for those slaves, for their

---

[118] Sen, A. *Op. cit.*

[119] Coase quoted Dawes' discovery in *The Nature of Firms*, but it did not seem to attract enough attention from Coase.

[120] Putterman, L. and Kroszner, R.S. eds. *The Economic Nature of the Firm*. Cambridge: Cambridge University Press, 2001.

incomes were not lower than those of free agricultural workers, and their life expectancy was "much higher than that of free urban industrial workers in the United States and Europe." Even so, the slaves still wanted to run away. "After the slaves were set free, many landlords tried to reorganize their working groups on a wage basis. Despite the fact that the wages paid to these free men exceeded 100% of what they had previously earned as slaves, such efforts never worked. The landlords found that as long as they were deprived of the power to use violence, it was impossible to maintain the working group system even if they were given extra wages."[121] Hence, Sen emphasizes that compared with market efficiency, man's freedom is a more prominent perspective,[122] which means personal freedom has the significance transcending income, efficiency and economic interests.

In real life, with the information revolution and the rise of the network economy, as well as the growth of the middle class and their gradual becoming the main social stratum, people's basic right to subsistence and economic security are no longer a problem. The longing for independence and autonomy, pursuit of a higher level, chasing after dreams and craving for space to realize one's value in spare time are becoming increasingly important in all kinds of firms (organizations), especially knowledge-intensive and intelligence-intensive firms (organizations). It has also led to big changes in the organizational structure and form of firms. Freelancers and SOHOs[123] are rapidly becoming popular in North America, Europe and other developed regions of the global economy. According to market analysts' survey, in the United States alone, home-based part-time jobs and freelance white-collar workers account for about 40% of the labor market. The pursuit of personal freedom has become a fashion of the new generation. Under the influence of this new trend, the "flat" and equal participatory management is gradually replacing the hierarchical bureaucratic management. The humanistic management concept,

[121] Sen, A. *Op. cit.*

[122] *Ibid.*

[123] SOHO (small office home office) refers to a new form of economic organization in which firms are set up in their own homes and business is carried out by relying on information equipment and computer communication networks.

which attaches importance to human value and personal freedom, has gradually replaced the non-humanistic management concept in which human is merely deemed as an inanimate tool to accomplish efficiency tasks. The core of humanistic management concept is to regard man as his own self, or, man himself is the highest essence of man, not just a factor of production or production resources. From this point of view, humanistic firm (organization) management has changed the bias of unilaterally emphasizing compliance and discipline in traditional management, but instead attached more importance on equal communication, personality independence, human initiative, creativity, and the realization of man's value. Management theory seems to be more keenly aware of this new trend and change than economic theory. Management theory has come to realize that "individual free space determines organizational efficiency."

2.11 The Human Value Ascension in Firm: From Physical Capital to Human Capital

In "non-humanist" Theory of the Firm, people, especially laborers, are only tools for making profits, while physical capital is the first and foremost factor of production. The neoclassical Harrod–Domar model attributes economic growth to the growth of physical capital and the ratio of physical capital to material output, namely $G = S / V$.[124] However, even within the framework of neoclassical mainstream economics, many researchers have found that physical capital alone cannot fully explain the efficiency of firms, let alone the growth of a country's national income, especially the endogenous economic growth of technological progress.

Professor Theodore W. Schultz, known as "father of human capital theory", winner of the 1979 Nobel Prize in Economics, explored the miracle of economic recovery and growth of Germany and Japan after the Second World War in his speech entitled *Investment in Human Capital* as president of the American Economic Association in 1960. He argued that the growth of national wealth in the two countries after the war was far

---

[124]Here, G is the rate of economic growth, S is the rate of capital accumulation (savings rate or investment rate), V is the efficiency of capital (investment) use, i.e., the ratio of capital to output.

greater than that of consumption of production factors such as physical capital and land, which meant a considerable part of output, namely the "unexplainable residual factor", cannot be explained by the improvement of material input or material input efficiency. That is to say, it is difficult to explain the economic miracle of Germany and Japan with physical capital as the first factor of production. Schultz believes human factor is the key to the economic miracles of Germany and Japan. Although the war destroyed physical capital, it did not destroy their relatively abundant human capital, which had brought about the two countries' high-quality labor force, high labor efficiency and rapid technological progress.

If Schultz has demonstrated the importance of human capital from a macro point of view, New Growth Theory with Romer and Lucas as the vanguards further explains that human capital is the first and foremost driving force of economic growth from the micro point of view — firm. In their theory, they make technological progress endogenous which was considered exogenous in traditional theory, highlight the pivot significance of human capital in economic growth. Romer has inherited and further developed Arrow's thought of "learning by doing" and "spillover effect" of knowledge as public goods, indicating that the accumulation of knowledge capital is the decisive factor for the long-term growth of firms; knowledge capital not only has its own increasing marginal productivity, but can also bring incremental income to physical capital, thus breaking the traditional bottleneck of decreasing marginal return on capital.[125] Lucas distinguishes the internal and external effect of human capital, put his stress on the external effect, which he believes is the core of the average human capital level of social labor force. He argues the external effect of human capital has not only the function of increasing returns but also spillover and diffusion effect, an important contribution to the productivity improvement of all factors of production.[126] It should be noted that Arrow's theory of "learning by doing" actually reveals the

[125]Romer, P. "Increasing Returns and Long-Run Growth", *Journal of Political Economy*, Vol. 94, No. 5 (1986), pp. 1002–1037.

[126]Lucas, R. "On the Mechanics of Economic Development", *Journal of Monetary Economics*, Vol. 22, No. 1 (1988), pp. 3–42.

vital importance of practice for the promotion of human capital and highlight the value of "human" as a practitioner in firms.

The rise of human capital theory in the 1970s and 1980s is not accidental. Rather it is inextricably linked with the rise of global knowledge economy. Knowledge economy or knowledge-based economy, taking human capital as the basic element and human knowledge innovation as the main source of growth, is strikingly different from industrial economy in that the latter regards physical capital as the basic element and physical capital accumulation as the main source of growth. In the industrialized era characterized by large machinery and mass production, the firm was an assembly-lined process-oriented firm. The employees working on the assembly line only needed to complete the operation process as ordered, just like a screw in a machine. Compliance is the basic requirement. Individual autonomy and creativity were neglected in the so-called scientific management, and even intentionally suppressed by rules and regulations. However, in the era of knowledge economy, diversification and differentiation have replaced simplification and standardization. Employees have gradually changed from manual workers to knowledge workers. People's initiative and creativity have increasingly become the main source of profits and competitiveness of firms. Since knowledge, initiative and creativity are inseparable from learning and practice, man, as the knowledge holder, user and creator (knowledge worker) is no longer the simple, mechanical, homogeneous and mutually replaceable laborer in traditional industrial society, but active, creative and capable in realizing their own value, and is also the "first factor of production" that promotes economic growth.

Admittedly, human capital theory still regards "human" as "capital", a tool of economic growth, and does not regard "human" as the purpose of economic growth. However, it has, after all, promoted the role and value of "human" within the framework of mainstream economics.

2.12 The Interest-Sharing and Inclusive Mechanism of Firm: From "Shareholder Primacy" to "Stakeholder Primacy"

With the rise of knowledge-based economy and the status promotion of human in the firm (organization), the concept of "entrepreneurs' firm" or "shareholders primacy" is challenged in both theoretical and practical aspects.

Firms are essentially human organizations and collections of various stakeholders, not just entrepreneurs' firms, or the mix of labor-capital relations. Stakeholders, in a narrow sense, are defined by Stanford Institute as people or groups that invest professional assets in firms.[127] In a broader sense, it is defined by Freeman as any group or individuals that can influence the achievement of organizational goals or are influenced by the goals.[128] In this sense, stakeholders include not only shareholders, managers, technicians, ordinary workers but also creditors, debtors, suppliers, sellers, consumers and other trading partners of firms, even relevant groups and pressure groups outside such as government departments, local residents, communities, media and environmentalists, as well as objects directly or indirectly affected by the business activities of firms such as natural environment and human offspring. Of course, they differ in the degree of closeness with the firm interests. Freeman divides them into three categories: ownership stakeholders, economic dependent stakeholders and social stakeholders.[129]

Compared with the traditional shareholder primacy, stakeholder primacy theory holds that the formation and development of any firm (organization) cannot be separated from the input or participation of various stakeholders, so the firm (organization) is commonly owned by all stakeholders; the firm is a system composed by many stakeholders. Therefore, firms (organizations) should pursue the overall interests of stakeholders, create wealth and value for all, so that all stakeholders instead of individual entity (like shareholders) can share profits.

Unlike Knight's view that only entrepreneurs (organizers) take risks and therefore they monopolize the residual of firms, stakeholder theory holds that all individuals or groups that make specific investments in the production activities actually all bear certain risks. Clarkson remarked that "stakeholders invest physical capital, human capital, financial capital

[127] Stanford Research Institute (1963), Internal Memorandum, http://www.ruf.rice.edu/-odw/.

[128] Freeman, R. E. *Strategic Management: A Stakeholder Approach.* Cambridge: Cambridge University Press, 1984.

[129] *Ibid.*

or something valuable in the firm, and thus bear some form of risks; or they bear risks from firm activities."[130] Stakeholder theory emphasizes the asset specificity of special human capital, so it also highlights the value and status of "human" as a special human capital in firms (organizations).

Since firms (organizations) are regarded to be commonly owned by stakeholders rather than "owned only by entrepreneurs", and all stakeholders are identified to bear certain firm risks as entrepreneurs (though they differ in ways and degrees of risk bearing), stakeholder theory reasonably requires all stakeholders to participate in decision making and interest sharing of firms (residual claims). In my opinion, the most valuable idea of Stakeholder Theory is that starting from Kant's philosophy, Freeman, the representative expert of stakeholder theory, states human is the goal rather than the tool of the firm (organization).

It is true that Stakeholder Theory has defects and shortcomings, and it is not a very complete and mature theory. However, the theory has expanded the vision and value of people in firms (organizations), emphasized interest sharing and inclusive benefit, and thus has reflected the new trend in the era of knowledge-based economy.

2.13 The Community of Free Individuals: Both Ideal and Practice

"The community of free men" is a conception of future communist social structure by Marx and Engels. It can better illustrate their vision and hope for the future society than public ownership and planned economy. They wrote in *Manifesto of the Communist Party* that "in place of the old bourgeois society, with its classes and class antagonisms, we shall have an association, in which the free development of each is the condition for the free development of all."[131] In 1894, when *New Century Weekly* asked Engels to briefly outline the basic ideas of the future socialist era, Engels

[130]Clarkson, M.A. "Stakeholder Framework for Analyzing and Evaluating Corporate Social Performance", *Academy of Management Review*, Vol. 20, No. 1 (1995), pp. 92–117.
[131]Marx, K. and Engels, F. Manifesto of the Communist Party, *Op. cit.*

emphasized this sentence again and asserted "I have found nothing except the following passage taken from *Manifesto of the Communist Party*."[132]

Establishing a "society in which the full and free development of every individual forms the ruling principle,"[133] i.e., establishing a community of free men is the ultimate goal and theoretical essence of Marxist social revolution. From the perspective of ultimate goal, all Marx's doctrines can be understood as "the doctrine of emancipating the whole mankind".[134] As is mentioned earlier, liberation and liberty are cognates, sharing the same root. Unfortunately, this idea has been intentionally or unintentionally forgotten or even misinterpreted for quite a long time. At the stage when the proletariat tried to seize power, it was understandable that people put more emphasis on class and class struggle, which was also the call of the time. At the initial stage of socialist construction, people did not have the existing socialist model to follow, and it was inevitable to regard public ownership and planned economy as the essential characteristics of socialism in the exploratory period. However, the most essential feature of communism is, after all, the full and free development of man, rather than the long-term class struggle between one class and another; nor is it the kind of planned economy that restrains individual autonomy and freedom and controls everything by state administration. Some people criticize the heated debate on "the community of free men" or the unusual interest in "the community of free men", but it's precisely because the profound thoughts of "the community of free men" have been ignored or distorted for such a long time.

Since the reform and opening-up, people have emancipated their minds and sought truth from facts. The emancipation of mind and the freedom of thought are the forerunners of freedom of action and freedom of practice. Especially after the establishment of the concept on "people-oriented" scientific development, Marx's thought of "full and free

---

[132]Engels, F. Engels to Giuseppe Canepa, *Karl Marx Selected Works in Two Volumes*. London: Lawrence and Wishart Limited, 1947.

[133]Marx, K. *Capital: A Critique of Political Economy*. Moscow: Progress Publishers, 1956.

[134]"In the final analysis, Marxist philosophy is a doctrine of emancipating the whole mankind." (Yu Wujin. *Practice and Freedom*. Wuhan: Wuhan University Press, 2010.), p. 18.

development of man" and "community of free men" have won more and more attention and affirmation, but there are also two noteworthy deviations.

The first is the tendency to replace "full and free development of man" with "full development of man". For a long time, there has been a trend that most articles only discuss full development, but intentionally or unintentionally avoid free development when talking about Marx's theory of human development. Some tend to replace the full and free development of man with the full development of man. The first reason is that there has been freedom-phobia for a long time in China's academia. Secondly, in the traditional political and economic thinking mode, full development denied the division of labor, professionalization, even market economy. In the context of long-term denial of market economy, full development is unilaterally highlighted. However, Marx's full development in its original sense denies only the compulsory division of labor, but not the voluntary division of labor, i.e., the division of labor based on free choice. In fact, full development doesn't imply people do everything, or the division of labor, social division and specialized production are extinct. The essential meaning of full development is that people can freely engage in the work they want to do. It also implies that people can choose not to engage in the work that they don't want to. Obviously, it includes division of labor and specialization.

Furthermore, in Marx's theory of the full and free development of man, which is of essential significance and more important between free development and full development? I believe it is free development rather than full development.

First, from the perspective of teleology, free development is of a higher level than full development. In a sense, full development is for people to fully realize freedom, or in Amartya Sen's words, to enhance people's capability to achieve substantial freedom. Perhaps, some may ask can we put it the other way around by saying free development is for full development? Definitely not. In Marx's theoretical system, the freedom for each and for all is the ultimate goal of human civilization development, but Marx has never given such a priority to full development.

Secondly, free development is the basic premise to achieving full development (note that basic premise does not mean free development serves for full development). Marx's full development refers mainly to the involuntary old-style division of labor, which brings about the alienation of labor. Marx and Engels remarked: "as long as man remains in natural society, that is, as long as a cleavage exists between the particular and the common interest, as long, therefore, as activity is not voluntarily, but naturally, divided, man's own deed becomes an alien power opposed to him."[135] How can we achieve full development (in Marx's words, each can become accomplished in any branch he wishes, society regulates the general production and thus makes it possible for me to do one thing today and another tomorrow)[136] rather than the abnormal, one-sided development bound by old-style division of labor? Marx believes that one of the most important ways is to gradually increase people's free time. He argued, the time which society is bound to devote to material production is shorter, and as a consequence, the time at its disposal for the free development, intellectual and social, of the individual is greater in proportion.[137] Only when people can freely control their time and develop freely can the so-called full development be realized. From this point of view, full development is only a by-product of free development.[138]

The second deviation is to regard the community of free men as a future ideal rather than a present practice.

---

[135] Marx, K. and Engels, F. *German Ideology. Op. cit.*

[136] *Ibid.*

[137] Marx, K. and Engels, F. Economic Manuscripts 1857–1858, *Karl Marx Selected Works in Two Volumes*. London: Lawrence and Wishart Limited, 1947.

[138] When Mr. Zhu Yongxin talked about the relationship between "personality education" and "full development" in education, he had a very insightful exposition, which was closely related to the "free development" and "full development" we discussed. "Every man is an individual, and every child is a unique individual," he said, "The best education should be tailored to the individual, and the best education should enable the individual to maximize his potential and personality. Then, we cannot use a single standard to require all children, nor can we simply stress the comprehensive development of morality, intelligence, physical fitness, aesthetics and labor. In fact, in the process of our education, many people are carrying on underdevelopment in a full way with the banner of full development, for full development is impossible both from the perspective of the time, space and capability of our education as well from the perspective of the personality of our children. Therefore, the best education should be the most personalized education. (Quoted from Wang Yao's "Education is a Poem", *Reading* No. 3, 2012.)

Emphasizing the practicality of the community of free men can avoid the tendency to regard it as only an ideal for the future which could be stored high up in the attic right now. In some people's eyes, the most basic personal freedom seems to be a luxury, let alone the community of free men. For GDP, for their so-called "development", individual freedom is often ignored, and organizations become powerful tools to limit individual freedom. Therefore, we emphasize the practicality of the community of free men. In the final analysis, we should emphasize that the basic purpose of modern organizations is to expand individual freedom and enhance individual's substantive freedom and capability, rather than alienate organizations into tools that limit individual freedom. The premise of the community of free men is free individuals. This is first and foremost personal freedom. In fact, without individual freedom, we can never talk about the freedom of all people, nor about the so-called freedom of the society as a whole, which is just as Engels put it: "It goes without saying that society cannot free itself unless every individual is freed."[139] It means we should strive for every individual's freedom before we realize the community of free men, and striving for every individual's freedom itself no doubt is a social practice. Community is a voluntary cooperation and organization on the basis of free individuals, and it is the unity of individual freedom and social freedom. In the final analysis, the purpose of union is to achieve freedom with freedom.

It is true that "mankind thus inevitably sets itself only such tasks as it can solve, since closer examination will always show that the task itself arises only when the material conditions for its solution are already present or at least in the process of formation."[140] From this perspective, the social practice of the community of free men is indeed a long historical process. Our subjective cognitive ability or our practical ability to act are restricted by nature, human society as well as every individual himself. In this regard, we are not free, or we are not free enough. The social practice

---

[139]Engels, F. *Anti-Dühring: Herr Eugen Dühring's Revolution in Science*. Moscow: Parogress Publishers, 1947.

[140]Marx, K. and Engels, F. Preface to a Critique on Political Economy, *Karl Marx Selected Works in Two Volumes*. London: Lawrence and Wishart Limited, 1947.

of the community of free men is to gradually eliminate such constraints and restrictions as to achieve more sufficient freedom.

2.14 Conclusion

This chapter has laid down the analytical framework, it is also the outline of the whole book. Its main purpose is to clarify the interactive relationship between organization and freedom, especially individual freedom.

Firstly, we must recognize that freedom is human nature, but at the same time it can and must be carried out in real life, which means freedom has not only the ontological meaning of "man is the highest essence of mankind" but also the practicality which is developed concretely in real life.

Secondly, although freedom is human nature, ideal and practice pursued by human society, as Rousseau put it, "Man was born free but always in fetters", which means that human freedom is always limited and relative. This is because not only human's cognitive and behavioral abilities are limited compared with nature but also more importantly, human beings must have a set of rules and regulations to restrict their behavior. In short, human's natural and social attributes determine that human's freedom will inevitably be restricted by natural and social conditions.

Thirdly, there are two kinds of restrictions on freedom by human rules and systems. The first is to better protect the freedom of the whole mankind, i.e., everybody's freedom, and expand the real space of human freedom. In other words, "exchange restriction for guarantee of freedom". The other is to deprive the freedom of the majority for the sake of the minority, whose freedom is based on the unfreedom of others. Whether freedom is a privilege of the minority or a right of the majority is the most important and fundamental dividing line.

Fourthly, from the perspective of the liberation of individual and mankind, the realization of freedom is an enduring historical process with no end. Freedom is both the primary purpose and principal means. In Marx's famous saying, "the realization of freedom with freedom" contains profound philosophy.

Fifthly, as a long-term and stable institutional arrangement of people's cooperative behavior and relationship, the most essential meaning of organization is that it can more effectively guarantee and realize individual freedom and expand the space of individual freedom. This is because: (1) the organization creates collective strength that individual labor does not have, which makes up for the limits of personal physical conditions, expands the space and time of individual labor; (2) the organization further deepens the division of labor, improves labor efficiency, obtains economies of scale that individual labor does not have, provide the necessary material basis and premise for the full realization of individual freedom; (3) organizations provide a platform for personal and social contacts, channels for knowledge complementation and exchange, thus greatly enhance the cognitive and behavioral ability of individuals to achieve freedom; (4) social security and punitive mechanisms provided by organizations can more effectively protect the boundary of individual freedom.

Sixthly, organizations, on the one hand, provide a platform to expand individual freedom space, on the other, can be alienated to become a powerful tool to restrict individual basic freedom because:

(1) the coercive force of an organization is far greater than that of an individual, and the organizer can forcibly deprive its members of their right to freedom by the adoption of force; (2) the division of labor within an organization may deepen the alienation of labor while promoting specialization and improving labor efficiency, making individuals more dependent on the organization and become slaves of the organization; (3) the operation of any organization needs authority, the opposite of which is compliance, obeying the will of others and being commanded by others; (4) in order to ensure unanimous will, organizations often require unanimous thought and speech, which may stifle the ideological freedom of its members.

Seventhly, Knight's Theory of the Firm interprets the relationship between employer and employee as a spontaneous and voluntary choice based on differences in ability and preference. Employees "trade freedom for security". But he cannot answer why some risk-biased individuals can only be employed because they are "free to have nothing". Moreover, he cannot explain how the differences in people's ability and preference are formed. The divergence between Knight and Marx is whether the division of employer and employee is caused by the differences in possession of property (means of production) or in personal ability and preference. However, in fact, Marx's analysis cannot fully explain why some individuals who are not "free to have nothing" in modern society choose to be employees rather than bosses when they have both alternatives. It should be noted that in the period when the middle class gradually becomes the backbone of the society, the process of intellectualization and capitalization of workers is accelerating, and employees (workers) are not all "free to have nothing". Many of them are fully qualified to make free choices between "independent production" and "being employed".

Eighthly, in neoclassical Theory of the Firm, labor and capital are mutually substitutable, homogeneous and undifferentiated factors of production. People in firms, especially workers, have disappeared. What we see is the undifferentiated factors of production and the inanimate functional relationship. "Firms are more like a series of cost-benefit curves than an organization." Especially in Taylor's *Scientific Management*, man as a living creature is described as a relatively simple machine to accomplish relatively simple tasks.

Ninthly, although New Institutionalism criticized neoclassical Theory of the Firm, it has gone further in the wrong direction in believing firms are a series of contract links, and the relationships between people, capital and labor in firms are totally submerged in the vast ocean of various contracts.

Tenthly, there are still some so-called non-mainstream voices in economics theory. They attach importance to the efficiency of firms but also to the significance of individual freedom. Especially with the growth of the middle class and its gradually becoming the backbone of the society, the pursuit of higher levels of individual freedom will bring a series of creative revolution in organizational form and structure.

Eleventhly, the rise of human capital theory in the 1970s and 1980s is not accidental, which is inevitably and inseparably linked with the rise of global knowledge economy. The theory of human capital promotes the role and value of human in firms (organizations) within the framework of mainstream economics.

Twelfthly, since the firm (organization) is regarded as a community of stakeholders, not just entrepreneur's firm, and it is recognized that all stakeholders bear certain risks like entrepreneurs, the theory reasonably requires all stakeholders to have the right to participate in major decision-making and to share the interests of firms (residual claim). The theory emphasizes sharing and inclusive benefit, which has reflected the new trend in the era of knowledge economy.

Thirteenthly, the community of free men is not only Marx and Engels' ideal about the future communist social organizational structure but also has realistic social practicality. Emphasizing the reality and practicality of the community of free men in the final analysis is to emphasize that the basic purpose of modern organizations is to expand individual freedom and enhance the capability of individuals to achieve substantive freedom on the basis of the scientific people-oriented concept.

Chapter 3

The Historical Context and Inherent Logic of the Transition of Agricultural Production Organizations in Contemporary China: Interpretation Based on Peasants' Freedom

Abstract

Following the basic analytical framework of "organization-freedom", the chapter tries to interpret the historical context and internal logic of the transition of agricultural production organizations since the founding of the PRC from the perspective of "realization of freedom with freedom", stressing that the household contract system of land in rural areas is the historical and logical starting point of the modernization of agricultural production organizations in the contemporary China.

3.1 The People's Commune System: A Basic Right of Collective Security at the Price of Peasants' Autonomy and Freedom of Choice

Since the reform and opening-up, changes of rural organizations and systems in contemporary China have become a "peaceful revolution". Since history cannot be separated, "the choices people made in the past have predetermined their choices possible now."[1] Therefore, to understand the profound changes in the rural economic and organizational systems since 1978, we should study the people's commune system by its historical background, internal motivation and contradictions, as well as the reason for its final disintegration.

The people's commune system is the final organizational form of the agricultural cooperative movement led by CPC and the government, so communization and cooperation can be regarded as two different stages of the same movement. Of the two stages, the crucial one is not the transition from advanced cooperatives to the people's communes, but the transition from individual households to primary cooperatives in the initial period, for although there are drastic changes in the external form of the transformation from advanced cooperatives to the people's commune, the contradictions and conflicts in essence are fewer than those caused by the transition from individual households to primary communes. Mao Zedong remarked at the Enlarged Meeting of Beidaihe Political Bureau held in August, 1958, "there is not as much danger in organizing communes as in organizing primary cooperatives. The key is primary cooperatives, from private ownership to public ownership. It's not that difficult to organize communes on the basis of primary cooperatives."[2]

The CPC succeeded in mobilizing the broad masses of peasants to join in or support the revolution by hinging on the land, which was vividly depicted in sayings like "Give the land back to the tiller" or "Overthrow the local despots and distribute their land to the masses". The founding of the People's Republic of China (PRC) and the launch and promotion of land reform ended China's feudal land ownership, which had lasted for thousands of years, and the country finally realized the dream of "giving the land back to the tiller" which had been dreamed of by peasants for thousands of years. Owner peasants became the most common form of rural micro-economic organization at that time, and China became the

---

[1] North, D.C. *Structure and Change in Economic History*. New York: W.W. Norton & Company, 1982.

[2] Bo Yibo. *Review on Several Major Decisions and Events*. Beijing: People's Publishing House, 1997, p. 770.

vast ocean of peasant economy with owner peasants as its main body.[3] But before long[4] why did the Communist Party of China (CPC) and the government urge a storm-like agricultural cooperative movement to transform private land into public land and individual peasants into members of cooperatives and communes?

From a macro perspective, at the beginning of the founding of the PRC, the country as a whole had not yet been unified, and Chiang Kai-shek Group withdrew to Taiwan. The capitalist countries led by the United States carried out policies of isolation, containment, encirclement, even aggression and provocation against China, while within the country, the national economy was backward, unemployment was high and all trades were totally underdeveloped. In face of domestic and foreign jeopardies, the only correct or inevitable strategy at that time was implementing the socialist heavy industry priority development strategy so as to realize the industrialization of the country in a relatively short period of time and build a relatively independent and complete industrial system, especially the national defense industry system. However, a sharp contradiction emerged in China's context of capital shortage and labor abundance. In order to ensure the implementation of the industrialization strategy, Chinese peasants had to make huge sacrifices, manifested in the fact that peasants, who accounted for the absolute majority of the population at that time, were the main "tributary" of the national industrialization. By using "price scissors", the state implicitly made the peasants pay a huge amount of "excess tax",[5] "similar to tribute in nature", for the national

---

[3] "Peasant economy with owner peasants as its main body" and "peasant economy with feudal land ownership as its basis and tenants as its main body" may be similar in operation form, but different in essence which cannot be equated.

[4] Another important reason for the rapid and large-scale advancement of the agricultural cooperative movement at that time was that a considerable part of the land of the poor peasants was allocated by the Party and the government during the period of the land reform, and their identity as owner peasants was endowed by the land reform, while the landlords and rich peasants were the class to be overthrown. Therefore, the most resistant to the agricultural cooperative movement at that time was the wealthy middle peasants, i.e., the traditional owner peasants.

[5] What is "price scissors"? In February 1929, *Resolution of the Joint Meeting of the Political Bureau of the CPC CENTRAL COMMITTEE and the Presidium of the Central*

industrialization. Secondly, in order to ensure the stability of cities, agriculture and countryside were used as the "reservoir" of numerous surplus laborers which couldn't be absorbed by industrialization. As can be seen from the above, there was a sharp, irreconcilable contradiction between the development strategy and individual peasants. How could you make sure individual peasants voluntarily hand in grains to the state at low prices?[6] How could you make sure rural population do not spontaneously flow into cities for employment but stay in the countryside? At the same time, under the premise of large-scale industrial drainage on agricultural surplus, how could you guarantee the basic right to subsistence of the broad masses of peasants, especially the poor peasants? In order to solve the contradictions, the state established strict urban and rural household registration management system and unified grain purchase and sale system. But in order to solve the problem fundamentally, peasants were organized through cooperative movement. The collectively owned agricultural cooperatives and later the people's communes were inevitable institutional arrangements and organizational choices.[7]

The author regards the people's commune system as "collective security guarantee for basic right to subsistence" for the following two reasons.

On the national level, the people's commune system guaranteed the high-speed industrialization of the country with priority on heavy

---

Supervision Committee has made it clear that when peasants buy industrial products, they pay more, while when they sell agricultural products, they get less. Stalin said, "This is because our country is backward and we have to produce a kind of" tribute. (Stalin. On the Danger of Right Deviation in the Party of the United Communist Party (Bolshevik), *Leninism*, People's Publishing House, 1964 edition, p. 282.)

[6] "The more we need food, the less they will sell," Chen noted in the early 1950s on the implementation of "grain purchase" [Chen Yun: Implementing Unified Purchase and Marketing of Grain, *Selected Works of Chen Yun's Manuscripts* (1949–1956): Beijing: People's Publishing House, 1982.] "They" here refers to individual peasants.

[7] More detailed expositions can be seen in Chapter 2 of Cao Yang's *Transfer of China's Agricultural Labor Force: An Analysis Based on System Change* (Central China Normal University Press, 1997); Lin Yifu, Cai Fang and Li Zhou's *Miracles of China: Development Strategy and Economic Reform* (Shanghai People's Publishing House, 1999); Wen Tiejun's *Research on China's Basic Rural Economic System* (Beijing: China Economic Press, 2000).

industry. It enabled China to establish a preliminary and complete industrial system (including the national defense industry system, which was of great importance at that time) and a national economic system as soon as possible from an extremely backward economy.[8] It played an extremely important role in guaranteeing the country's overall security and independent economic development.

On the rural level, the national heavy industry priority development strategy required peasants to make tremendous financial contributions and they were "squeezed" heavily. Nevertheless, a large number of surplus rural laborers couldn't be absorbed in employment, which undoubtedly further exacerbated the sharp contradiction between agricultural population and resources (especially land) in rural areas.[9] Under such circumstances, how to ensure the basic survival of the vast number of peasants, especially the poorer groups, was a major issue related to the stability of rural region and the stability of the regime. The people's commune system, through directly occupying, controlling and using the vast majority of the economic resources of rural areas (especially land and labor resources), had realized the equational distribution mode, guaranteed the priority of production and supply of basic subsistence goods and public goods, as well as established collective security guarantee system for basic right to subsistence.

The security guarantee of the system was displayed in many aspects. For example, grain ration and basic means of subsistence were distributed mainly by heads and supplemented by "work points". Other guarantees included "Five Guarantees Household" system and "Cooperative Medical Care" system and basic water conservancy in combat to natural disasters. In the extreme period of the people's commune, this kind of common guarantee had been carried out in various aspects in some places. For

---

[8]In 1952, China had a population of 574,820,000, a national income of RMB58.9 billion yuan, and an annual national income per capita of only RMB104 yuan.

[9]As for the pressure between population and resources, North regards it as the "core issue of economic history" (North, D.C. *Structure and Change in Economic History*. New York: W. W. Norton & Company, 1982.); Wen Tiejun regards the tension between human and land as the most basic national condition of China (Wen Tiejun. *Three Rural Issues and Institutional Change*. Beijing: China Economic Press, 2009).

example, Xushui County, once a typical people's commune in Hebei Province, tried to realize the "15 Guarantees Package".[10] At present, some places, which are commune systems in essence, have also developed this common security system into a wider supply system, e.g., Nanjie Village of Linying County in Henan Province.

[Case 3.1] Supply System and Public Welfare in Nanjie Village

The supply system of Nanjie Village began in 1986. From 1986 to 1994, from the initial water and electricity to 14 public welfare items, villagers there were provided free water, electricity, coal, gas, cooking oil, flour and holiday food. From nursery, primary school, middle school to university, all expenses were borne by the collective community. Entertainment, life insurance, epidemic prevention, medical expenses, family planning, agricultural taxes and rural reservations were also covered by the villages. During the Spring Festival of 1995, villagers were provided with 5 kilograms of pork (or beef), 2.5 kilograms of fish, 1 kilogram of chicken, 1 kilogram of eggs, 5 kilograms of rice, 2.5 kilograms of apples, 0.5 kilogram of sugar, 0.5 kilogram of melon seeds, 1 kilogram of jujube, 5 kilograms of tofu, 0.5 kilogram of millet oil, 2.5 kilograms of noodles, 1 bottle of wine, 1 dozen packs of cigarettes, 2.5 kilograms of walnuts, 1.5 kilograms of persimmon cake, 2.5 kilograms of onions, and other 29 kinds of stuff like spices, soy sauce, vinegar, anise, fennel, ginger and monosodium glutamate. Villagers didn't have to spend a penny on the festival preparation.

From 1993, Nanjie Village started to build high-standard residential buildings. Big suites, with a coverage of 92 square meters, had three bedrooms, one living room; small suites, with a coverage of 74 square meters, had two bedrooms and one living room. The apartments were equipped with central air-conditioning, 54-centimeter flat-right color TV sets branded "Changhong" and "Beijing", spring mattress beds, high and low cabinets, bedside cabinets and cooking utensils. Sun brand dual core LPG stove, Marlboro brand lampblack machine, and even LPG tank were brand-name products. Hot water baths were provided twice a week. A set of residential facilities added up to nearly RMB 80,000 yuan.

Immigrant workers working on Nanjie Street gradually enjoyed the supply service. They were provided with free staple food in the dining hall, their dormitory was spacious and bright, with eight people sharing one room and each occupying an area of 3.5 square meters. The room was equipped with central air conditioning, central heating, facilities like beds, quilts, washbasins, water bottles, teacups and cabinets. To go to work on South

[10]"15 Guarantees Package" of Xushui, Hebei Province, includes guarantee of food, clothes, housing, shoes, socks, towels, soap, lamp oil, matches, heating, bathing, hairdressing, movie, medical treatment and funeral expenses.

Street, workers just needed to take the change clothes. During the holidays, festival food was provided, workers could go home reuniting with their relatives. In the Spring Festival of 1995, each person was provided 5 kilograms of rice, 5 kilograms of apples, a box of instant noodles, a box of rice crust, two packages of fruit tea, one pack of beer and other food, costing nearly RMB130 yuan. In daily life, workers had free showers and haircuts.

—Nanjie Village Group: "The light of ideal — Nanjie locals talking about the construction of communist small communities", 1995, pp. 11–13 (abridged slightly)

Subsistence ethic, first coined by James Scott, means to guarantee the basic right to subsistence of all villagers, especially the weak groups, with the collective organizational strength in his study of rural organizations and rural societies in Southeast Asia. Scott argued that "all villagers have the right to minimum subsistence as long as the resources permit. The social power of subsistence ethic and its protection power for the poor vary from village to village. Generally speaking, the more developed the traditional organizations are, the stronger the protection will be."[11] Many scholars believe that the traditional Chinese countryside also has such subsistence ethic, which reflects the minimum moral requirements of villagers' mutual assistance". For example, when Li Huaiyin talked about the village regulations of Huolu County in Hebei Province in the early 20th century, he noted "subsistence ethic was more prominent in the turbulent 1920s when all kinds of apportionment increased sharply and the burden increased unprecedentedly. In order to ensure the survival of ordinary peasant households, local village communities even amended the old village rules to make the rich households bear more obligations." "What we see is that under the pressures of subsistence ethic, rich families and ordinary villagers both make compromises to overcome difficulties and maintain the subsistence of the village community."[12]

---

[11] Scott, J.C. *The Moral Economy of the Farmer: Rebellion and Subsistence in Southeast Asia.* New Heaven: Yale University Press, 1976.

[12] Li Huaiyin. "The Traditional Form of Rural Governance in China: An Example of Huolu County, Hebei Province", *China Rural Studies*, Vol. 1. Beijing: The Commercial Press, 2003.

Chairman Mao Zedong, as the supreme decision maker of the CPC and the state at that time, also endorsed the "subsistence ethic" of the traditional rural society. In the early days of the rise of the people's commune, Chairman Mao longed for public dining halls, free meals and supply system. He also appreciated Five-dou-rice Sect with strong farmer equalitarianism in the Three Kingdoms Period.[13] Protecting the right to subsistence of rural vulnerable groups was one of the most important reasons for Chairman Mao Zedong's endorsement to the people's commune system from the beginning to end. Therefore, in a certain sense, the people's commune system embodied the "subsistence ethic" and practiced this ethic nationwide in an institutionalized organizational framework.

3.2 Freedom is the Source of Efficiency: The Fundamental Reason for Collapse of the Commune

As mentioned above, people's commune as a collective guarantee system of the basic right to subsistence is the product of specific historical conditions, but at the same time, its establishment has also paid a very heavy price, the heaviest being the loss of peasants' right to management and free choice. In a conversation between Mao Zedong and Deng Zihui, there was a sentence with overtones, "peasants want freedom, and we want socialism". The essence of freedom here is peasants' right to management and free choice, while socialism refers to agricultural cooperation and agricultural cooperatives.[14]

In the primary cooperatives, peasants had certain property rights, so they could stake in land and important means of production (such as big livestock); even in the senior cooperatives, peasants nominally had

[13] Bo Yibo. *Reviews on Several Major Decisions and Events*. Beijing: People's Publishing House, 1997, pp. 767–768; pp. 801–802.

[14] Deng Xiaoping remarked: "What is socialism and what is Marxism? Our understanding of this issue in the past is not entirely clear." (Deng Xiaoping. Building Socialism with Chinese Characteristics. *Deng Xiaoping's Selected Works*, Vol. 3. Beijing: People's Publishing House, 1993.)

"freedom of withdrawal",[15] i.e., a certain freedom of choice. However, in the period of people's commune, property rights and freedom of choice were completely deprived. "There are no individual peasants but commune members." The people's commune, as an organization of unification, monopoly and integration of regime and society, had controls over not only economic resources but also political, social and cultural resources in an all-round way. The free space of individual peasants had been squeezed to minimum. We obtained socialism at the cost of peasants' freedom.

The direct consequence of the loss of peasants' right to management and freedom of choice is the decline of peasants' initiative and thus low efficiency of labor. Generally speaking, the collective production of the people's communes did not bring cohesive force, or "cooperative surplus" and "organizational income", which was supposed to exceed but turned out to be less than the total of individual labor force. That is to say, 1 plus 1 is not more than 2, but less than 2. An economic organization is difficult to sustain in the induced organizational change based on autonomy and volition that cannot bring organizational income and cooperative surplus more than the sum of individual labor force. Members of the such organization are likely to terminate this cooperation in the form of withdrawal or disbandment, which will result in the disintegration of the organization. However, in the mandatory organizational system change, especially those led and organized by government, the organizer may have other organizational gains which exceed economic efficiency, while the organized have no right to withdrawal. For example, the state, as the organizer of the people's commune, could incorporate such organizational incomes as national industrialization strategy, the stability of rural society and the substantial reduction of transaction costs with individual peasants. *The History of the Communist Party of China Volume II (1949–1978)*,

[15] According to the memory of Du Runsheng (Du Runsheng. *Autobiography of Du Runsheng: Account of Major Decision-making in China's Rural System Reform.* Beijing: People's Publishing House, 2005), from 1956 to 1957, the rural work departments of Liaoning, Anhui, Zhejiang, Jiangxi, Sichuan, Shaanxi, Henan and Hebei provinces reported that there was a problem of farmers' withdrawal from the community.

compiled by the Party History Research Office of the CPC Central Committee, wrote: "In order to implement the centralized purchase and distribution of grain, the State had to deal directly with hundreds of millions of peasants, verify the surplus grain of each household and mobilize each household to sell, the work of which could be tedious. It requires efforts like 'combing many small braids into a few larger ones', and basically organizing single household into cooperatives, so as to do an easier job in food acquisition, meet the demand for large quantities of grain and raw materials in industrial construction.[16] Thus, as far as the State is the organizer, the overall organizational benefits may still be greater than the organizational costs."

The low labor efficiency of peasants was rooted in the low labor initiatives caused by the loss of autonomy. Autonomy, according to March and Simon, is the right of individuals' freedom of action.[17] Autonomy is the basis and premise of individual's free choice. The income of the commune didn't exceed that of individual labor, members were discontent with "eating big pot of rice", or dissatisfied with the misdeeds of cadres and production teams. There was a strong resistance to the binding force of the commune. Getting "free rides" in collective action was prevalent, and commune members would naturally idle away the time, "working without putting efforts into it". If it was a free organization, peasants had basic autonomy and freedom of choice, of course, they would have resorted to "free exit" to express their will. Moreover, this "vote with feet" mechanism could also force organizations to improve management and efficiency. However, the people's commune was a government-led mandatory cooperative organization, which allowed neither "free entry" nor "free exit". Lin Yifu believed that the main reason for the failure of the people's commune lied in the deprivation of members' right to withdrawal. By adopting game theory, he explained the decline of commune efficiency:

---

[16] Party History Research Office of the CPC Central Committee. *History of the Communist Party of China*, Vol. 2 (1949–1978), Vol. 1. Beijing: Chinese Communist Party History Press, 2011, p. 229.

[17] March, J.G. and Simon, H.A. *Organizations*. New York: John Wiley & Sons, Inc., 1958.

"Due to the extreme difficulty in supervising production, the success of an agricultural cooperative or collective farm could only rely on a self-enforcing agreement among members". "This self-enforcing agreement can only be maintained through 'repeated game'. In a cooperative, if members have the freedom to withdraw, then the nature of the cooperative is a 'repeated game'. If the freedom of withdrawal is deprived, its nature has become a 'single shot game'. In this way, the self-enforcing agreement will not be maintained, the initiative of members will decline, and labor productivity will decline substantially."

Since "free exit" is not allowed, peasants can only vent their dissatisfaction and resistance into idleness in daily labor, which is a kind of "invisible exit". In general enterprise organizations, management can dismiss or expel employees to deter laziness or other opportunistic behaviors so as to maintain the overall labor efficiency. However, in the people's commune system, there was no freedom for farmer to withdraw, or for managers to dismiss or expel peasants. If the so-called "four categories" and "five categories"[18] were not sentenced by law, they must be supervised in the production team to carry out labor transformation, and grain rations were provided to maintain their basic right to subsistence. In conflicts between cadres and peasants of the commune, some farmer would say, "Dare you expel me from the commune?" Obviously, this was a typical "two-way lock- in" between peasants and communes.

In the context of New Institutionalism, the problem of idleness in collective labor is attributed to the subjective motivation of "free ride" inherent in the members of the organization, as well as the high cost of supervision caused by the external information asymmetry. However, in the people's commune system, idleness was mainly attributed to the narrow space of free choice caused by the "two-way lock-in" between peasants and the commune, which once again has proved "freedom is the source of efficiency".

---

[18]The so-called "four categories" of elements are landlords, rich farmers, counter-revolutionaries and bad elements; the "five categories" also include the Rightists.

Another strong proof that freedom can improve efficiency is the efficiency of the "household plots" at that time. In the system of agricultural production cooperatives and the people's communes, household plots had undergone a roundabout path of "loosening — confiscating — loosening again". Although it had been theoretically identified as "capitalist tail" or "capitalist remnant",[19] it was kept down because of its unique and irreplaceable contribution to the basic survival right of peasants at that time. Du Runsheng, who used to lead in agricultural production for a long time, wrote: "during that period, what impressed me most was the effect of the household plots policy on increasing production. Peasants have opposite attitudes towards household plots and collectively managed land, and their economic incomes from the two are different, too. The income of 0.2 mu household plot equals that of 1 mu of collective land, and the output of grain is at least twice as high, or even more. In many places of my hometown in Shanxi, the yield of household plots can reach 500 kilograms per mu. Local peasants told me household plots can make sure they're properly fed. I often think if the mechanism of household plots can be popularized, it may help pull the rural economy out of predicament."[20]

[Column 3.1] The Fate of Household Plots in the Periods of Agricultural Cooperative and the People's Communes

In October 1955, *Modeling Regulations on Agricultural Production Cooperatives (Draft)* was discussed and adopted in principle by the Sixth Plenary Session of the Seventh CPC CENTRAL COMMITTEE and it stipulated that "in order to meet the needs of members in planting vegetables or other horticultural crops, members should be allowed to have small plots of land for their own use." It also stipulated "the land

[19] Mao Zedong believed that household plot and livestock were "the remnants of capitalism". When he talked about the people's commune in 1958, he remarked that the commune is more socialistic than the co-operatives, and the remnants of capitalism (such as the household plot and livestock) can be gradually eliminated. Houses, chickens and ducks, small trees in front of and behind houses are still their own, and they will also be publicly owned in the future. (Bo Yibo. *Review of Several Major Decisions and Events*. Beijing: People's Publishing House, 1977).

[20] Du Runsheng. *Du Runsheng's Account: A Record of Major Policy-making Events in China's Rural Institutional Reform*. Beijing: People's Publishing House, 2005, p. 112.

kept by each population shall not exceed five percent of the average land owned by each population in the whole village." According to textual research, this is the first legal document of the central government on household plots. On June 25, 1957, at the 76th meeting of the Standing Committee of the First NPC, *Decision on Increasing Household Plots of Members of Agricultural Cooperatives* was adopted, which stipulated that the total quantity of farm land and feed land should not exceed 10% of the average land quantity of local people. However, after the people's commune, many places banned household plots. In August 1958, *Resolutions of the CPC CENTRAL COMMITTEE on the Establishment of the people's communes*, adopted at the Beidaihe Conference, proposed that "household plots may become collectively managed in the merger of the communes". In May and June of 1959, in order to survive the severe famine, central government resumed household plots by issuing successively several documents, e.g., *Five Urgent Instructions on Agriculture, Instructions on the Allocation of Household Plots for the Feeding of Pigs, Chickens, Ducks and Geese, Instructions on Four questions Concerning Household Plots, Raising Poultry and Livestock.* The quantity of household plots, still in accordance with the original articles of high-level communes, was neither more than nor less than 5% of each person's allocated land. However, after the wrong Anti-Rightist Movement launched at the Lushan Conference in 1959, household plots system was once again criticized and banned. In February 1960, the report entitled *On the Current Situation of Rural Public Canteens*, submitted by Guizhou Provincial Committee to the Central Committee, wrote: "In order to run a good canteen, household plots will inevitably be transferred to the charge of canteen." In March of the same year, on approving the petition, the CPC CENTRAL COMMITTEE ordered all localities to "follow suit and implement it without exception". However, with the further deterioration of food shortage and agriculture crisis, in November of the same year, the CPC CENTRAL COMMITTEE issued an *Emergency Directive on Current Policy on the people's communes*, which stipulated that "members should be allowed to operate a small amount of household plots", and stressed "in the future, members' household plots should not be confiscated or transferred arbitrarily." *The Draft of Amendments to the Rural People's Commune Work Regulations*, adopted in September 1962, stipulated that the total of "household plots, feed land and wasteland" could account for 5–10% of the arable land of the production brigade, and could not exceed 15% at most. During the period of "Cultural Revolution", the system was once again impacted. On November 23, 1967, "*People's Daily, Red Flag* and *The PLA Daily* published the article entitled *The Struggle of the Two Roads in Rural China*", which referred to the autonomies on rural market trade, household plots, self-financing and contracting production to households as "three-autonomies and one contract", and accused them of "attempting to disintegrate the socialist collective economy" and "carrying out the restoration of capitalism".

Household plots is the biggest "little freedom" that peasants retained in production and management during the period of the people's commune.

Peasants had the right of not only production management and decision-making but also possession of produces freely and completely. Therefore, it had greatly stimulated peasants' enthusiasm for production, "labor on household plots is lively, while on collective field is sluggish". This also proved once again the extreme importance of freedom on efficiency improvement. In addition, it had the special effect of improving soil and fertility. In 1962, Zhao Xiu, then Vice Minister of Agriculture, made an investigation in Inner Mongolia and found that peasants could transform the soil in their household plots and apply fertilizer extensively, even the poor soil could be made fertile. However, in some places, when the farmer had improved the soil, the rural community would take it back and replace it with poorer land. Unfortunately, those plots that had been transformed into good farmland once again were reduced to inferior farmland. The output of household plots still greatly exceeded the output of collective land. We have reached the conclusion that the organizational benefits of communes were less than the sums of individual labor incomes, the strongest proof being the contrast between efficiencies of individual labor in the household plots and collective field. Obviously, household plots were also an important historical resource for the later rural economic reform and the resumption of household management. In a sense, household contract of land can also be regarded as the expansion and universalization of household plots, and there is an inherent close logical relationship between the two.

[Column 3.2] Benefit Comparison between Household Plots and Collective Farming Land in the Period of the People's Commune

The term "household plots" refers to the land whose right of property is owned by the rural community while the right of use and benefits are owned by household peasants during the period of the people's commune. Generally, it only accounts for 5–10% of the total arable land area of production teams, but its output and economic benefits are strikingly higher than those of collective farming land of the same area.

According to surveys carried out by Huang Xiaojing and others of Fodian Village, Dingxian County, Hebei Province, during the period of the people's commune, peasants in this village spent 81% of the total working time on collective land, while the income from it only accounted for 39.46% of the total; the working time invested in the household plots only accounted for 11.38%, while the income was as high as 45.66%. Each labor force occupied an average of 6.01 mu of collective farming land and 0.42 mu of household plots.

The labor productivity of collective farmland was RMB0.47 yuan per capita, while that of household plot was RMB3.5 yuan per capita, 7.9 times that of the former.

In Wen Tiejun's visit to Meitan County, Guizhou Province, he cited Guo Wenyuan, former Secretary of the county Party Committee as saying that household plot accounted for about 7% of the total land, while the output accounted for 25% of the total output, and the yield per unit was 30–50% higher than that of collective land. Gan Jiaying from the villagers group of Xiaoji Bay Village, Gaoshan Administrative Village, Meijiang Town, said the household plot per capita was only 0.18 mu, his family owned 1.5 mu, but the income from it accounted for about 40% of the family's total, for the household plot was planted carefully and dedicatedly, the output twice as high as that of the collective land.

From 1972 to 1975, I, as an educated youth, was sent to the fourth production team of the second vegetable brigade of Chengguan Commune, Tongcheng County, Hubei Province, and witnessed the phenomenon of many commune members "working diligently on their household land and idled away on collective land". The vegetable output of the household plots was at least twice higher than that of the collective farming land, so that sometimes in order to cope with inspection from higher levels or visits from other places, household plots were showcased as collective farmland for its good output.

—Research Group on Rural Development in China. *Countryside, Economy and the Society*, Vol. 3. Knowledge Publishing House, 1985, p. 229; Wen Tiejun. *Research on Basic Rural Economic System in China.* China Economic Publishing House, 2000, pp. 218–219

[Column 3.3] The Eternal Sparkles of Household Plots

Hunger can drive people mad. At that time, the produce from farmer's own land was far from enough. In order to survive, villagers had to pick up hoes and rakes, and made use of every single space by reclaiming the ten side fields. What are ten side fields? They are river-side, bank-side, ditch-side, road-side, wall-side, land side, tomb-side and hill-side. On some ten side fields, such as river-side and ditch-side, there were still some feet for planting, while on others, such as wall-side, road-side and ridge-side, there were only inches. As long as crops could be planted, peasants were still competing for planting even one crop. But the loss often outweighed the gain. As we all know, grassland beside riverbanks and ditches is very important in consolidating embankments and preventing soil erosion, so peasants usually don't reclaim it, for if it is reclaimed, the grassland becomes cropland, riverbanks and ditches being damaged to varying degrees as a result. However, in those years, people didn't taken into account these factors, for though environment was precious, the price of life was more so. Don't underestimate ten side fields. It was a reserve besides household plots. Diligent peasants benefited a lot from ten side fields. When bags of soybeans, broad beans, sesame, mung beans, red beans, cowpeas and bitter corns came to market, it was the hungry city dwellers' big feast. If you were offered a handful of fried soybeans, fried broad beans on the verge of starving to death, it was like someone sending you charcoal in the snow. An anecdote goes like this: Mr. Wu Tiaogong, a famous professor in the Chinese Department of Nanjing Normal University (later changed to Nanjing Normal University), became very hungry in class. Though a disgrace on his scholarly dignity, he grabbed a carrot from his pocket, gobbled down and remarked, "it is the most delicious thing in the world. My greatest wish in life is neither papers nor positions, but to eat rice three meals a day, even if there are no dishes to go with it at all!"

It became a common phenomenon in the 1960s and 1970s that green branches and leaves growing on the household plots, but yellow and thin plants were found in the collective fields. In his new book entitled *1978: History Never Lingers*, Ling Zhijun has such a vivid description: Peasants can sow any crops on this narrow land according to their will, and they can own all the produces without the need to contribute to the rural community. Peasants labor with totally different frames of mind, which has resulted in strikingly different results. According to an official survey, the income of household plots ranges from RMB1,000 to 1,500 yuan per mu. If true, the household plots, accounting for 5% of the arable land in the country, provides at least 50% of the income of peasants. In some areas, the situation can be more embarrassing. For example, Zhao Xiu, then deputy minister of the Ministry of Agriculture under the State Council, was very surprised to find that the grain yields on the farm's household plots were 10 times higher than that of the commune. The reason was obvious: the collective farmland had to contribute public grain, the three-level cadres of commune brigade spared no efforts to get petty advantages, so the benefit for individual peasant was uncertain. At that time, peasants work for workpoints only, for there was no measurement of how many efforts you put into work or how many outputs you can produce. Socialist collectivization has bred a group of lazy men. While all the harvest on the household plots belongs to peasants themselves, so the input of peasants, both physical and intelligent, was thorough without any reserve. It was precisely for this reason that Comrade Deng Xiaoping conformed to the public opinion, supported Xiaogang Village in Anhui Province to take the lead in contracting production to households, and later to carry out the household contract system in the whole country. The year of 1978 witnessed the spring thunder of reform and opening-up in rural China.

The history of household plots ended after the practice of distributing farmland into households. Peasants put most of their energy into the big land, and household plots became a sideline literally. People just plowed and grew a few vegetables in their spare time. Some are abandoned, or used for other purposes like threshing, or as green belts for beautifying their houses. The demand for vegetables could be met by planting in big fields or purchase from groceries. However, the sparkle of the household plots will always shine in the hearts of Chinese peasants, for household plots, peculiar to China, has saved countless lives. It has left a deeper impression on peasants than the collective land, though it is now fading away like the candlelight in a starry night or little ripples of a calm river.

—*Changzhou Daily*, November 4, 2008

The low labor efficiency of the people's commune refers not only to the low initiatives of the members but also the "idleness" of the bureaucratic management of the communes, i.e., "insufficient management". In fact, in the people's commune system, neither the members nor the cadres had much freedom of choice. What, how much and how to grow on the land all came from the instructions of the upper strata. Because of the "two-way lock-in" between peasants and communes, cadres would not face the internal deterrence such as dismissal or expulsion commonly used in organizational management. In addition, the cadres of the brigade and the production team were usually natives, earning work points and grain rations. That is to say, their identity was in essence a peasant. Relatives, neighbors and sophisticated interpersonal relationship had also "softened" strict management. More importantly, the managers of communes lacked intrinsic incentives. Some researchers believed that effective supervision was needed to motivate managers, so that they could have the internal motivation, which was claim on economic surplus. The people's commune system has inherently excluded managers from obtaining economic surplus, so managers lacked a strong incentive. Zhou Qiren believed that the people's commune had canceled the managers' claim on economic surplus in the system arrangement, but it could not eliminate managers' demand for economic incentives. "Their incentives are ineffective, leading to the fact that collectivized economies of scale cannot be achieved at all."[21]

The long-term low labor efficiency, food crisis and agricultural crisis posed fatal threat to the collective guarantee of basic right to subsistence, undermining the rational foundation of the existence of the commune. According to authoritative data of the National Bureau of Statistics, compared with the year of 1976 when the "Cultural Revolution" ended, the annual per capita consumption of grain in 1976 was 191.5 kg, 13 kg lower than 204.5 kg in 1956, and the annual consumption of oil in 1976 was 1.6 kg, 0.95 kg lower than 2.55 kg in 1956. In 1976, the average net agricultural output value created by each agricultural laborer was RMB319 yuan, which was lower than RMB323 yuan in 1952, and the average grain produced by each agricultural laborer was 972 kg, which was also lower than 1031 kg in 1957. In addition, "according to the statistics of the State

[21] Zhou Qiren. "China's Rural Reform: Changes in the Relationship between the State and Land Ownership — A Review on the History of Economic System Changes", *China Social Sciences Quarterly* (Hong Kong), No. 6, 1995.

Ministry of Agriculture and Forestry in 1973, grain production in 72 counties remained at the level of the early liberation period; nearly one million production teams (about 20% of the total number of production teams across the country) distributed income below 40 yuan per capita annually on average. Those production teams basically did not have cash distribution, and some even had difficulty in maintaining simple reproduction."[22] In 1978, according to the ultra-low poverty standard of RMB100 yuan per capita income set by the Chinese government at that time, the poverty-stricken population in rural areas reached 250 million, accounting for 30.7% of the total rural population at that time.

In such prevalence of poverty, 800 million peasants were tightly tied to the land by the commune system for grain production, and such policies as "deforestation for cultivation", "destroying grass for cultivation", "enclosing lakes for cultivation" were carried out. However, cultivation didn't fulfill its task as vast peasants still couldn't be properly fed and clothed. Du Runsheng argued: "the fears of hunger aggravated peasants' doubts over the superiority of collective economy. However, in the people's communes with the unity of politics and society, members were not allowed to enter or exit freely, which blocked the way for members to make a living on their own and restricted their freedom to grow economy. Historically, peasants have always had the freedom to diversify and allocate their own resources. But in the period of the people's commune, their freedom was deprived. The result aggravated not only poverty in rural areas but also the shortage of consumer goods in cities. Chen Yun remarked that in the context of shortage of food, peasants concerned more about "eating rice or eating porridge" than "socialism or capitalism".[23] Practice has shown that the result of depriving peasants of their freedom, in the long run, can neither guarantee the most basic right to subsistence nor solve the essential problem of "food and clothing". Rural poverty expanded, spread and deteriorated. The collapse of the people's commune system is inevitable, i.e., it has the inherent inevitability of disintegration.

[22] Party History Research Office of the CPC Central Committee. *History of the CPC*, Vol. (1949–1978). Beijing: Chinese Communist Party History Press, 2011, p. 938.

[23] Du Runsheng. *Du Runsheng's Account: A Record of Major Policy-making Events in China's Rural Institutional Reform*. Beijing: People's Publishing House, 2005, p. 98.

3.3 Give Peasants the Freedom of Choice: The External Environment and Conditions for the Disintegration of the Commune

The long-term inability in solving the problem of food and clothing, and the failure in guaranteeing basic right to subsistence are the intrinsic reason of the inevitable disintegration of the people's commune system, but they are not the only reason. It should be said that 1959–1962 (historically known as the "Three-year Difficult Period") was the harshest period of the people's commune system. "The extreme shortage of grain, oil, vegetables and non-staple food seriously endangered the health and life of the people. In many places, urban and rural residents developed edema, the number of people suffering from hepatitis and gynecopathies was also climbing. There was a sharp increase in mortality and decrease in births. According to official statistics, the total population of the country in 1960 was 10 million less than that of the previous year. In Xinyang, Henan Province, nine counties had a mortality rate of more than 100 per thousand, several times that of normal years."[24] In such a severe situation, peasants' basic right to subsistence was not guaranteed, the rationality of people's communes was widely questioned both inside and outside the CPC. Despite the fact that it triggered a large-scale spontaneous wave of "contracting production to households" in rural areas throughout the country,[25] and that the spontaneous and free choice of peasants won support or consent by a large number of cadres at all levels (including Liu Shaoqi, Chen Yun and Deng Xiaoping, then members of Standing Committee of the Political

[24]Party History Research Office of CPC Central Committee. *History of the Communist Party of China*, Vol. II (1949–1978). Beijing: Chinese Communist Party History Press, 2011, p. 581.

[25]By the end of 1961, 91% of the total production teams in Anhui Province had implemented "contracted land". In fact, at this time, in addition to Anhui, Gansu, Zhejiang, Sichuan, Guangxi, Fujian, Guizhou, Guangdong, Hunan, Hebei, Liaoning, Jilin, Heilongjiang and other provinces and regions had also implemented various forms of production responsibility system, the percentage of which reached 40% in Guizhou, Guangxi and Fujian, 70% in Gansu, Zhejiang and Sichuan." [Party History Research Office of CPC Central Committee. *History of the Communist Party of China*, Volume II (1949–1978). Beijing: Chinese Communist Party History Press, 2011.], p. 611.

Bureau), it died down under political pressure of "giving priority to class struggle" and harsh criticism on "going solo".

"Contracting production to households" is, in the final analysis, a change demanded by the majority of peasants in rural collective economic organizations with an aim to striving for the autonomy of production and the right of free choice. In the words of peasants at that time, "it is impossible to go solo on the road of co-operation. Contracting production to households is a good choice."[26] Expressed in the language of modern economics, the essence of "contracting production to households" is a game between freedom and regulation within the framework of the people's commune system. At that time, some local leaders also saw this intentionally or unintentionally. Geng Qichang, former Party Secretary of Xinxiang County of Henan Province, believed that the collective way had restricted peasants and deprived them of their freedom. "After the agricultural cooperation, we took over the peasants' labor and they could not work freely; after the people's commune, we took over their life and living."[27] Therefore, the essence of "contracting production to households", which emerged in the agricultural cooperation in 1956 with twists and turns,[28] was to return some basic rights to peasants, so that they could become the entity of agricultural production. Although most peasants hoped to contract production to households at that time and quite a number of leading cadres from central to local government supported it, the

---

[26] Du Runsheng. *Du Runsheng's Account: A Record of Major Policy-making Events in China's Rural Institutional Reform*. Beijing: People's Publishing House, 2005, p. 91.

[27] *Ibid*., pp. 88–89.

[28] "In fact, since agricultural cooperation, whenever the Party proposed to adjust the production relationship within the agricultural collective economic organization, there were always farmers who spontaneously contracted production to their households. Although they were repeatedly prohibited, they would reappear once again." "During more than 20 years, farmers experimented with ideas like contracting production to group, contracting production to household and contracting labor to household, emerging three times with one before the anti rightist struggle in 1957, one before the anti-rightist struggle in 1959, and one before the Tenth Plenary Session of the Eighth Central Committee in 1962, though all of which were suppressed by subsequent political movements." [Party History Research Office of CPC Central Committee. *History of the Communist Party of China*, Volume II (1949–1978). Beijing: Chinese Communist Party History Press, 2011.], p. 611, p. 1036.

political atmosphere in the era of class struggle was tense and "contracting production to households" was severely criticized by Chairman Mao Zedong as "capitalist ideas" and "going solo". Deng Zihui once advocated conditional "four freedoms"[29] but was dismissed, for "trivial good deeds bring small benefits but make no contribution to the overall righteousness". Thus, it can be seen that without free and relaxed political atmosphere, peasants lacked the external environment of free choice and it was hard to strive for limited freedom even within the rural collective economic system.

Thanks to the end of the era from 1966 to 1976, China's political situation changed dramatically. By "emancipating the mind and seeking truth from facts", the political atmosphere was becoming freer and more relaxing. In this context, rural areas like Fengyang, Anhui Province, which used to be short of food supply, spontaneously started with "contracting production to households". Frankly speaking, there were differed opinions from the authorities, but differed opinions were allowed this time, as was described in the saying "you go ahead in your boulevard, while I cross my single-plank bridge".[30] Peasants' choice and trial were protected, "practice is the sole criterion for testing truth" and "square accounts after the autumn harvest" were advocated, so this time "contracting production to households" didn't die halfway, but instead gradually evolved to "big contract", i.e., to distribute collective land to peasants for individual management. The management mode was vividly depicted in the saying "to make enough contribution to the country, to retain enough for the rural community, and the rest is all our own". Chen Xiwen remarked: "Although

[29]Deng Zihui once referred to the "four freedoms" as the freedom of land tenancy, employment, trade and loan.

[30]At that time, Du Runsheng recorded the free debate of the upper level of the central government about "contracting production to household". The most vivid is what Chi Biqing, the Secretary of Guizhou provincial Party committee, said at that time: "you walk your boulevard, while I cross my single-plank wooden bridge." Wu Xiang, a reporter with the Xinhua news agency at that time, published an article "Boulevard and Single-plank Bridge" in *The People's Daily* on November 5, 1980, which described in detail the controversy at that time, and also explained the relatively loose and free political atmosphere at that time (Du Runsheng. *Du Runsheng's Account: A Record of Major Policy-making Events in China's Rural Institutional Reform*. Beijing: People's Publishing House, 2005).

there is only one-word difference between 'contracting labor to household' and 'contracting production to household', they differ strikingly in connotation." "In Contracting production to households, production teams are still the basic accounting unit, whereas peasants are the real business entity." "The management mode of 'big contract' not only thoroughly breaks the system of 'big pot rice' in which the production team unifies the control of products, business accounting and income distribution, but also reinforces the status of household as the entity of operation in agriculture and rural economy."[31]

The reinforcement of "contracting labor to household" will inevitably lead to the disintegration of the people's commune. The most important external condition here is to give peasants free options: they have the option of choosing land for household contract, or staying in collective management and production; they have the option of farming, or engaging in non-agricultural production; they have the option of employment in rural areas, or urban employment. The key factor here is to believe in peasants' rationality, judgment and creativity, respect their opportunities and rights of autonomy and free choice, including their opportunities of "learning by doing" and "trial and error".

It should also be remarked that the disintegration of the people's communes, as a way of "political and social integration", "unification" and monopolistic organizational structure, does not mean collective economic organizations with the nature of communes and centralized production and operation are not allowed to exist. In fact, over the past 30 years, there are still a number of collective economic organizations that adhere to the nature of communes and have developed quite well to some extent. For example, Nanjie Village in Linying County, Henan Province, Yakou Production Brigade in Zhongshan City, Guangdong Province, Zhoujiazhuang Township People's Commune in Jinzhou City, Hebei Province, and so on. Of course, the future direction of these organizations remains highly uncertain. Yakou production brigade in Zhongshan City, Guangdong Province, is on the verge of disintegration due to the

---

[31] Chen Xiwen, Zhao Yang and Luo Dan. 30 *Years Review and Prospect of China's Rural Reform*. Beijing: People's Publishing House, 2008, p. 63.

retirement of its Party Secretary Lu Hanman who firmly adhered to the belief of the people's commune.

There are other external conditions for the final disintegration.

Firstly, an independent and relatively complete industrial system and national economic system have been initially established in China. Indeed, the proportion of agricultural output value in GNP has dropped substantially, and the proportion of industrial output value has increased substantially. According to the data of the National Bureau of Statistics, compared with 1952, the proportion of agricultural output value dropped from 56.9% to 27.8% in 1978; accordingly, the proportion of industrial output value increased from 43.1% to 72.2%. It showed the so-called "accumulation stage of socialist primitive capital", in which industrialization of the country was realized by extracting agricultural surplus on a large scale, was completed and should also be ended. As a guarantee, the people's commune has fulfilled its historic mission of promoting industrialization by means of "supplementing industry with industry".

Secondly, with China's resumption of the legitimate seat in the United Nations as well as the icebreaking contact with the United States in diplomacy, China's international relations had greatly improved and the conditions for opening-up policy matured, providing a better external international environment for China's peaceful growth and development. In this context, the CPC and the central government adopted a realistic new understanding of the international situation, and resolutely replaced the judgment of "war and revolution" as the theme of the world in the past with "peace and development" at present. Due to the change of the view that "world war is imminent", and the establishment of an independent and relatively complete national defense industry system, the "war preparation" function innate in the people's commune system had fulfilled its historical mission.

Finally, the CPC and the central government abandoned the previous policy of "giving priority to class struggle" and established the policy of "taking economic construction as the core". Economic development, modernization and the improvement of people's living standards as promptly as possible, especially the living standards of the peasants who accounted for the majority of the population became the top priority of our work. Therefore, the people's commune system, as an organizational form that hindered the improvement of peasants living standards, had also come to an inevitable disintegration.

3.4 The Essence of the Rural Household Land Contract System: The Institutional Precondition for Peasants' "Free Realization of Freedom with Freedom"

Starting from poor rural areas, "contracting production to households" and the subsequent "big contract" can indeed be regarded as a "revolution driven by hunger". According to Du Runsheng, the first consent made by the central government after the year 1978 in "contracting production to households" was to allow peasants in poor areas to do so to "fill their stomachs". So "contracting production" was the precondition, while "to fill stomachs" was the goal. But it went far beyond ensuring "a full stomach", going far beyond solving the problem of hunger, as well as food and clothing.

Different from the top-down mandatory organizational change and institutional transition of people's commune, rural land household contract system was a bottom-up and gradually induced process. Moreover, its implementation didn't adopt the monopoly of "one size fits all" as the people's commune did, in which other forms of economic organization were not allowed to exist. Therefore, although it was the most basic economic system in the contemporary China, it was not the only one; peasants were the most common form of micro-economic organization, but not the only form, either. After its implementation, the form of rural micro-economic organization in China has changed from uniformity to diversity based on the household management of peasants.

The household contract system has ultimately ended the people's commune system because of its effect on increasing grain production and peasants' income, basically solving the problem of hunger which has long plagued the urban and rural population with immediate effects, and making the life of the vast majority of peasants better. From 1979 to 1984, agriculture had a bumper harvest for six consecutive years. In 1984, the total grain output reached 407.3 billion kilograms, a net increase of

100.75 billion kilograms from 304.75 billion kilograms in 1978, an average increase of 5% per year; in 1984, the total cotton output reached 6.258 billion kilograms, an increase of 1.88 times over that of 2.17 billion kilograms in 1978, an average increase of 19.3% per year. At the same time, according to the data of the National Bureau of Statistics, the average annual net income of peasants increased from RMB133.6 yuan in 1978 to 355 yuan in 1984, the actual net income increased by as high as 15.1 annually.[32] In light of the progress, the policy of centralized purchase and distribution of grain, which had lasted for more than 30 years, was finally abolished in the mid-1980s, and the history of urban residents purchasing food through food certificates and food coupons was ended.

With the same land and same laborers, why could the persistent problem of hunger be solved thoroughly in such a short period of time after the implementation of the rural land contract system? The reasons are of course manifold, but in the final analysis, the main reason is that peasants have become the real managers of land, which has motivated their initiatives and innovation.

At first, the household contract system was confined to the poorer areas where peasants without enough food had the strong urge to "fill their stomachs". However, with the prominence of its benefits, the more developed areas basically with enough to eat (such as the Yangtze River Delta and the Pearl River Delta) also implemented this policy. It means the significance goes far beyond solving the problem of hunger. In response to the question, Du Runsheng put it bluntly: "peasants need more autonomy and freedom." He quoted Jiangsu peasants who were economically well-off as saying, "we are not afraid of toil but afraid of being tied down together". Song Liying, senior director of Dazhai Brigade in Xiyang County, Shanxi Province, which was a model unit nationwide in the period of the people's commune, said after comparing situations before

[32]Although the rapid growth of agricultural production in this period cannot be solely attributed to the organizational and institutional change effect represented by "big contract", most researchers believe that the organizational and institutional change represented by "big contract" was the main reason for the rapid growth of agricultural production in this period.

and after the reform, "it is still better now that we are free in both production and life."[33]

If the land reform is the first liberation, liberating peasants from the bondage and dependence of feudal land ownership, then the rural land household contract system is the second liberation, liberating peasants from the bondage and dependence of the people's commune system. As mentioned in the second chapter of the book, freedom in its original sense means to get rid of the coercion of others and society, to relieve the attachment of personal relationship, to realize the independence of personality, and to make "man the highest essence of man". Liberty and liberation are cognates.

The most far-reaching, lasting and essential significance of rural land household contract system lies in that it provided a relatively broad and inclusive organizational and institutional platform for peasants to "realize freedom with freedom". The platform gave peasants two basic and crucial rights: one was land contractual right guaranteed by law, the other was freedom of labor.

3.5 The Land Contract Right: Interpretation Based on Peasants' Freedom

Since the reform and opening-up, the research literature on rural land contractual right has been abundant, but rarely on the perspective of peasants' freedom, or linking rural land contractual right with peasants' freedom.

According to Modern Property Rights theory, property rights are a group of right relations or "Bundle of Rights". Property rights include not only property ownership defined by law but also property possession, use, disposition and income rights in actual economic operations. In a sense, the rural land contractual right in the contemporary China is an incomplete or imperfect property rights. The farmer's land contractual right can be regarded as the actual possession or management right while the

[33]Tan Chengjian. *Dazhai: An Account of Famous Villages in China.* Zhengzhou: Central Plain Farmers Press, 1998, pp. 164–165.

ownership of the land is still in village community's hands. It is the separation of ownership and contractual right. Compared with collective ownership, contractual right is probably a more practical right in general. Over the past two decades, especially since the reform on rural taxes and fees, the policy orientation of the central government has been "to dilute ownership and reinforce management rights", which is reflected in the fact that households can actually occupy and use land during the contracting period, which has been extended repeatedly, from several years to 20 years, 30 years till permanency. More importantly, after the reform on taxes and fees, the contractor has got claims on almost all the land income, even various government subsidies for land (in reality subsides for contractor peasants). In contrast, because of the exemption of the "three commissions and five unifications", the collective community's benefit from the land income is almost zero. The author has always believed that in the "Bundle of Property Rights", the right to income is the most fundamental one. Ownership or management right without claims on income or even negative income is a meaningless right. In the state of "separation of two rights", the game between ownership and management rights (contractual rights) is essentially a game of interests, in essence, a game of the right to land income. In the contemporary rural areas of China, although the land contractual right is a more practical right in general, in some specific circumstances, ownership is in the leading position, for example, when rural collective land is requisitioned (for compulsory sale).

Farmer's land contractual right guaranteed by law is of great significance for peasants to realize their freedom freely. This is one of the two basic and crucial rights of peasants in the process of "realization of freedom with freedom".

Firstly, the farmer's land contractual right guarantees the peasants' basic right to subsistence, which is the basic premise for the existence of all freedom rights.

Many scholars have remarked that the current rural land contract system not only gives peasants the most basic means of production to engage in (land is the basis of agriculture) but also provides them with the most basic social security system within the framework of the current system. Huang Zongzhi remarked: "although agricultural income is very low, even the poorest peasants have the right to use the contracted land, which can act as a safety net for survival and avoid complete proletarianization."[34] As Malinowski said, all freedom must be based on the basic freedom of subsistence. "The eternal foundation of free expansion is the freedom of subsistence."[35] However, subsistence requires the most basic material conditions. Owning nothing is difficult to achieve real freedom of subsistence. The farmer's land contractual right prevents peasants from proletarianization, or, becoming "free to have nothing". With this kind of contract right, peasants can guarantee their basic survival of their families under normal conditions. It is true that peasant households are not the owners of the contracted land, but the villagers' committee, as the owner of land, cannot arbitrarily deprive households of land contractual rights. That is to say, the land contractual right has the state legal protection beyond collective ownership. *Law of the People's Republic of China on Rural Land Contracting* stipulates that "the state protects the long-term stability of rural land contracting relationship according to law"; "any organization or individual shall not deprive or illegally restrict members of rural collective economic organizations to contract land." "Any organization or individual" here includes the "villagers' committee" or "rural collective economic organization" as the "contracting party" or as the "owner" in jurisprudence. The Law clearly stipulates that "during the contractual period, the contracting party shall not recover the contracted land." In order to effectively protect peasants' land contracting rights, the central *No. 1 Document* in 2013 further explicitly requires "to reinforce registration and certification of rural land in order to "strengthen the property rights protection of management on farmland, forestland, etc."

The significance of property rights on freedom has been fully discussed by scholars at home and abroad. Mencius, ancient Chinese philosopher, said, "it's a universally acknowledged rule that people with property have perseverance, people without have no perseverance. If a man has no perseverance and let go of evil and luxury, he will go dissipated." Therefore, people's property is the basis of social stability and the realization of the people's real freedom. Locke, famous British philosopher in the modern times, emphasized the high consistency of the rights of life, liberty and

[34] Huang Zongzhi. *China's Recessive Agricultural Revolution*. Beijing: Law Press, 2010, p. 13.

[35] Malinowski, B. *Freedom and Civilization*. Bangalore: Mysore Press, 2014.

property in his *Two Treatises of Government*. Hume remarked more clearly: "Where there is no property, there is no liberty." In his book *Property as a Guarantor of Liberty*, Buchanan repeatedly emphasized that individual property rights were the basis and guarantor of individual liberty. Marx believes the roots of an employee's substantive unfreedom was being "free to have nothing"; in order to realize the "free development of each", it is necessary to establish "private ownership".[36]

Secondly, peasants' land contractual right gives peasants not only the right to operate and cultivate land but also the right not to operate or cultivate land by engaging in non-agricultural activities, which means it does not "tie down" peasants onto the land; instead it gives them liberty. Practice has shown on the basis of not giving up their land contractual right, peasants' liberty on "no tilling" is a very important right.

The separation of the rights of ownership, management and use is not uncommon in history both in China and abroad. Peasants, or agricultural producers, are usually those who cultivate land, while the entity of ownership is often diverse, including the state, manor owners, monasteries, merchants, landlords, village communities, clans, and also owner peasants. Therefore, land leasing or contracting, i.e., the so-called "separation of the two rights" of land ownership and management, is a very common practice in both historical and modern era at home and abroad.

The contemporary rural land contract system in China can also be regarded as a special land leasing relationship. Unlike many in history, which tied down peasants to land (land leasing and personal attachment were integrated), the land contractual right of contemporary Chinese peasants is a more liberal one. On the contracted land, peasants can make independent decisions on what to plant.

---

[36]"The capitalist mode of appropriation, the result of the capitalist mode of production, produces capitalist private property. This is the first negation of individual private property, as founded on the labor of the proprietor. But capitalist production begets, with the necessity of a natural process, its own negation. It is the negation of negation. This does not re-establish private property for the producer, but gives the producer individual property based on the achievements of the capitalist era, i.e., on co-operation and the possession in common of the land and of the means of production." Marx, K. *Capital: A Critique of Political Economy*. Moscow: Progress Publishers, 1956.

They can cultivate intensively and meticulously by investing a majority part of labor, time and energy, they can also regard land cultivation as a sideline, investing in a minority part of labor, time and energy; they can cultivate extensively, or even do not cultivate at all, i.e., land is left fallow. Before the reform on rural taxes and fees, "land being left fallow" was very common in provinces like Hubei, Hunan, Anhui and Jiangxi in central China, which actually was a kind of "silent protest", appealing to the government for changes and amendments to the current policy through "the liberty of not tilling". In retrospect, it is truly a key stimulus to promote the reform of rural taxes and fees. After the reform, there were still a small number of "being left fallow" phenomena in rural China for various reasons. For example, in my hometown, a small mountain village in Zhanqiao Town, Linxiang City, Hunan Province, many kinds of paddy fields (mostly inferior ones) in the past are now overgrown with weeds, which can be seen as "laying fallow" to some degree, or "quality abandonment", a rational choice of peasants, which is conducive to the conservation of soil fertility and the improvement of the ecological environment. If the income from grain cultivation increases, it is not difficult for such fallow land to be re-cultivated. The most effective way to solve the problem of abandonment of good farmland is the free circulation and trade of rural land contractual rights rather than administrative prohibitions.

[Column 3.4] Discussion on the Phenomenon of "Farmland Abandonment" in Rural Areas

Farmland abandonment means that the cultivated land is left fallow, without being converted for other economic purposes. Therefore, it's different from reclamation to forestland or grassland as advocated by the government.

China's arable land resources are scarce. Farmland abandonment means the scare land resources are left idle, which no doubt has drawn much concern. During the period of the people's commune, there were few "abandonment" phenomena, while reclaiming forestland, grassland and lake to farmland was prevalent. After the implementation of the household contract system, peasants have got certain freedom rights, including the freedom of no tilling. So came the "farmland abandonment", which, unfortunately, became the reason why some scholars criticized or even want to abolish rural land household contract system.

I believe behind the phenomenon is a real will expression of peasants' freedom of "no tilling", but the reasons underlying are very complicated.

Before the reform of rural taxes and fees, farmland abandonment was prevalent in some areas, especially in some major agricultural areas in central China. In essence, peasants were protesting in silence against the government policy, demanding a policy adjustment to the over occupation on land income by managers from a village or town level.

After the reform, small-scale, partial abandonment does exist. However, in order to attract the public's attention, some scholars and media made an undeserved hubbub about it. Our investigation shows that the land income has increased greatly, at least negative income has been eliminated, due to the lift on burdens of various taxes and fees attached to cultivated land, and the government subsidy. In this context, the existence of a small number of farmland abandonment is not an absolute bad thing. One of the obvious benefits is to conserve soil fertility and improve ecology. Of course, in order to ensure food security, we should keep vigilant on large-scale abandonment of good farmland, but the solution is not administrative prohibition, not the deprivation of peasants' freedom of choice, but to promote the circulation and trade of peasants' land contractual rights on a voluntary basis and abiding by market economic principles.

From a broader perspective, it is a very important right for peasants to have the freedom not to plant land without abandoning the right to contract, which means that peasants have the freedom to choose to engage in agricultural or non-agricultural business. It is a significant progress in peasants' free development compared with the "unfreedom" of the people's commune system which tied down peasants onto the land. At the same time, retaining land contractual right, peasants will be given the option to return to agriculture in case they failed in non-agricultural business, so that they could choose freely and safely, leaving room for trial and error. It is precisely because of the guarantee of land contractual right, or more generally, the alternative they can resort to that peasants can become more confident and practical in engaging in non-agricultural business and enjoy the freedom of not planting land.

Finally, the circulation and trade of peasants' land contractual right make the current rural land contract system more open and flexible, make the rural land resources better allocated, and further broaden the space for peasants' freedom.

Contracted land cannot be freely bought and sold by peasants, for villagers' committees rather than peasants are the ultimate owners of land, peasants cannot freely dispose of the common property. However, it does not mean land contractual right cannot be traded, transferred or sold, for they are not common property or public property right, but rather private property and private right. At the same time, this kind of private right is also a "bundle of rights". The right of contract and right of use (actual farming right) can also be separated. Of course, the premise of separation is the confirmation of the land contractual right as a private right that can be circulated and traded. If the contractual right is solidified, which means the contractor and the actual operator must be the same person, then no separation is allowed. Coase and other scholars believe even if the initial allocation of rights is inefficient, as long as the free exchange of rights is allowed, the optimal allocation of resources will eventually be realized. The transferable and transactable contractual right of rural land enables peasants to enjoy the freedom of not cultivating land without abandoning the right of contract or the land itself. It enables peasants or other economic organizations to obtain more arable land, form moderate operation scales, and improve the comparative benefits of cultivating land. This is undoubtedly a win–win solution of mutual benefits, and a rational choice for the optimal allocation of land resources and labor resources within the framework of the existing system.

It should be remarked that the premise of the current mainstream trade and circulation of rural land contractual right are "not to abandon the land contractual right", i.e., the contractor has the right to reclaim the right of use. If further developed, it is the complete transfer and transaction of land contractual right, i.e., the contractor permanently abandons the land contractual right. The so-called "exchange land contractual right for social security rights" is the final transaction, or "sell outright". Can peasants have such "sell outright"? Does land contractual right have to be used as transaction costs for peasants to enter cities and enjoy social security? There are differed opinions on this issue. The author will discuss it in detail in the next chapter.

The freedom granted by the current land contractual right is not absolute but relative with conditions and restrictions, some of which are reasonable and necessary. Restrictions are meant to guarantee peasants' basic right to subsistence. For example, peasants are not allowed to "sell outright" contractual rights before they settle down as real urban residents, get stable careers and incomes and enjoy the same social security right as urban residents do so to guarantee peasants' basic right to subsistence.

However, some restrictions are neither reasonable nor conducive to enhancing the capabilities of peasants to achieve substantial freedom. It highlights the inappropriate interference and infringement of public rights on private rights, which will be discussed in later part of this chapter. These interventions and violations have impaired peasants' rights to freedom.

According to the provisions of *The Law of the People's Republic of China on Rural Land Contracting*, "land" in the household contract system refers to farmland, forestland, grassland and other land used for agriculture by peasants collectively and by the State according to law. Farmland contracting is undoubtedly at the forefront of the rural land contract system due to the extreme importance of arable land in agriculture. At that time, the main contradiction was "to fill the stomach", which was closely related with arable land. Secondly, the contracting of farmland is simpler than that of forestland and grassland, and the externality of farmland is less complex than that of forestland and grassland. The grassland contract in pastoral areas and the collective forest land contract in rural areas are the inevitable continuation of the rural land contract system. Grassland and forestland have their particularities. Their contracting is essentially the same as farmland contracting, but there are discrepancies in paths, measures and methods.

[Column 3.5] Reform of Collective Forest Right in Rural Areas: Inevitable Continuation of Household Contract System

Over the past 60 years since the founding of the PRC, China's collective forest right system has experienced four stages, namely, "distributing forests and mountains to household" in the period of land reform, "forests and mountains joining in cooperatives" in the period of agricultural cooperatives, "collective ownership and unified management" in the period of people's commune, and "Three Determine's" in the period of reform and opening-up. However, with the gradual establishment of the socialist market economic system and the expansion and extension of the rural land household contract system, the drawbacks of China's forest right system have become increasingly prominent, namely, the property rights were not clarified, the operating entity was not identified, the management mechanism was inflexible and benefit distribution irrational, all of which had seriously hindered peasants' initiatives and productivity. At the same time, this kind of forest right system was in conflict with the relevant provisions of *Law of the People's Republic of China on Rural Land Contracting*.

In order to further reform on collective forest right system, the CPC CENTRAL COMMITTEE and the State Council issued *Decision on Accelerating Development of Forestry* on June 25, 2003, which put forward the overall requirements for the reform. On June 8, 2008, *Opinions on Promoting the Reform on Collective Forest Right System in an All-round Way* was issued, and it was decided to clarify property rights and the entity of contract in about five years.

A new round of forest right reform was summarized by peasants as "property rights determine the ownership of mountains, roots determine the growth of trees and aspirations determine people", so-called "Three Determine's". Its core is to clarify property rights, give peasants equal right to contract collective forestland with long-term stability. That is to say, under the premise of unchanged collective ownership of forestland, the right to use of forestland, the ownership, management, disposal and income of timber are returned to peasants' hands. There are 2.5 billion mu of collective forestland in China, involving the vital interests of 500 million peasants. Therefore, the reform of collective forest right is another significant change after the implementation of household contract system, and also its inevitable continuation.

3.6 Equational Contracting: Inheritance and Continuation of Guarantee for Peasants' Basic Right to Subsistence

Generally speaking, the people's commune system is an inefficient economic organization, but the function of collective guarantee for peasants' basic right to subsistence is still valuable. It has played an important role in preventing the polarization between the rich and the poor on the basis of the traditional "peasant economy" for thousands of years, especially in preventing the emergence of large-scale landless peasants, i.e., the "proletarian peasants" mentioned by Huang Zongzhi, and in ensuring the survival of the poor and disadvantaged groups in rural areas and maintaining the basic stability of the rural economy and society. Although household contract system disintegrates the people's commune as a monopolistic economic organization form of "the unity of politics and society", it has still maintained and continued the function of collective security of the basic subsistence right of peasants, i.e., equational contracting on the basis of collective ownership.

On the one hand, the collective guarantee for peasants' basic right to subsistence by the people's commune system is based on collective ownership, management and use of village community resources. The household contract system has changed management and use right rather than collective ownership. That is to say, the farmer's contract is the right of management and use, not the ultimate ownership of the land. Why should we implement the principle of equational contracting? The "equation" here, in fact, continues the function of collective guarantee for the basic right to subsistence. The logic behind it is there is no problem for peasants to ensure basic subsistence with equally divided resources under normal conditions. In other words, the premise of guarantee for basic subsistence is that they must have a certain number of land use rights that cannot be arbitrarily deprived by others (including the nominal owner "villagers' committee"), and incomes gained through land use right. As long as this bottom line is not broken, the basic right to subsistence of the vast majority of peasants, i.e., the problem of "food and clothing", will have more reliable material and resource security.

On the other hand, from the perspective of induced organizational and institutional changes, "choices people made in the past has predetermined their choices possible now" because of "path dependence". Reforms that completely break away from the past will cause the extreme sharpening of social contradictions and greatly increase the costs of reform, which will eventually hinder its advancement and can only be aborted halfway. Moreover, we can never completely break away from the past, or history, which is a more important factor to keep in mind. Marx believes "the new productivity and relations of production are not developed from nothing, or from the air, or from the fetus of presumed ideas that automatically set themselves up, but from within the existing process of production development and the traditional ownership relations that have been passed down, and developed as opposed to them."[37]

The basic social security function of peasants' land contractual right is further reflected and confirmed in the process of urbanization in recent years, especially in the process of "peasants becoming citizens". The premise of exchanging land contractual right for urban social security is their "equivalence", i.e., both of them have the "commonness" of

[37]Marx, K. Economic Manuscripts of 1857–1858. *Karl Marx Selected Works in Two Volumes*. London: Lawrence and Wishart Limited, 1947.

guarantee for basic right to subsistence. Whether they are "equivalent in value" or not may differ greatly in different regions.

[Column 3.6] Is it Feasible to Exchange Rural Land Guarantee for Urban Social Security?

It is an important policy measure to exchange "land guarantee" in rural areas for "social security" in cities. Although its comments differ, the progress in practice is still rapid.

Why can the two be exchanged? In essence they both have the social security function of the basic right to subsistence, although their intrinsic "value" may be different.

Owning contracted land in rural areas, or at least possessing the qualification and right of contracted land, is the most basic and major right owned by the vast majority of rural residents at present. Starting from the established institutional arrangement, following the principles of independence, volition and fair trade in market economy, and exchanging the rural "land guarantee" for the urban "social security", it is possible to break the "capital bottleneck" deadlock faced by the urban social security system in the process of "peasants' citizenization", and to carve out a path consistent with the market-oriented economic system reform in ways of social security transition.

The essence of market exchange is the mutual transfer of property rights between equal entities. Therefore, clear property rights are the basic premise of market exchange. If rural residents want to exchange the right to contract for the right to social security in cities, they need to first confirm their claims to the right. Secondly, they have to confirm their claim to "selling outright", i.e., whether the land contractual right is an exclusive "private right" and whether they have enough, sufficient and legitimate final disposal right (right to buy and sell). On this basis, they can freely choose whether to exchange for social security. If they choose to go to the city and enjoy the same social security benefits as urban residents, they can "sell outright" the land contractual right, and the proceeds will be converted into the initial fund of urban social security. Of course, they can choose not to. No organization or individual is authorized to "force peasants into the city".

Now many scholars think that peasants should go to the city and enjoy social security without giving up the right to rural land contract. It may be beneficial to peasants, but there are three defects in the reasoning.

First, urban social security is not a "free lunch". The biggest obstacle lies in where the "huge amount of money" comes from. Can central government and local governments at all levels cover such a huge expense at present? During my interview with several local government officials, they agreed "it's not lacking in good intentions but real capacity." Many city officials told the author that the current urban social security funds were already struggling to meet the needs of the existing urban residents, let alone the additional peasants. Furthermore, it is not a deprivation but an equal exchange of land guarantee for social security. As long as we adhere to the principle of independent and voluntary equal trade, this kind of exchange is "mutually beneficial and win–win cooperation", for through free exchange, we can not only solve the huge "gap" of urban social security funds but also promote the moderate scale operation of rural land. Some scholars suggest that the social security fund can be raised by issuing public bonds but which I cannot endorse. The current debt crisis in European countries is a good example. The experience of developed countries has told us social security expenditure is a "rigid" interest expenditure: easy to spend but hard to recover; easy to increase but difficult to reduce. The lesson should not be overlooked by our policy makers.

Secondly, supposing we can get social security without rescinding the right to contract, or rather, we can have both at the same time, who would possibly give up on such perfect opportunities, which, however, will inevitably lead to the flocking into cities beyond its capacity. *The World Development Report 1999/2000* issued by the World Bank stated that rural residents in some African countries had flocked into cities and shared in social welfare at no cost, which was very harmful to their economies. To exchange the right to land contract for urban social security is meant to prevent flocking into the city with no cost. Obviously, the right to contract is the cost that peasants have to pay.

Thirdly, even from the perspective of equality, if we do not give up the right to contract for social security, it's not necessarily fair. Compared with the peasants who choose to stay in rural areas, those peasants who enter cities have one more "urban social security right"; compared with the urban residents, they have one more "rural land contractual right".

In fact, it's common practice in Jiangsu, Zhejiang and other places to exchange rural land contractual right for urban social security right. For example, Jiaxing City, Zhejiang Province, known as the "Jiaxing model", launched a pilot reform named "Two Separations and Two Exchanges" in 2008: the separation of homestead and contracted land, the separation of immigration and land transfer; the exchange of homestead for urban residence, the exchange of contract right for urban social security. In practice, "Two Separations and Two Exchanges" have accelerated the substantial process of "peasants' citizenization", and also promoted the moderate scale management of rural land and the process of agricultural industrialization. According to the author's participation in the "three modernizations (new industrialization, new urbanization and agricultural modernization)" survey of Jianli County, Xiantao County, Hanchuan County and Daye County organized by the Agricultural Office of Hubei Province in September 2012, grassroots cadres generally reflected that even in the urbanization process at the county and township level, most peasants were willing to exchange rural land contractual right for social security right of cities and towns. At present, the major problem is the insufficient social security including the minimum living security, unemployment relief, medical security, pension security, etc. that can be traded for.

—Partly excerpted from Chapter 3, Section 7
of Cao Yang's *Research Report on Social Security of Rural
Non-agricultural Industry Groups in China*

It is undeniable that equational contracting is not the optimal allocation of land resources. According to classic economic theory, the most efficient resource allocation should adhere to the rule called "The highest bidder gets it." That is to say, the optimal allocation of land resources should ensure the highest land output rate, which requests the most productive peasants should have the right to land use. However, what about other peasants? If we can't guarantee that all peasants can obtain the average use right of the collective land within the scope of the village community, then it is against the principle of "equality", but more importantly, the basic subsistence right of peasants is lack of basic material guarantee. Therefore, we can understand why the central government has repeatedly stressed the long-term stability of land contractual right, while the government has never encouraged or endorsed the so-called "Two Fields System" (ration field + contracted field) which has taken both "equality" and "efficiency" into account. *The Law of the PRC on Rural Land Contracting* clearly stipulates: "During the period of contract, the contracting party shall not unilaterally terminate the contract, shall not force the contractor to give up or change contract and management rights in the guise of majority, and shall not take back the contracted land for bidding and contracting for the sake of the division of 'ration field' and 'contracted field', and shall not take back the contracted land to balance arrears. "

3.7 "Public Power": The Main Threat to "Private Power"

As is mentioned earlier, in contemporary China, the inalienable right of equational contracting is the most basic material condition to ensure the subsistence freedom of the broad masses of peasants, which is also the basic condition for all other freedoms". In the sense of jurisprudence, farmer's land contractual right is a kind of "legal private right" which is based on and surpasses the collective ownership of land, and is guaranteed by the state law. As a legal private right, it means this private right is guaranteed by law, or, by public power, for law is undoubtedly a kind of public power. However, public power has many forms or sources. In real life, we can see that the biggest threat to peasants' land contractual right often comes from public power of "quasi-government" at all levels, i.e., the public power from hierarchical governments and their affiliated departments challenging and violating the public power of the State law.

Firstly, peasants' land contractual right based on collective ownership is facing the threat of infringement from organizational owners.

In collective ownership of rural land, the identity of "owner" is vague and uncertain which brings about the inherent hidden danger of "owner" infringing on "contractor's" interests, or organizational owner infringing on the interests of individual owners. Jurisprudentially speaking, "rural community" is not an organization in strict legal sense, but a collective of all peasants in a specific area and an abstract collective group without legal personality. Therefore, in real life, there must be an entity of organization to act as owner or to perform the basic functions of owner. Although the current law prefers to regard agricultural production cooperatives and other rural collective economic organizations as owners, the entity of owner is in reality quasi-government[38] at the level of villagers' committees, or even township government due to the historical legacy of the people's commune system in which "politics and society were integrated", "three-level ownership was common", rural collective economic organizations which could cover all peasants in rural communities were rare.[39] In theory, peasants as contractors are also members of the owners. However, as a contractor, peasants are the real exclusive microeconomic entity, while as owners, individual peasants often only have abstract meaning of

[38]The villagers' committee is not a "first level government" but a "villagers' autonomous organization". However, in real life, the functions of the villagers' committee are more of the extension of the functions of the township level government, and there are not many functions that truly reflect "autonomy". So I tend to regard the villagers' committee as a "quasi government" rather than a "villagers' autonomous organization".

[39]Not all agricultural cooperatives and other rural economic organizations can act as the "owners" of rural land. In fact, the vast majority of various farmers' professional cooperatives and other rural economic organizations are not suitable to act as "owners". This is because such organizations do not cover all the farmers of the village community without difference. Therefore, only the kind of community-based rural economic organization that covers all residents of the village community can act as the "owner". From this point of view, if the economic organization acts as the collective "owner" of the rural community land, the "integration of politics and society" is inevitable and has inherent logical rationality.

ownership. In real life, villagers' committee and township government have the actual right to disposal of rural land. The individual farmer does not have much power in the transferring, leasing and trading of land, even if they oppose it, they are powerless and helpless. In fact, they are in the state of being "represented" voluntarily or involuntarily.

[Column 3.7] Who is the Owner of Land?

Article 10 of *The Constitution of the People's Republic of China* stipulates that "the land in rural and suburban areas is of collective ownership except that it belongs to the state as stipulated by law; homestead, household land and household hills are all of collective ownership." The question is, who does collective ownership refer to?

Article 10 of *Land Management Law of the People's Republic of China* establishes three "collective entities of peasants": village collective economic organizations or villagers' committees; rural collective economic organizations or groups; and rural collective economic organizations in townships (towns). However, there are only two farmer collective entities defined in Article 74, paragraph 2 of *General Principles of the Civil Law of PRC*, namely village farmer collective ownership and township farmer collective ownership. Among them, the land collectively owned by village peasants is managed by village agricultural production cooperatives and other agricultural collective economic organizations or "villagers' committees". "Villagers group" is not among the owners. There are two "farmer collective entities" identified in Article 12 of *The Law of the People's Republic of China on Land Contracting*, namely, "collective ownership of peasants" and "collective ownership of two or more rural collective economic organizations", "collective ownership of township peasants" are not included, which is different from *General Principles of Civil Law of the People's Republic of China.* But "villagers' groups" are given a seat, and "those who have belonged to two or more rural collectives in villages shall be contracted out by the rural collective economic organizations or villagers' groups in the villages." There are three peasants collective entities in *The Law of the People's Republic of China on Property Rights*, which is the same as *The Law of the People's Republic of China on Land Management.*

The three "owner entities" of "peasants collective ownership", namely, townships, villages and villagers' groups, obviously follow the legacy of "three-level ownership" of the people's communes, production brigades and production teams. Among them, the commune in the past and the township at present are not only the primary owner but also the primary government, which provides a convenient way for the transformation of collectively owned land into government-owned land. In fact, the villagers' committee at the village level is not a simple villagers' self-governance organization, but an organization with the function of "quasi-government". In the vast majority of rural areas in China, villagers' committee is more of an extension of government than an autonomous committee.

Secondly, peasants' land contractual right and even collective land ownership are facing the threat of public power from governments at all levels in the name of "public interest".

Because the current law stipulates that "the need of public interest" can be adopted as reasons for land expropriation, including rural collective ownership land,[40] and because of the lack of a clear definition of need of public interest, it can be arbitrarily interpreted and expanded, which deprives peasants of land contractual right and even farmer collective land in the name of public interest by local governments at all levels. Especially in the period of rapid industrialization and urbanization in China, land transfer fee is far higher than compensation for land acquisition, which has motivated local governments at all levels to try their best to transform rural collective land into state-owned urban land or construction land, and obtain huge land incomes from it. According to the data 2007 by Ministry of Land and Resources, "at present, local governments account for 80% of entities in land misuse cases, while individuals or enterprises account for 20%."[41]

If we examine it closer, we'll find the logic behind acquisition of collective land and violation of peasants' contract land for the sake of "public interest" is the presumption that public power is higher than private power. Although relevant laws stipulate that the expropriated land should be compensated, but such compensations cannot be parallel to "equivalent exchange" in the market. For a long time, the standard of compensation for land expropriation implemented by the state is multiplier method of output value, in which output value is the agricultural output value, a unilateral pricing of the government. The expropriated peasants have neither a say in pricing nor legal channels for bargaining. In fact, the price of land expropriation can neither reflect the intrinsic value of land nor the supply-demand relationship of market. In addition, there are also many intermediates who wish to grab a share in the compensation, so finally peasants can only get a pitiful fraction of the total compensation. According to Zhu Mingfen and

[40]Article 2 of the Land Management Law of PRC stipulates that "the state may levy or requisite land and compensate it in accordance with the law for the need of the public interest."

[41]*Shanghai Securities Daily*, July 13, 2007.

Changmin's discovery of land consolidation account in X Town, F County, Zhejiang Province in June 2010, "the compensation fee allocated by the county government to township government is RMB50,000 per mu, which dwindles to RMB20,000 per mu from township government to village government, and village community, as the owner of land, gets RMB12,000–13,000 per mu deducted the bidding cost of RMB7,000–8,000 per mu."[42] According to the investigation of Wen Tiejun, Lang Xiaojuan and Zheng Fengtian, the land issue is the most important cause of the current rural social conflicts, among which peasants' unfair compensation and their dissatisfaction with the illegality of land expropriation bear the brunt.[43]

[Column 3.8] Infringement of "Land Finance" on Peasants Basic Right to Subsistence

"Land finance", put it simpler, refers to the reliance of the local government on the incomes from the transfer of rights to land use to maintain local financial expenditure. Here, the right to use of land by local governments is often derived from the expropriation of collective ownership land as state-owned land. Moreover, the compensations paid by local governments to landless peasants are far lower than the income from the transfer of land use right, and the discrepancy has become a major source of local government revenue. Therefore, the benefit links brought about by "land finance" has in fact created a rolling development model of "land acquisition — land sale — tax collection — mortgage — land requisition". In this process, local governments, real estate developers and banks become the privileged groups, while landless peasants are the unprivileged group.

According to statistics of relevant departments, in the past 10 years, the income of land transfer has increased rapidly, and its proportion in local fiscal revenue has been increasing. Data shows that from 2001 to 2003, the income of land transfer reached RMB910 billion yuan, which was about 35% of the national local fiscal revenue in the same period; in 2009, it rose to RMB1.5 trillion yuan, which was equivalent to about 46% of the total revenue of local finance in the same period, accounting for 4–5% of GDP in that year. In 2010, the income of land transfer in the whole country exceeded RMB2 trillion yuan. In some areas, the proportion exceeded 50%, or even up to 80%. Even in economically developed areas like Beijing, in 2009, the land transfer fee income reached RMB92.8 billion yuan, accounting for 45.8% of the local fiscal revenue.

---

[42]Zhu Mingfen and Chang Min. "Analysis on the Characteristics and Attributes of the Recessive Market of Agricultural Land", *China Rural Economy*, No. 3, 2011, pp. 10–22.

[43]Wen Tiejun, Lang Xiaojuan and Zheng Fengtian. "Social Stability in Rural China and Its Characteristics: Based on the Investigation and Analysis of 1,765 Households in 100 Villages", *Management World*, No. 3, 2011, pp. 66–76.

Finally, the infringement of public power on private right is also manifested in various taxes and fees attached to land and apportionment.

The premise of land guaranteeing peasants' basic right to subsistence is that the income of land output can maintain peasants' basic survival needs. If the taxes and fees attached to the land exceed the income of the land output, or if the net income is negligible or even negative, peasants' basic right to subsistence cannot be effectively guaranteed. In peasants' words, "farming can't support a family".

The core of property rights, as a bundle of rights, is income right. If income is negative, the ownership of property rights will lose any practical significance, becoming a "burden of property rights". Before the reform on tax and fee in rural areas, farmland was abandoned, and land contractual right was transferred free of charge or was transferred with a loss sustained. The main reason was the heavy tax and fee burdens and the sparse, or even negative farming income.[44] Therefore, only by removing all kinds of tax and fee burdens can we ensure that the land has real, practical guarantee function rather than a nominal, illusory symbol. Of course, it is governments at all levels, including quasi-government like villagers' committee, that impose taxes and fees on land.

3.8 The Inherent Contradiction of Equational Contracting: A Challenge from the Dynamic Change of Rural Population[45]

The external threat of equational contracting mainly comes from the unrestricted public power; the internal threat is mainly the challenge of dynamic

[44]According to Wang Ximing's survey, before the tax reform in 2002, some township farmers in Hubei had the highest burden of 400 yuan per mu, i.e., 1 mu of land had to bear 400 yuan of various taxes and apportions, while the net income of 1 mu of land was less than 400 yuan. In 1998, Jingmen City, Hubei Province was approved by the municipal government to enter into the contract with farmers' burden of 147 yuan per mu and 233 yuan per capita, excluding various taxes and apportions added by county, township and village "hitchhiking". (China (Hainan) Research Institute of Reform and Development. *China Farmer Organization Construction*. Beijing: China Economic Press, 2005.), p. 198.

[45]The basic content of this section has been published. (Cao Yang. "Rural Land Inheritance System and Rural Land Community Ownership: Contradictions, Conflicts and Development Trend", *Theory Monthly*, No. 5, 2005.), pp. 5–9.

changes in rural population. The complete rural land system includes not only the current ownership system, namely the current land property rights arrangement but also the inheritance system, namely the future land property rights arrangement. In essence, the right of inheritance is the dynamic arrangement of current property rights, which determines the future of the current arrangement of property rights. Therefore, a comprehensive and prospective study of the institutional arrangement and evolution of property rights should not only focus on its current static pattern but also its future dynamic trend. In fact, there are two possibilities: one is that the arrangement of inheritance right is in accordance with the inherent logic of the current property rights arrangement, which will ensure the long-term stability; the other is that the arrangement of inheritance right is contrary to the inherent logic of the current property right system arrangement, then the conflicts will lead to the mutation of the existing property rights arrangement.

The current land tenure system in China's rural area, or the current land property rights, is arranged according to the rule of "the separation of two rights" in which the village community (collective) owns the ownership right and households own the management (contracting) right. That is the combination of the rural land village community (collective) ownership and household contracting system.

Collective ownership is the basis of collective guarantee of peasants' basic right to subsistence. It will inevitably lead to the equal sharing of land management right, or land use right, i.e., the equational contracting of rural land. First of all, land is the main (or even the only) public property in most rural areas. The villagers' equal ownership of the property is inevitably embodied in the equal right to use the land. In the final analysis, the form of management right depends on the form of ownership. Secondly, rural land has irreplaceable functions of employment insurance and minimal living security for rural residents at this stage, which is the "last line of defense" for rural social stability. In the serious Chinese context of a large population and small farmland, and the fact that the country cannot provide an integrated rural urban social security, the social security function of rural land has become more important and prominent. Therefore, it is difficult to fundamentally change the pattern of equational contracting.

The inheritance right system should also include the inheritance right to land ownership and land management. Although they restrict each other and have relative independence, in essence the inheritance system of land ownership determines that of land management right.

From the perspective of land ownership, the institutional arrangement of equational ownership of village community members excludes family inheritance of "son to father" from the jurisprudence, which is quite different from the traditional peasant economy in China, especially the owner peasant economy. To become a community landowner, a registered residence rather than blood ties is the primary qualification. Of course, consanguinity is also important in a sense, but it is not the sole factor, nor the decisive factor. Once you move out of the community, even if your ancestral family has lived in the community for generations, you will be excluded from any inheritance right (in contrast, you can still have equal inheritance right to your parents' family property); on the other hand, you have a right to inheritance once you have moved into a particular community and obtained residence registration, even if you don't know any of your neighbors. The community is more of a geographic than consanguineous concept. Admittedly, if your parents live in the community, and you continue to live in the community (even if you work in the city, but your registered residence is in the community), you will naturally have the qualifications of the community landowner, but please note that this is not inheriting your parents' qualifications. Even from the perspective of intergenerational inheritance of the community as a whole, the future generations of the community inherit their previous generations as a whole, which is not individual inheritance. This is because community property and community land have clear extensions and clear boundaries on the whole, but as far as individuals in the community are concerned, there is no specific community property and specific property corresponding to their ownership. Even if you are contracting for land, it is not owned by you or your family. You have only the right to use the land for a certain period of time, but no ownership, so current community land ownership logically excludes family inheritance, which is of the nature of private ownership or quasi-private ownership.

From the perspective of land management right, or land contractual right, the institutional arrangement should also exclude the inheritance of "son-to-father" from the innate logic angle. Although some scholars have been advocating complete land contractual right should include the right to use, transfer, inherit and mortgage, *The Law of the People's Republic of China on Rural Land Contracting* excludes the inheritance right. Article 50, the only one concerning the inheritance of land contractual rights, stipulates: "the contractual management right of land is acquired through bidding, auction, open consultation, etc., and if the contractor dies, the contractual income due to him shall be inherited in accordance with the provisions of *The Inheritance Law*; during the contracting period, his heir may continue to contract." It can be seen that the inheritance here is strictly limited, and is not the inheritance of land contractual right in the real sense. This is because community land is generally limited and constant, while the population of each family is variant. Some families have an increasing population, others a decreasing one. If we follow the rule of "father-to-son inheritance", the constant amount of land and changing population may lead to unequal contracting after some period of time, which is contradictory to the inherent logic of equational contracting by all community members. Therefore, the inherent rule of land community ownership inevitably requires the community to continuously adjust and reallocate the contractual land according to the changing population. This is how comes the phenomenon of "small changes every three years and big changes every five years". From historical experience, the reason why the German "Mark" with the ownership by village community could last for 1,500 years had been that it regularly adjusted the land distribution according to the change of family population. Its later change to the "hereditary system" of land leasehold was actually doomed to its final inevitable disintegration.

It is undeniable that the frequent adjustments take into account the principle of "equality" in which all members of the community enjoy land income equally, but it also seriously hinders the efficiency and brings about a series of sharp conflicts and problems:

First, the institutional arrangement has an incentive for population growth, which is unfavorable to population control in rural areas. This is because the right of equational contracting is closely associated with the population (especially men) of a household, the more population a household has, the more rights are obtained accordingly, which is an incentive to reproduce. Admittedly, many places have certain penalties for multiple births (such as fines or even deprivation of contractual right for a period of time). *Measures on the Administration of Social Maintenance Fees* levies social support fees on multiple-birth children who violate family planning regulations. Nevertheless, it is impossible for the government and society to punish multiple births for a lifetime. As a natural member of rural communities, children who have violated family planning rules will eventually become members of other communities. In most rural areas of China, the most important right is equational contracting right of land. From this perspective, equational contracting is no longer equal, for the incremental right and interest of multiple-birth households (increase in contractual land) are essentially a disguised deprivation of the right and interest of single-birth households (decrease in contractual land).

Secondly, due to the difficulty in increasing arable land (in fact land is constantly decreasing) and the continuous increase in population, equational contracting of land will inevitably lead to thinner arable land, less scale efficiency of land management, lower labor productivity of pure agriculture and more serious oppression of land by rural population.

Thirdly, due to the instability of land contractual right, the contractor lacks the initiative of long-term investment in land, so short-term predatory style of management is unavoidable, which damages the fertility of land and is not conducive to the sustainable development of land.

Fourthly, frequent changes of contracted land consume time and energy, increase cost of community organization and land adjustment, and thus increase the economic burdens of all members of the community.

It is precisely because of the above drawbacks that various approaches and methods have been explored in practice, which can be roughly divided into two categories: one is to stabilize farmer's contracted land and reduce the cost of land adjustment under the premises of community ownership and equational contracting. For example, in some places flexible land is preserved in advance for increased population; in some places the strategy of "settling accounts without land transactions" or "settling accounts with few land transactions" is adopted to make the system basically stable. Article 28 of *The Law of the People's Republic of China on Rural Land Contracting* stipulates that: "The following land shall be used for land adjustment or increased population: (1) flexible plot reserved by collective economic organizations adhering to law, (2) increased land through reclamation adhering to law, and (3) land returned by the contractor legitimately and voluntarily." The above methods can be regarded as technical ways of land adjustment, while other methods basically shake the foundation of community ownership and equational contracting, for they deviate from the inherent logic of community ownership.

Starting from 1987, Meitan, Guizhou Province, implemented the pilot scheme of land system reform, which clarified the entity of collective ownership, facilitated right to land use, stabilized investment expectations by excluding new births from access to land contracting. The scheme was simply summarized as "no increase for the newborn and no decrease for the deceased". In contrast to "small changes every three years and big changes every five years" in other areas, Meitan's reform has reiterated the policy that "the right to land use remains unchanged for 20 years regardless of increase or decrease of population during the contractual period". The reform remained open for things to come after 20 years.

The most obvious effect of the policy is to stabilize peasants' land expectations, motivate peasants to increase their investment in land, prevent land fragmentation and eliminate the cost of frequent adjustment. It has also exerted some, if not overall, influence on people's concept on reproduction. The Meitan experiment undoubtedly attracted great attention from the central authorities. In 1997, the CPC CENTRAL COMMITTEE issued the policy stipulating "land contractual period remains unchanged for 30 years", which fully affirmed the Meitan Experiment. Furthermore, on a national scale and for quite a long time, it has stabilized peasants' land contractual right and their land expectations with the authority of Central Government's documents. On August 29, 2002, *The Law of People's Republic of China on Rural Land Contracting*, adopted at the 29th meeting of the Standing Committee of the Ninth NPC, further clarified with the authority of the law: "The contractual period of arable land is 30 years. The contractual period of grassland is 30 to 50 years. The contractual period for forest land is 30 to 70 years; the contractual period for forest land with special trees may be extended with the approval of the forestry administrative department under the State Council."

However, there are still some uncertainties in *The Law of People's Republic of China on Rural Land Contracting*. For example, in "the state protects the long-term stability of rural land contracting relationship according to law", "long-term" means "30 years" (as far as arable land is concerned). Will it remain unchanged after 30 years? The most important issue here is how to define the inheritance right clearly. If not, it will lead to fluctuation after "30 years constancy". For example, Farmer A has two sons who have established their own businesses and divided their families after the contracting period of 30 years. Does Farmer A have the right to divide the land he contracted into two parts and pass them on to the two sons respectively? If the answer is yes, the problem of land fragmentation is not solved at all. The only difference is the right simply shifts from community to family. If the answer is no, does it mean his elder son should inherit it? Meanwhile, if the younger son still lives in the community, what will he do? Furthermore, if Farmer A is allowed to assign his existing contractual land to two sons, and Farmer B has only one son, it will mean that Farmer B's son's contracted land is twice as much as Farmer A's son's. If so, can such a disparity among community members (essentially the disparity in the rights and interests of community members) be called equational ownership or collective ownership?

Obviously, we have encountered an irreconcilable contradiction, a contradiction between the two basic principles established in the current Law. It is inconsistent with the inherent logic and cannot be solved. On the one hand, we need to maintain the community ownership, the core of which is equational contracting, so it necessarily requires that the land contracting right change with the population; on the other hand, we need to maintain the long-term stability of the land contracting relationship, the core of which is the departure of contracting right from population change. Obviously, there may be compatible coexistence between the institutional arrangement of the current land contractual period "30 years constancy" or even "long-term constancy" and that of the current land community ownership in the initial static configuration. However, there can't be dynamic compatibility due to the inherent logic conflict (unless all family members of peasants change synchronously). If the community ownership of rural land is to be maintained for a long time, i.e., the equal ownership of land by all members of the community stays constant, the right to contract must be adjusted according to the changes of population. It is impossible to keep the population unchanged for decades. Conversely, if we want to maintain the unchanged status of land contracting right, we must eliminate the uncertainty with the change of household population, which means equational contracting is difficult to maintain for a long time.[46] According to the survey results 24 years after the implementation of the policy called "no increase for the newborn and no decrease for the deceased" by Liu Shouying and Shao Xiazhen, equational contracting has in fact extinguished though rural land contracting system has continued. From 1987 to 2010, 120,000 new rural population in this county was not allowed to contract land. The landless population in rural areas accounted for 25% of the total population, and the number of households with landless population accounted for 84% in 2011. Obviously, the contracted land per household can no longer be averaged. The survey on 500 households showed households with landless population occupied less than half of arable land per capita than that of households without landless population: the former is 0.69 mu per capita, and the latter is 1.53 mu per capita.[47]

It is undeniable that though land contracting right is still the most important property rights of peasants, their appeal for "equality" is still strong. Liu Shouying and Shao Xiazhen's field survey showed that 93% of the respondents in Meitan, Guizhou Province agreed to redistribute land according to population, i.e., to return to the original pattern of equational contracting. On a national scale, since the second round of land contracting, 30–50% of the total land has been adjusted mainly due to population change, which has accounted for 63.5% of the total reasons for land transfer, far higher than the reasons of land expropriation (17.3%),

---

[46]To solve this contradiction, the author's idea is to implement the permanent tenancy system of land contracting (Cao Yang. "Rural Land Inheritance System and Community Ownership: Conflict and Development Trend — Reflection on '30 Years of Contractual Period Constancy' and the Implementation of the Permanent Tenancy System", *Theory Monthly*, 2005, No. 9.), pp. 5–9.

[47]Liu Shouying and Shao Xiazhen. "The Impact and Reflection of Meitan's 24-year Practice of 'No Increase for the Newborn and No Decrease for the Deceased'", *China Rural Discovery*, 2012, Winter.

land consolidation (13.3%) and due date (5.9%).[48] It also means that 30–50% of the villages have not strictly implemented the policy "no increase for the newborn and no decrease for the deceased" advocated by the central government.

3.9 Labor Freedom: A Key Right for Peasants' "Realization of Freedom with Freedom"

Since the disintegration of the people's commune and the implementation of the household contract system, the key right that peasants have obtained is the right to freedom of labor and right to land contract.

Under the system of collective labor and management of the people's commune, peasants didn't have control over their labor. In daily production activities, peasants had to wait for the production team to assign work. Peasants did what cadres ordered them to. They did not have the right to work independently and freely. Only after the completion of the collective work of the production team could they freely engage in work on household plot, or enjoy leisure.

After the implementation of the "big contract" system, peasants had the most freedom in their command of labor among the many production factors, for the command of land was limited by collective ownership, command of capital was restricted by the extreme scarcity of rural capital and difficulty of financing. As the *World Bank World Development Report 2003* pointed out, "labor is the most important factor in production and the most important assets of the people, especially the poor." Therefore, peasants' free control over their own labor is crucial to the effective allocation of labor resources.

From the unfreedom of labor in the commune system to the freedom of labor under the system of household contract, it is one of the key steps for peasants to realize their freedom with freedom. Only with the autonomous and free control over their own labor can there be the unique super-large-scale

---

[48]Yang Xuecheng and Zhao Ruiying. "Reflections on Rural Land Relations: Based on the Three Rural Household Surveys in Shandong Province from 1995 to 2008", *Management World*, No.3, 2008, pp. 53–61; Zhu Mingfen and Chang Min. "Analysis on the Hidden Market Characteristics and Their Attributes", *China Rural Economy*, No. 3, 2011.

transfer of agricultural labor force in Chinese history and even in the history of the world, the adjustment, optimization and upgrading of the economic structure of agriculture and rural areas, as well as the various forms of agricultural production organizations with different forms, like rich and colorful flowers blooming together.

The realization of "labor freedom" of Chinese peasants is a gradual historical process like the reform of China's overall economic system. The right to autonomous and free control over their labor is only the basic prerequisite to the realization of labor freedom. What is more important is a free economic and social environment which enables workers to realize labor freedom. In a sense, the process of economic and social reform in China's rural area, and even the whole country's economic and social reform, is a process of building an increasingly free economic and social environment for labor.

In 1979, *The Decisions of the CPC CENTRAL COMMITTEE on Several Questions Concerning Accelerating Agricultural Development* explicitly stipulated that "neither can farmland be distributed to single household... nor production be contracted to households", the freedom of labor began to be loosened within the framework of the collective economy of the people's communes, though. *The Decisions* pointed out "erroneous policies that are not conducive to giving full play to peasants' initiative for production and developing agricultural productivity should be corrected and revised resolutely." At the same time, *The Decisions* proposed that "peasants should be encouraged and supported in operating family sidelines, with an aim to increasing personal income and activating rural economy". Besides "operating in sidelines and increasing household incomes", the labor freedom at that time was more embodied in more autonomy on the part of production brigades, i.e., production teams (as well as production brigades) had more freedom in diversifying business and developing township enterprises. Individual peasants didn't have much freedom in engaging in non-agricultural industries, let alone starting business elsewhere. They needed approval from production teams and relevant departments, and they also needed to hold certificates. In 1980, Article 8 of *The Decisions of the CPC CENTRAL COMMITTEE on Several Questions Concerning Further Strengthening and Perfecting the Responsibility System for Agricultural Production* clearly stipulated that:

"We should give full play to the expertise of all kinds of handicraftsmen, peddlers and professionals in all walks of life, and organize them to participate in community enterprises and various collective sideline productions; individuals who engage in self-employed businesses may obtain approval from relevant departments to go out to work and operate with certificates."

In 1981, the Central Committee of CPC and the State Council transmitted *The Report on Activating Diversified Rural Operations* by the State Agricultural Commission, which was regarded an extremely important and even "milestone" document for Chinese peasants to realize freedom of labor. *The Report* clearly stated: "individual or cooperative engagement in industries like services, handicraft, aquaculture, transportation, etc., is greatly encouraged and supported. Any project suitable for individual management should be carried out by peasants themselves, and the production teams should organize and support it." In addition, *The Report* also pointed out that apart from busy seasons, semi-laborers and auxiliary laborers should be allowed to be exempted from collective work so that they can engage in household sidelines within their capabilities (i.e., to allow the existence of so-called "household personnel"). Obviously, *The Report* has opened the door for peasants to engage in all kinds of non-agricultural industries independently and freely. In addition, the extension of "household personnel" on the basis of "household plot" indicates that peasants have gained greater rights to labor freedom. When "household personnel" expands from semi-laborer and auxiliary laborer to full-time and main laborer, peasants' labor freedom has entered a new and higher starting point.

However, in the early stage of reform and opening-up, peasants' freedom of labor was mainly confined to the rural areas; peasants' cross-regional participation in secondary and tertiary industries, especially in large-and-medium-sized cities, was still regarded as a "forbidden zone" for a considerable period of time. The government's policy encouraged the development of township enterprises, diversified businesses and other non-agricultural industries in the countryside, i.e., "leave the land without leaving townships, enter factories without entering cities". Peasants' migration to cities for work and business, known as a "blind flow", was still blocked or restricted. At the institutional level, due to the disintegration of the people's communes, the main institutional barriers to restricting peasants' access to the city were the strict urban household registration management system and the grain purchase and marketing system. Only residents with urban household registration could purchase "ration grains" from state-owned grain stores with "grain purchase certificates". There was no legal free grain market in cities apart from illegal "black market". Without legal food supply, it became almost impossible for rural residents to have a long-term foothold in the city. Until 1984, the Central "No. 1 Document" only allowed the provinces, municipalities directly under the Central Government and autonomous regions to "select a number of towns for pilot projects and allow peasants to get employed there, do business and run services on the basis of taking care of their own rations to settle down in towns". Moreover, in October of the same year, the State Council issued *Notice on Peasants' Entry into Towns and Registration*, which clearly stipulated that only towns were open, excluding counties and cities.

[Column 3.9] Peasants' Spontaneous Employment in Cities and the So-called "Blind Flow"

In the process of industrialization and urbanization in all countries of the world, it is a common phenomenon that peasants enter cities for employment and become citizens. But in the period of planned economy in China, industrialization was not synchronized with urbanization, and peasants' entry into cities was severely restricted. Peasants' spontaneous employment in cities was regarded as a "blind flow", which vividly showed that Chinese peasants had neither freedom in employment nor freedom in residence and migration.

"Blind flow" was a specific concept in a specific historical period. It referred to the flow of labor and population from rural areas into cities (i.e., spontaneous and unplanned flow). In April 1953, the then Political Council issued *The Directive to Prevent the Blind Flow of Peasants into Cities*. According to textual research, it was the first time that the concept of "blind flow" was put forward in New China. In 1956, a large number of peasants spontaneously flocked into cities to make a living after the large-scale, storm-like agricultural cooperative movement, forming the so-called climax of "blind flow". In less than a year, the Central Committee and the Political Council issued four documents on countermeasures to "blind flow" in succession, in which the wording gradually weighed heavier from "to persuade" to "to prevent" and then "to curb". These four documents were: *The Directive of the Political Council on the Persuasion of Blind Flow* on December 30, 1956; *The Supplementary Directive of the Political Council on the Persuasion of Blind Flow* on March 2, 1957; *The Directive of the Political Council on the Prevention of Blind*

Rural Population Flow into the City on September 14, 1957; and the Central Committee of the CPC and the State Council issued on December 18, 1957 *Directive for Curbing the Blind Flow of the Rural Population*. The above directives ordered public security organs should strictly control household registration, grain departments should strictly prohibit the supply of food without urban household registration, peasants who blindly flowed into cities to get employed in industrial and mining enterprises must be repatriated to their origins, begging should be strictly prohibited, peasants should be prevented from abandoning agriculture for business, tickets should be strictly inspected along major railways, and civil affairs departments should be set up to take the lead in public security. Specialized agencies involving railway, transportation, commerce, grain and supervision departments were set up.

After the establishment of the people's commune system, rural labor and population were strictly restricted to the commune system. Coupled with the very strict household registration management system in urban and rural areas and unified purchase and distribution of grain products, the phenomenon of peasants' spontaneous influx into urban employment was basically eliminated. After the reform and opening-up, the people's communes were disintegrated, so the main organizational obstacles were eliminated. With the gradual loosening of various policies, the phenomenon began to emerge. In the 1980s, the influx of peasants into cities was still called "blind flow".

The abolition of unified purchase and distribution system and the emergence of free market were indeed double "benefits" for peasants' "freedom of labor". On the one hand, due to the abolition of "unified purchase", peasants were free to adjust their planting and agricultural structure, develop commercialized and market-oriented agriculture according to local conditions. On the other hand, thanks to the opening of grain market in cities, peasants no longer needed to bring their own rations when they went to cities for work and business, which cleared up a big obstacle for large-scale cross-regional migration.

Due to the rapid development of private enterprises, individual enterprises and all kinds of foreign-funded enterprises brought about by the reform of urban economic system, the rapid development of export-oriented, labor-intensive enterprises in China, especially in the southeastern coastal areas brought about by the industrial division of economic globalization, vast number of peasants obtained unprecedented freedom and opportunities in cross-regional mobility in history. However, for a long period of time, since the separation of urban–rural household residential registration system had not yet undergone fundamental changes, peasants did not have the freedom to settle down in the city. On the one hand, the city welcomed the "migrant workers" who could create wealth for the city; on the other hand, it did not grant "new citizens" access to social welfare. Peasants had the freedom to move to cities for labor and employment, but they had not yet become urban citizens. The "semi-freedom and semi-unfreedom" status posed various restrictions and constraints in urban employment and life. There were a series of "explicit discrimination" (like the household registration regulations for employment and education) and "implicit discrimination" (like verbal sarcasm and psychological repelling toward peasants). These restrictions, constraints and discrimination meant that peasants' freedom of labor in urban employment and life had not been truly fully realized. Generally speaking, labor freedom means not only workers have autonomous and free control over their labor, or freedom of labor entity but also the labor value of workers can be truly reflected, and workers can share the labor benefits they deserve. How to ensure the real realization of labor value? How to ensure workers share their own earnings? Practice has proved that it is more difficult and arduous than the realization of simple labor disposal.

The huge difference in labor remuneration between migrant workers and urban workers, especially the lack of social security for migrant workers, shows that the value of migrant workers' labor has not been truly reflected, and labor freedom is still inadequate. According to a comparative study between local workers and migrant workers in Shanghai conducted by a research team from China Economic Research Center of Peking University in 1998, the average labor cost ratio was as high as 5:1, which meant the total benefits migrant workers got was only 1/5 that of his Shanghai local counterparts. Wages of local workers were twice that of migrant workers, the remaining three times of the gap came from the "four funds" welfare including unemployment insurance, pension, medical insurance and housing provident that urban workers enjoyed while migrant workers didn't.[49] I conducted a large-scale survey of rural households at the end of 2001, and among the 820 migrant workers surveyed, only 38 enterprises paid the government-stipulated pension and

[49]"Urban Labor Market Task Force" of China Economic Research Center of Peking University. "Stratification and Integration of Urban Workers and Rural Migrant Workers", *Reform*, No. 4, 1998, pp. 99–110.

unemployment insurances, accounting for only 4.6% of the surveyed population. Some scholars have also made quantitative analysis on the discriminatory factors in the wage gap. Xie Sisheng and Yao Xianguo estimated that 55.2% of the wage gap was attributed to discrimination; Deng Quheng believed that the discriminatory factors accounted for 60%; Wang Meiyan showed with data that the discriminatory factors were as high as 76%.[50] It is undeniable that in recent years, due to the change of supply and demand in the employment market, wages of migrant workers have increased substantially. According to the data provided by the research group of the Rural Economic Research Center of the Ministry of Agriculture, the average monthly income of migrant workers in the first four years of *The Eleventh Five-Year Plan* period increased from RMB872 yuan to 1,417 yuan, an average annual increase of 12.9%. At the same time, under the coordination of the government, the situation of farmer workers enjoying various social security has also greatly improved. For example, the participation of migrant workers in endowment insurance reached about 15% on the whole. Although the coverage rate was still very low, it was a substantial increase over the past. Nevertheless, we should see that we have a long way to go before we truly realize the "equal pay for equal work" and "equal benefits within the same city" to ensure the full realization of the labor value of migrant workers, and to enhance the "freedom of labor" essentially.

Admittedly, according to Marx, before labor has become the "first need of human beings", labor is still the "means of livelihood" and the "freedom of labor" in general is relative and incomplete, which means there will inevitably be a phenomenon of "labor alienation" in society. People engage in labor mainly out of pressure of life and need for livelihood (subsistence) rather than voluntary volition. However, it is always a long process to move toward full "freedom of labor", which is impossible to

[50] Xie Sisheng and Yao Xianguo. "Quantitative Analysis of Wage Discrimination of Migrant Workers", *Rural Economy of China*, No. 4, 2006, pp. 49–55; Deng Quheng. "Income Gap between Urban and Migrant Laborers: Based on the Decomposition of Oaxaca-Blinder and Quantile Method", *Chinese Population Science*, No. 2, 2007, pp. 8–16; Wang Meiyan. "Wage Gap in Transitional Period: Quantitative Analysis of Discrimination", *Quantitative Economic, Technological and Economic Research*, No. 5, 2003, pp. 94–98.

achieve overnight due to economic and social conditions. "A journey of a thousand miles begins with a single step". Therefore, every progress of "freedom of labor" is an indispensable step to ultimate freedom.

[Column 3.10] Gradual Realization of Labor Freedom after Reform and Opening-Up

- After the implementation of household contract system, peasants gained the initial freedom to control their own labor.
- After the abolishment of rigid planting, peasants gained the freedom in planting.
- With the development of township enterprises, peasants gained the choice of "leaving the land without leaving hometowns".
- With access to cities on the condition of "taking care of one's own grain rations", peasants gained the right to limited urban employment.
- After the removal of constraints on grain market and labor market, peasants gained sufficient freedom of cross-regional employment.
- After the removal of constraints on urban household registration system, peasants gained the choice of transferring to a citizen.

3.10 Labor Freedom: A Basis and Premise of Voluntary Cooperation and Diversified Forms of Organization

Free labor is not the same as working alone. Working alone is only a formal freedom, which cannot achieve real freedom of labor. Marx remarked: "Man is a political animal in the most literal sense: he is not only a social animal, but an animal that can be individualized only with society"[51] Malinowski also remarked that "there is no freedom in individual action. Freedom only exists in organized groups based on a common goal, through joint cooperation and sharing fruits of labor."

Human cooperation and organization are the foundation and prerequisite for freedom, while labor freedom is the premise for voluntary cooperation and organization. In human history, only on the basis of labor freedom, can there be a wide range of forms and multiple levels of cooperation, as well as diversified forms of production organization with

---

[51] Marx, K. Introduction to A Critique of Political Economy. *Karl Marx Selected Works in Two Volumes*. London: Lawrence and Wishart Limited, 1947.

different characteristics. In a time when labor was not free, human cooperation was often compulsory, and the organizational form of cooperation single and rigid. The most obvious comparison in China is that of before and after the reform and opening-up. During the period of the people's commune, there were basically no other types of economic organizations, especially the spontaneous non-governmental organizations besides the people's communes, government-run supply and marketing cooperatives and credit cooperatives. As a highly monopolistic and unified economic, political and social organization, the people's commune excluded the existence of non-governmental organizations within the commune. Since the economic system reform has been carried out in the countryside and peasants have gained the basic right to freedom of labor, various types of economic organizations have emerged just like bamboo shoots springing up after a spring rain, forming a "hundreds of flowers blossoming" trend, and new forms of economic organizations are still coming out. Obviously, along with the gradual transition from unfreedom to freedom of labor, the form of economic organization in rural China has also changed from uniformity to diversity.

Why only on the basis of labor freedom can we have extensive cooperation with multi-forms and multi-levels? And why only in this way can we produce diversified forms of production organization with different characteristics?

First of all, labor freedom provides a broad social institutional space for different forms, different levels of cooperation and diversified economic organizations.

Labor freedom is not an isolated system of freedom, for there will inevitably be a series of supporting systems to make it complete. Similarly, if labor is not free, there will inevitably be a series of institutional arrangements that restrict its freedom. If labor is not free, workers are liable to economic compulsion or personal dependence that goes beyond economic compulsion, then many different types of free cooperation and spontaneous organizations from the civil society will lack the most basic labor resources, and even the necessary institutional protection and support. Furthermore, in the context of labor unfreedom, monopolists of labor resources, in order to maintain their monopolistic status, will try their best to strangle any labor freedom that can shake their status by using coercion.

Therefore, the kind of cooperation based on labor freedom, especially the spontaneous formation of non-governmental cooperative organizations, is difficult to function in such a system environment where labor resources are monopolized.

Secondly, freedom of labor nurtures extensive, various kinds of "organizers" (entrepreneurs), providing organizational talents for diversified organizational forms.

Marshall has long remarked that any cooperation and organization is not a simple accumulation and collection of personnel. It needs "organizers" to organize various factors of production (including labor factors, of course). Therefore, organization is the fourth factor of production besides labor, capital and land. In the context of unfreedom of labor, the society cannot provide the space and stage for the free emergence, growth and development of grassroots organizers. On the contrary, it will stifle any organizations, more specifically, the organizer, which is called "shoot the bird which takes the lead". Therefore, in the context of unfreedom of labor, organizers either come from the traditional family heritage, or from administrative order and selection, thus one of his/her most important duties is to maintain the monopoly of labor resources. Meanwhile, in the social and economic context of labor freedom, workers have the basic right to free movement and free choice, of course, they also have the authority to organize themselves or choose organizers. Due to the complexity of social economy, the different resource structures of different regions, periods and industries, as well as the differences in personality and ability of organizers, the recognition degree of different types of organizers will also vary among different types of workers, and the organizational forms of such autonomous, voluntary and spontaneous organizations are bound to differ greatly.

Finally, labor freedom provides basic labor resources guarantee for an open and competitive organizational structure, promoting the diversified development of economic organizational forms.

Diversity is always associated with inclusiveness and competition, while uniformity is followed by exclusiveness and monopoly. Diversified forms of economic organizations need an open, competitive and inclusive social environment, which encourages, at least tolerates, the coexistence and development of all kinds of economic organizations through competition and cooperation. All kinds of economic organizations need laborers and labor resources. On the one hand, the competition for labor resources promotes the flow of labor force, which is conducive to the effective allocation of labor resources, as well as the improvement of the value and status of laborers; on the other hand, it will motivate organizers to constantly improve management and efficiency. At the same time, open competition is closely connected with complementarity and cooperation among organizations, which is conducive to the development of differentiation and diversification. From a deeper level, an open, competitive, inclusive and diversified organizational structure provides a broad organizational and institutional platform for the comprehensive realization of labor freedom, because different types of economic organizations can better adapt to the heterogeneity of laborers and difference in needs and preferences of laborers. Moreover, this kind of adaptation cannot always be accomplished within once only. Multiple flow and comparison may be necessary. In addition, the quality and ability of laborers are constantly improving, so is the matching organizational form.

3.11 The Dual Economy and Society: Historical and Institutional Arrangement Restricting Peasants' Freedom

In China, peasants' inadequate labor freedom, especially the unequal treatment and employment discrimination they have suffered in urban area, mainly stems from dual economy and society as well as a series of corresponding institutional arrangements.

Lewis' dual economy refers to the existence of two distinct types of economic segments within an economy, in which the bulk of the economy is a labor intensive agricultural sector producing primarily products, and alongside this agricultural sector is a smaller manufacturing sector, which tends to have higher productivity. Before Lewis, Burke put forward the theory of "dual society", referring to the coexistence of traditional non-capitalist sectors and capitalist sectors from the suzerain, during his research trip in Indonesia, a former Dutch colony. It is generally believed that dual economy and dual society are the main characteristics of contemporary developing countries.

China, as the largest developing country in the world, is also prominent in dual economy and dual society. It should be noted that China's current status can be interpreted both from historical reasons, or "historical heritage", as well as institutional arrangements by the government in the planned economy period.

In the period of planned economy, China established a dual economy and society with "urban–rural divide" through rigid control over household registration to ensure heavy industry priority. "Urban–rural divide" was meant to divide urban and rural areas as two excluded geographical areas and implement different management policies through rigid administration (termed as "one country, two policies" by Lu Xueyi). The link between urban and rural areas was strictly limited within administrative plans, which prohibited the free flow of various factors of production, including labor resources. It should be underlined urban–rural divide was not meant for independent development of urban and rural areas as described in the saying "well water does not blend with river water", but for city's biased access to rural resources. The planned economy system transferred a large amount of agricultural surplus from agriculture and rural area through administrative instructions and channels to industries and cities, which further aggravated the existing imbalanced economic and social development, consolidating and reinforcing the dual structure.

China's reform is a "gradual" reform, in which the implementation of various measures is unsynchronized rather than synchronized. The reform of social management system is obviously lagging behind its economic system. When the rural labor market was liberalized, rural labor force could enter the city freely to engage in non-agricultural industries, for quite a long period of time urban household registration management system was not fundamentally loosened, which attributed to the discrimination of migrant workers, and was also the main institutional constraint on the full realization of peasants' labor freedom at this stage.

From a broader perspective, dual economy and dual society and their corresponding institutional arrangements have also restricted peasants' freedom in many ways, or, the capabilities to achieve freedom, as Sen has put it.

Firstly, dual economy and society worsens the rural "financial repression" and "financial discrimination" against peasants, which has explained peasants' lack of necessary financial capital support to enhance capabilities for substantive freedom.

In modern society, labor cannot create wealth in isolation. It needs to combine with capital to form a realistic production capacity. Therefore, no matter it is "capital hires labor" or "labor hires capital", employment must have capital as the necessary support. McKinnon remarked that in developing countries, "financial repression" was common mainly due to a "separated" economy and an "incomplete" market.[52] In China, the key feature of a separated economy is dual economy and society. It not only excludes the vast number of peasants from the normal financial market but also pumps the scarce capital resources from rural to urban areas on a large scale, forming a serious "financial anemia" for the countryside and peasants. According to statistics of relevant departments, state-owned commercial banks absorb a deposit of over RMB200 billion yuan in rural area every year, most of which flows into cities. Postal Savings Bank of China opens only deposit business, so more than RMB100 billion yuan of rural funds are transferred into cities every year. Even in rural credit cooperatives, their profit-seeking behavior makes a large amount of funds flow to cities. Compared with its urban counterpart, rural financial market has a small supply of funds, narrow supply channels in addition to a single financial institution, service and settlement. As a result, it's difficult for peasants and various agricultural and rural economic organizations to obtain financial support from the normal financial market. By the end of June 2009, there was 2,945 townships without a normal financial institution, 8,000 townships with only one bank outlets.[53] In this situation, peasants as well as agricultural and rural economic organizations can only resort to private banking, namely, private lending, illegal banks and pawnshops. However, the government's long-term control over access to financial market has suppressed the normal development of private banking. Although it complements normal financial institutions by alleviating to some extent the contradiction between supply and demand of rural funds,

[52]McKinnon, R.I. "Money and Capital in Economic Development", *The American Political Science Review*, Vol. 68, 1974.

[53]Fang Songhai, Wang Weinong and Huang Hanquan. "Research on Increasing Farmers' Income and Expanding Rural Consumption", *Management World*, No. 5, 2011, pp. 66–80.

it has been playing a game between "rationality" and "illegality", for it has not gained a legitimate status and is regarded as illegal "grassroots finance" without official recognition. At the same time, the loan interest rate of private banking is on general higher than that of formal financial institutions, so the borrowing cost of peasants as well as agricultural and rural economic organizations is higher than that of urban residents and economic organizations.

Secondly, dual economy and society have brought about a serious imbalance in the distribution of Common-pool Resources (CPRs) like education and health, resulting in a big difference in social investment on human capital, which has caused the lack in human capital support for peasants' capabilities to achieve substantive freedom.

Human capital, according to Schultz, is the knowledge, skills and abilities of workers. Human capital is not innate but rather acquired through education, training, health care, labor migration, "learning by doing", etc. So investment is crucial to human capital. The investment comes not only from individuals and families but also from the society, especially the investment of CPRs with strong externalities such as education and health, for which the government has a vital responsibility. In China, owing to dual economy and society and the corresponding institutional arrangements, the investment and distribution of CPRs such as education and health care are seriously imbalanced. To be exact, urban area is superior in the investment of funds, education and health facilities, distribution of education and health personnel. As far as education is concerned, according to the national sample survey of population changes in 2002, the proportion of illiterate rural population aged 6 years and above was as high as 13%, high school education only 6%, and college education merely 1%. The proportion of rural population with junior middle school and below was over 90%. By comparison, among the urban population aged 6 and above, the proportion of the population with high school and college education is 34%, five times higher than that of the rural population. As far as health care is concerned, in 2002, the number of hospital beds per 10,000 urban residents was 47.8, 6.5 times higher than that of rural area, which was only 7.4. The number of medical staff per 10,000 rural residents was 11.8, in urban areas it was 19.2, 1.6 times higher. From the comparison of per capita health care expenditure, in 2002, in urban area it was RMB568.4 yuan, 4.4 times of the 128.1 yuan in rural area. Because of the unequal share of medical and health resources, the annual mortality rate of rural residents was higher than that of urban residents for a long time. According to the data provided by *Report on China Human Development 2007–08* from Institute of Reform and Development of Hainan, although the gap in education resources was narrowed, in 2004, education expenditure per capita of rural students in primary school was RMB1,326 yuan, 33% lower than the 1,980 yuan of urban students; expenditure per capita in junior middle school was RMB1,487 yuan, 35% lower than the 2,288 yuan of urban students. In 2006, the total health expenditure per capita in China was RMB1,145.1 yuan in cities, 2.59 times of the 442.4 yuan in rural areas.

The upgrading of human capital is of great significance to the realization of people's substantive freedom, for it is one of the key factors to enhance people's capabilities. Sen reminds us that we should connect human capital with the capabilities to achieve substantive freedom. He remarked: "Human capital is a useful concept, but it's more important to view human beings from a broader perspective (breaking the equivalence between human and "wardrobe"). After recognizing the importance and effective scope of human capital, we must go beyond the concept, and adopt a perspective that is additive and inclusive rather than replaceable of the concept in any sense."[54] Obviously, the insufficient investment in human capital in rural area is a key factor for income disparity between urban and rural residents, as well as the lower cognitive and behavioral abilities of peasants, which has hindered the development of their capabilities to realize substantive freedom.

Finally, dual economy and society has brought about a serious imbalance of economic infrastructure like transportation, communications, tap water, power supply, sewage facilities, which also hinders the development of farmer's capabilities.

Infrastructure can be perceived both in a broad sense and narrow sense. The broad sense of infrastructure includes social facilities such as education, culture, health, sports and other general material conditions supporting social development. We refer only to infrastructure in a narrow sense,

[54] Sen, A. *Development as Freedom*. Palatine: Anchor Books, 2000.

i.e., economic infrastructure as defined in *The World Development Report 1994* by the World Bank: "These infrastructure include public facilities (electricity, communications, water supply, pipeline gas, sanitation and sewage system, solid waste collection and treatment system), public works (dams, irrigation, roads) and other transport sectors (railways, urban transport, seaports, waterways and airports)." In short, economic infrastructure is the material basis for providing public services for social production and people's lives. The public service system it provides is not only related to the operation and quality of people's production and life but also an indispensable public product to enhance people's capabilities to realize substantive freedom.

In China's dual economy and society, the distribution of infrastructure is also severely imbalanced between urban and rural area. Take tap water for an example. *The Outline of the Eleventh Five-Year Plan* stipulated rural tap water coverage reach 75% in 2010, but by the end of the "Eleventh Five-Year Plan", the coverage of Heilongjiang and Gansu Province was only 51%, and that of Shaanxi is 57%. "More than 200 million people drink unsafe water with excessive harmful substance. In some places, rural residents do not have access to tap water, drinking water has become a problem to be addressed, let alone the use of electronic appliances like washing machines."[55] There were rare sanitation facilities, sewage system and solid waste collection and treatment system. According to *Report of China Rural Internet Development 2008–09* by China Internet Information Center (CNNIC), Internet access rate of urban residents was 35.2%, and that of rural residents was 11.7%, among which more than a half was concentrated in the developed rural areas in the east. The Center's *Research Report on Users Behavior of Search Engines in China 2009* also revealed that by the end of June 2009, the proportion of urban and rural search engine users was 76.6:23.4, urban netizens over three times of rural netizens.

The lack of economic infrastructure has restricted peasants from realizing substantial freedom. For example, the inconvenience of transportation restricts the quick communication and contact between peasants and

---

[55] Fang Songhai, Wang Weinong and Huang Hanquan. "Research on Increasing Farmers' Income and Expanding Rural Consumption", *Managing the World*, No. 5, 2011, pp. 66–80.

the outside world, while the lack of Internet leads to information impairment and blockage, which has limited the ability of receiving and processing information.

In summary, the existence of dual economy and society makes the possession and enjoyment of both private goods and public goods of rural residents far lower than that of urban residents, which has led to the outcry of many scholars for equal "national treatment" for peasants.

3.12 Opportunities and Confusion in the Market: The External Environment for the "Market-Oriented Peasants" to Achieve Substantial Freedom

After the implementation of the household contract system, "peasant economy" still dominates in terms of its scale of production and operation, so some critics regarded this epoch-making reform as a historical retrogression and return to the traditional peasant economy.[56] This criticism equated similarity in form with similarity in essence. They ignored the profound changes in the macro-historical background of contemporary China's rural economic reform: the peasant household economy in contemporary China, or peasant economy, is household economy under the macro-background of China's overall transition to market economy. It retains the organizational form of small-scale household production and operation, but gradually changes the natural economic attribute of traditional self-sufficient peasant economy. In essence, peasant economy in contemporary China is "market-oriented" or in the process of "market-oriented" in terms of its developing trend.

China's traditional peasant economy has been closely linked with a self-sufficient natural economy for thousands of years. Small-scale household production was the external form of production organization, while

[56]For example, Professor He Xuefeng believes that "the land contract system in the early 1980s is not a revolutionary innovation in Chinese history, but a certain return to the farmland system before the primary cooperative in 1956, which is the norm of China's farmland system for thousands of years" (He Xuefeng. *Agriculture, Countryside and Farmers of China*, No. 1, 2004).

self-sufficiency was its essential internal economic characteristics. China's agricultural cooperative movement and the subsequent people's commune movement, with the mandatory way of "big grouping", organized the scattered peasants who had been grown on the basis of private ownership for thousands of years, but the movements hadn't touched the core, but rather strengthened its self-sufficiency in many ways. If the traditional individual peasant household was a "small and complete" self-sufficiency or semi-self-sufficiency, then the "large and public" people's commune was a "large and complete" self-sufficiency or semi-self-sufficiency. Although the basic micro-economic organizations had been made big and public, it was still closure or semi-closure in essence. Moreover, compared with the previous cooperatives, the commercialization, marketization and socialization of rural production had not been progressed but rather retrogressed. For example, the already-developed rural commodity economy in the Yangtze River Delta and the Pearl River Delta suffered a devastating blow. Many small towns used to prosper on their rural markets, later became bleak and desolate, which Mr. Fei Xiaotong had a vivid description. Li Xiannian, former Vice Premier and Minister of Finance of the State Council, described in an investigation report *Glimpses on the People's Commune* as follows: "In the past, many commodities which used to circulate among handicraft industry and agricultural cooperatives, agricultural cooperatives and peasants, have now become self-produced and self-consumed, and distributed directly within the community. What used to be made for sale has now made for its own needs; what used to be bought from the market can now be self-supplied." In short, in the period of the people's commune, the development of commodity economy was equated as development of capitalism. The so-called "blocking the road of capitalism" was essentially meant to block the road of commodity production and market economy. This theory and practice of regarding commodities and markets as evils greatly hindered the transformation of China's rural economy from a natural economy to a socialized market economy, leading to the stagnation of rural economy for a long time.

During the process of rural economic reform and the regeneration of farmer economy, the single vertical centralized form of production organization has been replaced by a decentralized form of family production organization. However, decentralized household management is not meant to disperse the "large and complete" self-sufficient closed economic system into the "small and complete" self-sufficient closed economic system. Compared with the traditional peasant economy, China's contemporary peasant household economy inherits the external economic organization form, whereas it is gradually changing and abandoning the internal attributes of the closed natural economy.

It is primarily due to changes of the external macroeconomic environment, and organizations have to adjust accordingly. China has established building a socialist market economic system as the ultimate goal of reform, and it will inevitably bring about marketization in all aspects of economic life. Rural area is no exception. Indeed, at the beginning of the implementation of the household contract system, most of the decentralized household management had features like being "small and complete", which seemed to be little different from the traditional peasant economy. However, this "small and complete" family management was only a temporary, transitional economic form in the process of a great historical change. It cannot represent the essential characteristics nor the future developing trend of the contemporary Chinese peasant household economy.

There are essential differences between the decentralization of contemporary household economy under the macroeconomic background of market economy and that of traditional peasant economy under the microeconomic background of natural economy. The traditional peasant economy was like "scattered sand": every household was a closed and isolated unit, lacking an internal economic link and cohesive force, so that they could "hear the sound of chickens and dogs of their neighbors, but won't see them in person till the end of life". Marx used the analogy of "a potato bag".[57] However, contemporary household economy is a kind of "net-

[57]"Every peasant household is almost self-sufficient and produces most of their own consumer goods directly, so they mostly get their means of living by exchanging with nature rather than by exchanging with society. A small plot of land, a farmer and a family; next to another plot of land, another farmer and another family. A group of such units forms a village; a group of such villages forms a province. Just like a bag of potatoes is composed of many potatoes." (Marx, K. The Eighteenth Brumaire of Louis Bonaparte, *Karl Marx Selected Works in Two Volumes*. London: Lawrence and Wishart Limited, 1947.)

work", in which individual household is connected by the link of market, reserving their independent status while relying on the market economy at the same time.

Market economy is an economic system in which many independent "economic men" trade freely. Compared with the self-sufficient natural economy, the division of labor, specialization and extensive trade and social cooperation brought about by market economy have led to higher labor efficiency and social productivity, creating more social wealth, a more solid material foundation for human pursuit of substantive freedom. In fact, freedom without material basis is only utopian freedom. "Of all history, the premise, namely, that men must be in a position to live in order to be able to "make history". But life involves before everything else eating and drinking, a habitation, clothing and many other things. The first historical act is thus the production of the means to satisfy these needs, the production of material life itself."[58] Historically speaking, market and freedom were closely connected. First of all, the free trade by "free men" was a reflection of freedom itself. "Denying people the opportunity to engage in trade through arbitrary restrictions can itself be a source of unfreedom."[59] Secondly, the efficiency of market economy comes from the free competition and cooperation of free "economic men" (free enterprises). The essence of market economy is a free economy. Finally, market economy provides a wide range of opportunities for free "economic men" to choose freely, providing a broader space for the development of people's personality and creativity.

Under the constraints of the people's commune system, low labor efficiency was mainly attributed to the lack of basic freedom, especially of labor freedom. In a single and standardized mandatory organizational form, there was only an "organizer" but no "individuals", and the society didn't provide peasants with the opportunity and platform to make choices and display their personality and creativity. After the reform of rural economic system, with the gradual and unprecedented advancement of marketization, the space of peasants' free choice has expanded greatly. Various types of "capable people" have emerged, and different types of

[58] Marx, K. and Engels, F. *German Ideology*. Moscow: Progress Publishers, 1968.
[59] Sen, A. *Op. cit.*

economic organizations have bloomed. To quote from *Manifesto of the Communist Party*, who could have imagined so many "capable men" are among our grassroots?

It is undeniable that the long-term natural, planned economy has resulted in the unfamiliarity with market and market economy of the majority of peasants, especially with the modern market economy. However, the craving for wealth through labor stimulated by market economy, the open horizon brought by labor mobility and the free choice of "free men", especially the repeated practice of "learning by doing", have accelerated their ability to understand, familiarize with and play by the rule of market.

[Column 3.11] "Learning by Doing": A Major Path of Growth for Economic Entity of Rural Micro-Market Economy

In 1962, American economist Kenneth Arrow put forward the concept of "learning by doing" in his paper entitled *The Economic Implications of "Learning by Doing*. In theory, Arrow's classic paper is the initial exploration on the endogenous process of technological progress in economic growth model, and thus Arrow has become a pioneer in endogenous economic growth model.

"Learning by doing" emphasizes the special significance of practice in technological progress and economic growth and implies the investment and accumulation of human capital have a way other than school education. "Learning by doing" is similar to Mao Zedong's strategy called "learning about war from war itself".

Peasants in China have entered the new market economy environment from the people's commune system. The way they gradually understand, familiarize with and finally learn to play by the rule of market cannot rely on books, meetings or schoolings. The only way is through "learning by doing". "True knowledge comes from practice." "Doing" can be a success or failure. Nevertheless, peasants can broaden horizon and accumulate experience, while experience is "a progressively increased productivity". Meanwhile, experience, as a kind of practical knowledge, is also a kind of public goods with "spillover effect". The diffusion of experience can save latecomers much time and cost.

Of course, market economy is not a paradise full of flowers, its mechanism far from perfect.

It has both opportunities and risks, which coexist in the market mechanism.

Firstly, household economy is an efficient production organization, but not an efficient circulation one. Facing the vast market, a single farmer has to deal with asymmetric information and high transaction cost, which constitute a sharp contradiction between "small production" and "big market".

Circulation and production are two major links in the process of social reproduction, which are both interrelated and relatively independent. In the social environment dominated by natural economy, as a self-sufficient and semi-self-sufficient farmer, circulation is only a minor supplement to the end of their production process. That is to say, he only puts a small part of the surplus agricultural products into circulation and exchange with others. Even if the exchange fails and the product cannot be sold, it won't make a big difference for the reproduction. As for the pre-production and mid-production links, he has little dependence on circulation, in essence, on others and society. However, in the context of market economy, the role of circulation has changed from a minor supplement to an indispensable, key link in the process of agricultural reproduction for "market-oriented" or "becoming market-oriented" peasants. This is because market-oriented agriculture essentially depends on modern agriculture with big market and big circulation. Market-oriented peasants produce agricultural products mainly for others and the society instead of their own. Therefore, whether a product can be sold and at what price it is sold are what Marx calls a fatal "thrilling leap". If the "leap" fails, it hurts the producer instead of the commodity itself. At the same time, the pre-production and mid-production link of market-oriented agriculture are also highly dependent on the market and circulation. For example, the purchase and circulation of seeds in pre-production period, pesticides and fertilizers in mid-production period have to rely on the market. Therefore, in the modern market economy, circulation has not simply acted as a medium of production and consumption, but has infiltrated into the whole process of production, improved the level and efficiency of market-oriented production, and guided producers to organize production in a market-oriented manner. It is in this sense that we can say that circulation determines production in market economy.

In the development of rural market economy, circulation is very important, but households are not a suitable and efficient circulation organization for the following reasons: (1) compared with production, circulation requires more accurate and fast market information, more extensive and convenient network, as well as transportation, warehousing and other infrastructure, which cannot be possibly supplied by individual household; (2) compared with production, circulation requires a larger economic scale, for example, large quantities of products. However, the produce of a single household is limited after all, unable to generate necessary or even minimum revenue of scale; (3) Production and circulation require different specialized knowledge and skills, requiring each farmer to have both competences is neither realistic nor economical, and it's in disconformity to the trend of specialized division of labor.

Since households are not an efficient circulation organization, how to connect peasants to the modern market system and make their production effectively integrate into market has become one of the priorities in the construction of modern agriculture under market economy, which is one of the biggest challenges faced by peasant economy.

Secondly, in the modern market economy, in order to truly become an efficient production organization, peasants must rely on a sound social service system, which is a public goods in a general sense. How to ensure the effective supply of public goods like social services is another big challenge faced by individual household.

Market economy is an open and socialized economy composed of numerous independent micro-economic entities (economic men) and connected by market networks. The efficiency of micro-economic entities stems not only from their own independent economic interests or the pursuit of maximizing those interests (the competition among economic men) but also from socialized cooperation and service system. Generally speaking, social services, as a public goods, is meant to meet the "aggregate social public needs" as the total of needs of all economic men, rather than an individual economic man. Therefore, an individual economic man, pursuing the maximization of his own interests, lacks the internal motivation to produce and provide public goods for others and the society. However, public goods are extremely important to the efficiency in the operation of socialized market economy. Therefore, how to ensure the supply of public goods on the basis of market economy has been a topic of constant concern in economic theory and practice since Adam Smith.

During the period of the people's commune, the commune and its subordinate production brigades and production teams were the main producer and provider of public goods. After its disintegration, however, an individual household were unlikely to act as supplier of public goods, while a suitable supplier had not yet been nurtured or supplemented, resulting in the absence of public goods supplier for a period of time. As a result, individual peasants were often in a disadvantaged position in face of the challenges from natural disasters and market economy, which had hindered the process of peasants' marketization and rural economy marketization to a great extent. For example, for quite a long period of time, the construction and maintenance of farmland and water conservancy facilities in a considerable part of rural area had been in a state of "three without's", namely, "without fund, without organization and without management", resulting in the blockage of ditches, the drying up of ponds and weirs, incompetence in coping with floods and droughts.

Thirdly, there is heterogeneity among peasants. Those peasants who are in disadvantaged position due to regional and human capital differences are often rendered incapable, helpless and hopeless in the market competition without a certain rescue and cooperation mechanism.

Market competition is a process of "survival of the fittest". Although it can promote social progress, unrestrained and cruel competition often does too much harm to the weak and vulnerable group, which is not conducive to the realization of the ideal of common prosperity, the construction of a harmonious society, and the pursuit of substantive freedom of everyone. Of course, to solve this problem is not to eliminate market competition, for to eliminate competition is to eliminate market economy. However, a rational society cannot let it go without control. Instead the society must establish a certain rescue and cooperation mechanism to help and protect the weak and vulnerable groups in market competition. Obviously, the establishment, perfection and development of such mechanism are beyond the capability of individual peasants. At present, the "complaints" and "criticisms" of some peasants toward market economy are largely due to the lack or imperfectness of such mechanisms.

Finally, the real market is neither harmonious nor perfect. The real market economy is a game of interests, in which strong interest groups seek benefits through their source of information, organization and even "discourse" advantages. Peasants, though large in number, are generally a disadvantaged group as a whole because of their weak organizational strength.

Marxism holds that everything people strive for is related to interests. Market economy is essentially a game of interests. Rational market economy is a benign and mutually beneficial game of interests, while irrational market economy is often a vicious one. The market economy in China is not yet a harmonious and rational one. Some powerful interest groups tend to use their information, organization and even discourse advantage to seek their benefits at the expense of benefits of others or the whole society. In this irrational game of interests, peasants as a whole, though large in number, is a weak group due to weak organizational strength and low degree of organization.

Michael Lipton, American economist, put forward the theory of "urban bias" in 1968 in his book *Why Poor People Stay Poor: Urban Bias in World Development*. He believes that in the game between urban and rural interest groups, the policy is always favorable to urban interest group, because peasants often have a weaker influence on government policy-making due to their higher cost of communication (dispersed residence), weak organizational strength and the common phenomenon of "free ride". That is to say, in the whole political system and policy-making system, the input pressure of rural residents is lower than that of urban residents, leading to an unfavorable condition for rural residents.

In China, peasants are the initiators of market-oriented reform, and in general, they are the beneficiaries as well. However, due to the shift of focus of China's economic system reform from rural to urban areas and the unbalanced progress of the reform, the traditional urban beneficiaries and beneficiaries strata, especially some vested interest groups and strata have, for a period of time, taken advantage of peasants' low degree of organization and weak organizational power to draft policies unfavorable to them, e.g., the discriminated policy of urban employment against peasants[60] especially the infringement of peasants' land right and interests behind "land finance". Therefore, how to win back their organizational

[60]For example, some urban governments have implemented the policy of "cleaning the cage for new birds", a typical discrimination against migrant workers, in which migrant workers are sacked for no good reason so that job vacancies can be left for urban workers to solve the problem of urban employment.

discourse power and their influence on policy-making in the interest game of market economy is a profound challenge faced by peasants.

3.13 The Triple Game between the Central Government, Local Government and Peasants: Participation and Interaction in Policy-Making by "Market-Oriented Peasants"

The economic system reform in contemporary China includes rural economic system reform, and it is essentially the institutional change promoted by the broad masses of the people for the "free realization of freedom". The ruling party and government, in the wake of the people's demand for change, create a pattern of "interaction between the masses and cadres" and "interaction between the upper and lower level". Therefore, it is partial to consider the reform process as a "government-led" institutional change. To put in strictly, it should be the "civil (market) and government-interactive" institutional change. The process of reform has also shown that the key to the smooth progress of reform lies in the positive interaction and rational game between the masses and the government. If they lack communication and cooperation, or irrational game emerges, it is difficult to promote the substantive reform process through either spontaneous force of the people or the coercion of the government. Worse still, it will lead to many social contradictions and various conflicts of interests.

In this process of "interaction between the upper and lower level" reform, the government's policy is undoubtedly a key factor influencing the economic decision-making of peasants. However, peasants are not passively accepting the government policy. In fact, they can also actively participate so as to direct policies favorable to their interests, thus forming a benign interaction and rational game between the two parties in the process of policy making.

Generally speaking, peasants' economic decision-making can be regarded as a rational "economic man" pursuing the maximization of their interests in the context of a certain natural, technical and institutional environment. Following this train of thought, government policy, as one of the major factors of the institutional environment, constitutes the external constraints on peasants' economic decision-making. Peasants will not only react rationally to the market environment as Schultz said but also to the policy environment. Stephen R. Boucher *et al.* studied how Mexican peasants who had become employed immigrants responded rationally to changes in immigration policies in the United States; Hennessy and Rehman and Uchida explored how government policies influenced peasants' economic decision-making behavior.[61]

The restriction and influence of government policy on peasants' economic decision-making is particularly important and prominent in the contemporary China, because the historical institutional changes in rural area are the result of peasants' spontaneous innovation and government-led promotion. Therefore, the interactive game undoubtedly becomes one of the key factors to the decision-making of peasants. The process of peasants' economic decision-making can be understood as the interactive game process between peasants and government policies in a sense. Following this train of thought, government policy is not only an exogenous variable but can also be internalized in the peasant household economic decision-making model, for the reason that government policy can be reflected in the income-cost curve and utility function of peasants, and the change of government policy will bring corresponding changes in the curve and function. Conversely, the economic behavior of peasants can also restrict, influence and even change the government policy to a large extent through a certain transmission mechanism.

Furthermore, government in modern society is not a single entity. In China, the government should at least be divided into two basic levels: the

[61] Boucher, S.R., A. Smith, J.E. Taylor and A. Yunez-Naude, "Impacts of Policy Reforms on the Supply of Mexican Labor to U.S. Farms: New Evidence from Mexico", *Review of Agricultural Economics*, Vol. 29, No. 1 (2007), pp. 4–16; Hennessy, T.C. and Tahir Rehman. "Assessing the Impact of the 'Decoupling' Reform of the Common Agricultural Policy on Irish Farmers' Off-farm Labor Market Participation Decisions", *Journal of Agricultural Economics*, Vol. 59, No. 1 (2008), pp. 41–56; Uchida, E., Scott Rozelle and Jintao Xu. "Conservation Payments, Liquidity Constraints and Off-farm Labor: Impact of the Grain-for-green Program on Rural House-holds in China," *American Journal of Agricultural Economics*, Vol. 91, No. 1 (2009), pp. 70–86.

central government and the local government.[62] Logically, if the economic decision-making is regarded as a dual interactive game between peasant households and the government (a single entity), it must meet one of the following two requirements: Firstly, the objective function, interest claims and even policy orientation of the central and local governments are completely consistent. Local governments do not have their own independent or relatively independent policies, and they are only the executor of central policies. Secondly, peasants are in a completely closed economic and social environment, so they cannot distinguish the policy differences between local government and central government due to sparse information and limited knowledge. The central government is very far away from them, and they can only deal with local governments. This is similar to the fact that before the reform and opening-up, when grass-roots people regarded the Secretary of the CPC branch as the incarnation of the CPC, in other words, the local Party branch represented the Central Committee.

However, in the reality of the contemporary China, neither of the above two assumptions are correct. Firstly, no matter whether it is interpreted as "federalism with Chinese characteristics" or "promotion championship model of local officials", the objective function, interest claims and even policy orientation of central and local governments are obviously not entirely consistent. The two have their own relatively independent interest claims. To put in vividly, the central government speaks standard Mandarin while the local government speaks local dialect. In order to maximize their respective interests, they play an interactive game at the policy level. Secondly, the peasant households are no longer traditional self-sufficient peasants, but "market-oriented" peasants or peasants in the process of becoming "market-oriented". Peasants can understand the differences in policies from central government and local government through television, newspapers, the Internet and other channels thanks to marketization, information technology and large-scale population and labor mobility, and they will also use these differences to maximize their own interests.

Thus, real life has shown us several possibilities: (1) The policy of central government and local government are highly consistent with the peasants' interests, and equilibrium of interests brings about equilibrium

---

[62]Local governments can also be divided into multiple levels, but this book will not elaborate on it.

of policies. No one is willing to change the established pattern of interests, so no party intends to change the policy. This is undoubtedly the most ideal "Pareto optimum state", a goal that governments have been striving to pursue. (2) The policy orientation of the central government is basically the same as that of the local government, but it is not in the best interest of peasants. Peasants tend to change the policy, but it's very difficult to do so. The situation before the reform on rural economic system could be regarded as this state. (3) The policy of local government is more beneficial to peasants, peasants can reach tacit understanding with local government, forming interest alliance and striving to urge the central government to revise its policy. (4) The local government policy is less beneficial to peasants than that of central government, then peasants can urge the local government to revise its policy through the central government. There are many examples of cases (3) and (4) in the institutional changes in rural China. For example, in the early stage of reform, the implementation of household contract production in Anhui rural area could be regarded as case (3). Local governments withstood the pressure of the official central document "no contracting production to households", supported or acquiesced in practice, and ultimately promoted the central government to revise its policy. In recent years, disputes over land property rights in many places are case (4), in which local governments violate peasants' right to land interest. As a result, peasants had no alternative but to appeal to the central government for justice. In short, the economic decision-making in reality is a triple game between peasants, local government and the central government rather than a simple double game between peasants and the government as a single entity.

In this triple game, how can peasants transmit their interest appeals to governments at all levels, especially the central government, to influence government policies? How can governments at all levels, especially the central government, truly understand and reflect peasants' interests and demands in the whole process of policy formulation, modification and perfection? It requires not only a democratic political system environment but also "organized" peasants.

Sen listed "political freedom" as the prerequisite to "instrumental freedom". Political freedom requires free and extensive participation in politics by the people. "Political and civil rights, especially those concerning freedom of discussion, debate, criticism and holding dissenting opinions, are core to the formulation of policy that is both open and can reflect public opinion."[63] To participate in the process of policy selection closely related to their own interests, peasants should not only have the right to know but also the right to express opinions before making decisions, the right to participate, supervise and evaluate, all of which are basic civil rights rather than bestowed rights. As far as feasibility is concerned, the core lies in the construction of systems and mechanisms, especially in the construction of channels of expression, transmission and feedback of people's appeals and opinions. It is undeniable that the infrastructure construction of "political freedom" in rural China lags far behind that of economic freedom.

Many a scholar has remarked that the low degree of organization is a major reason why peasants cannot safeguard their own interests and participate in the process of policy making by collective and organizational forces. Although the people's commune highly organized the peasants formally, most peasants were passively "organized" rather than actively "self-organize". Moreover, the people's commune was a "dual political and social organization" with its priority on the industrialization of heavy industry rather than an organization with an aim to safeguarding the interests of peasants. After the implementation of household contract system in rural area, how to organize peasants on the basis of market economy and free choice has become a major issue that needs to be seriously discussed and is related to the future direction of China's rural area and peasants. Undoubtedly, it's also a basic project for peasants to participate in the process of policy making.

3.14 The Future Trend of Institutional Change in Contemporary Rural China: Further Broadening the Institutional Space for Peasants' "Realization of Freedom with Freedom" and Increasing Peasants' "Capabilities" to Realize "Substantive Freedom"

The reform of the rural economic system in contemporary China has enabled the peasants to obtain two major rights, namely, the right to land

[63] Sen, A. *Op. cit.*

contract and the right to labor freedom. However, due to the dual economy and society, and the corresponding institutional arrangements, the opportunities and challenges of market economy coexist due to peasants' low degree of organization. The space for peasants to realize their freedom is yet to be broadened, which means the capabilities to realize substantive freedom needs to be strengthened urgently.

Although the history of human institutional change has undergone ups and downs, even short period of retrogression, the overall trend is toward civilization, modernization and freedom. Man's freedom is the ultimate criterion to measure the degree of human civilization and modernization. Therefore, we should adopt the yardstick of freedom instead of sole efficiency to view the reform of China's rural economic and social systems, the modernization process and the modernization of China's agricultural production organizations.

In general, the future trend of China's rural institutional and organizational changes is to further broaden the institutional space for peasants' realization of freedom with freedom and further enhance their capabilities to achieve substantive freedom. Around this overall goal, we also need a series of reforms as follows.

Firstly, we should further clarify the sanctity and inviolability of peasants' land contractual right as "private right", and give peasants more freedom in the transfer, trade and inheritance of land contractual right.

The rural land contractual right is the fundamental basis and property guarantee for the majority of peasants in contemporary China to realize their freedom. Although the income from contracted land is no longer the main source of income, and a considerable number of land contractors are no longer the direct operators on the land, land contractual right, as a "private right" peculiar to rural peasants instead of urban residents, has unique utility and function that cannot be replaced by other private properties. To guarantee the sanctity and inviolability of farmer's land contractual right, it's crucial to prevent the infringement and erosion from all kinds of "public power" through their privileges. Therefore, it is necessary to further amend *Law of the People's Republic of China on Rural Land Contracting* along the line of "strengthening contractual right, weakening property rights, standardizing expropriation right and loosening trading right" so as to eliminate legal basis for arbitrarily depriving peasants of their land contractual right. At the same time, peasants are given full freedom in the transfer, trade and inheritance of land contractual right. More specifically, peasants can be allowed to "sell outright" the land contractual right after entering the city, i.e., to exchange rural land contractual right for urban social security right. At the same time, son/daughter inheritance right of the land contractual right can be tried out in the countryside.

[Column 3.12] Suggestions on Amendment of the *Law of the People's Republic of China on Rural Land Contracting*

In Article 1, the term "peasants are granted long-term and protected right to land use" is amended as "peasants are granted long-term and protected right to land contract" in accordance with the actual separation of right to contract and right to use, and give peasants the freedom of retaining land contractual right without actually tilling soil.

Article 3 "Rural land that is not suitable for household contracting like barren mountains, ditches, hills and beaches can be contracted through bidding, auction and open consultation", and it is amended as "the real operator on rural land such as barren mountains, ditches, hills and beaches can be decided through bidding, auction and open consultation on the basis of the equitable determination of household contractors". Rural land such as barren mountains, gullies, hills and beaches is also the common property of all residents in rural communities. Granting households the contractual right does not contradict with the flexible land management and use methods; more importantly, it can prevent a small number of village cadres or government officials from using "property rights" or "public power" to infringe on the common property of all villagers.

Article 10 "The State protects the transfer of land contractual management right on the basis of law, voluntariness and compensation" is amended to "The State protects the transfer and trade of land contractual management right on the basis of law, voluntariness and compensation". The addition of "trade" here can give peasants more freedom in the disposal of land contractual right, including the right to "sell outright" land contractual right.

Article 18 "When contracting land in accordance with regulations, members of the collective economic organization shall exercise their right to contract land equally according to law, or may renounce their right to contract land on the basis of voluntariness", and it is amended as follows: "When contracting land in accordance with regulations, members of the collective economic organization shall exercise their right to contract land equally according to law, or may renounce their right to contract land on the basis of voluntariness and compensation". The additional "and compensation" here emphasizes the property rights attribute of the land contractual right. Peasants cannot and shouldn't be asked to give up the land contractual right without compensation.

Article 26 "During the contracting period, if the whole family of the contractor moves into a town or city, the contractor, at his own will, can retain or transfer the right to land contract according to law". "During the contracting period, if the whole family of the contractor moves to a town or city and become registered non-agricultural residents, the contractor should return the contracted arable land or grassland. If the contractor does not return it, the contracting party may recover it." The above two can be amended as "If the whole family of the contractor moves into a town or city, obtains the urban household registration and enjoys urban social security benefits, the contractor can sell outright the land contractual right to the contracting party on the basis of voluntariness and compensation." It is necessary to adapt to the practice of exchanging rural land guarantee for urban social security.

Article 33 deletes such wordings as "the transferee must have the ability of agricultural operation" and "under the same condition, members within the same collective economic organization shall enjoy priority", for they are in conflict with Article 34. Article 34 clearly stipulates "the entity of the transfer of land contractual management right is the contractor. The contractor has the right to decide whether or not the land contractual management right should be transferred and how it should be transferred according to law."

Article 46 deletes such wordings as "barren mountains, ditches, hills and beaches, etc. can be contracted directly through bidding, auction, open consultation". "Barren mountains, ditches, hills and beaches, etc." and "the right to land contract can be converted into shares among the members of the collective economic organization, and then contracted management or joint-stock operation can be carried out" are retained, which is the same as the amendment to Article 3.

Secondly, we should further reform the "urban–rural divide in household registration" to give peasants full freedom in residence and migration.

Up to now, the biggest institutional obstacle to the full realization of peasants' freedom is still "urban-rural divide in household registration". On the one hand, the second or even third generation of migrant workers are still rural residents in theory though they were born and grew up in cities. On the other hand, some governments force peasants to enter the city and become city dwellers in order to take over their land which is owned by village community and operated by peasants household. The above two phenomena are caused by one common reason — peasants' lack of freedom in residence and migration.

The core of the reform on household registration system is to retain its basic function of information collection while eliminate its regulatory function. The basic function is to record and retain the information of household population, while the division of "agricultural population" and "non-agricultural population", restricting population flow, migration and people's free choice of residence are the regulatory function attached to household registration by the planned economy. Admittedly, population movement and migration also need to be coordinated rather than controlled, for coordination is mainly about providing services, while control is meant to forbid or restrict against will.

Thirdly, we should further reform the "city biased" public service supply policy and implement the necessary inclination of public services to rural area so as to enhance the capabilities of peasants to achieve substantive freedom.

A major constraint on the realization of substantive freedom is the backwardness of rural public goods and public services, which affects the investment in and accumulation of human capital, the efficiency of rural investment as well as the living standard and quality.

The goal of reforming the "city-biased" public service supply is to "integrate urban and rural areas" on basic public services, i.e., all citizens, urban or rural, enjoy equal access to basic public services provided by the government. Since the rural public services lag far behind the city at the present stage, new public services should be provided to rural area so as to mitigate imbalance and finally realize equal treatment.

Fourthly, we should further improve the degree of peasants' "organization" and enhance their "discourse power" in policy making.

The freedom of "I" and "we" are closely linked, and the freedom of individual peasants is inseparable from the freedom of peasants as a whole. In the final analysis, the "organization" of peasants is to enhance the "capabilities" of realizing "substantive freedom" of peasants, not to control peasants.

The improvement of peasants' organizational level is undoubtedly conducive to the peasants' overall "discourse power" in the game of interests. In the past, some policies concerning peasants' interest were often formulated from the perspective of the city by "urban people", which no doubt harmed peasants' interest. Other policies, though well intentioned, didn't fulfil its expectation due to the lack of knowledge about the real needs of peasants. In essence, peasants lack discourse power or sufficient discourse power in decision making. The key to enhance peasants discourse power lies in the degree of peasants' organization. "We" peasants as a whole is undoubtedly more powerful than "I" as an individual farmer.

Fifthly, we should further promote democratic political and cultural construction in rural area and comprehensively enhance the capabilities of peasants to achieve substantive freedom.

Economic freedom inevitably requires political freedom, and it shall also rely on political freedom as a practical guarantee. Meanwhile, freedom is all rounded, going far beyond basic survival like food and clothing. Especially in the contemporary countryside where the problem of food and clothing has been primarily solved, peasants' demand for freedom will be broader and stronger. At the same time, the motivation of peasants' pursuit of further freedom is also the major driving force of rural reform, and the all-round and free development of peasants.

Chapter 4

Pluralism and Symbiosis: The Basic Framework of Agricultural Production Organizations in Contemporary China

Abstract

The free choice of the vast majority of peasants is the basic prerequisite to a pluralistic symbiotic structure in contemporary China's rural area. Conversely, the multi-symbiotic organization framework has provided a highly inclusive, open system and organizational space for peasants' free choices.

4.1 What is "Symbiosis"

More than 150 years ago, Alfred Marshall, scholar of economics and master of "economic mechanics" (neoclassicism), felt truly that "economic mechanics" might bring harm to the development of economic disciplines later on,[1] and prodigiously foresees a closer connection between economics and biology than that between economics and mechanics. "Economists should aim at economic biology, not economic mechanics," he said.

[1] "In the 100 years since Marshall's *Principles of Economics* was published," economics has become dramatically narrow and formalized as a discipline... They do not grasp and explain the real economic structure and process, but concentrate on building equations. (Hodgson, G.M. *Evolution and Institution: On Evolutionary Economics and the Evolution of Economics*. Cheltenham: Edward Elgar Pub, 1999.)

"Economists should learn from the recent experience in biology."[2] At present, there are two main trends in economic biology or, more precisely, in economics that uses relevant theories and concepts of biology to study social and economic phenomena. One is "evolutionary economics", based on Darwin's theory of evolution, the other is "symbiotic evolutionary economics", based on the theory and concept of symbiosis.[3]

"Symbiosis", originating from Greek, was first proposed by German Mycologist Anton de Bary in 1879. According to studies, symbiosis is a common phenomenon in the biological world, in which organisms with permanent material links live together in a given biosphere. In a certain sense, the concept of symbiosis is a correction to Darwinian evolutionism that overemphasizes species' uniqueness and survival competition. Instead it emphasizes the symbiotic relationship between species. However, symbiosis does not mean stagnation or closure. Symbiotic evolution can be seen as another evolutionary path, the coevolution of biological groups, the evolution of "cooperation and mutual benefits", "cooperation and win–win" or even "cooperation and multi-win" rather than the so-called "a life-or-death struggle" or "winners taking all". Hong Limin, Chinese scholar, remarked: "General biologists have a profound understanding of the complexity of biological interrelationship in a community. They have clearly revealed the mystery of an individual or group's victory or success, which lies in their ability to unite closely within the community rather than the intimidating ability of the strong. The rule can be applied to nature, to biological philosophy in humanistic sciences."[4]

After De Berry, biologists and scientists have carried out fruitful research on a series of extensive topics, such as "wide symbiosis", "narrow symbiosis", "symbiotic origin", "symbiotic evolution", "internal symbiosis", "external symbiosis" and "symbiotic interface". Professor Edward O. Wilson of Harvard University summarized three basic symbiosis patterns in natural organisms: group parasitism, partial symbiosis and

---

[2] Marshall, A. *Principles of Economics*. Andesite Press, 2015.

[3] "Symbiotic evolutionary economics" is put forward by the author, which is meant to differentiate from "evolutionary economics" popular in academic circle.

[4] Hong Limin. "The History, Present Situation and Prospect of Development of Symbiosis Concept", *Chinese Journal of Microecology*, Vol. 8, No. 4, 1996, pp. 50–54.

mutual symbiosis. Group parasitism refers to the phenomenon that one organism lives *in vivo* or *in vitro* another, depending on the latter metabolically to maintain life activities. It is only a special form of symbiosis. Partial symbiosis that is harmless to one side but beneficial to the other is not common; mutual symbiosis is the normal mode. The interpretation of symbiosis, according to *Unabridged Dictionary*, is: "a common phenomenon between organisms, generally referring to the relationship between two or more organisms living together, in which a species lives in vivo or in vitro another and is mutually beneficial to each other."

Professor Wilson further distinguished symmetrical mutual symbiosis and asymmetrical mutual symbiosis. Symmetrical mutual symbiosis is the most efficient, cohesive and stable mode of symbiosis that generates new energy based on division and cooperation of symbiotic units. Symbiotic interface has the function of symmetrical distribution among all symbiotic units, so that all units have the same evolutionary opportunity and cost, which lays down the foundation of symbiotic mechanism. In symbiosis process there are not only frequent bilateral exchanges but also a wide range of multilateral exchanges, which greatly increases energy and reduces costs. However, as an idealized model, symmetrical mutual symbiosis is not the most common one; the most common and influential one is the asymmetrical mutual symbiosis mode. The fundamental difference between the two is that the distribution of new energy among units is asymmetric under the influence of symbiotic interface.

Due to the similarity between biological ecosystem and human social economic system,[5] the concept of "symbiosis" has been widely used in the fields of philosophy, humanities and social sciences in recent decades. For example, Iwate Bookstore, Japan's prestigious academic publishing house, published eight volumes of *Lectures on New Philosophy*, of which Volume 6 was entitled *Symbiosis*. University of Tokyo established the International Exchange Center of Symbiosis Philosophy. Li Yan, Chinese scholar, summarized the following basic concepts of symbiosis philosophy: the concept

[5]"Another extremely important reason why biological thinking is relevant to economics is that both economic and biological system are extremely complex with structures and causal relationships that encompass both continuous change and great diversity." (Hodgson, G.M. *Evolution and Institution: On Evolutionary Economics and the Evolution of Economics.* Cheltenham: Edward Elgar Pub, 1999.)

of life (symbiosis means different organisms live closely together, so it's existential relationship between lives); the concept of process (continuity of time and tolerance of space, and the process of the creation of life and promotion of the realm are symbiotic); the concept of heterogeneous coexistence (heterogeneity is a universal, indispensable factor in the evolution system, and it's a basic condition for mutual symbiosis); the concept of neutralization (value orientation at the social level); the concept of relationship (symbiosis is essentially an existential relationship); and the concept of living (symbiosis is the coexistence of different lifestyles).[6]

The introduction of the concept "symbiosis" into economics and management began in the 1970s. Just like biological symbiosis is a tool for the analysis of interspecies relationship in biological population ecology, industrial symbiosis is an important tool for industrial ecology. In 1976, the United Nations Economic Commission for Europe put forward the initial conception of industrial symbiosis in a conference with a theme on "Technology and Production with No Waste".

Industrial symbiosis was regarded as a kind of cooperation between enterprises in utilizing waste and realizing clean production. However, the rich connotation goes far beyond that. Reid Lifest, editor-in-chief of *Journal of Industrial Ecology*, remarked "industrial symbiosis is not just about waste exchange between co-existing enterprises, but a comprehensive cooperation." Along this line of thinking, the concept of symbiosis in applied in industrial ecology, regional economy, circular economy, environmental management, enterprise clusters, ecological finance and other extensive fields. It has also gone deep into fields of social sciences, like sociology, politics and anthropology.

4.2 Symbiosis, Harmony, Inclusive Development and "The Realization Of Freedom with Freedom"

The concept of symbiosis embodies a harmonious coexistence between individuals and groups. Harmony, according to ancient Chinese philosophy, is the pursuit of unity and coexistence among different entities on the basis of diversity and heterogeneity. Here, heterogeneity is the premise, and

[6]Li Yan. "The Basic Concept of Symbiosis Philosophy", *Theory Learning*, No. 5, 2005, pp. 73–74.

harmony is the coexistence and tolerance built upon it. As can be seen from above, the traditional Chinese concept of harmony contains the modern sense of openness and inclusiveness. Confucius said, "A gentleman aims at harmony, but not at uniformity, while a villain aims at uniformity, but not at harmony," in which he affirmed the coexistence of diversity and heterogeneity, criticized the thought and behavior of defending those who belonged to his own fraction while attacking those who don't. Furthermore, other ancient Chinese philosophers put forward the idea of "harmony breeds everything", stressing diversity and heterogeneity are the basis and prerequisite to the survival and development of all creatures. In *State Tale — Zheng Tale*, "Harmony brings progress, while similarity brings no outcome. Respect for difference is harmony, so that everything can grow and flourish naturally." That is to say, only on the basis of heterogeneity and diversity, or difference and respect for difference, can everything flourish. Conversely, a high degree of identity, a rigid demand for similarity, quest water with water can bring nothing new, thus "similarity brings no outcome."

No matter it is symbiosis or harmony, the implicit premise is to recognize diversity, versatility and heterogeneity of the objective world. As to how to realize symbiosis and harmony under the premise of diversity, versality, heterogeneity and difference, inclusiveness is the key. If a pattern or a type were of high degree of identity, there would be no inclusiveness. Inclusiveness is meant to define one's subjectivity and pursue the maximization of one's own interests, while respecting the subjectivity of other individuals, groups and organizations, respecting their rights to pursue the maximization of interests. Therefore, we should abandon the thinking mode of "difference is hostility" or "solipsism", cherishing the broad mind as is depicted in the saying "all rivers run into the sea, its greatness contains everything."

Introducing the concept of inclusiveness into economic and social development is, in itself, inclusive growth and inclusive development. Asian Development Bank first proposed inclusive growth in 2007 in its *Report on Shared Growth for Social Harmony*. The essence of inclusive growth is shared growth and universally beneficial growth, with its core on sharing the fruits of growth equally and rationally among all social strata, avoiding polarization and unequal social distribution. Its goal is to promote the harmonious development of economy and society. Hu Jintao noted, "the ultimate purpose of achieving inclusive growth is to make economic globalization and economic development achievements benefit all countries, regions and people, as well as to achieve coordinated economic and social development in sustainable growth."[7]

Just as the connotation of economic development goes beyond economic growth, inclusive development has a broader content than inclusive growth. It includes sharing fruits of both economic and social development, as well as "five-pronged" coordinated development in economy, society, politics, culture and ecology. In his keynote speech entitled *Inclusive Development: Common Agenda and New Challenges* at Bo'ao Forum for Asia Annual Meeting in 2011, Hu Jintao gave a comprehensive explanation on the basic conception of the Chinese government, closely linking it with the building of a harmonious society.[8] According to Zeng Peiyan, vice chairman of Bo'ao Forum for Asia, inclusive development can be understood from four aspects: firstly, it is the development of equal opportunity and the sharing of achievements for all; secondly, it is the development of win–win and common progress for all countries and nations; thirdly, it is the interaction and equitable development of all kinds of civilizations; lastly, it is the harmonious coexistence of human beings, society and nature, development in a virtuous circle.

Symbiotic, harmonious and inclusive development has an internal logical connection, which is respect for every independent entity's legitimate interest and free choice on the basis of heterogeneity, pluralism and diversity, realization of inclusive, shared and universally beneficial development on the premise of common participation and equal opportunities so as to ensure every entity's interest and the common interests of different parties.

At a deeper level, symbiosis, harmony and inclusive development have similar connotation with the ideal and practice of man's pursuit of "realization of freedom with freedom". On the one hand, only by respecting and allowing people to choose freely can there be symbiosis on the basis

---

[7]Hu Jintao. "Deepening Exchanges and Cooperation to Achieve Inclusive Growth", *People's Daily*, September 16, 2010.

[8]The title of Mr. Hu Jintao's speech is *Promoting Common Development and Building a Harmonious Asia*.

of heterogeneity, pluralism and diversity; only by respecting and protecting people's opportunities and free choices can there be symbiosis and harmony as illustrated in the saying "getting along with others without agreeing with them"; and only by promoting the universal freedom of the masses can there be inclusive development of shared achievements and universal benefits. On the other hand, the ideal free economic and social environment we are pursuing is the essence of pluralistic symbiosis, pattern of interests, harmonious social atmosphere and the concept and practice of inclusive development. Only in such a free economic and social environment can people realize universal freedom in a full way, enhance the viable ability of "me" and "us" to realize "substantial freedom".

4.3 Pluralistic Symbiosis: The Basic Framework of Contemporary China's Rural Economic Organizations

In contemporary China, with the implementation of rural household contract system, peasants undoubtedly have become the most basic form of agricultural micro-economic organization. Due to basic national conditions of a large population and sparse farmland, and the inevitability of equational contracting of farmland, peasants in the contemporary China are generally so-called "owner peasants" in terms of the scale of rural land management. At the same time, along with the reform of rural marketization, the appropriate transfer of rural land and the process of rural economic and social development, various types of professional cooperatives, community cooperatives, peasants' professional associations, agricultural enterprises (especially leading enterprises in agricultural industrialization and agricultural joint-stock companies), family farms all come into existence, known as "a hundred flowers blooming together", showing a diversified organizational development trend intertwined with the "owner peasants" household economy.[9] There is no doubt that the form of

[9] "Adhere to the fundamental position of family management in agriculture, promote the innovative agricultural management mode, i.e., the common development of household, collective, cooperative and enterprise management." (*Decisions of the CPC CENTRAL*

production and organization has transformed from the sole people's commune system to a new stage of pluralism.

It should also be remarked that this diversified pattern is not closure or isolation as is illustrated in sayings like "the well water does not intrude into the river water", "a life-or-death struggle", "one defeats another", or "one destroys another". Instead, it is becoming increasingly obvious it is an interdependent, mutual developing symbiotic pattern under the influence of marketing, socialization and the Internet. We believe that pluralistic symbiosis is the basic framework of current and even 21st century agricultural production organization form in China. This pluralistic symbiotic framework has the following basic characteristics:

(1) Pluralism is the foundation and prerequisite to symbiosis, which reflects diversity, complexity and imbalance of China's rural economic and social development.

China has a large population and vast territory, and its economic and social development levels vary greatly. Some rural area of the Yangtze River Delta in eastern China (such as Huaxi village in Jiangyin, Jiangsu Province) is nearly one-century ahead of poor and remote mountainous villages in the northwest and southwest of China in terms of productivity. The people's commune system used to be applied to the whole country as a single organizational form, which has been proved a failure by practice. China's rural economic system reform was carried out in the late 1970s. In the later period of implementation, there indeed existed some top-down enforcement in some places, but it also retained some economic organizations with the people's commune nature (such as Nanjie Village of Linying County, Henan Province, Yakou Production Team of Zhongshan County, Guangdong Province, Zhouzhuang People's Commune of Jinzhou City, Hebei Province), allowing the presence of various types of economic organizations of different natures, without asserting "one size fits all". More importantly, the nature of rural household land contracting system is to give peasants the right to choose independently and freely, including the

COMMITTEE on Several Major Issues Concerning Comprehensively Deepening of Reform.)

right of trial and error, which provides a broader space for versatile, diverse and heterogeneous development. As the conditions of economy, society, culture, ecology and resources vary greatly in different regions, individuals and groups differ in economic status, human capital, interest orientation and value preference, the forms of economic organizations have to be different as well, forming a diversified and pluralistic pattern of symbiosis.

(2) Organizational symbiosis is based on recognizing and respecting the independent or relatively independent interest of different economic organizations and entities, on the premise of which we strive to pursue interest symbiosis and interest complementarity.

In pluralistic symbiotic framework, there are large-and-medium-sized economic organizations, such as leading enterprises in agricultural industrialization but also small-and-micro-sized entities, like owner peasants. In addition, there are relatively strong economic organizations, like agricultural joint-stock listed companies with extensive economic, social and political resources, and relatively weak economic organizations, like mutual aid organizations among the masses with no official background at all. However, no matter of what nature or type those economic organizations are, they have their own independent or relatively independent interests. If the big bullies the small, the strong bullies the weak, "winner takes all", there will be no organizational symbiosis at all. The foundation is the symbiosis of interests. Furthermore, it is "double wins" or even "multi wins" resulting from complementary interests.

Quoting from German philosopher Hegel, "everything that is reasonable". All sizes of economic organizations can complement, coexist and develop, because they have their unique comparative advantages in different fields or aspects. Conversely, no economic organization can excel in all aspects, which means they will be at a disadvantage in some aspect. For example, large supermarkets have economies of scale and information advantage in the circulation and sale of agricultural products. However, in organizing production, its efficiency is inferior to that of households because of high cost of supervision and far distance from the production scene. Household production has advantages of direct benefit and cost saving. The complementarity of interests, in fact, is the complementarity of advantages. It's more of "learning from each other's strengths" than "one party giving favor to the other". In fact, organizational symbiosis based on the complementarity of strengths and interests, instead of favors from one party to the others, is reliable and sustainable.

(3) The interface of organizational symbiosis is the environment of market economy, various kinds of organizations are the relatively independent dots in the network of marketization, socialization and modernization, without which there will be no organizational symbiosis in modern society.

Organizational symbiosis shall not be interpreted as a closed and isolated existence between various economic organizations, as is illustrated in the saying "two men live within hail but never visit each other" or "the well water does not blend with the river water". Neither is organizational symbiosis what Karl Marx called "potato economy", in which a bag of potatoes is composed by separate potatoes one by one. On the contrary, the essence of organizational symbiosis is mutual benefit and coexistence, and it's named "mutual symbiosis" by Professor Wilson. Therefore, the openness among units should be the prerequisite. Without openness, there's no worth mentioning material exchange, element exchange, information exchange between symbiotic units, let alone mutual benefits.

Contemporary China is different from either traditional rural China or the closed China in the planned economy period. The transformation of China's economy into a market one, its society into a modern and open one is an irreversible trend. In the market economy, the main elements connecting different economic organizations are no longer administrative channel or network, nor interpersonal network as in traditional society, but a market-oriented, socialized and modern network. Therefore, all economic organizations are relatively independent in the network, which cannot be separated and exist in a closed and isolated way. Even those with the nature of people's commune like Nanjie Village in Linying County, Henan Province cannot exist in a closed environment without market economy. In the so-called "outer circle inner square" Nanjie

Village, "outer circle" is, in the final analysis, the trend to be integrated into the market-oriented network and the market economy. Practice has shown that in modern society, without the market-oriented, socialized and modernized network, there'll be no organizational symbiosis.

(4) Organizational symbiosis is not stagnation or fossilization. Symbiosis does not exclude evolution. "Symbiotic evolution" is a harmonious state of evolution. It is an evolution of inclusive development.

Organizational symbiosis is not a long-term coexistence of the advanced and the backward, nor a stagnant and rigid situation. It emphasizes cooperation and inclusiveness, but it does not exclude competition. Therefore, symbiotic evolution will also adhere to the law of survival of the fittest. However, we cannot distinguish the advanced and the backward, the good and the bad with a single yardstick, standard or mode in the process; competition is not like "a life-or-death struggle", "who defeats whom", "who destroys whom" or "winner takes all". In short, the symbiotic evolution of diversified organizations is a process during which different economic organizations mutually benefit and universally grow. In essence it is inclusive development. Of course, with the requirement of the times, development of the situation and change of the environment, some economic organizations will rise, others will change, still others will perish. In a word, the forms of various economic organizations will not remain unchanged for a long time, but have different fates like life or death, prosperity or collapse. However, symbiotic evolution will never be attributed to the monopoly of unity or monotony. Monopoly, excluding diversity, pluralism and diversity, will deprive organizational symbiosis of its foundation and premise. Fundamentally, Marx' conception of "a community of free individuals" will have many forms of economic organizations, rather than a monopolistic model or a closed frame. A single pattern means little free choice or development. Therefore, the deeper essence of symbiotic evolution is "realization of freedom with freedom".

Table 4.1 is the form of various types of rural economic organizations in contemporary China summarized by the author. There is no doubt that the form in reality is more abundant than what the author has listed above.

Table 4.1. Different types of economic organizations in the contemporary Chinese village

Form of economic organizations	Content
Production organizations	Owner peasant households, large peasants, large breeders, family farms, private farms, collective farms, agricultural production cooperatives, agricultural production enterprises, rural land stock cooperatives, agricultural listed companies
Circulation organizations	Small vendors, brokers, agricultural retail markets, agricultural wholesale markets, modern grain logistics system, cold chain logistics for fresh agricultural products, supply and marketing cooperatives, futures market for agricultural products
Production service organizations	Farm keepers, professional households of plant protection, professional teams of plant protection, plant protection companies, professional households of agricultural machinery, agricultural machinery cooperatives, operation associations of agricultural machinery, professional service companies of agricultural machinery, leasing service companies of agricultural machinery, science and technology demonstration households, peasants' water cooperation organizations
Life service organizations	Biogas technology service stations, farmhouse restaurant and farmer tourist cooperatives
Financial service organizations	Rural Credit Cooperatives, Rural Land Credit Cooperatives, Rural Microfinance Organizations, Rural Credit Guarantee Organizations, Rural Community Banks
Comprehensive service organizations	Peasants' service agencies, rural community service centers, rural public service stations and rural information service centers
Equity transaction organizations	Land contractual management right transfer market, rural collective property right trading market, rural land bank
Strategic union organizations	Enterprise + peasant household, cooperative + peasant household, enterprise + cooperative + peasant household, supermarket + cooperative + peasant household, supermarket + base + peasant household, agricultural science and technology institute + agricultural enterprise + peasant household

4.4 Seeking Integration from Separation, Demanding Public from Private: A Case Study of Wenzhou, Zhejiang Province

Wenzhou is a prefecture-level city in southern Zhejiang Province, with a total area of 11,783.5 square kilometers, of which plains and mountains account for 17.5% and 78.2%, respectively. Witha large population and small farmland, the arable land per capita was only 0.53 mu (0.035 hectares) in 1978, the beginning of the rural economic system reform. It was obvious farmland couldn't support the population.

In the period of agricultural cooperation and the people's commune, Wenzhou among the earliest areas in China to create and implement rural household land contracting system so as to solve the problem of food shortage.[10] As early as in 1956, Yongjia county experimented with the reform of "contracting production to household" and "contracting work to household". Under the historical conditions at that time, the reform ended up with Li Yunhe, deputy secretary of the County Party committee who presided over the reform in the countryside at that time, rendered a "rightist" and expelled from the Party. However, just as the saying goes, "no prairie fire can destroy the grass, for it shoots up again with the spring breeze", at the end of the 1970s, Wenzhou peasants once again took the lead in carrying out the reform of household land contracting system. In addition, in the period of the people's commune, "Wenzhou's rural collective enterprises are negligible both in scale and quality. With the implementation of household contracting system, such small-scale collective cooperative enterprises rapidly collapsed."[11] After the reform of the rural economic system, the so-called collective management mode in Wenzhou

[10]The cases in this section are mainly from the investigation of Ruian, Yueqing, Yongjia, Wencheng and other counties affiliated to Wenzhou City, Zhejiang Province conducted by the research group on July 9–17, 2008. Yin Zuoliang, a member of the research group, presided over the investigation.

[11]As early as 1956, Yongjia County, under the jurisdiction of Wenzhou, tried to contract production to households, and the leaders concerned was later wrongly handled. On August 20, 1981, the 282nd Bulletin of the Secretariat of the CPC CENTRAL COMMITTEE published a letter entitled *The Grievances of Yongjia County in 1956 should Be Completely Redressed,* and an editorial note was added as "the first creation of this responsibility

existed in name only, collective economy was rendered an "empty shelf". It was widely believed that Wenzhou peasants only had the initiative to work alone, without the motivation and enthusiasm for cooperation. So came the saying "Wenzhou is an epitome of private economy".

However, after the reform and opening-up, the first new type of peasants' professional cooperatives in Zhejiang Province appeared in Tielong Township, Cangnan County, Wenzhou. On May 14, 1985, "Tielong Township Peasants' Service Society of Cangnan County" was formally established with a joint stock investment of RMB87,300 yuan from 135 shareholders, with the purpose of providing pre-production, mid-production and post-production services to peasants.[12] Entering the 21st century, farmer cooperative economic organizations and agricultural industrialization enterprises in Wenzhou have developed rapidly. According to the survey of Wenzhou Rural Work Office in 2008, there were 1,015 peasants' professional cooperative organizations and 53,300 members in 2007. Among them, 902 specialized cooperatives had a total membership of 41,600, income increased 1,192 yuan per capita, benefiting 284,000 peasants and connecting base areas of 724,800 mu (48,344 hectares). At the same time, leading enterprises of agricultural industrialization in Wenzhou were also developing rapidly. Up to October, 2008, the city had more than 200 leading agricultural enterprises with sale volume of over RMB5 million yuan, fixed assets RMB5 billion yuan, annual sales RMB13.9 billion yuan, profit RMB1 billion yuan, linking 850,000 mu (56,667 hectares) of planting and breeding bases, benefiting 350,000 peasants. Among them, there were 3 nation-level leading enterprises, 24 province-level leading enterprises and 116 municipal-level leading enterprises. According to the updated data of Wenzhou Agricultural Bureau in 2011, more than 2,000 cooperative economic organizations were established, such as professional associations, professional cooperatives and stock cooperatives, benefiting more than 300,000 peasants. There were 185 leading enterprises of agricultural industrialization above municipal level, 29 leading enterprises

---

system in that year" (Shi Jinchuan. *Institutional Change and Economic Development: Wenzhou Model Research*. Hangzhou: Zhejiang University Press, 2004), p. 469.

[12]Cangnan County regarded this cooperative the first peasants' cooperative in China (Cangnan News Network, October 16, 2008).

above province-level, and 4 leading enterprises at nation-level, including 12 enterprises with output value exceeding RMB100 million yuan; the total assets of enterprises are RMB5.73 billion yuan, with a base of 4,540,000 mu (302,667 hectares), benefiting 837,000 peasants. From the above data, we can see that Wenzhou has become one of the fastest growing area of China's rural professional cooperative organizations and leading enterprises in agricultural industrialization. Facts show that Wenzhou peasants have cherished not only the enthusiasm and creativity of "working alone" but also the initiative and passion of "cooperation" and "organization".

It should be emphasized the development of Wenzhou agricultural specialized cooperative organizations and agricultural industrialization enterprises has not led to the demise of the peasant household economy; on the contrary, it has promoted its prosperity and development. The reason is, in the final analysis, agricultural cooperatives, enterprises and various rural economic organizations in Wenzhou are well rooted in the inner needs of peasants' demand for economic development like "I want cooperation" and "I want organization", rather than external force like "I have to join in the cooperative" and "I have to join in the organization". For example, Tian Jinxin, director of the Rixin Rabbit Cooperative (former Shuangfeng Rabbit Cooperative) in Wencheng County, Wenzhou, summarized five intrinsic reasons why they started the cooperative: (1) Peasants who raised rabbits solely by themselves could not get the information of market supply and demand in time, the problem of sales difficulty was hard to tackle, and the risk of market operation was high. An increase in output couldn't bring about an increase in income. (2) Scale of breeding was small, sales ability was weak, and the economic return was poor. (3) Without standardized production, guaranteed product quality and brand effect, it was difficult to open up the market. (4) Low degree of intensification and organization was prone to the exploitation of middlemen. (5) Difficulty in obtaining pre-production, mid-production and post-production services resulted in high operating costs and low economic returns. The establishment of cooperatives was precisely for the sake of solving those problems that couldn't be solved by individuals instead of replacing the peasant households and returning to "the big group". Therefore, the fact that peasants became members of the cooperatives didn't change the nature of their family's private property, didn't rescind the longstanding right of contract management, or change the status of peasants as an independent economic entity. Cooperative and private sectors complement each other, peasant household economy and cooperative economic organizations, agricultural enterprises coexist. There is no such phenomenon as "who defeats whom" or "who destroys whom".

[Interview 4.1] Interview with Tian Jinxin

Interview time: July 12, 2008
Interview Venue: No. 11 Chengdong North Road, Dazhen Town, Wencheng County, Wenzhou
Interviewee: Tian Jinxin (born in 1966, male, Party member, college education, director of Rixin Rabbit Professional Cooperative, Wencheng County)

Q: What are the initial motivations of setting up of the cooperative?

A: Firstly, single household couldn't get timely access to information on market supply and demand. Failure in docking with large market led to sales difficulty and increased market management risks, so peasants often increased production without getting increased income. Secondly, the scale of breeding was small, sales ability was weak, and the economic efficiency was poor. Thirdly, lack in standardized production, guaranteed product quality and brand effect resulted in weak market competitiveness and market development. Fourthly, low degree of intensification, organization and cohesion led to poor market presence, which was also prone to the exploitation and control of middleman. Lastly, lack of pre-production, mid-production and post-production services caused high operation costs and low returns. Seven professional rabbit peasants originally set up a joint-stock cooperative, with the seven initiators as shareholders and other peasants as members. At present, there are 1,172 households in the cooperative. The establishment of cooperative can guarantee the quantity and quality of rabbits, for there's special personnel in every township in charge of the quality of rabbits, introducing the experience of big base (big rabbit farm) to household peasants. Thanks to the cooperative, "five standard's" can be achieved: standard yardstick, standard breeding rabbits, standard vaccine, standard breeding and standard sales. It can reduce not only the cost of breeding, but also peasants' burden, increasing peasants' income, achieving a certain scale of economy.

Q: How to deal with the relationship between the company and the cooperative?

A: The company and the cooperative are separate entities with independent accounting. Although there is an overlapping in personnel, the division of labor is clear and there is no interference between them. A contract is signed between the cooperative and households so that rights and obligations of the two parties are clarified, the minimum purchase is set but maximum is not. A lowest protective price is set, and the rest of the price will be decided by the market, so that peasants will not suffer loss in price. It can help peasants focus onto breeding without worrying about selling. From the perspective of the cooperative, if it wants to grow stronger, it should put the interests of peasants in the first place, and have their own processing enterprise and stable sales channels.

Q: What is the long-term goal of the company and cooperative?

A: The general goal is to turn the "little white rabbit" into a "golden phoenix", helping peasants become richer. The five-year plan (2010) will transform all rabbit peasants in Wencheng County into cooperative members, incorporate breeding, processing and marketing, optimize rabbit breeding, create Wencheng meat rabbit brand (registered trademark), eventually transform the cooperative into a joint-stock cooperative enterprise, and take the path of enterprise management.

Q: What are the advantages and disadvantages of the cooperative in the development process?

A: Advantages are mainly in the following aspects. Firstly, the state's policy support in the development of animal husbandry, for example, support in land use with the exemption of land use tax. Secondly, the quality of rabbit meat is superior and the market demand is high. Thirdly, it has won the trust of peasants, because the purpose of the cooperative is to serve rather than profit. It has provided preferential policy in breeding quantity, sales price and services in pre-production, mid-production and post-production process. The disadvantage is mainly a lack of specialized technical, managerial and marketing personnel, as well as miscalculations on the supply and demand of the market.

Q: What are the main obstacles to the development of the cooperative?

A: One of the main obstacles is the conflict between tax law and the cooperative regulation on taxation. Peasants do not have to pay tax on their own rabbit sales income, but they have to pay sales tax after joining the cooperative, which has affected their enthusiasm to join the cooperative. Another obstacle is the reluctancy of peasants to shoulder risks when the cooperative is in deficit, contrary to their desire to share in the revenues when it's making a profit. Conflicts in interest are unavoidable.

Q: How do you define the function of government in the development of the cooperative?

A: The government should mainly play the role of guidance and service rather than leadership and supervision. The stress should be laid on formulating policies and plans instead of interfering in the operation and management of the cooperative in various names.

Q: How does the cooperative cope with risks in the course of operation?

A: The cooperative tries to reduce risks firstly through insurance. Secondly, it seeks government support when in deficit. Since cooperative members are generally unwilling to take risks, the risks are mainly borne by shareholders of the company.

Q: How to straighten out the relationship between rights and obligations between company shareholders and cooperative members?

A: Rights and obligations between the company and the cooperative, cooperative and peasants are mainly clarified through the contract signed by both parties. It should be noted the company should serve for the members, and measures like secondary rebate and bonus are taken to encourage peasants' initiatives.

On the other hand, peasant households, the cooperative and agricultural enterprise, as independent or relatively independent coexisting economic entity, are inextricably connected, which is not an administration-dominated "forced marriage", but a market-oriented connection based on voluntariness, mutual benefits and contract (explicit agreement and implicit agreement). For example, in Case 4.1, Wencheng County rabbit peasants, Rixin Rabbit Professional Cooperative, Zhejiang Shuangfeng Food Co., Ltd. are such an "organizational symbiosis" based on the common interests of relevant stakeholders and secured by the contract as a legal guarantee. Case 4.2 gives an account of a "harmonious cooperation" between Taro Cooperative of Hushan, Yongjia County, taro peasants and related stakeholders based on their common interests.

[Case 4.1] Wenzhou Wencheng Rabbit "Organizational Symbiosis"

Wencheng County of Wenzhou is located in the southern mountainous area of Zhejiang Province. Mountainous area accounts for 82.5% of the total area, as is depicted in the saying "80 per cent mountains, 10 per cent water and 10 per cent farmland." Wencheng used to be an economically underdeveloped agricultural county. Entering the 21st century, in the context of its abundant forage and labor resources, long tradition and labor basis of rabbit breeding, the county's targeted rabbit breeding industry as a major means to readjusting agricultural structure and increasing peasants' income. The rabbit industry has developed rapidly. In this process, the county has formed an organizational symbiosis of breeding households, Rixin Rabbit Professional Cooperative, Zhejiang Shuangfeng Food Co., Ltd., working out a "farmer + a cooperative + a leading enterprise in agricultural industrialization" format.

First of all, Shuangfeng Food Co., Ltd. and the Rixin Rabbit Cooperative signed a purchase contract in which the cooperative should provide live rabbits according to the company's standards, the company guarantee to buy all at the contracted price. By so doing, the company, on the one hand, was guaranteed with stable, quality rabbits, and the peasants, on the other, were saved worries of sales difficulty. Secondly, Rixin Rabbit Cooperatives entered into tripartite contracts with rural (town) agricultural technology stations and peasants. Rural (town) agricultural technology stations were responsible for the technical guidance in rabbit breeding, so the cooperative and peasants paid technical guidance fees. It on the one hand provided scientific and technological support for peasants, and on the other broadened the space for scientific and technological coverage of rural (town) agricultural technology stations and their profit sources. Finally, the cooperative signed contracts with rabbit farms and peasants, in which the responsibilities, obligations and rights of both parties were stipulated. The farms and peasants were required to abide by "five standard's", namely, standard breeding rabbits, standard production, standard coding, standard vaccine and standard arrangement. On this basis, the cooperative undertook to make a unified acquisition, and fluctuate in line with the market when the price is good and set a minimum protection price when the price is bad.

This framework of "organizational symbiosis" enables stakeholders to make joint profits. First, peasants gain higher income. In 2007, there were 32,000 rabbit-breeding households in Wencheng County, with an average income of RMB2,188 yuan. The output value of rabbit industry accounted for 13.6% of the county's total agricultural output value, a key element for the local peasants, especially for those living in mountainous areas to get out of poverty. It's said "if you breed one rabbit, you don't have to worry about means of feeding your family; if you raise 10 rabbits, you don't have to worry about clothes and pants for your family; if you raise 100 rabbits, you are surely on the road to wealth." Secondly, the cooperative benefits. In 2007, Rixin Rabbit Professional Cooperative had an annual sales income of RMB24,520,000 yuan, secured a profit of RMB370,000 yuan; In 2008, it was awarded model farmer cooperative in Zhejiang Province. Thirdly, the company (enterprise) also benefits. Shuangfeng Food Co., Ltd. became the first manufacturer of organic rabbit pulp in China thanks to the guaranteed source and quality. Its products were awarded Famous Brand Product of Zhejiang Province. The trademark of "Shuangxi Phoenix" became Famous Trademark of Zhejiang Province. In 2008, the company achieved a gross output of RMB60,280,000 yuan, of which RMB4,950,000 yuan in profit and tax. It was named Pilot Enterprise in agricultural product processing of Zhejiang Province, Top Ten agricultural industrialization enterprise in Wenzhou City. Finally, also benefiting from it were local government, township (town) agricultural technology station and so on.

[Case 4.2] Wenzhou Yongjia County Taro Peasants and Hushan Taro Professional Cooperative's "Harmonious Cooperation"

Yongjia Hushan Taro Professional Cooperative was initiated and organized by 8 large households in taro planting and marketing in May 2003. Up till 2008, there were 325 members. At the same time, the number of covering households reached 2,115.

In our interviews with Ma Qingjie, head of the cooperative, he repeatedly noted they adhered to the concept of "harmonious cooperation", which included not only the internal implementation of "harmonious cooperative" construction program, but also external efforts to build a harmonious, cooperative relationship with taro peasants by striving to serve the community and fulfilling social responsibility of the cooperative.

The "harmonious cooperation" was embodied in the following aspects. (1) The cooperative was a poverty alleviation base for the disabled in both Yongjia county and Wenzhou municipal. In 2008, there were 16 members and 62 taro peasants with disabilities. Both disabled members and peasants could enjoy free seed supply, recycling, technical training, fertilizer subsidies, interest-subsidized loans, natural disaster compensation and free product packaging from the cooperative. The disabled members could receive a fixed annual salary of over RMB6,000 yuan, which was deposited into their personal savings account in Postal Savings Bank every quarter. In addition, the cooperative contributed RMB25,000 yuan a year to the five widowed and impoverished members of the disabled, insuring them with pension insurance. (2) The cooperative carried out the construction of "Harmonious Cooperative" internally, conducting annual evaluation of "Harmonious Star" in order to create a harmonious culture by helping members solve other difficulties besides cultivation. For example, when the two children of a cooperative member suffered from congenital heart disease, the cooperative raised RMB100,000 yuan of medical expenses through various channels. (3) The cooperative established a close, harmonious, mutually beneficial relationship with taro peasants. In 2006, the cooperative provided RMB160,000-yuan-worth taro seeds to members free of charge, provided technical training to 2,115 person-times, gave out over 1,500 free technical information brochures, signed recycle contracts with peasants of 3,600 mu (240 hectares), bought 5.4 million kilograms at a protective price. The cooperative also obtained RMB1 million-yuan loan from a credit cooperative that was then granted to taro peasants in the form of interest discount. It provided "five standard's" services, namely, standard production, standard brand, standard purchase and standard sales. (4) The Cooperative set up a website of "Chinese taro planting men" (www.zgxyr.com), opened a mailbox and blog for people engaged in taro planting in Hushan, and established a wider and opener relationship with the various stakeholder.

The two cases from Wenzhou give us some insights:

(1) The managements of peasant household, cooperative and agricultural company are not incompatible, but coexistent, complementary and mutually beneficial.

In traditional planned economy and the people's commune system, "public" and "private", "collective" and "individual" were often regarded as incompatible opposites, in sharp conflicts as was depicted in sayings like "who defeats whom" and "who destroys whom". Such a way of thinking still has a wide influence now. In the view of some scholars, the development of cooperative economy must change rural household-based land contracting system, abolish peasant household economy due to unilaterally and wrongly explaining Deng Xiaoping's thought of "Two leaps". Some people believed that in the long run, household contracting system was only an expediency. Therefore, in order to realize socialism, we should eventually develop a large-scale collective economy, using Nanjie Village of Linying County, Henan Province as an example of realizing the "Two leaps" ahead of schedule. Since the system was regarded as temporary rather than endurable, they put forward policy proposals that were meant to eliminate household management as soon as possible and return to the people's commune system, or other systems similar but with a different name.

Can managements of household, cooperative and enterprise of agricultural industrialization coexist and complement each other? It's pivotal to the future development both in theory and practice. Experience drawn from Wenzhou and other places has told us they can coexist and complement each other. The organizational structure is adapted to most rural areas in China and is welcomed by the majority of peasants. Therefore, it is also the foundation for the future development of China's agricultural production organization.

(2) Peasant household management will produce inherent demand for cooperation when it enters a certain stage. Cooperation based on household management has more vitality and sustainability than administrative command.

As mentioned earlier, the understanding of the rural household land contracting system in China should not be regarded only as a production organizational form of family management, but a broader organizational platform for peasants' realization of freedom with freedom from a deeper level. It gives peasants a wider space of free choice. To be specific, they can choose cooperation and organization based on their own interests, they can voluntarily abandon the right of management but retain the right of contract, or even completely abandon the contractual right of land and choose to become an urban resident. Compared with the administrative command of collectivization in the period of the people's commune, this kind of collective operation based on the inherent requirements of peasants will not develop very rapidly, and it is impossible to cover the whole country within a year like the people's commune. Surely enough in the process there will be ups and downs, "integration and division", "division and integration". However, in the long run, it will be more vigorous, more adaptable to the changes of external environment, so it will be more sustainable. The intrinsic interest needs of the micro-economic entity are "I want cooperation", "I want organization", not the extrinsic coercive "I have to join in the cooperative" or "I have to join in the organization". Practice has shown that the endogenous cooperative demand is the most fundamental driving force for the long-term development of various rural cooperative economic organizations.

(3) The key to the long-term coexistence of peasant household, cooperative and enterprise management is the complementarity and mutual benefit based on the independence of interests.

The key to the long-term symbiosis and coexistence lies in the complementary advantages of each entity and the formation of a mutually beneficial and win–win pattern based on the independence or relative independence of interests. Peasant households, cooperative and enterprise management have their own comparative advantages and disadvantages (see Table 4.2). Their symbiosis and coexistence, i.e., making best use of their advantages and bypassing their disadvantages, can form the optimal allocation of social and economic resources. Generally speaking, the labor achievement of peasants is closely related to their personal interests. It saves supervision costs and management costs, but lacks scale benefits, and the transaction cost in market circulation is on the high side. Cooperative operation has certain scale benefits, and can reflect the demand of equality and democracy, but the management cost is higher, and the "organizer" resources with the spirit of cooperation are scarce. Enterprise management has better returns to scale. Although the management cost is higher than that of peasants, it is lower than that of cooperatives. However, when dealing with peasants, the transaction cost is high, for enterprises usually have lower

Table 4.2. Contrast and comparison of the advantages and disadvantages of household, cooperative and enterprise management

	Advantages	Disadvantages
Household management	Inherent production initiatives, saving supervision and managing costs	High market circulation and transaction costs, low returns to scale, weak technological upgrading ability
Cooperative management	Certain extent of returns to scale, close relationships with peasants	Higher organization cost, scarce "organizer" resources, low organization stability
Enterprise management	Relatively high degree of returns to scale, lower organization cost than cooperatives	Weaker relationships with peasants than cooperatives

recognition among peasants than cooperatives. As could be seen from the above, only by cooperation of the three entities can we enlarge advantages, bypass disadvantages so as to share the benefits of cooperation.

4.5 State Ownership Open to Private Ownership: Case Studies of XPCC and HGBLR[13]

Xinjiang has a vast land with a total area of 1,664,900 square kilometer, accounting for 1/6 of China's total land area. That is why it is said that one will not know how expansive the motherland is until he arrives in Xinjiang. Xinjiang Production and Construction Corps (XPCC) is a "military and political enterprise" and the largest special economic and social organization, which garrisons the frontiers and stations troops to open up wasteland in China. According to 2006 data, the total land area of the entire corps was 7,456,300 hectares and the agricultural land was 4,198,600 hectares. The former includes 1,043,100 hectares of arable land, 65,200 hectares of garden plots, 443,900 hectares of woodlands, 2,426,500 hectares of pastures, 215,000 hectares of land for construction, 3,047,200 hectares of unused land and 219.900 hectares of other land.

XPCC is different from the small-scale production operation of the peasants in most parts of the country in that it has the superiority of large-scale operation of agricultural land.

[13]The actual data and cases of XPCC in this section are mainly the results of the field investigations of Xinjiang during Oct. 11 and 25, 2008 and in Sep. 2012 made by Cao Yang and Ma Xinzhi from the research team. The members visited a vegetable company and agricultural company (both are based in Shihezi City) of XPCC's Eighth Agricultural Division and Aksu-Based Science and Technology Company of the Third Platoon and the Fourteenth Platoon of the First Agricultural Division. They also made field visits to an apple grower at the Hongqipo Experimental Forest Farm in Wensu County and a date grower of the First Agricultural Division. They interviewed a peasant operating a land of 12,000 mu in Awati County. They also made investigations of the School of Economics and Trade of Shihezi University, Wujiaqu-Based Party School of the corps, Xinjiang Normal University, Xinjiang University of Finance and Economics and paid a visit to Wu Huiquan, head of the First Agricultural Division at that time.

[Case 4.3] The Science and Technology Company of TPFAD as a National Demonstration Base for Agricultural Modernization

The Science and Technology Company of the Third Platoon of the First Agricultural Division (TPFAD) was initially the Second Engineering Company established in early 1995 and reorganized into Science and Technology Company in 2003. It is now a national agricultural modernization demonstration zone with agricultural cultivation as the pillar industry.

The company currently has 18,000 mu of cultivated land, of which 12,000 mu is for cotton growth. The global mechanization rate of cotton growth is over 90% and huge domestically leading and world-class agricultural production systems in terms of automation, information and modernization were set up in cotton fields on a fairly large scale. It includes many sub-systems such as a visual agricultural information monitoring platform, an automatic monitoring system for crop pests and diseases, an automatic control system for cotton submembrane drip irrigation, an automatic monitoring system for irrigation water volume and a microcomputer-decided balanced fertilization system. In 2006, the company's 11,700 mu of land yielded 5.27 million kg of seed cotton.

It should be noted that the company with such an advanced mechanization and high-tech has also implemented the employee household land contract system. In 2007, 266 company employees contracted more than 60 mu per capita and obtained an annual income of RMB48,000 per capita.

For a long period of time, as a large agricultural production organization of a "paramilitary" nature with a special mission[14] of "garrisoning the frontiers and stationing troops to open up wasteland", the corps practiced a collective operation model of "comprehensive unification". The various regiments of the corps executed the policy of "unification of planning, production and distribution". Employees "went to work when the bell rang and received salaries monthly" with their products measured and evaluated in units and were rewarded with equal pays. Consequently, in spite of the vast agricultural land and the advanced agricultural

[14]"Garrisoning the frontiers and stationing troops to open up wasteland" are the historical heritage of China's development and defense of the frontiers for thousands of years. According to historical records, it has been an important national policy for the development of frontiers and the consolidation of frontier defense throughout dynasties. It was started by the central government on a large-scale in Xinjiang in the West Han Dynasty (202BC–8AD) and has continued up to today, playing an important historical role in unifying the country, consolidating border defense and promoting its social and economic development. In 1954, the Central People's Government decided to set up a production and construction corps in Xinjiang, which is an inheritance and development of this tradition under new historical circumstances" (from XPCC's website).

mechanization, the land output rate and per capita labor productivity were not high. In 1974, the corps' food, oil and meat were not self-sufficient and it became a major loss-making organization[15] in the country's agricultural sector, calling for 16.95 million kg of resold grains from the state. The "big agriculture" which had been warmly acclaimed found itself in a hopeless situation.

Since 1980s, the corps has been conducting reforms step by step in its operational management system in order to adapt to the change in the socialist market economy and get rid of its massive deficits and the extensive poverty on the part of its workers. The essential part of the reforms is to have the entity status of the farming households (employee families) established gradually in the micro-economy in the corps. For instance, the reforms adopt the households land contracting system characterized by establishing workers' household farms as the main body buttressed by developing developmental farms and courtyard economy, an economy in which peasants use their own residential courtyards and surrounding land to provide themselves and the public with agricultural products and related services. The reforms are conducted on a large scale in its 175 Tuanchang (typical regiments of XPCC), giving birth to a micro-level operational system involving over 700,000 employee household farms as the major force.

By now, an overwhelming share of land has been contracted by households,[16] and it is also true of livestocks, agricultural machinery, including large agricultural machinery (such as large agricultural harvesters). That many people think is inseparable. It has been privatized, sold to households or individual employees at fixed prices. This indicates that in such a big special agricultural production organization as XPCC, farming household economy incandescent with vitality can still survive and become the most basic level of microeconomic organizations. Meanwhile, as an organization, the corps has not broken up. Instead, its original functions are gradually transferring from management to service.

---

[15]In 1974, the corps lost RMB196 million and by 1975, the accumulated operating losses of more than 10 years reached RMB794 million, which led to the abolition of the corps in 1975. It was not restored until 1981.

[16]Different from China's rural land-based household contracting system, the corps' land is "state-owned" rather than "collectively owned".

As for unification, all its regiments generally require households for unification in crops to be planted, production standards, fertilization, plant protection and irrigation. The use of large agricultural machinery is arranged at the company level and the beneficiary households must pay to the farm machinery households at the market price. In addition, the corps makes centralized purchases of agricultural production materials, which is popular in that it ensures the quality of agricultural materials and reduces their prices. The corps has also proposed the goal of "order procurement of products", in the hope to further resolve the problem of the sale of farmer products, "a thrilling leap from merchandise to currency" in Marx's words.

In June, 2006, the corps' party committee clarified its overall framework of the basic management system, i.e., "household land contracting operation, a clear property right of each household, centralized procurement of agricultural materials and order procurement of products."[17] The first two embody division and the second two unification. Apparently, as a multi-level economic force, the corps plays functions similar to those of leading industrialized agricultural enterprises and specialized agricultural cooperatives. In the meantime, the corps has also vigorously developed various types of economic organizations such as joint-stock companies, group companies and leading industrialized agricultural enterprises. As of 2009, the corps had 13 listed companies such as Xinjiang Tianye, 61 key leading industrialized agricultural enterprises at national and corps' levels, of which 11 were of the national level.

In conclusion, farming household economy, company (enterprise) economy and corps economy of different types, and levels of economic organizations coexist in Xinjiang. It is a socialist market economic system with regional characteristics. In the integration of private ownership into state ownership, there are no such things as "who beats whom" nor "who destroys whom". Interestingly, some large privately owned farms in Xinjiang have borrowed the organizational symbiosis structure from the corps. They are mostly set up by contracting and developing vast wasteland (raw land). The common practice is that after land reclamation, the

[17]The author found at his investigation interviews that the practice of order procurement of products was still very problematic and the promotion was dissatisfactory.

owners will contract it in turn to farming households rather than practice centralized land operation themselves, resulting in big farms composed of small farms, i.e., a system of double-layered relatively independent economic entities.

We interviewed Mr. Wu, a peasant who had the use rights or contract rights of 12,000 mu of state-owned land in Awati County. He contracted the land he had developed to more than 50 peasants, over 20 mu on average. He required that all the peasants of the conjoined land should practice unification in plants (cotton), production standards, fertilization, plant protection, irrigation and deployment of large machinery. This means that he performed a number of "unification" functions similar to those of the corps.

XPCC's cases and experiences have the following implications. To start with, household-based farm operation applies to small and large-scale land operation as well as areas of either low or high mechanization of agriculture.

Some people hold that the rural household-based land contracting system and its family operation of land in China are the results of institutional arrangement as the last resort for rural people with small amounts of land. In other words, rural family operation is only applicable to small plots of land while collective land operation suits large plots. Therefore, they often equate large-scale operation with collective operation. When it comes to large-scale operation, they will criticize the rural family-based land operation for its limitations and try their best to change it. However, the cases of the reform conducted in XPCC and the similar reform in northeast state-owned large farms show that in terms of large-scale land operation, farming households and family-based farms are efficient microeconomic organizations and the window-dressing collective economic organizations tend to be extremely organization costly and low in productivity, which does not suit agricultural production.

A more popular view based on the theory of matching production relationships and productivity is that rural family-based land operation applies to the areas of low-level agricultural mechanization rather than those of high-level agricultural mechanization. However, the aforementioned cases demonstrate that rural family-based land operation also works with the areas of high-level agricultural mechanization. For example, XPCC's

Science and Technology Company of TPFAD in Case 4.3 is a national agricultural modernization demonstration zone with high-level agricultural mechanization and informatization. Nevertheless, it still implements the farm employee family-based land contracting system. TPFAD's leaders say that agricultural mechanization has improved year by year with decrease in labor intensity. As a result, the average land contracting area per employee has increased from 37 mu to 67 mu. This shows that agricultural mechanization can expand the scale of land that a rural family operates rather than do harm to it. The Heilongjiang Reclamation Area (North Wilderness) mentioned in Case 4.4 is another example. Although the comprehensive mechanization rate of field operation in the area has reached 94%, realizing a comprehensive agricultural mechanization, farming household-based operation is still the most suitable form of microeconomic organization.

[Case 4.4] Household-based Farms in North Wilderness

North Wilderness (NW), namely the Heilongjiang Reclamation Area (HRA), is the extra-large and most highly mechanized state-owned farm in the country except for XPCC. The comprehensive mechanization rate of field operation in the area has reached 94%, realizing overall agricultural mechanization at large.

In early 1985, when a full scale campaign of setting up family farms was launched in HRA, there was controversy surrounding whether household operation and family farms were compatible with agricultural mechanization and modernization. It was not until the end of the 1990s that family farm operation mechanism typified by self-sufficiencies in living expenses and production costs, and household-based land, machinery, accounting, profit and loss, and the two-tier operation system of large farms composed of small ones and a blend of unification and division were gradually improved and established. Now, more than 200,000 family farms have become the main force of micro-operation of this vast state-owned land. All the agricultural machinery including large agricultural machinery worth RMB several billions have been sold to family farms at fixed prices except 50 agricultural aircrafts. In addition, more than 40,000,000 mu of cultivated land was distributed among and operated by family farms.

Wang Mucun, simple and honest, was the first person to eat crabs (try something novel) in HRA. In 1958, he left the army and worked as a tractor driver in NW. Although he ended up each day completely worn out, he was still poor at the onset. In 1983, he returned to his hometown in Henan for the Spring Festival. He saw that all families there had become rich due to the booming household-based land contracting system and wished that he could "contract alone" in the reclamation area. His ideas were bought by the leadership of the farm. There were 5 people in his family and he contracted 2,200 mu of arable land, raised 1,000 laying hens and rented a set of farm tools. Lacking in workers, the family recruited two drivers and a farm hand. The eight of them got up early and went back home late, exerting their utmost. In the same year, despite flood, the first family farm in this area received a net profit of RMB27,000, three times that of the entire production team and was awarded the title of Model Family Farm by HGBLR. The large family photo is hung up in China Agricultural Exhibition Hall in Beijing.

Of the 859 farms located on the bank of the Ussuri River is Ge Bolin's family farm. In 1968 Ge left Jiamusi for this remote place, growing from an ordinary farm worker to a director and the party secretary of a branch of the farm. In the spring of 1985, he gave up his official position and led his wife, Lin Li, who gave up her leadership as a vice chairman of the farm union to operate a family farm. The initial operation was very tough. She used four wooden sticks to support a canvas and cooked for the farm workers with her feet in muddy water. Ge ran a tractor to dig trenches and opened up fields. In the first year, he opened up 2,000 mu of land but the next year it was flooded and in the third year he persisted. Today, after more than ten years, Ge's family has a farm of 7,000 mu of cultivated land, 2,000 mu of forest land and 900 mu of wetlands. He is also the first peasant in China to import large agricultural machinery and protect wetlands at his own expense. He exchanged 200 mu of cultivated land for wetlands that would be opened up by others. He spent RMB120,000 to repair its cofferdam and the wetlands were restored to the original state.

—Jia Hongtu, Looking up to You: North Wilderness, China's Big Barn, *People's Daily*, September 3, 2010

The second implication from the case of XPCC is that peasants' large-scale land operation must rely on extensive market-oriented and socialized services. The key to big agriculture is comprehensive socialized services rather than a one-sided pursuit of big microeconomic organizations.

Peasant households may be the main body of large-scale land operation but they must be modern market-oriented peasant households rather than self-sufficient ones. The reason is that with complete self-reliance the land that such a household can operate on its own is indeed extremely limited. Or it may plant more than it can harvest, resulting in a low land yield. Even if peasant households have modern agricultural machinery, it needs to be purchased from the market and requires specialized maintenance. In addition, products of large-scale land operation are not self-produced and self-consumed by the households. The products must rely on big market sales which transform them into the commodities that society needs.

Therefore, why modern market-oriented peasant households can operate large-scale land efficiently is that they rely on extensive and perfect market-oriented and socialized services. In this sense, the large-scale land operation forces are not peasant households alone, but rather a network of peasant households, markets and social needs.

"The stones from another mountain can help to grind jades." Internationally, the essence of the so-called "big agriculture" is the large scale of agricultural markets and socialized services rather than merely the large scale of the micro-forces of land operation. For example, the United States and Canada are publicly recognized as large modern agricultural models, but family farms are still the main body of agricultural micro-operation. However, the family farms are not self-sufficient and self-contained, but based on a wide range of market-oriented and social services. The latter is the very essence of "big agriculture".

[Case 4.5] American Family Farms, Agricultural Socialized Services and Big Modern Agriculture

The United States is the most developed country in the world today. It has a land area of 9,370,000 sq km, of which 187,000,000 hectares is cultivated land accounting for about 20% of the country's land area. It is rich in natural resources and enjoys unique production conditions, and advanced and developed science and technology. It is among the countries with the most developed agriculture, the highest agricultural labor productivity, the largest export of agricultural products and the strongest agricultural competitiveness in the world.

American agriculture is thought to be a typical big modern agriculture, but it is still family operation that prevails. Family farms are the most basic micro-economic body in American agriculture. At present, there are about 2 million family farms in America, and the average area of land operation per family farm is about 130 hectares (as opposed to less than 2 hectares per family farm for 95% of China's family-based operating area). In 2007, family farms had an average annual sale of $150,000.

In the United States, the specialized production of agriculture is reflected in the specialization of regional layout and the specialization of the division of labor in the family farm industry. In terms of regional specialization, America has formed nine big agricultural production industry belts including the North Central Corn Belt, the America Plains Wheat Belt and the South Cotton Belt. The specialized division of family farms within the industrial belts are basically consistent with that of the belts.

The socialized services of American agriculture are developed and fit in with highly specialized production.

They are mainly composed of four parts.

The first is specialized services involving agricultural production stages. There are a large number of agricultural machinery leasing companies and specialized companies that provide various productive services directly to farmers such as land-ploughing companies, sowing companies, cultivating companies, fertilizing companies, harvesting companies, warehousing companies, transportation companies, etc. These companies provide specialized quality specialized services to farmers throughout the whole process of production operation involving preparation for ploughing, sewing, fertilization, harvesting, storage and transportation. This production method of division of labor and specialized services can greatly reduce the input of capital and labor, and various costs of family farms, and increase progressively their production efficiency.

The second concerns plants protection and epidemic prevention services. Socialized agricultural services not only include specialized services for food production, but also extend to diseases and pests prevention and control on vegetables and fruit trees, and the sanitation and epidemic prevention involving poultry and animal husbandry. Based the pest information, epidemic situation notification, popular science publicization and consultation provided by the county agricultural technology promotion station, farmers will find promptly about pest and epidemic situations, notify specialized services companies or cooperatives and get timely and effective prevention and control services. If prevention and treatment are improper and cause any losses, farmers are justified in claiming reasonable compensations.

The next is promotion and application of new technology. The advantages of American agriculture, as is true of real estate industry, lie in the continuous updating, and rapid and widespread application of technologies. American agricultural technology is developing at such a fantastic pace that even farmers with relatively high technological literacy cannot quickly keep up with it. Therefore, they have to turn constantly to relevant services for help. For example, county agricultural technology promotion stations often organize training and demonstration activities to promote a new technology by teaching farmers to learn about and master the mechanism and operation methods of a new technology as soon as possible.

The fourth part is consulting services for management technology. The increasing efficiency of US farms depends to a large extent on the management and operation consulting services provided socially with regard to information, financial management and audit consulting, management, law, etc.

—Based on the relevant information sorted out by the author

The third implication with regard to XPCC is that it is necessary to build a comprehensive and improved market-oriented, socialized and modern services network, utilize and modify the traditional organizational structure to the maximum extent in order to reduce organizational costs.

Peasant households are efficient agricultural production organizations rather than efficient market circulation organizations nor efficient market-oriented and socialized services. There are many ways to build such efficient market-oriented and socialized services as can be newly constructed or introduced from foreign countries.

However, in given circumstances, it is more practicable and economical to utilize and transform existing and traditional organizational forms. The construction of a market-oriented, socialized networked organization is by no means a simple matter that can be accomplished overnight. It requires a lot of resources, time and high organizational costs. With more than 50 years of historical experiences, however, XPCC and HGBLRs' existing organizational structures provide such reliable, available and transformable organizational resources for the construction of a market-oriented socialized network. It is simply unnecessary to start from scratch and they can speed up networked organizations and reduce organizational costs.

In general, retrofitting an existing organizational structure is less costly and time-consuming than building a new one. Moreover, it can avoid social shocks that are too strong during the transition between the old and new systems, dissolve frictions and conflicts in terms of interests, facilitating the advancement of reforms. From a nationwide perspective, rural supply and marketing cooperatives, agricultural science and technology promotion stations, agricultural machinery stations and plants protection stations are all existing organizational resources that can be utilized and transformed.

4.6 Circulation-Promoted Production and Symbiosis of Large, Medium and Small Organizations: A Case Study of Peasants' Direct Contacts with Supermarkets

Linking peasant households and a supermarket (LPHS) is a new way of circulation in which large-scale supermarkets (merchants) contact agricultural production cooperatives or agricultural enterprises, which in turn sign contracts or intentional agreements with peasants according to which agricultural products are directly supplied by peasant households to supermarkets.

There are three types of relatively independent economic forces involved in this process, representing large, medium and small economic organizations, i.e., large commercial supermarkets, agricultural cooperatives or agricultural enterprises and peasant households. In general, large commercial supermarkets relate to a number of agricultural cooperatives or agricultural enterprises, which in turn are connected to a large number of peasant households. They form a two-pole radial organizational structure. By so doing, large commercial supermarkets are in fact indirectly linked to thousands of peasant households (Figure 4.1).

Why do large commercial supermarkets generally contact peasant households through agricultural cooperatives or agricultural enterprises without directly contacting them? The reason is that if large commercial supermarkets deal directly with thousands or even tens of thousands of peasant households to sign sales contracts, not only are transaction costs high, they are also difficult to supervise and follow up. Therefore, large supermarkets contact peasant households through agricultural cooperatives or agricultural enterprises, like combing tens of thousands of small pigtails into several large ones. This can greatly reduce transaction and supervision costs, and improve actual performance.

Why would agricultural cooperatives or agricultural enterprises prefer to act as agents of large supermarkets or as intermediaries rather than directly sell agricultural products? This is because agricultural cooperatives or agribusinesses lack the specialized advantages of large supermarkets in market circulation and commodity sales including infrastructure

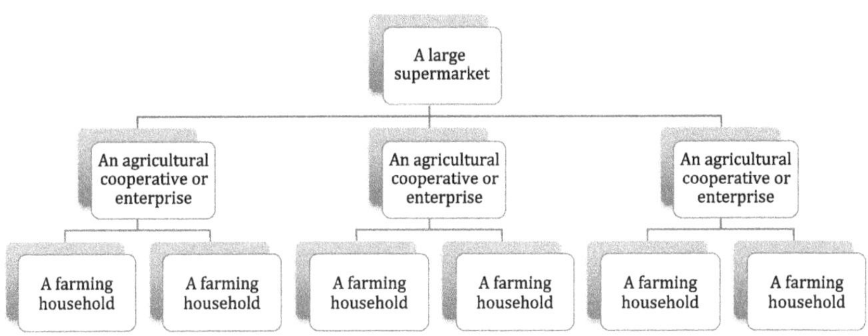

Figure 4.1. Framework of "Linking farming households and a supermarket"

advantages such as stores, warehousing, transportation, and venues as well as "soft" advantages in information, brands and sales techniques.

Why do large supermarkets, agricultural cooperatives or agricultural enterprises not produce by themselves, but organize or guide the production of thousands of scattered households? This is because peasant households, as direct producers of agricultural products, have internal incentives and therefore will economize on external supervision costs, hence the most efficient form of production organization. Conversely, if large supermarkets, agricultural cooperatives or agricultural businesses produce directly, the organization and supervision costs will be high. It simply does not pay off.

Why do peasants not sell their own agricultural products directly in the market, but instead turn to cooperatives and enterprises as intermediaries, and finally sell them in supermarkets? The reason is that although peasants are efficient production organizational forms, they lack the specialized advantages in market circulation and sales. When they produce and sell their own goods, apparently the circulation stage is saved and therefore, they not only get production profits but also get sales profits. However, if they are self-produced, sales cannot be guaranteed, and transaction and information search costs will increase remarkably. The costs will outweigh the benefits.

Table 4.3. Comparisons between advantages and disadvantages of large supermarkets, agricultural cooperatives or agricultural enterprises and peasant households

Organization	Organizational scale	Organizational advantages	Organizational disadvantages
Large supermarkets	Large	Sales, scale operation, market information	Direct production and direct contact with peasant households
Cooperatives or agricultural enterprises	Medium	Organizing and directing peasant households in production and agricultural product processing	Marketing
Peasant households	Small	Direct production	Marketing, market information

In conclusion, the pattern of complementary symbiosis of small, medium and large organizations is an organizational equilibrium formed by the interests of all stakeholders. It can leverage the strengths of all stakeholders to compensate for their deficiencies in order to maximize organizational synergy and surplus (see Table 4.3).

In the practice of "LPHS", the market guides production and circulation drives it. As specialized commercial circulation organizations, large supermarkets have unique advantages such as strong economic strength, prompt market information, wide sales channels (large supermarkets generally have many chain stores), strong storage and transportation capacity, and know "what markets and consumers need." Therefore, they play a leading role in the LPHS model. The role includes guiding agricultural product quality standards, agricultural production and circulation regulations, traceable agricultural product information management, etc.

Large supermarkets enter into purchase and sales contracts with agricultural cooperatives and agricultural enterprises, which in turn provide stable sources of supplies according to the safety and quality standards required by the supermarkets. They guarantee purchases at contract prices. On this basis, the agricultural cooperatives or agricultural enterprises then conclude contracts with the peasant households, organize and guide the normalization and standardization of the peasants' production, and guarantee the uniform purchase according to the contract price. Most of the agricultural products purchased directly enter the supermarkets, and some agricultural products enter them after being processed by agricultural cooperatives or agricultural enterprises, forming a seamless connection from "the field to the table".

The vitality of the LPHS model lies in all related stakeholders' sharing multi-party profits, thus forming a mutually beneficial symbiotic interest alliance relationship. First, fresh agricultural products are prone to damage and deterioration, and difficult to keep fresh and the practice of the model enables peasants to resolve the problem of selling agricultural products, especially the fresh agricultural products. Another feature is seasonal market concentration, resulting in sharp price fluctuations. A single household can control the production process to a certain extent, to ensure high and stable production, but it cannot control the overall market supply or market demands or market prices. The violent fluctuations in the market often lead to great losses to peasants. Even if the farms are high-yielding, it cannot ensure good incomes, for even a considerable part of the produces can only get rotten in the fields because they cannot be sold out, hence a great waste of social scarce resources. By means of LPHS, the households no longer have to find a market or sales channels for their agricultural products on their own, stabilizing the incomes with purchase and sales contracts and stable prices due to order agriculture. At the same time, under the guidance of agricultural cooperatives or agricultural enterprises, peasants implement regulated and standardized scientific production according to the requirements of the supermarkets, improve the quality of agricultural products, increase their values, enjoy a greater degree of agricultural labor productivity and land output rate, promoting the increase in incomes.

Secondly, agricultural cooperatives and agricultural enterprises gain a greater space for development as intermediaries between supermarkets and farming households. LPHS solves the problem of selling agricultural products and that of unstable sales prices. In addition, many supermarkets also provide "preferential policies of green channels" for the bulk agricultural and sideline products of agricultural cooperatives and agricultural enterprises to reach supermarkets. In addition, the zero entry fee policy also reduces the sales costs of agricultural cooperatives and agricultural enterprises. At the same time, through the linkage of peasants, agricultural cooperatives and agricultural enterprises can not only obtain certain organizational benefits but also provide stable and quality-assured sources for agricultural cooperatives and agricultural enterprises to develop agricultural products processing and deep processing. Once again, large supermarkets also make profits. This is mainly reflected in the reduction of unnecessary intermediate links and their information search costs, thus decreasing the cost of circulation. At the same time, large supermarkets ensure the quality and safety of agricultural products through the quality control of the whole process and win the trust of consumers and gain more market "popularity". The facts show that consumers who buy agricultural products in supermarkets will also purchase other items by the way, creating a purchase chain.

Finally, the majority of consumers also benefit. Since supermarkets have stricter quality control than fairs in general, consumers are more reassured. For example, Wuhan Zhongbai Chain Warehousing Supermarket Co., Ltd. (WZCWS) has established strict rules for agricultural and side-line product admission, "WZCWS Fresh Food Hygiene Management Regulations" and "WZCWS Quality and Safety Regulations for Vegetables", etc., for example. At the same time, due to the reduction of circulation links and costs, agricultural products in supermarkets are relatively cheap. Obviously, LPHS creates a community of interests for symbiosis of organizations. Peasant households, agricultural enterprises, agricultural cooperatives and supermarkets are relatively independent and interdependent. There are no such questions as "who destroys whom" and "who annexes whom". It is a win–win situation.

[Case 4.6] WZCWS-Dominated LPHS

WZCWS, established in 1997, is a wholly owned subsidiary of Wuhan Zhongbai Group Co., Ltd. (a listed company). At present, it has more than 120 supermarket outlets, not only across Hubei Province, but also in other provinces and cities such as Chongqing. It is the third largest supermarket chain in China.

WZCWS is one of the earliest large supermarkets in China which practice LPHS. As early as July, 2004, WZCWS was the first to put forward in the same industry at a national level the idea that agricultural products should enter supermarkets with no entrance fees. It gradually explored a variety of models of LPHS such as supermarkets plus bases plus peasant households, supermarkets plus cooperatives plus peasant households and supermarkets plus enterprises plus peasant households.

The first is supermarkets plus bases plus peasant households model. In 2006, WZCWS invested more than RMB5.8 million in Baiquan Farm in the Eastern West Lake District, Wuhan City and built a standardized fast-growing leafed vegetable production base with the highest specifications, the most advanced equipment and the largest radiated area throughout the city. Among them, the 110 mu greenhouse vegetable production area in its core area is equipped with independent sprinkler irrigation facilities, and all the drainage channels and field roads are hardened; the base also has a 30 mu reservoir and two supporting deep-water wells as water sources for washing and irrigating vegetables. The base cooperates with Wuhan General Vegetable Technical Service Station to jointly research on the supermarket's fresh market, and formulate enterprise standards for production, harvesting and circulation of fast growing leafed vegetables. At the same time, it uses standardized production procedures and plans according to which to arrange production and unify the input of production facilities and production materials to ensure the high standards of production procedures for product quality and the balance between supply and the demand of the market. In addition, the base has also tried the quality and safety traceability system for fast growing leafed vegetables so that the source can be traced, the flow can be tracked, the information can be stored and the products can be recalled to ensure their quality and safety. Then the vegetable peasants with rich experiences in vegetables production are required to plant and cultivate them according to the enterprise standards, and unification is required of the farming households in vegetable varieties, agricultural machinery operation, procurement, prices, packaging and brand. The guiding purchasing prices are determined with reference to the average selling prices of vegetables in the three preceding years to ensure that the peasants obtain stable incomes. Or the prices are set to go with the market so that peasants can roughly know the approximate benefits from growing vegetables every season.

The second is supermarkets plus cooperatives plus peasant households model. The Changjiadong Tea Specialized Cooperative in Changyang County of Hubei Province was established in 2008 and has a membership of 1,500 farming households. "Changjiadong Brand" and "Changyang Maojian" are officially identified as "Top Ten Provincially Famous Teas" by Hubei Province. In 2008, WZCWS and the cooperatives signed a LPHS contract and thereupon Changjiadong Brand and Changyang Maojian were directly procured by WZCWS, and the cooperatives organized and guided the production of tea peasants according to WZCWS' quality standards.

The third is supermarkets plus agricultural enterprises plus peasant households model. Juxin Modern Agriculture Development Co., Ltd. in Enshi, Hubei was registered in Nov., 2005 and based in Peak Village more than 1,800 m above sea level in Banqiao Town, Enshi City. The company practiced the model of "order agriculture", and developed from a high starting point a characteristic agricultural industry of growing high-altitude anti-season vegetables as its pillar with the features of standardization, scale and normalization. In 2007, through its successful cooperation with WZCWS Chain (Enshi) Supermarket Co., Ltd., it further broadened the market sales channels of its agricultural products.

At present, by means of LPHS models, the turnover of WZCWS has reached more than RMB4 billion, and more than 200,000 peasants are linked to bases, agricultural cooperatives and agricultural enterprises. In Hubei, LPHS has helped more than 40 kinds of agricultural products reach scale production via WZCWS.

In Jan., 2007, WZCWS' general manager Cheng Jun won the 2006 CCTV China Economics Annual Persons Nomination Award. The commentary by the jury reads: "He has set up supermarkets in townships, and has sickles and hoes distributed to thousands of villages and vegetables and fresh fruits purchased directly from the fields. 2006 witnessed the rise of a new countryside from supermarkets in central China."

—This case mainly draws on the author's investigations. Thanks to Cheng Jun for his relevant information and other help

The practice of LPHS has the following implications:

First of all, peasant households are efficient production organizations rather than efficient market circulation organizations. LPHS leads to the complementation between efficient production organizations and circulation organizations. This is an institutional arrangement for the organizational symbiosis and mutual benefits.

As far as agricultural production is concerned, especially the in-production of agricultural production, both Chinese and foreign experiences have proved that peasant households are efficient production organizations rather than efficient market circulation organizations. The reason is that market circulation requires specialized knowledge and infrastructure such as transportation and warehousing. It also requires extensive, accurate and prompt market information and an extensive market sales network missing among unrelated individual peasant households.

LPHS makes up for peasant households' weaknesses in market circulation, enabling them to focus on the production process proper and providing an alternative practicable way of linking "small peasants" and "big markets".

In addition, LPHS requires not only specialized production of individual farming households but also specialized regional agricultural production, which will effectively promote the improvement of specialized agricultural production in China.

As big commercial circulation organizations, objectively speaking, supermarkets require large quantity and scale to cut down on circulation and transaction costs when purchasing agricultural products. Large quantities of agricultural products cannot be produced nor supplied by a single farming household. Therefore, LPHS generally requires the same type or category of agricultural products to be planted and cultivated on conjoined plots of land, or bred likewise to form a specialized regional production layout.

The specialization of a regional production layout is a higher level of development based on the specialization of peasant households' production. It is often known as the "characteristic agriculture" of the region and its unique agricultural competitive advantage. Judging from the practices in the countryside, the development of the specialized regional production layout of agricultural products is relatively rapid where LPHS has developed fairly rapidly, resulting in a number of "characteristic villages", "characteristic townships" and "characteristic agricultural regions". For example, Jinan City of Shandong Province promoted the specialization of the regional production layout of agricultural products through LPHS and has set up characteristic production areas of agricultural products such as Millet Longshan Township, Covered Chive Western Suburb (chives that are grown in furrows in a sunny planting plot in winter and that are covered at night with horse dung and wheat bran which are taken off in the daytime) and Strawberry Zhang'er Village.

[Case 4.7] The development of Alpine Ecological Vegetable Base in Huoshaoping Township, Changyang County and LPHS

Huoshaoping Township is located in the central and western part of Changyang Tujia Nationality Autonomous County, Hubei Province, with an average altitude of 1,800 meters known as "natural refrigerator", for it has an average annual temperature of 7.6°C, a long period of snow and ice coverage and no obvious summer. The total area of the township is 105.5 square kilometers, including three villages and 18 villagers' groups.

Because of its unique natural conditions, Huoshaoping Township is an ideal place for the development of Alpine ecological green vegetables. However, for a long time, this unique production advantage was not brought into play. Peasants grew vegetables for their own use and their production was extremely limited. Obviously, the main obstacle restricting the development of eco-green vegetable was sales rather than production. The scale of market determined the scale of production.

Since the 1980s, in the wake of consumers' pursuit for green and ecological products, Huoshaoping Township began to develop Alpine ecological vegetables with opening-up market as its grasp, in the process of which LPHS played a key role. World famous supermarket Carrefour of France and WZCWS successively established business links with Huoshaoping Township, which has opened up a vast market for the mountain ecological green vegetables. Carrefour also hosted a week-long "Huoshaoping Township Vegetable Festival" in its Wuhan chain stores. At present, the planting base area in Huoshaoping Township has reached 80,000 mu, annual output over 250,000 tons, refrigeration processing capacity 3,000 tons per day, annual output value over RMB200 million yuan, accounting for about 70% of the total agricultural production value of the whole town. Huoshaoping has become the largest alpine ecological vegetable base in China. Its vegetables are sold well in more than 30 large and medium-sized cities such as Wuhan, Changsha, Guangzhou, Nanchang, Shanghai and Fuzhou through LPHS channels. They are also exported to Japan, Singapore, Thailand, Hong Kong, Taiwan and other countries and regions.

—On-the-spot investigation by our research group

(1) Agricultural products entering supermarkets have to meet standardized, green, health and safety requirements, which will promote the

normalization and standardization of peasants' production and agricultural production.

Compared with small farm product markets, supermarkets have stricter requirements for the quality of agricultural products, because they also shoulder the primary responsibility of safety and quality. According to the new trend of healthy, green and safe consumption in modern society, supermarkets generally make sure that the agricultural products are safe, secure and satisfying. Therefore, LPHS is neither a simple "buying whatever you sell" nor is it a simple sales platform for agricultural products. In fact, supermarkets often intervene directly or indirectly (through cooperatives, agricultural enterprises and other intermediary organizations) to guide peasants' production in ways like providing good varieties and technical guidance, restricting or prohibiting the use of pesticides and pollutants, as well as standardizing packaging. This is undoubtedly conducive to the normalization and standardization of peasants' production and agricultural production. At the same time, the specialization of regional layout also provides a favorable spatial environment.

(2) Peasants as small-and-micro-sized economic organizations, agricultural enterprises, agricultural cooperatives as medium-sized economic organizations, supermarkets as large-sized economic organizations, have their respective advantages and disadvantages. Only by complementarity and symbiosis, can all parties benefit.

Generally speaking, LPHS is not a direct connection between supermarkets and individual peasants, but an indirect one through specialized cooperatives or agricultural enterprises or bases. Therefore, there are at least three basic economic entities, namely, supermarkets, intermediary organizations and peasants. As a large-scale commercial circulation organization, supermarket is connected with dozens or even hundreds of agricultural specialized cooperatives and enterprises, which can be regarded as medium-sized economic organizations and are directly connected with hundreds of peasants. Therefore, supermarkets indirectly connect hundreds of or even thousands of peasants. Obviously, these three economic entities embody the coexistence of three types of organizations, namely, large, medium and small organizations. Why is it in symbiotic coexistence rather than vertical integration, as is depicted in the saying "big fish eat small fish, and small fish eat tiny shrimps"? This is because these three organizations have their own advantages and disadvantages, so symbiotic coexistence can enhance strengths to mitigate weaknesses so as to complement each other and achieve the best interests for all parties.

4.7 Peasants as the Entity, Multi-Party Participation, Organizational Symbiosis and Common Benefit: Cases from Rural Tourism

Rural tourism, which has existed since ancient times like the traditional "spring outing", is a kind of leisure tourism for people to travel to the countryside and the field. However, the rise of rural tourism as an industry is peculiar to modern society.

The rise of rural tourism industry in modern society has its objective inevitability. Firstly, in modern society, after the problem of "food and clothing" has been basically solved, people are trying to improve the quality of life and chasing a green, ecological and natural life. The expansion of urbanization has trapped most people in the "concrete jungle" for most of the time. While enjoying modern industrialized civilization, man is also alienating from the nature and confining his free mind. Pastoral scenery like lucid waters and lush mountains in the countryside can make up for what man has lost in the industrialized society, and better meet the spiritual needs for some who advocate nature and freedom. Secondly, in modern society, people's leisure time, or the increase in free time, provides sufficient time to guarantee people's participation in rural tourism, e.g., the general implementation of five-workday system, the increase and concentration of holidays (such as China's "small long vacation"), the gradual implementation of paid vacation system and the extension of various school holidays. Thirdly, in modern society, as people's understanding of the multi-function of agriculture expands and deepens, it has brought a series of profound changes in the industrial structure of agriculture. The functions of modern agriculture in maintaining ecological balance and biodiversity, maintaining original rural lifestyle, preserving cultural diversity heritage, inheriting traditional history and culture, and a series of new concepts of green, ecological and sustainable development of modern agriculture have also promoted and expanded rural tourism.

The rise of rural tourism in China also has its special significances.

(1) Rural tourism has a unique function in poverty alleviation and economic development to China's rural areas, especially remote mountain, lake and pastoral areas, old revolutionary base and ethnic minority areas.

A considerable parts of China's poverty-stricken areas are remote mountain, lake and pastoral areas with inconvenient transportation in the past, among which mostly are old revolutionary bases or ethnic minority areas. Such places have great difficulty in getting rid of poverty. However, despite all the disadvantages, they are "blessed by poverty" in that the under-development of industrialization has protected the ecological environment as well as rich natural tourism resources. At the same time, old revolutionary bases are abundant in red tourism resources, while ethnic minority areas boast of rich humanistic tourism resources due to their distinctive customs and traditions. Therefore, under the premise of protecting ecological environment, how to rationally utilize and develop various tourism resources have become a crucial method of poverty alleviation for those areas. In retrospect on the places of interest I have visited, I can recall such prototypes of "red tourism resources" as Jinggangshan Mountains in Jiangxi Province, Dabie Mountains in Hubei Province and Honghu Lake in Hubei Province, and typical examples of "tourism resources of ethnic minority groups" as Longji Terrace in Ping'an Village, Heping Township, Longsheng Autonomous County, Guangxi Province, "Thousand Miao Villages" in Leishan County, Miao and Dong Autonomous Prefecture, southeastern Guizhou Province, and "Grassland Tourism" in Hulunbeir, Inner Mongolia.

(2) Rural tourism can promote the construction and development of New Socialist Countryside in China.

To protect the natural scenery and ecological environment of the countryside is not to maintain the backward lifestyle, nor to refuse modern living facilities and conveniences. Rural areas also need electricity, highways, telephones, tap water, the Internet, as well as sanitary toilets, sewage and garbage treatment systems. These basic modern living facilities and material conditions are not only the indispensable "hardware" infrastructure for rural tourism but also the specific content of building a New Socialist Countryside. Practice has shown the development of rural tourism has brought about improvement on rural traffic and communications, sanitation, environmental governance and village landscapes, and ultimately the improvement on villagers' life quality, and promoted the construction of New Socialist Countryside.

[Case 4.8] The Evolution of Liujiashan Village

Liujiashan Village, located in the branch of Dabie Mountain, is the most remote administrative village with the highest altitude in Wuhan Province. It is also an old mountain village with a glorious revolutionary history, but it used to be the poorest village as well. In the past, there was no road in the village, so it was very difficult for villagers to go out of the mountain. A folk song went like this, "If you have a daughter/ never marry her to Liujiashan/ since you have ever heard the 24 sharp turns on the hillside there/ A man carries a plow on his back/ his wife following with lunch in her hand."

Although Liujiashan village is remote and poor, it is rich in tourism resources. First of all, the village is located at the top of the mountain, with green hill, lucid water and numerous natural landscapes. Thanks to its pleasant cool summer, it has become a favorite resort of people from Wuhan, which is nicknamed "stove" for its summer heat. Secondly, Liujiashan Village was once a major foothold of the Fifth Division of the New Fourth Army (NFA). Older generation of revolutionaries like Li Xiannian and Chen Shaomin had frequented here, so there were many red tourism resources. Finally, Liujiashan Village boasts of a history of nearly 1,000 years, numerous legends and profound historical and cultural heritage.

Since 2004, in the wake of "Rural Home Action Plan" of Wuhan City, Liujiashan Village introduced tourism developers in rural tourism, tremendous changes have taken place within a few years. The present Liujiashan Village has not only maintained the natural, ecological and primitive tradition, but also injected modern elements through "four networks and four changes", namely, the network of road, water, electricity and the Internet, and the change in water, toilet, shed and garbage dumping. The "Qingliangzhai Scenic Area" centered on the village has become a beautiful scenic spot for rural tourism in Wuhan, known as "Wuhan's Shennongjia", which receives over 10,000 tourists every year.

The development of rural tourism has brought about the transformation of the economic structure of Liujiashan village, with tourism becoming the leading and pillar industry of the village. The vast majority of villagers have on the way of prosperity by engaging in the tourism industry. For example, Liu Guofu, a villager in Liujiashan, said that in the past, his family with seven members contracted 3 mu of thin farmland. "The best harvest was only 300 kilograms of grain per mu, not to mention damages caused by wild boars and pecking birds. The family lived in constant fear of hunger." After the introduction of rural tourism, he "washed his feet ashore" and began to engage himself in tourism business by adapting his house into an "agritainment" (facilities for dining and boarding) with a beautiful name "Antique House". His farmland was planted with vegetables and fruits, with gross income of nearly RMB100,000 yuan a year. In the 20th century, the average annual income of the villagers was less than RMB1,000 yuan; in 2004, it was only RMB1,300 yuan; by 2010, it had exceeded RMB8,000 yuan.

—On the basis of on-the-spot investigation and relevant reports of the *Yangtze River Daily*

Rural tourism is a systematic project involving multi-industry (agriculture, forestry, transportation, catering, telecommunications, cultural performance, etc.), multi-field (rural planning, customs, economy, intangible heritage protection, ecological protection, etc.), and it's systematic project with multi-stakeholders (mainly peasants, tourism developers, travel agencies and government). Rural tourism resources, be it natural landscapes or cultural and historical heritages, are in theory CPRs of the region and should be shared by all villagers within the region rather than monopolized by a few individuals or interest groups. Therefore, the key to the harmonious and sustainable development of rural tourism is to build an "organizational symbiosis" and interest mechanism with multi-party participation, stakeholder benefit-sharing and resources sharing.

First of all, we should establish the concept of "peasants as the entity" in rural tourism development. Rural tourism resources are CPRs owned by all the villagers in the region. Therefore, local villagers should be the main beneficiaries of the development of rural tourism, and whether they can benefit from it is the ultimate criterion for its "people-orientation". Furthermore, the benefits gained by local villagers are the results of active participation, reasonable distribution and benefit sharing rather than "blessing" or "a slice" bestowed by developers or travel agencies. A large number of practical surveys has shown that in areas where rural tourism is not well developed, the interest allocation is often favorable to developers and travel agencies, while peasants' interests are neglected, so they block the scenic spots and cause damage to multi-party interests. The example given in Case 4.9 is a prototype of this phenomenon with conflict of interests as its major reason behind.

[Case 4.9] Recent Cases of Villagers Blocking Scenic Spots: Likeng Village, Wuyuan County, Jiangxi Province

It has only been over a decade since Wuyuan began developing its rural tourism, and it has turned from a small, desolate village to "the most beautiful village in China". The conflicts between local residents and scenic spot operators have been meandering for over a decade, with interest distribution as its core.

Likeng is but one of the villages in Wuyuan County, with a history of developing tourism for over ten years. In 2011, local people resorted to means of "non-cooperation" to confront the operator of the scenic spot. In the beginning, they shut out visitors and blocked their entry into the village, allowing no individual visitors or groups. Later villagers decided on taking turns to block the village gate with over 100 villagers per day who were mainly women or elderly people. The "non-violent non-cooperation" lasted for a whole month, from July 13 to August 13. The discontent of the villagers was not targeted at visitors but the managing agency — Wuyuan Tourism Co. Ltd.

They demanded an increase in the share of ticket revenue from 19% to 21%.

Longwan Village, Jingtai County, Gansu Province

Jintai Yellow River Stone Forest is located in the southeast of Jingtai County, Baiyin City, Gansu Province, neighboring Longwan Village, Zhongquan Township. Grotesque stone forest landscape featuring yellow glutenite is gradually formed during thousands of years of geological process. In 2004, the area was approved as National Geological Park by the Ministry of Land and Resources.

"During the park's operation period, the dispute between the park's operator and local residents was settled." Due to the escalating contradictions, villagers took drastic action to block scenic spots in the beginning of September 2011. A chain blocked the entrance to the park, and several farm tractors and motorcycles blocked the way into the scenic area. More than a dozen villagers sat on the floor in a row outside the gate. Their dissatisfaction was mainly over the operation right to some business projects in park.

Yuwan Village, Lianyungang City, Jiangsu Province

On August 21, 2009, Yuwan Scenic Area, a national 4A-level tourist attraction known as "Zhangjiajie in northern Jiangsu Province", was blocked by villagers in Lianyungang City, Jiangsu Province, which lasted until the afternoon of Aug. 23. The scenic spot was built solely by the villagers themselves in 1994 but was taken over by the government later, which had greatly hurt villagers' interest.

—The above cases are taken from relative news reports

Sharing ticket revenues is but one aspect of local people gaining benefits from rural tourism. As an independent economic entity, villagers take the initiative to participate in rural tourism in a variety of forms. The first is to set up "agritainment" restaurants and family hostels; the second is to produce, manufacture and sell agricultural and tourism products with local characteristics; and the third is to operate some small tourism projects, such as photography, boat cruising, horseback riding and camel riding. In addition, villagers can also work as developers, operators or employees of travel agencies to become wage workers, which is conducive to their income increase. In some developed area, revenues from tourism and related industries have become the major source of income for local residents.

Although it is not very common for peasants to organize and set up professional tourism cooperatives, it is also an organizational form to actively participate in rural tourism with the collective force. From the practice of various places, the advantages of establishing tourism professional cooperatives are: (1) to safeguard cooperative members and the interests of all villagers more effectively in negotiations with tourism developers, scenic operators and travel agencies through collective strength and organizational power; (2) to avoid disorderly and vicious competition among villagers for tourists, and formulate standards for tourism reception so as to safeguard the interests of both villagers and tourists. For example, after the establishment of the first tourism cooperative — Taohuayuan Agritainment Tourism Professional Cooperative in Tiankeng Village, Zaozhuang City of Shandong Province, the cooperative coordinated the arrangement of visitors, greatly avoiding conflicts caused by competing for customers. The cooperative also formulated the standard of reception by setting prices and prohibiting fraud, which was well received by customers; (3) to form a certain economy of scale and organize some large-scale tourism projects beyond the capabilities of individual households; (4) easier to obtain loans from banks or rural credit cooperatives as well as preferential support from local governments. However, from a practical point of view, the organizational cost of establishing tourism professional cooperatives is also very high. At the same time, difficulties needing to be addressed include how to handle the economic relationship between the cooperative and its members, among cooperative members, as well as between members and non-members. In many places, professional tourism cooperatives are only nominally "cooperatives" but private enterprises in essence. Generally speaking, even a tourism professional cooperative has been established, peasants are still the entities of independent accounting responsible for profits and losses. Rural tourism organizations, such as Nanjie Village in Linying County, Henan Province, which are totally collectively managed and exclude individual participation, are extremely rare. The Dazhai Village in Xiyang County, Shanxi Province, which was once famous throughout the country and I have personally visited, has a tourism company, but peasants are allowed to operate restaurants and sell local products individually.[18]

Secondly, tourism developers, scenic spot operators and travel agencies are also major participants in rural tourism, and they are stakeholders as well. It is undeniable that tourism developers are important to the development of rural tourism industry, and even play a key role in some cases, for prior development, tourism planning and capital investment are indispensable to the formulation of tourism industry and the growth of tourist attractions even in the cases of natural landscapes. For example, the necessary renovation of tourist attractions should be carried out, the protection and implementation of tourist safety should be enforced, roads and cable cars should be built in some mountains. In addition, all scenic spots need to build parking lots, public toilets and tap water, tourism advertising is necessary, too. The initiator of Liujiashan tourism in Case 4.8 is a developer named Yi Youqing. Without his early investment of tens of millions of yuan, the tourism industry would have never started up, and the evolution of Liujiashan village would have never become possible. Therefore, while recognizing that rural tourism resources are CPRs and interests gained should be distributed among stakeholders, we must also recognize the irreplaceable contribution made by entrepreneurs in developing tourism resources, and therefore, should give them the benefits they deserve.

[18] Dazhai Village in Xiyang County, Shanxi Province, was once an advanced model of the whole country in the period of the People's Commune — "Learn from Dazhai in Agriculture". At present, the collective economy of Dazhai still dominates, but the individual, private and family economy have made great progress. Agricultural production has been contracted out by households, allowing individuals to engage in private production. Individuals can own large and medium-sized means of production such as tractors and automobiles. When I visited Dazhai, I chatted with some villagers. The deepest impression was farmers had more freedom of choice. They could participate in the collective economy as well as private economy.

Generally speaking, tourism developers are often operators of scenic spots (of course, they can be separate entities as well). The incentive for their prior investment is the subsequent long-term operating income. It is undeniable that the conflict of interests in rural tourism are mainly concentrated between tourism developers, operators and local villagers. Insightful entrepreneurs are often good at dealing with relationships with local villagers. They know that only by guaranteeing local villagers' interest and creating a "harmonious" regional social environment, can enterprises gain long-term, stable and sustainable profits, which is a "win–win" pattern of "organizational symbiosis". On the contrary, bullying the small and the weak, or suppressing the will of villagers with the help of administrative forces will lead to inevitable "double-defeats" outcome. The phenomenon of local villagers blocking scenic spots mentioned in Case 4.9 is such an example.

The local government also plays an extremely important and irreplaceable role. As one of the major participants in the local rural tourism, the local government is also a stakeholder and should undoubtedly share the benefits. However, it has to be noted that the interest of the local government should be primarily social, followed by economic interest, and the two cannot be reversed. As far as rural tourism is concerned, "accessibility" is crucial, especially in remote areas. Like in the cases of "Longji Terrace" in Longsheng, Guangxi, and "Miao nationality village" in Xijiang, Guizhou Province, it is by no means within the capabilities of local villagers or developers to build the roads and highways, so the government should take on the responsibility. The highway of Liujiashan Village mentioned in Case 4.8 was invested and constructed by local government according to *Rural Home Construction Motion*. In addition, big projects such as power, water and the Internet are mainly government investments. In some poor areas where tourism resources are rich, the government develops rural tourism via poverty alleviation funds, which is an effective way to transform poverty alleviation from "aid" to "development", from "blood transfusion" to "hematopoiesis". In some places, in order to create "characteristic villages", the government encourages peasants to renovate their houses in a unified way through government subsidies. It will also promote the development of rural tourism and be welcomed by local villagers without compulsive force. For example, in the Red Pomegranate Village of East and West Lake District of Wuhan, the government renovated residential buildings in Hui-style architecture through villagers' voluntariness and government's subsidies. Practice has proved that this kind of government-led investment with peasants as the entity is more efficient, and causes fewer confrontations, which is a "win–win" institutional arrangement. However, if the government puts economic interest in the first place, the more it meddles or invisibly meddles in the management of tourism enterprises and attractions, or compete for interests with the people, the more likely it will cause a variety of confrontations. The three cases in Case 4.9 are more or less related to grabbing for profit on the part of the local government. Especially in Lianyungang Fishing Bay Scenic Spot, Jiangsu Province, the direct cause of the conflict was that the scenic spot, collectively developed by villagers, were forcibly taken over by the local government.

Finally, village-level organization or village committee, as a primary quasi-government, should also play an important role in organizing and coordinating rural tourism. Firstly, it should prevent villagers from competing for tourists in disorderly and vicious competition by drafting necessary rules and regulations. In most areas where rural tourism is carried out, there are no village cooperative economic organizations such as tourism professional cooperatives. Even in areas where there are tourism professional cooperatives, if the cooperatives do not cover all local residents, competition for tourists will still exist between members and non-members. Therefore, it is necessary for village committee to coordinate in the name of community organizations to reduce interest conflicts. For example, in Ping'an Village of Longsheng County, Guangxi Province (Longji Terrace scenic spot), the village committee demanded local residents take turns to receive visitors at the entrance so as to avoid disordered competition for customers, which was hailed by local villagers as "fair" and "practical", conducive to protecting the rights of the weak. Secondly, village committees should set up various systems and regulations to ensure the continuity of the ecological environment and the inheritance of traditional architecture and culture so that rural tourism resources with local characteristics will be preserved and long-term sustainable development can be maintained. For example, there are more than 800 ancient Miao stilted towers in Xijiang, Guizhou Province. They are the largest and most typical Miao stilted towers village community in China, known as the Open-air Miao Museum. In order to protect this Miao complex with a history of more than 2,000 years, the village committee and the Scenic Area Management Committee jointly formulated protection rules, and graded them according to the construction age, original style, architectural structure and fire safety of the tower. Buildings with higher scores won both material and spiritual rewards, greatly increasing residents' incentive to better protect towers. In addition, the scores on architecture, traditional culture and behavioral norm were regularly announced, rewards or punishments were given accordingly.

The cases of rural tourism in different places give us the following insights:

(1) On the basis of multi-party participation, benefit sharing is the core to the harmonious cooperation, co-existence and prosperity of all stakeholders.

As regional CPRs, the protection, development, utilization and management of rural tourism resources are a systemic project involving multiple participants and stakeholders, in which each party has its specialized and indispensable role and advantage, as well as its reasonable interest demand. Practice has shown that only through harmonious cooperation can all parties benefit each other, while sabotaging each other will cause injury to all parties. Therefore, in order to sustain long-term and harmonious rural tourism development, it is necessary to establish a cooperative and organizational mechanism for the coexistence of local villagers, tourism developers, scenic spot operators, travel agencies, local governments, village committees and other various stakeholders, taking into account the reasonable interests of all stakeholders, realizing harmonious cooperation based on benefit sharing and fair distribution of benefits.

(2) We should establish the concept of "villagers as the entity" to develop rural tourism from a "people-oriented" perspective, and to increase their income is the starting point and foothold of rural tourism development.

Rural tourism resources, as a kind of local and regional CPRs, should be owned by all villagers in the region. Therefore, to develop, utilize and manage rural tourism resources, we should give priority to the interest of villagers, and take their interest as the starting point and foothold for the development of rural tourism. Admittedly, tourism resources don't equal to tourism products, let alone tourism industry. Primitive tourism resources need to be developed, processed and reprocessed if they are to become tourism products. In this sense, decentralized villagers are not suitable to be the entity of tourism development. Of course, villagers can also organize, for example, tourism cooperatives for joint development. However, tourism cooperatives face such difficulties as high organizational costs and insufficient funds, so most rural tourism still needs to introduce developers with rich funds and experience, or the support from local government organizations. Whatever form of development will inevitably face the conflicts of interests among developers, scenic spot operators and the original owners of tourism resources (local villagers). At present, the disharmony in rural tourism is mainly due to the imbalance of the interests, or the infringement on the legitimate interests of local villagers. Therefore, the emphasis on "villagers as the entity" is well justified.

The emphasis is supposed to put villagers' interest in the first place, rather than turn rural tourism into profit source of some enterprise and local government, or even the "window dressing" of local government. Even if a developer has invested in the prior stage and obtained operating license, they should be prohibited from monopoly on all tourism resources, especially on projects which could have been managed by villagers independently, like "agritainment" restaurants, family hostel, etc.

(3) The major function of local government is to coordinate conflict, formulate rules, maintain order rather than engage in operation directly and "compete with villagers for profits".

Local government plays a major and irreplaceable role in the development of rural tourism, including capital investment of public infrastructure in the early stage and formulating tourism planning, etc. However, local government should be discouraged from acting as a direct operator, for its major duty is to coordinate efforts, formulate rules and maintain orders. Should dispute occur between developer, operator and travel agency, local government, as a "third party", can listen to the interest demand of the parties involved and settle their disputes. Cases from many places of interest show conflicts are often caused by disorientation of local government in that it either acts as operator competing with people for interests, or is biased to developer and operator, neglecting the legitimate rights and interests of villagers out of concern for its own interest or GDP-only view. Besides, local government, including village committee as a primary "quasi-government", should formulate necessary rules with its authoritativeness, including rules on protecting tourism resources, rules on developing and managing tourism resources, rules on protecting customers' rights and interest, etc. Such rules are formulated as to avoid predatory exploitation of resources for short-term interest by developer, operator and local people, prohibit disorderly, vicious competition, as well as maintain the sustainable development of tourism resources and create a harmonious tourism atmosphere.

4.8 Symbiosis Based on Mutual Benefits: A Case from Xinxing, Guangdong

In the early 1980s, four farming companies, namely, Guangdong Wens Food Co., Ltd. (then known as "Bamboo Animal Husbandry Co., Ltd.), Wen Muhui Chicken Company, Wen Shuhan Chicken Group and Gu ZhangHan Wanyi Company, were set up almost at the same time in Lezhu Town, Xinxing County, Guangdong Province. They are called "three Wens and one Gu" by the local people.

As the leading enterprise of agricultural industrialization, "three Wens and one Gu" adopted the organizational framework of "company + households" successively. It operated in the following mode: the company was responsible for chicken breeding, hatching, feed production and supply, epidemic prevention, technology development, the purchase and sale of product chickens, while peasants invested in chicken farms and equipment, engaged in daily feeding and quality control according to the company's standard. In a word, in this mode of "company + households", peasants utilized their advantage in production, assumed certain production risk rather than technological or market risk, thus avoided their disadvantage in market circulation and technology development. On the other side, the company, as the leading party in the "company + households" mode, was responsible for supply and service in pre-production stage, technological performance control in production stage, product quality control and sales in post-production stage. It undertook technological risks, market risks and overall operational risks but also saved a lot of investments in chicken farm construction, daily feeding cost, and supervision cost in production process. Therefore, this kind of cooperation was a win–win cooperation in which the advantages of both the company and peasants complemented each other and realized organizational symbiosis.

However, by the end of the 1990s and the beginning of the 21st century, "two Wens and one Gu" in the original "three Wens and one Gu" had gone bankrupt, while Wens Food Co. Ltd (Wens Group) grew into a large modern cross-industrial, cross-regional animal husbandry enterprise group with chicken-and-pig-raising as its leading industry, bio-pharmaceuticals and food processing as its sideline. It became a "National Key Leading Enterprise of Agricultural Industrialization", "Key High-tech Enterprise of National Torch Plan", "Benchmark Enterprise of 30 Years of Reform and Opening-up", "Guangdong Top 100 Private Enterprises" (ranked fourth). At present, the company has established more than 110 branches and subsidiaries in more than 20 provinces (cities, autonomous regions) including Guangdong. In 2007, the company became the first leading agricultural industrialization enterprise of RMB10 billion-yuan scale in Guangdong Province. In 2004, the company established Post-doctoral Research Workstation of Wen's Group. In 2007, it was approved to set up the Wen's Research Institute of Guangdong Province, undertaking research and development work of the national "Spark Plan", "863 Plan Project" and the national high-tech industrialization project of biological breeding. At present, the company is cooperating with over 40,000 peasants, including more than 30,000 chicken peasants. "Wen's Brand" was named the most influential animal husbandry brand of China in 2008.

Why have "three Wen's and one Gu", which started from the same place at almost the same time, engaged in the same industry and relied on the same organizational structure, diverged so greatly afterwards? The key lies in the equilibrium of interests: mutual benefits lead to co-existence, while conflicts of interests result in harm to all.

One of the secrets for Wen's Group's success is its decision-making organ's leadership skills at balancing interests of different stakeholders with an aim to coexistence and mutual benefits, which is particularly embodied in "dealing with the relationship with peasants", "always sticking to the rule of 'half-half' interest distribution with peasants, and guaranteeing both parties' interests". Therefore, "success is achieved in the interaction and 'win–win' cooperation is realized."[19] Even during the crisis of Hong Kong bird flu epidemic in the beginning of 1998, the company subsidized peasants with RMB1–2 yuan per chicken although the company itself was losing RMB1,300,000 yuan each day. The huge sacrifice has won trust and respect from peasants. According to statistics, in 2007, more than 365,500 peasants cooperating with Wen's Group made a profit of RMB1,135,000,000 yuan, with RMB31,000 yuan per household; in 2008, the average household profit rose to RMB34,000 yuan. In 2009, our team conducted an on-the-spot survey of in Luoding City, Guangdong Province, chicken peasants cooperating with Wen's Group (12 households surveyed) also confirmed that each chicken could make a profit of RMB1.5 yuan to 2 yuan. Each farmer raised about 10,000 chickens per batch, two batches to three batches per year. Moreover, peasants didn't need to worry about marketing and technology, and their income was relatively stable. In contrast, the other "two Wens and one Gu" failed due to their near-sighted opportunism. In order to grab for short-term interest, "they raised the price of feed and fertilizer arbitrarily, even failed in returning peasants' deposit and sales price in full," thus "became the target of resent". "Lack of leadership skills in building up a mutual trust and beneficial relationship, as well as bad reputations spread among farmers by word of mouth have resulted in the failure of the other 'two Wens and one Gu'."[20]

Besides the solid cooperation with peasants, Wen's Group takes good care of interests of other parties, including shareholders and employees within the Group, sales customers, as well as technological supporters.

---

[19] Wan Junyi. "Quasi-Vertical Integration, Relation Governance and Contract Implementation — Taking Wen's Model of Agricultural Industrialization as an Example", *Management World*, No. 12, 2008, pp. 93–102.

[20] *Ibid.*

For example, the Department of Animal Science of South China Agricultural University acquired a 10% stake in the form of technology equity in 1992, becoming the largest shareholder of the group at that time.

In the "organizational symbiosis" of "company + households" mode, we can draw some lessons from the different fates of "three Wen's and one Gu".

Firstly, only mutual benefit can establish long-term relationship, which is the basis of "company + households" cooperation.

Although there are many successful cases of "company + households" mode, we are never short of failed examples, either. Like in the case of "three Wen's and one Gu" mentioned above, failures triple success. Why are there so many failures? The main reason is the short-sighted opportunism, desire to benefit oneself at the cost of others and seek temporary satisfaction regardless of the consequences. The result of playing an unjust game is harm to both parties' interests and an inevitable end to cooperation. And the success of Wen's Group is the equilibrium of interests and beneficial symbiosis. Facts have shown that the trust and support of peasants are crucial to the long-term development of a company, and the interaction is two-way interaction rather than one-way blessing. Just as an executive of Wen's Group told us, "when a natural disaster strikes us, we choose to stand by the side of peasants, offering them our subsidies." "In converse, when the company is confronted with a crisis, peasants are generous in showing their understanding and support. It is the business philosophy of 'earnest cooperation and sincere harmony', as well as the mechanism for win–win cooperation that has fostered the "people harmony" basis for the company to weather through disasters and crises, realize fast, sustainable development."

Secondly, as the leading party of "company + households" mode, companies should put the long-term interest in priority, establish mutually beneficial relationships with peasants rather than bully them.

Compared with peasants, company, with stronger economic strengths, wider social relations and tougher ability to cope with risks, is the leading party in the "company + households" mode. It decides the destiny of the cooperation. Some companies, fully aware of their privileged position in the cooperation, never treat peasants as an equal partner. Instead, peasants are rendered vulnerable and exploitable target, subject to maltreatment and bully. When the market is good, prices are bottomed and when the market is bad, crises are transferred to peasants, who will, of course, take revenge by abandoning the company altogether. As a result, the "company + households" mode will dissipate. We should note the long-standing land contracting right has guaranteed peasants economic independence and relatively wide choices, so they will never put all the bets on one thing. If the cooperation is beneficial, they will go on playing the game; but if the other party is found playing foul, they will resolutely quit, or "become uncooperative".

4.9 Synchronous Development with Industrialization, Urbanization and Agricultural Modernization: A Case from the "Fuwa" Model in Jianli, Hubei[21]

"Fuwa model" is a prototype of the exploration in industrialization, urbanization and agricultural modernization in Hubei Province. As Li Hongzhong, secretary of Party Committee of Hubei Province, puts it, "we try to make Fuwa model a banner of synchronous development."

Fuwa Group, located in Xingou Town, Jianli county, grew from Yinxin Food & Oil company, a rice processing enterprise founded in 1993. Grasping the local advantage of "grain" resources and three precious opportunities,[22] the formerly small rice factory with no more than 10 workers has grown into a renowned food enterprise with nearly 3,000

[21]The case in this section mainly comes from the author's on-the-spot investigation with the Finance and Economics Office (FAO) of the Provincial Party Committee in 2012 as a special researcher of the "Research Institute of Agriculture, Countryside and Farmers" of Hubei Province, and relevant data was also collected for research. In particular, I would like to extend thanks to the Financial and Economics Office of the Hubei Provincial Party Committee (FAO) and Fuwa Group Company for their help.

[22]The first opportunity is the reform of the national grain circulation system, in which the leap from a small rice factory to a national leading enterprise of agricultural industrialization was realized; the second is the fast development of leisure food, in which the leap from rough rice processing to deep food processing was fulfilled; and the third is the Beijing Olympic Games. As the Olympic mascot "Fuwa" is similar to the "Fuwa" trademark registered by Fuwa Group in its early years, Fuwa Group has achieved a leap from making products to making brands (Peng Xianrong. "Fuwa Model — A Typical Case of Synchronized Development of 'Three Modernizations'", *Jingzhou Daily*, June 19, 2012).

employees. In 2001, the Group was recognized the first batch of national leading enterprises; in 2007, "Fuwa" rice was awarded China's Famous Brand Product. In 2011, the Group gained a sales revenue of RMB6.45 billion yuan, tax return RMB120 million yuan. Jianli County of Hubei Province, where Fuwa Group is located, is known for its rice production.

In 2011, its rice production reached RMB1.34 billion yuan. Despite its geological advantages and great production capability, Jianli county was a "fiscally poor county" due to its long-term restriction to production only, short industrial chain and low production revenue. Peasants' income was low, social contradiction was sharp in a period of time. Li Changping, who used to be a cadre in the township and once worked as secretary of Party Committee of Jianli county, wrote to the then Premier Zhu Rongji, telling him "how poor countryside is, how hard peasants' life is, how perilous our agriculture is!"

Fuwa Group is an enterprise starting from rice processing. Based on the advantages of Jianli's grain production, taking the refinement and deep processing of grain as the breakthrough and with an aim to squeezing out every bit utility of grain, the Group has vigorously extended and expanded the industrial chain of rice, maximized its added value so that this low-profit industry has been turned into a high-profit, extremely extensive industrial chain with very broad prospects for development. At present, the market share of Fuwa's Brown Rice Roll series ranks first in the country, and Snow Cake series ranks second. The group has undertaken or is going to extract rice protein and crystalline glucose from crushed rice in rice processing, to extract rice bran oil from rice bran, and to produce nutritious biscuits rich in dietary fiber from the residue of rice bran.

Thanks to the comprehensive utilization and wide market, the Group is now processing 800 million kilograms of grain annually, accounting for about 2/3 of Jianli County's grain output. In order to guarantee high quality of rice, the Group "subsidizes peasants, promotes agriculture and prospers countryside" through profits made from fine and deep processing and the economic strength gained thereinafter. According to the model of "company + base + households", the Group has signed 1.2 million mu of high-quality rice contract with 23 townships in the county with its purchase price over 10% higher than that of other markets in the neighborhood, and this alone has increased the annual income of peasants by about RMB200 million yuan, greatly encouraging peasants' initiative in production. The construction of the base has also brought about the optimization of rice varieties, nearly 70 rice varieties in the past are integrated into 5 major categories. At the same time, regional and standardized production of large acreage planting has been promoted. For example, in the demonstration area of high-quality rice, "five standard's" have been realized, namely, standard acreage planting, standard variety, standard formula fertilization, standard pest control and standard mechanical harvesting. In 2011, "five standard's" were carried out on the farmland of 240,000 mu. The construction of the base has also promoted the land circulation, accelerated the construction and renovation of farmland and water infrastructure, promoted the specialization, scale and intensive management of agricultural production, increased the level of mechanization, which reached 80% in the year 2011. In addition, Fuwa Group has also actively participated in the construction of specialized cooperatives through organizing (Futianxia Organic Rice Specialized Cooperative), merging (Longxin Agricultural Products Specialized Cooperative) and equity participating (Sanfeng Agricultural Machinery Cooperative). It has strived to explore the beneficial and win–win opportunities for peasants, cooperatives and enterprises. In recent years, the grain output of Jianli County has maintained an annual increase rate of over 8%. The company has been awarded the title of "National Pacesetter in Food Production" for several consecutive years. At the same time, the income of peasants has also increased considerably to net income RMB7,334 yuan per capita, higher than the average RMB6,898 yuan of Hubei Province in the same period.

The development of Fuwa Group has also promoted the urbanization of Xingou Town, and it has achieved the coordinated and synchronous development of both the enterprise and region (community), both industrialization and urbanization. At present, Fuwa Group has more than 2,600 regular employees and about 600 casual workers, more than half of whom come from nearby rural area. With stable work and income, these employees gradually move their families from the countryside to the cities and towns. Fuwa Group and Xingou Town Government have jointly developed the Fuwa community. By the end of 2012, more than 400 employees had moved in with their families. In addition, Fuwa Group gave special subsidy to those employees who had settled in Xingou Town by granting a one-off RMB5,000 yuan. At the same time, the development of Fuwa has also led a large number of related enterprises and supporting enterprises to settle down. Xingou has become an agricultural product processing industrial agglomeration area in Hubei Province and a national demonstration town for agricultural product processing. Population agglomeration also has promoted the development of the tertiary industries such as retail, transportation and logistics, catering and accommodation, culture and entertainment. Since 2000, the built-up area of Xingou Town has expanded from 2 square kilometers to 7 square kilometers, the urban residential population has increased from 15,000 to 64,000. The urbanization rate of Xingou Town has reached 54%, which exceeds the urbanization rate of Jianli County by 18.1%. With the economic strength of enterprises as support, the town construction has strived for complete functions and beautiful environment. In recent years, Fuwa Group alone has invested more than RMB300 million yuan in urban community projects.

We can gain the following insights from "Fuwa" model:

(1) In such counties (cities) as specialized in agriculture, especially those in grain production, we should give priority to the processing industry so as to connect industrial and agricultural modernization. The development of processing industry will spur planting (or aquaculture) industry, and the two will develop synchronously, realizing symbiosis and "win–win" cooperation. Its core is to set up interest- linking mechanism between enterprises and peasants.

Agricultural processing industry is of both "industrial" as well as "agricultural" nature. According to *China's Agricultural Science and Technology Policy*, issued jointly by 10 ministries and commissions including the State Science and Technology Commission and the Ministry of Agriculture in 1998, the processing industry of agricultural products is part of the modern agricultural system of the whole industrial chain in a broad sense. Therefore, the development of processing industry is the requirement of both agricultural industrialization and modernization. It is the bridge connecting the two. Due to a short production chain, low added value, extensive development and management, China's agriculture is called "weak industry" and "low-profit industry", while "Fuwa model" tells us that modern agriculture in the whole industrial chain can become a "strong industry" and "profitable industry" by stretching and expanding the agriculture industrial chain, "squeezing out every bit of utility" of rice and other agricultural products, fully exploiting, utilizing and enhancing its endogenous potential value through intensive development and management.

We must also note the strength of the processing industry is indispensable from the support of planting (or aquaculture) industry, the two being interdependent and mutually beneficial, symbiosis leading to win–win situation. "Fuwa model" tells us the development of processing industry can promote the synchronous, coordinated growth of planting industry, which is summarized as "the symbiosis of industry and agriculture" by Jingzhou Municipal Committee. Since the entity of processing industry is companies and the entity of planting industry is households, the core of symbiosis lies in interest linking-mechanism between companies and households. Starting from guaranteeing the self-interest of high-quality grain sources and based on the profit margin brought by deep and fine processing, Fuwa Group actively and consciously "subsidizes peasants, promotes agriculture and prospers countryside", and thus has forged a harmonious path hailed by companies, peasants and local government. In contrast, some agricultural counties (cities) regard agriculture as a "burden" and are keen to develop industries separate from agriculture. Industrialization and agricultural modernization have become "two separate paths", which have been proved ineffective in practice. Industry develops slowly, and agriculture is harmed, as well. Some processing enterprises treat planting (or aquaculture) peasants as the source of cheap raw material, tension is accumulated until conflicts erupt, which dooms their cooperation. For example, some companies, listed in the first batch of national leading agricultural industrialization enterprises together with Fuwa group, stagnated in their growth until they went bankrupt and was eliminated from the market. Although the reasons for their failure are manifold, the major one is their incapability to handle relationship with peasants. The example of "two Wens and one Gu" of Xinxing county, Guangdong Province mentioned above is a prototype of harming peasants and harming themselves.

(2) The growth of enterprise needs a certain spatial area, and the accumulation in towns and cities will promote rural urbanization. The virtuous

interaction between company (industry) growth and regional (community) growth will help realize "win–win" cooperation and interest symbiosis, a necessary condition of sustainable harmonious development.

We should never take the old path of "factories and chimneys can be seen in every village", or grow at the cost of agriculture and environment. Clustering in industrial park and township is an inevitable trend of new industrialization together with a coordinated, synchronous development of economy and ecology.

Urbanization is not simply moving people from rural to urban area. In some Latin American, South Asian and African countries, a large number of rural population flocked into cities and settled down in slums. Although the rate of urbanization was very high on the surface, it brought about a series of "urban disasters" such as serious polarization, widespread poverty and crime. It is obviously not our ideal urbanization. *The World Development Report 1999/2000* issued by the World Bank gives the following comments on urban disasters in African countries:

Urbanization is usually followed by income increase per capita, but some African countries are an exception.

From 1970 to 1995, the population grew at 4.7% annually in African countries, but the GDP per capita decreased by 0.7% annually.

"The urbanization without economic growth" in some African countries is caused by "welfare illness" to a large extent. Rural population flocking into cities is neither because of more job opportunities nor the possibility of finding a job in cities. Rather they are craving for various subsidies, reliefs and welfares that are peculiar to urban population. The biased welfare policy as well as discrimination against rural area have exacerbated the unproductive flow into cities.

To avoid unproductive flow to cities and "hollow urbanization", the prerequisite is to ensure the employment of new immigrants. Furthermore, the income of employment subtracting immigration cost must be higher than agricultural income. Only in this way can this urbanization be called "urbanization with economic growth" and the population flow "productive flow". But how to ensure employment? Besides self-employment, employment in a company could be an easier choice. Therefore, "employment is fundamental to people's wellbeing, and companies are basis of employment". If companies grow well, they can recruit a large number of workers, and urbanization becomes solid instead of "hollow". So we should give priority to company development in promoting urbanization.

A favorable regional (community) environment is also indispensable to healthy development of companies. We should note that local governments, especially governments at township level, don't have enough strength in urban construction and community construction due to limited fiscal ability. But without a favorable environment of community, industrial park or township, companies will find it hard to attract and keep talents as well as clients. So if a company is willing to invest part of its capital in the construction, renovation and upgrading of town (community) environment to make it more livable, it can acclaim not only good reputation from local residents, but also bigger support from the government and community, which is conducive to the company's long-term sustainable development, so it's "a big worth of small investment". In this sense, to increase the appeal of a city is also to increase the appeal of a company. "City" and "company" is a "community with a shared future".

Jingzhou municipal Party Committee summarized Fuwa model as "common symbiosis of industry and agriculture, common win–win cooperation of city and company, common prosperity of urban and rural area", which is insightful. The key word here is "common", while a shared interest is the core.

4.10 Combination of Forestry and Water Conservancy: A Case from the "Xiantao & Hongfu" New Countryside Construction Experimental Zone, Hubei[23]

Xianhong New Countryside Construction Experimental Zone (NCCEZ),[24] located in the central and southern part of Hubei Province, hinterland of

[23]The cases in this section are mainly from the investigation conducted by the research group in Honghu in September 2010. Thanks for the help provided by Honghu Municipal Water Conservancy Bureau, Honghu Forestry Bureau, Caoshi Town of Honghu City, and Hubei Changxing agricultural and Forestry Development Co., Ltd.

[24]In April 2008, Hubei provincial Party committee and provincial government decided to establish Xianhong New Countryside Construction Experimental Zone (NCCEZ). Luo Qingquan, then Secretary of the provincial Party Committee, was the leader of the leading group of NCCEZ. In July 2008, the provincial Party committee and provincial government

Jianghan Plain, centers on Xianhong Highway as its axis and extends around Honghu Lake, including Xiantao City, Honghu City, 23 towns affiliated to Jianli County (agencies, administrative areas and industrial parks), 729 administrative villages, with totally 313,400 households, a population of 1,232,200, arable land of 1,540,900 mu and aquaculture surface of 695,100 mu.

Known as "a land of fish and rice" in history, Xianhong area is the major production area of rice and aquatic products. At the same time, the area is called "water bag" due to its geographical feature of low terrain which is prone to floods and droughts, so water conservancy plays a key role in agricultural production. Water conservancy is multi-level CPRs based on covering or benefiting area. The management of big rivers and the construction of super large reservoir (e.g., Three Gorges Project) are nation-level CPRs. The governance of regional watershed, the construction, maintenance and management of small-and-medium-sized reservoir, the construction, maintenance and management of trunk canal are region-level CPRs. As far as rural water conservancy is concerned, public water sources, branch canal and canal network are typical CPRs at village level.

On the one hand, in the period of people's commune, almost all resources (land, labor and capital) were owned and used by the commune collectively, so there was no such a problem as "free ride" on the production, maintenance and operation of village-level CPRs like water conservancy, or, put it another way, external problems were solved internally. After the implementation of household contracting system, Xianhong region, like most other rural places, faced huge obstacles in this respect. An individual household, though fully aware of the extreme importance of water conservancy, was unable to handle it due to "lack in capital and initiative". "Lack of capital" referred to peasants' limited financial resources. Although some rich peasants had made a fortune by doing business in the village or outside, they were reluctant to invest in water conservancy, for agriculture was no longer their main undertaking and

---

officially issued the implementation outline of the overall planning which clearly proposed that it should be built into a pilot area in deepening rural reform, developing modern agriculture and building New Socialist Countryside.

for 64.5% of the whole population. So how to sustainably solve the problem of construction, maintenance and operation of water conservancy in the context of farmland household contracting system[26] became the most urgent problem influencing most population and with largest interests at stake.

Meanwhile, collective land resources in Xianhong experimental area were not fully, efficiently utilized. The most obvious sign was that the survival rate of collective forest land on both sides of irrigation ditch was extremely low. In the words of local peasants, "for the first year it's green, second yellow, third and fourth dead to see King of Hell". But the cost of planting and operation was disproportionately high. The investment in forestland didn't bring economical or ecological reward, even minus benefit, which, in local peasants' words, "to plant trees is to lose money" "year by year we plant trees without seeing a tree, year by year we cultivate forest without seeing a forest, either." As a result, the enthusiasm of afforestation was generally not high, and many villagers adopted a half-heated attitude toward planting trees. Departments and enterprises concerned also worried about finding forest resources in plain and water network areas, and the whole project was caught in big trouble.

However, breakthrough of a trouble means new opportunities. Faced with the dilemma, Xianhong experimental zone has creatively "combined" the two difficult problems of water conservancy and forestland through market operation, forging a new path called "connecting forest and water".

"Connecting forest and water" refers to trading the labor put in digging canals and ditches for the right to afforestation along the banks of river and ditch, or "digging for afforestation". To be specific, the village-level organization auctions and transfers the right to bank afforestation, slope management and canal usage, the income from which is used for

[26]Some scholars argue people's commune system is the most efficient in providing rural CPRs, especially in the construction water conservancy projects, because by expanding the scale of the organization, the people's commune has successfully saved the high transaction costs required in order to enjoy public services. However, these scholars do not seem to deny the high management costs of the people's commune system. Therefore, returning to the people's commune system is not a realistic choice.

mechanical digging and maintenance of canal networks. Practice has shown the market operation of "connecting forest and water" can "kill several birds with one stone", achieve "multi-party wins", realize good economic, social and ecological benefits. Luo Qingquan, former secretary of Hubei municipal CPC, remarked after inspecting "connecting forest and water" model of Caoshi town, Honghu city that the fresh and lively experiences grounded from the grassroots were often the "golden keys" to difficulties, "and when many other cadres are so perplexed by the problem of dredging canals, Honghu city has set us a very good example."

First of all, the problem of construction and maintenance of water conservancy which has baffled us for almost 30 years is well resolved from an institutional level, which helps promote the sustainable development of agriculture and countryside. According to statistics from departments concerned, till 2010 Honghu city alone dredged over 450 kilometers of canals and ditches through "connecting forest and water", which were now flowing lucid, fresh water in contrast to the previous polluted dead water overgrown with weeds and crowded with flies and mosquitos. The irrigation of farmland over 100,000 mu had also greatly improved. Among them, the earthwork volume dredged by Hubei Changxing Agriculture & Forestry Development Co. Ltd alone was equivalent to the total of that Honghu city had dredged in the past 10 years. Local peasants, without paying a coin, enjoyed good-quality water conservancy service which couldn't be imagined before, and a big trouble for over 20 years had been solved.

Secondly, "connecting forest and water" model effectively increases the survival rate of trees, changing the previous low survival rate and providing a wider space for afforestation in plain and water network areas. Since the management right of forest along the banks was transferred to a certain individual or company, the contractor, granted with clearer property rights, tightened up its management, so the survival and preservation rate of forests were greatly improved. According to statistics, it was about 30% before and over 90% after thanks to clearer property rights and good fertilizer from the silts dredged out of ditches, fully embodying the high-yield benefit of forestry. Xianhong region was a typical area of plain and water networks rich in canal, water and arable land but poor in forestland, so forestry development was restricted by insufficient land resources. By "connecting forest and water" model, as well as the extended "connecting forest and road" "connecting forest and tidal flat" and "connecting forest and bay", forestland resources were expanded. It forged a new path of afforestation and forestry in plain and water network area.

Finally, nature's self-resilience ability has been revived after silts are cleaned up and canals are linked. With the improvement of water ecological environment, the pollution of water resources in and around the village was curbed and schistosomiasis infection rate greatly inhibited. After the implementation of the mode, the village landscape was greatly improved, canals and distributaries became smooth, neat and tidy, human residential environment became better, and a harmonious pastoral picture of forest, farmland, road and canal was fully displayed. Besides, the problem of drinking water safety was solved, and the spread of schistosomiasis was inhibited. For example, 15 administrative villages affiliated to "Jinxiu Plum Garden" of Caoshi town, Honghu city, which implemented the mode earlier on, successfully brought the infection rate of schistosomiasis from 7.9% in 2006 to 2.1% in 2009, with the whole experimental area infection rate coming down from 7% to below 3%. Meanwhile, forest rangers were hired to watch out for behaviors like dumping garbage and polluted water into ditches, helping villagers form good behavior habit, which further proved good ecological environment was helpful to local customs building, and vice versa, local customs building was also beneficial to ecological environment.

The success of "connecting forest and water" model lies in the fact that it is an organizational symbiosis and win–win cooperation.

Firstly, the investment entity, or contractor, is no doubt a beneficiary. Hu Xingjiang, general manager of Hubei Changxing Agriculture & Forestry Development Co. Ltd which was the biggest investor, explained the dredging expense of an ordinary ditch was RMB70,000 yuan per kilometer, so it was RMB280,000 yuan for a 4-kilometer ditch. About 20,000 poplars could be planted on both banks. The cost of seedling, labor, fertilizer and management was RMB300,000 yuan, the principal and interest expenditure on a ten-year loan was RMB500,000 yuan. Calculated on 10-year timber cycle and a sales income of RMB100 yuan per timber, we could realize a sales revenue of RMB2 million yuan, and got a net profit of nearly RMB1 million yuan after subtracting a cost of RMB1.08 million yuan. Besides, the company got stable raw material supply for further processing, which was much more lucrative. The company was raising a medium-density fiberboard project with an expected annual output of 100,000 cubic meters, gradually forming an integrated forest-board industrial structure.

Secondly, local government and quasi-government at a village level (or collective economic organization at a village level) are also beneficiaries. Without expending a coin, they have not only solved the big problem of water conservancy which has baffled them for over 20 years, but also improved cadre-mass relationship and greatly increased forest coverage, making a good political achievement. Moreover, they can get a certain amount of rental for public service of the community.

Finally, peasant households (villagers) are undoubtedly and necessarily beneficiaries, a major criterion for the success of the mode. Their benefits are embodied in the following aspects. Firstly, peasants have increased production in grain and aquatic products and thus gained more income from the improvement of production condition without spending a penny. Secondly, peasants' residential and ecological environment have been greatly improved, their life quality upgraded. They are also provided with more growing space and job opportunities. For example, Hubei Changxing Agriculture & Forestry Development Co. Ltd. hired 268 regular workers in the recent two years, each earning a salary of RMB16,000 yuan. About 50,000 surplus labor made a revenue of RMB4.13 million yuan through creating and protecting forest. Over 2,200 households made a revenue of nearly RMB4 million yuan by interplanting melon and bean crops in 6,800 mu forestland.

We have to note that the implementation of the mode has also promoted "self-governance by peasants" and democratic political construction, popularized and strengthened stakeholders' legal consciousness. Questions like whether to implement and how to implement the mode are decided by all or the majority of villagers, and the villagers' congress has the final say. Just as some villagers said, now I came to realize how important my vote was! All the contracts signed between the village and the contractor required signatures and authorizations of all villagers concerned as a kept record, without which the contractor dare not start up. In the initial stage, there were indeed some villagers who cast doubt on the project and were opposed to it. Tried as cadres of village and township to persuade, they never resorted to force but chose to wait. On seeing the achievements with their own eyes, villagers were willing to participate. Mr. Zhang, deputy general manager of Hubei Changxing Agriculture & Forestry Development Co. Ltd, told us in the past we wooed villages for cooperation, "please authorize us to dredge canals and create forests"; now the cadres of village or town came to us for help, "please help us dredge canals and create forests". Consequently, the legal consciousness of villagers and contractors were raised, and the authority of contract recognized and respected by all. Just as some cadres of Honghu city said, it was truly a law popularization education, so villagers didn't have to appeal to higher authorities for help.[27]

Furthermore, the mode has provided new experience on market reform of rural CPRs, providing useful lessons for popularization nationwide.

(1) Can marketization become an alternative for rural CPRs supply?

In the "market-oriented" reform process, the undersupply of CPRs for social demand will be a long-term contradiction. Due to the dual economy and society, as well as the deep-rooted "city bias", the lagging behind and strong inadequacy of CPRs supply is prevalent in rural area.

Owing to the peculiarity of CPRs, beneficiaries often tend to get "free ride" or conceal information, so it's very difficult to realize "Lindahl equilibrium" in which beneficiaries provide CPRs through voluntary contribution and cost sharing. Therefore, government is expected to act as the supplier of CPRs through compulsory financing. However, two difficulties will emerge as the government is doing so. The first is high cost, low efficiency and possible corruption due to government's limitation in management and supervision. The second is government's limited financial resources. However, government's excessive concentration of financial resources will harm the initiative of private entrepreneurship, which is not conducive to the overall economic development. Therefore, whether we can provide CPRs more efficiently through private financing and market

[27]The cadres of Honghu City told us that up to now, there had not been a case of appealing.

force under the guidance of the government has become an inevitable exploration in the process of reform.

We cannot deny for some period of time we are overdoing the exploration. Governments tend to "push aside responsibility" and "unload the burden", pushing to the market some CPRs that shouldn't or cannot be marketized. But just as we can't refuse to eat in fear of choking, we cannot in turn conclude that no CPRs can be marketized, either. In China's context of big land area and huge population, government doesn't have the ability as well as the need to be the supplier of all CPRs. "Connecting forest and water" model by Xianhong experimental area proves by practice that the marketization of some CPRs is not only feasible but also the most efficient among all the alternatives.

(2) Which rural CPRs can be included into market operation domain?

Rural CPRs are a very extensive concept, with different features and levels, which needs to be handled accordingly instead of adopting a "one-size-fits-all" attitude. Such CPRs that are not suitable for market- oriented supply, like rural residents' minimum living security, basic pension, public education and basic medical care, shouldn't be pushed to the market nor "regionalized" or "urban-rural dualized". Instead the country, or at least the province should assume the major responsibilities to ensure common equality among people. On the other hand, such CPRs that are suitable for market operation with the space and potential for profits should be encouraged, supported and led to the market. Government shouldn't take over the responsibility, for it cannot handle it or handle it well. In other words, even if the government has the fiscal ability, such CPRs are encouraged to be marketized.

What are the basic features of rural CPRs that can be included into the domain of market operation? Firstly, they should have the dual nature of welfare and profitability, and the two should be able to complement each other. Taking "connecting forest and water" model as an example, "water" for irrigation is welfare, and "trees" on the banks have the space and potential for profitability. If we can combine the two together to make a "bundled" market operation, it will become a win–win choice, the profit of "trees" being used for the supply of "water". Secondly, the marketization of such CPRs can bring win–win results for the stakeholders. The success of "connecting forest and water" model is due to the fact that it can bring profits to all parties concerned, so it is supported by local government, investor, village-level organization and villagers. Of course, equilibrium of interests is a dynamic process, so we have to improve and perfect the distribution mechanism and system to maintain it for a long time. Finally, such CPRs can be easily inspected or supervised. People tend to worry that contractors, driven by motivations to maximize profit, may sell seconds at best quality prices, or cut corners in doing their work, harming the interest of the public. In other words, such CPRs that are not easily supervised or can be supervised but at a high price shouldn't go to market. In the above case, the dredging quality and the smoothness of the canal are easy to observe. Therefore, the cost of supervision is not high.

(3) What role has the local government played in the market operation?

Market operation can alleviate fiscal burden of local government, but it doesn't mean local government can assume the attitude of inaction, indulgence or "unloading the burden". Practice has shown government's appropriate interference is key to the success of the reform.

In the above case, the interference of local government is displayed in the following aspects. (a) Local government, as an authoritative external "third party", has played an irreplaceable role in guaranteeing the legitimate property rights and the performance of contracts. (b) Government's interference is to publicize, guide and support from a macro view so as to increase efficiency, improve service and create a good external environment. It is not to obstruct the free choice on the part of peasants or village-level organizations from a micro view. (c) As to contractors, they are not given other privileges than the necessary administrative support and favorable policy within the regulation of national policy, which is a sharp contrast to the many subsidies in tax and land granted by local government in the process of attracting investment.

(4) How to choose investment (contract) entity?

There are following categories of investment (contract) entity: The first is cadres in experimental area, who are familiar with national policy and have extensive social relations, so they have set a good example in the initial stage. The second is local peasants or villagers, who have economic strengths, willingness to contribute to hometown construction and wide business relations. They are usually risk biased. The third is individual business owner, who have economic strength and insight, ability in expanding business and organization. But they usually have their other major business occupations, so their participation is of a "trial" nature. The fourth is specialized enterprise. For example, Hubei Changxing Agriculture & Forestry Development Co. Ltd, a leading enterprise in agricultural industrialization and the first private company to create forest on Hubei plain and water network area, has contracted canals and ditches of over 300 villages affiliated to 20 towns and administrative regions of Honghu city, as well as part of villages from Jianli, Jiayu, Xiantao and Tianmen.

From the real effect of "connecting forest and water" model, it is the specialized enterprise and company that achieve the best result due to the following reasons: (a) They are more professional, standard and have economies of scale in canal and forest management, for they have specialized personnel and large machinery to guarantee quality. (b) They have strong financial strength and standard fiscal management system to guarantee capital input. Besides, financial institutions are more willing to lend them money. (c) They have similar investments in other villages in the hope of expanding business. A breach of contract in one village will spread to others, so "word of mouth" urges those companies to cherish their reputation more than anything else, so they seldom breach contracts. (4) Should such a breach of contract do happen, local government, village committee and villagers would be less obstructed by concerns of "locals" or "acquaintances" in finding and punishing the faulty party in question.

4.11 Community Co-Management Based on Stakeholders' Participation: A Case from YUEP Project[28]

"Yunnan Upland Eco-diversity Protection" project (YUEP project) is an international cooperation project funded by the Global Environment

[28]The cases in this section mainly come from Zhao Junchen and Luo Ronghuai's "Why the Democracy and Organizational Awareness of Poor Farmers Are So Strong", Zhao

Facility (GEF) and the United Nations Development Program (UNDP). In August 2001, two projects, Wuliangshan Nature Reserve in Shale Township, Nanjian Yi Autonomous County, Dali Bai Autonomous Prefecture and Houqing Yi Township, Yun County, Lincang District were officially launched.

In poor areas, the protection of ecology, nature and biodiversity is often contradictory with the subsistence of local villagers. Only by decreasing the over dependence on natural resources, can this contradiction be relieved and resolved. YUEP project aims to establish a sustainable, growing mechanism of poverty alleviation, development and natural protection by some amount of external financial input and an introduction of a new system design and community organizational form. Therefore, apart from the necessary technological support, the innovation of system design and organizational operation model is key to the success of YUEP project. "Community co-management based on stakeholders' participation" is an innovative organizational operation model with functions like regional ecological and bioresources protection, poverty alleviation and development. "It is a kind of management model in which stakeholders, with villagers as the entity, are organized according to an agreement, and protect, utilize the natural resources within the community, share the interests as well as risks in accordance to the agreement."[29]

"Villagers as the entity" is the basis for community co-management, which is not a slogan but should be embodied in a series of supporting system and regulation. For example, co-management committee at township-level and village-level community are elected by villagers directly. Important issues must be discussed and voted after the co-management committee inquire about opinions from all the villagers and stakeholders

Junchen and Song Yuan. "Farmers Grass-roots Financial Organizations Are the Core of Modern Agriculture and Modern Politics — A Case Study of Yunnan Academy of Social Sciences in Testing Natural Villagers' Fund of an International Project", China (Hainan) Institute of Reform and Development. *Construction of Chinese Farmers' Organizations*. Beijing: Economic Press China, 2005.

[29]Zhao Junchen and Luo Ronghuai. "Why the Democracy and Organizational Consciousness of Poor Farmers are So Strong". China (Hainan) Reform and Development Institute, ed. *China Farmer Organization Construction*. Beijing: Economic Press China, 2005, p. 171.

concerned. The natural resources in the community should be commonly developed and used by all villagers, especially those vulnerable groups like the poor and women, who are encouraged to participate through favorable policies to ensure they benefit from it. By August 2004, YUEP project had established two community co-management committees and 35 villagers' groups.

Multiple participation refers to the equal participation of all stakeholders, their legitimate interest should be respected and taken care of. To ensure the effective operation of co-management committee and groups they have to properly deal with the relationship with governments at all levels including "quasi government" like village committee and relationship with departments concerned, especially forestry resources management department. Practice tells us many conflicts stem from the interest contradiction between villagers and other stakeholders. "But in this model, the resolution of conflicts can often lead to a win–win situation." "Co-management committee can invite the two parties concerned to sit down, giving them a chance of communication, creating the atmosphere of negotiation, assisting in finding a way out." Besides, in YUEP project, GEF and UNDP, the international cooperation parties and sponsors of the project, are no doubt major stakeholders, too. Although they are not asking for economic returns, they have to make sure the funding is used effectively and efficiently, rather than wasted or embezzled. To ensure the implementation of the project and realization of the aid purpose is their interest demand. Therefore, it is important to deal with the relationship with the international sponsor, too.

Common participation and administration are the focus of community co-management. In the single management model of the past, villagers were viewed as the target of management, so villagers gamed with departments concerned for interests. For example, as to the forest resources of nature reserves, the government's "felling ban" and some villagers' "stealthy felling" had formed a "cat-and-mouse game" involving government personnel (forest rangers) and local villagers. The management cost was high but efficiency low. After the introduction of the model, villagers have become part of administrators rather than the target to be administrated. Since the rules are worked out by all and interests concern all, villagers will abide by them from their own interest. Even if some don't play by rule, they will be easily found out since everybody is watching. The management efficiency is far greater than that of the past.

In previous international programs, the program would terminate as soon as the funding period was due and the fund was exhausted. The most precious experience drawn from YUEP is it tries to nurture endogenous capacity for sustainable development within the experimental period. By August 2004, the funding period was due, but the program didn't stop. Instead it began to expand on the previous basis thanks to its precious legacy of a new system design and organizational operation model. Co-management model and organizational structure persist, even expand to neighboring regions.

A key element of its endogenous capacity is Community Protection and Development Fund (CPDF) established in the experimental period, covering the essential expense on co-management. CPDF is a long-term, paid and rolling private mutual fund managed by community co-management committee and village co-management groups. It's mainly used on business related to conservation of forest, ecology, nature and biodiversity. The basic unit of the fund is the natural village, which is owned, managed, supervised by the villagers and benefit them as well. Members should become shareholders before they are allowed to make loans.

CPDF is operated through microfinance to the household. Microfinance, small in amount and short in period, doesn't require mortgage and collateral but need group members to guarantee, help and supervise each other. Usually the loan term is within a year, but the specific period can be decided by villagers' congress or loan groups themselves. Although the loan interest rate is not low, which can prevent low-cost competition for scarce resources and ensure that the loan is used for the most needed and high-yielding projects, the default rate is extremely low due to familiarity between villagers, symmetrical and transparent information and strong mutual supervision.

The fund plays an important role in the community co-management model. First of all, it provides necessary financial support for the subsistence need and economic development of local villagers under the premise of protecting ecological resources and biodiversity, reduces the local villagers' actions of destroying mountain forest and biological resources such as "poaching" "stealthy felling" "deforestation and reclamation", alleviate poverty through green economy and ecological economy. Secondly, part of the loan interest can be used to maintain the normal operation of community co-management organization for its sustainable development.

Despite the turns and twists of "community co-management" model in the two experimental areas of Yunnan Province, the model, as a new organization and institutional operation mode, has been implemented in many areas, especially in nature reserves. In 2002, *Guidelines for Community Co-management of Nature Reserves*, issued by Department of Wildlife Protection of the State Forestry Administration, guides the practice in various nature reserves.

Natural, ecological and biological resources are undoubtedly CPRs of society. CPRs are a kind of resources that people share in a certain region, i.e., they can be used together and benefit all. However, due to the "dilemmas of collective action", in which the use and benefit of CPRs are often individualized, while the protection is public, the over-exploitation and over-utilization of CPRs based on individual interests will inevitably lead to what Garret Hardin called "the tragedy of the commons" or "the free use of CPRs will destroy all CPRs".

Then how to avoid "the tragedy of the commons"? How to effectively manage CPRs? Practice has shown that both complete private market management and complete state or public management in the form of administrative order have inherent drawbacks difficult to overcome. For example, private management requires to clarify all kinds of rights, including property rights, which is high in cost and impractical for some in technical sense. Administrative management by the government has inherent institutional defects, such as information asymmetry and bureaucratic inefficiency, and it lacks the micro-incentives for the protection of CPRs. Therefore, to get rid of the shackles of bipolar thinking of either "market" or "government" by creating a "third way" is an innovative thinking alternative for effective management of CPRs.

Elinor Ostrom, one of the laureates of the 2009 Nobel Prize for Economics and the first female Nobel Prize winner in Economics, published her famous work — *Governing the Commons: The Evolution of Institutions for Collective Action* on the basis of summarizing numerous cases of CPRs management in many countries of the world. As the Nobel Prize Committee for Economics noted in their announcement, the main reason for Elinor Ostrom's award is her insightful analysis on CPRs management.

Elinor Ostrom proposed a new way to administrate and manage CPRs through self-organization and self-governance. She believes that people who use CPRs together in a certain region are interdependent, they are stakeholders and have common interests. Therefore, they can organize themselves and govern independently through reasonable system design, cooperation and collective action, so as to realize sustainable common interest and "win–win" situation of resources protection and development in face of opportunist temptations like "free ride" and evading responsibility. Obviously, the theoretical basis of "community co-management" is Ostrom's management theory of CPRs autonomy.

According to Ostrom's theory, "community co-management" model characterized by self- organization and self-governance needs to overcome three major problems.

Firstly, who designs the model, i.e., the problem of system supply.

YUEP project is an international aid project. The system supply and organizational model being "external input", with advanced ideas, broad vision, and less internal interest involvement as its advantage, it can quickly break the "bottleneck" of organization and system. In this regard, "foreign monks chant better sutras". However, we also have to make the model internalized in order to ensure sustainable development. The success of the model in the poor mountainous areas of Yunnan is due to the harmonization of the input of its external ideas, systems and organizational models with the "local conditions", what Ostrom has stressed as rules should be coordinated with local conditions. Furthermore, the "external input" system and its organizational model should be "flexible" and evolving according to the local "local conditions" in order to adapt to the local resources, ecology, economy, politics and cultural environment.

Secondly, in the model, we have to address the problem of credible commitment, for "credibility" is crucial in collective action.

"Dilemmas of collective action" are largely due to the incredibility between individuals. The "cooperation" of collective action must be based on credible commitment, i.e., trust between individuals. The establishment and maintenance of this credibility mechanism is the result of multiple factors rather than a single factor.

The model of "community co-management" in Yunnan YUEP project experimental area is based on both "formal system" such as institution, rules, contracts as guarantees and the network factor of "acquaintance circle", knowing each other well in a traditional community. In addition, the cultural and moral factor of honesty in traditional society, as well as the primitive, simple customs in mountain society, are also crucial to the establishment and maintenance of credibility mechanism. In terms of modern institutional school, culture, morality, relations and customs can all be summed up as "informal institution". In the evolution of organization and system, "formal institution" is important, and "informal institution" plays an indispensable and irreplaceable role. It is the combination of the two that makes the credible commitment of YUEP project at a desirable level.

Finally, the model has to address the problem of mutual monitoring so as to curb opportunistic behaviors like "moral hazard" and "free ride".

Opportunistic behaviors, harming interests of others or units in order to benefit oneself, are main reasons for inefficiency or failure of collective action. Motivation of pursuing interest, asymmetrical information, especially loopholes in system design lure individuals to gain benefits from other people's efforts through deception, breach of contract (both "moral hazards"), or non-pay and underpay ("free ride"). If this opportunistic behavior is not curbed, it will spread like a contagion, and eventually lead to noncooperation, finally failure in collective action. Here, a major loophole of system design is the lack of mutual monitoring mechanism.

The "community management" model of Yunnan YUEP project, especially CPDF management, has solved the problem of mutual monitoring, and established a mutual monitoring mechanism which is more suitable to the regional conditions and people's conditions. CPDF takes loan group as the unit of mutual insurance, assistance and monitoring, which reduces risk, guarantees a high repayment rate of more than 90%. Since the community co-management group and "loan group" of CPDF are all based on natural villages, with "circle of acquaintances" as the boundary, information symmetry and transparency as its core, dishonest people will be marginalized from the "circle of acquaintances", disdained by relatives, friends and local villagers. With such a high cost of breach, people usually abide by rules, which saves much of monitoring cost and increases efficiency. Similarly, in this "acquaintance circle" of community co-management group, it's unlikely to get "free ride ", the behavior of benefiting from others' efforts are greatly restrained.

4.12 Conclusion: The Organizational Structure of Multiplex Symbiosis Provides Widely Inclusive System Space for Peasants' "Realization Of Freedom with Freedom"

The transition, from the "unification" of the people's commune system to the "diversification" of micro-economic organizations based on peasant household management, is an extremely important stage of development in the institutional change of China's agricultural and rural economic organizations. The basic pattern of agricultural and rural economic organization in the contemporary China is multiplex symbiosis based on family management and co-development, collective, cooperative and enterprise management. This basic organizational structure is the most suitable organizational structure for famers' realization of freedom with freedom for the present as well as for a long time to come.

Firstly, the microeconomic structure of multiplex symbiosis is in accordance with the multiplicity and diversity of rural economic and social development.

China is a big developing country. Regions differ greatly in economic and social development. For example, in 2010, net income of rural residents in Zhejiang Province was RMB11,303 yuan per capita, three times that of RMB3,472 yuan for Guizhou Province. Therefore, different regions should have different organizational structures according to the level of economic and social status of the region instead of a single framework or model. The premise of the microeconomic structure with multiplex symbiosis is to recognize multiplicity and diversity. It does not have a fixed organizational and institutional framework. Practice has proved that the structure has such strong adaptability, wide inclusiveness that it can be applied to small-scale households, large-scale family farms, agricultural professional cooperatives, agricultural joint-stock cooperatives, leading enterprises in agricultural industrialization, individual brokers, small vendors, agricultural products market and large supermarkets, like "hundreds of flowers blossoming together". The scale can be large or small, the form can be integrated or separate, the nature can be public or private. In a word, all kinds of economic organizations coexist in order to adapt to the diversity and difference of economic and social development in different rural areas.

Secondly, multiplex symbiosis of microeconomic organizations can adapt to China's different rural historic, cultural multiplicity and diversity.

China is a nation with multiple nationalities, religious beliefs and cultural forms. Even in Han nationality areas, there are Yongjia school in Wenzhou City, Zhejiang Province, Lingnan culture in Guangdong Province, Central Plains culture in Henan Province, Shangluo culture in Shaanxi Province and Jingchu culture in Hubei Province. The diversity and multiplicity of history and culture have a profound impact on the economic organization forms in different rural areas. Therefore, some micro-economic organizational forms suitable to Confucian cultural area are not necessarily suitable to Islamic cultural area or Tibetan Buddhist cultural area, and the rural organizational structure of Jiangsu and Zhejiang area with strong commercial culture may not suit rural area in the central and western regions. The multiplex symbiosis of micro-economic organization patterns respects not only the diversity and difference of economic and social development in different regions, but also the multiplicity of history and culture in different regions. Therefore, it has a relatively broad space for development.

Thirdly, the multiplex symbiosis of microeconomic organizations can adapt to the diversity and multiplicity of different resource endowments.

Different rural areas in China differ not only in economic, social, historical and cultural development but also in resource endowments. For example, places like Jiangsu Province and Zhejiang Province have a large population and small area, the arable land per capita is small; while places like the Xinjiang Uygur Autonomous Region and Heilongjiang Province have vast land and arable land per capita is large. Although there is little arable land in mountainous areas, there are abundant forest land resources. Although some areas have inconvenient transportation, they have good ecological environment and unique ecological resources. The difference of resource endowment determines the diversified industrial structure and organizational model. Generally speaking, the organizational structure must also be adapted to the pattern of local resource endowment.

Fourthly, the multiplex symbiosis of microeconomic organizations can adapt to the characteristics of vast number of peasants.

Although from the macro perspective, we often regard "peasants" as a whole, in fact, the individual peasants are not identical. Regardless of the overall regional differences among peasants in Jiangsu, Zhejiang, Qinghai-Tibet and Central Plains, even in the same region, say, in the same village, peasants differ in wealth, education, personality, interest and disposition. Organizations, in essence, are the collection of "individuals". Organizations are "a group of individuals", not "an individual". Human heterogeneity determines that different types of individuals have different demands on organizations. Different types of individuals need different organizational forms to adapt to and match with them. The fundamental defect of a single economic organization model is that it neglects the heterogeneous "individuals" in real life and tries to change all individuals into a single type of "organizational member".

Fifthly, the inclusiveness of "symbiosis evolution" can adapt to the constant changing and evolving of rural economic, social and cultural development, and can adapt to the changing and upgrading of peasants' human capital.

An important feature of contemporary China is that it is undergoing drastic changes. Such rapid, wide and profound changes are rare in the past thousands of years of Chinese history. Obviously, rigid organizational structure cannot adapt to the rapidly changing economic and social environment, let alone changing individuals. However, the organizational structure of multiplex symbiosis does not exclude evolution; instead it contains "symbiotic evolution". However, this kind of evolution is not like "who defeats whom" or "who destroys whom", and will not go to the monopoly of "unification"; but it is to make the multiplex symbiotic organizations constantly improving, renewing themselves and keeping pace with the times so as to adapt to the changing external economy on the premise of acknowledging heterogeneity and pluralism. The economic, social and cultural environment has also adapted to the changing individuals.

In a word, the vast number of peasants need organization. Peasants get "organized" in the final analysis is for "realization of freedom with freedom" and to enhance the "capability" of peasants to achieve "substantive freedom". Practice has shown that in contemporary China's rural areas, only the multiplex framework of symbiotic micro-economic organizations can provide a broad and inclusive system, as well as an organizational platform for the majority of peasants to achieve freedom with freedom, and to enhance the capabilities of the majority of peasants to achieve "substantive freedom".

Chapter 5

Transforming Small Farming: The Key to the Modernization of Agricultural Production Organizations in Contemporary China

Abstract

The key to the modernization of agricultural production organizations in contemporary China is transforming traditional small farming (SF) into modern marketized SF. The ultimate purpose is to enhance the capability approach of most peasants to achieve "fundamental freedom".

5.1 Definitions and Understanding of "Xiaonong"

The term "xiaonong" denotes small farming (SF) households, small agriculture and SF economy respectively. Its definition varies and can be classified roughly into three categories. The focus of the first type is on the individual ownership of small plots of land where farming is household-based and all family members farm on their own land. The typical feature of this type is that the owner, the operator and the actual farmer are one.

In contrast, the second type of definition is more general with a focus on the operational scale of farming. The main features are that farming households are the main farming forces with small-scale family-based operations but the land is not necessarily privately owned by the households. In this sense, "xiaonong" also includes the tenant peasants who rent the land from landlords and the farming households who share and contract small plots of land state-owned, collectively owned or village-owned. The most standard practice of classifying farming is measuring the size of the plot under agricultural operation. For example, arable land of less than 2 acres per household falls into the category of SF. In other words, "xiaonong" is virtually small-scale farming. "Another definition refers to limited resources in terms of land, capital, skills, labor forces, etc."[1]

Obviously, it is in this sense that farming household economy in the countryside in contemporary China is called "small farming economy".

The third type mainly emphasizes the operational subject of agriculture: Is it a household operation, corporate operation or collectivized operation? The so-called "modern SF system" in the countries where market economy is developed is also embodied in a household-based farm whose farming is operated in a modern (marketized) way. This definition does not pay special attention to the size of the operational farming land. As known to all, farming land of a household in the United States, Canada and some other countries is well above two acres (see Table 5.1).

All the three definitions point to household-based farming operation. In a traditional agricultural society, agricultural production relies mainly on manual labor due to underdeveloped science and technology excluding extensive agriculture, which is not output-oriented. As large-scale land operation entails massive employment of labor, household-based farming operation cannot but be of a small scale and therefore, household

Table 5.1. Different definitions of "xiaonong"

	Major features	Standard definitions
A self-cultivator	Land of individual ownership	Farming self-owned small plots of land operated on a household-basis
Traditional SF	Scale of operational land	Fairly small-scaled household land operation
Modern SF	Peasant household operation	Household farm operation in a modern (marketized) fashion

[1]Thapa, G. "Challenges and Opportunities for Small-Scale Agriculture During an Economic Transformation in Asia and Latin America", *Journal of China Rural Economy*, No. 12, 2010, pp. 77–87.

economy means small agricultural economy. However, in a modern society, grand-scale household-based farming is made possible without a massive employment owing to advances in science and technology, the promotion and application of mechanization, automation and informatization in agriculture, especially to the improvement and development of marketized agricultural production and socialized services. Good cases in point are privately-owned farms in the US, Canada and those in the Xinjiang Uygur Autonomous Region and Heilongjiang Province. Therefore, household-based economy does not necessarily mean small agricultural economy.

Theories of agricultural modernization in the early stage of industrialization chiefly drew on the experiences from British capitalized agriculture. It is thought to be an inevitable process institutionally and organizationally in which grand-scale capitalist market-oriented agriculture replaces small-scale feudalistic agriculture of natural economy and small agriculture. The large capitalist farm that employs multitudes of migrant workers is regarded as the only organization of production for big modern agriculture. Conversely, the "small-scale" household-based economy is doomed to disappear as a matter of course and as a result, the only way out for the households is to hire migrant workers. "There is no place for self-cultivating small peasants and SF in history either in Smith's idea of free economy or Ricardo's idea of national distribution. In their pictures of the future, such small peasants are bound to be overwhelmed by large-scale capitalist production."[2] Marx and Engels held the same views. Marx believed that "In the sphere of agriculture, modern industry has a more revolutionary effect than elsewhere for the reason that it annihilates the peasant, that bulwark of the old society, and replaces him by the wage-laborer."[3] Engels stated more explicitly: "The development of the capitalist form of production has cut the life-strings of small production in

[2]Dong, Z. "Historical Status of Modern Small Farming System — Review of the Discussions Concerning the 19th Century Marxism", in Yu, Keping, Li, Shenming and Wang Weiguang eds., *On Agriculture and Peasants and the Construction of New Countryside*. Beijing: Central Compilation & Translation Bureau Press, 2006, p. 46.

[3]Marx, K. *Capital: A Critique of Political Economy*, Vol. 1. Moscow: Progress Publishers, 1956.

agriculture; small production is irretrievably going to rack and ruin."[4] Huang Zongzhi, a Chinese-American scholar, pointed out that "A hypothesis put forward in the classic views of Smith and Marx is that small-scale household-based farming will decline as commercialization thrives."[5]

However, history does not evolve just in one direction. Along with the development of big capitalist agriculture, SF dominated by household-based agriculture and farms has gradually adapted to the development of modern science, technology and market economy. It has been transformed into modern SF with a tenacious vitality. "Modern SF system has an absolute superiority in the contemporary world."[6] In developing countries, SF undoubtedly is still the chief form of agricultural microeconomic organization. "It is estimated that there are 500 million SF households (with an operated land area of less than 2 hectares) in the world... In China and India alone, there are 193 and 93 million SF households respectively."[7] In countries with developed market economy, modern SF household-based farms still prevail in agricultural production organization. "In the United States, family farms account for more than 90% of the 2.1 million farms. In Denmark there are more than 120,000 peasant household-based farms. In other countries such as Japan where resources are relatively scarce, the agricultural operational and management system is built on family farms."[8]

Which is more efficient in the agricultural sector, corporate or collective "big production" or "small production" of peasant households? Is SF

---

[4]Engels, F. The Peasant Question in France and Germany. *Selected Works of Marx and Engels*, Vol. 3. Moscow: Progress Publishers, 1993.

[5]Huang, Z. *Small Household Farming and Rural Development in the Yangtze River Delta.* Beijing: Zhonghua Book Company, 2000, p. 44.

[6]Wen, L. "The Particularity of Agricultural Production and the Vitality of Household Self-Cultivated Farms", in Yu Keping, Li Shenming and Wang Weiguang eds., *On Agriculture and Peasants in the Construction of New Countryside.* Beijing: Central Compilation & Translation Bureau Press, 2006, p. 232.

[7]Thapa, G. "Challenges and Opportunities for Small Agriculture During an Economic Transformation in Asia and Latin America", *Journal of China Rural Economy*, No. 12, 2010, pp. 77–87.

[8]Huang, Z., Lin Jian, Zhang, D. *et al. Agricultural Modernization: Theory, Process and Approach.* Beijing: China Agricultural Press, 2003, p. 103.

economy "dying" in its historical course or retains its vigor in the new situation? In the past two centuries, there has been an extremely heated controversy surrounding them in the academia. As early as the 1970s, some scholars believed that "There is no tendency towards the large establishment in agrarian development and the large establishment is not always a superior form of production."[9] Although theories such as self-sufficient small peasants and labor and consumption equilibrium by Chayanov, rational small peasants and maximum utility by Schultz and Huang Zongzhi's "agricultural involution" pass entirely different judgments on the nature of SF economy, they all hold the idea backed up by evidence from diverse perspectives and layers that SF' economy is efficacious and can exist for a long time to come. Sen found in an empirical research that there is a negative correlation between the size of the peasant family and agricultural efficacy in India. This means that small-scale peasant household-based economy is more efficient than corporate or collective agricultural economy and large-scale peasant household-based economy.[10] Prosterman's empirical findings concerning more than a dozen developing countries including China also indicate that the profits from scale food production are not obvious and even if there is any, it is very limited whereas there are multitudes of evidences that scale food production is not economical.[11] Studies by Olinto and Burgess show that there are no economies of scale in agricultural production, but it may exist to some extent in the processing and sales of agricultural produces.[12]

Why is SF economy efficacious?

Many scholars have offered various explanations for this. To start with, the agricultural production cycle is long, the output is impacted by external factors unexpectedly, the supervision of labor is difficult and costly

[9] Kautsky, K. *The Agrarian Question*. London & Winchester: Zwan Publications, 1988.

[10] Sen, A. "An Aspect of Indian Agriculture", *Economic Weekly*, Vol. 14, No.(4–6) (1962), pp. 243–246. Sen, A., "Peasants and Dualism with or without Surplus Labor", *Journal of Political Economy*, Vol. 74 (1966), pp. 425–450.

[11] Prosterman, R. *et al.* "Scale Agriculture in China: Policy Appropriately Do", *China's Rural Observation*, Vol. 6, 1966, pp. 17–29.

[12] Boucher, S. R., Smith, A., J. E. Taylor *et al.* "Impacts of Policy Reforms on the Supply of Mexican Labor to U.S. Farms: New Evidence from Mexico", *Review of Agricultural Economics*, Vol. 29, No.1 (2007), pp. 4–16.

and the labor of household operators goes hand in hand with their own economic benefits so that the supervision problem may be resolved. That's how they can arouse greater enthusiasm for labor and improve efficiency. Moreover, "peasant households are characterized by less use of capital, greater use of labor and other household-owned resources, and usually higher multiple cropping and intercropping indices."[13] Therefore, there is a fairly high yield. That is only part of the story. Agriculture is an industry where economies of scale are not prominent in that land output rate is not inherently related to scale operation. Even if big agriculture has a higher agricultural labor productivity, its marginal productivity is lower. Weitz points out that agriculture is more than an occupation. It is a way of life endowed with special values, feelings and passions and goes far beyond the limitations of economic stimuli and organizational structures. Household farms have resolved their obvious conflicts with specialized agriculture and withstood the test of the transition from labor-intensive agriculture to capital-knowledge-intensive agriculture.[14]

It is undeniable that peasant household-based operation and SF economy including China's current rural household land contracting system are vulnerable to much criticism. Many scholars point out their limitations and drawbacks from different perspectives and dimensions.

- Lacking scale benefits.
- Impossibility of realizing agricultural mechanization.
- Lacking the motivation and capacity to make technological innovations.
- Resulting in an inadequate supply of public products in the rural area.
- Difficulty to confront market risks.
- Difficulty to protect the rights of peasants as a group due to their dispersion.
- A tendency for polarization.

---

[13]Ganesh, T. "Challenges and Opportunities for Small Agriculture During the Economic Transformation in Asia and Latin America", *Journal of China Rural Economy*, No. 12, 2010, pp. 77–86.

[14]Raanan, W. *From Peasant to Farmer — A Revolutionary Strategy for Development*. New York: Columbia University Press, 1971.

Some criticisms conflate SF economy of different natures and some mistake the problems arising from the development as permanent ones. Of course, some criticisms do make sense. However, the key point is that even if these criticisms are justified, will they inevitably lead to the replacement and inevitable demise of household-based operation and SF economy? Are the "substitutes" or alternative economic organizational forms bound to be superior? What's more, is it definitely true that given the retention of the independent business entities of peasant households, will these limitations and defects never be remedied, compensated for or alleviated even by an external transformation of SF as well as their internal transformation? Actually, a flawed and limited form of economic organization does not necessarily have to be supplanted or destroyed.

5.2 This "SF" is Not That "SF" — "Modern SF" is no "Traditional SF"

It is an undeniable fact that household-based agriculture has not been eliminated with the development of capitalist economy, industrialization and urbanization.

Whether in Japan and the Netherlands with smaller territories and greater populations, or the US, Canada and Australia famed for their vast territories or in France and Germany, where the proportion of land and population is moderate, the main form of agricultural production organizations is household-based farming rather than big capitalist farming operated by hiring migrant workers. Therefore, Smith and Marx's predictions that small peasant household-based economy would be eliminated and peasants would be replaced by "agricultural hired workers" have not been testified as history moves on. Nevertheless, we should be aware that the modern SF system is no traditional SF system and therefore, one should not be simplistically taken for the other. The reason is that they are identical or similar in forms but different essentially. Regrettably, many scholars including the two schools that hold the opposite views that "SF will disappear" and "SF will withstand the time" tend to conflate the two.

What are the essential differences between modern SF and traditional SF? In the final analysis, they differ in the degree of marketization and that of socialization. They are not merely differences in quantity such as the percentages of market shares, but differences in essence. The modern SF system is essentially marketized and socialized while the traditional SF system is self-sufficient and thus closed. Of course, the former cannot transform into the latter overnight. This is a long historical course that takes diverse paths with distinguishing characteristics in different countries and different historical periods.

The distinguishing feature of the traditional SF system, in a nutshell, is the "potato economy" that Marx once vividly compared it to: "Each individual peasant family is almost self-sufficient; it itself directly produces the major part of its consumption and thus acquires its means of life more through exchange with nature than in intercourse with society. The small holding, the peasant and his family; alongside them another small holding, another peasant and another family. A few score of these make up a village, and a few score of villages make up a Department ... much as potatoes in a sack form a sackful of potatoes." Obviously, the traditional has two fundamental features: dispersion based on individual, private or village or commune ownership and closedness based on the self or semi-self-sufficiency of natural economy. For a long time, especially since the establishment of the Chinese socialism, the focus of policy makers and theoretical circles has always been excessively on the "dispersion" of the traditional SF economy at the expense of the more essential closedness of natural economy.[15]

One of the purposes of China setting up agricultural cooperation and people's communization is to organize in a large collective the peasants who are like "a plate of loose sand" so that the disperse peasants can be transformed into "concentrated" members. However, it does not solve the problem of closedness of natural economy. Instead, it compounds the problem to a certain extent. The small but complete closedness of peasant household natural economy just turns into a big and complete closedness of the people's commune natural economy.

After the rural implementation of the household-based land contracting system in China, the concentrated members were transformed into

[15]Marx, K. The Eighteenth's Brumaire of Louis Bonaparte. *Karl Marx Selected Works*, Vol. 2. London: Lawrence and Wishart Limited, 1945.

disperse peasants. History seemed to have turned around and returned to its original starting point.[16] However, the fundamental transformation of a more important historical scene and the resultant fundamental changes in the internal mechanisms of the household-based farming system go unnoticed by some critics.

Is the SF in contemporary China still scattered and closed? On the whole and in terms of the development trend, the answer is of course "No". The author believes that the SF in contemporary China is marketized or being marketized. It means here that the decision-making of major economic moves of small peasant households is largely determined by market forces. Their economic moves depend on various market-oriented social service systems. They are getting increasingly widely involved in the market transaction process and the allocation of various economic resources, especially labor resources, is market-oriented.

SF being marketized means that the marketization of peasant households is a dynamic evolution. It reflects the participation of peasant households in market activities and the increasing dependence of the basic economic links such as production, consumption and exchange on the development trend of the market. If marketized SF means focusing on the degree of its development from the perspective of peasant households' participation in market operations, then the focus of SF being marketized is on the development trend from the perspective of a dynamic evolution.

In terms of patterns of phenomena, the SF in contemporary China is still decentralized. However, it is essentially different from the decentralized operation of traditional self-sufficient SF. The dispersion of the traditional SF is that of the potato economy like loose sand. The scattered points (the single small peasant households) are solitary and have no economic ties between them. There is no central cohesive power to connect them. In contrast, the dispersion of the SF marketized and being marketized in contemporary China is a kind of net-like dispersion. The scattered points are closely integrated into a large marketized and

[16]This vivid expression is found in a jingle of "after having been working hard for decades returning overnight to days before the old land reform" that was popular in the early days of the rural reform.

socialized network through various economic channels and ties. Any point is relatively independent but cannot be completely independent of the network. It can only survive and develop within it.

5.3 A Collectivized Approach to Transforming SF

As mentioned earlier, according to Smith, Ricardo, Marx and Engels, SF was bound to be eliminated. However, in Smith and Ricardo's viewpoints, it would be eliminated by large-scale capitalist farming. In contrast, Marx and Engels held that in addition to that, it would be supplanted by socialist cooperative and collectivized agriculture. In the actual course of socialism, either the collective farms of the Soviet Union or the people's communes before the land reform in China took the way of "eliminating SF" by collectivization.[17]

The socialism foreseen by Marx and Engels is based on highly developed social productivity of capitalism and large-scale socialized production. Therefore, in their view, replacing small agriculture and small production with big agriculture and production is the general trend in the development of socialist agriculture. In theory, the big agriculture of capitalism will have destroyed the "small agriculture" of "small-scale peasant economy" by then. Hereafter, socialism merely needs to transform the big agriculture and large farms of capitalist private ownership into big agriculture and big farms of socialist public ownership.

However, even in the developed capitalist countries, it took a long time for big agriculture to eliminate small agriculture. This suggests that for a long time, "small peasant household economy" can and will inevitably coexist with big capitalist agriculture. Marx pointed out that "Peasant agriculture on a small scale and the carrying on of independent handicrafts together form the basis of the feudal mode of production, and after the dissolution of that system continue side by side with the capitalist mode."[18]

---

[17] Although the theoretical community is aware of the difference between cooperation and collectivization, for a long time, they have been conflated both in the Soviet Union and China.

[18] Marx, K. *Capital: A Critique of Political Economy*, *Op. cit.*

How to treat the SF that will coexist with big capitalist agricultural production? In *The Peasant Question in France and Germany*, Engels elaborated on it, which was to have great impacts on socialist practice. First of all, Engels affirmed that the SF would inevitably die. "Our small peasant, like every other survival of a past mode of production, is hopelessly doomed."[19] In addition, Engels held that SF is the chief concern of all peasants and policies about them should be formulated accordingly. "Not only is he, of all peasants, the most important for Western Europe in general, but he is also the critical case that decides the entire question. Once we have clarified in our minds our attitude to the small peasant, we have all the data needed to determine our stand relative to the other constituent parts of the rural population."[20] Finally, Engels stressed that if the socialist political party takes power, "our task relative to the small peasant consists, in the first place, in effecting a transition of his private enterprise and private possession to cooperative ones, not forcibly but by dint of example and the proffer of social assistance for this purpose."[21]

Actually socialism did not win first in some countries that had been backward and underdeveloped rather than developed capitalist countries. Therefore, the main economic organizational forms that socialism was exposed to in the countryside were not "big agriculture" or "big farms" operated by hired workers in capitalist countries, but rather "the ownership of an overwhelming number of individual peasants."[22] Therefore, the main realistic task of socialism involving agriculture and rural areas was focused on how to address the issue of household-based peasants, i.e., how to reform them. Needless to say, the authentic socialist leaders such as Lenin, Stalin and Mao Zedong still adhered to Engels' fundamental idea, that is, transforming household-based peasants through collectivization, and the purpose and essence of so doing were to eliminate them.

---

[19]Engels, F. The Peasant Question in France and Germany. *Op. cit.*

[20]*Ibid.*

[21]*Ibid.*

[22]Mao Zedong. Agricultural Cooperation. *Mao Zedong's Collected Works*, Vol. 6, Beijing: People's Publishing House, 1999, p. 437.

It should also be pointed out that in socialist practice, there are political considerations in transforming household-based peasants and eliminating them through collectivization. Therefore, transforming household-based peasants and eliminating them are closely linked with the eradication of capitalist soil. Inheriting Lenin's thoughts, Mao held that after the land reform before the founding of the People's Republic of China, there was a conspicuous spontaneous tendency of capitalism in China's rural areas on the basis of the household-based peasant economy. "The spontaneous forces of capitalism in the countryside are developing daily. The new rich peasants can be seen everywhere and many wealthy middle-class peasants seek to turn themselves into rich peasants."[23]

The rich peasants here refer to the big household-based peasants of capitalism. Therefore, "the purpose of our socialist transformation of agriculture is to wipe out capitalism from its root in the vastest rural area." Obviously, according to Lenin and Mao's logic, transforming household-based peasants and eliminating them are not only trends of economic development but also out of a political need.

In a given historical period, political considerations even outweigh economic ones. Here it is an interesting question whether Lenin and Mao's view is consistent with that of Marx and Engels. The latter believed that capitalism destroys small production on a daily basis while Lenin and Mao Zedong held that small production produces capitalism constantly. Of course, the capitalism born out of SF economy will in turn eliminate it, which illustrates the historical dialectic process.

Judging from a bigger picture, the collectivizing path of eliminating household-based peasants is inherently related with the path of replacing market economy with planned economy. Traditional socialism rejects market economy and implements planned economy, on whose basis is adopted the national industrialization development strategy of giving priority to the development of heavy industry. Conversely, SF economy is considered to be incompatible with socialist industrialization and socialist planned economy.

Stalin said that SF economy and big socialist industry cannot coexist. "What, then, is the way out? The way out lies in making agriculture

---

[23] Mao Zedong. Agricultural Cooperation. *Mao Zedong's Collected Works*, Vol. 6, Beijing: People's Publishing House, 1999, p. 437.

large-scale."[24] Mao put it more explicitly: "Socialist industrialization cannot be carried out without agricultural cooperation."[25] Therefore, in the traditional socialist period when planned economy prevailed, whether in the Soviet Union or in China, SF economy (household-operated agriculture) had to be transformed into a collectivizing economy. Of course, this kind of transformation was not an exact copy of Engels' path of "example and the proffer of social assistance", for it relied more on government-led mandatory institutional changes and its political gains outweighed economic benefits.

5.4 Modern SF: A Marketized Approach to Transforming SF

Is household-operated agriculture small production inherently related to natural economy? Is household operation (household-based economy), a form of agricultural production organization, incompatible with commodity economy and market economy?

The answer is a sure "Yes" according to long-standing traditional Chinese thinking and concepts. Household-run agriculture is SF economy, which is in turn natural economy. This kind of absolute and rigid understanding has for a long time frightened people out of imagining a household-based economy related to big socialized production as well as commodity economy and market economy.

Factually, the American-style shows that small household-based farms without hiring migrant workers are highly likely to become specialized microeconomic organizations closely tied to markets. In the United States, produces by means of specialized production on family farms are mainly provided as commodities for markets. For various consumer items (including produces), household farms are mainly dependent on market supplies. For instance, they depend heavily on marketized and socialized

[24]Stalin, J. Issues Concerning Questions of Agrarian Policies in the U.S.S.R. *Selected Works of Stalin*, Vol. 12, Moscow: Foreign Languages Publishing House, 1954.
[25]Mao Zedong. *Op. cit.*, p. 431.

services in pre-production (seeds), in-production (fertilizers) and post-production (transportation), for example.

Therefore, the small-scale household operation is not necessarily of self-sufficient natural economy. Instead, it can become an organic chain and link in large-scale socialized production.

Conversely, large-scale agricultural organizations with centralized production and unified operation may be a "big and comprehensive" self-sufficient natural economy in nature. For example, the people's commune in China, which is characterized by a grand-scale and public ownership, is actually a fairly large-scale, self-sufficient natural economic organization. It rejects the relationship between merchandise and money and is distinct from Marx's big socialized production. Therefore, the scale of a production and operation organization is no justifiable basis for judging whether it is large-scale socialized production or small-scale production of natural economy.

Especially with the rapid development of contemporary science and technology, particularly information network technology, organizational forms of small-scale production and operation can be integrated into the network of big socialized production and become an organic node in socialized economy. It is true of not only agriculture but also industry and tertiary industries.

As famous futurist Alvin Toffler pointed out, "Today, we are beginning to realize that neither big or small is beautiful, but that appropriate scale, and the intelligent meshing of both big and small, is most beautiful." This is what is meant by "small-within-big is beautiful!"[26]

In fact, Marx believed that big agriculture was bound to replace small agriculture. The theory behind it is that large-scale socialized production would replace the small-scale production of natural economy and the operational scale of the agricultural organization has nothing to do with the essence of this theory. Regrettably, for a long time, we have been taking the form for the essence, understanding Marx's idea partially.

Another important matter is that just because SF economy and the production modes of market economy coexist in a society dominated by market economy does not mean "they by no means interact". Market economy will inevitably get inside SF economy and gradually transform in its own way the household-based agriculture of natural economy into household-based agriculture of market economy, i.e., convert "traditional SF" to "modern SF".

---

[26]Toffler, A. *The Third Wave*. New York: Bantam Books, Inc., 1980.

Therefore, SF economy dominated by market economy and that dominated by natural economy cannot be simplistically equated in that there is a tremendous or even essential change in both internal operational mechanisms and external operational environments. As Marx pointed out: "In every social formation, there is a specific kind of production which predominates over all the others and whose relations therefore determine their rank and influence. It is a general illuminant tingeing all other colors and modifying their specific features. It is a special ether determining the specific gravity of everything appearing in it."[27]

In short, the most fundamental difference between the market-oriented and the collectivizing approaches to transforming SF lies in the fact that the purpose and essence of the latter are to eliminate household farming operation while those of the former are to transform the traditional household farming operation into a modern one, or put it in other words, to supplant the traditional SF system with the modern one.

5.5 Quantitative Analysis of Marketization of Contemporary SF in China

China, in general, is in a transformational transition from traditional SF to modern marketized SF. It is keeping in step with that of entire Chinese economy from a dual economy to a modern unitary economy and from a planned economy to a modern market-oriented economy. More precisely, the transformation of SF is an integral part of the overall transformation of Chinese economy.

5.5.1 *A vertical metrological analysis of marketization of contemporary SF in China*[28]

The measurement factors of marketized SF are the marketization (commercialization) degree of produces by peasant households, the marketization rate of peasant household consumption expenditures, the marketization

[27] Marx, K. Introduction to a Contribution to the Critique of Political Economy. *Selected Works of Marx and Engels*, Vol. 1, Moscow: Progress Publishers, 1970.

[28] Team members Wang Chunchao and Hu Jiliang are the chief contributors to the quantitative analysis of this section.

degree of agricultural production services and the marketization degree of the labor force of peasant households.

5.5.1.1 *Commoditization rate of the production of major produces*

The commercialization degree of major produces by peasant households as basic production units is a vital factor in determining the marketization degree of peasant households. The commercialization degree of their produces goes up in proportion with the marketization degree of their production.

The commoditization rate of produces is the ratio of the average volume of produces sold by rural households per capita to the average volume of produces grown by rural households per capita multiplied by 100%.[29] In the actual measurement of the overall commercialization rate, are chosen the major agricultural produces of food, vegetables, pork, beef, mutton, eggs, aquatic products, etc. According to the findings of the rural household surveys by the National Bureau of Statistics over the years, since the rural reform in China, especially since the comprehensive implementation of the household contract responsibility system (agricultural production responsibility system in which a peasant household as a unit contracts land and other production materials and tasks), the overall commercialization rate of the household production of major agricultural produces increased steadily from 11.6% in 1981 to 69.7% in 2010, an increase of 58.1% (see Figure 5.1).

The commercialization speeds and current degrees of agricultural produces vary. For the necessities of peasants' daily consumption such as food, vegetables and other produces, the commoditization rate went up dramatically from merely 7.45% in 1981 to 71.74% in 2010 (see Figure 5.2), an increase of 64.29%. In addition, the commercialization rate of vegetables

[29]In the measurement of the overall commercialization rate of produces grown by rural household members, the total sum of produces grown by each household is the sum total of the produces sold and consumed based on the survey data from the National Bureau of Statistics. Although this measurement does not take into account the fact that rural families may grow a produce but consume the same type purchased from the market. Nevertheless, in terms of the overall balance between rural households' production and their consumption, this method can reflect the commercialization degree of produces grown in the country and sold in urban areas.

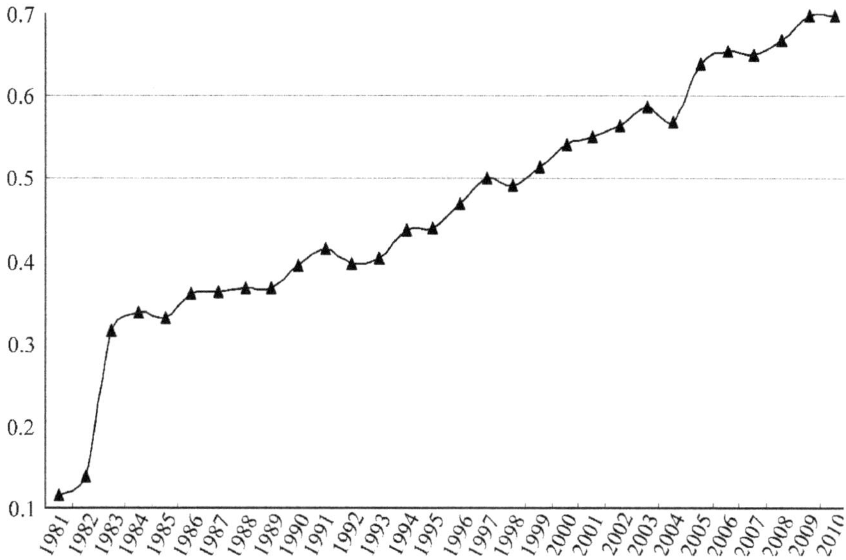

Figure 5.1. Changes in the overall commercialization rate of major produces of rural households in China (1981–2010)

Source: National Bureau of Statistics. *China Statistical Yearbook 2011*. Beijing: China Statistics Press, 2011.

Rural Social and Economic Survey Division of National Bureau of Statistics. *China Rural Statistical Yearbook 2011*. Beijing: China Statistics Press, 2011.

Rural Social and Economic Survey Division of National Bureau of Statistics. *China Rural Household Survey Yearbook 2011*. Beijing: China Statistics Press, 2011.

quickly reached 64.33%. In contrast, the commoditization rate of aquatic products fluctuated and rose relatively slowly. As for such mutually substitutable agricultural produces as pork, beef, mutton and eggs, the increase in their commercialization rates was relatively slow as against that of food and vegetables (see Figure 5.3). An important reason is that their initial commercialization rates were higher than those of food and vegetables.

5.5.1.2 *The marketization rate of rural household consumption expenditures*

Exposed to natural economy, the proportion of cash expenditures in basic consumption expenditures of rural households was extremely low. Just as Italian scholar Carlo Cipolla pointed out that peasants only go to the

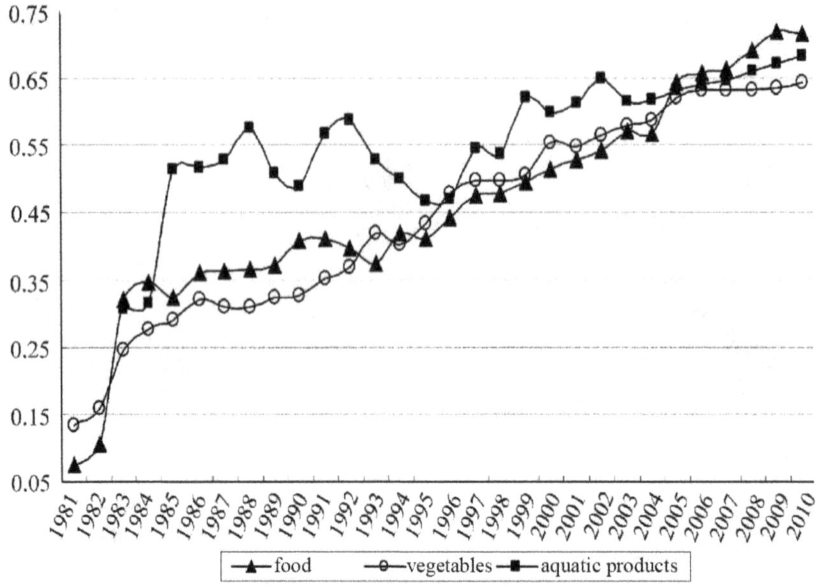

Figure 5.2. Changes in the commercialization rates of produces such as grain, vegetables and aquatic products of rural households in China (1981–2010)

Source: National Bureau of Statistics. *China Statistical Yearbook 2011*. Beijing: China Statistics Press, 2011.

Rural Social and Economic Survey Division of National Bureau of Statistics. *China Rural Statistical Yearbook 2011*. Beijing: China Statistics Press, 2011.

Rural Social and Economic Survey Division of National Bureau of Statistics. *China Rural Household Survey Yearbook 2011*. Beijing: China Statistics Press, 2011.

market for a small amount of what they need for life, which is an important feature of medieval economy. This is true of all places that have never experienced modern economic growth.[30]

Contemporary China is experiencing an unprecedented modern economic boom. This means that the transition has been accelerating from the traditional dualistic economic structure to the modern unitary economic structure. Along with this, small marketized peasants have been increasingly involved in consumption activities based on monetary expenditures

[30]Cipolla, Carlo M. *The Middle Ages, The Fontana Economic History of Europe*, Vol. 1. Glasgow: William Collins Sons & Co. Ltd., 1972.

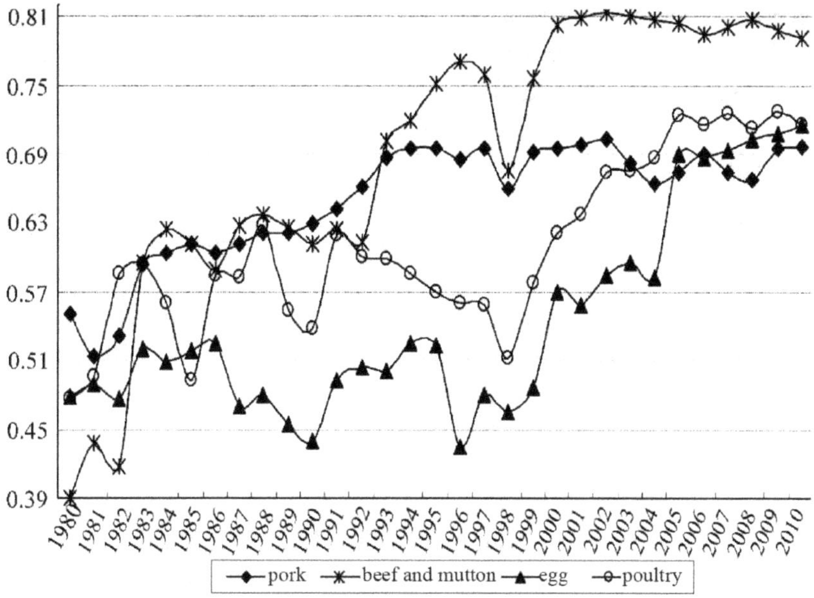

Figure 5.3. Changes in the commercialization rates of produces such as pork, beef and mutton, eggs and poultry of rural households in China (1980–2010)

Source: National Bureau of Statistics. *China Statistical Yearbook 2011.* Beijing: China Statistics Press, 2011.

Rural Social and Economic Survey Division of National Bureau of Statistics. *China Rural Statistical Yearbook 2011.* Beijing: China Statistics Press, 2011.

Rural Social and Economic Survey Division of National Bureau of Statistics. *China Rural Household Survey Yearbook 2011.* Beijing: China Statistics Press, 2011.

as the basic form. In order to continuously improve the overall household consumption effectiveness, there has been an increase in various cash consumption activities. In turn, peasant households' pursuit of consumption effectiveness has been replaced by a pursuit of monetary growth in real life. The marketization degree of peasants' consumption is embodied in their monetized consumption expenditures.

In order to describe the marketization evolution of rural household consumption expenditures in China, the marketization is measured according to the proportion of monetary payments in their rural consumption expenditures. The marketization rate of rural household consumption expenditures here is equated to the ratio of monetary payments of rural household consumptions to their consumption expenditures multiplied by 100%. Household consumption expenditures cover the costs of the main items including food, clothing, housing, household equipment and its services, transportation, communication, cultural and educational entertainments and their services, health care, other commodities and their services.

Overall, the marketization rate of peasant household consumption gradually increased from 51.7% in 1980 to 88.1% in 2010, an average annual increase of 1.2%. Among the various commodities consumed, the marketization of food consumption was the lowest (see Figure 5.4), but its marketization grew at a faster rate. The marketization rate of food consumption rose from 31.3% in 1980 to 72.9% in 2010. The average annual growth rate was 1.4%. The highest marketization rates of rural household consumption, those of the expenditures for transportation, communication, and cultural and educational entertainments had been close to 100% since 1980.[31] The marketization of peasant households in the basic consumption of shelter and clothing, closely related to life, had been rising steadily. The marketization rate of rural household consumption expenditures on shelter had been going up (see Figure 5.4) and that on clothing had been fairly high since 1980.

5.5.1.3 *Socialization of agricultural production services*

Agricultural production in a broad sense is a complete agricultural industrial chain including the three phases of pre-production, in-production and post-production. All the production work such as seed selection, breeding, plowing, transplanting (seeding), fertilization, management and harvesting was done mostly by the household-based labor force in traditional SF economy and a natural division of labor was made according to the gender and age of the family members alone. Seeds and fertilizers also came from the household, forming a closed internal circulation. Even households' cooperation and mutual assistance were mostly interchanges involving human and animal labor.

---

[31] The data are based on the findings from *China Rural Statistical Yearbook 2011* compiled by Rural Social and Economic Survey Division of National Bureau of Statistics published by China Statistics Press in 2011.

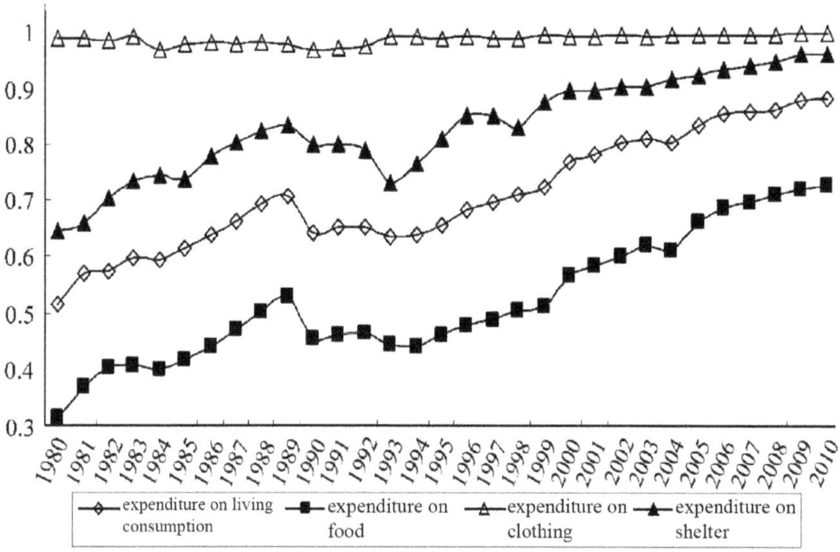

Figure 5.4. Changes in the marketization rate of rural households' consumption expenditures in China (1980–2010)

Source: Rural Social and Economic Survey Division of National Bureau of Statistics. *China Rural Statistical Yearbook 2011*. Beijing: China Statistics Press, 2011.

Rural Social and Economic Survey Division of National Bureau of Statistics. *China Rural Household Survey Yearbook 2011*. Beijing: China Statistics Press, 2011.

In contemporary China, however, peasants are dependent on the market and market-oriented social services in a considerable and increasing part of the above-mentioned production work such as seed selection, land plowing, plant protection and harvesting. They mostly purchase seeds, fertilizers and pesticides from markets. As a result, they have increasingly extensive ties with external markets, gradually forming an open market interchange system. This suggests that without market-oriented social service networks, Chinese peasants today would have much difficulty engaging in agricultural production.

Household use of power machinery gained increasing popularity in all links of agricultural production. There was an increase of 30.2% in the number of agricultural power machines owned by rural households in China from 11.6 per 100 households in 2000 to 15.1 in 2010 (see Figure 5.5).

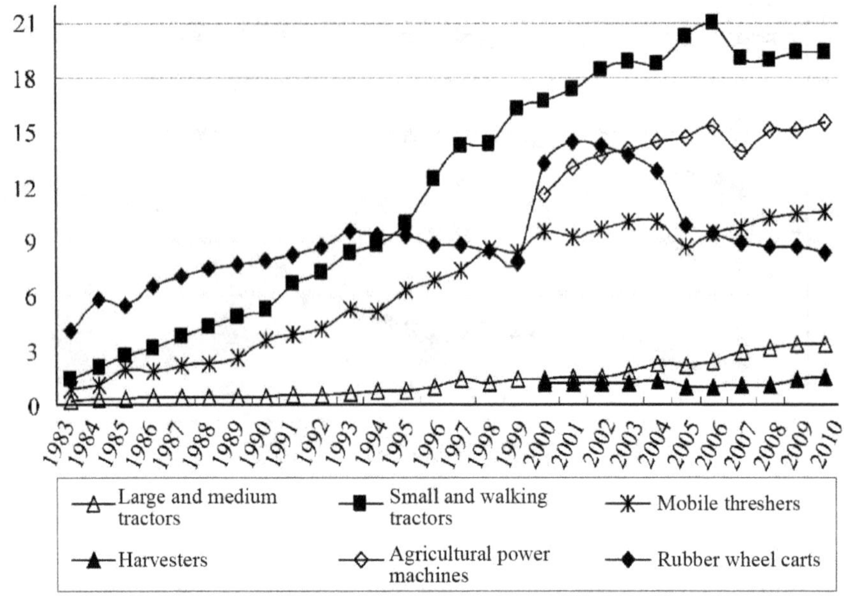

Figure 5.5. Changes in the socialization of agricultural production services (1983–2010)

Source: Rural Social and Economic Survey Division of National Bureau of Statistics. *China Rural Statistical Yearbook 2011*. Beijing: China Statistics Press, 2011.

Meanwhile, the average original value of agricultural fixed assets of peasant households in China increased from RMB4,673.1 per household in 2000 to RMB10,706.38 in 2010, an increase of 129.11%. This indicates that there was a greater increase in large and medium agricultural power machinery than the small-sized.

In fact, peasants' purchase of agricultural power machinery is not limited to their own use. In contemporary China, due to the limited scale of land operation, it is obviously an irrational economic behavior to purchase agricultural power machinery, especially large and medium-sized agricultural power machinery. Therefore, the increase in agricultural machinery per household actually led to a greater increase in the number of specialized households of agricultural machinery. It is estimated that during the period from the second half of May to the middle of June in 2012, the time for sowing, harvesting and caring, more than 510,000 harvesters were put to use for wheat harvesting, of which 325,000 were involved in cross-regional wheat harvesting, benefiting 96% of the major wheat producing areas such as Henan, Anhui, Shandong, Jiangsu and Hebei.[32] Throughout the harvesting period, more than 14 million sets of agricultural machinery and equipment were utilized in the fleeting harvesting and sowing periods. Over 90% of the national winter wheat harvesting was done by machinery.[33] The marketization rate had reached a fairly high level.

5.5.1.4 *The marketization rate of peasant household labor allocation*

Since 1986, labor input into peasant household's land operations has shown a decreasing trend while that outside it has been on the rise.[34] In 1986, the national average ratio of the labor input into household's land operations per household in rural areas to that outside was 5 to 0. By 2002, this ratio had been reduced from 2 to 0.16 (see Figure 5.6).

Obviously, the labor input outside household operations had been increasing rapidly. This indicates a rise in the employment of labor force attracted by posts of certain employment contract relationships in the country. It is an index of peasants' increasing involvement in the labor market. The labor force participated in employment contract labor in

[32] National Cross-regional Machine-Aided Wheat Harvesting Has Started, Xinhua, http://www.gov.cn/jrzg/2012-05/31/content_2150076.htm, May 31, 2012.

[33] Yu, W. and Yang Yuhua. There Will Be a Good National Summer Harvest of Grains. http://news.xinhuanet.com/2012-05/31/c_112086217.htm, May 31, 2012.

[34] From the planned economy period to the time since the reform and opening in 1985, China's rural household can be said to have not become a basic and important decision-making unit of operation in the true sense. Therefore, the author merely touches upon the household operations during 1979 and 1985 and focuses on the evolution of household labor employment since 1986. The amount of labor referred to here is explained in accordance with the Central Policy Office of the Central Committee of the Communist Party of China and the Office of the Rural Fixed Observation Point of the Ministry of Agriculture. It means "the cumulative number of labor days invested by men and women of working ages and a little younger or older ages who are directly engaged in the production and operation of agriculture, forestry, animal husbandry, etc., during the year."

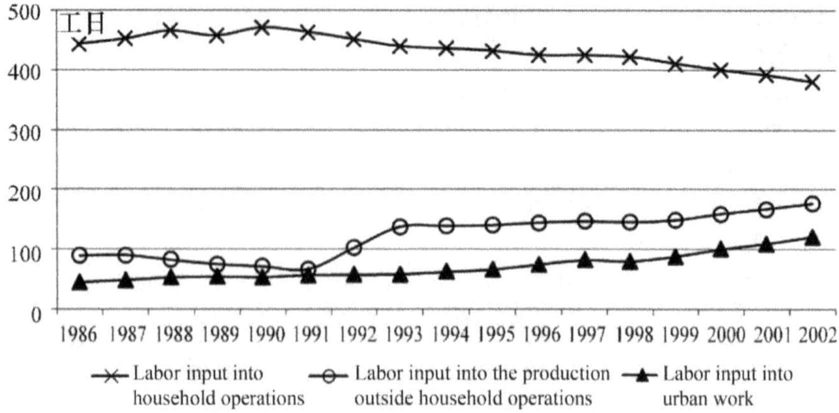

Figure 5.6. Changes in household labor input of rural households (1986–2002)[a]

Notes:

1. The amount of labor put into the production outside household operations is the sum total of the days of labor input into collective unified accounting units, unified operational township enterprises, unified operational village and group enterprises, township, village, group enterprises operated individually or in partnership and unified economic organizations.

2. 1992 data are the average of the data between 1991 and 1993; 1994 data are the average between 1993 and 1995.

[a]The data from 1986 to 2002 are the results of actual surveys. Since 2003, the focuses of the findings from the survey data released by the National Fixed Observation Point have been different. The data on rural labor were released according to industries rather than labor inputs into household operations, production outside household operations and urban work (see Figure 5.7). Quite like Figure 5.6, Figure 5.7 reflects the changes in the marketization of household labor.

Source: 1986–1990 data are cited from *Compilation of the Data on Typified National Rural Social and Economic Surveys 1986–1990* by the Central Government Policy Research Office and the Office of the Rural Fixed Observation Points of the Ministry of Agriculture. Beijing: CPC Central Party School Press, 1992, pp. 11–15.

1991–1999 data are cited from *Compilation of the Data on Typified National Rural Social and Economic Surveys (1986–1999)* by the Central Government Policy Research Office and the Office of the Rural Fixed Observation Points of the Ministry of Agriculture. Beijing: China Agriculture Press, 2001, pp. 77, 91, 92.

2000–2002 data are from *Compilation of Data from National Rural Fixed Observation Point Surveys (2000–2009)* by the Office of the Rural Fixed Observation Points of the Ministry of Agriculture. Beijing: China Agriculture Press, 2010, pp. 33, 47, 61.

various ways, and some did not necessarily have a formal labor contract. For example, long-term and short-term workers hired by family workshops might not have a formal labor contract. Nevertheless, this kind of

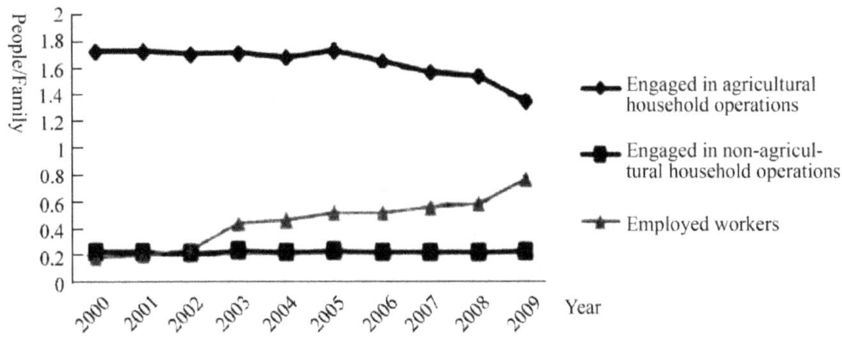

Figure 5.7. Industry-based national rural labor force (2000–2009)

Source: Office of Rural Fixed Observation Points of the Ministry of Agriculture. *Compilation of the Data from National Rural Fixed Observation Points Surveys 2000–2009.* Beijing: China Agriculture Press, 2010, p. 3.

employment also formed a contractual labor relationship essentially, which in turn constituted informal rural labor markets. As for informal urban labor markets, the main participants were mostly rural laborers.

The marketized decision-making concerning peasant household labor force employment is closely related to the intensified mobility of the labor force. The number employed in rural areas is shrinking rapidly in disproportion to the rural labor force taking temporary jobs in cities. According to the data from the follow-up surveys on peasant households released by the Ministry of Agriculture, 11.6% of the country's rural laborers went to work in different regions and the average employment size of temporary job-holders was 94 laborers per village in 1995. By 2009, the average number nationwide was 338.1 per village, accounting for 28.4% of the total rural labor force (see Figure 5.8).[35]

5.5.2 *Horizontal area metrological analysis of the marketization of SF in contemporary China*

Measuring the marketization of Chinese peasant households not only needs to be studied temporally but also spatially. The marketization of

[35]Ministry of Agriculture of the People's Republic of China, *2010 Report on China Agricultural Development.* Beijing: China Agriculture Press, 2010, p. 164.

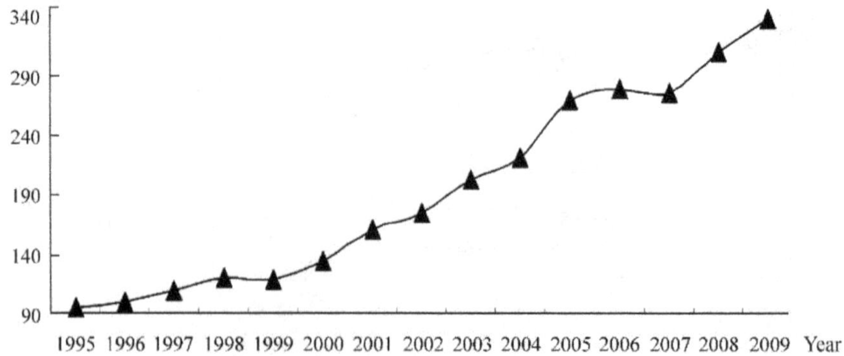

Figure 5.8. National growth of the labor force of temporary job-holders in each administrative village (1995–2009)

Source: Ministry of Agriculture of the People's Republic of China. Report on China Agricultural *Development*. Beijing: China Agricultural Press, 1996–2010.

different regions is influenced by their differences in agricultural production and operation conditions, economic development, humanistic and natural environments. A horizontal metrological contrastive study will be made of the marketization of peasant households in different regions in terms of the sources of incomes, household consumptions, household operations and labor allocations.

5.5.2.1 *The sources of incomes*

(Contrasts between different regions in the marketization degree of rural households' sources of incomes)

In traditional rural areas in China, the peasants lived a self-sufficient life or necessities were mostly used as barter. With the marketization of rural economy since the reform and opening-up, peasant households have been getting increasingly dependent on money. The monetization of incomes shows an essential transformation of traditional rural markets into modern ones. Therefore, the proportion of cash incomes from various income sources of rural residents generally reflects the degree of marketization of their income sources. For example, the nationwide degree of marketization of rural household income sources in 2011 reached

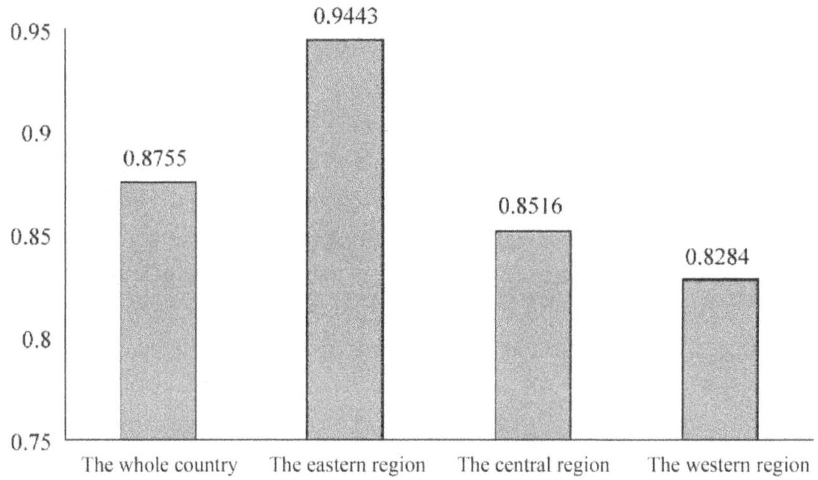

Figure 5.9. A contrast between different regions in the marketization degree of rural household income sources (2011)

Source: China Economic Net Statistics Database.

87.55%.[36] If Chinese peasant households are categorized according to geographical regions such as the eastern region, the central region and the western region of China, their marketization degrees are 94.43%, 85.16% and 82.84%, respectively (see Figure 5.9). The regional development of market economy is highly positively correlated with the marketization of rural household income sources.

5.5.2.2 *Peasant household consumptions*

(Contrasts between different regions in the marketization degree of rural household consumptions)

[36]The degree of marketization of rural household income sources here refers to the ratio of rural residents' cash incomes to the total incomes multiplied by 100%. This definition is adopted mainly because the greater part of their monetary income takes the form of cash. Its proportion highly reflects the degree of Chinese peasant households' monetary trading in markets, indicating in turn the extent to which they participate in marketization. Contrary to marketization is self-production, self-consumption or trading on a fairly small scale in a self-sufficient way or as barter.

The marketization of the overall consumptions of rural households is measured in line with the aforementioned definition. The data from peasant household surveys by the National Bureau of Statistics reveal that, in general, the marketization of rural household consumptions in various regions of China reached 83.5%, far beyond 50%, the critical point of the marketization of consumption expenditures. The horizontal contrasts show that the degree of the marketization of rural household consumption expenditures in China ranges from high to low in the order of the eastern, central and western regions (see Figure 5.10). The marketization degree of the eastern region was 89.6%, the highest of the three regions.

Most of the consumer goods were marketized while self-sufficient consumer goods accounted for a very small percentage. The percentage for the western region with the lowest marketization degree of rural household consumerization, was already 73.7%.

It is obvious that the Chinese peasant households relied heavily on market supplies rather than self-sufficiency for living consumptions. According to the surveys, the peasant households in the eastern region were largely dependent on market purchases for most staple foods

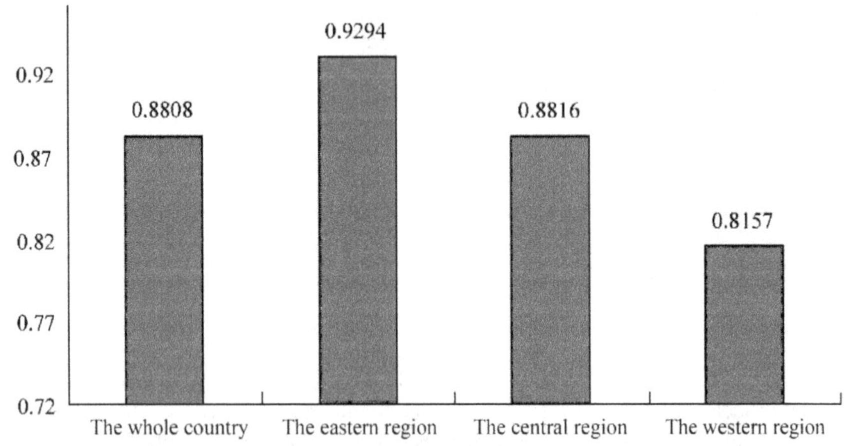

Figure 5.10. Contrasts between different regions in the marketization degree of rural household consumptions (2010)

Source: Rural Social Economic Survey Division of National Bureau of Statistics, *China Rural Household Survey Yearbook2011*. Beijing: China Statistics Press, 2011.

needed for daily consumptions. Therefore, they had entered into the stage of comprehensive marketization, changing from chiefly traditional natural exchanges to market exchanges. In contrast, the peasant household consumptions in the other two regions were in a transition to marketization.

5.5.2.3 *Household operations*

(Contrasts between different regions in the marketization degree of rural household operations)

The marketization degree of peasant household operations also varies geographically.[37] The degree embodies how closely rural households are tied to markets while engaging in various business activities. Judging from the input of family-run labor, capital and land, the ties between peasant household operations and various factor markets were getting increasingly strengthened and correspondingly, the operations were increasingly influenced by rural factor markets or product markets. Since rural household operations are core actions of their marketization, the degree of their connections with various markets has also become an important yardstick of their overall marketization. The order of the regional marketization degree from high to low in China was the eastern, the central and the western regions (see Figure 5.11).

5.5.2.4 *Labor allocation*

(Contrasts between different regions in rural household marketization degree of labor allocation)

The mobility degree of rural labor in contemporary China largely indicates the degree to which the labor is marketized. According to the basic rules of the demands and supplies in a labor market, the third industry is the most market-oriented followed by the secondary and then the primary industries.

[37]The marketization degree of peasant household operations here refers to the ratio of rural household's cash expenditures on operations to its total expenditures on operations.

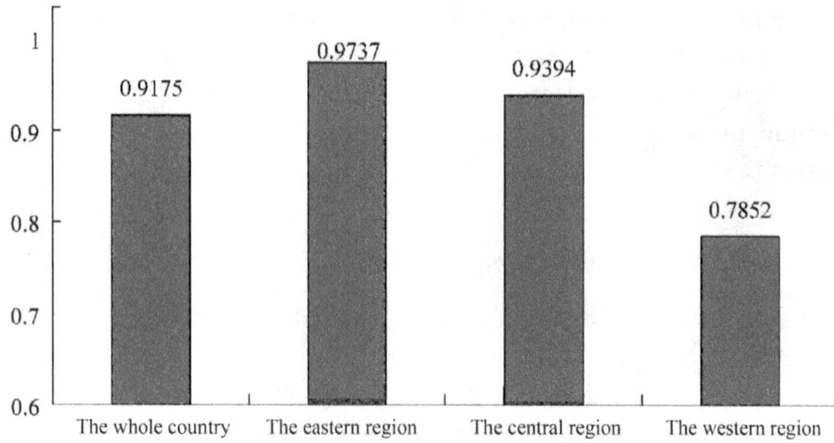

Figure 5.11. Contrasts between different regions in the marketization degree of rural household operations (2010)

Source: Rural Social Economic Survey Division of National Bureau of Statistics, *China Rural Household Survey Yearbook 2011*. Beijing: China Statistics Press, 2011.

A comparison was made about the proportions of the rural household labor force in labor employment in major industries in different regions of China. The results of the second national agricultural census show that the percentages of the rural household labor force involved in the tertiary industry in the three regions were 18.8%, 12.6% and 8.5%, respectively (see Figure 5.2). More rural household laborers in the eastern region were involved in a higher-level market-oriented employment in the tertiary industry than those in the central region followed by the western region. The percentages for the primary industry in the regions just took the reverse order. Based on the above-mentioned rural household labor employment in various industries, the marketization degrees of the regions went up in the order of the western, the central and the eastern regions (see Table 5.2).

The findings of the horizontal comparative analysis demonstrate a fairly great difference between regions in the marketization degree of rural households in China. In the respects of income sources, living consumptions, household operations and labor employment that embody the degrees, the eastern region comes first, the central region the second and the western region the last.

Table 5.2. National employment of the rural household labor force by industry in different regions (2006)

	National	Eastern	Central	Western
The sum total of rural laborers in industries (million)	47,852	17,652	13,043	13,927
The primary industry (percent)	70. 8	52. 4	76. 8	86. 3
The secondary industry (percent)	15. 6	28. 8	10. 6	5. 2
The tertiary industry (percent)	13. 6	18. 8	12. 6	8. 5

Source: Office of the Second National Agricultural Census Leading Group of the State Council & National Bureau of Statistics of the People's Republic of China. The Main National Data Bulletin of the Second National Agricultural Census (No. 5), February 27, 2008.

5.6 A Significant Reduction of the Number of Peasants — A Prerequisite for a Marketized Transformation of SF

The transformation of traditional self-sufficient and semi-sufficient rural households into modern, marketized and socialized peasants is not to fix them all on the soil. On the contrary, the prerequisite for it is to substantially cut down on the number of such peasants. In other words, only a large-scale transfer of the rural labor force can provide essential resources, and organizational and institutional space for the transformation.

The low level equilibrium trap into which the traditional agricultural society falls into stems from the imbalance between people and land, i.e., the imbalance between the population and the land resources. Since the major labor force in society is involved in farming and living on arable land, and in addition, production technology of traditional agricultural society has been long stagnant, the possession of arable land per capita determines the per capita food possession, peasants' living standards and the population carrying capacity of land.

In peacetime, traditional agricultural society has an inherently high rate of population growth due to various factors such as economy and culture, which leads to a geometrical growth of population. If the expansion of cultivated land cannot keep up with population growth, the conflict between man and land will get increasingly sharp. It will in turn intensify the conflict between population, and food and other living substances, and social conflicts. It seems as if only Malthus's so-called "positive suppression" or "negative suppression" could forcefully restore the balance between population and survival materials.

In traditional agricultural economic society in China, the crisis of cultivated land means a food crisis and an economic crisis of the entire society and therefore, land issue is the most essential problem of traditional agricultural society. "In the history of China, when the cycle of a population movement reached the nadir where the population was small while the land was relatively surplus, an average land system was easy to implement and the crisis of the total amount of cultivated land and the structural crisis were not very sharp. It was undoubtedly conducive to the development of productivity. However, once economy came back to normal and thrived, a massive population growth would compound the crisis of the total amount of cultivated land and the imbalance between population and land, which would in turn lead to a structural crisis. This would trigger off another round of wars and famines, which would lead to another sharp decline in population when a new round of cycles restarted."[38] As Marx remarked, "The unchangeableness of Asiatic societies is in such a striking contrast with the constant dissolution and re-founding of Asiatic States, and the never-ceasing changes of dynasty. The structure of the economic elements of society remains un-touched by the storm-clouds of the political sky."[39]

To break the weird cycle of the "Malthus Trap", a basic premise is to substantially reduce the number of the peasants living on arable land. Otherwise, the tension between man and land will not disappear and the self-sufficient agricultural society can never be changed fundamentally. Consequently, a modernized society with market economy cannot be built.

Obviously, if the vast majority of the social workforce is still composed of peasants, there will be no internal motivation for agricultural mechanization and the promotion and application of barrages of products of

---

[38] Cao, Y. *China's Transfer of Agricultural Labor Force: An Analysis Based on System Changes*. Huazhong Normal University Press, 1997, p. 23.

[39] Marx, K. *Capital: A Critique of Political Economy, Op. cit.*

agricultural science and technology. This is because they will further compound the tension between man and land. Moreover, the household self-produced agricultural produces generally can only suffice to maintain family consumptions, let alone the specialization and marketization of agriculture. Naturally, it will be difficult for non-agricultural industries to develop for lack of broad markets.

When it comes to world history, the beginning of British capitalism and Western modernization was coupled with a forced separation of multitudes of peasants from their land into cities. Although "the history of this, their expropriation, is written in the annals of mankind in letters of blood and fire",[40] after all, it initiated the process of capitalist modernization and transformed human society from agricultural to industrial.

China's socialist modernization course certainly cannot and should not repeat the history of depriving peasants of land and driving them into cities with force.[41] But drastically reducing the number of peasants is still the only way out for China's modernization. As Du Runsheng pointed out in 1988, if there was no change in the fact that 800 million people provided food for 200 million people, China's agriculture would go nowhere! Likewise, without the change, there would be no way out for China's modernization, either!

China's marketized transformation of SF went hand in hand with its large-scale agricultural labor transfer. The latter has so substantially reduced the number of agricultural laborers who made their living out of land that the extremely abundant labor resources were optimally allocated in a wider space. This greatly improved agricultural labor productivity as well as the efficiency of the labor allocation of the overall national economy. From pure peasant households with surplus labor in the past to households engaging in agriculture and part-time jobs and occupational peasant households (including big adequately self-employed agricultural households), Chinese peasants were gradually transformed into marketized peasants.

---

[40] *Ibid.*

[41] It is a pity that in some places the appropriation and drive still exist in the compulsory actions taken to drive them away from arable land in the name of "urbanization".

At the same time, however, with China's reform in urban and rural household registration systems lagging behind, there were still various institutional obstacles to the change of peasants into citizens. As a result, China's large-scale agricultural labor transfer failed to be accompanied correspondingly by its urbanization. This gave rise to the vulnerability and uncertainty of China's substantial decline in the number of peasants to some degree.

Figure 5.3 shows the changes in China's agricultural labor force in the past 30 years of reform and opening-up based on the data provided by the National Bureau of Statistics. It reflects to a certain extent the process of China's dramatic reduction of the number of peasants. "To a certain extent" suggests that the statistic findings fail to include the following changes.

A considerable part of part-time peasants are still counted as agricultural laborers. In fact, they only engage in agriculture partially or even they are not engaged in agriculture at all most of the time. If the calculation is conducted according to the time spent actually on agriculture, China's agricultural labor force might be smaller than the statistic findings indicate. Conversely, rural elderly people and minors in China who are not included in the labor statistics might engage in agriculture within a certain period of time. During the people's commune days, they were often counted as half-labor and auxiliary labor. Considering this factor, China's actual agricultural labor force might be underestimated (see Table 5.3).

Peasants who no longer engage in agriculture, or merely do it as part-time work maintain the right of contracting rural land. The transfer of agricultural labor is incomplete due to China's special national circumstances and special systems, which renders the process of the marketization of Chinese SF long and arduous and imbues it with distinctive "Chinese characteristics." With the collective ownership of rural land, peasants have no land of private ownership neither can they buy or sell it. The reliance on land sales and mergers to achieve agricultural scale operation is not legally backed up nor practically feasible in contemporary China.

However, the national policy that allows lengthening infinitely the rural household's land contracting right accentuates the operational right rather than ownership. The legal definition of rural land transfer (which means

Table 5.3. The changes in China's agricultural labor force (1978–2011)

Year	China's agricultural labor force (million)	Percentage	In comparison with the precious year	Changes in percentage
1978	28,318	70.5	−316	—
1979	28,634	69.8	488	−0.7
1980	29,122	68.7	655	−1.1
1981	29,777	68.1	1082	−0.6
1982	30,859	68.1	292	0
1983	31,151	67.1	−283	−1
1984	30,868	64	262	−3.1
1985	31,130	62.4	124	−1.6
1986	31,254	60.9	409	−1.5
1987	31,663	60.0	586	−0.9
1988	32,249	59.3	976	−0.7
1989	33,225	60.1	5689	0.8
1990	38,914	60.1	184	0
1991	39,098	59.7	−399	−0.4
1992	38,699	58.5	−1019	−1.2
1993	37,680	56.4	−1052	−2.1
1994	36,628	54.3	−1098	−2.1
1995	35,530	52.2	−710	−2.1
1996	34,820	50.5	20	−1.7
1997	34,840	49.9	337	−0.6
1998	35,177	49.8	591	−0.1
1999	35,768	50.1	275	0.3
2000	36,043	50.0	356	−0.1
2001	36,399	50.0	241	0
2002	36,640	50.0	−436	0
2003	36,204	49.1	−1374	−0.9
2004	34,830	46.9		−2.2
2005	33,442	44.8	−1388	−2.1
2006	31,941	42.6	−1501	−2.2
2007	30,731	40.8	−1210	−1.8
2008	29,923	39.6	−808	−1.2
2009	28,890	38.1	−1033	−1.5
2010	27,931	36.7	−959.5	−1.4
2011	26,594	34.8	−1336.5	−1.9

Note: Percentage here refers to the percentage of the agricultural labor force in the entire social workforce.
Source: 1978–2010 data are cited from the National Bureau of Statistics. *China Statistical Yearbook 2011*. Beijing: China Statistics Press, 2011. 2011 data are cited from the National Bureau of Statistics. "2011 National Economic and Social Development Statistical Bulletin of the People's Republic of China", Central Government Website (http://www.gov.cn/gzdt/2012-02/22/content_2073982.htm), February 22, 2012.

that a peasant who has contracted land has the right to lease its operational right to others and still retains the contracting right) is stipulated in *The Law of the People's Republic of China on Rural Land Contracting*. The promise and the definition provide necessary and limited institutional arrangements to promote the working of the markets for rural land transfer, a moderate scale operation of agricultural land and a substantial reduction of the number of peasants.

5.7 Land Transfer — A Progressive Route from Marketized SF with Chinese Characteristics to a Moderate Scale Operation

Promoting China's agricultural modernization on the basis of small agriculture rests with China's peculiar national situations and also draws on the experiences of some developed countries. However, this does not mean that the smallest scale of agricultural operation is the best. On the contrary, under the constraints of the existing resources, population, technologies and systems, expanding the scale of agricultural operation as much as possible is still an extremely important dimension of China's agricultural modernization process.

In order to speed up peasant urbanization, the author advocates permanent tenancy by which the land possession right and the land operational right may be in the hands of different people, the inheritance of the land contracting right by a single heir, one son or one daughter, and the use of rural land contracting rights to exchange for the social security rights of urban residents. A chief concern is to prevent the further subdivision and miniaturization of the scale of rural land operation to promote a moderate scale operation of small peasants on the basis of a substantial reduction of the number of peasants. Marketized SF is an inevitable choice for China's modernization of agriculture, but miniaturization of SF is a trend that must be prevented.

In some people's traditional mindsets, the scale operation of agriculture is immediately associated with collectivization. One of the superiorities of the people's communes that they cannot forget even today is the so-called scale operation, i.e., the so-called "big agriculture". As Wen Tiejun pointed out, "With low productivity, we practiced collective agricultural economy for scale operation. However, just such a simple addition as a hoe plus a sickle or the efforts of one peasant and another joined together was no progress in production relationships". Nevertheless, the author cannot agree with Wen Tiejun's another assertion that in the world, "no one can rely on the so-called market economy to achieve scale operation."[42]

China's trading and land operational right transfer under the collective ownership of rural land are essentially to promote and achieve a moderate scale land operation by means of market economy. On the basis of the separation between the rural land ownership and the contracting right, the trading and transfer of the land operation right finally lead to the separation of the three. The separation lays a necessary institutional foundation for the development of various forms of scale land operation and the promotion of an innovative agricultural operational approach to a coordinated development of household operation, collective operation, cooperative operation and enterprise operation, and the acceleration of the establishment of a new agricultural operational system.

Granted, in the early days, land transfer was not necessarily accompanied by the trading of the land operational right. For example, land contracting rights (actual farming rights) were freely transferred among relatives and friends. However, this kind of land transfer with traditional social favors gradually declined with the advances in rural marketization and was replaced by the transactions of market economy. Barrages of formal market organizations such as rural land property rights trading markets were established in some areas where land transfer was relatively developed, especially in the suburbs of large and medium cities. These factors made land transfer more standardized and scaled up.

In China, the rural land transfer, like the agricultural production organization forms, is conducted in various ways due to the diversity, differences and non-equilibrium of rural economic, social and cultural development. Land transfers of large-areas and patches tied up are mainly conducted in the peripheries of large and medium-sized cities. In contrast, however, in

[42]Wen, T. *Three Rural Issues and Institutional Changes*. Beijing: Economic Press China, 2009, p. 19.

most rural areas, the more common practice is land transfer conducted to a small extent and on a small scale between peasant households.

With China's grand-scale movements of the agricultural labor force and the deepening of the rural division of labor, a large proportion of peasants, especially the young ones, went out of their villages to take temporary jobs or do business. According to the findings of the investigations of Tianmen City in Hubei Province by the research group, there were nearly 550,000 rural laborers in the city in 2010, of which 350,000 went out to work all the year round.

What's more, they were mostly young or middle-aged. Their average age was 35 as against the average age of 50 of the rural laborers who stayed on the soil. Consequently, on the one hand, multitudes of young and middle-aged laborers who went out were unwilling and unable to cultivate the contracted land. Even if they reluctantly did, their way of increasing yields was merely increasing investments in land production and the land output rate was still extremely low. On the other hand, some peasants who stayed and tried to make a living out of farming suffered from a shortage of arable land and so they stayed idle, unable to find anything else to do.

The land transfer between peasant households undoubtedly alleviated the situation, making it possible for a more efficient allocation of land and labor resources. In 2011, the research group sampled 2,760 households in Tianmen City, of which 846 transferred their contracted land to others, accounting for 30.65%, the average cultivated area per household involved was 4.51 mu. Conversely, 581 households had cultivated land transfer from others, accounting for 21.05%, and the average land per household concerned was 4.93. Putting the two together, 1,427 households were involved in land transfer, accounting for 51.7% of the surveyed households. It is true that Tianmen may be one of the special cases of large-scale rural land transfers.

Nevertheless, on a national scale, by the first half of 2011, the total area of land operational rights transfer had reached 207 million mu, making up 16.2% of the total area of contracted cultivated land according to the statistics from the departments concerned.[43] This suggests that there was more land cultivated and operated by the laborers who actually engaged in agricultural production than the land contracted by peasant households.

[43] *Guangming Daily*. January 19, 2012, p. 14.

Therefore, the operational scale of the land operated by marketized small peasants in China was not as small as imagined, and, more importantly, with the further development of rural land transfer, the scale of land operation by peasant households is gradually expanding in China.

It is undeniable that in the initial stage of rural land transfer, it was often carried out in private and spontaneously between households. The transferor and the transferee tended to be relatives and friends. The transfer was mainly based on verbal commitments, seldom in the forms of contracts, documents and other formal documents. Therefore, it was essentially more of a mutual aid and assistance of a traditional agricultural acquaintance society and there was not yet any marketized transaction involving land transfer.

According to a 2006 survey on rural land transfer conducted by the Hubei Survey Team of the National Bureau of Statistics, 77.8% of the peasant households said that they had conducted their land transfers out of free will and 19.7% reported that their transfers were village-organized. Around 76% of the households said that there was only an oral agreement on the land transfer, 13.5% had signed land transfer contracts, and 6.7% had the deal affirmed through a third party.[44]

One of the important signs of the existence of marketized rural land transfer transactions is the fixation of the prices reached at transactions of regional land markets. Its further development was embodied in the emergence of normative land property rights transaction organizations such as centers for land property transfer transactions. Dacai Deng studied four different cases of Hongqi Village in Sichuan, Liyuantuan Village in Hebei, Lake Village in Hunan and Xiaogang Village in Anhui Province. They represented four distinguishing types of land transfer, indicating the multi-coexistence of land transfer models in China.

[Case 5.1] Multi-Coexistence of Rural Land Transfer Models in China

Dacai Deng from China Rural Research Institute of Huazhong Normal University looked into the land transfers conducted in Hongqi Village in Sichuan, Liyuantuan Village in

[44] Wang, C. and Li Zhaoneng. "The Predicament Regarding Rural Land Transfer: A Survey on Peasant Households from Hubei", *Journal of Huazhong Normal University*, No. 4, 2008, pp. 51–56.

Hebei, Lake Village in Hunan and Xiaogang Village in Anhui Province and classified them into four distinguishing types of rural land transfer in China.

The normative type of agricultural land transfer market is represented by Hongqi Village, Wanchun Town, Wenjiang District, Sichuan Province. The main sign of being "normative" is the establishment of a village-level center for agricultural land transfer services. The government requires that a contract should be signed about an agricultural land transfer, sent to the town and higher-level governments for review and approval before notarization.

However, the transactions conducted at the centers mainly concern the land transfers between peasant households and capital from elsewhere. The land transfers between the peasant households are still made by negotiations in private so that the transferee may elude paying regulation fees to village-level centers for land transfer services. Anyhow, land transfers in Hongqi Village are market-based transactions priced. 500 kg of rice is used as the basic measurement of the price and the market price of the year is used as the price basis for the rental price per mu.

The type of Liyuantun Village, Wei County, Hebei Province, is an example of an elementary rural land transfer market. It is "elementary" in that there is no such center and all transactions are negotiated in private between the peasant households involved without any help afore-mentioned in the first type. Nevertheless, the village has a reference land transfer price of RMB600 per mu. Even if land transfers take place between parents and children or other relatives and friends, the price remains fixed, "The price does not vary with the type of buyers."

Xiaogang Village in Fengyang County, Anhui Province, is a representative of the coexistence between market-based and non-market-based transfers. The former means that the price is market-based while the latter means the transfer is free.

There are land transfers in Lake Village, Hanshou County, Hunan Province but there is no land transfer market yet. This means that the land transfers between peasant households are free. Nevertheless, in 2001, the village leased 130 mu of low-lake fields to outsiders at the price of RMB120 per mu annually.

Deng, Dacai. "The Formation of Agricultural Land Transfer Markets Taking Hongqi Village, Liyuantun Village, lake Village and Xiaogang Village as Examples", *Journal of China Rural Observation*, No. 3, 2009.

Normative land property right transaction organizations came into existence as a matter of course as China's rural land transfer system matured as one type in the framework of China's multi-symbiotic rural economic organizations. After the reform and opening-up, the normative land property right transaction organizations developed rapidly from scratch. According to statistics, as of the first half of 2011, more than 800 counties (cities) and more than 12,000 townships and towns in China had established centers for land contractual operational right transfer services.

Market-oriented and normative land transfer transactions gradually become the main form of rural land transfers. Meanwhile, in some large and medium-sized cities such as Wuhan and Chongqing, the scope of the rural land property right transactions transcended that of peasant household land contractual right transactions to a broader space of land such as homesteads and the collectively owned land of rural economic organizations such as the four types of wasteland (barren mountains, gullies, hills and beaches) and collective forestry. Moreover, it also extended to a wide range of property rights such as rural collective economic organization equity and agricultural intellectual property rights. Chongqing even created land use indexes.

[Case 5.2] Wuhan Rural Comprehensive Property Exchange

Wuhan Rural Comprehensive Property Exchange (WRCPE) listed on April 30, 2009 is the first rural property exchange established in central China and the third in China after the first two set up in Chengdu and Chongqing.

The original intention of erecting WRCPE was to release the rural economic resources and various production factors in rural areas in order to marketize the factors, especially to change into money land operational rights and peasants' largest resources at their disposal, so as to increase their property incomes.

The products currently traded cover nine categories including rural land contractual operational rights, the use rights of four types of wasteland possessed by rural collective economic organizations, the aquaculture contracting operational rights of rural collective economic organizations, the use rights and ownership of rural collective forestry, agricultural intellectual property rights, rural collective economic organization equity, rural housing ownership, the use rights of rural idle homesteads and the use rights of agricultural production facilities.

WRCPE implements a "six unifications" regulation model. It covers unifications in transaction planning, transaction verification, information release, charging standards, supervision and administration, and platform improvement. They constitute the regulative system of rural property right transaction markets supervised by Wuhan Municipal Property Rights Transaction Supervision and Administration Committee. In order to regulate transactions, WRCPE has formulated 11 rules and regulations such as "Wuhan Rural Property Right Transaction Regulations (Trial)" and "Transaction Rules", and standardized more than 20 specific transaction rules.

In order to effectively protect peasants' land contractual rights, WRCPE stipulates that land operational right transactions and mortgages must be made according to the basic principles of peasants' willingness. When handling the transactions, WRCPE strictly follows the procedures and regulates the transaction contracts. If the enterprise that has purchased the land operational right plans to mortgage the right, it must obtain the consent of its original owner of the land contractual right and the land operational right before it finally signs a written contract. Simultaneously, WRCPE issues the transaction prices of land operational rights so that peasants can obtain reasonable revenues when they transfer their land operational rights. This not only regulates the mortgage but also avoids risks such as going against peasants' wishes, harming their interests, and guards them from loss of land and changes in agricultural land use, etc.

By the end of 2010, WRCPE had organized 526 transactions involving rural land contractual and operational rights amounting to RMB3.818 billion, involving 493,500 mu and 140,000 peasant households.

[Case 5.3] Chongqing's Reforms in the Rights of Using Urban and Rural Land and Land Ticket Transactions

Chongqing is the municipality with the largest area, the largest population and the clearest urban–rural economic structure in China. It is one of the pioneering experimental areas for the reform of urban and rural integrated planning, and established the first rural land exchange in the country guided by the principle of "urban and rural overall planning", initiated a new measure of "land ticket transaction" and launched the reform in the right of using urban and rural land with the same right, at the same price and in the same city.

Chongqing Rural Land Exchange (CRLE) practices the operation model of combining the "real" and the "virtual", that is, the combination of "four physicals" and "one virtual". The former refers to the transfer of four types of physical asset contractual and operational rights or use rights. They are the transfer of contractual and operational rights for agricultural production land, the transfer of contractual and operational rights or use rights for forestry land, the transfer of the right to use rural collective construction land such as peasants' homesteads, township and village enterprises' land, public facilities and infrastructure land and the transfer of the right of using rural unused land such as the four types of wasteland and their contractual and operational rights. The "virtual" refers to the "land ticket", that is, the transfer of the quotas of land use and is the most creative.

The so-called "land ticket" refers to the land use index generated after re-cultivation and land administration departments' rigorous inspection and examination of the rural collective construction land including rural homesteads and land for their ancillary facilities, township and village enterprises, rural public facilities and rural public welfares. Due to China's strict arable land protection system, there are strict index restrictions of industrial and other construction land, which makes land use indexes a very rare resource.

The "land ticket" transaction is essentially a market-based transaction of a land use index, and the ticket is an innovation which optimizes the allocation of urban and rural land resources under the constraints of the current system. Huang Qifan, then a member of the Standing Committee of Chongqing Municipal Committee and executive deputy mayor, summarized four points on the significance and role of the "land ticket" transaction.

First of all, the increase in urban construction land relates to the reduction of rural construction land. The total sum of urban and rural construction land does not increase and the total sum of arable land does not decrease. Compared with the existing "occupying construction land before converting construction land to arable land" model, the land quota transaction system is characterized with "cultivating land before using it". After converting rural construction land to arable land, new construction land will increase in cities, which will more forcibly and effectively protect arable land. On the one hand, rural idle land resources are re-cultivated in an orderly manner in accordance with the law, which solves the problem of waste rural construction land. On the other hand, the increase in urban construction land in well-paced proportion dissolves the shortage of urban construction land while the total sum of urban and rural construction land does not increase and the total sum of arable land does not decrease.

Secondly, public transfers of land completed at land exchanges in the form of land quotas make possible long-distance, large-scale exchanges of rural collective construction land, improve the value of land in rural areas, especially in remote rural areas so that urban areas may help rural areas and developed areas push the development of backward areas.

In addition, "land ticket" transactions are conducted in accordance with the national land system and protect peasants' rights for land possession, use and profits lawfully. The transactions do not change land ownership, or the current land system, and what's more, they blend the interests of the state, the collective and the peasants.

Last but not least, the transactions activate urban and rural factor markets and improve the urban and rural market systems. After the establishment of land exchanges, the long-distance and large-scale optimization of land resources converts the solidified land resources into movable capital.

According to statistics, between December 4, 2008 when CRLE was established and May 2010, 85 "land ticket" transactions were made, totaling 18,000 mu, with a turnover of RMB1.865 billion at an average transaction price of RMB103,600 per mu.

5.8 Industrialized Agriculture: A Radical but Cautious Transformation of SF

Judging from the transactions at centers for standardized rural land property right transactions in large and medium-sized cities, the demands far outnumber the supplies. They are chiefly made by various agricultural companies and industrial and commercial companies engaged in agricultural development (making investments in agriculture), which demand large patches of land. Although the land transferred concerns the four types of wastelands and collectively owned land including shared cultivated land, woodland, grassland and water surface of village collective ownership, the contracted land of peasant households makes up a greater percentage. For example, it accounts for 80% of the land transacted at WRCPE.

Excluding those cases of illegal use of agricultural land (such as real-estate development) in which agricultural land was converted to non-agricultural land, obtaining the operational rights of the transferred land by various agricultural companies is often followed up by large-scale, standardized land remediation for large-scale agricultural operations. A considerable part of the peasants who transfer their land become agricultural workers employed by the companies. Agriculture gets industrialized as the agricultural land is transformed into an agricultural workshop, the peasants become agricultural workers. This finds expression in a political term that many local government officials tend to use, "applying industrial thinking to big agriculture".

In terms of the main agricultural operational force, small peasants seem to have been eliminated in industrialized agriculture, that is, peasant households are no longer the *de facto* agricultural operational force. However, there are still some essential differences between the marketized and industrialized "elimination of small peasants" and the traditional elimination of small peasants by collectivizing them. Here are the distinctions.

They first differ in that peasant households are still the main owners of land contractual rights, with which they can obtain rental revenues from their land. The second distinction is that the transfer merely involves land operational rights of a certain period of time (within the contract period) rather than permanently. Therefore, they are entitled to "enter" and "exit", which means they are likely to become the main force of land operations, that is, become small peasants again. Finally, it is simply up to them to decide whether or not to become agricultural workers and agricultural companies are not entitled to force them to. The fact is that quite a lot of peasants who transfer their land operational rights do not become agricultural workers. In contrast, the people's commune-style of collectively eliminating small peasants was to use the administrative coercive means to permanently lock the peasants into membership of collective organizations, and completely eliminate them institutionally.

[Case 5.4] Agricultural Land Becomes Agricultural Workshops

Rows of greenhouses are like white oceans intersected with rows of cement roads in the fields with various facilities available such as irrigation sprinklers. This is what comes into view at Zhengxin Agricultural Science and Technology Park in Xinqiao Village, Haimen City, Jiangsu Province. Here fields have become standardized agricultural production workshops.

The park was established by Shanghai businessmen who invested RMB30 million in it. Now there are two fresh-keeping warehouses and 500 mu of distinctive vegetables are grown. The park has rent land from peasants' at a fixed rent per mu and peasants who lease the land are allowed to work with the company. According to a leader of Xinqiao Village, the pays that they get from the park range from RMB30 to RMB50 per day according to the labor intensity. The pays of the villagers who earn the most reach over RMB8,000 annually. A women villager Ms Qian, aged over 70, told reporters that since 2007, she had been doing odd jobs in the park and earned more than RMB5,000 in 2009.

—*Haimen Daily*, August 18, 2009

"Industrial and commercial capital invested in agriculture" is born with an inherent profit-seeking motive. The Fuwa Model of Jianli in Hubei Province expounded in the previous chapter has proved that modern agriculture in the whole industrial chain can grow into a profitable and strong industry. Other information concerned shows that supposing the purchase price of corn is RMB1,500 per ton, RMB500 more per ton will be obtained if the corn is processed into corn starch, RMB1,500 more if processed into corn juice and RMB2,500 more into protein powder. Therefore, the profit rate will be much higher than the national average profit rate of 5.47% of industrial enterprises in 2009. In addition, in recent years, with the government's barrages of preferential policies in favor of leading industrialized agricultural enterprises, industrial and commercial capital has much passion for expanding their fields into agriculture and rural areas.[45]

The policy of industrial and commercial capital invested in agriculture is very popular with local governments at all levels in that it makes up for the insufficiency of local governments' investments in agriculture and investment promotion is an important factor in the performance evaluation of the governments. Therefore, such investments enjoy many local governments' preferential policies applicable locally, including governments' land lease (the company that rents the land may keep its operational right for the length of time designated in the contract), or land transfers organized or coordinated by governments.

[45]Another major stimulus for the expansion is the cheap "enclosure" of land for real estate development. Since such an operation is mostly illegal and an issue of different nature, it will not be discussed in detail in this book.

Objectively speaking, there are some cases where this financial policy of transforming peasants into agricultural workers does work or work fairly well throughout the country. If the policy can indeed increase peasants' incomes and the increase is sustainable, they will be willing to adopt it. For example, some peasants in Jianli, Hubei Province, lease their land to Fuwa Company and worked as agricultural workers on its base. They calculate that from their leased land, they each can get per mu annually RMB680 revenues, RMB100 policy subsidies, and a pay translated into RMB480. In this way, the annual revenue from per mu is nearly RMB1,300 and in addition, it is labor-saving, risk-free and more cost-effective than farming.

Nevertheless, in spite of its advantages, this policy has been proved to have given rise to uncertainties and greater risks. However, the biggest risk is that if the company fails to operate, there will be a series of inevitable delicate problems. For instance, some companies used leased peasants-contracted land as a collateral for loans and their operational failure generated extremely complicated debt disputes. The land remediation projects left half-finished after the operational failures of some companies would take much money whether it was to return the land to its original state or would continue to remedy it, otherwise it would be difficult to proceed. Those who leased land to the company would find themselves in an embarrassing situation of receiving no rents nor any pays, and being incapable of getting back their land. A good case in point is the horrible situation in which the peasants in Qujiawan, Honghu Lake, Hubei Province, found themselves after the failure of the "Lantian Model" mentioned in Case 5.5. They handed over their land, fish ponds and even their houses to the company, and proudly became workers with it with monthly salaries. When the company went bankrupt suddenly, the peasants lost jobs, land and salaries.

Another more common phenomenon after the implementation of the financial policy is that some larger companies rent large areas of agricultural land in order to get plenty of land resources. With the assistance of local governments they demolish old villages to build new concentrated ones to obtain peasants' homesteads. After this large-scale old village-demolition, even if the peasants move into new houses before the company goes bankrupt, as is the case with Honghujiajiawan or put it another way, even if they can move into new houses, the overall costs of living for them will rise substantially.

If companies can provide new houses and new buildings as well as stable employment opportunities and salaries so that they can live a life of higher quality (with roads built, and water, electricity and internet available), most peasants will be pleased with it as a matter of course. However, if companies fail to operate, the peasants' employment will not be guaranteed, or the peasants' incomes will not be high enough, the increase in the costs of living in the new village buildings will affect their' living quality. Chen Xiwen made a very pertinent comment on this.

> This year on New Year's Day, General Secretary Xi Jinping went to a new village for investigations. The town and the city governments helped it to run a business. A company demolished all the houses in the village and funded its rectification flattening 500 mu of land including all the roads, pits and ponds within the entire village. The company allocated 140 mu of it to build a new village for the peasants. The beautifully built village is composed of identical two-storied townhouses equipped with heating, gas and tap water. The front and back yards with cement floors are adjacent to asphalt roads. The general secretary spent more than 20 minutes in the house of a four-generation family. The two-storied house is more than 180 square meter large and the family has two tractors. They live a life better than most urban residents. The general secretary talked happily with the family members.
>
> While taking his farewell, the general secretary told the old peasant, "I am pleased to see that you live in such a gorgeous house!" and added, "I have a question to ask and you please be truthful. I have just moved around your house. You no longer have any vegetable plot, neither do you have any open field to raise chickens and ducks. Since you moved into the new home, have the costs of living significantly increased?" It took the old man a long time to make sense of it. Then he replied, "You are so caring about us. But after moving in, even drinking water is not free anymore."
>
> The traditional village did not look good, but the peripheries of villages, the small patches around the fields and the courtyards were all places where the villagers could create wealth and make their living but now it is no longer the case. The old man was very happy to live in his townhouse. But

after he began to live in it, he realized that his actual incomes were reduced dramatically. How to solve such a problem? If there are new employment opportunities and higher incomes, this problem will be easy to solve. Otherwise it will be very troublesome.

All in all, that industrial and commercial capital is invested in agriculture transforms family farming into factory farming, arable land into agricultural workshops and peasants into agricultural workers. Especially in terms of the large scale demolition and new village construction, it is a radical agricultural land transfer approach as well as a radical SF-transforming approach. There are some successful or relatively successful cases but failures are commonplace. And the resultant troubles, especially the harm to the peasants, cannot be dissolved in a short period of time. Therefore, it is necessary to be cautious and prudent and advances such as the "great leap forward" should not be blindly promoted.

After a further analysis, it is found that industrialized "SF" may not necessarily enhance the feasibility of achieving substantial freedom. Of course, the author does not absolutely reject this kind of industrialized agriculture, but the primary premise is that "it is a matter of course", that is, it is the real demand of inherent economic development and the free choice of peasants.

[Case 5.5] The Failure of the Lantian Model in Qujiawan

Qujiawan is a remote township in Honghu City, Hubei Province. It was the center of the West Hunan–Hubei Revolutionary Base during the Second Revolutionary War. In 1994, the annual income per capita was less than RMB650 and it was one of the 21 most poverty-stricken old revolutionary-base townships in Hubei and one of the six poorest townships in the province.

In 1993, the party committee and the government of Qujiawan Township organized a special team to attract investments from all over the country. Qu Zhaoyu, president of Shenyang Lantian Company (LC), decided to come back to Qujiawan, his native place, and invest RMB5,000,000 in the construction of a refrigerating processing base there. In 1996, LC was listed and renowned as "the first stock of agriculture". Its headquarters moved from Shenyang to Honghu. Its main business converted to the cultivation, processing and sales of agricultural, sideline and aquatic products.

After 1998, under the impetus of Honghu Municipal Government and Qujiawan Township Government, Qujiawan Village successively transferred its land to the company on a large scale by means of "shareholding the joint venture" and cooperative development. The company paid 30% of its profits as land dividends to the village collective and had all the villagers work in the company. Meanwhile, with the help of the local government, the company carried out a large-scale demolition of villages to build a town for the villagers. In August 1999, Hubei Province held the "Symposium on Key Leading Industrialized Agricultural Enterprises in Hubei Province and Rural Policies" in Lantian Honghu Base to promote the "Lantian Model" in the whole province.

Chen Yongxian is a peasant of the seventh group of Chenwan Village, Qujiawan Township. His family contracted six mu of land and fish ponds, from which his family earned an annual net income of more than RMB4,000. After the land and the ponds were requisitioned by LC, he and his wife began to work with the company, earning a monthly income of over RMB1,000 altogether. In addition, they had to move out of the old house where they had lived for generations, and built a new house at a designated place in accordance with Lantian's unified town-building plan.

A cadre from Qujiawan Township recalled that the land requisition had not been easy. Many peasants were worried that they would lose their livelihood guarantee if the company requisitioned their land, fish ponds and houses. Therefore, many people did not buy the idea. In order to persuade them, the town cadres harvested the rape for them and sent the rapeseeds to their homes. Finally, under Lantian's financial temptations and the government's convictions, they had no choice but to surrender their land, fish ponds and houses to the company.

However, good times do not last. In Jan. 2002, due to fabricating profits, three senior executives of the Board of Directors, Bao Tian, chairman of the Board of Eco-Agriculture (formerly Lantian Joint Stock), Li Hongfu, director and financial controller, and, Wang Yiling, secretary of the board, were arrested by the public security organ for custody investigation. Qu Zhaoyu, president of China Lantian Corporation and former chairman of Lantian Joint Stock, was summoned from Beijing to Hubei for investigation. Lantian's core enterprise, Honghu Lantian Aquatic Products Development Co., Ltd. was paralyzed instantaneously.

It happened on the eve of the Spring Festival as a sudden and violent storm, which triggered an "earthquake" in Qujiawan. Xie Junsong, the concurrent mayor of Qujiawan Township, revealed that the news came like a bolt from the blue. Just a few years before, peasants had been talked into handing over their land and fish ponds to LC for unified operations. Thousands of peasants subsequently entered LC and became its workers. Now, if I suddenly tell them that something has gone wrong with it and they will get no salary, how can I explicate it to them?

"Since September last year, we have got no salaries. Even now, the company still owes me more than RMB3,000." Chen Yongxian complained. His greatest dissatisfaction with LC was that it had forced them to move out for a new town and new houses. "I didn't want to build a new house but the company took away my land by force. They promised each household RMB30,000 as house-building subsidies, but in the end it only gave me

RMB10,000, which could merely cover half of the building expenses, so I had to borrow upon usury to complete it. When the house was completed with much difficulty, there was no water nor electricity available, so we simply could not live in it."

Chen was not the most unfortunate. The street behind his house was called "Sad Street" by the peasants. The houses on either side, nearly 100, stayed simply uncompleted. Wood, plastic sheets, bamboo sheets and newspapers were utilized to block wind from all sides. As the old houses were demolished and there was no money to complete the new ones, some peasants lived in relatives' homes and some made it to live in uncompleted new ones. It was in rainy summer, and inside them raindrops ticked away. House-owners had to use basins, buckets and other utensils to hold rain from flooding the floors. According to a survey, most peasant households only got RMB5,000 from the company as house-building subsidies.

Due to the destruction of the irrigation canal and the original operational pattern, more than 1,700 mu of land requisitioned by LC was not re-cultivatable, and the four villages and two fisheries closely connected with LC involved a total of 1,336 households and 5,459 peasants who became jobless. They could neither go farming nor fishing. Even minimum living standards could not be guaranteed. LC had promised to subsidize RMB30,000 for each of the 1,665 peasant households which would vacate the land. A greater part of the subsidies were not paid. The houses of more than 100 households had not yet been completed, and some had just begun to have the foundation built. Nearly 7,000 workers of the company had not been paid for three to five months, and the payments for 24 infrastructure projects had not been settled. Nearly 1,500 migrant workers had not got wages. When the author and the research team members visited Qujiawan again in 2009, they still saw large patches of "uncompleted buildings".

The Lantian Storm triggered off a great shock and social unrest followed by such a burst of various complicated conflicts that the departments involved of the local party committees and governments had to exert their uttermost to clean up the mess.

In order to properly handle the Lantian problem, Hubei provincial government, Jingzhou and Honghu municipal governments sent investigative teams to Qujiawan. The Spring Festival was drawing near and in order to solve the problem that the workers had no money for the festival and to maintain social stability, the provincial and Jingzhou municipal governments allocated RMB6,000,000 and the company borrowed RMB3,000,000 to pay part of the arrears wages to the workers. And the civil affairs department allocated rice worth RMB50,000 and distributed it among the households.

After researches and investigations, the investigative teams decided to return to the workers the contracted fields and fish ponds whose operational patterns had not been completely broken, and contract to them the farmland and fish ponds remedied by the company at great expenses.

However, it was difficult to restore the land to the original state. The prime days of the company covered up the conflicts regarding land between the company and the surrounding village groups, capital and labour, and the disputes between the company and the surrounding counties and townships about waters and resources. After the "Lantian Storm", various conflicts such as water disputes, property rights, and fish pond recovery broke out unanimously, the pattern of people's interests needed re-adjusting and social order tended to fluctuate. Incidents of the masses besieging the local government and the company were not rare, and theft, looting and damage to the company's properties, though prohibited time and again, were fairly commonplace.

—This case is mainly based on "Honghu Qujiawan Township after the 'Lantian Storm'" by Chen Xinzhou and Li Changzheng (*Xinhua News Agency*, July 24, 2002) and the findings of the survey of Qujiawan Township in September 2009 by the author and his research team members

Different from turning arable land into agricultural workshops and turning peasants into agricultural workers, another approach is that after a large-scale, contiguous lease to the company of peasants' land for development and remediation, the agricultural company in turn leases the land to the peasants, and requires of them normative and standardized production. Here, the peasants are still the main productive force, whose autonomy of production is limited, that is, production is compelled to be carried out under the company's norms and guidance.

More importantly, under these circumstances, the peasants play a double translocation role. Initially the peasants lease the land operational right (contracting right) to the company with the peasants as lessors and the company as lessee. Afterwards, the company in turn leases the use or operational rights of the land that it has developed and remedied to the peasants with the company as the lessor and the peasants as the lessees.

It must be pointed out that the peasants might get the operational right of the land whose original contracting right they have transferred to the company, but more often than not it is not the case. In general, the scale of peasant households' operational land expands. This is because some of the peasants who have transferred their land do not contract land in the second round because they go out to work or do business, and after the companies' large-scale land development and remediation, the actual arable area expands. For example, in Xiliang Village, Shawan County to be mentioned in Case 5.6, the original 640 mu of land was expanded to 700 mu after extensive remediation, and the arable area increased by nearly 10%. In addition, large-scale remediation improves the quality of the arable land.

In real life, peasants' specialized cooperatives and rural community collective economic organizations play an important role in this lease-to-rent model. In some places, peasants first transfer their land contracting rights to village collectives or peasants' specialized cooperatives, which in turn lease them to agricultural companies. In some places, peasants' specialized cooperatives play the role of agricultural companies engaging in large-scale land remediation and development. In general, large agricultural companies do not favor direct transactions with peasant households on a one-to-one basis. The intermediation of village committees or peasants' specialized cooperatives is the best choice for agricultural companies to reduce transaction costs.

[Case 5.6] Contracting One Piece of Land and Getting Three Sources of Incomes — "Lease to Rent" that Increases Peasants' Incomes

"It is great to get two sources of incomes with the land transferred to an agricultural company," said excitedly Ke Changde, a villager from Xiliang Village, Shanghudi Township, Shawan County.

At the beginning of a year, Ke transferred his 33 mu of land at the price of RMB370 per mu to Shawan County Tunhe Tomato Sauce Factory which cultivates Heinz high-yield tomatoes to be harvested by machinery. The company paid Ke RMB145 per mu for field care. In early June, he helped the company to spray pesticide on 700 mu of tomatoes at the price of RMB2.5 per mu. So far, he has earned RMB25,000 from the company.

This year, Xiliang Village has adopted a land-patching-based operational planting mode. Under the initiative guidance of the township party committee and the township government, the village committee organized the transfer of the 700 mu of land from 21 peasant households in the village to an enterprise to apply the "lease to rent approach". It is found that the 700 mu was the village committee's expansion of the original 640 mu by eliminating some paths in the fields, greatly enhancing land utilization.

—Shawan County Government Network, August 24, 2009

5.9 A Feasible Way of a Marketized Transformation of SF: The Specialization of Agricultural Production Links Plus Scale Operations

A scale agricultural operation should include two meanings. First, the land operated by a single agricultural operation entity is large enough. Secondly, its agricultural production links are extensive enough. The two are related but not identical. In China, people pay more attention to the former. However, based on SF economy, the latter may be more important. With constraints in terms of designated resources and systems in China, the specialization of agricultural production links and their scale operations are also vital to the marketized transformation of SF.

As aforementioned, one essential distinction between marketized SF and self-sufficient SF lies in how dependent they are on market-oriented and socialized service networks. In terms of agricultural production, pre-production, in-production and post-production constitute a complete production chain. In a traditional agricultural society, the chain is basically operated independently and closed by individual peasant households. However, in a modern society, the division of labor concerns every production link, which means that every production link is likely to develop into an independent production sector. Obviously, it is necessary for an independent production sector to break through the operating restrictions of individual peasant households and serve multitudes of peasant households, conducting scale operations. Otherwise, it will generate no benefits nor can it survive.

Adam Smith long ago expounded on the impact of the specialization of agricultural production links on labor efficiency. In the opening of *An Inquiry into the Nature and Causes of the Wealth of Nations*, Smith used the pin manufacturing industry as an example to illustrate how the division of labor and factories' specialization of production links promoted the growth of labor productivity. He held that the "increase is owing to three circumstances: first, to the increase of dexterity in every particular workman; secondly, to the saving of the time which is commonly lost in passing from one species of work to another; and lastly, to the invention of a great number of machines which facilitate and abridge labor, and enable one man to do the work of many."[46] Therefore, why increase in agricultural productivity cannot keep pace with that in manufacturing may be that agriculture does not adopt a system of complete division of labor.[47]

[46] Smith, A. *An Inquiry into the Nature and Causes of the Wealth of Nations*, Vol. 1. Oxford: Clarendon Press, 1880.
[47] *Ibid.*

One of the fundamental differences between modern agriculture and traditional agriculture is that there are also a division of labor and specialized operation in production links in modern agriculture. As Smith said, "What is the work of one man in a rude state of society is generally that of several in an improved one."[48] This suggests that the ploughman, the harrower, the sower of the seed, and the reaper of the corn are often not the same person but different specialized people. The more developed modern agriculture is, the more developed the division of labor and specialized operations are in production links.

As Smith pointed out, the degree of division of labor is subject to exchange capacity and the size of the market. The reason why traditional SF economy cannot achieve division of labor and specialization in production links is that there is no such market demand in society. Conversely, modern SF economy achieves division of labor and specialized operations in production links due to such market demands of modern SF.

In China, as the land contracted by each peasant household is limited, there is a surplus of agricultural labor force. In this case, why should they subcontract production to others and buy their labor services? Won't they get idler as a result? The superficial formal logic is inadequate to address this issue, and so it is necessary to address it in terms of the profound changes that have taken place in China's rural areas.

From a macro perspective, China's super-large-scale migration of agricultural labor force enables a great part of the labor force of peasant households who have contracted land to be devoted to something other than agriculture, or chiefly concerned with something other than agriculture. If they do not transfer their land, they will have the actual and potential needs to purchase specialized services. It should be noted that "marketized SF households" are also rational (of course, this rationality is limited), since they tend to compare costs and profits instinctively. As long as the benefits from their non-agricultural work outweigh those from their agricultural production, they will be intrinsically motivated to purchase the services rather than do agricultural work "concurrently".

Taking into account land transfer, those households with a large area of arable land such as large grain growers simply cannot cultivate it fully on

---

[48] *Ibid.*

their own steam, and therefore, they also need to purchase the services. Meanwhile, due to the use of specialized machinery and equipment, and the specialized skills of the workers, some specialized services for agricultural production links improve the specialized production, or reduce costs. They are chiefly accountable for the demands for division of labor as well as specialized operations in the agricultural production links. For instance, in Jianli, Hubei Province, peasant households spend nearly RMB300 per mu cultivating seedlings themselves and having them transplanted. However, if they hire a specialized cooperative that has its own seedlings-cultivating factory with its own series of services ranging from seedlings-cultivation, machine insertion to offering instructions in the late period, they just need to spend a little over RMB200, saving RMB60–80 per mu. Moreover, the seedlings-cultivation done by the cooperative is superior and the machine insertion outdoes manual transplanting with a yield increase by about 50 kg per mu.

Judging from the practice across the country, the division of labor and specialized operations concerning the agricultural production links in China are still at an early stage on the whole. This is in line with China's overall process of marketizing SF. As far as food planting and growing industry is concerned, the specialized operations of seeding-cultivating, sowing (planting), harvesting and plant protection have developed rapidly. However, there is still a great potential and room for development in the division of labor and specialized operation in China's agricultural production links.

[Case 5.7] Specialized Outsourcing "in Pest Prevention and Control is Popular in Rural Hunan"

"In the past, we peasants prevented pests and diseases ourselves and none of us were well-acquainted with what medicine to utilize. This year, we are lucky to have "machine prevention teams" engaging in contracted drugs spraying. This both saves us much money and increases yields," Liu Dahui, a villager from Tongxinba Village, Deqiao Town, Dingcheng District, Changde City, Hunan Province, told a reporter in his field.

The reporter recently found at interviews conducted in the countryside in Hunan that "outsourcing" of pests and diseases prevention and control to specialized teams as Liu informed is beginning to gain popularity. According to Cheng Haibo, director of Hunan Provincial Department of Agriculture, more than 1,000 diversified pest and disease prevention and control services have been established throughout Hunan, involving over 12,000 specialized employees and over 3 million mu.

The reporter learned in Tongxinba Village that Changde Bangda Company engaged in pesticide business has set up a specialized plant protection station in the village. With advanced equipment and specialized employees, it provides full-course contracting services for specialized pests and diseases prevention and control. Its greatest advantages are to reduce costs and improve prevention and control by means of a scientific use of medicine. "Last year, the money we spent on pesticide for two seasons of rice was nearly RMB 200 per mu. However, this year, after contracting the prevention and control to the team, the cost is merely RMB90. The pesticide alone has saved us about RMB100 per mu, and if we suffer any loss, the company will compensate for it as written in the contract we have signed with the team. Therefore, it is a sure good bargain," said a villager Xie Ziqing.

This year, 514 mu of early rice in Tongxinba Village was involved in such services. According to calculations, the average yield per mu is 450 kg due to effective prevention and control, 50 kg more than the average yield of the land not involved. As a result, more late rice growers are willing to buy the services and the land involved now amounts to 1,108 mu. A leader of the company reveals that with peasants' increasing approval, the contracted area of the company has increased from three to four thousand mu last year to more than 80,000 mu this year.

At present, there are various service modes such as contracting by enterprises, agricultural technology stations and plant protection departments across Hunan. According to Li Yiping, an expert on plant protection in Hunan, some peasants in China have been long practicing "blind" pests and diseases prevention and control leading to a host of problems such as wrong selection of drugs, excessive use of them, mixed use of multiple drugs and discarding wastes as they please, for example. What's worse, the rural areas are generally farmed by the elderly and children, which results in poor prevention and control, increases the cost and affects the safety of produces and the ecological environment. Therefore, exploring the services of specialized prevention and control is of great significance.

—Ding Wenjie, *Xinhuanet*, August 10, 2008

[Case 5.8] Field-Sitters in Zongyang County, Anhui Province

In recent years, in the rural areas of Zongyang County, there have emerged multitudes of agricultural laborers, who provide field operation services for peasant households as an occupation. They mainly focus on the production needs of large grain growers and labor-insufficient households, giving them services of providing seeds, field care and harvesting, hence "field-sitters".

After household land contracted operation was practiced in rural areas, help among households was very commonplace, but it was confined to relatives, mainly in the form of exchange of labor. If one helped others to transplant one day, some day the latter would return the favor by harvesting rice for the household, for example. There was no need to pay for the labor, which is a typical mutual aid.

In recent years, "field-sitting" mutual aid here is a way in which market economy extensively permeates the countryside and the allocation of rural labor resources is market-oriented. Such an aid is fundamentally different from the former mutual aid in various ways.

First of all, "field-sitting" is clearly priced. Transplanting, spraying and harvesting are charged per mu, the fees ranging from RMB30 to RMB100. High fees rest with great labor intensity. For example, manual rice-harvesting (including placing the harvest into the warehouse) is charged RMB100 per mu. In this way, a "field-sitter" can earn about RMB50 daily and the annual income may reach RMB5,000–8,000.

Secondly, "field-sitters" work in groups. Since it is usually the big growers with hundreds or thousands of mu of land each who need such help, one project of field work will take tens of people to work simultaneously and therefore, field-sitters seldom work alone. A group leader (who plays the role somewhat similar to that of a contractor in construction industry) will be responsible for the negotiations about the fees and the required number of laborers before they begin to work as a team. At present, there is a field-sitting force of about 30,000 people in Zongyang County, forming more than 600 working teams whose members are bound together geographically or through kinship. The average number of a team is about 50 people. There is one or two such teams in each village of Qilin town of the county.

In addition, "field-sitting" mechanisms are flexible. The teams will go where they have business. They may even go out of their village, their township or even their county. It depends mainly on where big growers need laborers and where the contract signed by the team leader leads them. Numerous big growers from Chenyaohu Town and other places in Zongyang County have contracted land for rice-growing in other provinces and cities and that is why some teams even go all the way to work in Jiangsu, Zhejiang and other provinces.

—Based on reports on *Anhui Daily*

[Case 5.9] Grass-Cutting Households in Hulunbuir, Inner Mongolia

August and September are the grass-cutting periods in the Hulunbuir Prairie, Inner Mongolia. Herdsmen will prepare grass for cattle and sheep for the coming winter.

Grass-cutting used to be an arduous job. It was completed manually in the four procedures of hitting, smashing, stacking, and slapping with a scythe. Nowadays, grass-cutting there is generally done by machinery such as mowers, grass-gatherers and balers.

The author came to the Hulunbuir Prairie in Aug. 2011 and saw the mechanized grass-cutting and specialized grass-cutters. On a prairie in Erguna, the author had a short conversation with such a grass-cutter during his break.

Mr. Chen, about 40 years old, hails from a pastoral area in Baotou City. He told me that his household had got governmental machinery subsidies and spent about RMB200,000 purchasing all the tractors, mowers, grass-gatherers and balers. It wouldn't pay off if they were only used for the 200 mu of grassland that he had contracted and therefore he mainly used them to make a living by machine grass-cutting for other households. This year, it is dry in Baotou and the growth of grass suffers as a result. In contrast, there are abundant water resources, lush grasslands and great demands for grass-cutting in Hulunbeier. Piece wage is practiced for grass-cutting, RMB20 per bale. He can manage 80–100 bales a day, with a gross income of RMB1,600–2,000. Excluding fuel consumptions, accommodations, and meals, the net income is about RMB1,200 a day. The grassing season lasts about two months, and therefore, he can earn RMB80,000–100,000 annually. The purchase cost can be recovered in two to three years, but the two months is a trying period.

The Hulunbuir Prairie boasting of vast grasslands, is one of the four largest prairies in the world. The area of grasslands contracted by each herdsman household is more than 500 mu, and it is not uncommon for one household to contract thousands of mu. Many herdsmen tend to cut more grass for winter for their livestock and sell the surplus at RMB200 per bale in the market. Therefore, some herdsmen engage in growing "commodity grass" and get rich by selling it.

5.10 Can Agricultural Mechanization be Advanced on the Basis of Peasant Household Economy?

Agricultural mechanization is an integral part of agricultural modernization. After the implementation of China's rural household land-contracting system, agricultural mechanization progressed very slowly. Many researchers believed that it was hard for the small-scale operation of household contracted-land to be compatible with agricultural mechanization. In other words, the institutional arrangement of the rural household land-contracting system was not suitable for agricultural mechanization. Therefore, in order to promote agricultural mechanization, it was necessary to expand the scale of land operations and turn SF into big farming or collectivized agriculture. However, since the beginning of the 21st century, agricultural mechanization has made significant progress without fundamental changes in the household land-contracting system, which is the most basic institutional arrangement in rural areas. According to the authoritative data from the Agricultural Mechanization Regulation Department of the Ministry of Agriculture, by the end of 2009, the total agricultural machinery power in the country had reached 875,000,000 kw, with an average of 47.92 kw per 100 mu and 3.1 kw per agricultural laborer. The comprehensive mechanization level of plowing, planting and harvesting in China accounted for 49.13%. Among them, the comprehensive mechanization levels of the four staple food crops of wheat, rice, corn and soybeans were 89.37%, 55.33%, 60.24% and 68.68%, respectively.

This indicates that the agricultural machinery operation of the main staple crops exceeded manual operation, and mechanized production gradually gained a dominant position. Overall, since the beginning of the 21st century, China's agricultural mechanization has advanced from the initial to the intermediate stages.

It is traditionally thought that land concentration is the only way to realize agricultural mechanization and a powerful means to promote it. The small-scale operation of the household land-contracting system will hinder the application of advanced science and technology, especially agricultural machinery. Dong Hanying pointed out that agricultural mechanization "is not only the accumulation of machinery" and its development "depends to a certain extent on social conditions such as organizational management". Generally, economic and technological factors mainly influence the development of agricultural mechanization. At the same time, however, Dong also held that "the realization of agricultural mechanization requires a corresponding expansion of the scale of land operation, and they are in a mutually adaptative relationship."[49] Meng Fanqi and the research team of Study on a Moderate Scale of Farming Industry believed that small-scale rural production and operation are obstacles to agricultural mechanization. Therefore, "scale agricultural operation is a prerequisite for agricultural mechanization"[50]. Bai Yongxiu thought that small-scale land operation in China renders large-scale agricultural machinery useless and that it is difficult to improve mechanization.[51]

As agricultural mechanization develops on the basis of the household land-contracting system, some scholars criticize the idea that the expansion of land scale operation is a prerequisite for agricultural mechanization and explore approaches to agricultural mechanization from multiple perspectives. Yao Jianfu maintains that the degree of agricultural

[49]Dong, H. "Scale of Land Operation and Agricultural Mechanization", *China Rural Economy*, No. 8, 1986, pp. 50–53.

[50]Meng, Fanqi of the joint research group of "Study on a Moderate Scale of Farming Industry", "Issues of Developing Scale Agricultural Production and Operation", *Journal of China Rural Economy*, No. 1, 1987, pp. 26–31.

[51]Bai, Y. "Promote Moderate Scale Land Operation and Facilitate the Transformation of Economic Growth Mode", *Journal of Economic Reform*, No. 1, 1997.

mechanization depends on the specific conditions of a country or a region mainly including the country's demands for output, labor supplies, wage standards, land quantity and capital supplies. Land operation scale is not a necessary precondition.[52]

Liu Fengqin's research findings indicate with the development of rural economy have emerged a batch of peasant households engaging in "plowing, sowing and harvesting by agricultural machinery. They have increased the rate of agricultural mechanization, specialization and mobility of agricultural machinery. Liu contends that it is impossible to take a big pure mechanical farm-style agricultural development road under the current constraints in China. The existence of multitudes of small peasant households and their small-scale land operations do not hinder the development of agricultural mechanization."[53] Liu's point of view has in fact touched on the ways of realizing agricultural mechanization in a country like China, "which has a small land with a large population. Should the household land operational system be changed to adapt to the development of agricultural mechanization or *vice versa*?"

Furthermore, what are the criteria for the mechanization of agriculture which is essentially neither a simple accumulation of agricultural machinery nor the power of agricultural machinery, but rather the rate of agricultural machinery services that peasants are entitled to in all the agricultural production links. Or put it another way, it is the rate of the replacement of manpower with agricultural machinery in the links. In order to achieve this goal, households can purchase agricultural machinery by themselves and serve themselves within the family economic circle. They can also purchase specialized agricultural machinery services rather than purchase the machinery themselves and be agricultural machinery operators. In the

---

[52]Yao, J. "China's Agricultural Scale Operation and Agricultural Comprehensive Productivity — An Interview with Mr. Xu Xiaobai from Institute of Rural Development of University of Washington", *Journal of China's Agricultural Resources and Regional Planning*, Vol. 21, No. 5, 2000, pp. 19–21.

[53]Liu, F. "Study on the Scale of Agricultural Land Operation in China — A Case Study on Small-Scale land Operation", *Journal of Research on Financial and Economic Issues*, Vol. 239, No. 10, 2003. pp. 60–65. Liu, F. "Study on the Conditions and Effects of Scale Operation of Agricultural Land: Taking the Northeast Rural Area as an Example", *Journal of the Management World*, No. 9, 2006, pp. 71–81.

former case, the scale of household land operation is indeed a prerequisite for the adoption of agricultural mechanization. With a very small scale, the machine utilization rate is low, and so it is costly. However, the latter is more common in a specialized and marketized economy. The expansion of the scale of household land operation is conducive to the advancement of agricultural mechanization, but it is not a necessary condition. This means that agricultural mechanization can be carried out on the basis of decentralized small-scale household operations.

To examine the factors influencing agricultural mechanization, it is necessary to determine the criteria for it. Previous studies tend to reflect the level of agricultural mechanization through the indicators of the amount and power of agricultural machinery. However, as afore-mentioned, they are not the essential indicators. We will use the service rates of the agricultural machinery so that households can enjoy in all the links to represent the degree of agricultural mechanization. Taking into account the feasibility of acquiring the indicator, we will take a peasant household's expenditures on agricultural machinery services as a substitute indicator. It includes the total expenditures of a household for access to agricultural machinery services such as plowing, leveling and irrigation, and sowing, harvesting and transportation of crops. As for the agricultural machinery services provided by households themselves by purchasing agricultural machinery, we will monetize them according to the corresponding prices of marketized agricultural machinery services.

After the implementation of the household land-contracting system in rural areas in China, agricultural mechanization developed rapidly after a period of stagnation. Practice has proved that agricultural mechanization and the rural household land-contracting system are mutually compatible, which means that agricultural mechanization can be carried out within the institutional framework of the rural household land-contracting system. However, this entails the following fundamental changes. First of all, the goal of agricultural mechanization is not to pursue the amount of agricultural machinery owned by each peasant household, but to pursue a high service coverage rate of agricultural machinery in all the agricultural production links. Therefore, the promotion of agricultural mechanization should be chiefly based on specialized and marketized agricultural machinery services since what the vast majority of households need are specialized and marketized agricultural machinery services instead of purchasing the machinery themselves. This means that agricultural mechanization can be promoted through division of labor and specialization in all the links and the forces of specialized and marketized agricultural machinery services such as big agricultural machinery households, agricultural machinery production cooperatives and agricultural machinery leasing companies.

According to the authoritative data from the Agricultural Mechanization Regulation Department of the Ministry of Agriculture, by the end of 2009, the number of agricultural machinery households had reached 39.430 million (accounting for 15.35% of the total number of peasant households), of which 4.446 million engaged in specialized agricultural machinery operation services, making up for 11.33% of agricultural machinery households. There were 175,300 agricultural machinery operation services in the country employing 869,300 people. There were 14,902 specialized agricultural machinery cooperatives and 12,242 agricultural machinery operational services, each of which possessed an original value of agricultural machinery worth over RMB500,000. The total national revenues from agricultural mechanization services were RMB389.049 billion, of which RMB348.527 billion came from the total revenues of agricultural machinery households and the total revenues of agricultural machinery operational services amounted to RMB40.82 billion. The revenues from agricultural mechanization operation were RMB343.289 billion, accounting for 88.3% of the total revenues from agricultural mechanization services and operation. The inter-regional operation area of agricultural machinery reached 2,741.63 acres and the revenues reached RMB16.19 billion and the total profits from agricultural machinery operation was RMB14.634 billion.

[Case 5.10] Big Agricultural Machinery Owner Xiong Deyue from Yuanling

Xiong Deyue is a 35-year-old modern villager from Diping Group, Chiping Village, Lixi Township, Yuanling County, Hunan Province. With the party and the country's people-benefiting policies and scale land operations, her household has gradually turned out to be a big and leading wealthy agricultural machinery household with much machinery and comprehensive models of machinery in Yuanling County.

She is thought to be a very capable women in the eyes of the villagers in Lixi Township. In the past few years, she has spent altogether over RMB300,000 purchasing a

Shanghai New Holland SNH554 tractor equipped with a three-spade plow and a rotary tiller, a 4LZ – 1.8 double drum rapeseed combine harvester and a 4LZ-2.0 rice and oil dual-purpose combine harvester manufactured by Zhongji Nanfang Machinery Com. Ltd., two Fulaiwei 2Z-455 hand-held rice transplanters, a Huahui 3HH-36AP stretcher type motorized sprayer, a 3HH-15K frame type power sprayer, three modern agricultural 2BYF-6 rapeseed no-tillage direct seeding machine, a ride-on cultivator and a household mini rice machine.

In 2009, she adopted full mechanized operation, and contracted and operated 300 mu of rice fields, working on 1,500 mu of rice fields for others, including 600 mu of cross-regional rice fields. The total annual revenues from agricultural machinery operations reached more than RMB260,000, and the net revenues amounted to over RMB160,000.

—China Agricultural Mechanization Information Network, April 22, 2010

[Case 5.11] Modern Specialized Agricultural Machinery Cooperatives in Heilongjiang Province

Since 2008, ten modern specialized agricultural machinery cooperatives have been set up in Keshan, Baoqing, Mishan and the district of Ranghulu, Daqing City, Hailun, Bei'an, Fujin, Yilan, Bayan and Ning'an in Heilongjiang. They involve 85,600 peasants and 590,000 mu of arable land, 586,000 of which is under standardized operation with the degree of mechanization as high as 91%. The investments have reached RMB280 million and there are 76 large-horsepower tractors, 235 supporting agricultural tools, 83 harvesting machines and 10 pieces of plant protection machinery.

There are chiefly six types of cooperatives in Heilongjiang. The first type is cooperatives jointly initiated by townships and villages. The shares are distributed in terms of financial support funds, rural self-raised funds, capital in the form of machinery and peasants' investments.

The second is the integrated and upgraded cooperative whose founder is the former agricultural machinery cooperative, which sets up a new cooperative by integrating its assets, funds, talents and technologies. The shares are distributed according to financial support funds, the funds of the original agricultural machinery cooperative, investments in the form of machinery and peasants' investments.

The next is the big grower-dominated cooperative initiated by big grain growers and agricultural machinery owners, who invest more than 50% of the self-raised funds. The shares are composed of financial support funds, investments by big growers and machinery owners, and investments in the form of machinery.

The fourth is jointly initiated by villagers and the shares are composed of financial funds, peasants' investments and investments in the form of machinery.

Another type is the cooperative jointly initiated by office branches of reclamation areas and counties or farms and townships. The shares are composed of the investments by office branches of reclamation areas and counties or farms and townships, and investments in the form of machinery.

The sixth is the cooperative initiated by a leading enterprise, whose investments account for more than 50% of the self-raised funds. The shares consist of financial support funds, corporate investments, peasants' investments and investments in the form of land.

—"Investigation of the Pilot Project of Modern Specialized Agricultural Machinery Cooperatives in Heilongjiang Province", *China Agricultural Machinery Network*, March, 15, 2010.

[Case 5.12] Yanji Fumin Agricultural Machinery Leasing Co., Ltd. in Jilin Province

In October 2004, with a strong buttress from the Prefecture Agricultural Machinery Department, Yanji Bureau of Agricultural Machinery obtained a special national fund of RMB800,000 for agricultural machinery development, self-raised RMB500,000 and established Yanji Fumin Agricultural Machinery Leasing Co., Ltd. Now the company has over 50 large and medium-sized tractors, excavators, loaders, combine harvesters, tillage machines and seeding machines.

The establishment of the company has dissolved the shortage of rural laborers, reduced production costs, improved labor efficiency and is thus popular with peasants. Song Zhenbao, a peasant from Changsheng Village, Dongshengyong Township, Longjing City, said that he had contracted 7 acres of rice fields. Cutting, bundling, palletizing, transportation and threshing used to take at least a month but now it only takes three days. Manual harvesting costs RMB1,300 per acre but a combine harvester costs only RMB800–1000, saving RMB300–500. Cutting alone saves him more than RMB3,000. What's more, by using a combine harvester, a peasant can also grab the harvesting time and put new rice on the market 15–20 days earlier.

—*Yanbian Daily*, January 28, 2005

In addition, although the large-scale centralized operation of agricultural land is conducive to the advancement of agricultural mechanization, it is no prerequisite for it. Practice has proved so. Therefore, it is extremely dangerous to blindly use administrative means to promote agricultural mechanization through large-scale land transfers and land concentration with disregard to the basic national conditions of a great rural population and an insufficiency of land. That is to say, China's current focus is on how to promote agricultural mechanization on the basis of small-scale household land operation rather than change the basis in various ways to promote agricultural mechanization. Thirdly, a large-scale transfer of agricultural labor, a substantial increase in non-agricultural incomes of peasant households and the resulting increase in rural labor costs are among the decisive factors in pushing the replacement of manpower with agricultural machinery. Therefore, the promotion of the transfer of agricultural labor, the acceleration of national opening, the unification of labor markets and a substantial increase in the wages of laborers are extremely important to the acceleration of agricultural mechanization.

Finally, granted, agricultural mechanization must be chiefly driven by the internal forces of market mechanisms, but government policies are also of an irreplaceable importance. Therefore, in addition to the continued execution of various governmental policies such as agricultural machinery purchase subsidies and agricultural diesel subsidies conducive to the advancement of agricultural mechanization, it is necessary to further research new policies. It is of primary importance to study whether it is possible to provide peasant households with appropriate subsidies to purchase agricultural machinery services. Its distinguishing advantage is that it can encourage the specialized and marketized development of agricultural machinery services rather than the inefficient use of agricultural machinery caused by the purchase of agricultural machinery by all peasant households.

5.10.1 *Appendix: An empirical test to promote agricultural mechanization based on SF economy*[54]

In order to empirically test the various factors influencing agricultural mechanization on the basis of small-scale peasant household operations, our group organized a nation-wide rural survey by undergraduates and postgraduates from the College of Economics of Huazhong Normal University during the winter vacation in 2008. A total of 1,612 questionnaires were collected for this survey, and the total number of valid questionnaires was 1,362, accounting for 84.49%. The geographical distribution of the survey is extensive, covering 14 provinces, two municipalities and one autonomous region, 17 altogether, accounting for 54.84% nationally.[55] They include the large traditional agricultural provinces in the central area such as Henan, Hubei, Hunan, Anhui and Jiangxi, the main grain

[54] Hu Jiliang, a member of the research group, is a major contributor to the appendix.

[55] They are the provinces of Hubei, Hunan, Jiangxi, Henan, Sichuan, Shandong, Fujian, Guangdong, Zhejiang, Hainan, Hebei, Shanxi, Anhui and Jilin, the municipalities of Chongqing and Tianjin and Guangxi Autonomous Region.

producing area in the northeast like Jilin, the major western agricultural production areas that are relatively backward economically such as Chongqing, Sichuan, Guangxi and economically developed provinces on the southeastern coasts like Shandong, Fujian, Guangdong, Tianjin and Zhejiang. The survey is typically representative.

To examine the influencing factors of agricultural mechanization, it is necessary to determine the judging criteria. Previous studies generally used the two indicators of agricultural machinery and power as reflections of agricultural mechanization, but we believe that they are not essential. We use the rate of agricultural services open to peasant households in all agricultural production links to represent the degree of agricultural mechanization.

Considering the feasibility of acquiring the indicators, we use the household expenditures on agricultural machinery services as substitute indicators. They include the total expenditures for access to agricultural machinery services such as plowing, leveling and irrigation, and machinery operation for crops such as sowing, harvesting, and transportation. As for the agricultural machinery services provided by peasant households with their own agricultural machinery, we will sort it out according to the corresponding prices of agricultural machinery services purchased by peasant households.

Based on the above criteria, the following factors have impacts on China's current agricultural mechanization.

- **The age of the household head:** The head of the household is the family member that bears the main responsibility for the household operation and labor allocation. Therefore, the head's characteristics can influence its choice of and expenditures on agricultural machinery services. Logically speaking, the older the head, the greater the demand for agricultural machinery services. What accounts for this is that the older the head, the poorer the physical conditions, the less able to bear heavy manual labor, and the greater need to replace manpower with machinery. However, the actual survey results are contrary. The head's age is negatively correlated with the demand for agricultural machinery services. That is to say, under the same circumstances, the older the head, the smaller the demand. But why? One of the most important reasons may be that the older the head is, the smaller the opportunity he or she will have to work elsewhere. Therefore, with little opportunity to obtain non-agricultural incomes, the head tends to be confined to farming.

- **The education background of the household head:** The head's education background will influence his or her understanding, acceptance and application of knowledge and skills. Generally speaking, the head with a better education will be more flexible and open to a wider range of employment choices and so the opportunity cost of labor and employment is correspondingly high. They tend to choose tertiary industries such as business and operation, or working elsewhere.

The concurrent employment of such peasant households is fairly commonplace, and agriculture is no longer the main business for a considerable number of them. In particular, after the agricultural labor force has changed from "departing from the soil without leaving the hometown" to "leaving the soil and the hometown", the concurrent phenomenon of "going out to work after farming is done and doing farm work during the busy farming season" has given way to the specialized division of labor with greater comparative benefits.

After weighing the pros and cons of going back to farm work during busy farming seasons and staying out working (engaging in business), the laborers working outside tend to choose the latter, and as a result, for the farm work at home, they are likely to turn to specialized agricultural machinery services. Conversely, household heads with little education tend to have a lower opportunity cost of going out to work than pay for agricultural machinery services. Therefore, they are not highly motivated to have specialized and marketized agricultural machinery services and prefer engaging in agricultural production (see Table 5.4).

- **The head's gender:** In rural China, the vast majority of household heads are male. There are three main situations in which the woman is the head. The husband works elsewhere and is not registered in the village, or he has passed away or he lives in his wife's home. Overall, the gender of the head does not have a significant influence on the household's demand for agricultural machinery services.

- **The sizes of the family and its labor force:** The impact of the number of family members and laborers on agricultural machinery services is complicated and consequently their impact on the demand for agricultural machinery services is not clear. In general, a great number means that there is a large room for decision-making in the household labor allocation and as a result, there are many options. Different options create different demands for agricultural machinery services.
- **Actual arable area:** The actual arable area is an important factor in determining peasant households' expenditures on the services. The chances of their choosing the services increase with the expansion of the arable area. Especially where market economy is relatively developed and multitudes of rural laborers go out to work, the cost of rural labor has also risen sharply. For example, during the busy seasons, the daily wage of a rural laborer in Hubei Jianghan Plain has risen to more than RMB50, and in some areas, it is difficult to find a migrant worker even when the daily wage is RMB80. Therefore, compared with agricultural machinery services, the manual plus animal power model has no cost advantage. Therefore, with the ever-expanding scale of land operated by the households, there is a tendency toward increasing the expenditures on machinery services. Moreover, after the households' actual arable area reaches a certain size, they generally purchase agricultural machinery instead of relying on external services. It should be noted that the current increase mainly depends on the contracted reclaimed waste slopes, lands and beaches, and the formal or informal transfer of rural land, which has not changed the basic institutional framework of the household land-contracting operational system. In addition, in some areas with more labor and less land where most young and middle-aged laborers become migrant workers, the demand for agricultural machinery services is not weak.
- **Mountainous areas:** Machinery services, especially in the case of large and medium-sized agricultural machinery, are generally not suitable for mountainous areas. Therefore, the increase in mountainous areas will reduce the demand for agricultural machinery services. In China, with the implementation of the policy of returning farmlands to forests, mountains are generally transformed into land where grow

Table 5.4. Descriptive statistics of variables (Sample size: 1362)

Variables	Definitions and descriptions of variables	Minimum values	Maximum values	Mean	Standard deviations
Expenditures on machinery services	Actual expenditures on machinery services	0	30,400	784.212	1,520.575
Selection of service modes	Self-cultivation = 1, paid manual service = 2, machinery or machinery plus manual services = 3	0	3	2.5264	0.7993
Head's age	Actual age	17	87	47.9214	9.5660
Head's schooling	Illiteracy = 0, primary schooling = 1, junior high Schooling = 2, senior high schooling = 3, above senior high schooling = 4	0	4	1.8690	0.7918
Head's gender	Male = 1, female = 0	0	1	0.9589	0.1986
Size of the family	Actual size of the family	1	14	4.5102	1.4932
Number of laborers	Actual number of laborers	0	9	2.6433	1.1102
Actual arable area	Arable land area = contracted land + leased land + rented land	0	201.8	8.3466	11.3332
Hilly area	Actual farmed area	0	102	2.1220	8.2736
Total subsidies	Total subsidies = food subsidies + agricultural machinery subsidies + other subsidies	0	15,000	455.205	785.9983
Non-agricultural incomes	Non-agricultural incomes = working income + tertiary industry income + processing income	0	200,000	14,075.3	17,672.56

(*Continued*)

Table 5.4. (*Continued*)

Variables	Definitions and descriptions of variables	Minimum values	Maximum values	Mean	Standard deviations
Province, municipality and region	Sichuan, Chongqing and Guangxi = 1, Hubei, Hunan, Jiangxi and Anhui = 2, Guangdong, Fujian, Zhejiang and Hainan = 3, Henan, Hebei, Shanxi and Jilin = 4 Tianjin and Shandong = 5	1	5	2.3877	1.1082

fruit trees or trees to be used as wood. Apart from the need for mechanical services for large-scale felling of trees, in general, the operation of mountainous areas does not require too much machinery. In conclusion, mountainous areas and the expenditures on agricultural machinery services are negatively related.

- *Supporting agricultural subsidies*: The supporting agricultural subsidies here include various state-granted subsidies to peasant households such as direct subsidies for grain cultivation, improved seeds, agricultural machinery purchases and agricultural diesel. The second two subsidies are direct incentives for the households to purchase and use agricultural machinery services. The first two indirectly contribute to their demands for the services.
- *Non-agricultural incomes*: The households' non-agricultural incomes mainly include incomes they earn by engaging in secondary and tertiary industries and working elsewhere. They have direct or indirect effects on the demands for agricultural machinery services in many ways.

First of all, earning high non-agricultural incomes suggests the high opportunity costs of engaging in agriculture. Therefore, according to the principle of comparative benefits, they will spend more time on non-agricultural production than agricultural production and as a result, the production on arable land will mainly rely on specialized agricultural machinery services (Table 5.5).

Table 5.5. Regression results of the benchmark model (Sample size: 1362)

Variables	Model I	Model II	Model III	Model IV
Constant terms	5.0935***	5.0897***	4.9555***	4.9888***
	(1.4114)	(1.4106)	(1.3924)	(1.3924)
Head's age	−0.9856***	−0.9904***	−1.0014***	−0.9443***
	(0.3449)	(0.3427)	(0.3421)	(0.3391)
Head's education	0.1477*	0.1473*	0.1448*	0.1434*
	(0.0888)	(0.0887)	(0.0886)	(0.0886)
Head's gender	−0.2014	−0.2013		
	(0.3362)	(0.3360)		
Number of family members	0.029			
	(0.2200)			
Number of laborers	0.2853	0.2739	0.2741	
	(0.2372)	(0.2189)	(0.2188)	
Province, municipality and region	0.2200***	0.2203***	0.2204***	0.2169***
	(0.0616)	(0.0616)	(0.0616)	(0.0615)
Size of actual arable land	1.0496***	1.0474***	1.0444***	1.0724***
	(0.1128)	(0.1115)	(0.1113)	(0.1091)
Size of the hilly area	−0.3984***	−0.3988***	−0.3990***	−0.3924***
	(0.0774)	(0.0773)	(0.0773)	(0.0772)
Total subsidies	0.1427***	0.1428**	0.1425***	0.1415***
	(0.0234)	(0.0234)	(0.0234)	(0.0234)
Non-agricultural incomes	0.0538***	0.0536***	0.0530***	0.0548***
	(0.0156)	(0.0155)	(0.0155)	(0.0154)
Work place	−0.1751*	−0.1758*	−0.1753*	−0.1611*
	(0.0974)	(0.0972)	(0.0972)	(0.0965)
R_2	0.1777	0.1777	0.1775	0.1765
Adjusted R_2	0.1710	0.1716	0.1720	0.1716
F statistics	26.4430	29.1060	32.3166	36.1448

Note: *, **, *** signify the significance levels of 10%, 5% and 1%, respectively. The values in parentheses are standard errors.

Second, higher non-agricultural incomes are their financial guarantees to pay for the services. Besides, their increase in non-agricultural incomes also raises the labor cost of the whole society as well as that of the rural labor market. This drives rational peasants to replace manpower with machinery.

Finally, the non-agricultural incomes directly result from the transfer of agricultural labor, and the scale of agricultural labor transfer is a necessary prerequisite for the transfer of arable land and the expansion of the peasant households' actual farming areas. Non-agricultural employment opportunities and incomes are also necessary prerequisites for determining a moderate scale of land operation.

- **Locations:** Another important factor impacting peasant households' choice of mechanized services is the province where they are, i.e., the topographic features of the arable land. Generally speaking, mechanized farming works better with flat land with a lower cost than mountainous, hilly and fragmented land. As a result, expenditures on agricultural mechanization services in provinces in the North China Plain, the Northeast Plain and the Jianghan Plain are greater than in hilly and mountainous regions.

Paid manual service is no mechanized service, but it can be regarded as its echo. That is to say, if a peasant's household needs paid manual labor, he will seek cheap services in the market to help cultivate its land, therefore, the use of mechanical services can be an alternative, but it chooses manual service, which indicates that it has more advantages than machinery services. If the cost of mechanical services is lower, it will be a rational choice. Therefore, paid manual service is placed in the model as an independent variable, reflecting peasant households' implicit demand for machinery services.

5.10.1.1 *The empirical model and regression results*

The size of peasant households' expenditures on machinery services is mainly impacted by such variables as the characteristics of the head of the household, the number of family members and laborers, province and city, size of the actual cultivated land, state subsidies and non-agricultural incomes. There is a problem of heteroscedasticity due to the large size of the samples. Therefore, the non-virtual variables are logarithmically standardized here in an attempt to reduce the effects of heteroscedasticity. The benchmark model adopted is as follows:

$$
\begin{aligned}
EXP_i = \alpha &+ \beta_1 AGEi + \beta_2 EDU_i + \beta_3 SEX_i + \beta_4 POP_i + \beta_5 LAB_i \\
&+ \beta_6 PROV_i + \beta_7 LAND_i + \beta_8 MOUNT_i + \beta_9 SUB_i \\
&+ \beta_{10} INC_i + \beta_{11} SPOT_i + \beta_i
\end{aligned}
$$

EXP — expenditures on machinery services; *AGE* — age of the head of the household; *EDU* — education of the head; *SEX* — gender of the head; *POP* — the number of family members; *LAB* — the size of the labor force; *PROV* — the province from which laborers hail; *LAND* — size of the actual arable land; *MOUNT* — size of the mountainous area; *SUB* — Total subsidies; INC-non-agricultural incomes; and *SPOT* — the place where they go out to work.

The above model can only examine at a macro level what factors influence the households' expenditures on agricultural machinery services. The model has limitations that it is static in nature due to the cross-sectional data and cannot be utilized to study fully and profoundly the dynamic driving mechanisms behind the expenditures.

Two research perspectives can dissolve the defects to some extent. The first is collecting panel data to build a dynamic panel data model. This is the most scientific and reasonable solution, but the data are very difficult to collect. The second is directly employing the data collected in the aforementioned survey to construct a multi-decision model for a research on the driving mechanisms for households' selection of machinery services.

The model contains the micro-driving factors influencing households' decision-making and so it is also a feasible way to make up for the defects. Moreover, it can be contrasted with the benchmark model for its further verification. Based on the above analysis, a multi-ordered Logit model is established as follows:

y has j values, one of which is a reference value and when compared with it, other values can generate $j - 1$ non-redundant Logit models. For example, with $y = j$ as a reference category, all coefficients in the model are all zeros for the reference model. With $y = i$, its Logit model is:

$$\log\frac{P(y-i)}{P(y-j)} = \beta_i 0 + \beta_{i1}AGE_i + \beta_{i2}EDU_i + \beta_{i3}SEX_i + \beta_{i4}POP_i + \beta_{i5}LAB_i + \beta_{i6}PROV_i + \beta_{i7}LAND_i + \beta_{i8}MOUNT_i + \beta_{i9}SUB_i + \beta_{i10}INC_i + \beta_{i11}SPOT_i$$

Given the benchmark regression results, the factors which impact peasant households' expenditures on agricultural machinery services are mainly as follows.

The first factor influencing peasant households' expenditures on agricultural machinery services is the age of the household head which has a significant impact on the expenditures. If the estimated coefficient of the head's age is negative, it means that the older the head, the less he or she pays for agricultural machinery services. According to the survey data, the older the head, the less land he or she farms, and the smaller the chance the head stands of going out to work. Most of such households will choose self-cultivation and as a result, the expenditures on agricultural machinery services will be smaller. As shown in Table 5.6, there is a negative correlation between the head's age and the household's expenditures on machinery services.

The second factor is the educational background of the household head. The better the head is educated, the greater the expenditures on the services or vice versa. As shown in Table 5.7, there is a positive correlation between the household head's educational background and the expenditures on the services.

Table 5.6. Relationship between the age of the household head and its expenditures on machinery services

Age	Sample size	Average size of arable land (mu)	Average expenditures on mechanical operation (RMB)
Under 40	228	9.67	960.10
40–49	547	8.35	808.47
50–59	414	8.12	713.38
60–69	118	7.21	630.64
70 and over	33	5.96	561.45

Table 5.7. The relationship between the household head's educational background and the expenditures on agricultural machinery services

Educational background	Sample size	Average size of cultivated land (mu)	Average expenditures on mechanical operation (RMB)
Illiteracy	43	9.17	614.51
Schooling	378	8.15	684.71
Junior high schooling	673	8.53	837.86
Senior high schooling	249	8.11	805.82
Above senior high school education	19	6.28	854.17

The third factor is the province where the peasant household resides. In areas where economy is underdeveloped and which are mostly hilly or mountainous such as Sichuan, Chongqing, Guangxi, and central Hunan, Hubei, Anhui and Jiangxi, expenditures on mechanical farming services are smaller. In contrast, in the northern economically developed areas and the North China Plain like Shandong, Tianjin, Henan, Hebei, Shanxi and Jilin, the expenditures are significantly greater than elsewhere. The south-eastern coastal region is economically developed, but there is less land used for farming than other regions and for that matter, the land is mostly hilly and mountainous. The expenditures on mechanical farming services here are just between the other two types.

The next factor is the actual size of the peasant household's cultivated land, which has a significant positive impact on its expenditures on agricultural machinery services. According to the survey data, the Pearson correlation coefficient between the size of the actual cultivated land and the expenditures on agricultural machinery services is 0.7511, demonstrating a high positive correlation. This indicates that the households with more actual cultivated land tend to have greater expenditures on the services.

Another factor is the size of the mountainous area that a household cultivates, which has a significant negative impact. According to the survey data, the Pearson correlation coefficient between the actual size of the mountainous farming area and the expenditures on agricultural machinery

Table 5.8. Regression results of the multivariate decision-making (reference) model

Variables	Model I	Model II	Model III	Model IV
Age of the head	−0.0202***	−0.204***	−0.0124***	−0.0193***
	(0.0070)	(0.0070)	(0.0041)	(0.0068)
Education of the head	0.2098**	0.2097**	0.1147**	0.2241***
	(0.0832)	(0.0830)	(0.0485)	(0.0826)
Gender of the head	0.0102			
	(0.2910)			
Number of family members	−0.0126			
	(0.0502)			
Number of laborers	0.1010	0.0922	0.0465	
	(0.0730)	(0.0641)	(0.0366)	
Province, municipality or region	0.5482***	0.5484***	0.3043***	0.5553***
	(0.0716)	(0.0715)	(0.0384)	(0.0711)
Size of actual arable land	0.0213*	0.0212*	0.0126*	0.0252**
	(0.0128)	(0.0128)	(0.0071)	(0.0128)
Size of the hilly area	−0.0068	−0.0068		
	(0.0068)	(0.0068)		
Total subsidies	0.0004**	0.0004**	0.0002**	0.0004***
	(0.0002)	(0.0002)	(0.0001)	(0.0002)
Non-agricultural incomes	0.000007	0.000006	0.000003	0.000001**
	(0.000004)	(0.000004)	(0.000002)	(0.000004)
Work place	−0.0671	−0.0699		
	(0.1343)	(0.1338)		
limit_2: C (12) Critical limit_2: C(12)	−0.2579	−0.2457	−0.2217	−0.3069
	(0.5125)	(0.4522)	(0.2662)	(0.4421)
limit_3: C (13) Critical limit_3: C(13)	0.2634	0.2756	0.0806	−0.2079
	(0.5124)	(0.4521)	(0.2660)	(0.4419)
Pseudo R	0.0653	0.0653	0.06311	0.6624
-2LL	958.4946	958.5269	962.9380	969.2133
LR	134.0320	133.9676	129.7318	137.5199

Notes: (1) *, ** and *** indicate the significance levels of 10%, 5% and 1%, respectively.

(2) Model I is the regression results containing all the independent variables. Models I–IV are the results of the stepwise regressions with the insignificant variables removed one by one according to their significance.

(3) The values in parentheses are standard errors.

services is –0.0292, showing a weak negative correlation. This indicates that the mountainous geomorphological feature affects the use of agricultural machinery.

The six factor is the non-agricultural incomes of the peasant household which is positively correlated with the services. The higher the non-agricultural incomes, the greater the expenditures on the services. At this stage, it is fairly commonplace that Chinese peasants take part-time jobs, and the rise of non-agricultural incomes has led to an increase in the opportunity cost of labor. In the case of constant or falling prices of machinery services, rational peasants are bound to supplant manual labor with machinery, which increases their expenditures on machinery services. The promotion of agricultural mechanization by agricultural non-agricultural incomes mainly reflects the irreversible power of the market, an "invisible hand" .

The seventh factor is the state's agricultural subsidy policy, which plays a certain positive role in promoting agricultural mechanization. It covers agricultural machinery purchase subsidies and agricultural diesel subsidies, which directly promote the development of agricultural mechanization while grain growth subsidies and improved seed subsidies play a more indirect role. The subsidies reflect the role of the government's "visible hand" (see Table 5.8).

5.11 How to Promote Agricultural Technology on the Basis of Peasant Household Economy

Professor Schultz, 1979 Nobel Prize winner in economics, pointed out in *Transforming Traditional Agriculture* that the key to transforming traditional agriculture is to introduce modern agricultural production factors, whose core is technological progress. Professor Schultz pointed out that as to modern economic growth, whether it stems from agriculture or other economic sectors, the application of technology is undoubtedly a key variable and it is likely that traditional agriculture is strongly resistant internally to any changes in technology.[56] Therefore, the establishment of institutions, mechanisms and organizational forms that can promote

[56] Schultz, T.W. *Transforming Traditional Agriculture.* Chicago and London: The University of Chicago Press, 1983.

technological advances is an indispensable and powerful means of transforming traditional SF. In 2012, No. 1 Central Document says: "In the long run, the fundamental way out to achieve sustainable and stable development of agriculture and ensure an effective supply of agricultural products is the application of science and technology. With the distinguishing features of being public, basic and social, agricultural science and technology are the essential supports of ensuring national food security, inevitable choices to break through the limits of resources and environment, and also the decisive power of accelerating modern agricultural advances."

According to *The Law of the People's Republic of China on Agricultural Technology Promotion* promulgated in 1993, promoting agricultural technology refers to "the application of agricultural technology to pre-in-post agricultural production through trials, demonstrations, trainings, guidance and consulting services." By agricultural technology here is meant "the scientific research achievements and practical techniques applied to planting, forestry, animal husbandry and fishery. They include techniques involving breeding of improved varieties, application of fertilizers, pests and diseases prevention and control, cultivation and culture, processing of agricultural and sideline products, preservation, storage and transportation, agricultural machinery and aeronautical aviation, farmland water conservancy, soil improvement, soil and water conservation, rural water supply and energy use, and agricultural environmental protection, operation and management, and agrometeorology."

Obviously, the promotion of agricultural technology here is a highly inclusive concept. In a certain sense, it is also a kind of social public product and a kind of input from the society and the government into modern agricultural production factors. It falls into the category of supplying modern production elements in Schultz's theoretical framework. He held that the economic growth of agricultural sector in poor countries depends mainly on the availability and the prices of modern (non-traditional) agricultural factors. In a true sense, their suppliers control the key to the growth.[57]

It is undeniable that at the onset of the implementation of the peasant household land contracting system, the rural agricultural technology promotion system established on the basis of the people's commune system encountered a universal crisis of survival. It underwent an overall negation

[57] *Ibid.*

of peasant household economy. Among the reasons are the so-called "governmental buttress stoppage, loss of the technical staff and technological network break-down", which led some scholars to doubt whether the application of agricultural science and technology could be promoted on the basis of peasant household economy.

Can the application of agricultural science and technology be promoted on the basis of peasant household economy? Here are two options. One is "going back" and the other is "jumping out". The latter means transforming the traditional mechanisms and organizational forms of promoting agricultural production technology based on planned economy and the people's commune system and replacing them with new mechanisms and organizational forms that adapt to market economy and peasant household economy.

When it comes to the needs, which is in a greater demand for agricultural technology, peasant households or members of the people's commune? The latter were not independent production and operation entities. Even the production team, the production brigade or even the commune had to take the instructions from their superiors as to what to plant and how to plant to a large extent. Therefore, the agricultural technology promotion at that time was essentially an external intervention. The big collective pot of the people's commune system inactivated the inherent need of the members (ordinary peasants) for science and technology. After the reform of the rural economic system, peasant households in contemporary China became independent production and operation entities, whose economic benefits were closely bound to their economic interests. Therefore, judging from the theory that the "economic man" aims to maximize his own interests, they are supposed to be intrinsically motivated for the needs of science and technology, especially what works with them.

A sample survey on the households' need for comprehensive social services was conducted by Kong Xiangzhi's research group. Here are the rankings from high to low. The services they need concern technological information (78.6%), price information (69.3%), policy and legal information (56%), credit rating (34.2%), credit (loan) guarantee (31.9%), introducing loan channels (31.6%), organizing household collective loans (24.5%) and organizing peasants to go out to work (20.8%).[58] However,

[58] Kong, X. *Supplies-and-Demands-Based Researches on China's Agricultural Socialization Services*. Beijing: China Renmin University Press, 2009, p. 64.

there is an undeniable fact that for those peasant households who take agriculture as a "side job" and are contented with growing their own food, do not have strong demands for agricultural science and technology, or they are not very concerned about promoting agricultural technology. According to our rural field surveys, those specialized agricultural households including specialized farming and breeding households have the strongest demands for applicable agricultural technologies. Agricultural cooperatives and enterprises also have strong demands for the technologies. A good case in point is Hou Anjie, a famous big grain grower or rather an agricultural entrepreneur in Daye City, Hubei Province, who has hired four permanent agricultural technological experts[59] for advice on agricultural production.

According to reports by *People's Daily Online* reporters Feng Hua and Chen Renze, Gansu big grain growers are responsible for the experiments, demonstrations and promotion of more than 70% of over 260 new technologies, products and improved produces in the province. Huang Chaosong, a big grain grower in The Guangxi Zhuang Autonomous Region, has been utilizing since 2004 new technologies for grain production such as rice no-till cultivation, standardized production, soil testing, formulated fertilization, and integrated pests and diseases prevention and control. Under his leadership, the application rate of new agricultural production technologies in the whole village has reached more than 85%.[60] In fact, in contrast with big grain growers, specialists in vegetables, fruit, trees, flowers, and breeders of aquatic products and livestock tend to have greater demands for science and technology and may impose much higher standards on them.

[59]Hou Anjie is a peasant from Dajipu Town, Daye City, Hubei Province, and a nationally renowned big grain grower, the "food king". After 2001, he contracted a large area of land through various types of land transfers. By 2008, he had contracted 20,300 mu of land, 16,800 mu of which was rice fields. In order to ensure benefits, he has employed four agricultural technological experts. They are rice expert and agronomist Pan Xishu, rice expert and senior agricultural technological promotion researcher Zhou Kaijing, vegetable expert and senior agronomist Mei Hongbiao and forestry expert and senior engineer Zhou Zhixi.

[60]Feng, H. and Chen Renze. "A Big Grain Grower's Ecstasy and Expectations — A Report from the Front Line of Agricultural Production", *People's Network*, February 11, 2011.

[Case 5.13] Reliance on Science and Technology Makes Wang Xianrong a Grape Prince in Hunan

In 1968, Wang Xianrong was born in Zengjiagang Village, Yongfeng Township, Li County, Hunan Province. He failed in the college entrance examinations in 1986. In October the same year, Wang and some of his classmates went on a releaving trip to Sichuan. While visiting the local agricultural market in Leshan, the local giant grape caught his full attention. He gave the grape seller RMB20 as the fee for his guide to Jianguo Vineyard in Leshan City. It is a grape base of Professor Chen Jianguo from Southwest Agricultural University. Wang tracked down the professor and sincerely requested to learn under the teacher. He studied conscientiously breeding, cultivation, pruning, pests and disease prevention and control, picking and storage, and practiced what he had learnt. In the winter of 1987, he returned to his hometown with the 2000 Kyoto grape seedlings that Professor Chen had presented to him at his departure and set up his enterprise.

In 1993, Wang made some achievements in grape growth when a contagious disease called black pox that had never been heard of before spread in the vineyards of Wang and other growers under his leadership. He turned for help to Hunan Provincial Department of Agriculture and rushed into many offices. After twists and turns, he got help from Bai Wenyun, a researcher at the Institute of Diseases and Insects affiliated to the provincial Bureau of Agriculture and Economics. Bai referred Wang to Professor Shi Xuehui from Hunan Agricultural University. Professor Shi spent the night organizing experts to discuss 7 sets of treatments. They did work.

Since 1993, Professor Shi has been giving long-term and patient technical guidance to Wang's grape enterprise. They also co-authored the book *Annual Management Technology for Grape Quality and High Yield.*

After 2007, Wang launched an all-round scientific and technological cooperation with Hunan Agricultural University to extend the grape industry chain, developed the Vitis davidii Wine Series and founded the Hunan Shenzhou Manor Wine Industry Co., Ltd.

Wang Xianrong, who is fully aware of the importance of science and technology, is always leading his folks to live a life of plenty. For more than 20 years, he has provided free technical consultations and services for grape growers in and outside the province by offering training courses, on-site guidance, and making multimedia courseware, benefiting more than 580,000 person-times. He has won the honorary titles of "Young Spark Leaders", "Excellent National Rural Practical Talents" and "Hunan Provincial Model Workers". He is also a winner of the first "Yuan Longping Science and Technology Award" and was a representative of the 17th National Congress of the Communist Party of China.

This case is based on the information involved obtained by the author when he visited the Hunan Shenzhou Manor Wine Industry Co., Ltd. during the "Huxiang Agricultural, Rural and Peasant Forum" held in Changde, Hunan Province in October 2009.

In the case of supply, agricultural technology promotion is essentially a public product with a strong external positive effect because "as a materialized carrier of agricultural technology, most agricultural technological products have the non-exclusive and non-competitive features characteristic of general public products. First, the production of agricultural technologically materialized products is first of all the production of biological products. Their self-propagation characteristics determine their non-exclusive feature. Second, a peasant household's adoption of an agricultural technology and its materialized products will not restrict other households' adoption, hence, non-competitiveness."[61]

Therefore, governments at all levels have major or even "leading" responsibilities in the promotion of agricultural technology. However, it does not mean that they will run the whole show. Practice has proved that under their leadership, the establishment of a multi-symbiotic agricultural technology promotion organizational network is a vibrant and inclusive realistic choice compatible with market economy.

The network includes the top-down agricultural technology promotion system of five levels ranging from state, province, city, county to township involving agricultural research and educational units, agricultural enterprises, rural cooperative economic organizations, science and technology associations and agricultural supply and marketing cooperatives at all levels, special agricultural science and technology commissioners and agricultural science and technology demonstration households.

It should be noted that the marketized peasants' demand for agricultural technology is indeed extremely utilitarian, and they just need applicable technologies rather than advanced technologies. That is to say, they perform instinctively revenue cost assessments of adopting new technologies. Only those really beneficial to them are likely to be accepted. However, the adoption of new technologies is often risky, especially in the initial experimental promotion stage. Therefore, whether there is a group of new technology testers who dare to take risks and can afford to take risks is particularly critical to the promotion.

When the people's commune system was implemented, agricultural technology promotion was a process of giving and receiving an external

---

[61] Chen, Y. and Wu Haitao. *Agricultural Technology Diffusion and Peasant Households' Economic Action*. Wuhan: Hubei People's Publishing House, 2010, pp. 8–9.

input of administrative instructions. The risks were undertaken by collective economic organizations. A peasant had neither the intrinsic motivation to promote the application of agricultural technology nor was subjected to fear and external pressures of taking risks. The advantage of this system is that the promotion is less likely to come across organizational barriers and so is relatively fast and easy but it can hardly inspire internal motivation and shows no regard for costs.

After the implementation of the household land contracting system, peasant households, especially those who were mainly engaged in agriculture, were eager for technologies applicable to them and had inherent motivations to promote them, but they were also afraid of taking risks or being unable to afford them. If the pioneers could bear the high costs of the trial period, solving the key problems that might arise from the new technologies' local adaptability, for example, and in addition, their practice proved to be highly effective, the majority of the peasant households would follow suit as a matter of course. As a result, their promotion would be quick on the basis of low costs and high profits. The majority of the peasants firmly believed that "Seeing is believing" and so in the actual promotion, the demonstration of local "acquaintances" was more effective than any external publicity. Obviously, they were imitators and followers and the "pioneers", "pace-setters" and "demonstrators" were in the minority.

How to cultivate such people? Internally they must be "adventurous", adequately educated and equipped with prerequisite technical skills, and financially well-off and psychologically sound against odds. Regarding external environment, society, especially governments at all levels, have an obligation and responsibility to use various policies and measures to stimulate such people for innovations and reduce the risks of making innovations.

Selecting some households as agricultural science and technology demonstration households is an organizational means by which the governments foster the "pioneers", "pace-setters" and "demonstrators" of agricultural technology promotion. It is also an organizational innovation of exploring the organizational network of agricultural technology promotion on the basis of peasant household economy when market economy prevails. These households are generally those in the area who are relatively well-educated and mainly engage in agricultural production. Many of them are big local agricultural households and agricultural technicians and self-taught local "experts". According to the 2004 Opinions of the Ministry of Agriculture on the Promotion of the Application of Agricultural Science and Technology to Peasant Households, the governments "buttressed technology demonstration households and achieved the goal of providing improved seeds, technologies, agricultural machinery and information for the households by means of tilt policies, direct subsidies, science and technology trainings for the application of agricultural science and technology, expert guidance and microfinance. Obviously, these special governmental incentives have spurred the enthusiasm of agricultural technology demonstration households for new agricultural technologies and also reduced the risks and costs of their pioneering trials.

Of course, the key to cultivating agricultural science and technology demonstration households is "demonstration", that is, "the leadership to popularize and impart the knowledge and skills to surrounding households". Plenty of actual surveys show that in rural areas, when something new such as a new technology, a new product and a new mode of production is under promotion, talks alone can hardly persuade the peasants, however hard you try. But if acquaintances in the local area do it, do it well and make money from it, then, you don't need to say anything and they will follow suit. This is where the role and significance of such practice lies. This accounts for the practice of having science and technology demonstration households.

[Case 5.14] Agricultural Science and Technology Demonstration Householder Deng Pingyun

Deng Pingyun is a peasant from Daping Village, Yantian Township, Wugang City, Hunan Province. He went to a vocational school when young. In 2011, his household was chosen to be an "Agricultural Science and Technology Demonstration Household" in Wugang City.

Deng has been taking growing rice as the main source of the family's incomes. He works hard with new agricultural technologies. In 2010, he took two new technology training courses sponsored by the Municipal Bureau of Agriculture. He centered on rice directional wide and narrow row cultivation techniques and rice soil testing and formula fertilization techniques. Through hard work and systematic study, Deng applied what he had learned to his 12 mu of contracted rice field.

The average yield was 90 kg more per mu than before, and he earned nearly RMB 3,000 more than before. After being designated as the "Agricultural Science and Technology Demonstration Household" in Wugang City in 2011, he selected the new rice type Y Liangyou No. 1 and Y Liangyou No. 7 under the technical guidance of agricultural technical instructors. By adopting new agricultural technologies such as scientific water-fertilizing management, integrated pests and diseases prevention and control, soil testing and formula fertilization, he saved labor costs by more than RMB1,200, and his rice yield increased. In 2011, the rice yield for one season reached 635 kg per mu, 67 kg more than in 2010 with a net income increase of RMB4,600.

As a demonstrator, Deng enthusiastically helps other villagers and ardently promotes new agricultural technologies. He patiently introduces to neighboring villagers the rice production technology essentials and experiences in soil testing and formula fertilization, and specialized knowledge on crop pests and diseases control. He is consulted about various technical problems more than 300 times annually. As a result, his shop for agricultural materials has become a science and technology park where villagers acquire knowledge of agricultural science and technology and discuss new agricultural technologies. It plays a good role of activating others and changing many of their traditional modes of farming. Now, he has been elected by the villagers as the director of the village committee.

—*China Agricultural Promotion Network*

However, it takes more than demonstrators to promote agricultural technologies. As a systematic project, it requires a multiple cooperation to form an organizational network of multiple complementary symbioses. Agricultural enterprises and cooperative economic organizations have great demands for applicable agricultural technologies. Compared with the demonstrators, they have greater economic strengths, technological absorption capacity and technological development capability. Especially in the organizational forms such as leading agricultural industrialized enterprises plus peasant households and agricultural cooperatives plus peasant households, the enterprises and cooperatives bear the risks and costs of technology development and promotion, which accelerates the popularization and application of new technologies among the households. For example, in the organizational cooperation model of leading agricultural industrialized enterprises plus peasant households plus bases, households organize production according to the technical quality and standards unified and normalized by the enterprise. This provides a feasible organizational guarantee for the promotion of new technologies, new products and new production methods.

The government-established-and-supervised nationwide five-leveled agricultural technology promotion and services system is headed by the Center for the National Agricultural Technology Promotion and Services established in 1995. The system is the backbone system of the agricultural technology promotion organizational network led by the Chinese government. It evolved out of the agricultural technology promotion system covering the whole country during the people's commune period. Since a series of market mechanisms-introducing reforms, it has been gradually developing along the line of "strengthening the public welfare functions and invigorating operational services" to adapt to the need of building China's rural market economy on the basis of peasant household economy.

This kind of marketized transformation conducted on the basis of traditional organizational structures undoubtedly saves organizational costs, but it is very difficult to achieve a complete change in mechanisms in that the deep-rooted interest relationships behind the traditional system are hard to straighten out. One of the typical problems is that "public welfare functions" and "operational services" are "unified", leading to the conflation of the two types. Consequently, the former is often abducted by the latter and becomes the means of making profits adopted by the basic-level promotion stations and institutes.

Some useful explorations have been carried out across the country of how to establish a new agricultural technology promotion model in line with the marketized operation under the leadership of the governments. The Shaanxi "Dali Model" to be discussed in Case 5.15 is quite typical and has great social impacts. It is carried on *Guangming Daily* with a large concentrated coverage. It shows that the marketized operation of the practical agricultural technologies that is led by the governments and that peasants need badly is not only feasible but also more beneficial than the governments' running-all administration.

[Case 5.15] Shaanxi Dali's New Model for Agricultural Science and Technology Promotion Network

Dali County is a typical large agricultural county in Weinan City, Shaanxi Province. It has 26 townships and towns, 415 administrative villages, more than 1.5 million mu of arable land and a population of 750,000. For a long time after the reform of the rural system, like most rural areas in the country, the promotion of agricultural science and technology in Dali was trapped in a situation of "nets and lines break up and people are gone".

How to construct a new model for agricultural science and technology promotion network in a market economy environment? Dali made a useful exploration called the "Dali Model".

One characteristic of the model is the interoperability of the agricultural materials chain operation network and the agricultural technology services network, which organically combine the public welfare agricultural technology services with the marketized agricultural materials operation. As far as the organizational structure is concerned, it uses the Shaanxi Limin Agricultural Materials Chain Company as a platform to integrate various agricultural science and technology services, and the public welfare services out of the county's science and technology resources and the marketized operational services, developing a marketized operational mode of combining government, enterprises, peasant households and science and technology experts.

The company buttresses public welfare agricultural science and technology services with the profits from agricultural materials operation and in turn, utilizes the extensiveness and pertinence of agricultural science and technology services and the trust of peasants in the services to increase the profits from agricultural materials operation. The model of "government guidance, peasants making the orders, science and technology delivering them, enterprises paying for them" and "the chain of agricultural materials and agricultural technology services" has made possible the mutual benefits and win–win for all the stakeholders including peasants, agricultural science and technology personnel, enterprises and the government.

Meanwhile, Dali County has also set up an information network suitable for agricultural science and technology promotion services with modern information technological means such as "Science and Technology 110 (a mechanism of assigning special science and technology commissioners to villages)" and messages sent on smart-phones and videos. The technological network and the integration of technology, materials and information have built a new model of networked agricultural science and technology promotion based on market economy.

At present, there are agricultural technical service expert groups, special township commissioners and village-hired technicians in Dali County, forming an agricultural science and technology services network covering every village in the county. It provides agricultural forecasting, soil testing, formula fertilization and many other free agricultural technology services. What is more, the "last kilometer" problem that has been affecting the agricultural technology promotion has been effectively resolved.

Based on reports concerned from *Guangming Daily* and related materials provided by Shaanxi Dali County Government Network

5.12 Modern Agriculture: Who Will Be the Growers? — The Fundamental Key to Transforming SF is Cultivating New Types of Peasants

After the large-scale transfer of agricultural labor force, who will be the growers? This is a major social concern and a fundamental issue of agricultural modernization.

Abundant survey data show that there are clear distinctions between the transferred labor force, that is, the labor force going out to work, and the labor force staying in the countryside. For example, our 2011 survey in Tianmen, Hubei, found that the average age of migrant workers was 35 while that of the staying laborers was 50. The average schooling of the former was 8.5 years whereas that of the latter was 6.7. This indicates that the peasants who stay behind are older and not as well-educated as those going out. It is true elsewhere in the country.

Li Min and Zhao Liange found in the data of a follow-up survey lasting from 2003 to 2008 on the fixed rural households collected by the Liaoning Provincial Rural Social and Economic Investigation Team that there is a significant aging trend in the agricultural labor force. The laborers under 40 dropped from 38.7% in 2003 to 33.2% in 2008. In contrast, the laborers over 50 rose from 32.3% in 2003 to 38.1% in 2008.[62] Since the young labor force is generally better educated, the aging suggests poor schooling.

The fact that mainly the poorly educated elderly engage in agriculture seems to indicate that being a peasant is a very low-tech occupation, hence "Everyone can be a peasant." In the contemporary rural areas of China, in the households that take agriculture as a "side job", the young members go out to work and the few mu of contracted land is mostly attended by the elderly, women and children at home, the so-called "993861 troops" ("99" stands for the aged, "38" for women and "61" children). This has caused a widespread concern. Who can be counted on for the realization of agricultural modernization?

However, one should seek hope in worries. We have found from investigations that the "993861 troops" are not the main agricultural producers, or rather, they are not actual agricultural producers. Among the troops, the vast majority of the children are not engaged in agricultural production, and many old people and women only attend the land rather than actually farm it. Our surveys demonstrate that much of their agricultural production is actually "outsourced" to others, that is, they rely on specialized agricultural laborers for the production. Tilling, sowing, transplanting and harvesting are done by specialized agricultural machinery households or specialized teams and pests and diseases prevention and control are conducted by specialized plant protection teams or plant protection companies, for example. That is to say,

[62]Li, M. and Zhao Liange. "The Impacts of Rural Labor Mobility on the Aging of Agricultural Labor Force", *Journal of China Rural Economy*, No. 9, 2010, pp. 68–75.

those who are engaged in the specialized production of agricultural production chains are the actual agricultural laborers. Such people as agricultural machine operators and plant protection workers are generally younger and better educated. From this perspective, a general conclusion cannot be reached that the quality of agricultural laborers is getting increasingly low.

Judging from the tendency of development, the industry of modern agriculture is not technically low, but instead, it will be increasingly technical and knowledge-intensive. As Qian Xuesen, a deceased pre-eminent Chinese scientist, predicted in the mid-1980s, the sixth industrial revolution in the 21st century would be a modern biotechnology revolution and the main battlefield would be "big agriculture". Therefore, modern agriculture will be a highly knowledge-technology-intensive industry. It will inevitably require talents and labor forces that suit it. Therefore, as agricultural labor forces are drastically reduced, modern agriculture will require increasing science and technology literacy in them.

Judging from the experiences of developed countries, modern agricultural workers must have good comprehensive qualities, and therefore not everyone can be a qualified peasant. For example, in many European countries, one must obtain a "green certificate" to be a peasant and to obtain it, one needs to take a specialized or a job training and pass rigorous examinations.

[Case 5.16] Green Certificates in Denmark

Denmark is one of the oldest kingdoms in Europe and its agriculture has a long history and has always been an important industry in Denmark.

Although Danish agriculture relies heavily on small private household farms, not everyone is qualified to engage in agriculture. According to the Danish law, one who wants to purchase a farm of more than 30 acres must be a green certificate holder, who is eligible for a loan and enjoy from the government an interest subsidy worth 10% of the expenditures on the purchase of the land, European Community's economic subsidies for environmental protection and other preferential favors. Even a farmer's children must obtain a Band II green certificate to engage in agriculture.

Green Certificates in Denmark are divided into five bands.

Band I Certificate is an apprenticeship certificate for agricultural vocational education, equivalent to an agricultural vocational junior high school diploma in China.

A Band II Certificate is granted to a Band I Certificate holder who has graduated after another 3-year study when the holder is eligible to operate a farm.

For a Band III Certificate, one must have an experience and get involved in a period of about 3-month of off-the-job study.

A Band IV Certificate is obtained after a Band II Certificate holder studies in an agricultural school for 3 years so that he may be eligible to be employed to operate a farm elsewhere.

A Band IV Certificate holder can go to an agricultural university and obtain a Band V Certificate after graduation when he can become an agricultural engineer.

The following green certificate system for agriculture has just been established in China. This certificate, also called a technical post certificate, is a technical qualification certificate for Chinese peasants. At present, its implementation scope covers cropping, animal husbandry and veterinary, aquatic production, agricultural machinery management, rural cooperative economic management, rural energy and environmental protection, etc. The system is in line with the development of big agriculture.

It is undeniable that at the present stage in China, it is an unrealistic fantasy to require all agricultural laborers engaged in agriculture to obtain a green certificate, but the system can be practiced to train a batch of modern peasants for the development of modern agriculture. At present, the targets of the system are mainly the specialized agricultural production personnel with junior and senior high school education, and the personnel of the socialized agricultural service system such as village cadres, specialized households, technology demonstration households and peasants engaging in some technical work. They are not in the majority of current agricultural laborers, but they represent their future. Here is the description of the new type of peasants reported on Page 5 of *Guangming Daily* on November 8, 2011.

Our former impression of a peasant was a man with "one mu of land, two cows and the wife and children around him". However, with the development of modern agriculture, this tender but self-contented dream is no longer the pursuit of the rural youth, hence, an essential change in the concept of "peasant".

Recently, at the 18th China Yangling Agricultural High-Tech Achievements Expo in Yangling, Shaanxi Province, the exhibits of large eggplants as tall as half a human, pumpkins weighing 130 kg, peppers of diverse colors, mushrooms growing in pots, etc., replace the traditional simple images. They present the public with the tremendous changes brought about by science and technology.

The peasants who bring their produces to the expo are no longer "rustics". They are fashionable, professional and self-confident. At the expo, they are busy communicating with various agricultural experts from all over the world. They exchange all kinds of information such as successful models and experiences concerning domestic and international application of information technology to promote agricultural production and operation, rural science and technology promotion, agricultural materials and agricultural products marketing services and the education of science and technology in the countryside.

—*Guangming Daily*, November 8, 2011, p. 5

There are two fundamental approaches to cultivating vocational peasants as evidenced in actual cases in many places. The first is promoting rural land transfer, cultivating households of specialized agricultural production and developing household farms. The second is promoting the specialization of agricultural production links, and cultivating and developing various types of specialized agricultural production organizations.

Who will farm the land in the future? The best solution is the cultivation of "vocational peasants" based on all the present agricultural labor forces' free will rather than bind them to the land as permanent peasants. In addition, non-peasants, urban people and college students should be allowed to freely choose to become vocational peasants.

[Case 5.17] Post-85 College Students as Peasants

More than a dozen college students born after 1985 work as peasants in the high-efficiency agro-ecological park in Xidong Street, Zouping County, Shandong Province. They have been here from all over the country in recent years to be engaged in efficient agricultural production. They are involved in breeding, cultivation and care of vegetables, research on and development of horticultural seedlings and growing seedlings in the park, and application to production new technologies such as water-saving irrigation and three-dimensional cultivation.

—*China Youth Daily*, December 20, 2012 p. 1

5.13 Summary (The Ultimate Purpose of Reforming SF is to Enhance the Capability Approach to Achieving Substantial Freedom)

Contemporary Chinese agricultural production organizations take a multi-symbiotic structural pattern based on peasant household operations. Transforming SF is the key to realizing the modernization of agricultural production organizations and even achieving comprehensive agricultural modernization.

Transforming SF on the basis of market economy is not to eliminate it. Throughout the history of world agricultural development, especially the history of agricultural modernization in developed countries, the modern SF system is still a microeconomic foundation of modern agriculture. Of course, the modern and the traditional systems are much alike in form, but entirely different essentially. The latter is loose sand as described in Marx's potato economy while the former is closely linked to a large marketized network by means of a variety of economic channels and ties. Therefore, modern SF is marketized SF.

Transforming traditional SF into marketized SF is a key link in the modernization of contemporary Chinese agricultural production organizations. However, it is not the ultimate purpose of the transformation. Actually, the ultimate purpose is to improve the capability approach of the majority of farmers to achieve "substantial freedom" rather than marketize SF. Granted, the transformation is indeed an inevitable requirement of the development of rural market economy and an objective trend that no one can will against. In this respect, marketizing SF is irreversible, but the ultimate goal does not mean that the higher the marketization, the better.

Not everything needs to be marketized and the marketization here is no pan-marketization. The marketization that undermines the goal is not desirable. Therefore, in the course of the transformation, the governments and society also have important responsibilities, and it is not right that everything is market-oriented. That is to say, in some respects and realms, the governments and society should take the place of the market.

The premise for the marketized SF reform is to significantly reduce the farming forces. Only their large-scale transfer can provide essential resources, and organizational and institutional space for the marketized reform. Practice has shown that China's marketized SF reform has proceeded along with China's large-scale agricultural labor transfer. The very large-scale agricultural labor transfer has substantially reduced the size of the agricultural laborers who live on the land for life so that China's extremely abundant labor resources can be optimally allocated in a wider space. The transfer is also conducive to the gradual transformation of Chinese peasants into small marketized peasants. However, due to the lag of the reform of China's urban and rural household registration system, there are still various institutional obstacles to the transformation of peasants into citizens. Consequently, the transfer has not been accompanied by a corresponding peasant citizenization process, which renders the large-scale reduction vulnerable and uncertain.

China's current trading and transfer of land operational rights (contracting rights) under the premise of the same collective ownership of rural land is a realistic and feasible approach to gradually promoting moderate scale land operation through market economy based on marketized SF. With adherence to the basic principles of peasants' voluntary and free choice and multiple symbiosis, it is certain that the goal is realizable of steadily promoting the moderate scale land operation with Chinese characteristics under the premise of a long-term household land-contracting system.

Industrial and commercial investments in agriculture transform household farming into factory farming, agricultural land into agricultural workshops and peasants into agricultural workers. They are radical ways of agricultural land transfers and SF reforms. There are certainly some successful or fairly successful cases across the country, but there are many lessons to take from failures. The consequence, especially the harm to the peasants, cannot be dissolved in a short time. Therefore, it is necessary to be prudent and careful, and great leaps forward should be forbidden. Look deeper into them and it will be found that practice shows that this radical approach may not necessarily enhance the capability approach of peasants to achieving substantial freedom.

Under the specific resource and institutional constraints in China, the specialization and large-scale operation of agricultural production links are also key dimensions of the marketized SF reform. It should be noted that in many parts of China, a considerable portion of household agricultural production is actually outsourced to others in the multi-agricultural production links done by specialized agricultural laborers, who are likely to gradually grow into the main force of China's future agricultural production.

Agricultural mechanization is an important aspect of enhancing peasants' substantial freedom and capability approach. In China, efforts should be made to study how to promote agricultural mechanization on the basis of marketized SF instead of changing the household operation approach to achieve agricultural mechanization. In a market economy environment, the goal of agricultural mechanization is not to pursue the self-sufficiency of agricultural machinery, but the coverage of agricultural machinery services in all agricultural production links. Therefore, the promotion of agricultural mechanization should focus on specialized and marketized agricultural machinery services. Most households do not need to purchase agricultural machinery, but purchase the services instead.

Establishing systems, mechanisms and organizational forms that can bring about technological changes and promote technological progress is an indispensable and powerful marketized means of transforming traditional SF. Therefore, it is necessary to replace the traditional mechanisms and organizational forms of agricultural production technology promotion based on planned economy and the people's commune system with new ones that adapt to market economy and household economy. Practice has proved that setting a multi-symbiotic agricultural technology promotion organizational network under the leadership of the governments is a vigorous, inclusive and realistic choice compatible with market economy. In this regard, special attention should be paid to the role played by agricultural science and technology household demonstrators as pioneers, pace setters and demonstrators in agricultural technology promotion.

The key to marketized transformation of SF is to cultivate more and more new types of peasants to solve the problem of "Who will farm the land in the future?" In terms of development, modern agriculture is not an industry of low technology, but rather an industry that requires increasing high-tech knowledge. Therefore, while agricultural labor is transferred on a large scale and the size of agricultural labor force is reduced, modern agriculture needs increasing high qualities in the labor forces. There are two approaches to cultivating new types of peasants, in other words, vocational peasants. The first is promoting rural land transfer and cultivating households engaging in specialized agricultural production to develop family farms. Another approach is propelling the specialization of agricultural production links and cultivating and developing various types of specialized agricultural production organizations.

Chapter 6

Who Organizes Peasant Cooperative Organizations and Whom to Organize?

Abstract

"Organizing", or the "organizationalization" of peasants, is not to restrain their freedom, but to provide broader organizational and institutional platforms for them to "freely achieve freedom". In this sense, the peasant cooperative economic organizations, especially the specialized peasant cooperatives, provide a freely selectable organizational model for the "organizationalization" of peasants and for the peasants to enhance their "capability approach" to "substantial freedom".

6.1 Does Marketized SF Need Cooperative Economic Organizations?

Do the Chinese peasants who were liberated from the people's commune system more than 30 years ago and who have obtained independent operational rights and rights of free choices still need cooperation and cooperative economic organizations? Some scholars believe that Chinese peasants are "good at individual work rather than cooperation".[1] In particular,

[1] "Their inherent weakness is that they cannot cooperate well. They know their immediate interests but cannot foresee the common interests of different households built on the basis of long-term interests. Consequently, they cannot establish on the basis of equal consultation various forms of economic unions beyond the household. In other words, the common interests of the villagers exist objectively rather than subjectively." (Cao, J. *China on the*

peasants have an internal fear of cooperation due to the sequela of the people's commune system by which they are collectivized and organizationalized. The proposition that Chinese peasants are "good at individual work rather than cooperation" has caused heated controversy in academia. Most scholars maintain that neither "good at individual work or good at cooperation" should not be discussed in an inch-deep way. Either of them should be economically and institutionally contextualized. According to a theoretical linguistic analysis of economics, they each can be regarded as a behavioral preference. In the theoretical paradigm of neoclassical economics, preference stability is an external basic assumption and premise. However, the stability must be based on the stability of the socio-economic and institutional environment. After all, human economic behavior mainly depends on specific historical scenarios and the economic and institutional environment rather than heredities.

Under the potato economy (a bag of potatoes is a bunch of single potatoes) of the traditional agricultural society, peasant households engage in agriculture in a disperse and self-sufficient way. In the narrow specific radius of social interactions, "My household will produce what yours do" and "My household will consume what yours do." The high homogeneity of production and consumption structures makes it difficult to deepen social division of labor. Consequently, economic cooperation based on social division of labor lacks internal motivations and social needs. In this particular economic and social environment, "work by individual households" is the mainstream. However, even in the traditional agricultural society where self-sufficiency prevails, there is mutual assistance and cooperation to a certain degree, in different forms and at different levels among peasants. But such mutual assistance and cooperation are difficult to develop into a stable and standardized form of cooperative economic organization. That is to say, with traditional peasants' cooperation, it is difficult to form cooperatives.

However, China today is no longer a traditional rustic country and the countryside is no longer a traditional self-sufficient farming society. So contemporary Chinese peasants are not the traditional self-sufficient

---

Riverside of the Yellow River. Shanghai: Shanghai Literature and Art Publishing House, 2000, p. 167.)

peasants closed to the outside world. After the reform of the implementation of the household land-contracting system for all peasant households in China, should the countryside and peasants get increasingly atomic, isolated and closed or gradually become more marketized, socialized and open? In the former case, the atomic peasants lack the internal motivation and micro-foundation for economic cooperation while in the case of the latter, the marketized and socialized peasants have inherent needs and internal motivations for cooperation. It is true that peasants' need to cooperate mutually is closely related to joining in specialized cooperatives and other peasant cooperative economic organizations, but they should not be conflated. This point will be discussed in more detail in Section 6.11 of this chapter.

In fact, the marketization of contemporary Chinese SF, or the marketization of the entire rural economy are mutually complementary to peasants' needs for cooperation and the development of peasants' cooperative economic organizations. The World Bank's research report "Peasants' Specialized Associations in China: Review and Policy Recommendations" released in 2006 clearly states: "That peasants take actions to form their own societies and associations to help them confront barrages of challenges has much to do with the popularization of commercialized agricultural production under market economy." "For the small peasant households faced with the challenges of rapid market development, the best solution for them is probably better organizing themselves for cooperation."

Why are household-based peasants marketized or being marketized under market economy in greater need of economic cooperation, and why do they in turn need to establish diversified types of peasant cooperative economic organizations? The World Bank report gives the following reasons.

- "Market development requires an increase in production scale, and this leaves in disadvantage Chinese peasants, who are scattered and have only a small size of land."
- "Meeting new market needs puts higher demands on technical services and supports, which cannot be provided by existing agricultural technology promotion and service departments."
- The contracts are beyond the supply capacity of individual laborers.

- Agricultural materials can be procured at good prices.
- Peasants can gain access to more attention of public/non-public service departments or more public/non-public services.
- Collective investments can generate a larger economic expansion than that of an individual peasant household.
- Cooperation can improve the overall negotiating ability of peasants and provide an important feedback mechanism for dialogues with governments so that they can participate more fully in policy decision-making and their implementation.
- A peasant cooperative economic organization can establish a new social network for peasant households to be connected and combined to reduce the transaction costs of development.
- It is conducive to combat against poverty in rural areas and the alleviation of the marginalization of socially disadvantaged groups.
- It can help to build a good inclusive society.
- It can raise peasants' awareness of democracy.

The World Bank report also reads that given the series of structural changes that have taken place in China, SF marketized and being marketized calls for cooperation, and in turn, it is necessary and urgent to establish cooperative economic organizations.

Many structural changes are accompanied by market opening. One outcome of these changes is the increase in the optimal economic size of agricultural production. In turn, these changes make it difficult for individual peasants with small, scattered land to remain competitive in the market. The driving forces behind the changes include the following factors.

The first is that China's entry into the World Trade Organization has changed the balance of the domestic markets. Under the earlier policy of self-sufficiency in food, many peasants mainly depended on growing grain for their livelihood and did not need to produce diversified items. Now under the framework of the World Trade Organization, China's grain market is open to the outside world, and now food prices are influenced by international markets. Meanwhile, China's entry has also created opportunities for its industries with comparative advantages such as animal husbandry, aquatic products and horticultural products, but they must measure up to rigorous quality standards. It is completely beyond the small-scale peasant households who are used to traditional production methods whether it is to produce a certificate that indicates that the product reaches the standards, or to meet the needs of the global market in terms of quantity.

The next factor is that the vertical integration of the food supply chain has rapidly deepened, and some industries are already under the control of just a few large companies. In order to meet the needs of the emerging middle class, the number of chain stores and supermarkets is constantly rising, which also promotes the integration of the supply chain. Modern supermarkets, convenience stores, mega-marts and member stores, and retail models that never appeared in China before the early 1990s, now account for 30% of urban food sales and the number is going up by 30–40% annually. This tendency is getting increasingly pronounced because of China's urbanization and the expansion of the supermarket chain to the central and western regions, small cities and towns. Meanwhile, local governments, especially the municipal governments, are gradually having traditional free markets closed in the name of food safety and improving the city image. Chain supermarkets purchase large quantities of quality commodities whose production is standardized and moratoria are permissible, which is beneficial to suppliers with abundant supplies and large-scale production lines. Small producers are unable to enter the high value-added markets, as if separated from the consumers by an insurmountable wall.

The third factor that brings about the changes is that consumers are getting increasingly particular, no longer just satisfied with varieties of products or seasonal supplies from which to choose. For example, they are more and more aware of food safety. Producers can make high profits from producing high-quality off-season fruits and vegetables, but large quantities of the same products are required due to many factors including freezing and other transportation infrastructures. They are all favorable to large-scale producers rather than small growers. Varieties of certification standards have been introduced due to concerns about food safety, but the costs and work to meet them are mostly beyond individual small households.

Chinese scholars Zhang Xiaoshan and Yuan Peng discussed theoretically the background and necessity of the rise of peasants' cooperatives after the reform of the rural economic system in China. They accounted for it in four respects. First, the ineffective market mechanisms put scattered small peasant households at a disadvantage in the market. Second, the distortion of resource distribution caused by information asymmetry added to peasants' blindness in terms of production, purchase and sales. Moreover, as the supplies of agricultural produces grew from insufficiency to surplus, it got more and more difficult to achieve the values of produces. Finally, primary agricultural produces kept declining in the share of the final prices of agricultural produces. They reach the conclusion that "When the market situation is severe and the external environment is unfavorable to the development of commercialized agriculture, peasants tend to get organized in various forms of alliance and cooperation in order to counterbalance diversified economic forces in the market so that they may enter the market unanimously at lower costs and in faster ways."[2]

Practices show that the development of rural cooperative economic organizations and the degree of the marketization of rural economy are clearly in proportion to the degree of the marketization of peasants (household-based peasants). In China, rural market economy is the most developed in the Yangtze River Delta Region and it is also here that China's rural cooperative economic organizations are fastest-growing and relatively normalized. According to a joint survey conducted by the Rural Economic Research Department of the Center for Development and Research of the State Council and the Agriculture Department of the Ministry of Finance in 2005, peasant households in Taizhou, Zhejiang, which joined agricultural cooperative economic organizations, accounted for 27% of the peasant households of the city, much higher than the national average of 9.8% over the same period. Across the world, "It is common that more peasants join cooperatives in more agriculturally developed countries. Each peasant household in the United States joins an

---

[2]Zhang, X. and Yuan Peng. *The Theory of Cooperative Economic and the Practice of Chinese Peasants Cooperatives*. Beijing: Capital University of Economics and Business Press, 2009, pp. 131–134.

average of 2.6 cooperatives. More than 90% of the peasants in France and the Netherlands have joined agricultural cooperatives. Around 98% of the peasants in Denmark are members of agricultural cooperatives and each joins an average of 3.6 cooperatives. In Japan, South Korea, Australia, and New Zealand, more than 90% have done so."[3]

6.2 A Bewilderment: Why do Cooperatives Lack Attraction to and Cohesion of Peasants?

The experiences of countries around the world and the practice in various parts of China indicate that peasants' cooperative economic organizations do bring to small peasant households in a marketized economic system scale incomes and cooperation benefits that are not available otherwise. At the end of 2004, China (Hainan) Reform and Development Research Institute and International Republican Institute jointly held a "China International Forum on Peasants' Organizations" in Haikou. Chi Fulin, Chairman of the Federation of Social Sciences in Hainan Province, wrote in the introduction to the proceedings of the conference that "According to the latest information released by the Ministry of Agriculture, the per capita annual net incomes of peasant households that are members of cooperative economic organizations are usually 10–40% higher than those who are not."

Ample empirical investigations demonstrate that their entry into the organizations do ensure them great economic benefits, reduce market uncertainties and avoid market risks. For example, according to the findings of the investigations made by the research group, the members of Hushan Xiangyu Specialized Cooperative in Yongshan County, Zhejiang, have an average annual income of over RMB300 more than other peasants who are not. This is also the case with the cooperative members in Cangnan County, Zhejiang, according to the statistics.

However, in actual economic life, the development of China's rural cooperative economic organizations is not smooth enough. In 2004, a

[3]Han, J. *Surveys of Specialized Peasant Cooperatives in China*. Shanghai: Shanghai Far East Publishing House, 2007, p. 192.

national sample survey organized by the China (Hainan) Reform and Development Research Institute shows that the villages with cooperative economic organizations accounted for only 7.18% of the surveyed villages, which means that in more than 90% villages there was no cooperative. During the winter vacation in 2008, the research group organized undergraduate and postgraduate students from the Economics College of Huazhong Normal University to conduct a questionnaire survey of 1,612 (recovering 1,362 valid questionnaires) peasant households in 14 provinces, two municipalities and one autonomous region.[4] The findings are that peasant households who had joined rural cooperative economic organizations or those associated with rural cooperative economic organizations accounted for only 2.5% of the surveyed households.

After the promulgation of *The Law of the People's Republic of China on Specialized Peasant Cooperatives* in 2006, specialized peasant cooperatives seemed to have entered a period of rapid development under the impetus of the governments at all levels." At the end of June 2011, there were 446,000 specialized peasant cooperatives registered in the industrial and commercial sector and 30 million peasant households were cooperative members, accounting for about 12% of peasant households in the country. Some provinces (municipalities and autonomous regions) announced that cooperatives had been established in all their villages, and some promised that they would exert their utmost to set up cooperatives in all their villages within one or two years.[5] In January 2012, the number of specialized peasant cooperatives in the central part of Hubei reached 20,245, a year-on-year growth of 55.63% and their registered capital amounted to RMB24.663 billion, a year-on-year increase as high as 57.3%.

However, behind the data on the fantastic growth of cooperatives, as Pan Jin pointed out, "After in-depth investigations, it is found that specialized peasant cooperatives have not been positively recognized by the majority of peasants, who are stunned and indifferent to them. Even in the

---

[4]They are Hubei, Hunan, Jiangxi, Henan, Sichuan, Shandong, Fujian, Guangdong, Zhejiang, Tianjin, Hainan, Hebei, Shanxi, Anhui, Chongqing, Guangxi and Jilin.

[5]Pan, J. "Specialized Peasants' Cooperatives in China: Interpretation of Data", *Journal of China Rural Observation*, No. 6, 2011, pp. 2–12.

areas where cooperatives have developed to a certain extent, still a large number of peasant households have not joined any. Of the established cooperatives, a considerable number are no longer operating and even multitudes of operating cooperatives have taken on features incompatible with the existing rules of cooperatives."[6]

They indicate that peasant specialized cooperatives actually have not developed so well as reflected in official data, actually far from them. "Fake cooperatives" and "pseudo-cooperatives", and the phenomena of "being cooperativized" and "being made a member" are widespread in some areas.[7] That is to say, even after the promulgation of *The Law of the People's Republic of China on Specialized Peasants Cooperatives* with the governments' ardent promotion of their development, China's rural cooperative economic organizations still have "a narrow coverage, are run on a small scale and so lack attraction to and cohesion of peasants".

It seems to be a paradox that since "peasant households who have joined cooperative economic organizations earn annually net incomes per capita usually 10–40% higher than other peasant households," why do cooperative economic organizations still "lack attraction to and cohesion of farmers?"

What accounts for the problem? Is it that peasants have an insufficient demand for cooperative economic organizations, or is it that they offer weak supplies or both? Or is it that there are other economic organizations such as an agricultural enterprise that can perform such functions of rural cooperative economic organizations that they may have been replaced and squeezed out?

The following part of the chapter will first discuss many supply issues of peasants' cooperative economic organizations including the possibility of rural enterprises, especially private rural enterprises, replacing peasants' cooperative economic organizations. The second to be discussed will

---

[6] *Ibid.*

[7] Pan provided many examples: "According to an employee of the agricultural economic station in a suburban district of a municipality, 50% of the over 500 cooperatives did not carry out any activities." "Had the author not visited some peasant households according to their names provided, they might not have known that they are already members of a cooperative."

be some reasons for their needs of peasants' cooperative economic organizations, for example, must peasants join such an organization for the sake of cooperation?

6.3 Peasants Cooperative Entrepreneurs: Very Scarce Organizational Resources

According to the theoretical framework of Marshall, a pre-eminent economist, particularly versed in neoclassical economics, entrepreneurs are the personified productive element "organization", or the organizers who organize productive elements. They brave or take business risks, collect the capital and labor needed for business, arrange or "budget" the general operation and supervise details.[8]

Another renowned economist Schumpeter defines entrepreneurs from the perspective of innovators. He believes that entrepreneurs are people who take the new combination of production elements as their basic function. The so-called new combination of production elements includes adopting a new product or a new feature of a product, or a new production method, opening-up a new market, gaining access to or controlling a new supply source of raw materials or semi-finished products and creating a new organization of any kind of industry.[9]

The entrepreneurs in the eyes of Marshall and Schumpeter are not identical, nevertheless, they have much in common. As far as the development of China's rural economy is concerned, one called an organizer of an enterprise is one who creates a new combination of economic resources. In a specific sense, organization is innovation.

As organizers or innovators, entrepreneurs are a very scarce economic resource. This is because they are a special type of human resources. They not only need to be keen observers of opportunities but also need to be decisive enough to take them. They also need to be tough in the case of risks but also need the courage to take risks. They not only need to be able to disrupt the old balance but also creative enough to strike up a new one.

---

[8] Marshall, A. *Principles of Economics*. New York: Macmillan Publishers Limited, 2013.
[9] Schumpeter, J.A. The Theory of Economic Development. University Park: Transaction Publishers, 1982.

They not only need to manage the internal staff, coordinating internal relations but also have the ability to develop outward and to communicate with external connections.

These diversified special traits of entrepreneurs, or special human capital, can be obtained not by common monetary investments, nor copied in batches simply by general school education or training institutions. They need long-term tempering in tenacity and perseverance as well as individual aptitudes. As an old Chinese saying goes, "A thousand troops are easy to get, but one general is hard to find."

Entrepreneurs are scarce and cooperative entrepreneurs as a special kind of entrepreneurs, who organize peasants' cooperation, are even more scarce. This is because they need to have some more special qualities in addition to the basic qualities of entrepreneurs.

To start with, they need to identify and practice the concept and value of cooperation. The main business goal of an ordinary entrepreneur is to maximize the profits of the company. Although modern enterprises have increasingly highlighted the interests of the stakeholders concerned, the interests of the shareholders of the company are still placed at a central position.

However, in the case of a cooperative economic organization, as is emphasized by the International Cooperative Alliance, "Capital is the servant of the cooperative rather than its owner." Therefore, its business objectives are more focused on the sharing of interests by all the members. From this perspective, the maxim of the cooperative economic organization is "efficiency in addition to equality", or "equality and efficiency stressed alike". It is different from an ordinary enterprise whose pursuit is maximal efficiency. This means that the entrepreneur of a cooperative economic organization, or the organizer and the intermediary of the cooperative economic organizations is in a strict sense only a member of the organization. It is not his private enterprise or private company. The organizer is not justified to material benefits much higher than other members. Therefore, material benefits alone can hardly stimulate entrepreneurs with entrepreneurial talents to engage in peasant cooperation and set up peasants' cooperatives.

Obviously, an entrepreneur of a rural cooperative economic organization should pursue dedication such as altruism and putting greater weight on organizational interests. Or according to the analytical framework of the mainstream economic theory, among the objective functions of maximizing personal interests are a greater proportion of non-material and spiritual benefits such as the recognition of and belief in the value of cooperation, doing good to the hometown and the happiness of enjoying a good reputation and social respect.

The second quality is that an entrepreneur is in greater need to pursue democratic management and should be more adept at handling and balancing interpersonal relationships within the organization. An important principle of cooperative economic organizations is democratic management, that is, all members participate in the decision-making of major events on an equal footing and it is emphasized that the principle concerning the decision-making power of all members is "one person, one vote", rather than the stock company's "one share, one vote".

Therefore, an entrepreneur of a cooperative economic organization must be adroit at communicating with a all members when making major decisions by persuading, guiding and maintaining good interpersonal relationships with them all. Therefore, the personal ethics of an entrepreneur and members' trust in the entrepreneur are more important to the entrepreneur than ordinary entrepreneurs. Agricultural expert He Huili had her article entitled "What Do We Learn from the Peasants' Cooperatives in Lishu County?" carried on the website of "Baixin Window". She used some fresh and vivid local language of the leaders of specialized peasants' cooperatives in Lishu County, Jilin Province to describe some characteristics of the entrepreneurs in rural cooperative economic organizations: "Having a business mind and a bodhisattva's heart", and being "a maniac and a fool".

[Column 6.1] What Kind of Leader Does the Cooperative Need?

The peasant elites in point mainly refer to those who have a firm belief in cooperation and selfless dedication, certain practical skills and a macroscopic grasp of the market and policies. None of the leaders of the peasants' cooperatives we have visited are paid or given any allowances. Zhang Shuxiang, chairman of Xiajia Village Cooperative, revealed that the heads should play leading roles that are the key to running a cooperative. They work in a down-to-earth manner and have no intention of personal gains. In the early days of cooperatives, some of the expenses were mostly covered by the directors themselves.

In the long run, the expenses will be covered by the revenues of the cooperative, but in the early days of the venture, it is thrift and diligence that are emphasized. She believes that whoever wants to do anything should initially learn to be a good heart and set a good example for the members to follow and convince them completely. She has rich technical experiences in feed, epidemic prevention, etc. and is good at market predictions, hence the fame of having “a business mind and a good heart”.

Jiang Zhiguo, chairman of Yanjia Village Cooperative, holds that only the “crazy and foolish” will run cooperatives. By “crazy” is meant that one is obsessed with cooperation to such a degree that ordinary people can hardly understand and the so-called “foolish” suggests that the backbone members of cooperatives do altruistic deeds like a living Lei Feng (God’ fool) in a society where personal interests are prized. Since Jiang became the chairman engaged in mutual fund assistance two years ago, he has helped the members to dissolve shortages of funds. He himself has contributed a lot of money to the cooperative because the interest income of mutual funds is insufficient for its expenses. He already has a small farming vehicle, but he is obliged to take the lead in raising funds to buy a large agricultural vehicle, which can help its members with farming mechanization.

Guojia Cooperative has persisted for four to five years due to the central role played by several core members led by Chairman Guo Lianwei, whose nickname is “a forever hold-out”. He used to be a barefooted doctor in his village. When he finally found that a cooperative could lead people from poverty to wealth and happiness in the convictions that a cooperative is the protector of peasants, he began to make use of his expertise in medical skills in an arduous exploration of ways of cooperation in medicine, education and guarantee for the aged.

Another good case in point is Zhou Bin, chairman of Taiping Cooperative, and Zhou He, its supervisor, who are versed in the national policies about “countryside, agriculture and peasants” and the guiding documents in support of peasants’ cooperation. They have also mastered excellent production techniques in farming and breeding, and have learnt from many-year experiences and lessons in cooperation how to use benefits to facilitate cooperation between and among peasants. They have also found effective ways for national financial and insurance industries to serve peasants. They have exerted their uttermost to pioneer new ways of cooperation.

An ordinary member sings a song to eulogize the two leaders.

“Who doesn’t have parents and brothers and sisters, who doesn’t have his/her kernal family? Who doesn’t want to settle down and live happily, who wants to get involved in troubles and disputes?” Just because of the moral obligations on their iron shoulders, how many times have they passed by their houses without getting in?

“You have a mind as broad as the sea and a body as tall as a mountain, willing to be a seed dedicated to others. There are ups and downs on the zig-zag road of cooperation. You withstand cold winters and sultry summers and nothing on earth like bitterness and misery can scare you away.”

> In a sense, it is people's character that determines what they do. It is the dedication and capacities of the leaders of the cooperatives that are the chief forces behind their survival and development.
>
> —He Huili. "What Do We Learn from the Peasants' Cooperatives in Lishu County?", website of *Baixin Window*

Needless to say, rare are the ideal entrepreneurs of peasant cooperative economic organizations in real life. This is also one of the most important reasons for the insufficiency of rural cooperative economic organizations in China. As German scholars say, there will be no cooperatives without cooperative entrepreneurs. This is because even if the majority of farmers have the needs and desires for cooperatives, if no one comes out to organize it, they cannot turn into a real-life organization.

In my opinion, benefiting the people does not equate completely with selflessness. The two are not incompatible actually. The key lies in how to balance public and private or cooperative and personal interests. Of course, compared with private entrepreneurs, the entrepreneurs of cooperative economic organizations must sacrifice more personal interests and have sort of dedication. However, people cannot ask too much of them or even blame them for their reasonable, legitimate and moderate pursuit of personal interests. Ancient Chinese philosophers have long before recognized that "One cannot catch fish in clear water."

6.4 Organizational and Operational Costs of Peasants' Cooperative Economic Organizations: A Comparison with Private Enterprises

The lack of peasants' cooperative economic organizations stems from the scarcity of entrepreneurs as well as relatively high organizational and operational costs. Moreover, there are close causal relationships between them. The scarcity contributes to the high costs, which, in turn, further adds to the scarcity.

In contrast with rural private enterprises, what accounts for the high organizational and operational costs is mainly as follows.

First of all, peasants' spontaneous establishment of cooperative economic organizations is a process of collective consultation and bargaining. It is much more difficult to reach consensus for a cooperative-establishing agreement than that for a rural private enterprise. The reason is that there are higher negotiation and formation costs and even if it is a government-intermediated action without any administrative coercive force, there are also high costs for mobilizing and persuading peasant households to voluntarily join the cooperative. In contrast, a private enterprise can recruit its labor in the market. It is not very difficult to enlist ordinary laborers at a labor market in China with an overall oversupply of labor.

Secondly, cooperative economic organizations implement a member open system in which cooperative members have greater enter and exit freedom, which is not conducive for the cooperatives to maintain long-term stability and development and an even more deadly threat to those cooperatives with large indivisible assets. Therefore, it is very difficult for cooperative economic organizations to perform scale operation. In contrast, the property system of an enterprise or a company is relatively stable. As long as the system and rules restrict the free exit right of a few key members, the mobility of an individual ordinary worker has no substantial impact on the long-term stable operation of the enterprise.

In addition, cooperative economic organizations implement the system of "one person, one vote", democratic decision-making and democratic management. Although it can raise the members' awareness of democratic participation, reduce the information asymmetry in the principal-agent structure and the agent infringing the interests of the principals, but it also adds to decision-making costs and decrease in decision-making efficiency. Especially with ever-changing market situations and fierce market competitions, a lengthy and inefficient decision-making process will lead to inefficiencies in the production and operation of the organizations. Conversely, the decision-making power of private enterprises is concentrated in the hands of a few people, but the decision-making costs are lower, the response to the market is quicker and so the decision-making efficiency is higher.

Fourthly, in order to control capital-dominated labor, cooperatives generally implement the system of internal shareholdings and profits return of their members and restrict external shareholdings and share-based gains. Although this is beneficial to the centripetal force of cooperative members, it also adds to the difficulty of external financing of cooperatives, which is not conducive to their expansion. In contrast, enterprises or companies generally do not restrict external investments and in addition, dividends can stimulate and attract external investments with economic interests, which is undoubtedly beneficial to corporate financing and the expansion of business.

Furthermore, the income distribution of the cooperative organizations is mainly labor-based. Therefore, it tends to be relatively average within the organizations and the income gap among managers, technicians and ordinary workers is small, which is beneficial to harmony between members and reduces the conflict concerning interests within the organization, but it also weakens the role of the incentive mechanism of personal interests, and it is likely that "able members will drop out" when "lazy members get average incomes".

Finally, within the organization, the proceeds stemming from supervision are shared by all members and thus have a public nature, but the costs of supervision are of a private nature. The benefits and costs brought by supervision to supervisors are in disproportion and consequently a weak supervision within the cooperative economic organization becomes commonplace.

6.5 Policy Benefits: The Necessity of Governmental Support

Given the aforementioned greater scarcity and higher organizational and operational costs with regard to peasants' cooperative economic organizations, rural enterprises and companies out-number and out-size them in China. In order to encourage their development, reduce the costs and improve organizational benefits, governments often give them a variety of special policy supports, the so-called "policy benefits". Duan Yingbi pointed out: "The experiences of countries around the world show that the development of peasants' cooperative economic organizations entails the buttresses of the government."[10] In their studies of the development of a

[10]Duan, Y. "Preface: Concerns for and Studies of the Issues of the Improvements of Peasant Organizations", in China (Hainan) Reform and Development Research Institute, eds. *China's Improvements of Peasant. Organizations*. Beijing: Economic Press China, 2005, p. 2.

new generation of cooperative economic organizations in the United States, Andrea Harris, Brenda Stefanson and Murray Fulton discover that even in the United States, a country with a deep-rooted liberal culture, the government also plays an indispensable and irreplaceable role in the process of the generation and development of agricultural cooperative economic organizations. Their research findings all indicate that the process relies heavily on governmental supports in terms of systems and policies.

Why are government buttresses, and institutional and policy supports required? A reasonable explanation is that the institutional limitations inherent in peasants' cooperative economic organizations often put them at a disadvantage in a completely equal free competition environment and so they are difficult to develop rapidly.

Here, the governments support peasants' cooperative economic organizations and give them special "policy benefits" out of a consideration of political and social benefits rather than that of economic efficiency, or they are rather a kind of equilibrium between the interests of interest groups and between policy games. For example, the United States exempted the full tax burden of peasants' cooperatives at the end of the 19th century and it was not until 1951 that some agricultural cooperatives were taxed, but the tax collected was only one third of that imposed on industrial and commercial enterprises. In France, the government gives certain investment subsidies to peasants' cooperatives in the initial period and tax incentives after the establishment, guiding peasants to join them effectively through policies. In Italy, if peasants' cooperatives purchase agricultural machinery by taking loans from the national bank, they will be exempt from the capital reserve that ordinary enterprises must pay (accounting for 30% of the total capital of the enterprise). Moreover, the state can also invest in the construction of agricultural water conservancies according to the plans of peasants' cooperatives. After completion, they will be handed over to the cooperatives for collective use. In addition, in many developed countries such as the United States, there are national legislations that give agricultural cooperatives some legal monopoly on the sale of their produces so that they can legally monopolize some profits.

[Column 6.2] Policy Supports for Cooperatives in Some Developed Countries

America: In 1922, the US Congress passed the Capper-Volstead Act, stipulating that all types of peasants involved in agricultural production can establish associations and other organizations in the form of shares or non-shares and collectively engage in agricultural produces' processing, sale and other activities. The passage affirms the basic norms and legal status of American cooperatives, hence the Charter of Cooperatives. In addition, the act provides a limited antitrust immunity for US agricultural cooperatives, giving them a certain degree of legal monopoly on the sale of agricultural products. In 1926, the Congress passed the law of Sale of Agricultural Products, and the Ministry of Agriculture set up the Cooperative Sales Office, which gradually developed into the current American Center for Agricultural Cooperative Services.

In order to support the development of peasants' cooperatives, the American government exempted the entire tax of the cooperatives at the end of the 19th century. It was not until 1951 that taxes were imposed on some agricultural cooperatives, but the tax was only one third of that on industrial and commercial enterprises. In addition, the government has varieties of subsidies for agricultural cooperatives such as direct subsidies, sales subsidies, long-term agricultural subsidies and crop insurance subsidies.

France: In 1945, the French government promoted the establishment of the National Union of Specialized Peasants' Cooperatives. The Law on the Organization of Agricultural Production Economy and Agricultural Cooperation Charter were promulgated in 1962 and 1972, respectively, to facilitate the development and improvement of agricultural cooperatives.

When various specialized peasants' cooperatives were founded, the government gave certain investment subsidies. For example, when a jointly used agricultural machinery cooperative was established, the government gave it a start-up subsidy of around 30,000 euros. Financial aids, tax rebates and other policy assistance are given to agricultural common economic organizations. Financial subsidies are given to sales cooperatives, for 3 years after the establishment and priority for funding is given.

At the same time, the French government implements different preferential policies for members of specialized peasants' cooperatives. For example, tax exemptions are granted to cooperatives that only conduct business with and serve the members and tax stamps are exempt from registration for grain cooperatives. In addition, agricultural production, procurement cooperatives and agricultural production, processing, storage and sales cooperatives are exempted from company tax (worth 35–38% of their net production value), 50% of the real estate tax and the product tax levied according to the type of industry.

Germany: Newly established agricultural cooperatives are entitled to entrepreneurship funding for 5 years covering labor costs, purchase of office equipment and consultation fees. The initial funding ratio is 60%, and drops year by year. Within 7 years the cooperatives are eligible to investment subsidies. For instance, regarding the operating investment costs in procurement, processing, sales, warehousing, packaging, etc., the maximum funding is 35% of the total investments, but no more than 3% of its sales revenues. Meanwhile, the investments out of the after-tax profits are exempt from income tax, the agricultural cooperatives can be exempted from business tax and motor vehicle tax and cooperatives that provide consulting services, agricultural machinery rental and other services for agricultural enterprises are exempt from corporate tax.

Japan: After the Second World War, in November 1947, the Japanese government formulated the "Agricultural Synergy Combination Law" and after the National Agricultural Association Central Committee was established in 1954, a three-level organizational system was constituted. It consists of grassroots agricultural associations, county economic associations and the National Agricultural Association Central Committee.

After the Second World War, the Japanese government designated agricultural associations main conduits for the purchase and sale of grain and agricultural materials and granted them legal monopoly rights. Since 1961, the associations have assisted the government in the operation of special agricultural funds such as agricultural modernization funds.

In China, Article 8 of *The Law of the People's Republic of China on Specialized Peasants' Cooperatives* stipulates: "The state promotes the development of specialized peasants' cooperatives through financial supports, tax incentives, and measures such as financial, scientific and technological, talent buttresses, and industrial policy guidance." Meanwhile, "The state encourages and supports all sectors of society to provide services for specialized peasants' cooperatives".

The seventh chapter of *The Law of the People's Republic of China on Specialized Peasants' Cooperatives* specifically enumerates the following supportive policies of the government: "Article 49: the state supports the development of agricultural and rural economic construction projects, and can entrust them to suitable specialized peasants' cooperatives involved." "Article 50: the central and local finance departments should arrange funds to support specialized peasants' cooperatives in information, training, agricultural produce quality standards and certification, agricultural production infrastructure construction, marketing and technology promotion services. Priority support should be given to specialized peasants' cooperatives in ethnic, remote and poverty-stricken areas and specialized peasants' cooperatives that produce important agricultural produce urgently needed by the country and society." "Article 51: national policy-based financial institutions should provide multi-channel financial support for specialized peasants' cooperatives in various forms ... The state encourages commercial financial institutions to provide financial services for specialized peasants' cooperatives by various means." "Article 52: specialized peasants' cooperatives are entitled to corresponding tax incentives for agricultural production, processing, circulation, services and other agriculture-related economic activities as stipulated by the state."

That specialized peasants' cooperatives can gain access to these special "policy benefits" from the government has given rise to a considerable number of so-called "fake plate cooperatives" in real life. They are cooperatives by name, but factually rural enterprises and companies by nature, most of which are private enterprises and private companies, some of which are even urban enterprises and companies. This is illustrated by a pig transport cooperative in Shandong, a case provided by Zhang Xiaoshan and Yuan Peng. "This cooperative is actually a family partnership."[11] Named specialized peasants' cooperatives, the enterprises and companies purport to exploit various governmental preferential policies on specialized peasants' cooperatives, that is, to obtain policy benefits including various financial subsidies. Furthermore, the fake plated cooperatives can circumvent some taxes and fees, and enjoy the cooperative construction project benefits, financial loan concessions, tax incentives, etc. Many local governments also support or acquiesce in the enterprises and companies taking the names of specialized peasants' cooperatives. They are done chiefly out of considerations for political achievements. Therefore, the number of specialized peasants' cooperatives counted by local governments is often falsified.

However, it is more common that specialized peasants' cooperatives draw on and introduce some institutional elements and operational mechanisms of enterprises and companies to attract more people of entrepreneurship to run the cooperatives, which reduces their organizational and operational costs. In addition, the specialized peasants' cooperatives established by agricultural enterprises and companies cannot simply be taken as fake plate cooperatives. In real life, this is an extremely important way for China to expand the resources of the organizers of specialized peasants' cooperatives.

---

[11] Zhang, X. and Peng Yuan. *The Theory of Cooperative Economics and the Practice of Chinese Peasants' Cooperatives*. Beijing: Capital University of Economics and Business Press, 2009, pp. 4–5.

If the rigid international standards (the International Cooperative Alliance Standards) are used to judge China's current specialized peasants' cooperatives, it should be said that there are not many standard cooperatives. This has led to debates on international standards and local characteristics of agricultural cooperative economic organizations.

6.6 Specialized Peasants' Cooperative Economic Organizations: International Standards vs Local Features

China's current peasants' economic cooperation organizations originated from China, but they also draw on international experiences. Although traditional rural China also has peasants' cooperative practice, it has not developed any relatively standardized cooperatives, and also lacks a systematic theory of cooperative economic. Therefore, with the "Western wind going eastward", China's early theory of cooperative economic originated from the West and is introduced rather than endogenous. According to the "international standards", the establishment of cooperative economic organizations in a normative manner is the consensus and wish of many people who actively promote the cooperation movement.

However, the practice of cooperative economic organizations in China does not operate in accordance with the norms of "international standards." According to Chen Yixin, the vast majority of the cooperatives in China which were copies of the West in the late 19th and early 20th centuries were not cooperatives in the strict sense, but rather the cooperatives that Chinese intellectuals had softened, improved and localized and rid of the revolutionary elements of cooperativism in the West.[12]

The agricultural cooperative movement launched in the 1950s went to the other extreme of the revolution. The governments promoted cooperation by force, i.e., peasants were "cooperativized" and "targeted" for

[12]Huang, Z. and Shao Ke, "The Nature of Cooperatives and Its Drift", *Journal of Zhejiang University*, No. 4 (2009). Pan, J. "Specialized Peasants' Cooperatives in China: Behind the Data", *Journal of China Rural Watch*, No. 6, 2011. Zhang, X. and Yuan Peng. *Theory of Cooperative Economic and Practice of Chinese Peasants' Cooperatives*. Beijing: Capital University of Economics and Business Press, Vol. 39, 2009, pp. 11–16; pp. 2–12.

cooperation, which ran against the basic principles such as peasants' voluntary cooperation, freedom of entry and exit and democratic regulation advocated by the International Cooperative Alliance. Since the rural reform and opening-up in the late 1970s, peasants' cooperative economic organizations, most of which are various types of specialized peasants' cooperatives, have been flourishing with the rise of rural economic marketization.

However, strictly judged by the international standards, most of these organizations are deviations and alienations and put in the words of Huang Zuhui and Shao Ke, the nature of the cooperative is "drifting" and in Pan Jin's words, "a large number of cooperatives are not consistent with the current regulations by nature." Zhang and Yuan asked more directly: "Are the cooperatives developed in the way we expect?"

What accounts for the "drift" and the inconsistency? Why is there such a big gap? An extremely important reason lies in the multilateral diversified development of these cooperative economic organizations in contemporary China. Duan Yingbi once pointed out: "Currently China's cooperatives vary widely with one common characteristic that many people, including leaders at all levels, have a concept of 'cooperatives' in their minds."[13] That is to say, the peasants' cooperatives in contemporary China are extremely different, especially when each has its strong local characteristics, hence the localization of peasants' cooperatives. The impossible existence of uniform specialized peasants' organizations and peasants' cooperative economic organizations is attributed to differences in geographical features, resource endowments, economic and social development stages, and, still further, in culture and the personal perceptions of local government leaders, cooperative organizers and cooperative members. Adherence to the rigid "international standards" will block the practice and the development of cooperative economic organizations. Changes made according to local characteristics will make it and remaining unchanged will get "nowhere".

---

[13]Duan, Y. "Preface: Concerns for and Studies of the Issues of Peasants' Organizations", in China (Hainan) Reform and Development Research Institute, eds. *Improvements of China Peasants' Organization*, China Economic Press, 2005, p. 2.

Since the reform and opening-up, all kinds of Chinese peasants' cooperative economic organizations have experienced the non-standardized and then gradually standardized development with diversification maintained. Peasants' cooperative economic organizations in many places were initially not confined to any international standard framework, but just "crossed the river by feeling stones". For example, the joint-stock cooperatives in the rural areas of southern Jiangsu can be regarded either as joint-stock enterprises or classified into cooperative economic organizations.

Factually, western cooperatives are not identical, either. Likewise, with no adherence to the rigid international standards, many deviate from them and make innovations based on their national characteristics. For example, the new generation of peasants' cooperatives in the United States, which began to appear in the 1980s, is a modified form of cooperative economic organizations that absorbs some of the advantages of joint-stock companies and, therefore, more effectively dissolves the problem of fairly high cooperative organizational and operational costs.

[Case 6.1] America's New Generation of Peasants' Cooperatives

Due to the fairly high organizational and operational costs of traditional peasants' cooperatives, the new development of contemporary America's market economy has outgrown some of the cooperative principles that people have adhered to, hence, the halt of the development of traditional cooperatives. That's why after the 1980s, a new generation of peasants' cooperatives emerged. Compared with the traditional cooperatives, the new generation has the following distinguishing features.

The first is that the chief goal of traditional cooperatives is to sell bulk agricultural produces, helping households get over sales difficulties while that of the new generation is to enhance the added values of agricultural produces.

Secondly, the members of the traditional cooperatives are free to join and exit from cooperatives whereas the new generation of cooperatives has a certain degree of closure mainly reflected in the following facts. The new generation determines the total equity, the number of members acceptable according to the reasonable scale of operations, and the produce quota according to the number of shares held by the members. Members can retire, but they cannot withdraw their shares. Their shares or residual claim can be transferred internally so that the share capital remains relatively stable.

The third feature is that in terms of financing mechanisms, the new generation generally introduces joint-stock companies' practice of raising social capital by allowing external funds to participate in shareholding so as to expand the scope of fundraising.

The next characteristic is that as for decision-making management mechanisms, the new generation does not strictly follow the traditional cooperatives' one-person-one-vote system, but adopt the method of allocating voting rights according to the size of investments.

Another feature is that the new generation allows external experts to implement a specialized management of cooperatives.

However, too much emphasis on local characteristics will go to the other extreme, that is, the organization just has the name of a cooperative but is not by nature. Essentially, the so-called "local characteristics" castrate the essence of cooperative economic organizations. Will the essential properties of cooperatives "drift"? This involves a key question of what the properties are.

We believe that a cooperative has three properties. The first is the voluntary nature of the joining and the exit of the members. It is true that in order to maintain the relative stability of cooperatives in actual operations, there is a certain degree of restrictions on the joining and the exit, but essentially, they should be voluntary rather than mandatory. The second is the democratic management. The word "cooperative" denotes the cooperation of all members and therefore, its management must involve the participation of all members. The third is the sharing of interests by all. Cooperatives are, in the final analysis, established in the common interests of all members in the first place. Therefore, the benefits of cooperatives should be shared by all members. In these three essential provisions, voluntariness is the basic premise, democratic management the general means and the sharing of interests the ultimate purpose.

Some basic principles of specialized peasants' cooperatives and various types of cooperative economic organizations should develop with time as a matter of course. However, if the essential properties get completely lost, they will be no cooperative economic organizations at all. That is to say, without the peculiar properties, the cooperative economic organization does not need to have the name as if it were different from other economic organizations. Even the new generation of cooperatives in the United States with the essential nature of a joint-stock company maintains some of the characteristics of cooperatives that are different from those of an ordinary enterprise, that is, maintains the essential properties of cooperatives. "First, it is an enterprise owned by both the investors and the targets of the services, agricultural producers, who have the same identity in the enterprise." "Second, although the profits of the new generation of cooperatives are returned according to the shares that the members hold, the shareholdings of the members are linked to the trading quota of the agricultural produces at a given ratio. This is actually the indirect surplus returned in proportion to the transaction amount. Third, one or several shareholders in a common joint-stock enterprise are often in a controlling position, which is not permissive in a new generation of cooperatives."[14]

6.7 Governments as Organizers: Path Dependence in China

According to the international standards, cooperatives should be independent social self-governing organizations freely established by the people and independent of governmental departments. Nevertheless, it is undeniable that the vast majority of the rural cooperative economic organizations in China, including various types of specialized peasants' cooperatives and associations, are either directly founded and pushed by governments, or intricately linked with governmental departments. Rare are the so-called standard and purely civil cooperative economic organizations that are entirely self-organized by peasants and have no connection whatsoever with governments. Essentially it is attributed to the unique national characteristics of contemporary China and a path dependence defined by a historical context.

After the reform and opening-up, especially in the initial stage of the development of China's new rural cooperative economic organizations, the spontaneous cooperative economic entrepreneurs from the private sector were extremely scarce, hence the "organizer bottleneck" in the development of cooperative economic organizations. In order to promote the development of various types of the organizations, the governments used their unique organizational advantages and authority and acted as their organizers.

---

[14]Zhang, X. "Preface", in Du, Yintang, eds. *Cooperatives: A Modern Enterprise System in Agriculture*. Nanchang: Jiangxi People's Publishing House, 2002, p. 3.

The first government organizational form was that government-related departments or companies under governments' control (such as tobacco companies) directly led and organized various types of rural specialized cooperative economic organizations. At the onset and in the initial stage of the development of new cooperative economic organizations after the rural economic reform, governmental departments involved such as science associations at all levels, agricultural economic administrative stations, supply and marketing cooperatives, tobacco bureaus, and agricultural machinery bureaus often initiated various types of cooperative economic organizations in rural areas or acted as intermediaries. Some of these organizations were affiliated with these governmental departments and the heads of the organizations were often the cadres directly appointed by the departments. For example, "Surveys show that the development of the cooperatives in Jingyan County has obvious government-driven characteristics on the grounds that the leading members of most cooperatives are government officials or cadres from village-level organizations."[15]

The second form is that the governments arrange and plan top-down tasks under their administrative hierarchical structures, especially by forcing village cadres to play a leading role in setting up cooperative economic organizations. A World Bank research report says: "It is usually the governments rather than peasants themselves that decide to set up peasants' organizations. The accentuation and stress of the central government on their development put the establishment of peasants' associations on local governments' top agendas. The traditional practice of local government officials to achieve policy objectives is to set quantitative targets, issue orders and assign tasks to governmental departments involved. Many scholars believe that because peasants' organizations are a relatively new form of innovation, it is necessary for governmental departments to provide guidance and encouragement to help them get organized and the governments should play a role in nurturing a new-type of organizations."[16]

---

[15] Han, J., ed. *Surveys of Specialized Peasants' Cooperative in China*. Shanghai: Shanghai Far East Publishing House, 2007, p. 118.

[16] World Bank. *Specialized Peasants' Associations in China: Review and Policy Recommendations*. Beijing: China Agricultural Press, 2006.

Using the unique organizational resources and advantages of the governments to organize specialized cooperatives, associations and other peasants' cooperative economic organizations is a major way or a major experience in contemporary China of accelerating the development of rural cooperative economic organizations. However, it is also accountable for the deviations of the international standards or a major cause of the drift and the alienation of the cooperative economic organizations in China. Of this there are two different interpretations: "On the one hand, the establishment of peasants' organizations can be interpreted as the result of taking governments' orders and therefore, the organizations are not peasants-initiated. On the other hand, this result may indicate that initiatives and supports from the governments or possibly third parties are necessary to the initiation of the establishment of such organizations."[17]

[Case 6.2] Experiences of Developing Specialized Peasants' Cooperatives in XX County, Inner Mongolia

The first experience is that cadres promote the establishment of the specialized peasants' cooperatives by playing the double function of leading and mobilizing peasants. Cadres at all levels play the function fully in leading and participating in, guiding, and promoting the establishment and development of the cooperatives. The leadership in the establishment of cooperatives is an important annual assessment indicator for administrative village cadres. Establishing the cooperatives and their standardization are among the annual task objectives of the township and town cadres assigned to be responsible for a given village. In addition, pushing, supporting and serving specialized peasants' cooperatives are among the buttresses of the units at township or town levels which are assigned the tasks to help given villages. Among the 305 cooperatives in the county, 46% of them were set up under the leadership of village leaders, 23% under the promotion of party organizations at all levels, 16% with the support of cadres at all levels and 15% spontaneously by peasants themselves.

—An excerpt from the official website of the government of *XX County, Inner Mongolia*

According to the aforementioned investigations, rare are the rural cooperative economic organizations directly established and organized by the local governments apart from the involvement of "village committees" which are at a "quasi-government level". Conversely, common are the rural cooperative economic organizations set up under the leadership of

[17] *Ibid.*

governmental departments involved, or quasi-governmental departments concerned, or government-run companies and governmental enterprises and institutions. Good cases in point are all kinds of specialized peasants' cooperatives for the production and marketing of agricultural produces initiated by supply and marketing cooperatives, the specialized tobacco cooperatives whose establishment was initiated with the government-owned tobacco companies or tobacco bureaus as the intermediaries, various types of specialized peasants' associations by the science and technology associations at all levels and specialized agricultural machinery cooperatives by agricultural machinery companies and stations, etc.

Special attention should go to two types of specialized peasants' cooperatives organized by the governmental departments involved. The first type concerns the cooperatives organized with local supply and marketing cooperatives as the main organizers. In 1995, the State Council issued the "No. 5 Document", stating that it is necessary to actively develop specialized rural cooperatives with the support from supply and marketing cooperatives. Propelled by the document, the specialized peasants' cooperatives established by supply and marketing cooperatives at all levels developed rapidly across the country. According to the authoritative data from the National Federation of Supply and Marketing Cooperatives, by the end of 2010, the number of such cooperatives had reached 54,817.

Due to the special nature of tobacco monopoly, the specialized peasants' tobacco cooperatives established under the leadership of the state monopoly tobacco companies or bureaus were quite commonplace in some major tobacco growing areas, achieving fairly good results. For example, in 2010, 20 key tobacco-producing villages were selected to establish specialized peasants' tobacco cooperatives in Enshi, Hubei Province, creating a new pattern of modern agricultural tobacco organizations composed of tobacco companies, tobacco cooperatives and tobacco peasants. The approach of "production by peasant households served by the cooperative" better solved the problem of organizing disperse tobacco peasants and obtained a moderate scale operation and standardized production. Practice has proved that tobacco companies organizing specialized peasants' tobacco cooperatives ensures a rigorous implementation of the national tobacco monopoly policies and the interests of the majority of tobacco peasants, and betters the interests, resulting in a win–win cooperation.

[Case 6.3] The Tobacco Leaf Cooperative of Shandang Village, Le'an Town, Jiangxi Province, Whose Establishment was Initiated and Promoted by the Tobacco Leaf Bureau of the County

Shandang Village is under the jurisdiction of Shandang Town, Le'an County, Jiangxi Province. In 2002, the village began to experiment with tobacco cultivation. By 2004, the tobacco-growing area had reached 128 mu, but the average yield of tobacco peasants was only worth RMB1,500 per mu. The meagre benefits diminished their enthusiasm. In 2005, tobacco growth in the village sank into a morass. At this critical moment, the tobacco bureau and the tobacco office of the county had people involved go to the village for investigations and decided to help the village committee to establish a tobacco leaf cooperative composed of tobacco peasants. By 2007, the tobacco-growing area had increased to 346 mu, and the number of tobacco peasant households had gone up to 33.

In Jan. 2007, under the impetus of the Tobacco Bureau of Le'an County, the Branch Committee of the Chinese Communist Party and the Self-Government Committee of the village, Shandang Village held a village conference of tobacco peasants at which five people with high prestige, a good knowledge of technology, the courage and competence for work, and great enthusiasm about the development of flue-cured tobacco production were elected to constitute a tobacco leaf cooperative council. A tobacco peasant was elected president of the board of directors, and the village party secretary honorary president. The cooperative's charter got improved, and on a voluntary basis, the 33 tobacco peasant households were divided into 10 joint mutual aid groups (three to five households formed one group). In accordance with the principles of equality, mutual assistance and a mutually favorable exchange, the tobacco peasants in each group exchanged labor for labor and helped each other during the production of tobacco leaves without a group leader. Each of the cooperative directors including the presidents were responsible for guiding the tobacco production of two groups. A new operating model was created (see Figure 6.1) with directors and joint mutual aid groups added to the traditional operation model of a company plus peasant households.

Due to the clear division of labor, personal responsibility and the remarkable increase in the rate of varieties of technical measures taken such as material transportation, technical training and field demonstrations, the yield and quality of tobacco went up so much that tobacco peasants' enthusiasm was further stimulated. In 2008, the tobacco growing area in the village stretched to 736 mu, and the number of cooperative members rose to 45 households and 61 in 2009. The new members freely joined the original 10 groups according to the principle of the similar size of tobacco growing areas. Another five households were elected and added to the cooperative council. According to production needs, five more groups were added to the cooperative (the sowing and seedling group, the

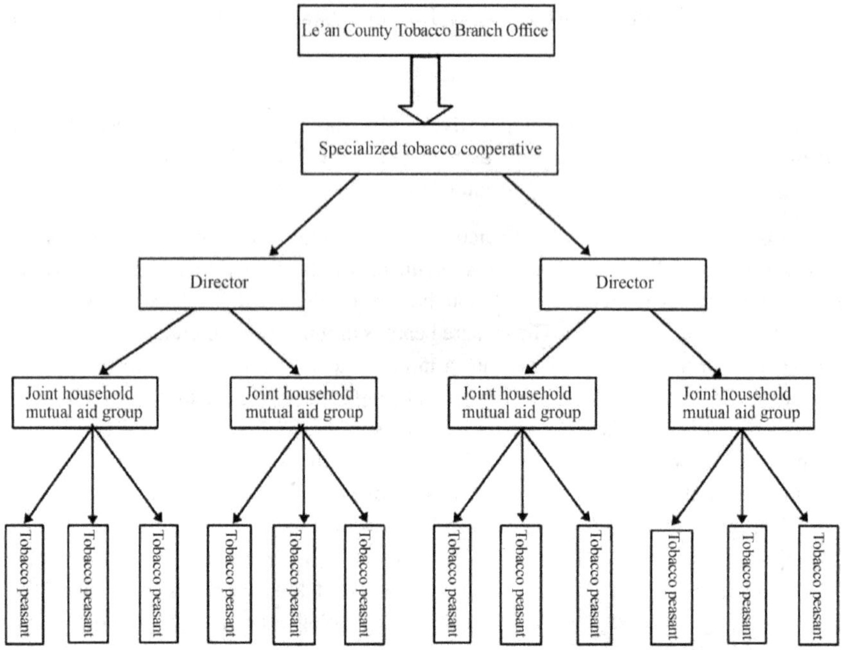

Figure 6.1. Diagram of the operational mode of a specialized tobacco cooperative

machine-farming group, the plant-protecting group, the picking and baking group, and the grading and tying group).

—An excerpt from Zhou, Dongliang, Zeng, Min, You, Gaoliang *et al.* "An Investigative Report on Tobacco Cooperatives in Shandang Village, Le'an County, Jiangxi Province", *Online Tobacco Specials*, April 29, 2009

[Case 6.4] The Supply and Marketing Cooperative of Jiayu County, Hubei Province, Led in the Establishment of Various Rural Cooperative Economic Organizations

Jiayu County is located on the southern bank of the middle reach of the Yangtze River in southeastern Hubei Province. It covers an area of 1,017 square kilometer and is under the jurisdiction of Xianning City, Hubei Province. It is adjacent to Wuhan on the north and rich in rivers and lakes, and boasts of fertile land and abundant products, hence the name of the

"Beautiful South, a land of milk and honey". Since it is a large county for vegetable production, it is also known as the vegetable garden of Wuhan.

Since 1995, Jiayu County Supply and Marketing Cooperative (JCSMC) has been actively implementing the "No. 5 Document" issued by China's National Development and Reform Commission and vigorously led and participated in the improvement of various rural cooperative economic organizations and made remarkable achievements. By the beginning of 2010, under JCSMC there were five specialized associations such as Agricultural Produce Brokers' Association and Agricultural Production Materials Association, 25 village-level comprehensive service agencies and 22 multiple specialized cooperatives involving vegetables, tea, fruit, agricultural materials, cotton, etc., of which specialized vegetable cooperatives made up approximately 50%. Based on them was established the Federation of Rural Cooperative Economic Organizations (FRCEO) co-located with JCSMC, that is, the same staff with two organization names.

There were two types of rural specialized cooperatives whose establishment was initiated and supported by JCSMC.

The first type was based on the existent grassroots' cooperatives. JCSMC relied on the advantages of the township or town-level grassroots' supply and marketing cooperatives in information technology, infrastructure and AI networks. It initiated and supported the establishment of specialized cooperatives involving leading industries or peculiar products by absorbing peasants' shareholdings on a voluntary basis. Good cases in point are the Xinjie Specialized Vegetable Cooperative and the Guanqiao Specialized Tea and Hemp Cooperative.

The second was the specialized cooperative jointly run by JCSMC and the village. Under JCSMC's instructions, such joint cooperatives were built on administrative villages or natural villages and led by competent villagers selected by village leaders or villagers themselves. The examples are the vegetable cooperatives established in Wangjiayue Village, Xinjie Town and Siyi Village, Panjiawan Town.

In addition, JCSMC actively guided able rural people to form specialized cooperatives spontaneously, the Specialized Fruit Cooperative in Luxi Town for example and provided them with timely guidance on production technologies, market information, etc.

JCSMC set up a specialized cooperative led by a JCSMC deputy director to be better acquainted with the county's production, sales and market conditions of agricultural products, release market information and guide the production and sales of specialty products of the county's specialized cooperatives. It arranged market surveys in rural areas and other places all the year round, released irregularly the market information collected with its own Internet equipment to the county's specialized cooperatives to serve the peasants and guide their production.

—This case comes from the author's field survey and thanks are extended to JCSMC for the information provided

6.8 The Boundary of Governments-Dominated Cooperation: The Inviolability of Peasants' Freedom of Choice

It is undeniable that due to the path dependence ascribed to China's special national conditions, the governments play an important role in the development of China's rural cooperative economic organizations. Especially in the early days, their role was difficult to be replaced by other organizers and to some extent they dissolved the scarcity of the resources of China's rural cooperative economic entrepreneurs and reduced the organizational costs of rural cooperative economic organizations. However, the special organizers of the governments were prone to over-engage and thus did harm to the healthy and rational development of rural cooperative economic organizations.

The governments' over-involvement stems from the deep-rooted administrative order-issuing and campaign-launching working approaches of the planned economy period. Their impacts still work even today. The standard practice is that initially high-standard plan indicators are fixed and followed by much publicity, "establish a cooperative economic organization in every village" and "have the vast majority of peasants join a cooperative", for example. Subsequently, the top-down task is decomposed through the determination of the indicators assessing the performance the leaders and the cadres of all levels who are bound to villages and even households. Granted, the government documents and leadership speeches state the principle of peasants' voluntariness, but with political performance closely related to the promotion of local government leadership and administrative staffs as well as the assessment focused on the outcomes rather than the process, it is not rare that in the actual campaign-launching organizational process, peasants are said to have joined the cooperative unknowingly themselves. It should be noted that even today peasants are haunted by the sequelae of the agricultural cooperative process of the 20th century when peasants were made cooperative members unknowingly. Unable to distinguish the current specialized peasants' cooperative and the peasants' cooperative economic organization from the past people's commune, a considerable number of peasants will be frightened even at the mention of "cooperative". What is even worse, the campaign-launching working methods are often simplistic and rude, causing misunderstanding, fear and dissatisfaction among the peasants. This is evidenced in Case 6.5 provided by Chen Wenlie and Ma Dejun of the research team, who made investigations in Hainan Tibetan Autonomous Prefecture in Qinghai. Some herdsmen sold out their cattle and sheep, and private properties out of instinctive fears of the development of the cooperatives, which echoed what had happened during the campaign of the agricultural cooperation in the 20th century.

[Case 6.5] Over-reaction of Herdsmen in Hainan Tibetan Autonomous Prefecture, Qinghai to Being Made Cooperative Members

Hainan Tibetan Autonomous Prefecture is located in the eastern part of Qinghai Province. It is to the south of the famous Qinghai Lake, hence, Hainan (the south to the lake). It covers an area of 44,500 sq km, accounting for 6.18% of Qinghai and its average elevation is over 3,000 m above sea level.

Hainan's economy is relatively backward. Local governments believe that nomadism represents a backward mode of production and hope that the herdsmen will be organized through cooperatives and settle down. Moreover, with the establishment of cooperatives, local governments can also obtain more financial bolstering from higher-level governments, make political achievements and win recognition from higher-level governments.

Conversely, most herdsmen were not highly motivated to join cooperatives as they held that nomadism and living around waters and amidst pastures were the most secure means of livelihood. Some herdsmen believed that joining cooperatives means returning to the previous commune era when their assets were confiscated. Consequently, some herdsmen simply sold their own livestock below reasonable prices.

Hearing the news that a group of herdsmen in Chana Village of Gonghe County sold their livestock and pastures, we went there accompanied by local government officials to look into it. At first the herdsmen were scared and refused to admit the transactions. They did not tell the truth until after we told them that all that we wanted to do was to find out what had happened and the invited living Buddhas in local monasteries explained our purpose to them. A herdsman named Caixiang Renzeng told us that when they heard that the government had decided to have a cooperative established, they all thought that all their livestock would be communized as in the former people's commune days. Some of them had more cattle and sheep than others and felt that they would lose rather than gain. So they started selling their livestock, and finally grass hills and pastures. We reasoned with them and explained the distinctions between the specialized peasants' cooperatives and the people's communes. By setting up cooperatives, the governments meant to do them good. At this, he responded with a blank expression that they were living a good life and did not want to be subjected to any change anymore!

—By the investigators of the team, Chen Wenlie from School of Economics and Ma Dejun from School of Public Administration of Qinghai University for Nationalities

Another manifestation of the governments' over-engagement is that governmental departments concerned, government-related companies, enterprises and institutions practice monopoly in their own interests in the name of building rural cooperative economic. According to Public Choice Theory, they are also "economists" with their own independent economic interests. In the planned economy period, they exploited their administrative privilege to exercise a long-term interest monopoly and their interests were heavily impacted and challenged by the development of market economy after the reform and opening-up. In particular, cooperative economic organizations privately formed spontaneously are very likely to enter the economic fields that they have long monopolized, threatening their economic interests. In response, they tend to exploit their organizational advantages to suppress the development of private peasants' cooperative economic organizations or to grip them in their hands so that they can maintain their monopoly in the name of cooperatives and enjoy the policy benefits that the state grants to cooperatives. Obviously, such over-engagement is a natural choice in their interest games.

Despite their organizational advantages that non-governmental organizations are not entitled to, they are susceptible to some congenital institutional defects such as bureaucratic malpractices and inefficiencies. In addition, even in the period of economic transformation, they still retain to different degree and in their respective different fields more or less, bigger or smaller administrative privileges such as the administrative approval power and the monopoly franchise. Their administrative power converted into monopoly power with regard to economic affairs is prone to give rise to institutional discrimination against other economic entities and do harm to their legitimate rights and interests. This is not only detrimental to the improvement of overall economic efficiency but also violates the principle of fair and just competition in market economy.

During our investigations, some specialized agricultural machinery households complained to us unless they joined the cooperatives organized by the county agricultural machinery bureau or the rural agricultural machinery station, they would run into weird trouble regarding agricultural machinery subsidies, technical training and outbound operations. Some peasants complained that the specialized cooperatives organized by the supply and marketing cooperative monopolized the sources of materials and markets, suppressed the proper commercial circulation in which non-cooperative peasants and those in other specialized peasants' cooperatives get involved. Some peasants who had joined the cooperatives formed by the supply and marketing cooperatives protested that some good posts and benefits of their cooperatives were always divided among the close connections of the cooperatives. In summary, although the government-led cooperation was indeed necessary and justifiable in given periods of time, there should be an insurmountable red line that the peasants' freedom of choice is inviolable and peasants should not be forced to join a cooperative. The coercion is embodied in both the hard campaign-launching administrative orders and the soft exploitation of economic monopoly.

6.9 Able Organizers: Rural Cooperative Economic Organizations are No Pure Unions of the Weak

Although rural cooperative economic organizations are advocated as unions of the weak, in actual life, if organizations are not government-led, most of the organizers of various types of rural cooperative economic organizations are able rural people, the relatively capable rather than the so-called weak. Therefore, specialized peasants' cooperatives and other rural cooperative economic organizations are not unions of the weak in that its organizers are strong. The self-organizations of the weak are extremely rare.

A greater part of the able people as the organizers are village cadres including the former village cadres. As aforementioned, the extreme scarcity of the special human resources is chiefly accountable for the insufficiency of rural cooperative economic organizations in China. In a Chinese socio-economic environment where governments play special roles and functions, especially in the early stages of the reform and opening-up and the development of rural cooperative economic organizations, some current or former rural cadres and public officials including those retired, who converted from leadership to business or played both roles, became an extremely important source of the organizers of China's rural cooperative economic organizations.

According to a survey conducted by Kong Xiangzhi' group from Renmin University of China on 33 specialized peasants' cooperatives in the provinces of Shandong, Shanxi and Shaanxi, 16 heads of the cooperatives were rural cadres, accounting for as high as 48.5%.[18] For instance, the president of Shandong Wucheng Peasants' Science and Technology Information Service Association was a retired former manager of the county's agricultural production material company, the president of Shaanxi Liquan County Peasants' Fruit Association is a two-term member of the municipal Chinese People's Political Consultative Conference (CPPCC) and the chairman of Qi County Yuanquan Green Vegetable Cooperative in Shanxi is a deputy branch party secretary and director of the women committee of her village. Another good case in point is Ye Yiguo, founder and director of the board of directors of Zhejiang Sanmen County Specialized Seafood Cooperative, who is a former director of the county's supply and marketing cooperative and a former director of the county commercial bureau. Yao Fengjun, a deputy director of the Laohekou Municipal Bureau of Fruit Trees to be mentioned in Case 6.6, is an ardent organizer of specialized peasants' cooperatives. It is reported that the heads of 7 out of the 19 specialized peasants' cooperatives registered for business and commerce in 2008 in Xinfeng County, Jiangxi Province, are village branch party secretaries. More typically, all the 256 village branch party secretaries in Xuyi County, Jiangsu Province, led or were involved in the establishment of specialized peasants' cooperatives.

[Case 6.6] An Ardent Organizer of Specialized Peasants' Cooperatives

Yao Fengjun is an agronomist and a former deputy director of Laohekou Municipal Bureau of Fruit Trees. In 2001, he retired from leadership and in May, Yao and his wife moved from the lively city to the Lilou township seedlings experimental base, Baihuashan Forest Farm, in order to guide the fruit peasants to set up a fruit sales association. 2004 saw the

[18] Kong, Xiangzhi, eds. *China's Agricultural Socialization Services: Research Based on Supply and Demand*, Beijing: China Renmin University Press, 2009, p. 144.

establishment of Laohekou Municipal Chunyu Specialized Peasants Association of Seedlings and Fruit (CSPASF).

Yao proceeded to organize the peasants to establish a higher-level specialized peasants' cooperative on the basis of the association. He visited the peasants, bringing home to them the power of cooperation and cohesion, enabling them to have a strong faith in cooperation and guiding them along the road of cooperation. He summoned the members of the association to a meeting, where he claimed: "We are to set up a cooperative in order to lead all to live a well-off life." Carried away by his true feelings, the members raised RMB 300,000, were registered at the Municipal Bureau of Industry and Commerce (BIC) and established the CSPASF in Mar. 2006. It is the first specialized peasants' cooperative in Laohekou City (a county-level city) and the first in Xiangfan City (currently named Xiangyang City under whose jurisdiction is Laohekou City).

At the inaugural meeting, Lao Yao was unanimously recommended to be the cooperative party branch secretary and the technical director.

At the onset, insufficient funding was the major concern. Yao invested in the development of the cooperative the RMB200,000 that he had earned out of his technical instruction and promotion of excellent varieties in Henan a few years before. In order to help the fruit peasants (members of the cooperative) to master the seedling technologies more quickly, he spent RMB30,000 of his own purchasing cameras, computers, and editing and burning equipment. He shot 20 promotional episodes of the compiled traits of the 76 new varieties introduced and their cultivation management techniques, carved into 2,000 CDs to be given away to the fruit peasants and members for free. He also bought 3,000 technical books for them. In addition, he ran technical training programs for the adjacent townships, training 12,000 people (times).

In 2012, the cooperative was awarded the First Batch of National Specialized Peasants' Demonstration Cooperatives in China.

—Yao Fengjun, a former deputy director of the Laohekou Municipal Bureau of Fruit Trees

[Case 6.7] All Village Branch Party Secretaries in Xuyi Led or Were Involved in the Establishment of Specialized Peasants' Cooperatives

Xuyi County is located in the lower reaches of the Huai River and on the southern bank of the Hongze Lake.

It has a total area of 2,483 sq km and 256 administrative villages under its jurisdiction.

In the process of guiding the development of specialized peasants' cooperatives, Xuyi BIC takes measures to ensure that village cadres, especially village branch party secretaries, play their roles and guide them to participate in the establishment and the betterment of the cooperatives.

The first measure is providing counseling and training. Since 2008, the bureau has been actively assisting the organization department of the county party committee in training the village branch party secretaries and directors in batches about the rules regulating specialized peasants' cooperatives. The laws and the specialized knowledge on the training course cover the selection of entrepreneurial projects and operational organization forms, the application for business licenses, the signing of contracts and the registration of trademarks. "Baby-sitting" services are provided for village organizations with entrepreneurial intentions.

The second is physical persuasion. Given that all the village branch party secretaries undertake projects and are competent for operations, the bureau assigned its employees involved to the villages to persuade the secretaries to participate or lead in persuading peasant households producing and operating produces of the same types to set up specialized peasants' cooperatives. Luo Laibo, the branch party secretary of Honghu Village, Guantan Town, used to drive tractors to transport goods together with 100-odd local agricultural machinery operators. Then, the transportation market for walking tractors shrank and many of them stayed idle at home. Therefore, the officials from the Sanhe Branch of BIC visited Luo at the beginning of the year, persuading him to lead the agricultural machinery operators to establish a specialized peasants' machinery cooperative. After over half a year of preparations, Honghu Village set up an agricultural specialized peasants' machinery cooperative composed of 209 agricultural machine operators and with 228 supporting agricultural machines. Due to low fees and good services, it undertakes mechanical farming, planting, harvesting and irrigation services for more than 3,000 peasants of the town and its surrounding areas. Each operator can earn more than RMB100 daily.

The third measure is solving problems and raising efficiency. Whenever a village branch party secretary is encountered with a tough problem in running a cooperative, the BIC will provide him with functional services. At the end of 2007, the bureau bolstered Chen Yuren, the branch Party secretary of Getan Village of Huaihe Town, to organize 59 peasants to set up the Xuyi Specialized Peasants' Vegetable Cooperative engaging in the sales of 22,000 mu of vegetables of more than 3,000 households in Getan Village and three adjacent villages. In response to the initial poor sales and low revenues, some officials from the Shancheng Branch of the BIC went to diagnose the problems. Afterwards they helped the cooperative apply for the registered trademark of Getan, trained 25 vegetable brokers and started field vegetable markets, attracting vegetable merchants from elsewhere. For over one year, the cooperative sold 100,000 tons of vegetables and the vegetable peasant households each increased their income by over RMB10,000.

Now by participating in or leading in the establishment of specialized peasants' cooperatives, all the 256 branch party secretaries have embarked on the road to prosperity with the peasant households.

—Jiangsu Provincial Bureau of Industry and Commerce, "The Xuyi Bureau of Industry and Commerce Guides All the County Village Branch Party Secretaries in the Development of Specialized Peasants' Cooperatives", September 9, 2010

Rural cadres and higher-level public officials do have their own unique advantages in human resources as "organizers" of rural cooperative economic organizations. The reason is that in a developing country under transition like China, the major concern to establish rural cooperative economic organizations is their rapports with governments at all levels and the corresponding governmental agencies. The current or former village cadres and higher-level national cadres are all in office or have such experience and therefore, have a relatively large network of connections from governments and are better acquainted with governmental policies. They have better access to all kinds of supports including policy concessions, land leases, loan acquisitions, etc., from governments at all levels, the township-level and county-level in particular, for cooperative economic organizations. They can even get a full set of baby-sitting-like services as mentioned in Case 6.7. The case of the Fuping County Kenong Fruit Cooperative of Shaanxi Province provided by Kong Xiangzhi's research group shows that "The organizers did much preliminary publicity before the establishment of the cooperative. The person in charge, a former government official, is a vice president of the cooperative. They first went to publicize cooperatives in all the townships and towns of the county, where they first mobilized the able persons in each village, some of whom he had developed friendship with in his previous work."[19]

Relation, defined according to institutional economics, refers to an informal institutional arrangement, and a kind of social capital. In China's specific institutional environment, having or not relations, especially with governmental departments and government officials, tends to be the pivotal factor determining the success or failure of rural cooperative economic organizations. This is because good relations can establish a mutual trust, which reduces the external transaction costs of cooperative economic organizations and fills the power vacuum and bridge the institutional gaps of the transition period. However, too much emphasis on them has negative impacts. For example, it may lead to cooperatives' complete attachment to the governments at the expense of their independence as well as all forms of corruption and distorted markets.

---

[19]Kong, X. eds. *Research on Socialized Agricultural Services Based on Supply and Demand in China*. Beijing: China Renmin University Press, 2009, p. 116.

As rural cooperative economic organizers, in addition to these officials, the able people also include a very large host of major specialized peasant households, technology demonstration households, market brokers and self-employed entrepreneurs who have kept mushrooming since the reform and opening-up. The main advantage of the former is in political relations and that of the latter in markets and economy. Among the heads of the 33 specialized peasants' cooperatives surveyed in Shandong, Shanxi, and Shaanxi by Kong Xiangzhi's research team, six were technically able people, four major growing and breeding households, two brokers, and one corporate leader, totaling 13 people altogether, who were a bit fewer than village cadres, totaling 16, but they far outnumbered ordinary peasants, merely four of them.

Specialized peasant households are the peasant households who first implemented social division of labor after the rural economic reform, engaged in specialized production and had their operations market-oriented in rural areas. Specialized peasant households would develop into big specialized peasant households at a given stage. The "big" here mainly refers to the scale of their specialized operations. They would indeed feel the limitations of single-household operations when they grew big enough. A further expansion would entail either setting up a private company or leading in establishing a cooperative economic organization. Judging from the findings of the surveys, the proportion of setting up private enterprises was greater than cooperative economic organizations.

[Case 6.8] From Big Grain-Growing Peasant Households to Specialized Grain-Growing Cooperatives

Chen Shiluo, a peasant from Ningxiang County, Hunan Province, graduated from a secondary school. After taking odd jobs and engaging in business elsewhere for many years, he was still nostalgic. Therefore, he resolutely returned, contracted land and started scale grain-growing, turning out to be a big grain grower. In 2010, he contracted more than 500 mu of rice fields.

In 2011, Chen led in the establishment of the Ningxiang Daofeng Specialized Grain-Growing Cooperative. It was mainly composed of 18 big grain-growing households connecting nearly 300 peasant households from 13 townships such as Maple Bridge and Batang. The planting area was over 54,000 mu.

—China Research Network of Peasants' Cooperation

The results of multitudes of surveys indicate that peasants' cooperative economic organizations set up through the intermediation by brokers were also fairly commonplace. In general, rural brokers are a group of people who dare to take risks in markets. The earliest batch of them started with the so-called "speculation" and grew into major product marketers. Their main advantage is their acquaintance with the market and closeness to peasants, hence one of the bridges linking "small-scale" peasant households and big markets. Therefore, that brokers lead in the establishment of specialized peasant's cooperatives can solve the sales problems that arise after the peasants engage in scale farming or breeding. For example, in Jintan, Jiangsu Province, peasant brokers play a key role in the specialized peasant's cooperatives. The Rulin Aquatic Professional Cooperative in Changzhou, Jiangsu Province, has 168 members and operates more than 6,500 mu of water area. Guo Caisheng, chairman of the board of directors, was selected Top Ten Agricultural Produce Brokers in Changzhou. Mao Jun, the head of the Specialized Golden Tea Cooperative and three other specialized cooperatives, were among the First Zhejiang 100 Best Agricultural Product Brokers. The results of the survey conducted in 2005 by the Development Research Center of the State Council and the Agriculture Department of the Ministry of Finance show that "Almost all cooperatives in Taizhou were established to solve sales problems."[20]

[Case 6.9] Brokers Led in Establishing Cooperatives in Qunzhong Village, Hailun City, Heilongjiang Province

Since the establishment of the Featured Crops Production Cooperative in 2002 in Qunzhong Village, Yonghe Township, Hailun City, Heilongjiang Province, the peasants' self-produced green corns have been earning at least RMB0.12 more per ear than before through unified quick freezing and sales by the cooperative. In 2004, with other things unchanged, the per capita income of cooperative members was RMB360 higher than the villagers who did not join the cooperative.

The production cooperative of the Qunzhong Village was set up under the leadership of a broker. At the Spring Festival of 2000, Dong Wei, a peasant agent in the village, saw that frozen corns were sold at the price of RMB1 per ear in Daqing City. He calculated that at least 35,000 ears could be processed per mu and with RMB1 per ear, the benefits

[20]Han, J. eds. *Surveys of Specialized Peasants' Cooperatives in China*. Shanghai: Shanghai Far East Publisher, 2007, p. 65.

would outnumber those of a factory. After returning home, he immediately consulted experts and purchased corn seeds. In the same year, he planted sweet sticky corns in all his contracted fields. After autumn, the corns were quickly frozen and put into the Daqing market. They soon sold out. That year, his income from farming exceeded RMB10,000 for the first time. The next year, he planted 75 mu of "quick-frozen" corns with a couple of relatives and had another bumper harvest and a higher income. Under his leadership, by 2002, 42 peasant households in his village grew quick-frozen corns in an area of 150 mu. The huge market and villagers' faith in him made it a matter-of-course that he led in establishing a specialized cooperative.

The cooperative's exploration of raising the degree of peasant's organization was so beneficial and the results were so positive that the cooperative received much attention immediately after its birth. After investigations and argumentation, the municipal supply and marketing cooperative helped the cooperative establish a green pollution-free food production base, register the agricultural product trademark Xiangyu Brand and set up a specialized processing factory to increase the incomes of the peasant households. They invested RMB300,000 in their procurement of high-pressure steam boilers and unified the product standards by supplanting the original backward iron pot boiling processing method with direct modern autoclaving after picking before cold storage and quick freezing. The cooperative also initiated full-time quality inspection to ensure that the sizes of the corns were uniform and the corn steep liquor was suitable.

With the cooperative's improvement of the products' quality, their sales increased remarkably and they entered international markets. In the past few years, 3.5 million quick-frozen ears have all hit the Korean markets, generating RMB1.2 million for its members. Its produces have got diversified and there are five kinds of produces such as quick-frozen melons, potatoes and millet in addition to quick-frozen corns. By now, many peasants from other villages have offered to join Dong's cooperative.

—*Heilongjiang Daily*, September 12, 2005

6.10 Private Entrepreneurs — Cooperative Organizers: Role Positioning and Role Conversions

Rural private entrepreneurs are undoubtedly the able and powerful people in the countryside. They and the organizers of cooperative economic organizations can be regarded as rural entrepreneurs in a broad sense. Nevertheless, different in nature and roles, they should not be conflated. As discussed in the third section of this chapter, the latter need to be more dedicated and cooperative than the former, and therefore are a scarcer resource of entrepreneurs.

Why should private entrepreneurs organize and establish specialized peasants' cooperatives, or other types of rural cooperative economic organizations? The motivations and reasons may vary from person to person. Except for the cooperative and the private enterprise that are the same and one which are named such in order to capture governmental policy benefits, the private entrepreneurs who organize and establish specialized peasants' cooperatives can be roughly divided into two types.

The first type refers to those who completely convert to organizers of specialized peasants' cooperatives or other types of rural cooperative economic organizations. They completely desert their private businesses to focus on the cooperatives and even turn their hard-earned private properties into the cooperatives or the organizations. Judging from the investigations, this is a relatively rare type.

What do they pursue?

Despite their differences in life experience and inner growth, they have one thing in common that the spiritual values of engaging in cooperative economic outweighs that of personal materialistic gains. The investigations indicate that the cultural sources backing up their spiritual values are diversified. They include the desire for a good reputation, the wish of benefiting villagers and winning honor for their ancestors, repaying villagers' kindness, rewarding villagers' recognition and respect, and of course the internalized communism and collectivism through education after the founding of the People's Republic of China and belief in Buddhism and Islam with which they think the cooperative cause is in line. It should be pointed out that the rural private entrepreneurs here may not necessarily have established their enterprises in their hometowns. Actual surveys indicate that most of such entrepreneurs were wage earners.

After many years of hard work elsewhere, they accumulated some capital and market and management experiences before they set up their own enterprises or companies. Many local governments used affection, nostalgia, and friendship to attract them to set up enterprises back home, hence the so-called "home-returning project". The vast majority of these returned private entrepreneurs went back to start private enterprises and some returned and worked as village branch party secretaries or village committee directors. They either established or led in establishing specialized peasants' cooperatives, or village-level collective enterprises. For example, in Tongcheng County, Hubei Province, known for its home-returning project, more than 200 such entrepreneurs have returned from Shenzhen and Dongguan of Guangdong, Shanghai and other places in recent years. Their investments account for 70% of the investments in the county and most of them have started their own enterprises.

However, Li Jinlin, the current branch party secretary of Baota Village in Juanshui Town, is an exception. He graduated from Wuhan University in 1988 and after working in a governmental department and a large state-owned enterprise for four years, he began to engage in business in 1992. Working hard for many years, he established a high-tech enterprise in Shanghai with an annual sales revenue of over RMB100 million and a profit and tax of over RMB10 million. His father served as the branch party secretary of Baota Village in Juanshui Town for 22 years until he passed away in 2006. Under his leadership, the village's collective economy developed rapidly and it became the "star village" of the county. In order to sustain its development and under the repeated urge and persistence of his father as well as the sincerity of the chief leaders of the Tongcheng County Committee, who went to Shanghai to invite him many times, Li Jinlin returned to his hometown in 2006 before his father died. He initially served as the director of the collective emery cloth factory of the village and later its branch party secretary. Meanwhile, his company in Shanghai employed three professional managers for an annual salary of RMB1 million each. He transformed himself from a private entrepreneur to a leader of the village collective economic organization. Another example is Zheng Zhong, a private entrepreneur to be mentioned in Case 6.10, who returned from Chongqing to his hometown to lead the villagers in setting up a peasant's cooperative.

[Case 6.10] Zheng Zhong: from a Private Entrepreneur to the Chairman of a Cooperative

Zheng Zhong was born in Wangping Village, Guandang Town, Shayang County, Hubei Province. He ran a company elsewhere for many years. He was a deputy general manager of Yinzu Ancient Architecture and Garden Engineering Co., Ltd. in Hubei Province, general manager of its Chongqing Branch and the vice executive president of Hubei Chamber of Commerce in Chongqing.

Wangping Village covers an area of 507 acres including 3,357 mu of arable land. It has nine villager groups and 308 households under its jurisdiction. The village mainly grew rice and rapeseed and had no other sideline occupation or business. What is worse, it was a poor place with traffic inconvenience.

Zheng has a strong native complex. After getting rich, he did not forget the villagers. Before returning to his hometown to establish the cooperative, he donated a total of RMB3.67 million to build roads, bridges, welfare homes and drill wells in his hometown. He returned annually and gave the villagers New Year money, but this could not fundamentally rid his hometown of poverty. In 2010, in response to the "home-returning project" in Hubei Province, he returned with RMB100 million, and registered the Shayang Zhengzhong Modern Specialized Pastoral Ecological Agriculture Peasants' Cooperative. All the 308 households in the village joined it and he was the cooperative director.

The cooperative and the village committee joined efforts in the establishment and operation of the cooperative. They contracted land about 2,000 mu including the land owned by the village collectively, and the newly added land after the village was removed was transferred to the cooperative with an annual rent of RMB2 million. Capital management was adopted and half of the rent went to the cooperative's shareholding and operation for dividend incomes.

At present, Wangping Village has completed the transfer of contiguous land and centralized remediation of all its land, set up a complete water conservancy system, modern water-saving sprinkler irrigation facilities and more than 1,000 modern vegetable greenhouses, and planted more than 100 varieties of organic vegetables and fruit, four vertical and four horizontal roads and the first part of a new rural community for the 308 households. The village is planning to build a Chinese ecological garden and the first water town brand in Hubei with ecology-friendly breeding and processing, and eco-tourism services as two wings by constituting a whole ecological industrial chain of ecological agriculture, processing industry and service industry.

The private entrepreneurs who lead and organize the establishment of specialized peasants' cooperatives tend to run both their enterprises and the cooperatives simultaneously. They fall into two types. The first type focuses more on the cooperatives than their own businesses, transiting from private entrepreneurs to cooperative organizers. However, they are outnumbered by the second type of entrepreneurs, who are more concentrated on their enterprises. This is the type in which leading companies intermediate the organization of specialized peasants' cooperatives which will be the focus of the next section. The personal actions of the leading entrepreneurs and the corporate actions of the leading companies are essentially the same.

6.11 Leading Enterprises Organize and Lead Specialized Peasants' Cooperatives: A Chinese Experience or a Variation of Cooperatives?

It is commonplace across the country that leading enterprises, especially leading agricultural industrialized enterprises, lead and organize the establishment of specialized peasants' cooperatives. This is an organizational form of specialized peasants' cooperatives that many local governments zealously advocate. Good cases in point are many large-scale specialized peasants' cooperatives in Hubei Province such as Chunhui Model, Tianhui Model and Fuwa Model.

Generally speaking, the enterprise tends to act as a legal person member of the cooperative, who controls and dominates it. The enterprise and the cooperative are two independent or relatively independent economic entities in terms of jurisprudence, but the head of the enterprise or the manager appointed by the enterprise is usually the head of the cooperative, which is largely in line with the company's development strategy. Some cooperatives are essentially intermediaries linking enterprises and multitudes of peasant households.

There are roughly several reasons why companies are willing to play an intermediary role in the formation of specialized peasants' cooperatives.

First, as aforementioned, the establishment of specialized peasants' cooperatives is entitled to governmental "policy benefits", and the entrepreneurs of leading enterprises as "rational economic people" will naturally embrace such low-cost and profitable opportunities. As Zhang Xiaoshan and Yuan Peng pointed out, "When a policy is issued, it is the strong groups in relation to the preferential policy that first seize the opportunity, fully exploiting it, and it is true of the establishment of cooperatives." "That leading enterprises join in or lead the establishment of a cooperative is interest-driven, which is economically justified."[21]

Second, for most agro-processing enterprises, an important goal of helping with the organization of the specialized peasants' cooperatives is

---

[21] Zhang, X. and Yuan Peng. *The Theory of Cooperative Economic and the Practice of Chinese Peasants' Cooperatives*. Beijing: Capital University of Economics and Business Press, 2009, p. 9.

to secure stable, reliable and quality-assured sources of primary agricultural products. As for agricultural product circulation enterprises, it is necessary to ensure adequate barrages of supplies of agricultural products while maintaining a legal monopoly in a specific regional market bolstered by governmental preferential policies.

Third, the operating model in which leading enterprises directly cooperate with peasant households has the obvious defects of high transactional costs and peasants' low trust in the enterprises, which is prone to trigger off direct conflicts of interests. Conversely, the operating model of major enterprises helping with the establishment of peasants' cooperatives can reduce the costs of dealing with peasants and establish a buffer zone regarding the interests of enterprises and peasants. It is conducive to the coordination and balance of interests between enterprises and peasants. In addition, the establishment of the cooperatives generates a certain sense of ideological superiority. Specialized peasants' cooperatives seem to be more socialistic than private enterprises and in turn, gain access to a series of political or social gains, which enables leading companies, especially the entrepreneurs, to expand their political and social impacts.

The fifth reason is that some private entrepreneurs desire both to maintain their own private enterprises and repay the kindness of their village folks. The establishment supported by leading companies is thought to be an ideal choice benefiting both private entrepreneurs and the cooperatives.

Local governments think highly of and encourage such cooperation. Many of them have issued relevant documents to encourage leading industrialized agricultural enterprises to lead in the establishment of specialized peasants' cooperatives and formulated a series of incentive preferential policies. From the perspectives of institutional economics and government economics, local governments are also "rational economic people". Encouraging such establishments is a rational choice for local governments which can reap economic, political and social benefits from the encouragement.

As mentioned before, the organizational resources are scarce. In order for local governments to get actively involved in the development of specialized peasants' cooperatives in response to the call of the central government and other higher-level governments, the key is breaking through the bottleneck of the scarcity of organizers. Obviously, the entrepreneurs of leading enterprises are rare cooperative organizers with economic strength and organizational and managerial skills. Therefore, the leading enterprise-leading model plays a very important role in the nationwide development of specialized peasants' cooperatives. Furthermore, specialized peasants' cooperatives relying on leading enterprises develop relatively stably, and the latter's economic strengths can ensure a sustainable operation and development of the former. The leaders of many local governments have told us that without the buttresses of leading enterprises, the cooperatives will be deficient in necessary financial bolstering for their routine operation. Some of the cooperatives formed solely by peasants themselves, especially various types of peasants' associations, tend to last merely one year or two for lack of funds.

On the author's investigation tour of Jingmen City, Hubei Province, a head of a chicken association told me that the initial funding of the association was RMB1,000 from the county's Association for Science and Technology. He originally envisaged maintaining its operation on membership fees, but after one year of actual operation, few members offered to pay them. When asked for the fees, they would make various excuses. They just waited for others to take the lead and none paid eventually. The head was very pessimistic about how long the association could hold out. Nevertheless, he was a fairly optimistic person. According to him, this was the case with all other associations. In contrast, it was relatively easy to solve the problem of operating funds for specialized peasants' cooperatives whose establishment was initiated by companies and enterprises.

[Case 6.11] Qionglai Jinli Industrial Com., Ltd. in Sichuan Led in the Establishment of Jinli Specialized Pig Cooperative

Sichuan Qionglai Jinli Specialized Pig Cooperative (JSPC) was established in Aug. 2005 with the Qionglai Jinli Industrial Com., Ltd. (QJICL) as the major leader. Established in 1994, the company has developed into a modern group company of meat processing, sales of frozen pork and meat products, animal husbandry and feed processing. In 2008, it was listed as a major enterprise and a major group company in Chengdu. In order to guarantee the quality and number of pigs, the QJICL established the JSPC with the assistance of the local government. The general manager of the QJICL acted as chairman of

JSPC and the appointed vice chairman was a 60-year-old former village branch party secretary.

Soon after the establishment of the cooperative, the municipal governments of Chengdu and Qionglai, and the QJICL invested RMB400,000 each and the breeding peasant households invested a rolling capital contribution of RMB200,000 with RMB1 per pig. With the RMB1 million, a risk guarantee fund was set up. Both the annual operating expenses of the cooperative which exceeds RMB1 million and the salaries of the 16 staff members of six offices are provided by the QJICL with the QJICL as the first-class finance and the JSPC as the second-class finance.

The cooperative has established a membership conference and holds a member meeting annually. The chairman responsibility system is implemented at the intervals and actually the chairman has the major decision-making power of the cooperative because the supervisory board of the cooperative consisting of six big pig breeding households fails to play its supervisory role.

—Liao, Zujun, Zhao, Lu and Ling Yuzhi, "Research on the Development of the Cooperative Whose Establishment Was Led by a Leading Company — A Case Study of Qionglai Jinli Specialized Pig Industrial Cooperative", *China Cooperative Economic Review*, No. 2, 2010

The third benefit is that in general, the specialized peasants' cooperatives that leading industrialized agricultural enterprises, especially the state, provincial (municipalities, autonomous region-level) industrialized agricultural leading enterprises, have the features of a large scale operation, a wide coverage, leading potential, and fairly standardized operation and management. Therefore, a considerable number of them are "standard cooperatives" and "model cooperatives" set by local governments.

Needless to say, such cooperatives are not commonplace in the history of the development of international cooperative movements, nor is it the model advocated by the International Cooperative Alliance (ICA). It is China-specific to develop leading industrialized agricultural enterprises and encourage them to lead the establishment of specialized peasants' cooperatives. The Chinese experiences are fairly in line with China's rural development and that of Chinese specialized peasants' cooperatives. In addition, there have emerged a number of typical models with regional and local characteristics. For example, in the large agricultural province Hubei, specialized peasants' cooperatives have developed rapidly in recent years. In January 2012, the provincial number of cooperatives reached 20,245, a year-on-year increase of 55.63%, 18.01% higher than the national increase over the same period.

In the development of specialized peasants' cooperatives in Hubei, the leadership of key enterprises is conspicuous and there are some innovative breakthroughs. For example, the "Chunhui Model" to be discussed in Case 6.12 reflects the characteristic "group" of specialized peasants' cooperatives, that is, a leading enterprise leads a group of specialized peasants' cooperatives, which have their own features each. The "Tianhui Model" in Case 6.13 provides the experiences of a major enterprise leading in the founding of many specialized peasants' cooperatives and forming a cooperative alliance.

[Case 6.12] Chunhui Model of a Group of Specialized Peasants' Cooperatives

Chunhui Group (CG) in Hubei is a large-scale private enterprise with the characteristics of the combination of workers and peasants, unity of the urban and the rural and the integration of the first, the second, and the third industries. It mainly engages in research on high-quality rice seeds and grain cultivation, acquisition, storage, processing, trade and real estate development, hotel catering, and tourism services. Currently it has 17 subsidiaries with the total assets of RMB860 million and nearly 1,000 employees.

In recent years, CG has signed a total of 66,000 mu through land transfer agreements in counties and cities such as Xiaonan, Hanchuan, Yunmeng and Anlu, and together with tens of thousands of peasant households established Hubei Longgang Land Shareholding Cooperative (HLLSC), Hubei Chunhui Specialized Agricultural Machinery Cooperative (HCSAMC), Chunhui Japonica Rice Cooperative (CJRC) and Chunhui Fragrant Rice Cooperative (CFRC). They are of three types.

HLLSC is an independent market entity and an economic entity jointly established by the villagers and the collectives of Longgang Village, Tongchang Village, Dongqiao Village and Pengqiao Village, and CG Weiye Chunhui Rice Industry Co., Ltd (WCRICL). Converted into shares are the use right of the village collectives' reserved land, the operational right of the contracted land of the peasant households and WCRICL' agricultural machinery. The cooperative has 669 members (shareholders) with the total assets of RMB10.62 million and a total of 11,773.73 shares. The village collective and peasants get shares by investing 6004.6 mu of land, one share per mu, RMB902.02 per share. Thus 6004.6 shares translate into RMB5,416,300.

Land transfer is conducted almost throughout Longgang Village, which has the largest number of shares involving 4,000 mu and 474 households, accounting for 92.4% of all the contracting households in the village. Therefore, it is called Longgang Model and Whole Village Transfer Model. It is particularly worth mentioning that the peasants' land transfer is entirely voluntary. 37 households are unwilling to transfer their land or all of it for the time being and their decisions are respected.

Chunhui Specialized Agricultural Machinery Cooperative (CSAMC) is the largest agricultural machinery cooperative in Hubei with the branches of Anlu, Yunmeng and Zhuhu. It has a membership of 153, 327 (sets of) agricultural machinery models, an agricultural machinery farm of 80 mu, an office building of 1,200 sq m, a center for agricultural machinery repairs of 400 sq m and a parking shed, a fuel reserve station, a staff accommodation, a canteen and other supporting facilities with total assets of over RMB40 million. The cooperative has a smart greenhouse nursery factory covering an area of 15 mu with a total investment of RMB20 million. It adopts an intelligent management control system, through which workers can sit in the office monitoring and controlling the humidity, temperature and illuminance of each greenhouse. Next to it a large 120 ton/6–7-hour grain drying plant is being built mainly to solve the problem of a bumper rice harvest with a difficult drying during harvesting seasons and to reduce rice losses in rainy days. The cooperative adheres to the development concept of "integrating resources, developing agriculture through science and technology, scale operation, the middle region taking the lead and occupying the leading position in the country". It has transferred concentrated areas of 20,000 mu, on part of which has been built the "10,000 mu of Fragrant Rice Production Demonstration Base" and practices a unified operation and management of the whole process of production and sales.

The distinguishing feature of the CJRC is unified production management, actually a strengthened management of production processes. Its core base has a membership of over 200 peasant households and occupies 6,200 mu, involving over 20,000 mu. Instead of land transfers, it engages in production management and acquisition, implementing the unification of cultivation, breeding, machine insertion, fertilization, irrigation, machine harvesting, acquisition and settlement. They are coordinated by a management team of 56 hired field workers. All the services carried out by the cooperative to its members are not charged on the spot, instead, they are book-kept by field workers and one-off deductions are made after the autumn acquisition. In addition, the prices for agricultural materials and the fees for machinery services provided are lower than at the market while the price for the acquisition from the membership is RMB0.1 to RMB0.2 higher per kilo. If the output at the time of the acquisition does not meet the minimum amount, members can seek compensations from the cooperative. If the acquisition price is lower than at the market, they may refuse to sell their products to the cooperative and pay for the production. Since these provisions ensure that all farming peasants have gains from multi-sources at no risks, they were eager to join the cooperative as staunch supporters and advocates.

In short, the four CJRC cooperatives fall into three main categories characterized with land shares, agricultural machinery shares and unified management respectively. Their structures are compact, semi-compact and flexible. The cooperatives and the neighboring peasant households have established the relationships of fixed and flexible links. Some of the top cooperative managers are the chairman of the group or management is entrusted to second-level or even third-level institutions for management. Some of the operations are unified, others are a blend of unification and division. The distribution of benefits is either diversified or uniform. As for the right of speech, generally it just depends. The members may have a greater final say than the boss or vice versa. Relying on the CGRICL of CG as the leader, the four cooperatives as entities of investment, management and service have intrinsically inseparable relations and each has its own operation as a completely independent market entity. CG can be viewed as a "big view garden" of land transfer, scale operation and specialized cooperation in Hubei.

—Excerpted from "A Modern Agricultural Banner — A Survey of a Group of the Chunhui Group Specialized Peasants' Cooperatives in Hubei", He, Hongwei, Yu, Aimin and Huang Jianjun, eds., *Hubei Agricultural Information Network*, September 14, 2011

[Case 6.13] Tianhui Model of Co-Forming Cooperatives

On Jan. 15, 2012, the Tianhui Cultivation and Breeding Specialized Cooperative (TCBSC) in Hubei was jointly initiated, and registered by Wuhan Tianhui Bio-Engineering Co., Ltd (WTBCL) and the Dongfeng Farm Cultivation and Breeding Specialized Cooperative of Taizi Town, Yangxin County. Later, a cooperative community was formed when a host of cooperatives joined the TCBSC. They were Rare Tea Specialized Cooperative in Enshi City, the Wild Mountain Top Edible Fungus Growing Specialized Cooperative in Jingmen City, Nongxin Edible Fungus Specialized Cooperative and the Healthy Mushroom Specialized Cooperative in Nanzhang County, the Zhengfeng Hongshan Vegetable and Sedges Cooperative in Wuhan, the Luyuan Planting and Growing Specialized Cooperative in Xian'an District, Xianning City, etc. According to the official website of the Tianhui Cooperative Community (TCC), as of December 2012, 40 more cooperatives applied to join it.

Tang Hongquan, TCC's main sponsor and the TBCL's chairman said: "If peasant households can be compared to street vendors, then, specialized cooperatives are small shops and the community we set up is a supermarket with unified management for the sake of modern, scale, intensive, and informatized operation." The TCC is a large-scale comprehensive cooperative economic organization formed to achieve common aspirations and interests. According to the principle of voluntariness, it takes the specialized cooperatives as its basic members and main service targets and through shareholdings they form a community of interests, which participate in competitions outside and engage in good services inside.

Relying on the staunch supports from the enterprise and more than 80 domestic first-class experts and consultants, the TCC focuses on building a strong service system — the Service Center for Cultivation and Breeding, the Service Center for Procurement and Supply of Green Production Materials, the Service Center for Green Agricultural Produces' Safety Monitoring and Brand Marketing, etc.

However, that leading enterprises take the lead in setting up peasants' specialized cooperatives with the assets of the enterprise and cooperatives intersected and overlapped, if not handled properly, will give rise to various problems that do not meet the "international standards" of cooperatives, or even violate *The Law of the People's Republic of China on Specialized Peasants' Cooperatives*. This is chiefly embodied in the fact that leading enterprises turn out to be the actual controllers of specialized peasants' cooperatives, which become their vassals. Sufficient survey findings demonstrate that it is very commonplace that the cooperative with a shareholding system is controlled by a private entrepreneur and one or a few major shareholders. For example, a Zhejiang University research group found that based on 442 cooperatives it had surveyed, the average share of the largest shareholder's contribution to the cooperative's total investments accounted for 29.4%, and the share of the largest shareholder's contribution of 25% of the cooperatives exceeded 30%, some even reached 100%. As mentioned earlier, even the new generation of cooperatives in the United States does not allow a minority holding. That a leading enterprise controls the cooperative and a cooperative is controlled by one or a few shareholders is another main reason for the deviation of China's current rural cooperative economic organizations, especially the specialized peasants' cooperatives, from the so-called international standards, and their alienation.

In order to prevent the dominance of an enterprise, or a company or a small number of individual shareholders from controlling the cooperative, Article 15 of *The Law of the People's Republic of China on Specialized Peasants' Cooperatives* stipulates: "Peasants should at least account for 80% of the membership of a specialized peasants' cooperative. Only one member from an enterprise or institution or a social association is permitted to join a cooperative of fewer than 20 people. For a cooperative whose membership exceeds 20, people from any of them shall make up no more than 5%."

In order to prevent the minority from holding and in turn violating the democratic management principle of the cooperative, Article 17 of *The Law of the People's Republic of China on Specialized Peasants' Cooperatives* provides: "At the membership conference of a specialized peasants' cooperative, the election and voting are implemented according to the one-person-one-vote principle on the premise that any member is entitled to one basic voting right." But in order to ensure the interests of the major shareholders, the clause provides an additional voting right: "Members with a larger amount of capital contribution or number of transactions with the cooperative are entitled to additional voting rights in accordance with the provisions in the cooperative charter. The additional votes shall not make up for more than 20% of the votes of the membership. The names of the members who enjoy additional voting rights and the percentage shall be announced at the membership conference held to the members present."

In addition, "The charter may limit the extent of the additional voting rights." According to our investigations made in Zhejiang, Hubei and other provinces, the fairly normalized cooperatives adhere to the above provisions at least in form. For example, Huang Zeqiang, the legal representative and the largest funder of Rui'an Meiyu Specialized Vegetables Cooperative set up in 2008 in Zhejiang, contributed 16.71% of the investments; the second investor, Hong Zuocun, 15.65%, 7 people each 10 or more than 10%, 4 people below 10% and Chen Chiyou contributed RMB 600, the smallest investment, only 0.2% of the total capital contribution. According to Article 11 that "In principle, regarding a member's capital contribution, a single member (including one from a corporal organization or an association) shall contribute no more than 20% of the total investments of the membership and the percentage of the total funds contributed by the members engaged in production shall be above 50%. Another example is the 8 promoters and funders of the Hushan Taro Specialized Peasants' Cooperative in Yongjia County, Zhejiang Province, who each contributed the same amount of capital, each accounting for 12.5% of the shares. Meanwhile, it also has 268 non-shareholder members."

Article 12 stipulates: "With regard to the election and voting of the membership conference, the one-person-one-vote system shall be implemented and each member shall have one basic voting right. When it comes to the decisions about the disposal of the cooperative's major assets, investments in the establishment of economic entities, external guarantees, and production and operation, no more than two votes concerning additional voting rights (the total number shall not exceed 20% of the total number of votes of the membership) are allowed the member who contributes more than 40% of the total capital investments in the cooperative or whose transactions account for more than 40% of the cooperative's total amount. The names of the members who enjoy additional voting rights and the percentage shall be announced at the conference to the members present."

6.12 Whom to Organize: Specialized Peasant Households or the Impoverished?

A popular view is that a cooperative is the union of the weak. As pointed out earlier, however, the organizers of cooperatives are not at all weak. In reality, the organizers of all rural cooperative economic organizations in contemporary China are either governments and leading enterprises or strong and capable people in rural areas. Then, are the members weak? Is it true that one or several strong people have led and organized groups of the weak to set up their specialized peasants' cooperatives and all other rural cooperative economic organizations? This may not be the case.

On a close analysis of the membership, be it a specialized peasants' cooperative or a specialized association of peasants, the vast majority are specialized peasants' households rather than poor local peasant households. Generally speaking, the specialized peasants' households are fairly wealthy or moderately rich local peasant households. In conclusion, relatively speaking, rural cooperative economic organizations are not composed of the weak in rural areas.

In fact, it is still difficult for poor peasants to join a specialized peasants' cooperative or a specialized peasants' association in that most specialized peasants' cooperatives and associations have some membership thresholds. For example, specialized agricultural machinery cooperatives generally require that the peasant households have their own private agricultural machinery, specialized planting and breeding cooperatives require that the peasant households reach a certain scale of planting and breeding and joint-stock cooperatives require a certain amount of share capital. They tend to keep away the poorest local peasant households. The Rural Economic Research Department of the Center for Development Research of the State Council and the Agriculture Department of the Ministry of Finance conducted a survey of 75 peasants' cooperatives in Jingyan County, Sichuan Province in 2005. The findings indicate that most

Table 6.1. The membership requirements for the admission into 75 cooperatives in Jingyan County

	Is a specialized breeding peasant household	Reaches a minimum scale of production	Has shipping capability	Is technically competent	Products reach certain quality requirements	Has specialized machinery	Pays a new member fee	Pays an annual fee
Sum total	62	61	36	35	24	1	21	15
Rabbit farming	32	35	26	10	10	—	—	—
Sericulture	13	15	14	11	—	—	13	10
Pig breeding	2	1	1	1	—	—	—	—
Fruit industry	7	3	5	5	3	—	4	3
Crops	4	3	2	3	—	1	2	—
Circulation industry	2	2	1	—	—	—	—	1
Association of science and technology	2	2	1	2	—	—	2	1

Source: Han, J. eds. *Surveys of Chinese Specialized Peasants' Cooperatives*. Shanghai: Shanghai Far East Publishing House, 2007, p. 95.

cooperatives required that the applicant should be a specialized breeding household, technically competent and have shipping ability, and that the production should reach a certain scale and the products should meet certain quality requirements.

There is a distinction between members and connected peasant households in some specialized peasants' cooperatives. Many poor peasant households may be classified into connected households rather than members. It should be noted that between them there are distinct differences in the distributions of rights and interests regarding the cooperatives. For instance, a specialized peasants' cooperative can acquire agricultural products from connected households and help them to solve sales problems. However, generally the latter are not entitled to the surplus benefits distributed among the membership at the cooperative's secondary distribution. Neither can they attend its membership conference nor have any voting or discourse right in major matters concerning the cooperative. The Hushan Taro Cooperative mentioned in Case 4.2 absorbed 16 disabled members as it is a poverty alleviation base buttressed by the municipal and county governments. Such admission is a premise on which the cooperative can become the base, which enables it to receive funding and policy supports from the departments concerned (Table 6.1).

It is inherently and logically justified that specialized peasants' cooperatives are chiefly composed of specialized peasants rather than poor ones. As is defined in *The Law of the People's Republic of China on Specialized Peasants' Cooperatives*, "A specialized peasants' cooperative is a mutual aid economic organization out of voluntary cooperation for democratic management based on rural households contracted operation. It is composed of production operators of similar agricultural products or the providers and users of the same agricultural production, operation and services." The word same here has the implication of specialization. In fact, only specialized peasant households have common needs such as the market development of same agricultural products, technological development and training, standardized production and brand unification, etc. It is the common needs based on specialization that are the catalysts of the establishment of specialized peasants' cooperatives. Therefore, their main function is promoting the scale and organization of specialized rural production rather than alleviating poverty.

It is found that specialized rural production and markets prevail where specialized peasants' cooperatives and various types of rural cooperative economic organizations are fairly developed. Good cases in point are the areas such as Zhejiang, Jiangsu, and Shandong Provinces where peasants are relatively wealthy. In contrast, the counterparts in poorer areas are underdeveloped. For them, the practicable approaches to the elimination of poverty may be peasants leaving the village to work elsewhere, setting up small self-employed and private enterprises. After an inspection of a specialized peasants' cooperative in a coastal area of China, a British researcher on cooperatives pointed out: "The reform of the cooperative economic better enables peasants wealthier and with more entrepreneurial traits to seek new market opportunities, but it has proved to be getting increasingly difficult to create a kind of mechanism which protects and even adds to the interests of poor peasants."[22]

The specialized peasants' cooperative is not the most suitable form of poverty-alleviating organization in China in terms of systems and policies. Its major function is promoting specialized and commercialized production in rural areas. The main beneficiaries are relatively specialized wealthy peasants. Therefore, we believe that the cultivation of the formation and development of the rural middle class actually outweighs poverty alleviation.

6.13 Does Peasant Cooperation Have only the Form of Joining a Cooperative Economic Organization?

Except for a solitary individual in a closed, isolated environment, anyone in society needs to interact and cooperate with others. In this sense, it is human to be cooperative and egoistic. Even Robinson, who drifted onto an isolated island, cooperated with Friday when the latter got there. As aforementioned, peasants in traditional society of potato economy cooperated in different ways at various levels despite an economic life of self-sufficiency.

[22]Zhang, X. and Yuan Peng. *Theory of Cooperative Economic and Practice of Chinese Peasants' Cooperatives*. Beijing: Capital University of Economics and Business Press, 2009, p. 7.

Why do the marketized peasants or those to be marketized have strong needs for cooperation is that peasants cannot survive without cooperation since they have been plunged into a marketized and socialized modern network consciously or unconsciously, voluntarily or involuntarily.

Must peasants join cooperatives or other similar peasant cooperative economic organizations for the sake of peasant cooperation? Not necessarily. They provide an alternative form of economic organization for peasants' cooperation, which is not unique and exclusive.

In fact, to date, the vast majority of rural households in China have not joined a cooperative or organization yet. However, the breadth and depth of peasants' cooperation have far exceeded the age of the people's commune when "everyone was a member of the people's commune". In terms of scope, marketized or being marketized peasants have broken down the narrow boundaries of villages and townships through various types of market transactions. The vision of economic exchanges and economic cooperation has extended to large domestic markets and even international markets. Regarding degree, peasants' cooperation is more than a simple mutual labor assistance in that it is embodied in a combination of various production factors such as financial, technical and information cooperation.

As is pointed out in Chapter Four, in rural areas of contemporary China there has appeared a multi-symbiotic economic organizational pattern that diverse economic entities and various economic organizations are in a relatively independent and interconnected coexistence. Connection means cooperation, which does not require one to join a given cooperative economic organization. For example, a peasant household can join a specialized peasants' cooperative, give as a member its products to the cooperative, which in turn sells them to an agricultural processing enterprise or a supermarket. Peasant households, especially big specialized production households, can sign long-term contracts directly with agricultural product processing enterprises or supermarkets without necessarily joining a cooperative. In real life, peasants can choose peasants' cooperation from the forms of cooperative plus peasant households and a leading enterprise plus peasant households. It is true that some scholars strongly advocate the cooperative model of "cooperative plus peasant households and belittle that of a leading enterprise (company) and peasant households."[23] They appeal that "Governmental policies should rather support specialized peasants' cooperatives than the company plus peasant households model."[24]

However, in actual economic operations, the cooperative model of "leading enterprise (company) plus peasant households" still surpasses that of "cooperative plus peasant households" in number and scale. Although the former has declined while the latter has increased since the promulgation of *The Law of the People's Republic of China on Specialized Peasants' Cooperatives* in 2006, the overall pattern has not changed significantly.

Why is it that peasants want cooperation while it is uncommon to join a cooperative? Apart from the insufficiency of cooperatives, they hardly need cooperatives. Here, their needs for cooperation and a cooperative should not be conflated. That is to say, there are other paths to meet the needs for cooperation and specialized peasants' cooperatives or other types of cooperative economic organizations are simply among the alternatives.

That peasants join the above-mentioned organizations according to the principle of voluntariness will be of course both beneficial and costly. Whether to join or not depends on a variety of factors. From the perspectives of free will and organization, their entry into a cooperative is subject to the rules and regulations of cooperatives, which means losing a certain degree of individual decision-making power in production and operation. Multitudes of peasants are perspicacious about which outweighs which. As rational economic people, they will be willing to join a cooperative at such a cost if a broader and higher level of freedom will be obtained such as greater material and financial freedom due to more realistic economic security and increase in incomes and the freedom to get more spare time by averting the risk of sales problems, saving trading time and worries

[23]"The model of company (organization and market) plus peasant households has become infamous." Wang, J. *The Rise of Rural Cooperative Economic Organizations*. Beijing: Economic Press China, No. 3, 2005, p. 130.

[24]Du, Y. "Impacts of Industrialized Agricultural Operation and Peasants Organizational Innovations on Peasants' Incomes", *China Rural Observation*, No. 3, 2005, pp. 9–18.

about production and operation. However, so far, many specialized peasants' cooperatives and other types of rural cooperative economic organizations have been unable to promise peasants stable and credible expectations. This means that the loss of partial freedom cannot be counterbalanced by a sure broader and higher level of freedom. That is why a considerable number of peasants take a wait-and-see attitude.

Consequently, peasants' trust in specialized cooperatives, their intermediaries or heads in particular, becomes a determining factor due to the uncertainties of expectations and for lack of reliable promises. In our survey, when asked at interviews why they did not join cooperatives, most of them would reply that they had no faith in them. They had the least trust in the leader or head, for he was egoistic. Neither did they trust other cooperative members. Another common response was that "I enjoy my freedom and don't want to be controlled by others". This indicates that actually they had a strong awareness of self-reliance and freedom. Without expected and credible practical benefits and substantial freedom promised to peasants, it was very difficult for these organizations to attract them.

The experiences of developed countries demonstrate that joining a cooperative offers peasants more substantive freedom rather than constrain it. For example, in the United States and Denmark, each farmer joins an average of 2.6 and 3.6 cooperatives, respectively, and is therefore not fixed to or locked in any. Farmers still have a high degree of economic independence and freedom of choice. Joining a cooperative means a mere combination of part of the economic functions of the members rather than their belonging to cooperatives. Therefore, they hold that "Cooperatives combines business rather than people".

6.14 A Freely Selectable Organizational Model to Enhance Peasants' Capability Approach to Substantial Freedom

Marketized peasant households are in greater need for economic cooperation than the traditional self-sufficient and the semi-sufficient. The marketization process of small peasants or that of the entire rural economy goes hand in hand with their needs for cooperation and the development of peasants' cooperative economic organizations.

There are two factors accountable for the insufficiency of peasants' cooperative economic organizations in China. They are the scarcity of entrepreneurs and fairly high organizational and operational costs. Moreover, the two have a close reciprocal causal relationship that the scarcity contributes heavily to the high costs, which, in turn, further aggravates the scarcity.

Exploiting governments' unique organizational authority and advantages is the main approach to the acceleration of the development of rural cooperative economic organizations as well as a major reason for their deviation or "drift" from international standards in contemporary China. However, it is undeniable that it is due to the path dependence in China's special national context that governments play an important role irreplaceable in the development of cooperative economic in rural China, make up to some extent for the extreme scarcity and reduce the organizational costs. Meanwhile, governments as special organizers are prone to over-involvement, doing harm to a healthy and rational development of the organizations. Therefore, government-led cooperation should not break the boundaries that peasants have inviolable free choices and should not be coerced into cooperation.

Although the rural cooperative economic organizations are advocated as the combinations of the weak, in actual life, apart from the leadership of governments or leading enterprises, most organizers are able peasants, that is, the relatively strong rather than the weak. Therefore, the organizations are no simple unity of the weak in that the organizers are strong.

Cadres at all levels make up a great percentage of the able people in the capacity of organizers. Another important part of the organizers are varieties of major specialized households, technology demonstration households, market brokers, private entrepreneurs, etc., generated during the reform and opening. The former's main advantages as organizers lie in political and connectional aspects and the latter in markets and economy. It is characteristic of China that leading enterprises, especially industrialized agricultural leading enterprises, take the lead in setting up specialized peasants' cooperatives nationwide. It is an organizational model of specialized peasants' cooperatives advocated by many local governments. Generally, when a leading enterprise leads in the establishment of such a cooperative, the enterprise tends to be the legal person member who takes control and assumes dominance. Although enterprises and cooperatives are jurisprudentially two independent or relatively independent economic entities, enterprise leaders or enterprise-appointed administrators always assume leadership of the cooperatives, which is largely subject to enterprise development strategies. Some cooperatives are essentially intermediate organizations connecting enterprises and peasant households.

The assets of such enterprises and cooperatives are cross-sectioned and overlapped, which will, if not handled properly, bring about various outcomes that do not meet the "international standards" of cooperatives, or even violate *The Law of the People's Republic of China on Specialized Peasants' Cooperatives*. This may be another important reason for their deviation and the so-called alienation.

On a close analysis, it is found that a greater part of the membership of specialized peasants' cooperative or associations is not poor local peasant households, but rather specialized ones. Generally speaking, they are relatively rich or moderately rich localities, which means, relatively speaking, the members are not the rurally weak. One conclusion drawn is that the specialized peasants' cooperative is not the most appropriate form of poverty-alleviating organization as its major functions are promoting the development of rural specialized production with relatively wealthy specialized peasant households as main beneficiaries. Therefore, bolstering the formation and development of the rural middle class by establishing specialized peasants' cooperatives is an alternative organizational approach.

Specialized peasants' cooperatives, or other similar rural cooperative economic organizations, though a freely selectable form of organization for economic cooperation among most peasants, are not the only and exclusive forms of organization. Therefore, granted, rural cooperative economic organizations play an important role in the organization of peasants, but their functions should not be overstated. Essentially, the organization of them is not to restrain their freedom, but instead to provide a broader organizational and institutional platform for them to freely obtain their freedom. Peasants' cooperative economic organizations, especially specialized peasants' cooperatives, only provide one freely selectable organizational model for the peasants to attain capability approach to achieving substantial freedom.

Chapter 7

Networking in the Modernization of Agricultural Production Organizations in Contemporary China

Abstract

The transformation from the uniformation of the people's commune system to the diversification of household-based operation was a great leap forward in the changes in China's agricultural system of productive organization. Nevertheless, diversification does not mean modernization. In modern society, without marketization, socialization and modern networking, the diversified organizational structure cannot effectively ensure that peasants achieve freedom as a matter of course. In response to the demands of the informatization-led agricultural modernization of modern society, the focus and strategic inclination of the further development of China's modernization of agricultural productive organizations are on and to the construction of the networked organizational group for a new leap from diverse to networked with the ultimate goal to improve peasants' capability approach to realizing substantial freedom.

7.1 What Is Meant by *Wangluo*?

"*Wang* (net) can be defined as a crisscross organization or system in Cihai (an authoritative Chinese dictionary), composed of unstructured nodes and their interactions." "*Luo*" has a similar meaning. Cihai defines "*luo*" as a net that means connecting and intertwining. In short, a network is not a single point, nor is it simply a space or an isolated line. Instead, it is an organic combination and a holistic and systematic coordination of and interactions between them all. Therefore, a network has four basic properties: connectivity, systematicness, coordination and interactivity.

Networking is universal in nature, the human self and the entire human society. Therefore, networking research and analysis are widely applicable to natural science, human body science and social sciences.

Biological population in nature utilizes networking organization methods to a great extent. Therefore, research on biological networking is a cutting-edge research in today's biological science. According to the introduction of Institute of Frontier Interdisciplinary Research of Peking University, starting from the nature of the overall dynamics of the regulatory networking of proteins and genes in cells, research on biological networking studies the stability, polymorphism, dynamic properties and evolutionary laws of biological networking, seeks universal laws of biological networking design and dynamics, and verifies or modifies them through cell biology experiments.

Traditional Chinese meridian science can be regarded as a network science about human body systems. The meridian theory holds that like a straight path, the meridian, the backbone of the meridian system, runs horizontally and links inside and outside. In contrast, "*Luo*", which refers to networks, are tiny intricate branches off the meridian into all parts of the body. The meridian and the branches constitute a unified whole, maintaining the coordination and balance of the human body's functional vitality. The occurrence of any disease lies in their destruction.

It is undeniable that the wide application and dissemination of the concept of networking in modern society are attributed to the popularity of the Internet brought by the development of modern information technology. Network in people's daily language generally refers to the Internet. "Got online today?" has become a popular greeting like "How are you?" and various network expressions have gained wide popularity. The Internet is quietly changing the way people produce and live and even the way they think, which, in turn, changes human society. Our era is becoming an era of informationalization and networking. A network system has the basic features of an organic combination of "points", "surfaces" and "lines", overall coordination and interaction, and resources sharing.

Technically, as the Internet is a platform for the transmission of information resources, their reception, connection, and even information resources sharing, networking and informationization are closely related. Nevertheless, the network system is not confined to the information system. Its essential features are also embodied in the modern systems of transportation, logistics, infrastructure, etc. A further expansion of the concept networking has reached the fields of humanities and social sciences stretching from material networking to social networking. Social anthropologists long before proposed the concept of social networking. Mitchell defined it as a specific type of relationships that connect a series of people, things, or events.[1] Obviously, this definition equates social network to social relationships. Famous American sociologist Mark Granovetter adopted the path of connection in terms of weak relationships and strong relationships in response to Polanyi's Theory of Embedded Systems and developed it. He believed that economic behavior is embedded in social structures and the core social structures are the social networks in people's lives. Granovetter criticized the narrow "economic man" analysis paradigm of prevailing Western economics, and supplemented and improved its analytical framework with man in connections. He believed that trust, social relations, and social networking are the basic factors that influence people's economic behavior and economic decisions. He compared theatre fire with family fire, and explained how people inevitably fell into the collective prisoner's dilemma in the theater fire case due to distant relationships and lack of trust, and how the family avoided the so-called prisoner's dilemma in the case of the family fire owing to close relationships and mutual trust.[2]

With the further expansion of social relations, the concepts of social resources and social capital, which are closer to economic terms, have gradually been incorporated into the analysis framework of social networks and further into that of modern economics. Social network theory provides a brand-new picture against which to view our society. It regards

---

[1]Mitchell, J.C., eds. *Social Networks in Urban Situations*.Manchester: Manchester University Press, 1969.

[2]Mark, G. *Embeddedness: Social Networks and Economic Action*, trans. Luo Jiade. Beijing: Social Sciences Academic Press, 2007.

society as a network diagram. There are many nodes in it which are connected by line segments, i.e., social connections. Individuals can take advantage of this network to maintain a certain social identity and establish social contacts so as to obtain corresponding resources. The social resources generated by social relations and networks put in terms commonly used in modern economics are "social capital" thought to exist in social relations and networks and categorized as the third type of capital in addition to economic and human capital. As such, it can increase value and bring future benefits to the owners. As Lin Nan's put it, social capital is "a resource that is invested in social relations in an attempt to be rewarded in markets and dwells in social structures, flows through purposeful actions."[3] Nevertheless, as a product of social relations and social networks, it is different from purely private belongings due to its nature of public goods or quasi-public goods. Therefore, in addition to its increase in personal interests, it is also an extremely important resource for stimulating collective actions and increasing supplies of public goods quasi-public goods.

In a sense, a social network is a sort of virtual network different from what we usually call the virtual world of the network in that it is virtual as opposed to the material network. After all, social networks are distinct from material networks such as the Internet, transportation networks and logistics networks as the latter involve tangible, visible and accessible buildings, machines, equipment, roads, pipelines or accurately measurable currents, information flows, etc. Although many scholars at home and abroad strive to quantify various types of relationships of social networks, the author always believes that they are essentially immeasurable, or are difficult to measure accurately. This is the essential difference between social science and natural science. Of course, just because social networks can be regarded as virtual networks in a certain sense does not mean that the relationships, structures, functions, and systems revealed through social network analyses are imaginary. On the contrary, they actually exist in people's socio-economic life, impacting their economic behaviors and decisions.

---

[3]Lin, N. *Social Capital: A Theory of Social Structure and Action.* Cambridge: Cambridge University Press, 2002.

7.2 Modern Networks: The Interdependence and Mix of Modern Materials and Social Networks

Modern networks defined in this book is a concept used in a fairly broad sense covering not only modern material networks such as the Internet, infrastructure, logistics, etc., but also modern social networks such as modern organizations, interpersonal relationships and so on. They can be viewed as the hardware and the software of modern networks respectively.

Modern society is often referred to as a network society. In spite of their various definitions of network society, scholars have reached a basic consensus that modern networks have an extremely significant impact on modern society and penetrate into all facets of social life. Modern networks are, of course, dependent on the development of modern information technology. It is true that networking has objectively long existed in nature and human society, but the modern network is a new social form resultant from the information technology revolution, accentuating the importance of information as a most important economic resource. Information promotes the conversion of human society to a society of information-and-knowledge-based economy. If the invention of the steam engine, electric power, automobiles, etc., in industrialized society mainly liberates human physical strength, extends and expands human physical fitness, then the information technology revolution, the invention of computers, the Internet, etc., mainly liberate human brain power in information society. They extend and expand the functions of human thinking organs and intelligence, hence a revolution of the human mind. Many scholars hold that human civilization has experienced nomadic, agricultural, industrial and network economies, the last one of which is the economic form that reaches the highest degree of human development.

The Internet, one of the main representatives of the modern information technology revolution, is the foundation of modern networks. As a platform where countless independent nodes are interconnected, interdependent and interactive, it has the essential characteristics of information and resources sharing. Independent nodes, equal participation, free interactions, open platforms and sharing of information and resources are the basic characteristics of the Internet and a modern network economy based on it.

Modern network economy manifests itself as a physical network with a material content. It is the hardware and material carrier of modern network economy. Without it, there would be no modern network or modern network economy. However, modern network economy is more than such a physical network. As is pointed out by David Clark, a senior researcher at the Computer Science Lab of Massachusetts Institute of Technology, "It's not enough to think of the network as merely a connection between computers. More importantly, it links the users. Therefore, its biggest success is not technical but its impact on people."[4] In this sense, modern network economy connects people with the help of these material and physical networks. The essence of information and resources sharing is still people's sharing of interests.

The software and the hardware, and the material network and the social network are interdependent. The more developed the material network is, the more nodes there will be in the network, the more social dimensions will be involved in modern network economy, the greater influence it will have on society, and the more attractive it will be to people. As a result, the modern social network based on the material network will, in turn, get more developed and improved. Conversely, the more people utilize modern networks, the more independent nodes there will be in them and the more extensive and strong people's demands for them will be. According to the rule of decreasing marginal costs (increasing marginal revenues) of network economy, the larger the network scale is, the more network nodes there will be, the smaller the total and marginal costs will be, and the larger the total and marginal revenues will be, which will further accelerate the development of material networks. No doubt, this is a typical positive feedback mechanism: material networks and social networks are mutually adaptive and supportive, and therefore develop unanimously.

Physical and social networks are not only interdependent but are also integrated. For example, modern online banking develops with the advances in information network technology, the Internet as well as social

---

[4]RFC, No. 1336. RFC is the abbreviation of Request for Comments. It is a series of numbered documents of collected information about the Internet and an authoritative source of information sponsored by the Internet Society (ISOC) for the Internet industry.

dealt with here only in so far as they are the personifications of economic categories, the bearers of particular class-relations and interests."[8] Therefore, in Marx's view, the essence of the market is "the sum total of all the mutual relations of commodity-owners."[9] Based on modern social network analysis methods, all commodity owners are the different nodes within this market-oriented network and the sum total of all the interrelationships between the commodity owners constitute a systematic market network. Neo-institutionalists Eirik Furubotn and Rudolf Richter also believe that "Market is a (more or less) contractual network of relationships between individuals or organized groups of individuals."[10]

Market networks are different from social networks in that after all, people's market relationships cannot exhaust all of their social relationships. No matter how extensive the marketization of human society is and how profound the connotation, marketization cannot cover the entire social and economic life of human beings. Therefore, strictly speaking, the market network is only one type of human social network. In a certain sense, as social group animals, people are bound to be related where they are together and there must be social structures and mechanisms that connect them. Therefore, there must be social networks adaptive to them.

Fei Xiaotong, one of the renowned founders of Chinese sociology and anthropology, once described the interpersonal network based on the differential pattern of hierarchy of Chinese traditional agricultural society as another type of social network. He believed that in the social structure of traditional rural China there are differences as well as hierarchies. "In the differential pattern of hierarchy, social relationships radiate from each individual to others, hence an increase in personal connections. The social margin is a network of individual connections" which the author calls an interpersonal network.[11] It is a subjective social network of a traditional

---

[8] Marx, K. *Capital: A Critique of Political Economy*, Vol. 1. Moscow: Progress Publishers, 1956.

[9] *Ibid.*

[10] Furubotn, E. and Richter, R. *New Institutional Economics: An Analysis Paradigm of Transaction Costs*, trans. Jiang Lianqiang and Luo Changyuan, Shanghai: Shanghai Sanlian Bookstore and Shanghai People's Publishing House, 2006.

[11] Fei, X. *Fertility System in Rural China*. Beijing: Peking University Press, 2004.

agricultural society. What are the major and fundamental differences between market and interpersonal networks?

First, the statuses of the social participants (network nodes) in the two types of networks are grossly different. In market networks, the legal statuses of market participants, i.e., stakeholders, are equal. The primary premise is the independence of microeconomic entities and the equality in the legal statuses among the entities. As Marx put it, "A commodity is a born leveller."[12] Interpersonal networks with hierarchical differences, however, are based on the differences in status. The so-called ethics are the hierarchical differences. Fei stated, "The essence of ethics is distinction, which is embodied systematically in *The Book of Rites* in the ten ethical aspects with regard to ghosts and gods, monarch and ministers, father and sons, nobles and subjects, relatives and relations, official titles and salaries, man and wife, political and non-political affairs, the old and the young, and the superiors and the inferiors."[13] That is to say, in this pattern, people have differences and inequality in identity and status.

Second, the two types of social networks have fundamental differences in economic foundation and structure.

Although the microeconomic entities in market networks have equal legal statuses, they differ in production structure and the possession structure of economic resources, hence heterogeneity. Obviously, it is necessary and possible only for the producers of different commodities and the owners of different resources to exchange commodities and property rights. That is to say, market networks are built on commercialized and specialized production, and social division of labor, i.e., differences in economic structure. In interpersonal networks, in spite of the differences in identity and status, the production and consumption structures, and even the overall economic structure of the entire society tend to be homogeneous and non-hierarchal. Here are illustrations of the self-sufficient small peasant economy in a given area. "Their field of production, the small allotment of land that each cultivates, allows no room for a division of labor… We have the allocated patch of land, the farmer and

[12] Marx, K. *Capital: A Critique of Political Economy*, *Op. cit.*

[13] Fei, X. *Fertility System in Rural China*. Beijing: Peking University Press, 2004.

his family, alongside of that, another allocated patch of land, another farmer and another family."[14] Therefore, due to similar production and consumption structures, and similar products produced in the same production methods, no exchange is necessary and consequently markets are of no use.

In addition, the two types of social networks use different media to connect social participants.

Within market networks various stakeholders are chiefly connected by commodity exchanges and property rights transactions. Social interactions and exchanges of such commodities as personified products, and such property rights as personified rights can be made with strangers without their producers or owners through the intermediations of merchants, brokers and property rights trading agencies, market circulations and market trading channels. Here, "The persons' economic character masks are mere personifications of the economic relations as whose carriers they confront each other."[15] Therefore, the participants in market networks need the market trading rules that are provided in contracts, laws and institutions and that all participants must comply with. Institutions and rules are above human connections and interpersonal relationships. In comparison, social interactions in interpersonal networks count on physical presence rather than materialized carriers and intermediaries. In such so-called "acquaintance society" networks, the degree of being acquainted and the distance of "relationships" exemplify Granovetter's strong and weak relationships. In short, human connections and interpersonal relationships are the decisive factors in social intercourse.

Finally, there is a distinct difference in coverage between the two types of social networks.

As the exchange within market networks does not require physical presence, its coverage is much larger than the limited one in the interpersonal networks. As market networks can break down blood bonds, and even geographical and ethnical boundaries, the configuration of production, consumption and production factors tends to get

[14]Marx, K. The Eighteenth Brumaire of Louis Bonaparte. *Karl Marx Selected Works*, Vol. 2. London: Lawrence and Wishart Limited, 1945.

[15]Marx, K. *Capital: A Critique of Political Economy*, *Op. cit.*

increasingly cosmopolitan and international. Obviously, market networks can virtually infinitely expand and have unlimited potentials to develop. Comparatively speaking, interpersonal networks can only be limited to such relatively narrow geographical and spatial areas as "acquaintance societies" or "semi acquaintance societies". For example, in the French countryside of a traditional society, "A normal geographical margin of a farmer in contact with the outside world is 25 km long, a round trip distance a farmer can manage within a day. During 1811–1820 in Le Bleymard, Lozere Province, the places where nearly one third of the married couples had lived before marriage were no more than one km apart and hardly any couple had lived more than 20 *km* away"[16] (see Table 7.1).

The interpersonal network in the differential pattern of hierarchy of traditional agricultural society is the prevailing social network. However, in traditional agricultural society, market networks also exist on a limited scope and in limited fields as there are an underdeveloped social division of labor and a non-mainstream commodity production and circulation. In traditional agricultural society, a considerable part of commodity production and circulation is confined to small local markets such as local bazaars where transactions are confined to acquaintance circles. This suggests that the underdeveloped local market network also has certain characteristics of interpersonal networks. As Marx pointed out, "In every social formation there is a specific kind of production which predominates over all the others and whose relations therefore determine their rank and influence. It is a general illuminant tingeing all other colors and modifying their specific features."[17]

In modern society dominated by market economy, the market network is undoubtedly the dominant social network, but it is not the only one. Especially in the rural areas of contemporary China, market economy is advancing in all directions, but traditional self-sufficient and semi-sufficient economy still occupies a certain proportion. Therefore, the

---

[16] Xu, P. The Reform of French Rural Areas in the Second Half of the 19th Century and the Transformation of Traditional Peasants into Neoterics, *World History*, No. 2, 1994, pp. 34–41.

[17] Marx, K. Introduction to a Contribution to the Critique of Political Economy. *Selected Works of Marx and Engels*, Vol. 1, Moscow: Progress Publishers, 1970.

Table 7.1. Comparisons between market and interpersonal networks

	Market networks	Social networks
Participant's social status	Independence and equality	Attachment and inequality
Production structure	Heterogeneity	Non-hierarchal
Social media	Materialized products	Physical presence
Codes of communication	Contracts and institutions	Interpersonal relationships
Communicative margin	free space	Acquaintance society

social network of contemporary rural China is a network of the market network blended with the traditional social network. On the one hand, peasants in contemporary China have become or are getting to be marketized peasants and the market network has become or is getting to be the major force predominating over peasants' social network.

The predicaments and difficulties encountered by the vast majority of peasants in the process of marketization are largely ascribed to the incomplete, imperfect and underdeveloped market network in rural areas. On the other hand, peasants in contemporary China generally are not oversocialized as described by Granovetter, but rather under-socialized. Therefore, the interpersonal relationship network of traditional agricultural society continues to influence peasants' economic behaviors, decision-making, and even social behavior and decision-making. The impact is not only manifested in traditional production and life but also the fact that peasants often enter the market through the "acquaintance relationship network" to make up for the imperfect and underdeveloped market network, resulting in the blend of interpersonal relationship and market networks. The traditional interpersonal relationship network is integrated or penetrates into the modern market network. Although it cannot be said to be peculiar to China,[18] at any rate, the role it plays in contemporary China has a very significant impact on China's modernization process. Plunged into a "stranger society" of market economy, the vast number of

[18]Quite a few Western scholars such as Wank & David, Xin & Pearce, Gold, and Guthire & Wank believe that connection is a phenomenon unique to China, assuming that the Chinese connection differs from that in the English context. In response, they use *guanxi* instead in their English treatises.

peasants used to rural traditional "acquaintance society" can hardly adapt to it when "guanxi" (connection) can help them with various tough problems. For example, "acquaintance circles" can save peasants many costs in job-hunting in cities. Therefore, in the process of rural labor's migration, traditional interpersonal networks of rural people, relatives, classmates, and acquaintances are often more important and useful than market networks.

In 2011, it was found that more than 80% of the 3,392 migrant workers we surveyed in Tianmen City of Hubei Province got employed through interpersonal networks of relatives, fellow villagers, classmates and acquaintances while only about 10% found their jobs through market channels such as labor markets and employment agencies (see Table 7.2 for specific data). In the case of capital lending and financing, due to financial suppression and discrimination in the economic and social structures of the coexistence of modern industry and traditional agriculture, informal financing through various *guanxis* often exceeds formal financial markets. Abundant empirical studies indicate that, either willingly or in actual actions, peasants are more inclined to take loans from informal financial institutions through private "networks" while only 32% do so from formal financial organizations.

However, there are two sides to everything. Relying too much on and over-emphasizing *guanxi* may distort market networks and hinder their growth, development and improvement. What is even worse, over-reliance and over-emphasis on it will pollute the market economy environment to a certain extent, engendering unfair competition and various types of corruption. One important reason is that when governments at all levels and government officials still control a greater part of economic and social resources, too utilitarian *guanxi* tends to contribute heavily to government-business conspiracies and power-money transactions, leading people to use scarce economic resources in non-productive activities and establish rapports with the officials and benefit from them.

In modern society, there is another kind of social network different from the market network and the interpersonal network of traditional agricultural society. This is the enterprise relationship network that we will discuss below.

Table 7.2. Channels for migrant workers from Tianmen City, Hubei to find jobs

Through the referral of	Person-times	Percentage
Fellow villagers	1,165	29.18
Relatives and relations	1,680	42.08
Fellows and schoolmates	356	8.92
Employment agencies	55	1.38
Governments	45	1.13
Personal applications at labor markets	187	4.68
TV broadcast networks	10	0.25
On-the-spot applications	298	7.46
Others	196	4.91
Sum	3,992	100

7.4 Internal Corporal Relationship Networks in Market Economy

As mentioned earlier, in market economy, all social networks are not market networks. An enterprise is the most basic microeconomic entity in market economy, whose internal relationships may be said to be a blend of market networks and special interpersonal networks. Adam Smith revealed the significance of the division of labor to the increase in labor productivity. "The greatest improvement in the productive powers of labor, and the greater part of the skill, dexterity, and judgment with which it is anywhere directed, or applied, seem to have been the effects of the division of labor."[19] However, he did not distinguish the social division of labor from the division of labor within the enterprise and consequently he did not clearly distinguish the external and internal relationships of the enterprise. Marx was one of the first scholars who realized that there is an essential difference between social and corporal divisions of labor. He clearly pointed out: "In spite of the numerous analogies and links connecting them, division of labor in the interior of a society, and that in the interior of a workshop, differ not only in degree, but also in kind."[20] He discussed

[19] Smith, A. *An Inquiry into The Nature and Causes of the Wealth of Nations*, Vol. 1. Oxford: Clarendon Press, 1880.

[20] Marx, K. *Capital: A Critique of Political Economy*, *Op. cit.*

in detail their difference in nature and characteristics in the fourth part of Chapter 12 of the first volume of *Capital*. He first listed four types of division of labor. "If we keep labor alone in view, we may designate the separation of social production into its main divisions or genera — *viz*., agriculture, industries, etc., as division of labor in general, and the splitting up of these genera into species and sub-species, as division of labor in particular, and the division of labor within the workshop as division of labor in singular or in detail… After further development within a tribe, there springs up naturally a division of labor, caused by differences of sex and age, a division that is consequently based on a purely physiological foundation."[21] More importantly, in contrast, the division of labor in the workshop implies concentration of the means of production in the hands of one capitalist. The division of labor in society implies the dispersion of the means of production among many independent producers of communities. The division of labor within the society brings into contact independent commodity-producers, who acknowledge no other authority but that of competition. In contrast, regarding the internal division of labor within a factory, the capitalist has absolute authority over the workers, which means that the relationship within the factory is one between orders and obedience.

Unlike the market network formed by social division of labor, the interpersonal relations network within an enterprise appears to be similar to the interpersonal network in the differential pattern of hierarchy of traditional agricultural society. Senior managers, grass-roots managers, technicians, foremen and workers in an enterprise are different in roles with a command–subordinate relationship between the senior and inferiors. The multi-leveled vertical hierarchy constitutes a pyramid-shaped power structure. However, on close analysis, the interpersonal network within the enterprise is in many ways fundamentally different from the interpersonal network of traditional agricultural society. First of all, the interpersonal network in a differential pattern of hierarchy results from the undeveloped social division of labor. Moreover, this type of interpersonal network is a subjectivity-based social network of the entire society, the so-called home and country homomorphism. In contrast, the division of labor within

[21] *Ibid*.

enterprises of market economy is the result and catalyst of the development of social division of labor. Marx pointed out: "Since the production and the circulation of commodities are the general prerequisites of the capitalist mode of production, division of labor in manufacture requires that division of labor in society at large should previously have attained a certain degree of development.[22] In turn, its division of labor will have a counter effect, developing and strengthening the social division of labor. In essence, the "command-obedience" and "pyramid" interpersonal relationship network within an enterprise is not a subjective social network of the entire market economy society, but rather a social network subject to the market network dominated by overall economy, not the other way around.

Secondly, the roles of various types of personnel within the enterprise, or their locations in the corporate relations network, are defined by market contracts. In this sense, this kind of enterprise's interpersonal relations network can be a network connected by market contracts with some characteristics of market networks. The market network lights all types of social networks in a market-oriented social form. Jensen and Meckling held that in extreme cases an enterprise is just a connection of a series of contractual relationships.[23] Therefore, the spatial and temporal scope and the natures of functions with regard to internal command-obedience relations, are all strictly limited, rather than simply personally determined. For example, beyond the workplace, working hours and work itself, managers have no business to require the employees to obey orders. Conversely, the interpersonal network in the differential pattern of hierarchy of traditional agricultural society has nothing to do with market contracts as feudal ethics govern people's entire life with the interpersonal network and personal attachment extremely overlapped.

Finally, the internal relations network is not fixed and closed due to many factors. The first is the personnel mobility including both vertical movements within the enterprise such as promotions and horizontal movements outside it like resignation, dismissal and job hopping. The

[22] *Ibid.*

[23] Jensen, M. and W. Meckling. "Theory of the Firm: Managerial Behavior, Agency Costs and Ownership Structure", *Journal of Financial Economics*, Vol. 3, No. 4 (1976), pp. 305–360.

second is that the power structure within the company is under constant adjustment. The interpersonal relations network in traditional agricultural society is relatively fixed. The born hierarchal relationships such as father–son and uncle–nephew define people's roles and positions in interpersonal relationships. Changes in the roles and positions, for example, the son becomes the father and the daughter-in-law becomes a mother-in-law, take a long trying time rather than a free mobility.

It is necessary to distinguish the relations networks within an enterprise and the interpersonal relations networks of traditional agricultural society since currently some scholars who are keen on social network analyses tend to conflate their essential differences and regard them as one. Granted, the interpersonal relations network within an enterprise is extremely closely related to the market network viewed as the universal light in a society dominated by market economy, but after all, they are not identical. Marx saw in his time that the two developed in opposite directions. "The less authority presides over the division of labor inside society, the more the division of labor develops inside the workshop, and the more it is subjected there to the authority of a single person. Thus, authority in the workshop and authority in society, in relation to the division of labor, are in inverse ratio to each other."[24] However, in today's modern network economy era, drastic changes take place in the power structure and the relations network within enterprises with the development of knowledge economy and the waves of the information revolution. The power hierarchy inside enterprises has got increasingly flattened, and democracy is getting more and more prevalent rather than totalitarianism. This means that people inside enterprises, especially the majority of workers have raised their value and status and gained more independence and equality, and meanwhile the internal relations network gets closer to the market network, which is experiencing many significant and even substantial changes. For example, the interactions between market participants are not merely transactions between ruthless strangers since the development of modern information technology and modern networks has greatly expanded people's acquaintance relations circle. Even far apart, they can become acquaintances through modern networks when trust, cooperation,

[24] Marx, K. *The Poverty of Philosophy*. Moscow: Progress Publishers, 1955.

mutual benefit, and symbiosis are getting increasingly important in the market network. These changes mean that the market network and the corporate relations network are infiltrating each other when a new pattern of networked organizational groups in modern network economy is gradually taking shape.

7.5 Networked Organizational Groups in the Era of Modern Network Economy

A networked organizational group, or, in a popular term today, a networked organization, is a new form of economic organizations in the modern networked economy era, or an organizational structure of a higher level. In a certain sense, it can be viewed as a new organizational pattern formed by the mutual penetration of the market network and the internal relations network of the enterprise. Networked organizations arose from the barrages of new economy waves of knowledge economy, information economy and networked economy embodied in the information technology revolution. With the emergence of the Internet, the pyramid-shaped internal organization hierarchy based on industrialized society was challenged by the information revolution triggered by the "information superhighway", the development and flourishing of virtual economy and networked economy coupled with the informatization and globalization of social economy. Due to the interweaving and complexity of the social, natural and ecological environments across the world as well as the growing uncertainty of human society, traditional enterprise hierarchal organizations with planning and control as the core functions were rendered clearly unable to adapt to the new era. The reason for it is that the capacity of the corporal hierarchal organization to control and process information is no more adaptive to the decision-making environment where information rapidly changes and explodes. Meanwhile, the information revolution, the application and popularization of network technology and the rapid development of modern networked economy have made possible the sharing of information and resources in human society in a wider sense and in turn individual free space is expanded in an unprecedented way. They provide a more practical technical and material foundation and a wider world for human society to better display individuality and realize freedom more freely. The old balance of power based on information monopoly, fortifying information asymmetry, and obedience and authority has been broken and a new networked organization relationship based on information disclosure, transparency, sharing, and more freedom and equality is developing. It is in this sense that the rise of networked organizations is a revolution in organizational theory and practice.

First, the networked organization is not a corporal organization in a sense of traditional industrialization, nor is it a vertically integrated enterprise merger and reorganization in a traditional sense. Instead, it is a "community of interests" or "strategic organization alliance" formed by the connection of many independent or relatively independent individuals and legal persons (networked nodes). Its operation does not rely on the traditional top-down hierarchal control, nor is it a pure market transaction between strangers. The operation of the networked organization is based on the common interests, goals and mutual trust of the networked nodes and is a multiple connection of stakeholders stemming from long-term cooperation and responsibility, and mutual benefit. Therefore, the networked organization is a more complicated new social economic organizational form that transcends the dichotomy between market and enterprise in Coase's sense. Outside the enterprise, that is, between the enterprises, it transcends the market transaction relationship and incorporates long-term trust into cooperation while within the enterprise, it transcends the simple pyramid-shaped management framework and incorporates participation and sharing, effecting more extensive and equal autonomous exchanges and cooperation.

Second, in light of organizational ecology, the networked organization can be considered an organizational ecosystem, or economic ecosystem. By organizational ecosystem is meant the ecological environment of organizational groups and the state of their internal relationships.

Regarding the organizational group, regardless of size, "group" is emphasized rather than an individual organization. Strictly speaking, it encompasses all organizations that share a common ecological environment in a given time and space and within a given boundary. In this sense, the networked organization is also an organizational group, which makes it a research focus of organizational ecology today. It must also be pointed out that organizational ecology emphasizes the organizational ecological niche, that is, the collection of all resources that support the common survival of an organizational group. It also emphasizes the density of relationships between organizations, which tends to shape the internal structure and direct its dynamic evolution. The two terms are two important concepts that can be applied to studying modern networked organizations.

Third, each "node" in the networked organization, that is, the single independent organization and related stakeholders constituting the organization, still retains the status of independent economic entities on an equal footing in a legal sense. Therefore, equality is an important sign that distinguishes between the "cooperative relationship" of a network organization and the subordinate relationship of a hierarchical organization. It also means that different from the integration of the merger of property rights, the network organization is the combination of assets (including tangible and intangible assets, and also physical and human assets) that crosses the restriction of property rights (ownership). It is true that not all independent economic entities and economic organizations in a networked organization are of the same size and economic power. On the contrary, in most networked organizations often co-exist large, medium and small organizations. Therefore, the diversification and differentiation of various economic organizations are the prerequisites for the existence of networked organizational groups and should not undermine the independence of and equality between the organizations.

Fourth, given independence and equality, the management of the networked organization needs to establish flexible mechanisms which render possible comprehensive involvement, equal negotiation and democratic decision-making for all parties concerned. In contrast to the traditional hierarchal "rigid" management characterized by command-obedience, the flexible management puts weight on humanitarization and humanization, the sharing of information, resources and benefits as well as the autonomy and creativity of economic entities. Of course, flexible management does not absolutely exclude authority neither can any independent economic entity do anything unconstrained. Its authority rests with the consensus and shared responsibility of all parties and therefore any individual entities which do otherwise will be jointly punished, marginalized and even expelled by the organizational group.

Fifth, the networked organization is essentially open and dynamic. Compared with a traditional corporal organization, it is extremely inclusive and has relatively flexible organization mechanisms that accommodate many participants and obtain mutual benefit, interactions and win-win results. Therefore, its boundary is essentially open. Any individuals, legal persons, and organizations with common interests, goals and willingness to assume common responsibilities can enter it fairly freely. Conversely, anyone unwilling to be subject to its rules can withdraw.

7.6 Networked Organization Theory: A Challenge to Traditional Business Theories

The research on enterprise-dominated economic organizations has always been the mainstream of the research on economic organizations since in standard microeconomics, the enterprise is the basic economic unit of production while the household is that of consumption.[25] In a sense, the vertical bureaucratic organization within the enterprise and the horizontal market connection between enterprises are the ordinate and abscissa of a research on enterprises. The latter can also be regarded as the external organizational structure of the enterprise. Competition and monopoly are the focuses and cores of theoretical researches in this field and the survival competition of the "survival of the fittest" is their keynote while mutually beneficial cooperation and reciprocal symbiosis between business organizations, especially the symbiotic evolution of organizational groups have been generally neglected or downplayed in mainstream economics.

The tradition of Smith and Marx regards the enterprise as a productive organization based on specialization and social division of labor, and the enterprise replaces individual production with organized production.[26] In *An Inquiry into the Nature and Causes of the Wealth of Nations,* Smith explained how companies use the benefits of specialization and division of labor to

[25] Louis, P. and Randall, K., eds. *The Economic Nature of the Firm.* Cambridge: Cambridge University Press, 1987.

[26] Simon also held a similar view. The process in which members of an organization join it is that of replacing their individual goals with those of the organization.

increase labor productivity and in turn national wealth. Marx discussed in detail in *Capital* how companies evolve from simple collaboration, workshop handicraft to factory systems on the basis of social division of labor and internal division of labor. According to them, the market is the external environment of the company's production and operation and the scale of the division of labor and even the size of the company are subject to the size of the market. It is the expansion of the market that promotes the development of division of labor, manufacturing and enterprises. And in turn, the latter promotes further expansion of the market. In short, Smith and Marx emphasized the complementarities and interactions of the coexistence and prosperity between the enterprise and the market rather than mutual replacement.

In his classic thesis "The Nature of the Firm", Coase took transactional costs as his theoretical basis and regarded the firm as "a substitute of the market, a kind of transactional organization different from the market." In his theoretical framework, "The distinguishing mark of the firm is the supersession of the price mechanism."[27] The firm and the market are integrated into a bipolar organizational system framework on the same plane. The comparison between market transactional costs and corporate organizational costs determines the size of the firm. Obviously, Coase was different from Smith and Marx. His focus was on the mutual replacement of the firm and the market rather than the coexistence and prosperity of the two based on their complementarities and interactions.

Coase's new institutional analysis greatly expanded the field of researches on enterprises (organizations), but it was also questioned and challenged in three dimensions.

The first challenge came from the enterprise capability theory holders represented by Pensose, Richardson, Prahalad and Hamel. They inherited the basic ideas of Smith and Marshall explaining the growth of the company from within the company, insisting on the key idea that the essence of the company is productive organization (productive resource assembly) rather than transactional organization. Prahalad and Hamel explicitly put forward the concept of core competitiveness of the enterprise. In their opinion, it is the unique and lasting heterogeneous capability of an enterprise stemming from its accumulated knowledge acquired during a

[27]Coase, R. "The Nature of the Firm", *Economica*, No. 4 (1937), pp. 386–405.

long-term production and operation. The acquisition and development of this ability come from the long-term accumulation and evolution of the company as a productive organization, which cannot be explained by Coase's concept of transactional costs.

The second challenge mainly came from the pan-market school[28] within the neo-institutional economics. It believed that Coase did not consistently implement the concept of transactional costs. For example, Zhang Wuchang held that "It is not entirely correct to say that enterprises replace markets. To be accurate, it is one contract that replaces another".[29] In other words, factor markets have replaced intermediate product markets. This means that in the eyes of these economists, the enterprise is still only a special form of the market, and the enterprise in nature is also a contractual organization, a series of cohesive contractual relationships. Therefore, they actually contended that the enterprise and the market are not what Coase calls "the two poles of the economic organization system". Instead, the market is a general form of economic organization, and the enterprise is just a special form of it.

The third challenge stemmed from the theory of networked organization. It maintained that Coase's corporate and market dichotomy organization analysis framework cannot well explain the many new economic organization phenomena such as industrial clusters, network economies, service outsourcing, organizational boundary elasticity, strategic alliances, enterprises plus peasant households, etc. Porter believed that an industrial cluster is a kind of spatial accumulation economy of closely linked criss-crossing network relationships between enterprises of different scales and levels of labor and cooperation. It can neither be equated with the market nor the traditional enterprise, but a new spatial economic organization form lying between the market and the corporate hierarchy.[30] Adhering to the idea of Coase's transactional costs, Williamson argued that under the premise of limited rationality and opportunistic behavior, the choice of the economic organization form mainly depends on asset

---

[28] It is the author's generalization of this group of scholars, open to criticism from the academic circle, I hope.

[29] Zhang, W. *Interpretations of Economy*. Beijing: The Commercial Press, 2000, p. 363.

[30] Porter, M. E. *The Competitive Advantage of Nations*. New York: The Free Press, 1998.

specificity, transactional frequency and uncertainty. Therefore, there is actually a middle-tier organization between the enterprise and the market.[31] This suggests that even following the classification logic of Coase's organizational structure, real life is a three-leveled organizational structure of markets, corporate networks and corporate hierarchies as Larsen said, rather than a bipolar organizational structure of the enterprise and the market. The networked organization here has some characteristics of the enterprise and the market as Coase held. It is more stable than the market organization and more flexible than the hierarchal organization, hence a handshake between the invisible and visible hands.[32] This means that whether in the market (outside the enterprise) or inside the enterprise, market mechanisms and enterprise organization mechanisms coexist. That is to say, the market and the enterprise are not mutually opposite or replaceable, but complementary, connected, and integrated. They ultimately lead to complex and rich networked structures and diverse institutional organizations to deal with other enterprises.

The theory of networked organization has an internal logical connection with the theory of organizational symbiosis discussed in Chapter 4 of this book, or in other words, they are internally related and compatible in theory.

First, the theory of networked organization and the theory of organizational symbiosis both rose and developed in the wave of new economy (knowledge economy) represented by the information technology revolution, and closely related to the research on a series of new economic phenomena in the new era.

It is true that the concept of symbiosis and that of network may date far back. They go back to ancient Greece and Rome in the West and the Spring and Autumn Period and the Warring States Period (770–221 B.C.) in China. However, it is in recent decades that the two theories have received widespread attention from the whole society, and exerted greater academic and practical influences. With the wave of knowledge economy

[31] Williamson, O. *The Economic Institutions of Capitalism: Firms, Markets, Relational Contracting*. New York: The Free Press, 1985.

[32] Larson, R. "The Handshake between Invisible and Visible Hands", *International Studies of Management and Organization*, Vol. 23 (1993), pp. 87–107.

triggered by the information technology revolution, there have been barrages of economic novelties such as network economy, virtual economy, ecological economy, circular economy, green economy, industrial clusters and service outsourcing since the 1970s. A series of essential changes have taken place in traditional corporate and organizational structures with the boundaries between markets and enterprises getting increasingly blurred. Under the impact of new economy, traditional organization and business theories can hardly explain new economic practices. It is against this macro background that the theory of organizational symbiosis and the theory of networked organization have emerged. They offer new and more convincing explanations for a series of new economic phenomena in new economy from new perspectives by applying new theoretical analysis frameworks.

Secondly, the two theories have the same or similar philosophical basis. Therefore, their analysis frameworks share the same or similar concepts and categories to some extent.

Different from traditional business theories based on classical mechanics, the two theories embody the economic biology paradigm, according to which, they place more emphasis on diversity, cooperation, and symbiosis rather than live-or-die competition of Darwinism. Based on the new philosophical concepts of symbiosis, harmony and inclusive development, the two theories stress the complementarities, mutual benefits and standing coexistence of heterogeneous economic entities and heterogeneous economic organizations rather than homogeneous mergers and vertical or horizontal integration. In addition, with the same or similar philosophical basis, they share some identical or similar concepts and categories in their analysis frameworks such as mutual benefits, cooperation, trust, community of interests and so on.

Nevertheless, the theories differ in some respects, especially in their definitions of market. The theory of networked organization, the one proposed by Williamson in particular, still upholds the Coase tradition to a large extent, contending that the market is parallel to the enterprise and that they have point to point or pole to pole relationships while the networked organization is regarded as the third pole or the blend of the two poles. The theory of organizational symbiosis regards the market as a symbiotic interface and enterprises and other different economic organizations as symbiotic units. According to this theory, the symbiotic interface is the medium and carrier for the transmission of matter, information and energy between the symbiotic units. This means that the relationship between the enterprise and the market is an unparallel point to surface relationship rather than a parallel point to point or a pole to pole relationship. In the terms that many economists prefer, the market is an ocean, and enterprises are independent islands and islands are in oceans, which connect islands. This point and surface relationship between the enterprise and the market seems closer to Smith's tradition.

As mentioned earlier, organizational symbiosis does not suggest a long-term coexistence of the advanced and the backward or "well water and river water" nor absolutely exclude competition and the survival of the fittest. Symbiosis is also a type of evolution. Symbiotic evolution means the evolution of organizational groups rather than monolithic evolution in which one organization eliminates another.

7.7 Enlightenments from Modern Networks and Networked Organizations to Modern SF

As aforementioned, agricultural modernization in the contemporary world has not given rise to the demise of household farms and agriculture. On the contrary, the experiences from developed countries have proved that agricultural modernization can be based on the modern SF system. However, while emphasizing the system, it is necessary to realize that without modern networks and networked organizational groups, the modern SF system would be non-existent. Some scholars advocating it often place too much weight on the clarification of household property rights, directness of benefits, economization on supervisional costs and the privatization efficiency function of preventing any members from getting average incomes, and neglect another source of the efficiency of modern SF, i.e., marketization, socialization, modern networks behind the efficiency and the pluralistic symbiosis organizational groups connected by the modern networks.

The Netherlands is reputed as a model of modern SF with high efficiency by the international academic community. For many years it has been ranking first in the world in land productivity, the agricultural product export rate, and the per capita agricultural exchange rate. Known as the king of small peasants for its household farms taken as the major force of the micro-foundation for agricultural economy, it has no self-sufficient household farms. Its highly efficient market-oriented family farms (modern SF) are based on a good agricultural infrastructure system, a developed agricultural product processing system, a perfect agricultural product circulation system, a well-organized peasant cooperation system and a system of the trinity of agriculture, education and scientific research. These systems constitute a relatively complete modern network, based on which is a complete and developed networked organizational group. For example, "The Netherlands has world-class networked high-standard water conservancy and flood protection facilities."[33] It boasts of an extremely developed and integrative public transportation network of land, sea and aviation, a food and beverage manufacturing industry that can process more than 60% of the country's agricultural products and multitudes of imported primary agricultural products into high value-added consumer goods, and various types of agricultural cooperatives and agricultural cooperative economy organizations. What is more, it has an efficient, developed and perfect agricultural product circulation network, a network of agricultural knowledge, creation and promotion, and a highly organized peasant cooperation system.

Agriculture in the Netherlands is so specialized and marketized that it is highly dependent on the world market for vast bulk of imports and exports. Therefore, an efficient, developed and improved agricultural product distribution network inevitably becomes the lifeline of Dutch agriculture. A good case in point is the Dutch flower industry, which ranks first in the world. The Netherlands is the world-famous floral kingdom and its flower exports have long accounted for about 50% of the world market. In order to ensure that Dutch flowers are exported quickly and conveniently to all parts of the world, the Netherlands has formed a flower auction-centered circulation network, connecting many stakeholders such as flower management companies, flower farms, flower cooperatives,

---

[33]The altitude of Dutch high-standard flood prevention dams and inland dams has reached 2,800 km ranking the first in flood prevention standards, capable of beating the fiercest flood of 1,250 years and some dykes even 10,000 years.

flower wholesalers, flower dealers, and even flower consumers. For example, the world's largest flower auction market the Aalsmeer Flower Auction (AFA) is a stock consortium of more than 500 flower farms, flower management companies, and specialized flower cooperatives in the Netherlands. It also connects more than 500 large wholesalers and over 150 export companies. It is through this type of "networked" organizational group and "big circulation network" where the interests of multiple parties coexist and reciprocate that the Dutch family farms have achieved a perfect seamless connection with the world market.

[Case 7.1] The Dutch Flower Auction Industry

The Netherlands is the world's largest flower exporter, whose flower exports account for 40%–50% of the world's flower markets. Its flower auction industry budded in the late 19th century. Family farms, the main producers of Dutch flowers, do not sell their own products. Instead, as members of auction houses, they send all their products to the auctions.

There are seven flower auction markets, among which, the AFA is the largest with sales accounting for 43% of the country. The auction markets do not have the ownership of the auctioned goods, but only provide sellers and buyers with trading places as efficient as possible. Auction markets only help to find suitable trading partners for both supply and demand. It would be hard to imagine, without them, how thousands of flower farmers in the Netherlands could sell flowers to the world within a day. Likewise, without them, dealers from all over the world could not purchase flowers from thousands of flower farmers in the Netherlands at reasonable prices. Flower auction markets are open five days a week and auctions begin at 6:30. All flowers for auctions will be delivered to the markets early in the morning or evening the day before the auctions start. The transportation can be done by the flower farmers themselves, who tend to pay specialized transportation companies for the deliveries. Reaching the auction markets, the flowers get into a huge cold storage via a conveyor belt. There is a product quality inspection office in the cold storage and the inventory, where, auctions' quality inspectors perform a quality inspection of each batch of flowers and write the results on delivery notes.

Merchandise auctions are conducted in a Dutch fashion that the auction prices go from high to low. The auction clock has a huge "clock face" with the following information. (1) The name of the producer; (2) the product name, the inspection number, the location code, the location (row and column) in the cold storage and the number of products (the number of trolleys), the number of trolleys that each container can hold; (3) the unit price: guilder and cent; (4) sales conditions: purchaser code, minimum limit, number of purchasers, number of units sold, trolley codes at auction, etc. It is said that each auction clock can complete 1,500 transactions per hour. Payment is made immediately once flowers are sold and beyond the payment desk there are multiple banks where buyers can transfer money with convenience.

The purchasers usually pack up the flowers according to the users' requirements. In most cases, flowers and plants go together for a bouquet. The assembled bouquets are packed in cartons or plastic boxes and shipped to the shipping center of the auction market, where there is a customs and phytosanitary station. Trucks drive the air containers loaded with flowers to Schiphol Airport or European countries at the fastest speed. Everything is done by the auction markets for one goal: the flowers and plants sold every morning must appear in flower shops in countries and regions such as Europe, America, and Japan that night or the next day.

—Based on Li Weimin's *The Miracle of Dutch Agriculture*

The Netherlands also has a world-class agricultural education and scientific research system, the Agricultural Knowledge Creation and Promotion Network, as the foundation of modern agriculture. This network combining researches on agricultural science and technology, promotion and education is chiefly composed of agricultural colleges and universities (the most famous is Wageningen Agricultural University), the Academy of Agricultural Sciences, 34 regional research centers throughout the country, farming households' cooperatives and agricultural cooperatives. This networked organizational group for the creation and dissemination of agricultural knowledge not only enables the Dutch agricultural science and technology to lead the world flower markets but also effectively solves the problems of organic integration of agricultural science and technology research, promotion, and application, trains the new-type peasants to develop modern science and technology literacy and has successfully answered the question of "who will farm" in modern society.

It must also be pointed out that the highly developed modern network of the Netherlands is a combination of interdependent highly developed physical and social networks. The Netherlands is called the lowland country by its citizens in that about one-fourth of the country is below sea level. Coupled with the lowlands about only one meter above sea level, one-third of the country is vulnerable to tidal invasions or river flooding. In their lasting struggle against floods, the Dutch, wisely dug deep ditches on the low-lying plains, drained the water, and opened up arable land known as "polders". It could not have been attained by a single farming household for it took cooperation and organization in the form of a community of interests. Therefore, the polders laid the foundation for the Dutch solidarity and cooperation, getting rooted in the Dutch culture as the national spirit known for the Polder Model.

As many scholars have pointed out, the Polder Model, which plays an important role in the so-called "Dutch Miracle", emphasizes the solidarity of the economic entities and the tradition of cooperation, and forms a community of shared interests characterized by the complementarities and interactions between multi-economic entities, and their symbiosis and common prosperity made possible by modern networks.

The Polder Model has a long history, on whose basis Dutch peasants are highly organized. In the Netherlands, various peasant cooperatives and other cooperative economic organizations are well developed, diversified and have an extremely wide coverage. There is cooperation in production, processing, circulation and sales of agricultural products, and technology, information and loans. Although highly organized, Dutch farmers are not fixed or "locked" in any cooperative. They generally join three–five cooperatives, and maintain a long-term and stable cooperative relationship with the first cooperative for shared interests and bound responsibilities. In the meantime, they also get different types of services and help from other cooperatives. This peasant's non-linear net-like connection with cooperative economic organizations ensures the independence of farming households and their status as a major economic force.

In summary, without a highly developed modern network and a symbiotic and prosperous networked organizational group, Dutch family farms could not have accomplished much, however powerful they might be. The modern Dutch agricultural production organization model is not simply represented by privatized family farms, but rather a blend of family farms and modern networks. It is a networked organizational group composed of family farms, agricultural product processing enterprises, agricultural product trading markets, agricultural auction markets and wholesalers, peasants' cooperatives, peasants' cooperative banks, agricultural associations, research institutions of agriculture and education and governments.

The Soviet Union has proved the extreme importance of modern networks and networked organizational groups in modern agriculture with a counter case. It has a vast territory, with a per capita arable land area of 0.86 acre, equivalent to 2.4 times the world's per capita arable land area.

However, due to the planned economy and a series of wrong policies, agricultural production in the Soviet Union stagnated for a long time. In 1950, its total grain output was 6.48 million tons, lower than the 7.25 million tons in 1913 during the Tsarist Period, changing from a grain exporter to a major grain importer. The state-owned farms and collective farms, on which the Soviet agricultural microeconomic organizations were based, were a form of large-scale agricultural production organization extremely inefficient but not low in mechanization. For a long time, its agricultural labor productivity was only 20–25% of that of the United States although the cultivation and harvesting of its food crops were fully mechanized, and the comprehensive mechanization rate of the livestock industry reached 70–80%. This demonstrates that rich land resources as well as agricultural mechanization are not equivalent to modern agriculture.

In the late 1980s, after the disintegration of the Soviet Union, Russia began the reform of the agricultural microeconomic organizations by following the examples of the European and American modern SF and learning the successful experiences of the rural household land contracting system in China. At the end of 1991, the then Russian President Yeltsin issued a presidential decree on "Emergency Measures for the Implementation of Land Reforms in the Russian Federation". It set out the general principles of Russian agricultural reform, and called for the reorganization and re-registration of collective and state-owned farms within one year. Its goal was to develop one million household farms in rural Russia to form a rural middle class with modern small peasants as the main force. On October 27, 1993, he signed the presidential decree "The Regulation of Land Relationships and the Development of Land Reforms", which stipulates that land owners have the right to sell their land. On March 7, 1996, he signed the presidential decree "The Realization of the Land Rights of Citizens under the Constitution", reaffirming the rights of land owners to freely control their land share, including selling, leasing and giving it away. However, initially Russia's reforms in agriculture did not receive positive responses from the vast majority of farmers as expected by the reformers in charge. According to relevant data, less than 2% of the farmers positively responded to the implementation of the land lease system in the late 1980s. In 1994, after Russia passed the private law on agricultural land, only 6% of the farm households individually had family farms on 5%

of agricultural land. "In Russia, this type of peasant household (farm) economy did not develop much, neither did peasant households become the main force of agricultural production."[34] Meanwhile, the privatization reform of state-owned and collective farms not only did not improve the efficiency of Russian agriculture significantly at the onset, but caused a decline in total agricultural output instead. "Against an average annual increase of 10% in China's total agricultural output in the early years of their reform, Russian agriculture underwent a severe recession."[35]

Why did Russia's privatization reform of establishing modern SF not lead to the improvement of Russian agricultural efficiency and the development of agricultural economy, but instead caused a decline in agricultural output and a serious recession in agriculture? According to Zhou Qiren's analysis, it lacked an effective production support system constructed according to the marketization principle. Lu Nanquan explicated more clearly, "Russia is unlike the United States, which has developed timely available agricultural social services."[36] The services and the system are essentially the marketized, socialized and modern networks buttressing the networked organizational groups based on modern networks mentioned before. In modern society, without the modern networks (support systems), and the networked organizational groups under market economy where agricultural production has reached a certain stage, neither public-owned big agriculture (collective farms), or privately owned small farms (family farms) can get anywhere. For example, Russia's family farms not only operated large-scale land but also had a high degree of mechanization. They did require timely and convenient mechanical maintenance services and fast oil distribution services. They also needed comprehensive and developed agricultural product storage and transportation services, convenient and guaranteed credit support. Without these basic production support systems and networked organizational groups, the

[34] Lu, N. "Russian Agricultural Reform and Its Implications." *China Social Science Network*, December 22, 2011.

[35] Zhou, Q. Property Rights Reform and New Commercial Organizations: A Comparison of Agricultural Reforms Between China and Russia. *Property Rights and Institutional Change: An Empirical Study of China's Reform*, Beijing: Peking University Press, 2004.

[36] Lu, N. "Russia's Agricultural Reform and Its Implications." *China Social Science Network*, December 22, 2011.

production and management of family farms would be in trouble, which could not be dissolved simply by privatization.

The cases of the Netherlands and Russia indicate that the form of microeconomic organization is very important for modern agriculture, but at a certain stage of its development, modern networks and networked organizational groups may be more important. China's agricultural and rural modernization should first address the issue of microeconomic organizations and proceed to the next top priority of the acceleration of the construction and improvement of modern networks and networked organizational groups.

7.8 Informationalization Leads Agricultural Modernization: China's Agricultural Production Organization Model Changes from Diversification to Networking

Since the rural household land contracting system was implemented, the small-scale production and operation of peasant household economy (small peasant economy) has once again been the basic organizational form of China's rural micro-economy. In the early days of the reform, high-level policy makers, mainstream media and the general public viewed the system as an expedient measure to adapt to backward productivity in rural China, especially in poor areas, and few people associated it with agricultural modernization. Even today, many people are still dubious about whether peasant households may turn out to be the basic economic organizational form of modern agriculture. However, the super-strong adaptability of peasant household economy shows that there is no irreconcilable internal conflict between agricultural modernization and peasant household economy. Even in areas where labor per capita is rich in land resources and the degree of agricultural mechanization is high, No. 3 Company of Science and Technology of No. 1 Division of Agriculture of the Xinjiang Production and Construction Corps, and Heilongjiang Land Reclamation Bureau for example, as is aforementioned in this book, peasant household-based operation is still the best option in terms of the configuration of agricultural resources.

Finding the right major rural microeconomic force is undoubtedly one of the core parts of China's rural economic system reform and has brought about tremendous changes in China's agriculture and rural economy. However, doing the right thing, i.e., transforming the rural microeconomic organizational form from the uniformity of the people's commune system to "diversification" based on household operation is only the first step to the modernization of agriculture and agricultural productive organizations. It is not all there is to the modernization, let alone its completion. In modern society, especially when it has entered a new stage of information and networked economy, household-based farming will never get far even if it has a short-term efficiency advantage with no modern networks or networked organizational groups to support it. With merely the private ownership efficiency of family farming and the diversification of agricultural production organizations, it is impossible to achieve the full modernization of agriculture including the modernization of agricultural production organizations.

In terms of origin, peasant households, which can become the basic organizational form of agricultural modernization, are by no means the peasant households representing the traditional agricultural society's potato economy as described by Marx, but rather the marketized peasant households of modern networked economy, i.e., modern small peasants. In Western developed countries, the typical representative of modern SF is the family farm. In China, great advances have been made in recent years in making family farms a form of new agricultural operation. Closer observations reveal that the organizational carrier of contemporary Chinese agricultural modernization is not merely represented in peasant households and family farms. It is an organizational structure of diversity and multiple symbiosis.

In this diversified organizational structure, each organization (symbiotic unit) is an independent or relatively independent economic entity and has its own independent or relatively independent economic interests. Therefore, its essential characteristic lies in its diversified interests. In the structure, different organizations have different functions and comparative advantages. The heterogeneity of functions constitutes the basis for their complementarities, and the synthesis of different comparative advantages forms comprehensive competitive advantages.

However, a diversified organization does not necessarily form a comprehensive competitive advantage with complementary functions. The structure may stagnate in a "diversified and scattered" state for a long time, forming no organizational synergy. Therefore, the key to comprehensive competitive advantages with complementary functions is building networked organizational groups complementary and mutually beneficial, sharing resources and benefits. It will create returns of nexus economy peculiar to modern networked economy. Compared with previous linear cooperation, the integrative economic benefits originating from networked cooperation will produce a new and higher level of cooperation value and cooperation surplus. More importantly, they are no benefits which belong to any single economic organization and which any single economic entity can monopolize and enjoy alone, i.e., winner-take-all, but rather benefits that are shared by all economic organizations and stakeholders of the networked organizational group. In it, the sustainable long-term development of any party depends on that of all other parties, which forms a gain-and-loss-for-all-involved relationship within a symbiosis. The short-sighted egoistic behavior (opportunistic behavior) that Williamson described as harming partners at the loss of their values may be beneficial to one for a while, but will undermine the symbiosis within the networked organizational group, which will be detrimental to all the cooperating parties including oneself.

A developed and perfect modern network is indispensable to the integration of diversified organizations into a networked organizational group of modern networked economy. This modern network is equivalent to the symbiotic interface of the symbiosis theory. By symbiotic interface is meant the internal mechanism working behind the relationships between the symbiotic units (equivalent to the nodes in the network theory). It is the medium, channel or carrier for the transmission of matter, information and energy between the units and the foundation for the establishment and development of symbiotic relationships, having direct constraining impacts on the formation and upgradation of the symbiotic energy. According to the modern networked organization theory, in a modern networked economy environment, diversified economic organizations and networks are closely integrated, to be exact, the former is based on the latter. A networked organizational group is a harmonious economic community of various types of economic organizations connected by modern networks. In the community all unit-like economic entities are complementary and interactive, and share resources and benefits.

In China, with the reform of the rural economic system, the micro-economic organization of agriculture and rural areas has shifted from the "uniformity" of the people's commune system to diversity based on peasant household operation. However, globally, the diversified economic organization structure of agriculture in contemporary China and rural areas is diversified but scattered, and the construction of networked organizational groups has just begun, and is, therefore, still underdeveloped. This is chiefly ascribed to China's imperfect modern rural networks, which renders impossible the building of complete and developed networked organizational groups. The lack and imperfection of modern networks and networked organizational groups have become the main obstacles to the development of China's agriculture, rural economy and modernization.

Nevertheless, there is no consensus surrounding the main constraints on and obstacles to the development of China's agriculture and rural economy, and modern construction.

Holding that the most severe constraint on China's agricultural modernization is still microeconomic organizations, quite a number of scholars continue to focus on and encourage reconstruction of microeconomic organizations. Whichever is advocated, further privatization reform, re-collectivization or re-cooperation, or nationalization, it seems that there is great divergence, but they have one thought in common that further experiments should be made again with the form of China's rural micro-economic organizations.

There is no denial that the form of micro-economic organizations in rural China today is somewhat incompatible with the development of the socialist market economic system and therefore, it is indeed necessary to further deepen the reform. However, in general, the multi-symbiotic organization structure based on peasant household economy in China is a highly inclusive and open organization structure generally adaptable to the promotion of the marketization of China's rural economy and development of agricultural modernization. The main current problem is that China's pluralistic and symbiotic agricultural economic organization structure is still in a diversified but scattered state with no developed networked organizational groups to count on. In other words, there is a diversified organizational structure in the rural areas of contemporary China, but it is not networked yet. Consequently, there is more competition among various types of economic organizations than cooperation and even if there is any, it is difficult to establish standardized networked organizations of modern networked economy for lack of tied interests and appropriate institutions and mechanisms. Compared with developed countries, China's agricultural and rural microeconomic organizations may be more diversified, but because of the lack and the imperfection, the degree of the organization of peasants is fairly low, even lower is the level of reorganization of various types of rural economic organizations.

The aforementioned factors give rise to the following consequences: (1) The production potentials of peasant household economy and various types of economic organizations are severely restricted by production technology and physical infrastructure (due to the lack of modern networks) on the one hand and markets and institutions (for lack of networked organizational groups) on the other hand. (2) Trust among various economic organizations (including peasant households) and interest linkage are inadequate and external transaction costs are high. (3) Information and resources cannot be shared among various types of economic organizations (including peasant households), resulting in a closed use of social and economic resources and great waste of them. (4) There are no systems and mechanisms for benefit sharing among various types of economic organizations (including peasant households), triggering off frictions and conflicts of interests, leading to losses of interests of all parties involved to different extents.

Therefore, the goal to further the reform of rural economic organizations is not to rebuild microeconomic organizations, nor to further privatize, nationalize, or re-cooperate or collectivize, but rather to promote and perfect the networkitization of the multi-symbiotic organizational structure after stabilizing the rural household land contracting system in order to form networked economic organizational groups compatible with the development of socialist market economy and modern networked economy. In short, the aim of the further reform and development of China's rural economic organizations should be to stabilize the rural household land contracting system, allow the market to freely choose from diverse and symbiotic agricultural production organizational forms, and focus on building agricultural and rural networked organizational groups.

Judging from the history of the reform of China's rural economic system, during the late 1970s and early 1980s, the bottlenecks and major conflicts that restricted and hindered China's agricultural and rural development were indeed uniformity and rigidity of the microeconomic organizations resulting from the people's commune system. Without fundamental reforms in the basic economic system and organizational framework, the transformation of China's agriculture and rural economy into a socialist market economy could not have begun, neither could China's agriculture and rural modernization process. Therefore, the reconstruction of microeconomic organizations from the uniformity of the people's commune system to the diversity of micro-economic organizational forms to lay a micro-economic foundation for rural market economy, agricultural and rural modernization was bound to be the focus of the reform and the major concern of the governments-dominated economic reform. After the two-way bottom-up and top-down interactions and the joint efforts of the people and governments at the turn of the 21st century, a pluralistic symbiotic organizational pattern based on peasant household economy can be said to have been essentially established and the task of reorganization basically completed.

Since the beginning of the 21st century, there have been changes in the main bottlenecks and conflicts hindering China's agricultural and rural economic development. Now the underdeveloped and imperfect modern networks and networked organizational groups are the main bottlenecks and major conflicts restricting China's agriculture, rural economic development and modernization, and will continue to be so for a long time to come.

The political report of the 18th National Congress of the Communist Party of China proposed the "four simultaneous developments of new industrialization, informationization, urbanization, and agricultural modernization." Informatization and networkitization are closely tied and mutually inseparable. Information economy is networked economy. "Informatization leads agricultural modernization" should not be limited to technical aspects such as the access of every village and every household to telecommunication and the Internet "(of course, this is very important, too), but more attention should be paid to the all-round profound reforms in the agricultural production economic organization models resulting from modern information economy and modern networked economy." Here, "lead" is an extremely important keyword. It means guiding and directing future development. The transformation of agricultural production organizational forms from diversification to networkitization is a living embodiment of informatization leading agricultural modernization and modern networked economy leading an all-round and profound transformation of agricultural production organizational models.

7.9 China's Lack and Imperfection of Modern Networks in Agriculture and the Countryside

Since the networked organizational group of modern networked economy must be based on modern networks, this part will first analyze the *status quo* of China's agriculture and rural modern networks.

The first is the lack and imperfection of agricultural production infrastructure networks.

Agricultural production infrastructure is the material condition and guarantee for agricultural production. Put in the terms used in 2009 CG Document No. 1, it can also be called the "material support system for modern agricultural production." Why networks are particularly emphasized here is that the agricultural infrastructure is systematic and inherently related to the increase of overall benefits.

In 1958, Chairman Mao Zedong proposed the famous eight-character constitution of agriculture, i.e., "water, soil, fertilizer, seed, dense planting, conservation, labor, reformed tools and field management." Among them, water and soil are the two most important basic material conditions for agricultural production. "Water is the lifeblood of agriculture" and "Soil is the foundation of agriculture". Agriculture is an industry where land resources are the objects of production. Their quality has a decisive influence on agricultural production. In the 2011 No. 1 Central Document "The Decision on Accelerating the Water Conservancy

Reform and Development", it is stated that "Water conservancy is an indispensable primary condition for modern agricultural construction, an irreplaceable foundation for economic and social development, and an integral guarantee system for the improvement of the ecological environment. It has the properties of being publicly beneficial, basic and strategic." Therefore, water and soil remediation are the top priorities in the construction and improvement of the modern agricultural production infrastructure network.

Since ancient times, water and soil remediation has been a public product of Chinese agricultural flourishing and national prosperity, hence an important responsibility of the governments. As cross-regional large-scale water and soil remediation is an extremely external activity, it is beyond individual farmers and collective efforts at negotiation and organization are very costly and therefore, governments become the organizers as a matter of course. *The History of Chinese Philosophy* edited by Xiao Shafu and Li Jinquan holds that it is the fight of Da Yu (an ancient Chinese tribal leader) against floods that contributed heavily to the establishment of China's slavery state. "Politically he united the chiefs of all clans under his leadership and established flood prevention institutions. Organizationally, he led his people to use earth to block flood for national welfare, divided the territory in line with the distribution of clans and mobilized labor accordingly. Economically, he gave away the fruits of the victory over flood according to official positions. In this way, the original organization that safeguarded the common interests in terms of irrigation evolved into China's first slavery state." Marx thought that "Artificial irrigation by canals and waterworks is the basis of Oriental agriculture... This prime necessity of an economical and common use of water, which in the Occident drove private enterprises to voluntary association as in Flanders and Italy, necessitated in the Orient, where civilization was too low and the territorial extent too vast to call into life voluntary association, the interference of the centralizing power of government, hence an economic function devolved upon all Asiatic governments."[37]

[37]Marx, K. British Rule in India. *Selected Works of Marx and Engels*, Vol. 2. London: Lawrence and Wishart Limited., 1945.

In modern society, water and soil remediation is still of special significance to agricultural production and even entire national economy. Studies on the "Comprehensive Scientific Investigations of Soil and Water Loss and Ecological Security in China" conducted from July 2005 to November 2008 show that the economic loss caused by soil and water losses to China translated into approximately 3.5% of GDP. If the GDP of RMB51.44 trillion in 2010 were used as the basis, the economic loss due to soil erosion would be 1.8 trillion annually. Relevant statistics also indicate that China's crop areas affected by various natural disasters such as droughts, floods and other natural disasters each year reach 50 million acres, involving 400 million people and resulting in an economic loss of over RMB200 billion. If droughts and floods are the biggest natural disasters that threaten China's agricultural production, soil quality degradation due to soil salinization, nutrient depletion, soil pollution, soil acidification and degradation of soil structure will threaten China's agricultural production in the long run.

In contrast with the dominant loss of agricultural output caused by the lack of drought resistance and drainage capacity due to insufficient water conservancy facilities, the damage to agricultural output caused by the degradation of soil quality is a relatively slow and "hidden" process, which tends to go unnoticed. Therefore, to some extent, the treatment of soil outweighs but is more difficult than that of water. Our investigations show that in many places, treating soil was interpreted as simply flattening land while the more substantially improving soil quality is neglected. Given the short-term policy effects of local leadership's pursuit of political performance, large-scale land leveling is loud and vigorous, and is liable to be conspicuous while improving soil quality takes a long time, and its effect is yet to appear in a long time to come. This accounts chiefly for greater stress on engineering construction than soil fertilization. Under China's current national contextualization, governments-led public product construction is bound to be absent if it is not put on governments' top agenda. It is true that the 2004 No. 1 Central Document repeatedly accentuates the soil fertilizing project and the Ministry of Agriculture also formulated the "Plan for Fertile Soil Infrastructure Construction 2006–2010", but the degradation of agricultural land quality in China has not been essentially reversed. More reasons run as follows. (1) The increase in soil fertility requires the application of organic fertilizers such as farm manure, less use of chemical fertilizers and an adjustment of the fertilizer structure. However, the short-term yield increase effect of chemical fertilizers outdoes that of farmyard manure and they are convenient to use, and relatively clean and hygienic. Conversely the collection, processing, and use of farmyard manure are more complicated and inconvenient, and the short-term yield increase effects are not as good. Consequently, peasants prefer chemical fertilizers and are reluctant to adjust the fertilization structure as large numbers of young and middle-aged farming laborers go out to work.[38]

(2) Enhancing soil fertility requires land to lie fallow for a period of rest rather than over-utilization. For example, the United States and the European Union have formulated a policy on fallow farmland, which is regarded as an important part of sustainable agriculture as fallow land helps maintain the carbon content of the soil and thus reduces soil erosion. As fallow land is hardly mentioned in China for lack of arable land resources, the reverse is the case. A single season is replaced by a double season, which in turn is changed to a triple season for a maximal use (in fact, squeezing) of land. This spells the decline of land fertility, which can only be compensated by the heavy use of chemical fertilizers, which exacerbate soil compaction. It makes for further degradation of soil quality and forms a vicious circle.

(3) In addition to agricultural pollution and domestic waste emissions, industrial pollution has further aggravated rural soil quality in China and posed a serious threat to China's food safety due to the lag of environmental protection policies in China's industrialization process and some local authorities' short-term policy proclivity to GDP at thc cost of anti-pollution. According to incomplete statistics, currently there are about 150 million mu of arable land polluted in the country (mostly concentrated in the more industrialized areas such as the Pearl River Delta and the Yangtze

[38] In many rural areas such as Hubei and Hunan, peasants generally do not use chemical fertilizers or pesticides on their own rations as rural people have become aware of the concepts of green and environmental protection but for the sake of outstanding short-term increase in yield, they use chemical fertilizers and pesticides in the fields whose output is for sale on the market.

River Delta) including 32.5 million mu polluted by sewage irrigation, two million mu used as solid waste storage and ruined, totaling about one tenth of the total national arable land area. According to the data reported at the 2009 China High-Level Food Safety Forum, at least 20 million acres of arable land was contaminated by heavy metals, accounting for one sixth of China's arable land.

(4) In the process of industrialization and urbanization, the cultivated land occupied by non-agricultural construction is mostly high-quality land on the edges of cities and towns, and much is vegetable land. Although the newly cultivated land can offset the decline in the amount of arable land, it is difficult to make up for its drop in the overall quality.

(5) Some scholars point out that the expectations of Chinese peasants' unstable land contracting rights also account for the decline in agricultural land soil fertility. After the implementation of the peasant household land contracting system in rural areas, water and soil treatments were stagnant for a period of time due to the absence of investors. As public products with extremely strong externalities, they must rely on government investments at both central and local levels as well as private investments guided by government policies. At the same time, as a systematic project to build and improve the material supporting network of modern agricultural production, the treatments must be comprehensively coordinated to gain overall effective benefits. A good case in point is the water irrigation network where large and medium-sized trunk canals, branch canals connecting villages, and bucket canals and ditches connecting farmlands constitute a complete irrigation system. Failure of any link will reduce the overall irrigation benefits. According to statistics from parties concerned, by the end of 2009, the effective irrigated area of farmland across the country was 889 million mu, accounting for 49% of the country's total arable land area and producing 75% of the country's grain and over 90% of cash crops. However, more than 80% of large and medium-sized irrigation areas have been functioning for more than 30 years, and the facilities are aging and seriously in disrepair. Consequently, the damage rate of backbone facilities in large-scale irrigation areas nationwide is nearly 40%, and the rate of trunk and branch canals in good conditions in small and medium-sized irrigation areas is only about 50%. Especially the

bucket canals and ditches at the end of the canal system in the irrigation area, that is, the capillaries of farmland water conservancy system, are mostly silted and blocked, which seriously affects the flood control and drought resistance functions of farmland water conservancy and in turn agricultural output.

The second is the lack and imperfection of modern agricultural product processing networks.

Modern agriculture is no weak industry. One of the keys in the transition from weak to strong is extending the agricultural industry chain and maximizing the added value of agricultural products, hence, the special significance of the agricultural product processing networks to strong agriculture. The experiences of the Netherlands have proved that a highly developed agricultural product processing network (system) is an important pillar of an agricultural power. Its strong agricultural product processing industry not only greatly enhances the value of agricultural output but also provides strong industrial support for labor employment and foreign exchange earnings from agricultural products.

An extremely important reason for weak Chinese agriculture is that the processing capacity of agricultural products in China needs improvement. The facilities for primary (rough) processing are crude, the methods are primitive and technologies are backward. There is only a short chain with a narrow coverage for the finishing and deep processing and the technologies are underdeveloped and what is even worse, the comprehensive utilization efficiency is low. All these factors contribute to the huge losses of agricultural products and their low added value, which directly hinders the growth of China's agricultural output value and in turn the increase in peasants' incomes. According to experts' estimate, the post-natal loss rates of grain, potatoes, fruit, and vegetables in China are 7–11%, 15–20%, 15–20% and 20–25%, respectively, much higher than the average losses in developed countries, translating into over RMB300 billion equivalent to a waste of the inputs and outputs of more than 100 million mu of arable land. Data show that the most important agricultural value-added part in developed countries lies in the processing and the transformation links. For example, in the composition of the total value of agricultural products in the United States, the added value of the circulation and the processing links is 3.6 times that created in the production links. The ratio of agricultural product processing value to agricultural output value is 3.7:1 in developed countries while that in China is only 0.43:1, which means that the added value of agricultural products of the same variety in China is far lower. Cui Guoqiang's empirical analysis on the impact of agricultural products processing industry on peasants' income growth by means of Granger's causality test, co-integration analysis, and the error correction model based on the 1992–2008 data from Henan, shows that for every 1% increase in the value added of agricultural processing industry, the per capita net income of peasants will increase by 0.955447%.[39]

In China, the low value of agricultural products results from the short value chain and its insufficient development and utilization attributed to the imperfect and underdeveloped agricultural product processing network. For example, in Hubei, the output of catfish accounts for about 40% of the output of freshwater aquatic products, but at the market price, it can only sell for a bit over RMB2 per 500 mg. If the industrial chain of catfish processing is extended and all the fish scales, skins and fish bones are exploited, the value of catfish can increase to more than RMB40 per 500 mg, an increase of 20 times. In addition, China's deep grain-processing accounts for less than 8% of the total output as against over 70% in developed countries, which means that for the same amount of food, China's total value is far lower than that of developed countries. Therefore, China is still just a "big agricultural country", a large country producing agricultural products as the output of primary agricultural products such as wheat, rice, cotton, vegetables, livestock products, and aquatic products ranks first in the world. Nevertheless, China is not yet a strong agricultural country due to the very low utilization rate of agricultural products. In the long run, adding agricultural value and increasing peasants' incomes cannot be pinned on the price increase of primary agricultural products or the output increase of agricultural products. Instead, the greater potentials lie in the extension of agricultural product value chains and the increase in agricultural products' added value.

---

[39]Cui, G. "An Empirical Study on the Impact of Agricultural Product Processing Industry on Peasants' Income Growth in Henan Province", *Acta Agriculturae Jiangxi*, No. 2, 1994, pp. 159–160, 167.

From a broader perspective, a networked agricultural product processing industry not only includes the production system of primary (rough) processing, finish machining and deep processing of agricultural products but also the technical development system, the production organization system and the product quality control system. Especially now that people pay increasing attention to food safety, health and nutrition, it is of vital importance to establish a comprehensive food quality production and control network from sources, which is urgent after the occurrence of barrages of major agricultural product quality safety incidents such as" Sanlu Milk Powder Incident. Without quality standards and safety, individual agricultural product processing companies may benefit for a while, but the pollution of the entire market environment and the loss of the trust of consumers will eventually lead to the harm to the overall interests of the agricultural product processing industry. For example, after the Sanlu Incident was exposed, China's dairy industry suffered such "unprecedented calamities" that a large backlog of domestic milk powder was unsalable, and many dairy products companies either stopped production or closed down. In terms of imports and exports alone, China's dairy products exports in 2008 fell by 10.4% as against an import increase by 17.4%.

In contrast with the efforts governments make to push the development of agricultural product processing enterprises, their buttress for the construction and improvement of the public networks of the agricultural product processing quality standard system and safety system appears to be inadequate. Judging from the *status quo*, there are relevant laws and regulations to be further improved, corresponding government agencies to be further integrated and strengthened, and technical standards and quality control measures to be further bettered. What is absent is their unity for integrated communication by combining them into a modern network system covering all aspects including the production, processing, distribution and consumption of agricultural products. With the absence, responsibilities are not clearly defined in the fragmentary control system, which triggers off a general crisis of trust in agricultural products, hence the deadliest threat to the healthy development of China's agricultural processing industry. Under market economy, social trust is more important than capital and technology for the development of any industry, especially the agricultural product processing industry concerning people's health and safety.

The third is the absence and imperfection of modern agricultural product circulation networks.

In market economy, especially when agricultural product market constraints are getting increasingly severe, the construction of a large agricultural product circulation network is of special significance. Developed logistics industry, an unblocked information network and a sound market system ensure a modern commercialization and marketization of agriculture and tie small peasants and big markets under China's current institutional framework. Therefore, the 2004 No. 1 Central Documents repeatedly emphasizes that it is necessary to strengthen the improvement of rural circulation infrastructure, develop modern circulation approaches and new circulation formats, speed up the construction of rural informatization, establish unimpeded agricultural and rural information networks, cultivate diversified and multi-leveled market circulation entities to build an open, competitive and unified market system.

According to the experiences of developed countries, the modern agricultural product circulation network must be based on modern logistics industry and information networks. For example, the Netherlands not only has integrative water, land and air-born transportation and logistics networks, complete storage and distribution facilities and systems but also extremely developed information networks including electronic information ordering systems and virtual electronic agricultural product logistics supply chains. Not only does the United States have a developed agricultural logistics infrastructure where roads can reach every rural household but also 90% of farming households have access to information network facilities, contributing heavily to a developed agricultural e-commerce.

There was no modern "logistics" concept at all during the planned economy period in China when the circulation of agricultural products was restricted to the closed and narrow channels of administrative instructions. With China's transition from planned economy to market economy and market circulation playing a more and more important role in social and economic life, it took some time before modern logistics got established in China. However, there is still a big gap between China and developed countries here. Agricultural product logistics is an important branch of modern logistics and due to the difficulty in keeping products fresh, uniform standards, product packaging, and storage and transportation, it is more difficult and slower to develop in China compared with industrial product logistics. The reasons run as follows. First, China's agricultural product logistics is still mainly self-operated while in developed countries it is chiefly entrusted to specialized third-party logistics. Secondly, it is mainly done at room temperature or by means of natural logistics and unprocessed fresh products account for the greatest percentage due to China's underdeveloped agricultural processing industry. In developed countries, however, the cold chain system of agricultural products mainly characterized by refrigerated and low-temperature storage and transportation accounts for a large proportion and that is also true of processed agricultural products. Thirdly, the infrastructure of China's agricultural product logistics is still relatively backward. For lack of a comprehensive transportation network, perfect storage and distribution facilities, many agricultural products cannot be transported nor stored. In addition, the level of the standardization of agricultural products in China is low, but standardization is an important technical support for the development of modern logistics industry. What is more, the information network of China's agricultural product logistics is still underdeveloped and consequently the lack of information leads to the backlog of agricultural products in one place and shortages in others, and periodic market turbulences occur due to the follow-suit cultivation of agricultural products. Overall, China's agricultural product logistics industry is still in the initial stage of modern logistics and the informationization of agricultural product logistics has just begun with much yet to be done before the construction of a large agricultural product distribution network. That is why the circulation of China's agricultural products is characterized by many links, high costs and heavy losses. For example, the loss rate of Chinese fruit and vegetables in picking, transportation and storage is as high as 25–30%, while that in developed countries is generally controlled below 5%, and only 1–2% in the United States. This suggests that in China large numbers of vegetables and fruit rot and deteriorate in the circulation process, which not only wastes valuable resources (including land, manpower, etc.) but also becomes a source of pollution. Therefore, building a modern agricultural product logistics network to save logistics costs and reduce agricultural product logistics losses means an increase in actual effective supply of agricultural products and land rebuilt.

The key feature of a large-scale agricultural product circulation network is an unblocked openness to ensure smooth flows of goods. Currently China's agricultural products are difficult to sell because of high prices, especially in recent years when the prices of urban vegetables remain high due to the backlog of vegetables in the producing areas, and multitudes of vegetables rot in the producing areas and circulation links, which exposes many problems in the circulation process of agricultural products in China.[40] The contributing factors are various tangible and intangible barriers and obstacles regarding systems, policies, rules and management. First, the costs of the circulation links are too many and too high. Second, there are too many unnecessary circulation links lacking in fast, convenient, wide and accessible network channels. Third is that the infrastructure for the networked circulation of agricultural products is so backward that the agricultural product circulation is too long and the decay rate is too high. Fourthly, the construction of agricultural product information network lags behind, resulting in information occlusion, inaccessibility and lag. Too many half-way obstructions and stoppages in the circulation process cause poor circulation or excessively high circulation costs, which does harm to the interests of both consumers and producers. Granted, China's agricultural production is relatively advantageous because of its low land and labor costs in comparison with that of developed countries, but due to insufficient and imperfect large agricultural product circulation networks, the circulation costs are much higher and the advantage in low production costs is offset by the disadvantage in high circulation costs. Case 7.2 shows that the production cost of green onions is only RMB0.5 per catty, but the final sales price is as high as RMB5. The circulation and sales costs are three times the production costs.

[40]For a long time, the circulation loss of vegetables in China has been very severe, and the decay rate of fruit and vegetables has been as high as 20–30% with an annual loss of over RMB100 billion (see the announcement of the National Development and Reform Commission and the Ministry of Agriculture about printing and issuing the 2011–2020 National Vegetable Industry Development Plan).

[Case 7.2] Tracking the High Prices of Green Onions

After the 2012 Spring Festival, the prices of green onions in Beijing soared up to RMB10 per kg, and even as high as RMB10 every two onions. Reporters conducted a tracking investigation from where onions grew to where they sold to look into the extremely high prices.

In an onion field in Luxiang Town, Jinshan District, Shanghai, more than 20 peasants are digging green onions. The man directing them is named Xu Qilong, a vegetable wholesaler from Xinfadi Market of Beijing. During the gap period of onion production in the north from Jan. to Mar. every year, Xu will purchase green onions from Shanghai and deliver them to Beijing. Now, he is procuring onions from a field of about 11 mu at the price of RMB3 per kg.

Xu is buying them from an onion dealer Shi Jiahu. The dealer, commonly known as the "land contracting boss", negotiates the prices with the peasant households when the green onions are planted, contracts the sales of all the green onions and resells them to wholesalers in other places during the harvest season. The real planter of the green onions that Shi Jiahu has contracted is a 42-year-old peasant Zhang Changqing.

Zhang is not a local peasant in Shanghai and grows onions through land transfer. The rent per mu is RMB1,000 and other expenses cover RMB150 for cultivating land, RMB120 for buying seeds, RMB800 for fertilizers and pesticides, and the labor cost of having onions sliced. The actual income from per mu is only just a few hundred Chinese yuan. Xu's more than 60,000 kg of green onions is shipped from Shanghai to Xinfadi Market in Beijing. His son Xu Kechao is responsible for receiving and trading in the onion processing area in Xinfadi. He has to have the leaves and soil outside the onions removed and net onions repackaged before selling them to the next batch of wholesalers. With regard to the 60,000 kg of green onions, excluding RMB7,000 transportation fees, RMB500 loading and unloading fees, RMB2,000 market administrative fees and RMB6,000 processing fees, and considering that the net onion yield is merely 60%, the costs increase by RMB3 per kg.

Xu's onions will be sold to the next level of onion wholesalers, who will then sell them to the retailers directly dealing with consumers. Li is a green onion wholesaler and will wholesale 2,000 kg at RMB6 per kg, ship them to Dongchang Lihua Vegetable Wholesale Market in Chaoyang District of Beijing and sell them to vegetable retailers. Li said that as for the 2,000 kg that he would sell, he estimated that he could make RMB200, excluding RMB60 shipping fees, RMB60 market administrative fees, booth fees and the losses due to fallen leaves.

Retailers told us that they could earn RMB1 per kg, excluding fallen leaves and booth fees. If their onions could not sell the day they had purchased them, they would sell at a reduced price. Other reports said that the monthly rent in 2011 for a store of less than 30 sq m in Beijing Xinfadi Vegetable Wholesale Market was RMB3,000, and rose to RMB7,500 in 2012 when the rent for a 7 sq m booth in an ordinary Beijing vegetable market was RMB2,800 per month and the utility bill was RMB100 per month.

—Based on the relevant reports on *China News Network* on March 31, 2012

The fourth is the deficiency and imperfection of modern agriculture and rural financial service networks. The role of finance in modern society is what blood is to the human body. One of the bottlenecks in the development of agriculture and rural economy in contemporary China stems from serious financial restraints. It is undeniable that chasing profits is the essence of capital. Since the profits from agriculture are lower than non-agriculture and the rural profits are lower than the urban, it is only too natural that funds flow from agriculture to non-agriculture and from rural to urban, which is in line with the basic principle of the capital flow in market economy. However, without financial buttress, modern agriculture will grow and develop with difficulty and without the pillar of modern agriculture, it will be difficult for modern economy to develop healthily and sustainably. This means that, at this stage in China, if nothing is done to restrict a full market allocation of finance and finance is regarded as pure private belongings, there will be inevitably a shortage of agricultural and rural financial supplies, which can hardly satisfy the needs of the development of modern agriculture, and the financial needs of the overall rural economic and social development.

An important function of governments is to rectify market failures and make up for market defects. The rural financial service network is essentially a "public product" whose provision is government-led rather than a "private product". Of course, it does not follow that governments are the main suppliers of funds in the rural financial system. The planned economy period witnessed the insufficient financial supplies, the "shortage" and "deficiency" of rural finance, which could not be dissolved by the government-monopolized rural finance. The lessons from the past should be an enlightenment on the present. Government-led here means that governments' responsibility is to provide planning and guidance, appropriate policies and an innovative institutional environment in order to build and improve a financial service network suitable for agricultural and rural economic and social development. Obviously, governments are the main suppliers of a rural financial system and environment rather than rural financial funds.

Where can governments make a breakthrough to innovate the institutional environment for agricultural and rural financial development? Practice has proved that the entry point is to reform and innovate the rural financial system. Governments cannot coerce financial institutions with the independent legal person economic status into operating at a loss in rural areas. They should not even deprive a state-controlled agricultural bank of or restrict its independent operation and decision-making power in accordance with company rules and regulations.

In terms of self-employment and self-financing, and rational economic people, it is inherently rational for large and medium-sized commercial banks such as Agricultural Bank to contract rural services, and close and switch rural outlets. A fundamental reason here is that due to asymmetric information and the pyramid-shaped organizational structure, the national or large regional financial institutions are not suitable for the rural areas of contemporary China.

Therefore, the cultivation and development of rural financial institutions more suitable for rural economic and social development are the keys to building and improving rural financial service networks. Marshall pointed out long ago, "A private banker, who has spent all his life in the neighborhood of his bank can often safely lend on mere personal security, where a manager of a branch of a great joint stock bank, who has no direct personal acquaintance with his client, could not. It is to be hoped that the supersession of small banks by branches of large banks will not leave small farmers and other traders in time of difficulty with little recourse."[41] This means that small and micro local financial institutions, which are down-to-earth or have comparative information advantages, can better satisfy the needs of agricultural and rural economic development. Therefore, the 2004 No. 1 Central Document states that "It is of importance to accelerate the reform and innovation of the rural financial system in accordance with the requirements to increase loans to peasants and enterprises and improve rural financial services on the basis of practical rural and farmers' needs."

[41] Marshall, A. *Money Credit and Commerce*. London: Macmillan & Co. Limited, 1923.

China's rural financial service networks should copy the agricultural production organizational structure of pluralism and symbiosis in China. Large and medium-sized commercial banks such as Agricultural Bank will not completely withdraw from agriculture and rural areas. Under the guidance of market mechanisms, they will focus on developing their own key financing fields such as financing agricultural listed companies and leading industrialized agricultural enterprises. Policy banks like agricultural development banks should make a point of expanding the scope of services to agriculture and rural areas in accordance with the national policy requirements. Through the classification reform, some rural credit cooperatives[42] will be restructured into villages or township banks and others will be transformed into real rural credit cooperative institutions. Now are emerging across the country small rural or even micro-finance organizations such as village and town banks, microfinance companies and small loans guarantee companies, which are getting to be the main forces of rural financial service networks. There are also postal savings banks, agricultural commercial insurance companies, agricultural policy insurance companies, various types of peasants' mutual aid organizations of funds, etc. In short, the structural framework of rural financial service networks in the future will assume a pattern characterized by the coexistence of large, medium, small and micro financial institutions, the overlapping and integration of multiple forms of ownership, and the coexistence and complementarities of multiple businesses.

The keys to the innovation of pluralistic and symbiotic rural financial organizations are the cultivation and development of small and micro local rural financial organizations. The 2004 No. 1 Central Document states that "It is important to encourage places where conditions permit and under the premise of strict supervision and effective prevention of financial risks to establish financial organizations of various ownerships that directly serve agriculture, countryside and peasants by actively attracting social and foreign capital." The 2006 No. 1 Central Document also puts forward that "On the premise of ensuring sufficient capital, strict financial supervision and the establishment of a reasonable and effective exit mechanism,

[42]The 2005 No. 1 Central Document hopes that rural credit cooperatives will become the pillar of rural financial services, but now it is not realistic yet.

efforts should be made to encourage the establishment of community-owned financial institutions of multiple ownerships in the county, allowing the shareholding of private and foreign capital, and to vigorously cultivate small loan organizations initiated by natural persons, corporate legal persons or mass organizational legal persons." The 2008 No. 1 Central Document clarifies that "The pilot work should be accelerated concerning the promotion, adjustment and relaxation of the entry-permissive policies on banking financial institutions in rural areas." On the basis of policy pilots, the 2010 No. 1 Central Document further states that "Actions should be taken to accelerate the cultivation of village and town banks, loan companies and rural funds cooperatives of mutual aid, and orderly develop small loan organizations and guide the social funds to invest in the establishment of various types of new financial organizations that adapt to needs involving agriculture, countryside and peasants (ACP)." The 2012 No. 1 Central Document makes more specific provisions that "It is necessary to develop a diversified rural financial structure, encourage private capital to enter rural financial services and support commercial banks to set up village and town banks in counties in the central and western regions." It also announces a number of special policies to support the development of rural finance. "Things should be done to improve differentiated supervision policies in line with the characteristics of rural banking and financial institutions and businesses, to appropriately increase the risk tolerance of agricultural loans, and to implement a moderately loose market access and flexible deposits loan ratio policies."

Why is it that the emerging rural community-based financial institutions represented by village and town banks rather than the rural credit cooperatives on which high hopes have always been placed, will become the main body of China's future rural financial service networks? The key reason is that the former is more adaptable to the development of China's rural market economy in the future while in the case of the latter, in spite of the several rural reforms carried out so far, its endogenous institutional disadvantages under the traditional planned economy system are difficult to eliminate completely. Therefore, part of the rural credit cooperatives will be transformed into village and town banks, and the others will convert to real rural financial cooperative institutions. Moreover, compared with national or large regional banks such as Agricultural Bank, new rural community financial organizations such as village and town banks have the advantages and features of simplicity in the organizational structure, low organizational costs, flexible operating mechanisms and more symmetrical rural information.

The authoritative data from the Fourth China Rural Bank Development Forum reveal that as of the end of the first quarter of 2011, a total of 552 new rural financial institutions had been established nationwide, of which 448 were opened and 104 were been planned. 40% of them were in the eastern region and 60% in the central and western regions. Among the 448 opened, there were 400 village banks, accounting for 89%, 9 small loan companies, 2% and 39 rural mutual aid cooperatives of funds, 9%. The new rural financial institutions opened had a paid-in capital of RMB23 billion, and various loan balances were RMB73.3 billion, of which 83.4% were targeted at peasants, and small and micro enterprises in rural areas. Although the overall size and coverage of new rural financial institutions represented by village and town banks were much smaller than that of rural credit cooperatives, their operating performance far outdid the latter. The overall weighted capital adequacy ratio of new rural financial institutions opened was 30.5% and the non-performing loan ratio was only 0.12%. Factually, reforms were also carried out in rural credit cooperatives. As of 2011, 155 rural commercial banks and 210 rural cooperative banks were separated from the original rural credit cooperative system. These restructured and new-type rural financial institutions will jointly build rural financial service networks by being mutually complementary and blending.

[Case 7.3] The Rise of Village and Town Banks in Wenzhou

Wenzhou is one of the areas where private economy and capital are most active in China. It is also a pilot area where innovations are made in rural financial organizations and systems in China to form rural financial service networks that meet the requirements of the development of market economy.

In Mar. 2009, the first village and town bank in Wenzhou, Yongjia Hengsheng Village and Town Bank was established, in May, Cangnan Jianxin Village and Town Bank and in the first half of the following year, Yueqing United Village and Town Bank, ushering formally in the tremendous development of rural banks in Wenzhou.

The banks stuck to the market positioning of "supporting agriculture, small businesses and various forms of organizations". Their financial services were targeted at ACP, and businesses and individuals whose services were not covered by the state-owned and joint-stock commercial banks. As of the end of Sep. 2010, the average loan taken from the first three village and town banks was around RMB700,000, lower than the relevant indicators of local state-owned and joint-stock commercial banks, and covered some clients not served by traditional banks. The loans involving peasants amounted to RMB 13.4751 billion, accounting for 70% of the balance of various loans.

The competitive atmosphere of financial services in the pilot areas was heightened by the establishment of village and town banks characterized with the unique business methods and philosophy of "specialized products, localized employees, community-centered outlets and market-oriented evaluation". Some local financial institutions also began to adjust development strategies, reform incentive mechanisms, transform management processes, innovate service types and simplify service procedures, which promoted the joint improvement of the service level of financial institutions in the pilot areas, and brought about the "catfish effect" of village banks. Since village and town banks had great potentialities and a broad market, they had been keeping the attention of private capital since the trial began, and became the preference of Wenzhou private capital for its entrance into banking industry. The Wenzhou Banking Supervisory Branch Bureau took the opportunity to guide good private capital to participate in the pilot reform and greatly increased the proportion of private enterprises' investments and shareholdings. As of the beginning of 2011, the first three villages and town banks introduced private capital of RMB346 million, accounting for 63% of the total equity. The input of private capital changed the "external circulation" of funds to "internal circulation", making the pilot reform one of the effective ways for governmental departments to guide and regulate private capital. Meanwhile, village and town banks occupied part of the private lending market, which also exerted a good demonstration effect on the external circulation of private assets and private borrowers' codes of conduct.

On Mar. 28, 2012, the executive meeting of the State Council decided that Wenzhou be a pilot area for the comprehensive financial reform, and identified 12 major tasks for the reform, the second of which was to accelerate the development of new financial organizations. Wenzhou obtained two important reform pilot rights in the development of village and town banks, i.e., private capital could act as the sponsor of a village and town bank and small qualified loan companies could be converted to village and town banks. According to the person in charge of the Wenzhou Finance Office, in the next 3–5 years, 50 village and town banks will be established in Wenzhou, which will basically cover all central towns. In addition, Wenzhou village and town banks have gone beyond Wenzhou. For example, in Jun 2010, with the Cangnan Rural Cooperative Bank as the main sponsor, Hengxing Village and Town Bank was established in Fuding, Fujian Province.

—Based on "Wenzhou Village and Town Bank Pilot Project Has Exerted Multiple Effects" on *Economic Daily*, February 18, 2011 and relevant reports

The fifth is the lack and imperfection of modern agricultural and rural science and technology service networks.

The 2012 No. 1 Central document states that "In science and technology lies the fundamental way out to achieve sustainable and stable agricultural development and ensure a standing effective supply of agricultural products. Agricultural science and technology, markedly public, basic, and social, are the primary buttresses for national food security, an inevitable choice to break through the limitations of resources and the environment, and the decisive power to speed up the growth of modern agriculture."

Based on the experiences of developed countries, the agricultural science and technology service network integrates knowledge innovation, popularization and promotion. The innovation here, if understood in a narrow sense, can be regarded as original agricultural science and technology, including new agricultural scientific principles, the discovery of new varieties, the application of new production methods, etc. In Schumpeter's broad sense, they also include the innovation of systems and organizations and the development of new markets. As a networked agricultural science and technology service system, the popularization and promotion of agricultural science and technology knowledge are more important than knowledge innovation in a certain sense. Without them, the results of innovation might not be able to get out of the laboratory, out of the test field, or might be silent in papers and research reports, failing to exert actual benefits and form realistic productivity. According to the research of some scholars, the average conversion rate of China's agricultural scientific and technological achievements is only 30–40%, which is far lower than the 65–85% of developed countries. Among the intertwined factors, the most important are undoubtedly the incomplete and weak networked agricultural science and technology promotion system, and poor scientific and technological achievements transformation channels.

China's current agricultural technology promotion system, led by government agencies, was chiefly generated during the planned economy period. Although it has been reformed several times since the reform and opening-up, its disadvantages still exist. (1) The administrative functions of the government's agricultural technology promotion department outweigh its business functions, which severely affects the promotion. (2) Solely dependent on government funding, the promotion funds are seriously inadequate, unable to push the promotion after deducing capitation. (3) The staff structure is seriously unbalanced in that professional talents are drained and aging while non-professionals are redundant. (4) Because agricultural research, education, and promotion are under the administration of different governmental departments, system barriers lead to a departmental division and consequently research results and practical demands are disconnected.

It should be noted that the promotion is both for public welfare and market-oriented. Government-leadership does not mean that governments monopolize or that they arrange everything. Instead, they should reinforce the reform of the promotion system in accordance with the basic principle of "strengthening public welfare functions and activating business services." The current focuses are on the establishment of government-led and diversified agricultural technology promotion organizational groups in line with the demands of the development of a socialist market economy and agricultural science and technology service networks blending agricultural science and technology, their education and promotion to satisfy peasants' scientific and technological needs.

7.10 Difficulty in Transforming Diversified Economic Organizations into Networked Organizational Groups

The organizational structure of multiple symbiosis is the foundation and premise for the formation and the development of networked organizational groups, but it does not follow that the formation will occur as a matter of course. In terms of type and quantity, China's current forms of agricultural production organizations outnumber those of many developed or even all developed countries put together. They are indeed pluralistic and diversified like "a hundred flowers bloom together." However, in terms of the level of the development of networked organizational groups, there is still a giant gap between them and those in developed countries in the West such as the Netherlands and the United States. This suggests that the transformation from diversity to networking is the major development direction of China's future agriculture and the modernization of rural economic organizations.

"The journey of a thousand miles begins with the first step." At present, the patterns of companies plus peasant households, cooperatives plus peasant households, companies plus cooperatives plus peasant households and supermarkets plus companies plus cooperatives plus peasant households are commonplace across the country. They direct the initial development of China's agriculture and the rural networked organizational groups and also show that the formation and construction of the groups are no abstract matter nor out of reach. Nevertheless, virtually, the networking of the plus type is still in its infancy in most regions of China, and overall, its development is only at an initial level. The reasons run as follows.

First, most peasant households in China are still outside any networked organizational groups. Whether willing and conscious or not, most peasants in China are inevitably involved in market economy and have become or are becoming market-oriented. Nevertheless, they are still unorganized when encountered with the markets, hence small peasants versus big markets. Peasants' organization is a natural choice to dissolve the conflict between them.

There are two basic paths for peasants' organization. The first is collective organization that eliminates small peasants and the second is networked organization based on the modern SF system. The former is represented by the people's communes of the 20th century in China while the latter the Dutch example mentioned earlier in this chapter.

In China, the vast number of peasants will not consent to revert to the people's communes.[43] Therefore, the realistic and feasible approach is the organization of the majority of peasants through marketization, socialization, modern networking and networked organizational groups so that they can truly become modern marketized small peasants. In the groups, they can both maintain the status of independent economic entities and be organized peasants. They can enter the market with the power of cooperation and organization to achieve effective docking of organized and networked small peasants with large markets. The current problem is that peasant households' economic dominance has been basically established through the household land contracting system. However, the construction of rural networked organizations is merely budding, and most peasants are

[43]The author talked with many peasants including many of their relatives. Critical of and dissatisfied with the current rural policies and many phenomena in the countryside, none of them were willing to return to the original people's commune system in that the two biggest problems with it were insufficient food and freedom.

yet to be integrated into a group, resulting in the confusion and inadaptability of most unorganized and vulnerable small peasants in the face of large markets.

Secondly, there are quite a few "plus" networked organizations, which are only linked in form with no substantive interest connection and benefit sharing.

At present, multitudes of the aforementioned plus groups lack substantive connection. The most extreme form of the so-called formal connection is reflected in some falsified reported figures, word games fabricated by some local leaders in pursuit of political achievements. More forms tend to be meetings and agreements signed followed up by no actual organizational actions nor substantial cooperation and therefore, the signed agreements are no more than pieces of empty paper.

Third, even if some plus groups do take actions, the connection needs deepening. There is no denying that there are typical models of good or relatively good plus networked organizational groups. These economic entities have initially developed a pattern of complementary functions and advantages among themselves and benefit symbiosis and sharing. Nevertheless, even most of them are still at a low level of connection. This is highlighted in the following aspects. The first is the lack of endogenous, long-term and sustainable interest linkage and benefit-sharing mechanisms. The plus connection tends to stay at a short-term cooperative level where temporary measures and short-term agreements have become the main means of connection. The second is that there are only expedient rules and regulations that vary with the targeted people for lack of normative and sustainable institutional guarantees. Investigations find that some plus connection often depends on the personal connections of several leaders and their influence on ordinary peasants. This leads to some changes in connection and cooperation with changes in their personnel relations. Third, the coverage of networked organizations is not extensive as their radiation is not extensive. Most of China's agricultural and rural networked organizational groups are still confined to small areas. So far, there are no networked organizational groups similar to the Dutch florist industry's flower auctions that act as the centers and ties, connecting many stakeholders, neither are there any influential networked organizational groups such as the Japan Agricultural Association.

Then, what accounts for the low level of China's development of agricultural and rural networked organizations?

First, the lack and imperfection of China's agricultural and rural modern networks make for the lack of the prerequisite material foundation for the development of networked organizational groups.

Organizations must adapt to the environment, which largely determines the forms of the organizations. As mentioned earlier, modern networks are the material foundation that supports the development of networked organizational groups. In China, especially in the vast rural areas, the lack and imperfection of modern networks is an important reason why networked organizational groups develop with difficulty and even if they are developed, it is difficult to advance to a higher level. For example, with no large-scale modern agricultural product circulation networks when peasant households' fresh characteristic agricultural products cannot be shipped out nor preserved, it will be unlikely to form networked organizational groups composed of multitudes of stakeholders and based on characteristic agricultural products (such as Dutch flowers). In addition, without well-developed and perfect agricultural machinery distribution, repair and service networks, the agricultural community of machinery stakeholders cannot be formed. Without water irrigation networks connecting the main canal to the fields, it is difficult for water users, providers and pipe attendants to form a community of stakeholders in water irrigation. What is more, without modern transportation and information networks, the networked organizational group can only be confined to a fairly small geographical area covered by the networks.

Secondly, a healthy and sustainable development of networked organizational groups requires a high degree of trust in various economic entities. For lack of trust mechanisms, the development of China's agricultural and rural networked organizational groups is in want of necessary social capital support.

A networked organizational group is an organizational form in which all stakeholders' functions and advantages are complementary, and interests and benefits are linked and shared, involving inclusive development. The main impetus to the support of a smooth operation of this organizational form is not the traditional pyramid-like, top-down and command–obedience relationship, but the mutual trust of economic entities and stakeholders in the organizational group based on common interests. A current fatal obstacle to the development of the plus networked organizations in rural China is the lack of such social trust mechanisms. For lack of trust, networked organizational groups are compelled to pay extremely difficult negotiational and organizational costs before the connection and pay more for precautions and supervision after it if economic entities are on guard against each other. Moreover, if they are prone to break up and drop out at any time, there will be great uncertainties in connection and cooperation when it is very difficult to enter into a long-term, stable, and sustainable strategic cooperation. Both theory and practice show that trust is highly negatively correlated with opportunistic behavior. In a socio-economic environment where trust mechanisms are lacking, opportunistic behavior is bound to flood, and the cooperative and organizational costs are extremely high when it is difficult to form standardized networked organizations based on long-term and comprehensive interests.

7.11 Leading and Joint Forces: Two Basic Points for Building and Improving China's Modern Networks in Agriculture and the Countryside

Globally, the modern network is a typical public good with extremely strong externalities. The increase in network nodes, network users and economic entities joining the network, expands its scale effect, benefits it as a whole, and greatly reduces the informational and transactional costs of each economic entity. Therefore, with the expansion of the network scale and coverage, network economy obviously increases the incomes and decreases the costs. According to Metcalfe Law, the value of the network is proportional to the square of the number of the network users, that is, V = n2 ("V" represents the total value of the network, and "n" represents the number of users). This means that the network effect increases exponentially with the increase in network users. The more network users and consumers, the stronger the network effect. Obviously, the economic implication of Metcalfe's Law lies in positive externality.

Because network effects are positively related to the size of networks, modern networks are extremely open and inclusive. Newly-entered

Internet users, that is, the new Internet economy entities, will not affect standing users' (the standing Internet economy entities) use and consumption of the networks but instead the new users will increase the old users' use and consumption as well as the functions and efficiency of the networks. This demonstrates that modern networks have the obvious features of non-competitive consumption and non-exclusive benefits. At the same time, the network effects are also closely related to the unblocking of material and information flows within the networks. The greater the material and the information flows in the networks, the faster the flow rate and the greater the network effects. Whether the flows are unblocked depends on whether the network systems and their functions work well. Therefore, the more complete and developed the networks, the more potent the systems and functions, and, in turn, the greater the network effects.

As modern networks are public goods with extremely strong externalities, their construction and improvement in agricultural and rural areas are beyond any single peasant household, enterprise, or agricultural cooperative economic organization. Markets tend to fail mostly in the case of a public good with externalities. "According to economists' deduction, the areas where market mechanisms fail are where the public sector or governments need to play a role."[44] Therefore, governments should play and can play a role in the construction and improvement of the agricultural and rural modernization networks. As has been pointed out earlier, their construction and improvement, including the construction of modern networked organizational groups adaptive to them, are the focuses of China's agricultural and rural reform and development for a long time to come. They must also be the focuses of the Party and governments' agricultural and rural work.

Of course, the governments may play different roles in various ways and with diverse effects. There is a continuum between the two poles of complete government monopoly and complete government *laissez-faire*. In the case of the construction and improvement in agricultural and modern rural networks in contemporary China, the governments play a leading role, whereby, it is vital to mobilize peasants, enterprises, various types of

[44] Gao, P. and Cui Jun. *Public Sector Economics*. Beijing: China Renmin University of Press, 2004, p. 13.

cooperative economic organizations and the whole society to join their efforts in the building and improvement. Here, the leadership and the joint efforts play a decisive role.

By leadership is meant the overall leadership and guidance. Therefore, the primary responsibilities of the governments are general planning and overall arrangements. At the core of the planning is its being comprehensive, systematic and forward-looking in the construction and improvement. Of course, initially this may not be necessarily the case. However, they must be required of the construction and improvement, the latter in particular. Since modern networks are public products with extremely strong externalities, their systematic planning cannot be made by a single economic entity out of its own interests, including any single department of the governments. Therefore, the governments (not a governmental department), as managers and coordinators of the economic life of the whole society, have an unshirkable responsibility and in modern society, only the governments can make this overall planning in the role of subjects. It must be pointed out that what we call the agricultural and modern rural networks are by no means separated from modern urban networks. In essence, they are an integral part of the modern networks of the entire country. Therefore, their construction and improvement must be integrated into the global networks including the urban and the rural, and designed by the central government at the top. According to the annual No. 1 Central Document since 2004, it has been compulsory to develop a new pattern of integrated urban and rural economic and social development by taking comprehensive measures, adhering to the overall strategy of urban and rural development and unifying the leadership in the comprehensive economic and social development.

Another important responsibility of the governments is that they must act as the major investment bodies, the most important, too, for the construction and improvement of modern agricultural and rural networks. Public products are where the governments chiefly make investments due to their basic characteristics of benefiting the whole society. Moreover, as highly external public products, the networks have a vital bearing on the interests of hundreds of millions of peasants, which used to be the weakest government investment area. Therefore, in the 21st century, it is necessary for the governments to take the investments in the construction of modern agricultural and rural networks as the top priority and make investments in its favor. The 2007 No. 1 Central Document emphasizes that "Governments at all levels must effectively shift the focus of infrastructure construction and social undertaking development to rural areas where the state's new funding for education, health, culture and other undertakings, and the increase in investments in fixed assets should be focused and the proportion of government land transfer revenues should gradually be increased. In order to establish stable growth mechanisms for the investments in ARP and actively adjust the structure of fiscal expenditures, the investment structure of fixed assets and the credit distribution structure, the central and county-level fiscal authorities must increase the total annual agricultural input by a greater percentage than the regular fiscal revenues in order to obtain a stable source of funds as soon as possible for the new rural construction."

The third role of the government leadership lies in the policy guidance. The governments should formulate appropriate policies and create a good investment environment to guide various social and economic entities and social capital to invest in the construction of agricultural and rural networks.

Take the innovation in agricultural science and technology for example. It is a public product with extremely strong externalities characterized with significant publicity, basicness and sociality. Therefore, government-leadership plays a key role chiefly in the following respects. (1) The governments plan the developmental direction of agricultural science and technology and establish national and regional agricultural science and technology innovation systems. (2) The governments are the main investors to ensure the prerequisite capital investments in agricultural science and technology, the basic, cutting-edge and public welfare research on agriculture in particular. (3) The governments create a good scientific research environment and formulate appropriate preferential policies to attract all kinds of talents to participate in the research. (4) The governments build a good investment-friendly environment and lay down appropriate preferential policies to guide social capital to invest in scientific and technological innovations in agriculture.

However, it does not follow that government leadership should cover everything as, after all, the body of specific agricultural science and technology research and development is not the governments but specific innovators (innovation teams) are agricultural science and technology researchers instead. They mainly work in agriculture or agriculture-related education and research institutes, agro-related companies and there are individual researchers in society as well. Compared with universities and research institutes, the technological innovation of enterprises is more focused on practical technologies, especially the research on and development of practical technologies with broad market application prospects. Opening-up the market with innovations and gaining new sources of profits are the basic driving forces for technological innovation in enterprises. Therefore, through system reforms and policy formulations, and by inspiring enterprises' motivations for maximum profits, the governments' leading role is to guide and promote enterprises to become the mainstay of agricultural technological innovation in cooperation with universities and research institutes by being complementary in terms of functions and advantages. Of course, these two should not become two skins that do not interact with each other. How to eliminate the current institutional obstacles and how to establish their collaborative innovation mechanisms are important tasks to be carried out through China's reform of the agricultural science and technology innovation system, and they are also system and mechanism problems to be resolved by the governments. The Wuhan National Agricultural Science and Technology Park to be mentioned in Case 7.4 is an exploration of the governments as a "policy guide" to use market mechanisms to promote collaborative innovation.

[Case 7.4] Wuhan National Agricultural Science and Technology Park

Wuhan accommodates multitudes of Chinese universities and research institutes. Around the South Lake are numerous agricultural education and research institutions such as Huazhong Agricultural University, Hubei Academy of Agricultural Sciences and Wuhan Academy of Agricultural Sciences. Near the lake are universities such as Wuhan University, Huazhong University of Science and Technology, and Huazhong Normal University, which accommodate many agriculture-related disciplines and majors. Around the South Lake gather multitudes of agricultural science and technology talents and as many as six academicians in agriculture of Chinese Academy of Sciences and Chinese

Academy of Engineering. They are Zhang Qifa, director of the State Key Laboratory of Crop Genetic Improvement, Fu Tingdong, an expert in rape genetics and breeding, Zhu Yingguo, plant genetics, Chen Huanchun, animal infectious diseases, Xiong Yuanzhu, animal genetics and breeding, and Deng Xiuxin, fruit tree science.

For a long time before 1998, these agricultural researchers were confined to high-wall-encompassed buildings and their research merely lived in theses and laboratories, or small-scale experimental fields. Their scientific and technological advantages in agriculture were not transformed into industrial and product advantages. In 1998, Wuhan South Lake Agricultural High-Tech Industrial Park was established under the promotion of Hubei Provincial Government and Wuhan Municipal Government in order to dissolve the separation of scientific research from industries and push the organic combination of industries, universities and research institutes. In 2001, the park was merged into Wuhan East Lake High-Tech Development Zone and was approved as a national agricultural science and technology park by the Ministry of Science and Technology in Sep. 2001.

The basic aim of the park was to incubate enterprises and transform achievements in the hope of using the park as a platform to attract agricultural science and technology talents to establish or integrate themselves into agricultural science and technology enterprises, which were expected to effectively transform agricultural science and technology achievements. It formulated a series of preferential policies to achieve this end. For example, "capital investments in the forms of patented technology, scientific and technological achievements, equity and other non- monetary properties can amount to as much as 70% of the registered capital of the enterprise." For a technology-based enterprise established with intellectual property rights, "a unit-funded inventor or a chief implementer may hold the company's shares as an individual." "For enterprises' cooperation funds for scientific research projects granted to universities and research institutions, 10% subsidies will be given to the enterprises" and "for biology enterprises, universities, and scientific research institutions in the park that obtain new crop varieties, veterinary drugs, pesticides and other new products certificates are given a one-time subsidy from RMB100,000 to RMB1 million." "The revenues obtained by agricultural high-tech enterprises engaging in technology transfers, technology development and related technical consulting and technical services are exempted from business tax after approval" and "necessary financial supports are given to high-level talents for innovation and establishing businesses and those of them who meet the requirements can attain as much as RMB100,000 to RMB100 million as funding supports".

By the first half of 2012, the park had transformed more than 1,000 agricultural scientific and technological achievements and incubated, established and introduced over 330 agricultural enterprises. The Advanced Agricultural Biological Park within the park had introduced five academician-led projects, the Center for China Seed Life Science and Technology, the Bayer Biological Science Laboratory of Germany and the Bayer Wuhan Center for Crop Science, and Israeli Schrader (a world-renowned incubator company), British Intertek (the world's largest agricultural, food, drug quality testing and certification institution) and other well-known domestic and foreign scientific and technological institutions and technology companies. In recent years, relying on the enterprises in the park, four provincial centers for engineering technology research and six provincial centers for enterprise technology have been established, and four industrial technology innovation alliances have been formed under the intermediation of the enterprises in the park.

—The author is a member of the Expert Advisory Committee of Hubei Agricultural Science and Technology Park. This case is based on the information about the park and the author's field work

Of course, the governmental leadership does not mean governmental monopoly or sole responsibility. The governments are the main investors in the construction of modern agricultural and rural networks, but they are not and should not be the only investors. It must be noticed that the investments in the construction of modern agricultural and rural networks are so huge that they are beyond the governments whose financial resources are limited. Therefore, it is necessary to encourage and guide various types of social capital to be invested in the construction so as to create combined multi-input mechanisms involving many social forces under the leadership of the governments. The governments' basic responsibilities are to design systems, formulate sound policies and create a good atmosphere so that peasant households, agricultural enterprises, various types of rural cooperative economic organizations, various social and economic organizations in urban and rural areas and all other social forces can actively and voluntarily engage in the construction. The key to making them voluntary is to find the point of convergence between social interests and individual (organizational) interests and to guide the coincidence between maximizing private economic entities' own interests (self-values) and the provision of the social benefits of public products. Famous German philosopher Hegel once pointed out: "A State is then well constituted and internally powerful when the private interest of its citizens is one with the common interest of the State."[45] Therefore, the core of coordination is the integration of the microeconomic private interests of the entities and the overall social interests. In this regard, the central government has taken a series of measures. For example, the 2004 No. 1 Central Document stresses that "Individual rural industrial and commercial households and private enterprises can enter into the

[45] Hegel, G.W.F. *The Philosophy of History*. New York: Penguin Random House, 1990.

industries and fields such as infrastructure, public utilities unforbidden by laws and regulations. Bolstering should be given to them in terms of taxation, investments and financing, and use of resources and talent policies." "Various economic levers such as taxation, interest discounts and subsidies should be utilized to encourage and guide various social capital to invest in agriculture and rural areas." The 2007 No. 1 Central Document states that "Creations should be continuously made of agricultural investment channels so that diversified investment mechanisms can gradually take shape where peasants can become active in investments and labor, the governments can continue to increase investments and social forces may get extensively involved." It also suggests that "A comprehensive use should be made of taxation, subsidies, equity, interest discounts, guarantees and other means to create a good environment for social forces to invest in the construction of modern agriculture and that enterprises which donate money and invest in the construction of rural public welfare facilities should enjoy corresponding preferential tax policies." The 2013 No. 1 Central Document further proposes that "Social capital should be encouraged to invest in the construction of a new countryside and all sectors and industries should formulate development plans, organize projects and take the initiative to mainly favor rural areas with increased investments", and "Enterprises should be encouraged to make multiple investments to get involved in the construction of rural production and living infrastructure."

However, government investments have institutional defects such as low efficiency and vulnerability to corruption. That is to say, even the governments should make full use of market mechanisms in their investments to encourage and guide the active participation of private economic entities, and curb institutional corruption and improve investment efficiency through systems and mechanisms. For example, the governments should act as investment subjects, but not necessarily as the construction and operational subjects. They can select the subjects of construction and operation of public products through various means such as signing agreements and contracts, and giving authorizations. The new public management theory believes that the shift from direct government supply to selective supply that relies on market operations can dissolve or reduce the overburden of public finances, the waste of common pool resources, the inefficiency in public services, low quality, etc.

It is of necessity to clearly define government and private investments with reasonably divided responsibilities. The governments should not compete with the private for profits or intrude into the areas that should be exclusive to private investors and operators. For example, with regard to the construction and improvement of agricultural product processing networks, the focuses of government policies and investments are not to overslant social resources toward merely a few enterprises including state-owned and leading industrialized agricultural enterprises. Instead, the bolstering should go to the construction of quality and safety networks of agricultural products processing, which are public products in nature. The aim is to safeguard the overall and long-term interests of agricultural products processing industry and the whole society. On this basis, the governments should formulate inclusive bolstering policies favoring all agricultural product processing enterprises of all ownerships and create a good market competition environment to arouse the inner enthusiasm in private enterprises for investments in and operation of agricultural processing industry.

7.12 Construction and Improvement of Deep-Level Trust Mechanisms: Basic Social Projects for the Construction of Networked Organizational Groups in China's Agriculture and Rural Areas

A modern network counts on a modern organizational structure and is bound to give birth to modern organizational structures compatible with it, which turn out to be networked organizational groups according to the experiences of developed countries. They can be regarded as long-term, stable and mutually beneficial relationships networks, where each independent economic entity will get to be highly dependent and devoted mutually and have repeated interactions, generating interdependent symbiotic effects. However, this must be built on a great trust among organizations, economic entities and stakeholders. The short and classic definition of trust from Niklas Luhmann, a famous German sociologist, is that "Trust is to simplify cooperative relations between people." Translated into the language of modern institutional economics, trust can be seen as a tool to save transactional, management and supervisional costs.

Trust requires not only the extra-legal constraints of laws, contracts, and rules but also the self-discipline constraints stemming from culture and morality. The deep-seated factor regarding the establishment of networked organizational groups where all economic organizations and entities are mutually reliable and have their interests bound involves building indispensable trust mechanisms. In contemporary rural China, a diversified organizational structure has not yet engendered tightly integrated and well-developed networked organizational groups. Among the most critical factors is the lack and imperfection of trust mechanisms in the entire society. In our survey, distrust is often the first reason why people reject cooperation and the most important reason that hinders the formation and development of networked organizational groups.

Trust is a public product as well as a social resource. It is the foundation and premise for any social cooperation, especially sustainable long-term cooperation. Chinese traditional culture prizes honesty, which is blended with trust. Honesty is thought to be one's internal moral quality and trust its externalization, suggesting that trust is built on honesty. Actually, since ancient times across the world, honesty has been thought to be an ethical and moral standard. It is culturally universal in that it is the basic value maxim for the cooperation between various social entities and for the formation of voluntary organizations. Without it, whole society would fall into a "prisoner's dilemma". In fact, without it, there would be no cooperation and even if there is any, it can only be a one-shot deal. Trust is a universal value foundation for any society to operate smoothly and a universal culture, but trust mechanisms are specific to socioeconomic environments and change with time. In a society where self-sufficient small peasant economy prevails, people's production and life are locked in a closed acquaintance circle, where the external deterrents of maintaining trust are the social interaction rules that have evolved out of the strict hierarchy and marginalization by society for an individual breach of contract and dishonesty, and where the inherent factor in maintaining trust is the ideological (moral) constraints of traditional culture. "Credit counts." However, in a market economy environment, the market subjects that people face are often a "stranger society", which transcends a narrow space, and the counterparty to the transaction is not an acquaintance, or even a stranger due to social openness and mobility. This gives rise to the ineffectiveness of a series of rules that maintain trust in a traditional acquaintance circle. Meanwhile, there are also profound changes in people's internal ideological (moral) constraints. For example, traditional Chinese farming culture preferred farming to business and despised the pursuit of profits while market economy is based on the pursuit of rational economic men for the maximization of their own interests. Therefore, with the cooperation and trust under the conditions of market economy, the parties involved in the transaction and the cooperation must adhere to the principle of mutual benefits, respecting the other parties' pursuit of their own interests. Adam Smith believes that human beings have a general tendency to trade with each other, and such cooperation is based on mutual benefits driven by an egoistic motivation. "That you give me that which I want, and you shall have this which you want, is the meaning of every such offer."[46]

Mutually beneficial cooperation will result in a win-win situation for two or more parties as a matter of course. Therefore, it is symbiotic cooperation in essence based on diversity, variety and difference. It excludes by nature the monopoly of complete unification and differs from a fierce competition of life or death nor "The winner takes all". The concept and practice that treat market economy as a bullying arena is only a crude hopeless stage that only exists in a certain economic and social environment of market economy. According to Chinese economist Wu Jinglian, this is a bad market economy, which does not represent the nature of a rational market economy nor the development trend of market economy.

China is in a special period of dual transformation from a binary economic and social structure where a modern society and a traditional one co-exist and to a modern unary economic and social structure, and from a traditional planned economic system to a modern market economic system. Consequently, the previous trust mechanisms based on traditional society and the planned economy system were attacked or disintegrated

---

[46] Smith, A. *An Inquiry into the Nature and Causes of the Wealth of Nations*, Vol. 1. Oxford: Clarendon Press, 1880.

while new trust mechanisms compatible with modern society and modern market economy are yet to be established, hence a vacuum period of a lack of trust. With people's enhanced sense of independence and autonomy went their mistrust in the authorities that they once had faith in or even followed blindly, including organizations, individuals, rules and values. Society seems to be immersed in an atmosphere of "You can believe in no one except yourself." With the absence of the new trust restraint mechanisms, untrustworthy people benefit from their deceptions and get away with them, which has further polluted the trust environment of the entire society. Distrust can be more contagious than trust, as evidences show that the inspiration of trust tends to require long-term communication, understanding and cooperation while the collapse of trust may merely take one breach of contract and one loss of trust within an instant. Judging from the actual situation of rural areas in contemporary China, one breach of contract or dishonesty on the part of any parties is accountable for the great amount of unsustainable cooperation involving companies plus peasant households, cooperatives plus peasant households and companies plus cooperatives plus peasant households. Many peasant households are unwilling to cooperate and one of the fundamental reasons is the too high cost of cooperation, for which the general distrust is accountable.

Building new social trust mechanisms matching market economy is one of the most tough, long-term and complex tasks in the modernization of contemporary China. It is also the most important social foundation project for the construction of networked organizational groups in rural China. The mechanisms must be built on the independence of various economic entities and the reasonable pursuit of their own interests. Therefore, the project is economic rather than charitable, and market-oriented rather than planned. Meanwhile, in addition to self-interests, it puts more emphasis on mutual and common benefits. The pursuit of one's own interests entails the respect of the other transaction parties' pursuits of their own interests and the interests of society. Therefore, all stakeholders must bind themselves with honesty, which means keeping the commitments to other transaction parties and society, i.e., respecting others and society in terms of interests.

How can all market economy entities be kept honest and trustworthy? A key approach is enhancing the value of a good fame, i.e., increasing the benefits from trustworthiness and the cost of dishonesty. Here is how.

First and foremost, it is important to set up constraint systems and rules that punish the dishonest parties so that the cost of dishonesty may outweigh its benefits so that, in a micro sense, the motive of economic entities for interest can curb distrust. From a macro perspective, the most important thing is to strengthen the legal system and especially the enforcement of the law to provide a strong legal guarantee for the trust mechanisms. When it comes to the organizational groups, it is necessary to formulate binding systems and rules, especially severe disciplinary measures and means targeted at untrustworthy persons including expulsion from the organizational groups.

Secondly, it is of special significance to the construction of social integrity networks to raise the value of reputation. Some people are dishonest because of the low cost. In an open and mobile society, they can "shoot and run for another place", that is, deceive people in one place and then move to deceive people in another place. Integrity network mechanisms for the whole society are equivalent to establishing a social file for the distrustful behavior of the distrustful, which will greatly increase the cost of distrust and remarkably raise the value of a good fame across geographical and temporal limits. This will, in turn, help create a social environment where it pays off to be honest.

Of course, it is inadequate to rely solely on external disciplines as self-discipline is more essential and important in a certain sense. There are costs for systems and rules, and the construction and improvement of social integrity networks. External disciplines concern a series of management and operation costs with regard to law enforcement agencies and information collection, processing and release agencies, law-executors, information processors, supervisors and screeners. If most people cannot exercise self-discipline, the restraining costs will be very high, and there will be even more losses than gains. Self-discipline is a moral restraint deep-rooted mentally and culturally. Trust mechanisms can be truly established in the whole society when most people are highly aware that dishonesty is shameful and cherish a good fame the way they value life.

Since social trust mechanisms are also public products and have extremely obvious positive externalities, the governments are highly responsible for their establishment and improvement in three respects. First, the governments should serve as the main suppliers for institutions and rules about the establishment. The institutions including various laws, rules and contracts, provide people with basic norms for organization and cooperation to maintain trust with social restraints by protecting those who are honest and punishing those who are not. Second, the governments must act as the morality preachers by taking advantage of their control of the mainstream ideology and various media resources to publicize honesty and gradually imbue people with the idea of honesty, and making a point of so doing for a long time to come. Third, they must set themselves up as examples of integrity. Practice has proved that governmental integrity is the foundation of social integrity. If the governments tell lies, they will do a much greater harm to social trust than the ordinary people. The construction of rural networked organizational groups in contemporary China requires social trust mechanisms as its important prerequisite and foundation and in turn, the former is also conducive to the reconstruction of the latter. The groups not only transcend the pyramid-shaped vertical administrative relationships but also the horizontal relationships of market transactions. Based on the maintenance of the independence of various economic entities is established in essence a long-term, standardized and stable strategic cooperation alliance between organizations and between people. Therefore, the networked organizational groups not only adhere to the basic principle that trust mechanisms must ensure that the economic entities are entitled to independence, equality and free choices under the conditions of market economy but also incorporate a long-term and stable trust relationship into a harmonious society. In contrast with the strangers' society of market economy, the networked organizational groups can expand the acquaintance relationship circle in market transactions with the aid of modern transportation and communication networks. This renders people's cooperation and mutual trust more stable and sustainable, avoiding or reducing the risk of uncertainties in transactions with strangers. In contrast with the acquaintance society characterized with interpersonal relationships of the traditional differential pattern of hierarchy, the groups are open rather than closed with the economic entities independent, equal, and free rather than hierarchal and connections-dependent so that the trust mechanisms can adapt to the modern market economic development and better satisfy the humanistic requirements of modernization.

Practice indicates that in the countries and regions where the networked organizational groups are relatively developed and complete, social trust mechanisms are relatively sound and complete, and cases of dishonesty and breach of contracts are rare. For example, in the Netherlands, economic entities could not survive without modern networks and the networked organizational groups and therefore, will be marginalized due to dishonesty and breach of contracts by the groups and actually by the whole society, hence a high cost of distrust. Conversely, with honesty and trustworthiness, they can maximize the networked returns of nexus economy.

7.13 The Development of China's Agricultural Production Organizations from Uniformity, Diversification to Networking

The turn of the 1970s and the 1980s saw a thorough reform in the rural economic system in China. Its focus was on the reconstruction of microeconomic organizations by getting them right. The essential significance of the reform was to provide a broad range of freely selectable organizational foundations for an inclusive institutional space for the majority of peasants to achieve their freedom freely and improve their capability approach to substantial freedom.

Regarding the development of the agricultural production organizations, the reform then shifted from uniformity to diversification. The people's commune was a uniform, exclusive and monopolistic organization, a political and communal unity, within which other forms of economic organization were forbidden, let alone any forms of independent peasant household economy. "There were only commune members and no individual peasants whatsoever." The implementation of the rural peasant household land-contracting system broke the monopoly of the extensive unification of the people's communes. The peasant household economy gained a rebirth where the peasant household became the most basic form of microeconomic organization in the countryside. However, rural economic reform did not replace the uniformity of the communes with the uniformity of the peasant households, which, as the basic form of rural microeconomic organization, was not the only one. The essence of China's rural reform is to allow the majority of peasants to choose from much freely instead of simply dividing the land into households. As the majority of peasants have the basic right to choose freely, various microeconomic organizations have sprung up when the rural areas of contemporary China assume a symbiotic pattern of diverse economic organizations, in which the operations of families, collectives, cooperatives and companies develop side by side. This suggests that the form of economic organization in rural China has advanced from uniformity to diversification.

Nevertheless, diversity is not equivalent to modernization. The experiences of developed countries and China's 30-odd years of practice demonstrate that the right microeconomic organization and the diversification of its form alone cannot guarantee the modernization of agriculture and rural areas. In market economy where social ties are getting increasingly strengthened, modern society has entered a new era of information economy and networked economy.

Without modern networks and networked organizational groups compatible with modern market economy and networked economy, peasant households in a diversified organizational structure and any single microeconomic organization will have difficulty taking hold in a growing market of increasing uncertainty.

The key issue in China's tough agricultural and rural modernization does not lie in whether we have the right microeconomic organizations, but in the incomplete and underdeveloped modern agricultural and rural networks. Networked organizational groups are yet to evolve out of diversified organizational forms. The reason is that the diversified organizations are still small and isolated, chaotically competing for limited socio-economic resources and market share. Obviously, small peasant households and diversified but isolated organizations are hardly adaptive to large markets.

Only organization can dissolve their conflict. However, it cannot slide back into the uniformity of people's communes. Instead, it must rely on modern market economy and the multiple symbiosis of various organizations in line with the development of information economy and networked economy of modern society. Therefore, networkitization is an inevitable choice for organizations. This suggests that China's rural economic organizations will further develop from diversification to networkitization.

Informatization-led agricultural modernization was proposed in the political report of the 18th National Congress of the Communist Party of China. It should not be limited to the technical aspect that "Smart-phones and the Internet are accessible to every village and all households". A greater focus should be on all-round tremendous changes in the agricultural production organization model that will be brought about by modern information economy and networked economy. The transformation from diversification to networkitization is a concrete manifestation of the reforms of informatization-led agricultural modernization and the agricultural production organization model led by modern networked economy.

There has appeared across China organizational cooperation in the forms of companies plus peasant households, cooperatives plus peasant households, companies plus cooperatives plus peasant households, etc. They have ushered in the initial development of China's rural production organizations from diversification to networkitization with much room for further improvement. However, "the journey of a thousand miles begins with the first step". The modernization of China's rural microeconomic organizations has begun to enter a new stage from diversification to networkitization.

Since modern networks are essentially social public products with extremely strong externalities, the governmental leadership in their construction and improvement is inevitable as a matter of course. Nevertheless, it does not mean governments arrange all. Therefore, under the governmental leadership, it is necessary to mobilize peasants, enterprises, various types of cooperative economic organizations and the entire society to join efforts to build and improve modern networks. In short, the governmental leadership and the economic stakeholders involved are the two pillars in the building and the improvement of modern networks regarding agriculture and rural areas in China.

Modern networks must be bolstered by a modern organizational structure and will inevitably give birth to a modern organizational structure suitable for it, i.e., networked organizational groups. In order to constitute the groups where all economic entities rely on each other, coexist in co-prosperity, the deep-seated factor is the establishment of trust mechanisms for the whole society. Practice shows that building the new social trust mechanisms compatible with market economy and networked economy is a most difficult, long-term and complicated task in the modernization of contemporary China and a most important social foundation project for the construction of networked organizational groups in the rural areas of contemporary China.

The reform of China's rural economic organizational model, be it a transformation from uniformity to diversity or from diversity to networkitization, is essentially aimed at improving the capability approach of the majority of peasants to substantial freedom. The key to the former is the establishment of the independence and the right of the free choices of multiple economic entities and at the core is the protection of the freedom of individual economic entities. The transformation of the latter is to further emphasize the freedom of the whole society on the basis of the freedom of individual economic entities, and the latter is essential to the enhancement of the freedom of the former. The purpose of emphasizing social freedom in the process of networkitization is not to suppress or constrain individual freedom with social freedom, let alone replace it with so-called social freedom, but better strengthen and protect personal freedom with social freedom.

Afterword

When I submitted this book as the final result of the major project, I was not relieved at all. The project lasted for 5 years. Its completion was delayed due to my dissatisfaction with the result and therefore, many issues called for further research. However, another delay was insensible in that even if I had been allowed another five years or more, it would still be uncertain whether I would achieve a full satisfaction. Moreover, new questions that require exploration may far outnumber those resolved or answered. Therefore, I have to live with the sub-optimal and long for criticism as well as help from colleagues.

Strictly speaking, this book is only part of the achievements of the project, which is a thematic summary. As a supplement to the book, there are resultant monographs of four sub-projects, which respectively discuss peasant households (Wang Chunchao. *Chinese Peasants' Employment Decision and Labor Mobility*. Beijing: People's Publishing House, 2010), agricultural cooperatives (Chang Ming. *Institutional Environment and the Development of China's Agricultural Cooperative Economic Organizations*), agricultural listed companies (Hu Jiliang. *Research on Governmental Policies and Performance of Agricultural Listed Companies*) and the relationship between governments and firms in ethnic minority areas (Chen Wenlie. *A Study on the Relationship between Private Firms and the Governments in the Western Ethnic Areas of China — Based on an informal Institutional Perspective*. Beijing: Economic Management Press, 2013). They are four important aspects closely related to the theme. Some of these four monographs have been published and gained some recognition from academic colleagues. For example, Wang Chunchao's *Chinese Peasants' Employment Decision and Labor Mobility* entered into the "University Social Science Library" of the Ministry of Education and won the nomination award of the Fifth China Rural Development Award and the third prize of the Sixth University Humanities and Social Sciences

Outstanding Achievement of the Ministry of Education. In addition, the research group also published four English papers, three of which were carried in SSCI journals. At the same time, 21 papers were published in domestic journals such as *Management World*, *China's Rural Economy* and *Economic Trends*, among which 16 papers were published in CSSCI journals, and many were reprinted by *Xinhua Digest*, *Academic Digest* of Liberal Arts in Colleges and Universities and collected in Renmin University's ⟨⟨Copy Edition of the Materials from Periodicals for Reference⟩⟩ in Libraries.

I would like to thank all the members of the research group. They are Wang Chunchao from the School of Economics of Jinan University, Hu Jiliang from the School of Economics and Business Administration of Central China Normal University (CCNU), Chen Wenlie and Zhang Shihua from the School of Economics of Qinghai University for Nationalities (QUFN), Li Runguo from Shenhua Co. Ltd., Chang Ming from the Industrial Development Office of the National Supply and Marketing Federation, Yin Zuoliang from Jingmen Institute of Technology, Ma Xinzhi from the School of Economics and Management of Xinjiang University, Wu Chao'an from Hubei Provincial Youth League Committee, Ma Dejun from the School of Public Management of QUFN and Li Mingfeng from the School of Public Management of CCNU. Some of my graduate students, He Wei, Gao Song, Ding Zhifeng, Zhong Jun, Shang Ying, Yu Zhen, Fan Zhengan and Li Jing also participated in the research work. As the second person in charge of the research group, Dr. Wang Chunchao assisted me to do a lot of work for the project, both during his doctoral study in CCNU and during his work in Jinan University. Dr. Hu Jiliang has undertaken many trisvial affairs. Obviously, without the concerted efforts of all members of the research group, the completion of the project would be impossible.

In 2014, this book entered the National Library of Philosophy and Social Sciences. I am grateful to the review experts for their recognition of the book and valuable suggestions for its revision and the Chinese Social Science Press for recommending this book. Finally, I am appreciative of CCNU and its School of Economics and Business Administration where I work.

References

Chinese Monographs

Bo Yibo. Reviews on Several Major Decisions and Events. Beijing: People's Publishing House, 1997.

Cao Jinqing. *China by the Yellow River*. Shanghai: Shanghai Literature and Art Press, 2000.

Cao Yang. *A Study on the Forms of Contemporary Rural Microeconomic Organizations*. Beijing: China Social Sciences Press, 2007.

Cao Yang. *Research Report on Social Security of Rural Non-agricultural Industrial Groups in China*. Beijing: China Social Sciences Press, 2006.

Cao Yang. *China's Transfer of Agricultural Labor Force: An Analysis Based on System Changes*. Shanghai: Huazhong Normal University Press, 1997.

Chen Xiwen, Zhao Yang and Luo Dan. *30 Years Review and Prospect of China's Rural Reform*. Beijing: People's Publishing House, 2008.

Chen, Yuping and Wu Haitao. Agricultural Technology Diffusion and Peasant Households' Economic Behaviors. Wuhan: Hubei People's Publishing House, 2010.

China (Hainan) Reform and Research Institute. China Farmer Organization Construction. Beijing: China Economic Press, 2005.

China (Hainan) Reform and Research Institute. China Human Development Report 2007/2008: Basic Public Services Benefiting 1.3 Billion People. China Translation and Publication Corporation, 2008.

China Rural Development Research Group. Countryside, Economy and Society, Vol. 3. Knowledge Press, 1985.

Cihai (Miniature Edition). Shanghai: Shanghai Dictionary Press, 1989.

Decision of the CCCPC on Several Major Issues of Comprehensively Deepening Reform. Beijing: People's Publishing House, 2013.

Deng Xiaoping. *Deng Xiaoping's Selected Works*, Vol. 3. Beijing: People's Publishing House, 1993.

Du Runsheng's Account: A Record of Major Policy-making Events in China's Rural Institutional Reform. Beijing: People's Publishing House, 2005.

Du Yintang, ed. *Cooperatives: Modern Enterprise System in Agriculture*. Jiangxi People's Publishing House, 2002.

Fei Xiaotong on the Construction of Small Towns. Beijing: Qunyan Press, 2000.

Fei, Xiaotong. *Fertility System in Rural China*. Beijing: Beijing University Press, 2004.

Gao, Peiyong and Cui Jun. *Public Sector Economics*. Beijing: Renmin University of China Press, 2004.

Guo Hongdong and Zhang Ruojian. *Surveys on Chinese Farmers' Professional Cooperatives*. Hangzhou: Zhejiang University Press, 2010.

Han Jun, ed. *Surveys of Specialized Peasants' Cooperatives in China*. Shanghai: Shanghai Far East Publisher, 2007.

Han Shuifa. *Kant Biography*. Hebei: People's Publishing House, 1997.

Huang Zongzhi. *China's Recessive Agricultural Revolution*. Beijing: Law Press, 2010.

Huang Zongzhi. *Small Scale Household-Based Farming and Rural Development in the Yangtze River Delta*. Shanghai: Zhonghua Book Company Limited, 2000.

Huang, Zuhui, Lin Jian, Zhang Dongping *et al*. *Agricultural Modernization: Theory, Process and Approach*. Beijing: China Agricultural Press, 2003.

Hu Jintao. *To Uphold High the Great Banner of Socialism with Chinese Characteristics and Strive for the New Victory of Building a Well-off Society in an All-round Way — Report on the Seventeenth National Congress of the Communist Party of China*. Beijing: People's Publishing House, 2007.

Hu Jintao. *Unswervingly Following the Road of Socialism with Chinese Characteristics and Striving for Building a Well-off Society in an All-round Way — Report at the 18th National Congress of the CPC*. Beijing: People's Publishing House, 2012.

Kong, Xiangzhi, eds. *Research on Agricultural Socialized Services Based on Supply and Demand in China.* Beijing: Renmin University of China Press, 2009.

Kuang Jili, ed. *Speech Appreciation of Famous Jurists.* Shandong: People's Publishing House, 1995.

Law of the People's Republic of China on Agricultural Technology Popularization. Beijing: People's Publishing House, 1993.

Law of the People's Republic of China on Farmers' Specialized Cooperatives. Beijing: People's Publishing House, 2006.

Law of the People's Republic of China on Land Administration. Beijing: People's Publishing House, 2004.

Law of the People's Republic of China on Rural Land Contract. Beijing: People's Publishing House, 2002.

Li Dan. *Understanding Peasant China.* Jiangsu: People's Publishing House, 2008.

Li Gefei, ed. *Chinese Dictionary (Simplified Edition).* Hubei: Dictionaries Publishing House, Sichuan Dictionaries Publishing House, 1996.

Li Weimin. *Agricultural Miracle in Holland.* Beijing: China Agricultural Science and Technology Press, 2003.

Lin Yifu, Cai Fang and Li Zhou. *China's Miracle: Development Strategy and Economic Reform.* Shanghai: People's Publishing House, 1999.

Lin Yifu. *System. Technology and China's Agricultural Development.* Shanghai: People's Publishing House, 1994.

Liu Lingling. *The Final Part of the Research Report on China's Rural Financial Development by Tsinghua University of Economics and Management (2006–2010).* Tsinghua: Tsinghua University Press, 2010.

Lu Xueyi. *On Agriculture, Countryside and Farmers in Contemporary China.* Beijing: Social Sciences Literature Press, 2002.

Luo Biliang. *System Logic of Economic Organization.* Shanxi: Economic Publishing House, 2000.

Ni Hongxing. *Non Trade Concerns and Trade Liberalization of Agricultural Products.* Beijing: China Agricultural University Press, 2003.

Party History Research Office of the CCCPC. *History of the CPC*, Vol. 2 (1949–1978) (Vols. 1 and 2). Beijing: Party History Press of the CPC, 2011.

Qi Liang. *Western Liberal Tradition*. Guangdong: People's Publishing House, 2003.

Qu Futian *et al*. *Research on Rural Land Problems in the Process of Industrialization and Urbanization in China*. Beijing: Economic Science Press, 2010.

Selected Works of Chen Yun's Manuscripts (1949–1956). Beijing: People's Publishing House, 1982.

Shi Jinchuan. *Institutional Change and Economic Development: Wenzhou Model Research*. Hangzhou: Zhejiang University Press, 2004.

Tan Chengjian. *Dazhai — An Account of Famous Villages in China*. Beijing: Central Plain Farmers Press, 1998.

Tan Chongtai, ed. *New Trends in Development Economics*. Wuhan: Wuhan University Press, 1999.

The Literature Research Office of the CCCPC. Selected and Compiled Important Documents Since the Third Plenary Session. Beijing: People's Publishing House, 1982.

Wang Bing. *Modern Market Theory — Economics of Market*. Hubei: People's Publishing House, 2003.

Wang Chunchao. *Employment Decision and Labor Mobility of Chinese Farmers*. Beijing: People's Publishing House, 2010.

Wang Jingxin. *The Rise of Rural Cooperative Economy Organizations*. Beijing: China Economic Publishing House, 2005.

Wen Tiejun. *Research on China's Basic Rural Economic System*. Beijing: China Economic Press, 2000.

Wen Tiejun. *Three Rural Issues and Institutional Changes*. Beijing: China Economic Publishing House, 2009.

Xiao Jianfu and Li Jinquan, ed. *History of Chinese Philosophy*. Beijing: People's Publishing House, 1999.

Xuanxingyun and Wang Chunfa. *Perspective of Agricultural Modernization in Western Countries*. Shanghai: Far East Press, 1998.

Yu Wujin. *Practice and Freedom*. Wuhan: Wuhan University Press, 2010.

Zhang Peigang, ed. *New Development Economics*. Henan: People's Publishing House, 1999.

Zhang Peigang. *Agriculture and Industrialization*. Huazhong: Huazhong University of Science and Technology Press, 2002.

Zhang Wuchang. *Interpretations of Economy*. Beijing: Commercial Press, 2000.

Zhang Xiaoshan and Yuan Peng. *Cooperative Economic Theory and Practice of Chinese Peasants' Cooperatives*. Beijing: Capital University of Economics and Business Press, 2009.

Zhou Chaomin, ed. *Network Economy and Management*. Shanghai: People's Publishing House, 2008.

Chinese Papers

Analysis and Research Group of Rural Economic Research Center of the Ministry of Agriculture. "Challenges and Choices Faced by Agriculture and Rural Development during the 12th Five Year Plan Period", *China Rural Economy*, No. 8, 2010, pp. 4–13.

Bai, Yongxiu. "Promote Moderate Scale Land Operation and Facilitate the Transformation of Economic Growth Mode", *Journal of Economic Reform*, No. 1, 1997, pp. 47–50.

Cao Yang and Hu Jiliang. "Agricultural Mechanization under China's Land Household Contract System — Based on the Survey Data of 17 Provinces (Districts and Cities) in China." *China Rural Economy*, No. 1, 2010, pp. 57–65.

Cao Yang. "External Environment Constrains Farmers' Rational Decision-making as "Economic Man" — Report on Investigation and Analysis of Thousands of Rural Households in Mainland China," China Rural Research (Vol. 2002). Beijing: China Social Sciences Press, 2003, pp. 274–295.

Cao Yang. "Reflections on Several Issues of 'Hypothesis of Economic Man'." *Jianghan Forum*, No. 1, 2009, pp. 46–50.

Cao Yang. "Rural Land Inheritance System and Rural Land Community Ownership: Contradictions, Conflicts and Development Trend", *Theory Monthly*, Vol. 9, 2005, pp. 5–9.

Cao Yang. "The Position and Value of 'Freedom' in Marx's Theory of 'Human Development'." *Economic Trends*, No. 1, 2012, pp. 72–75.

Chen Xiwen. How to Coordinate China's Urban and Rural Development. *China Rural Discovery*, Vol. 13, Hunan: People's Publishing House, 2010, pp. 6–11.

Chen Yixin. "Dissemination and Influence of Western Cooperativism in China in the Early 20th Century", *Journal of Historical Research*, No. 6, 2001, pp. 89–102.

Chen Yun. Implementing Unified Purchase and Marketing of Grain. *Selected Works of Chen Yun's Manuscript (1949–1956).* Beijing: People's Publishing House, 1982, pp. 189–203.

China Internet Network Information Center. 2008–2009 China Rural Internet Development Survey Report.

China Internet Network Information Center. 2009 China Search Engine User Behavior Research Report.

Cui Guoqiang. "An Empirical Study on the Impact of Agricultural Product Processing Industry on Peasants' Income Growth in Henan Province", *Acta Agriculture Jiangxi*, No. 4, 2010, pp. 159–160.

Deng Dacai. "How to Form the Rural Land Transfer Market — Case Studies from Hongqi Village, Liyuantun Village, Hucun Village and Xiaogang Village", *China Rural Observation*, No. 3, 2009, pp. 26–35.

Deng Quheng. "Income Gap between Urban and Migrant Laborers: Based on the Decomposition of Oaxaca-Blinder and Quantile Method. Chinese Population Science", No. 2, 2007, pp. 8–16.

Deng Xiaoping. Building Socialism with Chinese Characteristics. *Deng Xiaoping's Selected Works*, Vol. 3. Beijing: People's Publishing House, 1993, pp. 62–66.

Deng Xiaoping. Plans and Markets Are Both Methods for Developing Productive Forces. *Selected Works of Deng Xiaoping*, Vol. 3. Beijing: People's Publishing House, 1993, p. 203.

Dong, Hanying. "Scale of Land Operation and Agricultural Mechanization", *China Rural Economy*, No. 8, pp. 50–53.

Dong, Zhenghua. "Historical Status of Modern Small-Scale Farming System — Review of the Discussions Concerning the 19th Century Marxism", in Yu Keping, Li Shenming and Wang Weiguang eds. *On Agriculture and Peasants and the Construction of New Countryside.* Beijing: Central Compilation & Translation Bureau Press, 2006.

Du, Yintang, "Impacts of Agricultural Industrialized Operation and Peasants Organizational Innovations on Peasants' Incomes", *China Rural Observation*, No. 3, 2005, pp. 9–18.

Fang Songhai, Wang Weinong and Huang Hanquan. "Research on Increasing Farmers' Income and Expanding Rural Consumption", *Managing the World*, No. 5, 2011, pp. 66–80.

Feng, Hua and Chen Renze. "A Big Grain Grower's Ecstasy and Expectations — A Report from the Front Line of Agricultural Production", *People's Network*, February 11, 2011.

Ganesh Thapa. "Challenges and Opportunities Faced by Small and Medium-sized Agriculture in the Process of Economic Transformation in Asia and Latin America", *China Rural Economy*, No. 12, 2010, pp. 77–86.

Guo Lulai. "Institutional Economics of Cooperative System and Practice of Professional Association", *China Rural Observation*, No. 4, 2001, pp. 36–48.

He Lixin and Pan Chunyang. "Understanding China's "Easterlin Paradox": Income Gap, Unequal Opportunities and National Well-being", *The World of Management*, No. 8, 2011, pp. 11–22.

Hong Limin. "The History, Present Situation and Prospect of Development of Symbiosis Concept", *Chinese Journal of Microecology*, Vol. 8, No. 4, 1996, pp. 50–54.

Hu Jintao. Deepening Exchanges and Cooperation to Achieve Inclusive Growth. *People's Daily*, September 16, 2010.

Huang, Zuhui and Shao Ke, "Nature of the Cooperative and Its Drift", *Journal of Zhejiang University*, No. 4, 2009, pp. 12–17.

Li Chunhai, Zhang Wen and Peng MuQing. "Research Status and Guidance of Agricultural Industry Cluster: Perspective of Organizational Innovation", *China Rural Economy*, No. 3, 2011, pp. 49–58.

Li Huaiyin. "The Traditional Form of Rural Governance in China: An Example of Huolu County, Hebei Province", *China Rural Studies*, Vol. 1. Beijing: Commercial Press, 2003.

Li Yan. "The Basic Concept of Symbiotic Philosophy", *Theory Learning*, No. 5, 2005, pp. 73–74.

Li, Min and Zhao Liange, "The Impact of Rural Labor Mobility on the Aging of Agricultural Labor Force", *Journal of China Rural Economy*, No. 9, 2010, pp. 68–75.

Liao, Zujun, Zhao, Lu and Ling Yuzhi. "Research on the Development of the Cooperative Whose Establishment Was Led by a Leading Company — A Case Study of Qionglai Jinli Specialized Pig Industrial Cooperative", *China Cooperative Economic Review*, No. 2, 2010.

Liu Shouying and Shao Xiazhen. The Impact and Reflection of Meitan's 24-year Practice of "No Increase for the Newborn and No Decrease for the Deceased", *China Rural Discovery*, 2012, Winter.

Liu, Fengqin. "Study on the Conditions and Effects of Scale Operation of Agricultural Land: Taking the Northeast Rural Area as an Example", *Journal of the Management World*, No. 9, 2006, pp. 71–79.

Liu, Fengqin. "Study on the Scale of Agricultural Land Operation in China — A Case Study on Small-Scale land Operation", *Journal of Research on Financial and Economic Issues*, No. 10, 2003, pp. 60–65.

Lu Xun. *Advantages and Disadvantages of Electricity, Pseudo-Freedom Statement*. People's Literature Publishing House, 1995, pp. 8–9.

Lu, Nanquan. "Russia's Agricultural Reform and Its Implications", *China Social Science Network*, December 22, 2011.

Luo Biliang. "Peasant Cooperative Organizations: Laziness, Supervision and Guarantee Mechanism", *China Rural Observation*, No. 2, 2007, pp. 26–37.

Luo Xingzuo and He Xuefeng. "Organizational Basis of Rural Water Conservancy", *Xuehai*, No. 6, 2003, pp. 38–44.

Ma Xiaoqing and Huang Zuhui. "A Comparative Study on the Difference of Farmers' Credit Demand and Financing Preference — Based on a Questionnaire of 588 Farmers in Jiangsu Province", *Journal of Nanjing Agricultural University*, No. 1, 2010, pp. 57–63.

Mao Zedong. Agricultural Cooperation. *Selected Works of Mao Zedong*, Vol. 5. Beijing: People's Publishing House, 1977, pp. 168–194.

Mao Zedong. On People's Democratic Dictatorship. *Selected Works of Mao Zedong*, Vol. 4. Beijing: People's Publishing House, 1991, pp. 1468–1482.

Meng, Fanqi and the joint research group of "Study on a Moderate Scale of Farming Industry". "Issues of Developing Scale Agricultural Production and Operation", *Journal of China Rural Economy*, No. 1, 1987, pp. 26–31.

No.1 Document issued by the Central Government in 2004–2014.

Pan, Jin. "Specialized Peasants' Cooperatives in China: Interpretation of Data", *Journal of China Rural Observation*, No. 6, 2011, pp. 2–11.

Tan Xuewen. "Modern Agriculture, Post-modern Agriculture and Ecological Agriculture" — "Two Types of Countryside" and

Ecological Agriculture and the Fifth International Symposium on the Comparison of Agricultural Modernization in China", *China Rural Economy*, No. 2, 2010, pp. 92–95.

"Urban Labor Market Task Force" of China Economic Research Center of Peking University. "Stratification and Integration of Urban Workers and Rural Migrant Workers." Reform, No. 4, 1998, pp. 99–110.

Wan Junyi, "Quasi-Vertical Integration, Relation Governance and Contract Implementation — Taking Wen's Model of Agricultural Industrialization as an Example", *Management World*, No. 12, 2008, pp. 93–102.

Wang Meiyan. "Wage Gap in Transitional Period: Quantitative Analysis of Discrimination", Quantitative Economic, Technological and Economic Research, No. 5, 2003, pp. 94–98.

Wang Yao. Education is a Poem. *Reading*, Vol. 3, 2012, pp. 96–101.

Wang, Chunchao and Li Zhaoneng, "The Predicament Regarding Rural Land Transfer: A Survey on Peasant Households from Hubei", *Journal of Huazhong Normal University*, No. 4, 2008, pp. 51–56.

Wen Tiejun, Lang Xiaojuan and Zheng Fengtian. "Social Stability in Rural China and Its Characteristics: Based on the Investigation and Analysis of 1,765 Households in 100 Villages", *Management World*, Vol. 3, 2011, pp. 66–76.

Wen, Lipeng. "The Particularity of Agricultural Production and the Vitality of Household Self-Cultivated Farms", in Yu, Keping, Li, Shenming and Wang Weiguang, eds. *On Agriculture and Peasants in the Construction of New Countryside*. Beijing: Central Compilation & Translation Bureau Press, 2006, pp. 278–282.

Wu Xiang. "Boulevard and Single-plank Bridge", *People's Daily*, November 5, 1980.

Wu Yunli. "Analysis of the Transformation Factors of Agricultural Scientific and Technological Achievements", *Journal of Southwest Agricultural University*, No. 3, 2000, pp. 278–282.

Xi Jinping. Speech at the First Session of the Twelfth National People's Congress. *People's Daily*, March 17, 2013.

Xiao Guoliang. Contemplation on Company. *Reading*, No. 2, 2011, pp. 11–17.

Xie Sisheng and Yao Xianguo. "Quantitative Analysis of Wage Discrimination of Migrant Workers", *Rural Economy of China*, No. 4, 2006, pp. 49–55.

Xu, Ping. "The Reform of French Rural Areas in the Second Half of the 19th Century and the Transformation of Traditional Peasants into Neoterics", *World History*, No. 2, 1994, pp. 34–41.

Yang Xuecheng and Zhao Ruiying. "Reflections on Rural Land Relations: Based on the Three Rural Household Surveys in Shandong Province from 1995 to 2008", *Management World*, No. 3, 2008, pp. 53–61.

Yao, Jianfu. "China's Agricultural Scale Operation and Agricultural Comprehensive Productivity — An Interview with Mr. Xu Xiaobai from Institute of Rural Development of University of Washington", *Journal of China's Agricultural Resources and Regional Planning*, No. 5, pp. 22–24.

Yu Hai and Huang Jikun. "Stability of Land Rights, Land Circulation and Sustainable Utilization of Agricultural Land Resources", *Economic Research*, No. 9, 2003, pp. 82–91.

Zhou Li'an. "Local Officials in China: Research on Promoting Championship Mode", *Economic Research*, No.7, 2007, pp. 36–50.

Zhou Qiren. "China's Rural Reform: Changes in the Relationship between the State and Land Ownership — A Review on the History of Economic System Changes", China Social Sciences Quarterly (Hong Kong), No. 6, 1995.

Zhu Mingfen and Chang Min. "Analysis on the Characteristics and Attributes of the Recessive Market of Agricultural Land", *China Rural Economy*, No.11, 2011, pp. 10–22.

Zhu Shouyin, Zhang Zhaoxin, Zhang Haiyang and Wang Chengxian. "Supply and Demand of China's Rural Financial Market — Taking Traditional Agricultural Areas as an Example", *Management World*, No. 3, 2003, pp. 88–95.

Translated Chinese Works

Acton, L. *Freedom and Power*. Scotts Valley: CreateSpace Independent Publishing Platform, 2013.

Arendt, H. *The Freedom to Be Free: From Thinking Without a Banister*. New York: Vintage Books, 2018.

Becker, G.S. *An Economic Analysis of the Family*. Dublin: Economic and Social Research Institute, 1986.

Boucher, S.R., Smith, A., Taylor J.E. *et al*. "Impacts of Policy Reforms on the Supply of Mexican Labor to U.S. Farms New Evidence from Mexico", *Review of Agricultural Economics*, Vol. 29, No. 1, 2007, pp. 4–16.

Breit, William & Ransom, Roger L. *The Academic Scribblers*. Princeton: Princeton University Press, 1999.

Buchanan, J.M. *Property As a Guarantor of Liberty*. Northampton: Edward Elgar Pub, 1993.

Cassirer, E. *An Essay on Man*. New York: Bantam Books, 1970.

Chandler Jr., A.D. *The Visible Hand: The Managerial Revolution in American Business*. Cambridge: Harvard University Press, 1993.

Cipolla, C., ed. *The Middle Ages, The Fontana Economic History of Europe*, Vol. 1. Glasgow: William Collins Sons & Co. Ltd., 1972.

Coase, R. "The Nature of the Firm", *Economica*, No. 4 (1937), pp. 386–405.

Concise Encyclopedia Britannica, Vol. 9. Beijing: China Encyclopedia Press, 1986.

Drucker, P.F. *Innovation and Entrepreneurship*. Sanford: Collins Press, 1993.

Dye, T.R. *Understanding Public Policy*. London: Pearson, 2012.

Engels, F. *Anti-Dühring: Herr Eugen Dühring's Revolution in Science*. Warsaw: Progress Publishers, 1947.

Engels, F. Engels to Giuseppe Canepa. *Karl Marx Selected Works*, Vol. 2. London: Lawrence and Wishart Limited, 1947.

Engels, F. The Peasant Question in France and Germany. *Selected Works of Marx and Engels*, Vol. 3 Moscow: Progress Publishers, 1993.

Foster, J. and Metcalf, J.S. eds. *Frontier of Evolutionary Economics*. London: Edward Elgar Pub, 2001.

Furubotn, E. and Richter, R. *New Institutional Economics: An Analysis Paradigm of Transaction Cost*, trans. Jiang Lianqiang and Luo Changyuan. Shanghai: Shanghai Sanlian Bookstore and Shanghai People's Publishing House, 2006.

Granovetter, M. *Embeddedness: Social Networks and Economic Action*, tran. Luo Jiade. Beijing: Social Sciences Academic Press (China), 2007.

Hegel, G.W.F. *The Philosophy of History*. New York: Penguin Random House US,1990.

Hendrikse, G. *Economics and Management of Organizations*. New York: McGraw-Hill, 2003.

Hobbes, T. *Leviathan*. Eugene: The University of Oregon Press, 1999.

Hodgson, G.M. *Evolution and Institution: On Evolutionary Economics and the Evolution of Economics*. Cheltenham: Edward Elgar Pub, 1999.

Höffe, O. *Political Justice: Foundations for a Critical Philosophy of Law and the State*. Hoboken: Wiley, 1995.

Jensen, M. and Meckling, W. "Theory of the Firm: Managerial Behavior, Agency Costs and Ownership Structure", *Journal of Financial Economics*, Vol. 3, No. 4 (1976), pp. 305–360.

Kant, I. *The Critique of Pure Reason*. Midland Park: Pinnacle Press, 2017.

Kautsky, K. *The Agrarian Question*. London and Winchester: Zwan Publications, 1988.

Kindelberg, C.P. and Herrick, B. ed. *Economic Development*. New York: McGraw-Hill Education, 1977.

Larson, R. "The Handshake between Invisible and Visible Hands", *International Studies of Management and Organization*, Vol. 23 (1993), pp. 87–107.

Lin Chonggeng and Spencer, M., ed. *Medium-and-long-term Development and Transformation of China's Economy: Thoughts and Suggestions from an International Perspective*. Beijing: CITIC Press, 2011.

Lin, N. *Social Capital: A Theory of Social Structure and Action*. Cambridge: Cambridge University Press, 2002.

Locke, J. *Two Treatises of Government*. Scotts Valley: CreateSpace Independent Publishing Platform, 2015.

Louis, P. and Randall, K. eds. *The Economic Nature of the Firm*. Cambridge: Cambridge University Press, 1987.

Mach, J. and Simon, H. *Organizations*. Hoboken: Wiley-Blackwell, 1993.

Malinowski, B. *Freedom and Civilization*. Bangalore: Mysore Press, 2014.

Marshall, A. *Money Credit, and Commerce*. London: Macmillan & Co., Limited, 1923.

Marshall, A. *Principles of Economics*. New York: Macmillan Publishers Limited, 2013.

Marx, K. and Engels, F. Economic Manuscripts 1857–1858. *Karl Marx Selected Works*, Vol. 2. London: Lawrence and Wishart Limited, 1947.

Marx, K. and Engels, F. Manifesto of the Communist Party. *Karl Marx Selected Works*, Vol. 1. London: Lawrence and Wishart Limited, 1947.

Marx, K. *Capital: A Critique of Political Economy*. Moscow: Progress Publishers, 1956.

Marx, K. *Economic and Philosophic Manuscripts of 1844*. Eastford: Martino Fine Books, 2011.

Marx, K. Proceedings of the Sixth Rhine Province Assembly. *Karl Marx & Frederick Engels: Collected Works*. New York: Intl Pub Co. Inc, 1996.

Marx, K. The Eighteenth Brumaire of Louis Bonaparte. *Karl Marx Selected Works*, Vol. 2. London: Lawrence and Wishart Limited, 1947.

Marx, K. The Rule of Britain in India. *Karl Marx Selected Works*, Vol. 2. London: Lawrence and Wishart Limited, 1947.

Marx, K. These on Feuerbach. *The German Ideology*. Moscow: Progress Publishers, 1968.

Maslow, A.H. *A Theory of Human Motivation*. Eastford: Martino Fine Books, 2013.

McConnell, C. and Brue, S. *Economics: Principles, Problems and Policies*. New York: McGraw-Hill Education, 2014.

McKinnon, R.I. "Money and Capital in Economic Development", *The American Political Science Review*, Vol. 68, 1974.

Meier, G. and Stiglitz, J. eds. *Frontiers of Development Economics: The Future in Perspective*. Oxford: Oxford University Press, 2000.

Mitchell, J.C., eds. *Social Networks in Urban Situations*. Manchester: Manchester University Press, 1969.

Montesquieu. *The Spirit of the Laws*. Cambridge: Cambridge University Press, 1989.

North, D.C. *Structure and Change in Economic History*. New York: W. W. Norton & Company, 1982.

Ostrom, E. *Governing the Commons: The Evolution of Institutions for Collective Action*. Cambridge: Cambridge University Press, 2015.

Pearce, D.W. *The MIT Dictionary of Modern Economics*. Cambridge: MIT Press, 1987.

Porter, M.E. *The Competitive Advantage of Nations*. New York: The Free Press, 1998.

Prosterman, R. *et al*. "Scale Agriculture in China: Policy Appropriately Do", *China's Rural Observation*, 1966, pp. 17–29.

Robbins, S.P. and Coulter, M.K. *Management*. London: Pearson, 2004.

Rousseau, J.-J. *The Social Contract*. Washington, D.C.: Henry Regnery Company, 1954.

Sandel, M. *Justice: What's the Right Thing to Do*. New York: Farrar, Straus and Giroux, 2010.

Schultz, T.W. *Investment in Human Capital*. London: Collier-Macmillan, 1971.

Schultz, T.W. *Transforming Traditional Agriculture*. Chicago and London: The University of Chicago Press, 1983.

Schumpeter, J.A. *The Theory of Economic Development*. University Park: Transaction Publishers, 1982.

Sen, A. "An Aspect of Indian Agriculture", *Economic Weekly*, Vol. 14, No. (4–6) (1962), pp. 243–246.

Sen, A. "Peasants and Dualism with or without Surplus Labor", *Journal of Political Economy*, 74, 1966, pp. 425–450.

Sen, A. *Development as Freedom*. Palatine: Anchor Books, 2000.

Smith, A. *An Inquiry into the Nature and Causes of the Wealth of Nations*, Vol. 1. Oxford: Clarendon, 1880.

Stalin, J. Issues Concerning Questions of Agrarian Policies in the U.S.S.R. *Selected Works of Stalin*, Vol. 12. Moscow: Foreign Languages Publishing House, 1954.

Thapa, G. "Challenges and Opportunities for Small Agriculture During an Economic Transformation in Asia and Latin America", *China Rural Economy*, No. 12, 2010.

Tocqueville, A. de. *The Old Regime and the Revolution*. Chicago: The University of Chicago Press, 1998.

Toffler, A. *The Third Wave*, New York: Bantam Books, Inc, 1980.

Weitz, R. *From Peasant to Farmer — A Revolutionary Strategy for Development*. New York: Columbia University Press, 1971.

Williamson, O. *The Economic Institutions of Capitalism: Firms, Markets, Relational Contracting*. New York: The Free Press, 1985.

World Bank. *1994 World Development Report: Providing Infrastructure for Development*. Beijing: China Finance and Economics Press, 1994.

World Bank. *China Farmers Association: Review and Policy Recommendations*. Beijing: China Agriculture Press, 2006.

World Bank. *Specialized Peasants' Associations in China: Review and Policy Recommendations*. Beijing: China Agricultural Press, 2006.

World Bank. *World Development Report 2003: Changing Sustainable Development in the World (Improving System Growth Mode and Quality of Life)*. Beijing: China Finance and Economics Press, 2003.

English Literature

Boucher, S.R., Smith, A., Taylor, J.E. and Yunez-Naude, A. "Impacts of Policy Reforms on the Supply of Mexican Labor to U.S. Farms: New Evidence from Mexico", *Review of Agricultural Economics*, Vol. 29, No. 1 (2007), pp. 4–16.

Clarkson, M.A. "Stakeholder Framework for Analyzing and Evaluating Corporate Social Performance", *Academy of Management Review*, Vol. 20, No. 1 (1995), pp. 92–117.

Coase, R. "The Nature of the Firm", *Economica*, Vol. 4, No. 16 (1937), pp. 386–405.

Easterlin, R. *Does Economic Growth Improve the Human Lot? Some Empirical Evidence, Nations and Households in Economic Growth*. New York: Academic Press, 1974.

Freeman, R.E. *Strategic Management: A Stakeholder Approach*. Cambridge: Cambridge University Press, 1984.

Gold, T., Guthrie, D. and Wank, D., eds. *Social Connections in China: Institutions Culture and the Changing Nature of Guanxi*. Cambridge: University of Cambridge Press, 2002.

Granovetter, M. "Economic Action and Social Structure: The Problem of Embeddedness", *The American Journal of Sociology*, Vol. 91, No. 3 (1985), pp. 481–510.

Habermas. Modernity — An Incomplete Project. Paul Rabinow and William M. Sullivan eds. *Interpretive Social Science: Second Look*. California: University of California Press, 1979.

Hennessy, T.C. and Rehman, T. "Assessing the Impact of the 'Decoupling' Reform of the Common Agricultural Policy on Irish Farmers'

Off-farm Labor Market Participation Decisions", *Journal of Agricultural Economics*, Vol. 59, No. 1 (2008), pp. 41–56.

Jensen, M. and Meckling, W. "Theory of the Firm: Managerial Behavior, Agency Costs, and Ownership Structure", *Journal of Financial Economics*, Vol. 3, No. 4 (1976), pp. 305–360.

Kaight, F. *Risk, Uncertainty and Profit*. New York: Houghton Mifflin Co., 1921.

Kornai, J. *By Force of Thought-Irregular Memoirs of an Intellectual Journey*. Cambridge, Massachusetts and London, England: The MIT Press, 2005.

Lang, R. *The Transformation of Organizations in East Germany and Eastern Europe: Unsolved Questions and Problem Areas for Research*. Munich: Mering Hampp, 1996.

Lazonick, W. "The Integration of Theory and History: Methodology and Ideology in Schumperter's Economics", in Magnusson, L. ed. *Evolutionary and Neo-Schumpeterian Approaches to Economics*. New York: Springer-Verlag, 1994, pp. 245–263.

Lipton, M. *Why Poor People Stay Poor: Urban Bias in World Development*. Harvard: Harvard University Press, 1977.

Locke, J. *Two Treatises of Government*. Cambridge: Cambridge University Press, 1960.

Lucas, R. "North-Holland on the Mechanics of Economic Development", *Journal of Monetary Economics*, Vol. 22, No. 1 (1988), pp. 3–42.

Mabel Ping-Hua Lee. *The Economic History of China*. New York: AMS Press, 1969.

March, J.G. and Simon, H. A. *Organizations*. Hoboken: John Wiley & Sons Inc., 1958.

Meier, G.M. ed. *Leading Issues in Economic Development*. Oxford: Oxford University Press, 1984.

Mitchell, J.C. ed. *Social Networks in Urban Situations*. Manchester: Manchester University, 1969.

Prosterman, R. *et al.* "Scale Agriculture in China: Policy Appropriately Do?" *China's Rural Observation*, Vol. 6 (1996), pp. 17–29.

Qian, Y. and Roland, G. "Federalism and the Soft Budget Constraint", *American Economic Review*, Vol. 77 (1998), pp. 265–284.

Romer, P. "Increasing Returns and Long-Run Growth", *Journal of Political Economy*, Vol. 94, No. 5 (1986), pp. 1002–1037.

Scott, J.C. *The Moral Economy of the Peasant: Rebellion and Subsistence in Southeast Asia*. New Heaven: Yale University Press, 1976.

Sen, A. "An Aspect of Indian Agriculture", *Economic Weekly*, Vol. 14, No. 4–6 (1962), pp. 243–246.

Sen, A. "Peasants and Dualism with or without Surplus Labor", *Journal of Political Economy*, Vol. 74 (1966), pp. 425–450.

Simon, H.A. *Models of Man*. New York: John Wiley and Sons, 1957.

Uchida, E., Rozelle, S. and Jintao Xu. "Conservation Payments, Liquidity Constraints and Off-farm Labor: Impact of the Grain-for-green Program on Rural Households in China", *American Journal of Agricultural Economics*, Vol. 91, No. 1 (2009), pp. 70–86.

Wagner, D.G. and Berger, J. "Do Sociological Theories Grow?" *American Journal of Sociology*, Vol. 90, No. 4 (1985), pp. 692–728.

Wank, D.L. "The Institutional Process of Market Clienteles: Guanxi and Private Business in a South China City", *The China Quarterly*, Vol. 9 (1996).

Wilson, E.O. *Sociobiology: The New Synthesis*. Cambridge, Massachusetts: Harvard University Press, 1975.

Xin, K. and Pearce, J. "Guanxi: Connections as Substitute for Formal Institutional Support", *Academy of Management Journal*, Vol. 39 (1996), pp. 1641–1658.

Index

N

CPSIA information can be obtained
at www.ICGtesting.com
Printed in the USA
JSHW011147300323
39281JS00001B/66